Bill Cooke

Bill Cooke was born and raised in Kenya. Since 1965 he has lived in the United Kingdom and New Zealand. Cooke's previous books include *Heathen in Godzone:Seventy Years of Rationalism in New Zealand* (NZARH, 1998), and *A Rebel to His Last Breath: Joseph McCabe and Rationalism* (Prometheus, 2001) He is Editor-in-Chief of *The Open Society*, the official journal of the NZ Association of Rationalists & Humanists.

While writing this book, Cooke was Senior Lecturer at the School of Visual Arts, University of Auckland at Manukau, in New Zealand. He has since taken the position of International Director of the Center for Inquiry, based at Amherst, New York. He is also visiting Assistant Professor of Philosophy at the University of Buffalo.

Bill Cooke is married to Bobbie Douglas Cooke, an artist. When not writing on the history of humanism, Cooke trawls second hand bookshops, writes an art column, and enjoys unheathily large quantities of curry and red wine.

The
Blasphemy Depot

A Hundred Years of the Rationalist Press Association

Bill Cooke

Rationalist Press Association

First published in Great Britain in 2003
By the Rationalist Press Association

© Bill Cooke

All rights reserved. No part of this publication may be reproduced, stored in a retrieval system, or transmitted, in any form and by any means, electronic, mechanical, photocopying, recording or otherwise, without the prior permission of both the copyright owner and the above publisher.

ISBN 0 301 00302 5

Printed in Great Britain by RAP, Clock Street
Hollinwood, Oldham, OL9 7LY

For Bobbie

Contents

Foreword by Edward Royle		1
Preface and Acknowledgements		3
Chapter 1	The Gathering of the Infidels	5
Chapter 2	The Blasphemy Depot	32
Chapter 3	War and Change	74
Chapter 4	Change and War	103
Chapter 5	The Humanist Labyrinth	136
Chapter 6	A Voice in the Wilderness	170
Chapter 7	Rationalism, Humanism, and the Retreat from Spencer	201
Chapter 8	Eupraxophy in Action	234
Epilogue	The Summing Up	266

Appendices

1:	Works Published by Watts & Co since 1890	268
2:	Honorary Associates	320
3:	Office Holders	326
4:	Books or Issues Featured as Supplements of the *Literary Guide*, 1893-1907	328
5:	Topics and Speakers at Rationalist Press Association conferences, 1945-2001	330

Endnotes	335
Bibliography	354
Index	367

Foreword

One day a half-educated youth was visiting his aunt and uncle, first generation primary school teachers with a reputation for being 'on the left'. Like many in their situation, growing into maturity after the Great War, they supported the Labour Party, trespassed on Kinder Scout and – to compound their lack of orthodoxy – married at Cross Street Unitarian Chapel in Manchester. And theirs was a house with books. The youth recalls seeing neatly arranged on one long shelf a row of small, evenly-sized, yellowish-orange volumes with black lettering and the black outline of Rodin's Thinker towards the bottom of the spine. In this way I first met the Thinker's Library, and its publisher, Watts & Co. for the Rationalist Press Association.

Many years later, when that same aunt pointed me in the direction of Holyoake House at the Co-operative Union in Manchester where I began my research of British freethought, I met the Rationalist Press Association again, this time through my work on its first Chairman, George Jacob Holyoake. Over the next few years, as my researches deepened and became more extensive, I found my way to Islington High Street with its library, extensive run of back numbers of the *Agnostic Annual* and the *Literary Guide*, and the generous supportive scholarship of Nicolas Walter. The history of the RPA was badly served. True, David Tribe had included a few references to it and provided the context in his *100 Years of Freethought* (1967) and Susan Budd had devoted two sections of her thesis to the Rationalists and the RPA, published in 1977 in *Varieties of Unbelief*. This was at that date the only treatment of the subject to be written out-of-house, and the fullest since Adam Gowans Whyte's little jubilee volume, *The Story of the RPA* (1949). Despite being a founder of the RPA, and later vice-Chairman and Literary Adviser, Whyte modestly did not get into his own index, nor into Susan Budd's, though he took his rightful place in the best early history, F.J. Gould's *The Pioneers of Johnson's Court* (1929). This latter, though, was little more than a series of excellent short pen and photographic portraits of the men who made the RPA the successful publishing concern it had become by 1929.

Begun in 1890 as the Propagandist Press Committee, the concern evolved into the Rationalist Press Committee and then, in 1899, the Rationalist Press Association. The driving force behind this venture was Charles Albert Watts, publishing heir to a tradition which had begun in the early years of the nineteenth century with Richard Carlile, James Watson, G.J. and Austin Holyoake and then his father, Charles Watts. Unlike the others, Charles Albert was a publisher, not a writer, though his impact was such that the British Library has catalogued all the father's works under the son's name. The RPA was an innovation of the greatest importance for the history of publishing, pioneering where Victor Gollancz's Left Book Club and Penguin Books were to follow in the inter-war years: it was a book club and it published serious books at unheard-of low prices. Watts had a good sense of the market, but even he must have been surprised by the volume which enabled the RPA to make an early impact of enormous proportions, the publication of Joseph McCabe's translation of Ernst Haeckel's *The Riddle of the Universe* (1900). This set the Association on an upward path which lasted until the Great War but which proved difficult to sustain thereafter as other publishers offered the sincerest form of flattery.

That story is now told for the first time in Bill Cooke's work. His aim is to set out the achievements and the ideas of the RPA, but he does not shy away from the difficulties and the controversies, and he is no respecter of persons. Few of the leading figures of the Association lacked feet of clay, which are unblushingly exposed. Rationalists should desire no other. 'The Association,' states Susan Budd (p.125) 'has not acted as a social movement with a distinctive set of ideas and aims but as an organization which tries to increase the influence of a certain way of looking at the world by presenting a body of information from which, it is believed, certain conclusions will inescapably emerge.' Readers of the present work will find this amply exemplified: rationalism is a method of travel, not a fixed destination, and all manner of men and women have chosen to travel together in the RPA over the past hundred years. Though the future may now appear uncertain and the destination obscure, the mode of travel is still intact and remains the one that best guarantees the onward journey in safety, despite the dark clouds of unreason which still hang overhead.

That this centenary volume is a little late may be due to Nicolas Walter's habit of breaking off from the major task which should have been in hand to pen another letter to the press, exposing some public stupidity and driving home the message of reason in the world of folly, but thanks to Bill Cooke we can now have both the memory of those sharp epistolary exchanges and a history of the RPA. Nicolas's letters are seen in this history as his greatest achievement. What they meant to him and the Association can be summed up in a query he sent me shortly before he died. He asked me to identify the following quotation:

> But words are things, and a small drop of ink,
> Falling like dew, upon a thought, produces
> That which makes thousands, perhaps millions, think.

The answer, which he may never have received, is George Gordon, Lord Byron. These words of wisdom may serve as a summary of the work not only of Nicolas Walter but of all his contemporaries and predecessors, pioneers of Johnson's Court, Islington High Street and Theobald's Road, for whose history now read on.

Edward Royle
York, December 2002

Preface

This book began with a death. It was originally to have been written by Nicolas Walter, who will figure prominently before this book is done. Sadly, Walter had hardly begun the book when he died in March 2000. All he had managed to complete by the time of his death was a couple of articles outlining the history of the RPA for the *New Humanist* and a few pages of notes.

The writing of this history seemed too important to be left undone, however, so I wrote to the RPA a couple of months after Walter's death and offered to take the project over. Having recently completed an intellectual biography of Joseph McCabe, a long-standing RPA activist and author, this history seemed the logical next step for me. That writing a history of a London-based organisation is possible when living at the other end of the world is testimony to the RPA's tremendous influence. The New Zealand Association of Rationalists & Humanists, one of the RPA's most successful satellite organisations, has a substantial and well organised collection of RPA material, which was used extensively for this book.

At the beginning of 2001 the RPA funded a research trip to London where I was given unrestricted access to all its archives. Minutes for the organisation go back to 1934, although there are some disconcerting gaps in the middle of the 1960s and again between 1973 and 1986. The situation is less promising with regards to correspondence. Very little from before the 1950s has survived, although what has survived is of first-rate interest and importance. A great deal of the early RPA material was destroyed by a fire in London in 1944. The library of Charles Watts, the RPA's founder, was also destroyed in this fire and it is possible that that is where the early minutes met their demise. Frequent moves, often to smaller premises, account for the loss of much of the other material the historian might have counted on. The RPA had not long moved their archive from Islington to Conway Hall when I arrived in January 2001, and was also in need of some work.

Acknowledgements

During my research visit to London I was able to more or less squat at the combined library of the RPA and South Place Ethical Society (SPES) at Conway Hall. As well as paying for my fare to Britain, the RPA took the trouble to provide me with comfortable and convenient accommodation. Jim Herrick, *New Humanist* editor, John Metcalf, Company Secretary and Dr Shirley Dent, Assistant Editor, all went out of their way to help and make my stay as productive and enjoyable as possible. The office-holders of SPES even took pity of my crouching over a small laptop and sped up their timetable for purchasing a computer for the library, which I then used for the duration of my visit. They were also very generous with their time and with their photocopier, which got a bit of a thrashing. They even took me out to dinner.

Manukau Institute of Technology, where I worked as Senior Lecturer at the School of Visual Arts, was also generous in providing me with some financial assistance and a laptop computer for my research trip, for which I am grateful.

I conducted interviews with three past and current chairmen of the Board of Directors. Antony Chapman, David Pollock and Ivor Russell all went out of their way to find time to speak to me. David Pollock went further and provided me with substantial information from his own records that were absent in the RPA archives. He continued to provide significant assistance and criticism for many months after my return to New Zealand. Professor G A Wells took time and trouble to answer a very lengthy letter I wrote to him. Regrettably, Christopher Macy, editor of the *New Humanist* between 1971 and 1975, decided not to participate in this exercise until it was too late. An unexpected bonus was the support of Mary Vidal, widow of Hector Hawton, a very prominent RPA office holder from the 1940s to 1970s. Mrs Vidal read over relevant chapters and undertook some time-consuming research despite only recently having recovered from an operation.

The final manuscript was read very thoroughly by David Tribe and David Ross. David Tribe is author of *100 Years of Freethought, President Charles Bradlaugh, MP, Nucleoethics* and a large number of smaller publications and articles on aspects of freethought history. David Ross is Treasurer of the New Zealand Association of Rationalists and Humanists and editor of that association's monthly newsletter. Both men are hugely well read in freethought history and have a superb understanding of English grammar. Much of the readability of this manuscript is due to them. I am also grateful to Professor Emeritus Kenneth Maddock for some timely and relevant advice on matters related to anthropological questions as they appear in this book.

While in London, George Leslie was most generous in providing me with some rare nineteenth-century rationalist material. I assured him that they would indeed be going to a good home. Wayne Facer, a New Zealander then in London, also made a point to find me at Conway Hall and give me some relevant material. I have received valuable assistance from Nigel Sinnott and Dr Ralph Biddington, both historians of freethought based in Melbourne, Australia. I am also grateful to Tim Binga of the Center of Inquiry Library in Buffalo, New York, and Norman Bacrac, editor of the *Ethical Record*, the journal of the South Place Ethical Society for assistance in compiling Appendix One.

As usual, none of these people, or the RPA, is responsible for the opinions expressed in this book. They are my responsibility.

Bill Cooke
Buffalo, March 2003

Chapter 1

The Gathering of the Infidels

'The lecturer wins his thousands, the writer his tens of thousands.'
F J Gould, 1889

The freethought movement around the world can boast some of the longest-standing organisations and publications, some of the most interesting personalities, and some of the most fascinating tales of the modern era. But, for a variety of reasons, little mention is made of them. Even where another story would be enriched by recounting its dealings with the movement, even if the story is to the disadvantage of the freethought movement, a cone of silence hangs over freethought history. There are few more telling examples of this than the Rationalist Press Association, for the RPA has the added disadvantage of beginning its story when most studies of nineteenth century freethought are coming to an end. Most histories of freethought activity in Britain focus on the 1860s to the 1880s; the years when George Jacob Holyoake and Charles Bradlaugh were active. The 1890s and 1900s are often covered hastily as an epilogue to those stirring times. The following summary is typical: 'By the turn of the century the Secularists had already dwindled and divided. The Rationalist Press Association survived, but as a pioneer book club, not as an active Freethinking society. The Positivists had virtually disappeared.'(1)

But the Rationalist Press Association has done so much more than merely survive. The RPA cannot simply be dismissed as an epilogue to the study of nineteenth century freethought. The fact that this history is being written after a hundred years of activity is sufficient proof of that. It is true, however, that the RPA involved a change in direction from earlier freethought organisations. Two new directions in fact. On the one hand the RPA was designed to be a mass impact organisation without necessarily being a mass membership organisation. And on the other, it popularised the term 'rationalism' into the movement. We shall follow both those developments in this chapter.

But of course the RPA did not arise in a vacuum. What were the intellectual conditions of the time? Through the course of the nineteenth century Britain changed almost out of recognition, with the churches feeling the sharp edge of these changes. Toward the end of his life, J M Robertson (1856-1933), one of the freethought movement's most accomplished historians, concluded that 'in the course of a century, a religion which had confidently been founded on Revelation…transmuted, for comparatively instructed people, in this and other countries, into a religion stripped of these foundations and formulas.' (2) In the wake of this doctrinal confusion, Robertson concluded that the churches had come to emphasise their role as social organisations in their efforts to retain their congregations.

For a while it was fashionable to deride freethought historians as somehow outmoded in their methodology and reasoning. This attitude partially explains why freethought history has been so scandalously neglected. Owen Chadwick, in his celebrated work, *The Secularisation of the European Mind in the 19th Century*, is a typical example. Chadwick dismisses Robertson and others like him as 'old-fashioned', mainly for their alleged want of a sociological perspective. (3) Chadwick is scornful of those who claim 'reason' is the cause of secularisation. He seems little bothered that Robertson made no such claim. Showing an admirable sociological perspective, Robertson finished his work with a warning for his readers: 'For this survey has taught us, if anything, that history, like science, is a perpetual reconstruction, and that what may rationally be regarded as a true summary at any period is the outcome of the whole intellectual effort of the age.'(4) Robertson's final words are a warning that rationalists are no less prone to error or free from the need for revision and criticism than anyone else.

As against this awareness of sociological and historical perspective, Chadwick finishes his book with a piece of theological rhetoric. Was it a bigger act of faith in 1900 than in 1800, he asks, 'to trust that all the hairs of your head were numbered, and that not a sparrow shall fall to the ground without a purpose? For all the shipwrecks and railway accidents, for all the natural selection or Marxist theory, it is not certain that the answer to that question is in the affirmative.'(5) Chadwick is straining to ignore that it *was* in fact much harder for tens of thousands of people to believe such things as acts of faith in 1900 that it had been in 1800. As Chadwick himself conceded: 'The Victorian father goes to church. The Edwardian son stays at home.'(6) Even more galling for religious conservatives like Chadwick is that many of those Edwardian sons (and, worse still, daughters) read rationalist material while they stayed at home. It is not a simple question of reason having won the day; no rationalist scholar has ever suggested that. It had more to do with traditional supernaturalist interpretations of events no longer being credible. The naturalist interpretations offered by rationalist scholars were found by intelligent readers to be more convincing than dogmatic and supernaturalist formulae. And it's important to bear in mind that rationalists were by no means all outside the church. Given all this, it is Chadwick's work which appears outdated rather than Robertson's. Moreover, it is Chadwick's criticisms which are out of date, rather than Robertson's, as we will see in Chapter Three.

Even the enemies of rationalism felt obliged to recognise its successes. John F Hurst, DD, wrote a long attack on rationalism, which he saw as a pernicious attack on the church from within. When Hurst was writing (1867) rationalists were generally understood to refer to reformist theologians and Higher Criticism scholars – Christians to a man. Hurst began his book challenging 'Deism, and even Atheism itself, to furnish proof of a more malignant antipathy to some of the cardinal doctrines of the common faith of Christendom than Rationalism has produced in certain of its exponents, and which we will strive to expose in future pages of this book.'(7) Yet even Hurst had, at the end of his book, to acknowledge that 'The most critical and accurate of the Rationalists have, in almost every case, told us some truth which the professed friends of the Church might have been compelled to seek for centuries without success.'(8) So while Chadwick may well think that simple supernaturalistic faith was just as credible in 1900 as in 1800, Christian scholars of the time seemed not to think so.

It is beyond the task of this work to trace the main movements of nineteenth century secularisation. But we need to recall a few significant developments in order to appreciate the conditions in which the RPA arose. For the Church of England, the nineteenth century was a testing time. In his otherwise devout history of the Anglicans, Stephen Neill acknowledged that so much about the nineteenth-century Church of England 'was indefensible that complacency was impossible.' (9) In the face of protracted opposition from religious conservatives, a Commission of Inquiry into church revenues and abuses was appointed in 1831, which led to the creation of a permanent Ecclesiastical Commission to deal with abuses and inequalities in endowments and income. Far more serious still, it became apparent after a count of attendance of religious worship was taken in 1851 that the churches were in trouble. Even a historian as well disposed to the Church as P T Marsh was compelled to describe the census as a 'jolting disappointment' to the Established Church. (10) Of the 7,261,032 who attended a religious service, fully 3,177,208 of them were attending service in a chapel of one the many Nonconformist denominations. This was an impressive figure, given the long history of petty discriminations and social condescension Nonconformism had suffered in Britain.

But once that shock had passed, an even more dreadful realisation came over those who studied the figures. Where were the 5,288,294 people who could not be accounted for at any place of worship? The poor of Britain had been drifting to the cities for decades, but church construction and the realigning of ecclesiastical boundaries had not kept pace with the changes. But more important even than that: the Christian message was losing its hold. Religious leaders were shocked to find that a very large section of the urban poor of England were not attending church at all. They had to face the prospect that, in Marsh's words, 'England was not even a Christian let alone Anglican country.'(11) It was those non-churched urban poor who became the backbone of the various secularist and freethought organisations around Britain in the second half of the nineteenth century.

The churches were also giving ground in the battle of ideas. In the second half of the nineteenth century, the Church was in disarray in several important areas. The publication of *Essays and Reviews* in 1860 rivalled Darwin's *Origin of Species* the year previously for the level of controversial heat generated. *Essays and Reviews* was a series of seven essays, all by capable theologians and churchmen. Each contributor was accountable for his own work only. The unsigned note to the reader advised that:

> The Volume, it is hoped, will be received as an attempt to illustrate the advantage derivable to the cause of religious and moral truth, from a free handling, in a becoming spirit, of subjects peculiarly liable to suffer by the repetition of conventional language, and from traditional methods of treatment. (12)

Here were some of the rationalists against whom John Hurst raged. How people responded to that claim and to the essays written in that spirit has helped determine the chasm between religious liberals and traditionalists that remains a central feature of most Christian churches to this day. The book was condemned by Convocation and no fewer than eleven thousand clergymen signed a declaration of loyalty to all the old dogmas. The authors were branded the 'Seven against Christ'. A second declaration, inspired by two senior churchmen and aiming to defend free inquiry, was never published as it failed to gather adequate support. (13) Frederick Temple, one of the essayists, was later subjected to a torrid campaign against his ordination as Bishop of Exeter, which reached the Judicial Committee of the Privy Council. Two other contributors were initially found guilty of heresy, and only later acquitted on appeal to the same Judicial Committee of the Privy Council. Neither was this the only example of persecution of learning. In 1877 the General Assembly of the Free Church in Scotland voted by a large majority to deprive William Robertson Smith (1846-1894) of his chair at Aberdeen University for making public the latest findings of German higher criticism. Not content with that, he was then hounded by a series of libel charges; libel in this context meaning publishing material detrimental to established Christian dogma. (14)

The painful struggle of the churches in the nineteenth century was not limited to disputes among academics. One disturbance, over the level of ritual appropriate in a Church of England service, had to go to parliament for resolution. The Public Worship Regulation Act of 1874 failed to crush the ritualists within the church's ranks, despite the provision in the Act for imprisoning clergymen who conducted services with unseemly popish flair. The Church had also failed to prevent the atheist Charles Bradlaugh taking his seat in parliament. Bradlaugh (1833-1891) was a brilliant speaker and campaigner for freethought who, by the middle 1860s had become Britain's leading atheist. Bradlaugh's work, and the more general publication of scientific and other developments, were diverting people's attention to new and more interesting fields. Each new development in science and biblical criticism undermined an important point of church doctrine and belief. In nearly every case, the churches first adopted a stance of obscurantist opposition, only later on to make some accommodation with the ever-growing pile of evidence for the new viewpoint. The extended argument over evolution was only the most prominent of these debates from which the churches emerged badly scarred. The Church of England, in fact, had only retained its status as the established religion of the nation because fewer people cared enough to devote their time to the issue. (15)

Even when the churches attempted a counterattack, things often did not go as planned. In 1871 the Christian Evidence Society instigated a series of lectures to address several issues where opinion seemed to be moving away from church orthodoxy. Senior churchmen delivered lectures on evolution, science and materialism and related questions, but were replied to by a series of tracts from someone going by the name of 'Julian'. There was at the time a lot of speculation as to who 'Julian' was, but it was clear that he was a knowledgeable man. 'Julian' also contributed a series of articles for the *Agnostic Annual*. Long after his death, it was revealed that 'Julian' was Dr Ebenezer Cobham Brewer (1810-1897), sceptical churchman and compiler of a number of popular reference works, the best known being his *Dictionary of Phrase and Fable*, which is still in print. (16) The Rationalist Press Committee printed several 'Julian' pamphlets. The quality of the 'Julian' replies and the speculation as to his identity completely overshadowed the Christian Evidence Society tracts and lectures. The church, it seemed, could not act as a united voice, let alone vanquish the voices of the infidels.

Despite this, efforts continued to be made. In response to the success of freethought publications among the working people, the Society for the Promotion of Christian Knowledge (SPCK) felt the need to widen its activities to include the refuting of freethought tracts. In 1870, the SPCK established a Christian Evidence Committee and provided it with a generous budget. Over the next few years the committee was quite successful, producing 28 publications, 19 of them being cheap tracts for non-specialist readers. But it soon ran into trouble with its own reactionaries. In 1877 the committee published a work by the Rev. Brownlow Maitland called *The Argument from Prophecy*, which sought to salvage aspects of the popular argument that Old Testament prophecies served as proof for the New Testament's authenticity. This argument had been decisively undermined by Biblical criticism, and Brownlow's book angered many of his co-religionists by conceding too much of the argument. After this, the Christian Evidence Committee was neutered and little effective work came from that source.

The war of words

In the same year that the spirit of censorship got the better of the SPCK, Charles Bradlaugh and Annie Besant (1847-1933) began a publishing venture of their own. The Freethought Publishing Company was set up originally with the purpose of ensuring the birth control tract *The Fruits of Philosophy* continued to be published. Originally published in the United States in 1832, this work by an American physician, Charles Knowlton (1800-1850) had already enjoyed a long and controversial career. The robust sales of *The Fruits of Philosophy* was a welcome boost to the hitherto modestly funded Freethought Publishing Company. On the strength of those sales, it went on to publish Annie Besant's *My Path to Atheism* (1877) a collection of Bradlaugh's works, and an imposing series called the International Library of Science and Freethought. Included in this series were Ludwig Büchner's *Mind in Animals*, Ernst Haeckel's *The Pedigree of Man and Other Essays*, and *The Student's Darwin*, by Edward Aveling. Only in 1890, after his partnership with Annie Besant had dissolved and with his own health clearly failing, did Bradlaugh divest himself of the Freethought Publishing Company. Bradlaugh's paper, the *National Reformer*, continued operating until 1893, two years after his death.

Unnoticed amid the glare of Bradlaugh's career, Charles Watts (1836-1906), the son of a Wesleyan cobbler, was also involving himself in the difficult world of freethought printing and publishing. Born and raised in Bristol, Watts became a freethinker after hearing the colourful freethought orator Charles Southwell (1814-1860). Once in London, Watts took employment with the firm that printed Bradlaugh's material, run by Austin Holyoake (1826-1874), younger brother of the veteran secularist George Jacob Holyoake (1817-1906). After a while he was working on the *National Reformer*, a paper Bradlaugh had controlled since 1862, until the two men had a major disagreement over the merits of publishing

Knowlton's *The Fruits of Philosophy*. Bradlaugh and his new-found comrade Annie Besant, were keen to continue the publication of the pamphlet. Walter Arnstein, the historian of the Knowlton trial, has observed that there was little incentive for Bradlaugh to publish a profoundly controversial tract, particularly at a time when he was trying to get into parliament. So why did they publish it? Arnstein's conclusion will doubtless be mocked by postmodernists and others who sneer at principle being offered as a reason for an action. The fact remains that Bradlaugh and Besant published Knowlton's work because they were committed to the principle of freedom of expression, notwithstanding the potential damage to their careers. (17) Watts, on the other hand, felt it was not worth jeopardising Bradlaugh's or his own future in printing such a tract. As the printer of the tract, Watts was the person in the line of fire, and he pleaded guilty to printing an obscene work. Bradlaugh and Besant were furious and resolved to publish the work themselves, in defiance of the law. This resulted in their trial, which became a significant milestone in nineteenth-century British history. Bradlaugh never forgave Watts, considering him a coward. Watts, in turn, remained suspicious of what he interpreted as dogmatism and extremism for the remainder of his life.

The disagreement between Bradlaugh and Watts over their attitudes toward *The Fruits of Philosophy* goes to the heart of the division in the freethought movement around the world, then and now. People like Bradlaugh see their role relative to religion essentially as a combat role. Angered by the many errors in religious truth claims and motivated by injustices experienced at the hand of religious intolerance, they see their task as the elimination of error. But other people within the freethought movement have a different focus. They are more likely to appreciate the inclusive, nurturing elements in religion, and seek to recreate some of that spirit in the freethought movement, minus, of course, the dogmatism and error. Colin Campbell has posited these two types as abolitionists and substitutionists. (18) Bradlaugh and his followers had more of the features of the abolitionist strand in freethought. Charles Watts and his friends had more features of the substitutionist strand of the movement. Both are legitimate and honourable facets of international freethought, but relations between exponents of each of these strands have often been tense, as this history will recall.

The principal figure from the nineteenth century to represent the less combative, substitutionist strand of freethought was George Jacob Holyoake. Not surprisingly, Holyoake and Bradlaugh had an uneasy relationship. Holyoake never really came to terms with what he saw as Bradlaugh's brashness and aggressiveness. And Bradlaugh couldn't see beyond what he saw as Holyoake's willingness to loosen his principles so as to retain the esteem of his wealthy friends. Holyoake was opposed to secularism becoming associated with the controversial issue of birth control. Bradlaugh called himself an atheist, Holyoake disliked the term. This, too, was to have long-term consequences.

With these titanic struggles going on it is not to be wondered at that Watts's new venture attracted no publicity. On the premature death of Austin Holyoake in 1874, Watts took the firm over, changing the firm's name in 1880 to C Watts and later again to C A Watts & Co. The fledgling company remained at 17 Johnson's Court, the same cramped building off Fleet Street where Watts had begun work in his youth. As the Freethought Publishing Company was at its height, Watts &

Co had to struggle to remain solvent, so, not surprisingly, Watts turned to Bradlaugh's rivals for business. For ten or so years from its foundation in 1880, Watts & Co survived by printing the various works of William Stewart Ross (1844-1906), better known at the time by his pseudonym 'Saladin'. Ross was a bitter critic of Bradlaugh and strongly disliked the term 'atheist'.

Watts also took part in forming the British Secular Union, which was intended to rival Bradlaugh's National Secular Society. After the trial over *The Fruits of Philosophy*, there had been an attempt to limit Bradlaugh's power as president of the National Secular Society. It was unsuccessful and the losers of that struggle left to form the British Secular Union (BSU). The president of the BSU was the Marquis of Queensbury, whose place in history has since been guaranteed, thanks not to his advocacy of freethought, but to his harassment of Oscar Wilde and passion for boxing. In a little aside in the *Literary Guide* in 1887, Watts noted that the Marquis of Queensbury 'than whom Scotland possesses no more heroic or daring son' had offered to subscribe £3000 to Stanley's expedition into Africa, on the condition that he could join the party. (19) Stanley, it seemed, decided that travelling in darkest Africa with the Marquis was not worth £3000.

Marquis or no Marquis, the British Secular Union failed to take root. The Marquis was succeeded as president by Charles Watts, but when Watts left for Canada in 1884 the BSU quickly collapsed. Two years earlier, Watts had handed over his small publishing venture to his son. Charles Albert Watts (1858-1946) was only 24 years old when he took over the firm, but he was already a veteran in the trade, with twelve years' experience. He had been apprenticed aged twelve as a 'printer's devil' to Austin Holyoake at Johnson's Court. Young Charles Albert's apprenticeship was a severe one. He worked from 8.00am to 8.00pm five days a week and then from 8.00am to 6.00pm on Saturdays. Each week of his first year's apprenticeship the twelve year old was given a shilling as good-conduct money. Only in his second year did he actually receive a wage; six shillings a week rising by two shillings a week each year until the seven-year apprenticeship ended. Fortunately for young Charles Albert, Austin Holyoake was a kindly and skilled taskmaster. By the time he took the firm over Charles Albert was skilled in all aspects of the printer's trade. This was one of two most important differences between this small and underfunded freethought publishing firm and every other small and underfunded freethought publishing firm that had come and gone before it. Up until then freethought publishing ventures had simply been means by which freethought titans could ensure their works reached the public. Charles Albert Watts was not a titan, but unlike his predecessors, he understood intimately the processes, and the costs, of publishing as an industry. The second of the two principal differences between Watts's venture and every other freethought publishing venture was Watts's personality. He was, as we have said, not a titan of the Bradlaugh mould. But he had another personal strength, one which would prove invaluable to the continued prosperity of the RPA. Constance Dowman, longtime secretary and Director of the RPA, understood Watts perfectly when she described him as 'a very modest man who had the ability to gather around him many eminent people who had faith in his vision of what the RPA could achieve.' (20) Watts's intimate knowledge of the industry and his ability to inspire confidence and loyalty were the crucial factors for the initial success of the RPA.

Despite his father's difficulties, there is no record of young Charles Albert Watts inheriting any personal animosity toward Charles Bradlaugh, although J M Robertson, the first significant historian of nineteenth-century freethought, described Watts, correctly, as an 'inheritor of the Holyoake tradition'. (21) While it is true that Watts was an inheritor of the Holyoake tradition by inclination, it is also true that he worked with Charles Bradlaugh and his supporters for his entire life without conflict. While still a child, Watts was often sent as runner to Bradlaugh's lodgings in Turner Street, off Commercial Road in East London to hand the big man the proofs for the *National Reformer*. Watts recalled Bradlaugh 'invariably had cheery words for me, and...once ventured to prophesy that in the years to come I should work hand-in-hand with his son – a hope never realised.' (22) On Bradlaugh's death Watts wrote:

> Charles Bradlaugh was without a peer. He had faults - grievous ones. But his virtues were so transcendent, his personality so awe-inspiring, that posterity will lightly pass over, if it does not affect to be ignorant of, his foibles. The Freethought Party, especially, will be ungrudgingly grateful for his splendid and truly herculean labours on its behalf. It will be very difficult, if not impossible, to fill his place. (23)

And so it proved. But while he was generous to Bradlaugh's memory and followers, Watts was unequivocally of the tradition exemplified by Spencer, Holyoake and Huxley. These three men provided the philosophy, the terminology, the attitude to religion and the organisational emphases that built and sustained the RPA. Nowhere is this more clear than in his preference for the term 'agnostic'. The use of this term was liberating for freethinkers of Watts's stamp. Both theism and atheism were seen as two sides of the same coin. They both rested, so the agnostic account went, on unprovable and unverifiable declarations. The agnostic, by contrast, was seen as avoiding intellectual pretentiousness and tailoring one's belief to what one can actually know. One of Watts's first ventures was *The Agnostic Annual 1884* which included articles from a wide range of freethinkers of different stripes including T H Huxley, Ernst Haeckel, the leading German populariser of Darwinism, and Francis W Newman, Cardinal Newman's brother and a liberal theist.

It is one of the ironies of this history that Watts got on very well with Bradlaugh, whose emphases he did not share, and had a torrid time, originally at least, with T H Huxley (1825-1895), whose emphases he did share. In September 1883 Watts wrote to Huxley announcing the forthcoming *Agnostic Annual* and asked Huxley for a statement on agnosticism. Watts was nothing if not polite. 'I make so bold as to appeal to you for your generous advice and assistance because I am convinced that you are desirous of guiding and influencing the thought of the nation, to which you have already rendered such incalculable service.' (24) Huxley wrote back and Watts duly featured his account in the *Annual*. To Watts's great pleasure, the *Annual* quickly sold out and he then wrote to Huxley once more asking to 'amplify your brief remarks' for a second printing being planned.

One can imagine Watts's shock when Huxley wrote back a month later complaining of his letter being included in the *Annual*. Watts's reply was almost obsequious, so anxious was he to mollify the great man. It hadn't occurred to Watts that Huxley would not realise that the correspondence was due to be published. While he hadn't specifically said it was meant for publication, Watts could be forgiven for thinking that his referring to influencing the thought of the nation could only mean that it was to be published. Huxley remained unmollified and sent a series of rude letters to Watts and a letter to the press complaining of his treatment at Watts's hands. This was too much for Watts, who now lost his temper.

> Up to this time I have treated you with all deference and delicacy...Your most insulting and discourteous letter of yesterday, however, shows me that you have mistaken politeness for weakness, and forbearance for an admission of wrong-doing on my part, and has impelled me, in justification of my conduct, to take a far other course than that which at first, out of deference to you, I was disposed to take. (25)

Watts then published a second edition of the *Agnostic Annual* and included the correspondence between the two. Watts felt strongly that Huxley had misrepresented the facts of the case in his public letter on the matter and had brought the reputation of freethinkers into disrepute.

Every historian who has written of this affair has accepted Huxley's account of it. The best-known recent example of this can be found in Adrian Desmond's otherwise superbly researched intellectual biography of Huxley. After a few sentences placing Watts in context, Desmond portrays Watts & Co as seeking to 'trade on agnosticism's respectability', promising their readers 'intellectual upward mobility' by virtue of agnosticism's ability to penetrate the Establishment. But in the very next sentence, Desmond completely undermines this sanguine picture by accusing Watts of questionable street ethics. 'Piracy was still part of street publishing: Watts canvassed Huxley's views and coolly printed his reply without leave in the first *Agnostic Annual* in November 1883.' (26) In his notes on this affair, Desmond speaks of Watts 'still using Huxley's name to catch writers of Karl Pearson's calibre.' (27) Desmond's analysis of this episode is inaccurate and unfair. If Watts was so keen for respectability and the approval of middle class readers (which he was) it seems extraordinary that he should stoop to the very practices which were calculated to bring the movement into disrepute with the same people. And if Watts was shamelessly trading on Huxley's name ten years after this, why did Huxley give the RPA rights over his work *Possibilities and Impossibilities?* And if Watts had behaved so badly, why did Huxley's widow and son both go out of their way to further the RPA's cause in the years to come, as we shall see in the next chapter? Furthermore, if Watts was that keen to trade on the respectability of Huxley's term 'agnosticism', it seems odd that he should be party to rejecting the term agnostic in favour of 'rationalist' when he came to found the RPA. Desmond's errors here are the simple result of not studying Watts's side of the affair sufficiently closely. Were historians to recognise the value of the RPA as an historical resource, these sorts of errors would be avoided.

The difficulty Watts had in persuading the rich and famous to participate in the *Agnostic Annual* and other publishing activities is symptomatic of his lowly social standing. And the fuss Huxley made did nothing to make life easier for Watts. That Watts succeeded in attracting quite widespread support is because people warmed to him and trusted his judgment. Given Watts's social disadvantages, his achievement is all the more outstanding. The *Agnostic Annual* was to become the *RPA Annual*, then the *Rationalist Annual*, and then *Question*. It appeared without a break from 1884 until 1980 and included some of the greatest intellects of the century of its existence.

Watts was determined to raise the general profile of agnosticism and viewed the *Annual* as the best medium through which this could be done. Introducing the symposium on agnosticism in the very first *Annual*, Watts had this to say:

> Agnosticism, while opposed to both Atheism and Theism, comprises within its teachings the essence of every liberal system, and, by recognising and utilising the good in the various dominant religions, it facilitates and renders easier the transition from mental darkness to intellectual light. (28)

The following year Watts began two more publications, both monthlies. The flagship of the two was *The Agnostic*, which aimed to become the leading mouthpiece for the secularist-agnostic wing of British freethought. But it was not to be – *The Agnostic* was born in January of 1885 and died in December of the same year. Part of the problem had been an objection from William Stewart Ross, Watts's irascible ally. Ross objected that *The Agnostic* looked very much like a rival publication to his own *Secular Review*. So in December 1885 Watts succumbed to what he later called Ross's 'imperious objections' and closed *The Agnostic* down. (29) But a month earlier Watts had begun a more modest publication that couldn't be said to rival Ross's publication, or anyone else's. *Watts's Literary Guide* was an eight-page factsheet-cum-advertising leaflet with the simple task of announcing and reviewing new freethought works, most of which were Watts & Co's own publications. The *Guide* also gave comprehensive summaries of books by leading thinkers, for those who could not afford to buy them. It even promised to keep readers up with the latest literary gossip.

Watts's Literary Guide achieved a degree of success. Like the other freethought journals, it ran articles of interest to a variety of heterodox opinion, but it was less shrill than many of its predecessors and rivals. But the point of difference in Watts's enterprise was his notices and reviews of publications of interest to freethinkers. It is difficult to appreciate in an era of globalisation and information overload quite how closed and restricted this information was. Respectable journals steered clear of drawing attention to freethought works for fear of attracting clerical condemnation, a frequently-resorted-to weapon. Even journals sympathetic to aspects of freethought preferred the discussion to be reserved for middle class readers, who, it was thought, could handle the consequences of the loss of religious faith better than the lower orders. Watts frequently complained of periodicals refusing to place his advertisements. One journal refused to run an advertisement for Watts's anthology called *Why Live a Moral Life?* on the grounds that it would serve as an invitation to immorality! (30)

Watts's Literary Guide bridged this gap. Convinced freethinkers could read it with pleasure, while respectable men and women, people with reputations to lose, could also be kept informed about the latest rationalist publications without being exposed to vulgar criticism. It was in this area of keeping readers informed that

Watts's Literary Guide was innovative. Beginning in 1893, a supplement to the journal was added which gave an outline of a work thought to be of interest to the readers. Any of these works would have been priced beyond the range of the poorer readers, while the wealthier readers could use the supplements as a guide to purchasing, much as review journals do now. The supplements were lengthy summaries and analyses of a new book or, less frequently, a topical issue relevant to freethought. For instance, in July 1897, F J Gould outlined the plan for moral instruction which had got him in such trouble with the Christian education authorities. The last of the supplements, written by Constance Plumptre, appeared in the October 1907 issue of the *Guide* and surveyed the attitudes of prominent authors of the day toward women. A full list of the topics treated in this way appears in Appendix Four. It reveals an interesting chronicle of rationalist priorities. By the time the last supplement appeared in October 1907, the RPA had come up with an even more innovative way of getting quality material to poorer readers.

But Watts was more than aware of the limitations to the growth he could achieve on his own resources alone. Despite having found for himself a sustainable niche, Watts saw that any growth of his venture would be fatally circumscribed by lack of money. His firm had an extensive stock of books and pamphlets on various aspects of freethought on its lists, but he could see that a lot more could be done. So, in November 1889 he ran an advertisement in *Watts's Literary Guide* announcing a Propagandist Press Fund and called for donations. Watts obviously had been made aware of the existence of willing donors; all that was needed was the mechanism for the donors to give their money in confidence.

> What is needed is organisation of the forces of liberal thought. We have intellect on our side, and we have money, if it be properly sought. At present well-to-do members of the Party are perplexed how best to help the movement, and with security that their endowment shall be strictly used in accordance with their wishes. (31)

Under the discriminatory law of Victorian England, bequests could not be given to organisations opposed to Christianity, or for anti-Christian purposes without fear of their being set aside. The only safe avenue was to bequeath the money directly to the individual, which, understandably, donors were reluctant to do. Watts's solution was the creation of a Propagandist Press Fund. It would be the purpose of such a committee to:

> direct and supervise all expenditure, and…render a detailed account of its labours. For many years our work will be mainly in the direction of disseminating literature, and it is work which is always most remunerative and most permanent in its results. There is no blinking the fact that the conductors of the movement, probably because they are such, are without worldly riches, and often their struggles to continue the propaganda to which they have consecrated their lives are truly pitiable and disheartening. Their self-respect forbids begging, and yet without money they are comparatively impotent. Authors sometimes expect - and rightly - to be remunerated; the printer and paper-maker will be paid; and advertising needs capital. With a good fund to meet this initial outlay, our publications would ultimately be

made to pay for their production, and thus a tremendous impetus would be given to liberal thought. Who will be the first to start the Propagandist Press Fund? (32)

Ninety per cent of such appeals are stillborn, either because the readers don't have the money to donate to the cause, no matter how worthy, or else they don't have sufficient confidence that the people running the advertisement would use the money wisely. Even Watts's first attempt, an Agnostic Press Fund in 1885, had not been a success. But now, having gathered together a reliable and trustworthy band of colleagues, and having proved his competence and honesty, wealthy acquaintances were prepared to put money forward for his venture.

The response was encouraging, as Watts must have known it was going to be. The first of the letters he reproduced in the following issue was from his friend, F J Gould, who supported the idea. 'Many will read a pamphlet who would never dream of visiting a Secular Hall. At the quiet fireside, arguments strike home which might be dissipated by the excitement of a public debate. The lecturer wins his thousands, the writer his tens of thousands.' (33) Most of the letters coming in were accompanied by donations, usually of about ten pounds.

By June 1890 the fund reached £121 and Watts decided it was time to bring together a committee of people to administer it. The following month, July 2 1890, three of Watts's friends joined him in his cramped offices at 17 Johnson's Court, just off Fleet Street, and established the Propagandist Press Committee. The aim of the committee was 'to assist in securing the amendment of the law which sanctions the confiscation of property left for anti-theological purposes, and to promote the issuing, advertising, and circulation of publications devoted to Freethought and Advanced Religious Reform'. (34) It is important to appreciate, more than a century later, that the Propagandist Press Committee was originally established to secure a change in the law regarding bequests and only after that was it devoted to the publication of freethought works. One of the PPC's first actions was to establish the Liberty of Bequest Committee. While this committee did not last long, its activists campaigned unceasingly, and in the end, successfully, to change this discriminatory legislation.

It is important to have some understanding of the people Watts gathered around him if we are to appreciate the flavour of this distinctly unpropitious venture. We must start by mentioning a person who was not at the first meeting. George Jacob Holyoake was asked by Watts to chair the Propagandist Press Committee. Holyoake agreed but was prevented from attending by illness. This was yet another of a large number of committees devoted to some aspect of freethought that Holyoake had been involved in over a career spanning six decades. But the choice of Holyoake was deliberate. As the most respected rival of Bradlaugh in the freethought movement, Holyoake was essential to providing the committee with the gravitas Watts knew it needed. And Holyoake represented the style of freethought Watts and his colleagues most admired.

Holyoake began his adult life as a disciple of Robert Owen (1771-1858). While on Owenite duty in Cheltenham in 1842, he was arrested for blasphemy and spent six months in prison. Blasphemy in 1842 amounted to an off-hand remark about the Deity being put on half-pay while so many of his creatures on earth were so afflicted. Holyoake was to spend the rest of his life in the service of various reformist causes. When Watts asked him to chair the Propagandist Press Committee, Holyoake was a veteran of the long and successful campaign to build up an effective co-operative movement which could permit the working classes to improve their position on the strength of their own limited resources. Holyoake was also the creator of the secularist movement, the record of which was less successful. As we have already noted, there had been a plethora of secularist organisations, causes and crises, but by the end of the 1880s the movement had largely petered out. Much of the original battle had been won, and many secularists had moved on to the socialist movement, to fight what many saw as the battle of the future – that between capital and labour. Joseph McCabe, Holyoake's biographer, described Holyoake's position in 1890 in these terms:

> The hundred interests in secular causes that he had once thought to bind up in one organisation were now entrusted to a hundred intent and specialist bodies. The one thing that remained was the criticism of what he believed to be erroneous religious traditions, in a broad, cultured, refined way, and with a care to impart positive education while older views were being modified or removed. (35)

This was why Holyoake was asked to chair the Propagandist Press Committee's meetings, and why he accepted. Holyoake was the oldest of the originators of the PPC, but of the people who were actually at the first meeting, the oldest was in fact Richard Bithell (1821-1902). Aged 69 when the PPC first met, Bithell was seen by his younger colleagues as venerable and genial. He had written two books exploring aspects of agnosticism, in 1883 and again in 1887. The eldest of eleven children (of whom four died in childhood), Bithell was not sufficiently robust to follow his father's occupation as blacksmith. Fortunately for him, he qualified for assistance to be given an education, which went on to levels his father must have wondered about. Bithell eventually earned a doctorate from study at Göttingen and London Universities and from 1865 worked in the Rothschild Bank. His was a reverent agnosticism. Bithell was opposed only to the theology of the Christian Church, in all other respects he spoke and thought in theological terms. Bithell continued to be closely involved in church affairs, despite having abandoned Christian theology. He took the cause of agnosticism seriously. Men of science, Bithell wrote in 1883,

> know also that the truly devout man of science worships a greater, more awful and withal more beneficent Deity than the self-satisfied formalist or the illiterate devotee could ever form a conception of; and it is their constant aim to make their disciples see that there is no possible way of getting to know more of that great Being, the unknown Cause of all things, but by studying the manner in which He reveals and manifests Himself. Whether these manifestations are called the ways of Providence, or the Laws of Nature, or the phenomena of the Universe, is a matter of small importance. (36)

It is a testimony to the changes forced upon the churches that, a century later, this could have been written by an archbishop or a New Ager. Bithell outdid Holyoake in his dislike for atheism; in fact Bithell's strongest words were reserved for atheism, which he described as 'as repugnant to the sentiments of the true Agnostic as are any of the false certitudes embodied in the professions of religious sects.' (37) His hostility toward the radicals within the wider Freethought movement was also behind his work in establishing the RPA. In an article in 1897, Bithell asked the question 'why do prominent freethinkers remain aloof from taking part actively in Rationalist organisations?' His answer was clear. In a thinly veiled attack on *The Freethinker* and its editor, G W Foote (1850-1915), Bithell lamented the trend to pander to the baser elements of the movement. Such literature 'is characterised by scurrility and vulgarity, and a coarseness of language which repels reflective men, and causes them to hold themselves aloof from our movement.' (38) Bithell assured readers that the Rationalist Press Committee was fully alive to this trend and made it quite clear that the committee was not in the business of publishing that sort of material. Charles Watts senior agreed. In his essay, *The Meaning of Rationalism*, Watts insisted that 'injudicious advocacy does more harm to a good cause than open antagonism. Gentleness is one of the greatest virtues, and to promulgate our opinions in what is conventionally, but very appropriately, termed a gentlemanly manner is to give them a stamp of amiability.'(39)

Only three years earlier Foote had run into trouble when he accused a liberal clergyman, Rev. Hugh Price Hughes of contriving a story about the conversion of an atheist shoemaker. Such stories were common and usually apocryphal, but it was Foote's bad luck that this one was true. But Foote then converted bad luck into bad judgment when he refused to retract his story and apologise. Hughes was a personal friend of George Jacob Holyoake, and relations between his friends and supporters and the remaining core of Bradlaugh supporters sank to a new low. It was the aim of Watts, Holyoake, Bithell and others not to operate as Foote and *The Freethinker* did. At the very first meeting of the Propagandist Press Committee, Bithell donated the entire stock, 700 copies, of his book *Agnostic Problems*, for the committee to dispose of.

Of all the men who formed the Propagandist Press Committee, none was more important to Charles Albert Watts than his lifelong friend Frederick James Gould (1855-1938). Like his colleagues, Gould strenuously avoided the term atheist, and like Bithell, this was because he genuinely and consistently was not an atheist. He described himself in his autobiography as 'half a Rationalist, if not more.'(40) Gould had been brought up as a fervent evangelical and even after he lost his faith he never lost his zeal for proselytising. Gould was, like Bithell a reverent agnostic. Soon after arriving in London he became active in the East London Ethical Society, where he developed his ideas on moral education. After 1902 he became a member of the Positivist Church, an institution founded by Richard Congreve (1818-1899) and guided by the writings of Auguste Comte (1798-1857). By the time he was writing his autobiography in the early twenties, Gould was a true Positivist.

> I do not reject the God-doctrine because it appears untrue. I reject it because it is not noble enough for the human To-day. For Yesterday I deem it was indispensable; and so it still is for the souls that dwell in Yesterday's circle of thought. We live on the threshold of a

magnificent age of creation, fellowship, aesthetic, [sic] and expansion; and for such an age the God-idea is too limited, too formal, too bureaucratic. Hence I take no interest in niggling and jealous debates as to whether the term "Atheist" or "Agnostic" is the more proper badge of a progressive intellect. Oh! Let us all – God-worshippers, Atheists and Agnostics – hasten to greater discoveries and more spacious uplands. (41)

It has become easy and even fashionable to look down one's nose at this sort of unreal optimism. But Gould, who had lost a daughter aged only six and a half in 1893 and was to lose his son in the Great War, was not a stranger to suffering and was still able late in his life to see goodness in being human. Gould's lifelong preoccupation, not surprisingly, was education, and most of his written work was of a pedagogical nature.

Gould had known Watts for eight years when he took his seat on the PPC in 1890. He had gone to the pokey little office at 17 Johnson's Court in 1882 with a pamphlet on the Home Rule issue he wanted Watts to publish. Gould doesn't mention whether the pamphlet was in fact published, but a lifelong friendship between the two men was struck during that visit. The following January Watts wrote up Gould's very first lecture, given to the Peckham and Dulwich branch of the National Secular Society. Gould spoke on 'The New Pilgrim's Progress from Christianity to Secularism' and Watts was writing for Saladin's *Secular Review*. The friendship between Watts and Gould was one of the crucial axes of the first three decades of the RPA. It was Watts who was instrumental in getting Gould's first book published. *The Children's Book of Moral Lessons* had already been rejected by a couple of publishing houses when Watts approached two of his personal friends and borrowed the money to finance getting the book published. The book sold well without being a runaway success. It did more than enough for Watts to repay his friends their investments and justify their confidence in his judgment.

Gould's interest in moral education stayed with him for the rest of his life, brought on by his conflict with the London School Board, which branded him a blasphemer in 1888 for his heterodox views on religion. Gould eventually resigned from the board in 1896 rather than continue to give religious lessons. This had happened to a freethinker in 1889 as well. Arthur B Moss was only reinstated to his position on the London School Board following action from Annie Besant. In 1897, a year after his resignation, Gould was involved in the establishment of the Moral Instruction League and it was with this organisation's needs in mind that he wrote his first books of moral instruction. The objections of people like Moss and Gould were not against ethical instruction of the young – Gould's whole career was devoted to providing such instruction – but to ethical instruction being confused with Christian indoctrination. A century later this confusion is still being made.

Most of Gould's books make for heavy reading a century later, although his *Children's Book of Moral Lessons*, which went through four volumes, were genuinely warm and humane works. Gould wrote about a wide range of universal values and introduced the reader to the Buddha, Muhammad, Jesus,

Confucius, Newton and a wide range of peoples around the world. Gould's programme of moral instruction was humane and civilised and remarkably contemporary in its emphases.

> The true basis of moral instruction lies in the doctrine that humanity is a social organism composed of self-respecting members. We have a Common Life, a Common Civilisation, a Common Welfare...With ever-increasing clearness the child should learn that his personal duty is a part of his civic duty, that right conduct obeys a social demand, that the good citizen makes the good city, that public prosperity is built upon individual integrity. (42)

Gould then outlined what to him were the basic tenets of an enlightened programme of moral instruction. They remind one strongly of Confucian humanism. They ran like this:

- self-respect, self-control, self-help
- truth and truthfulness
- kindness
- work, duty and honour
- good habits
- mutual dependence and the social organism
- disinterested application of justice
- the work of the state and the citizen
- co-operation and peace
- study of nature and of art
- enjoyment of play

His books of moral lessons consisted in thematically arranged stories and anecdotes which highlighted some particular value. To take a couple of randomly-chosen examples, Gould praises the gentleness of the Burmese towards animals. 'In England,' he wrote, 'we are obliged to have a Society for the Prevention of Cruelty to Animals. The Burmese do not need such a society.' (43) When writing of heroism, Gould's approach was equally gentle.

> A little girl was carrying a big baby. Someone asked her if the baby was not very heavy. She smiled and said, "Oh, no, he is not heavy; he is my brother." He did not seem heavy because he was her brother. There was something heroic in the girl. I think – and I hope you think – that little girls, as well as kings and warriors, can have the heroic spirit in their hearts. (44)

Decades later, and as part of a spirit of rebellion against rationality, this old story was retold in one of Bob Dylan's songs. While Dylan is undoubtedly cooler than F J Gould, it was the rationalist who retold the story first. Gould's whole career was centred on his theories of moral instruction and he was not without influence. The first volume of the *Children's Book of Moral Lessons* sold over 46,000 copies and was translated into Arabic, Hindi, Italian and Polish. In 1913 Gould toured India as the guest of the government of Bombay, speaking to teachers, education administrators and students. We might now see these books as too 'nice' but that says as much about us as it does about Gould. His campaign for a method of moral instruction shorn of exclusivist theology was a central part of the RPA programme in its earlier years. And it was in the interests of that exclusivist theology that Church of England and Roman Catholic leaders in Cheshire collaborated in 1905 to have Gould's book withdrawn from school libraries.

Gould was 35 when he sat down at the first meeting of the PPC, but he was ten years older than Frederick Millar (1865-1933), the youngest person at the table. Millar was a regular contributor to Ross's *Agnostic Journal* and an active debater and speaker. With evident relief, Watts noted that it is 'probable that, had he [Millar] never read and diligently studied Herbert Spencer's works, he would have thrown in his lot with the destructive school of Freethought represented by Mr G W Foote.' (45) But his real interest was what we would now call libertarianism. The year before joining the Propagandist Press Committee, Millar had lectured to the Leicester Secular Society on aspects of individualism. Millar, along with his friend Wordsworth Donisthorpe, was involved in the Liberty and Property Defence League. At the end of 1890 Millar debated Annie Besant on 'Individualism versus Socialism' and the following year he co-edited *The Liberty Annual*, published by Watts & Co. While Millar remained a rationalist his entire life, his work for organised rationalism did not last long. In 1893 he assumed the editorship of another new Watts & Co venture, a periodical called *Liberty Review*, which he edited until it folded in 1909. It was symptomatic of the times that, for the youngest of the founding members of the Propagandist Press Committee, it was politics and socialism (albeit in his case, opposition to) rather than religion and rationalism that ended up capturing Millar's energies.

It is interesting to consider these people in the light of the point consistently made by historians that the RPA signalled some sort of decline in the prospects of organised freethought. The nineteenth century had seen a variety of freethought organisations come and go. Little societies, in the words of the prominent freethought historian, Edward Royle, 'were formed and dissolved, amalgamated and sundered, in a ceaseless ebb and flow.'(46) The lives of these organisations rarely outlived that of the personality who founded them. Few people were more aware of this than the prominent freethinkers of the time. How did the pioneers of Johnson's Court (as Gould later portrayed them) see their role?

Adam Gowans Whyte, an earlier historian of the RPA, addressed the question. 'To some extent,' he wrote, 'the new policy was dictated by events; the meagre results and the frequent failures that had attended previous enterprises demanded a fresh missionary technique.'(47) The men who formed the PPC recognised that the age of freethought titans was over, and that their methods were no longer the most effective. The complete failure of the British Secular Union and the decline of the National Secular Society could attest to that. It was time to expand freethought activities. The lecture hall was no longer enough. As Gould had said, the lecturer will win his thousands, but the writer will win his tens of thousands. Britain was now a society of near-universal literacy and that vast reading public needed to be catered for. In other words the creators of the RPA were well aware of the changing situation in Britain at the time and recognised that a new style of freethought advocacy was needed. Far from being a retreat from a golden past, the founders of the RPA were preparing for a new future.

The choices for freethinking people at the time were either the in-your-face style of anti-Christian polemic favoured by the National Secular Society or the dissembling attitude of many intellectuals who, while having shed religious beliefs themselves, were reluctant to publicly criticise religion or to see the traditional consolations withdrawn from the uneducated. George Eliot, Leslie Stephen, Matthew Arnold, J S Mill, Herbert Spencer, Grant Allen, Karl Pearson, John Morley and even T H Huxley were all content that the status quo should be preserved for the general population. Their reticence was, to some extent at least, conditioned by their complete unwillingness to be associated with the style and tactics of the National Secular Society. And towards the end of the century this was compounded by a recoiling among such people from the socialism that was becoming more popular among the poor. It was Charles Watts' genius to see that a new type of organisation, free from political attachments and with a quite different style of advocacy, could draw in the support of this sort of person.

But does this mean that the RPA was a retreat from the freethought movement's working class roots? Noel Annan is one historian who has claimed that the rationalist movement began life as a middle class organisation, in contrast to most of its freethought predecessors. In his first biography of Sir Leslie Stephen, Annan observed that the middle class rationalists recognised that, while they shared some important religious and ethical views with the working class secularists and atheists, they did not share the political radicalism that often accompanied those views. (48) And on top of that, the middle class rationalists saw more future for themselves with Liberalism, whereas their working class colleagues were turning more and more to socialism.

This is true, but is not completely and entirely true. Some of the founders of the RPA were from the middle class. But it is also true that others were from significantly more modest backgrounds, and had grafted their way into what could, at a pinch, be seen as a middle class way of life. The Watts family is a case in point. Even more important, however, is that the RPA's vision was never restricted to a middle class audience. On the contrary, most of its greatest successes involved reaching the large working class readership. It was Watts's ability to satisfy both his working class freethought veterans *and* his middle class rationalist readers that was the secret to the survival of the RPA. It was also the chief legacy Watts and the RPA inherited from George Jacob Holyoake and the secularist tradition he had done so much to create. And neither would it be accurate to portray the National Secular Society as exclusively a working class organisation. While most of its members were from the working classes, most of its leadership from families of self-employed artisans and small businessmen, people with strong links to the Liberal party. (49)

In describing the RPA as a predominantly middle class organisation which decided to specialise in publishing, there is also an implication that it was less radical than its predecessors. Again, there are elements of truth in this, but it is far from entirely the case. It is worth remembering that some of the most stirring memories the founders of the PPC would have had involved struggles concerning publishing. Was it not the struggles of Richard Carlile (1790-1843) who went to prison several times (as did many of those who worked with him) for daring to publish forbidden material and for defying the so-called taxes on knowledge?

While it is true that the founders of the RPA were generally middle class men who favoured the evolutionary approach to social reform, it would be quite wrong to see them all as unadventurous or conformist. The history of freethought publishing is every bit as radical and just as studded with martyrs and heroes as is the history of freethought organisations.

Two incidents will help to illustrate the problems in bracketing the RPA as exclusively bourgeois and anti-militant. The first is that Watts was not afraid to publish aggressive works. One such book, *Antidotes to Superstition* by George Henry Martin, published in 1891 was marketed in *Watts's Literary Guide* as 'aggressively anti-Christian'. The militants obviously agreed as the book was favourably reviewed in Bradlaugh's paper, the *National Reformer*. And secondly, the RPA did not jump at each opportunity to attack the militant wing of freethought, even when it was their mentor George Jacob Holyoake who wanted to conduct such an attack. In the July 1896 issue of the *Literary Guide*, notice was given of a new work by Holyoake called *The Warpath of Opinion: Strange Things Thereon, as Shown in the "Life of Bradlaugh" and the "Memoirs" of Linton*. The *Guide* could not disguise its unease about the book, which it described as 'a series of biographical chapters, in the course of which Mr Holyoake corrects many statements concerning himself in Mrs Bonner's Life of her distinguished father. The book is a curiosity in many ways, particularly from a literary standpoint.' (50) This was a polite way of saying that *Warpath of Opinion* was an intemperate and divisive response to the biography of Bradlaugh. Evidently, Watts and his colleagues had second thoughts about this book, and in the interests of the unity of the movement, applied pressure to the old man.

> Mr G J Holyoake has yielded to the solicitations of many friends and decided not to publish his *Warpath of Opinion*. The book dealt with certain statements in the *Life of Charles Bradlaugh* which he considers inaccurate and misleading, and it also narrated some remarkable experiences in his advocacy of unpopular opinions. Necessarily personal reflection was inevitable, and this might have been used to the disadvantage of Rationalism. Mr Holyoake has acted wisely and magnanimously in refusing to provide weapons of attack for those unfriendly to the movement with which his name is honourably identified. (51)

Even Joseph McCabe, Holyoake's disciple and admirer, recognised the weakness of the *Warpath of Opinion*. The work revealed the nerves of 'an aged, ailing, and injured man.' (52) So, while the RPC was clear in its differences with the followers of Bradlaugh, Foote and *The Freethinker*, they had no wish to score points against them. *The Warpath of Opinion* was eventually published, though not by the RPA.

Why Rationalism?

We need now to ask why these men took on the term 'rationalism'? Obviously some change was necessary. Having become a successful propagandist committee, it was clear that the next step should be to assert more openly the nature of the propaganda being produced. But why, for instance did they not use the term 'secularism'? This was Holyoake's own term, which had by 1890 an honourable record of struggle without having been seen as dogmatic or unduly sectarian. The problem with secularism was that it was visibly on the wane by 1890. Secularism had shown itself to have no answer to socialism in the battle for the hearts and minds of the working men who made up the core of the movement. What is more, following the demise of the British Secular Union the only nationwide secularist organisation was the National Secular Society, which was exactly the sort of organisation the founders of the RPA did not want to use as a model. Under the leadership of Foote, the National Secular Society (NSS) had become the guardian of the memory of Charles Bradlaugh and, in the minds of Holyoake, Watts, Gould and Bithell, exhibited precisely the type of dogmatism and extremism they thought injurious to the movement.

If secularism was not a viable contender, why was agnosticism not used? After all, agnosticism was genuinely thought to be the term of the future. It was held to avoid the dogmatism of atheism, to be philosophically defensible, and acceptable to middle class members in a way that 'atheism' was not. But it was becoming more widely appreciated that agnosticism, too, had its problems. As a result of the clerical counterattacks against the term, agnostics were feeling evermore obliged to defend themselves from the charge that agnosticism meant ignorance.

> It should be distinctly understood that Agnosticism is not to be in any way confounded with ignorance, as that word is used in every day life. Herein consists one of the errors into which our orthodox opponents are continually falling. They use the words "Agnosticism" and "general ignorance" as if they were synonymous, which is misleading, to say the least of it – that is, unless the latter term be employed as the direct antithesis of omniscience. (53)

This passage comes from the elder Watts, but similar sentiments can be found in Bithell's writings. It was largely as a response to these sorts of criticisms that the defenders of agnosticism strove to develop the positive side of the term. Far from an admission of ignorance, the second wave of agnostic apologetics stressed its unity with the scientific method. Twenty years after originally coining the term, T H Huxley wrote:

> Agnosticism, in fact, is not a creed, but a method, the essence of which lies in the rigorous application of a single principle. That principle is of great antiquity; it is as old as Socrates; as old as the writer who said "Try all things, hold fast by that which is good;" it is the foundation of the Reformation, which should be able to give a reason for the faith that is in him; it is the great principle of Descartes; it is the fundamental axiom of modern science: In matters of the intellect, follow your reason as far as it will take you, without regard to any other consideration. And negatively: In matters of the intellect, do not pretend that conclusions are certain which are not demonstrated or demonstrable. (54)

So by the time the PPC had formed, agnosticism was being portrayed more as a method than as a creed. But it must have occurred to the PPC that if this was the case, then why not use a term which more completely signified method? Here is where the term 'rationalism' would have had its appeal. 'Rationalism' was attractive to these men because of its tying in positive knowledge with the means by which the knowledge is gained. Moreover, it did all this while remaining committed to the central principle of agnosticism. 'Rationalism,' wrote Charles Watts, 'does not deny the existence of God or a future life. Upon such topics it is not thought rational to dogmatise. Where knowledge is absent, to either affirm or deny is sheer presumption.' (55)

Having retained what they saw as the chief advantages of agnosticism while also having eliminated its principal disadvantage, 'rationalism' also allowed the founders of the RPA to focus on what was their chief area of interest. Holyoake observed that rationalism 'advises what is useful to society without asking whether it is religious or not. It makes morality the sole business of life, and declares that, from the cradle to the grave, man should be guided by reason and regulated by science.'(56) So, unlike 'atheism' or 'secularism,' or even 'agnosticism,' 'rationalism' could allow the discussion of an issue without it necessarily involving a split between religionists and non-religionists. Rather, the split would be between those who use their reason and those who do not. Holyoake had written in these terms in his book *Rationalism: A Treatise for the Times* almost half a century previously. Holyoake's life work had been to turn infidelity 'from a strident protest into a fundamental question of personal choice under a new banner.' (57) This is very much what Watts and his friends wanted to do as well. And, of course, by adopting the word 'rationalism' the founders of the RPA could honour Holyoake and avoid more unpleasantness with the irascible old Huxley.

Holyoake spoke of morality as the sole business of life. Watts said the same thing when he said that 'ethical culture is essential to well-being.'(58) These men desired that the path to a moral society be open to all people, and that contributions to such a society can be made by all people, regardless of their religious opinions. All that was needed was goodwill and the capacity to reason. Rationalism was the ideal term for the purposes of the founders of the RPA.

Gould claimed to have suggested the word to the committee, a point conceded by the other veterans. (98) But while this is superficially true, it is also true that rationalism was in vogue at the time. It was in the air. We have already encountered Holyoake's celebration and John Hurst's criticism of rationalism. It is inconceivable that men of the stamp of Gould, Holyoake and Bithell were unfamiliar with Hurst's work, which would have been 26 years old in 1893. Hurst, as we have seen, was in no doubt about the pernicious nature of rationalist criticism, but he repeatedly conceded that its criticism has been useful to the church. 'Church history was crude and ill-written before the Rationalists expended their toil and learning upon it.' 'The Rationalistic divines have also been the indirect means of a better estimate of the life of Christ.'(60)

It was in this sense that 'rationalism' was the term of the hour. None of the founders of the PPC was fundamentally opposed to religion per se; it was dogma, the claims of revelation, and static formulae which they opposed. In 1865, two years before Hurst's attack, William Edward Hartpole Lecky had written what proved to be a massively influential work called *History of the Rise and Influence of the Spirit of Rationalism in Europe*. Lecky (1838-1903) got to the heart of the matter for the founders of the RPC when he declared that disinclination to believe in miracles is 'so emphatically the distinctive mark of Rationalism that with most persons it is the only conception the word conveys.'(61) Lecky understood, in a way rationalists then and now are not credited with, that it is not a simple reason/unreason split. The 'binary oppositions', which postmodernists insist rationalists are addicted to, find no place here. Lecky writes:

> No mind, it is true, was ever altogether free from distorting influences; but in the struggle between reason and the affections which lead to truth, as in the struggle between the will and the desires which leads to virtue, every effort is crowned with a measure of success, and innumerable gradations of progress are manifested. (62)

The founders of the Rationalist Press Committee sought a more radical criticism of the church than Hurst or even Lecky would have considered positive; a criticism Gould, Bithell and Holyoake would have seen as in the name of 'true religion', which now might be best understood as the essential goodness which unites us all and informs our essential humanity. But while their approach was more radical than Lecky or Hurst, it was less radical than that of the National Secular Society. The founders of the RPA did not see themselves as enemies of religion in general or Christianity in particular. This constituted their main point of difference with Foote and the NSS. After a criticism of Foote's approach, *Watts's Literary Guide* put the RPC mission in these terms:

> If Freethought is to continue to make headway, it must frankly recognise the moral worth of Christianity - aye, even the Salvation Army. In making this conclusion our warfare against dogma and superstition is made considerably easier; and, after all, the extinction of these twin monsters is the high purpose of our propaganda.' (63)

So, with these thoughts in mind, the Propagandist Press Committee changed its name in March 1893 to the Rationalist Press Committee. At the time, of course, this change would not have been as portentous as the historian is inclined to suggest. The committee carried on pretty much as before. And given its modest financial base, the PPC/RPC did an impressive job. As well as continuing to print the *Literary Guide* (*Watts's* having been dropped in October 1894), several books were published as well. Among the titles it was responsible for having published were Bithell's *Agnostic Problems*, Gould's *Concise History of Religion*, T H Huxley's essay, *Possibilities and Impossibilities* and a survey called *Modern Rationalism* by a young man who had recently seceded from the Roman Catholic Church. His name was Joseph McCabe. There was also a large number of pamphlets.

The RPC also attracted publicity over its role in advocating a non-theological moral instruction in London's schools. Gould produced a pamphlet in 1894 entitled *Religion in Board Schools* which advocated precisely this sort of non-theological moral instruction. The London School Board had branded Gould as a heretic in 1888 after a similar proposal. The *Daily Chronicle* saw fit to castigate

Gould's work as 'a disgraceful attack on the Christian faith', but more broad minded religionists welcomed the pamphlet, including the prominent Unitarian Page Hopps and J Allanson Picton (1832-1910), an heretical churchman and educator. By virtue of this activity, the Rationalist Press Committee continued to attract friends and readers.

The formation of the Rationalist Press Association

Having dealt with the *why* and the *who*, it now remains only to ask why the Rationalist Press Committee became the Rationalist Press Association *when* it did. Without doubt the main reason was the discovery made by G W Foote that formal establishment of a company would enable the secularists to receive bequests without fear of confiscation. As we have noted, it was another of the petty legal discriminations of the time that bequests made to freethought organisations were usually disallowed by the law courts. It simply wasn't credited that a morally sound person would want to make a legacy to a freethought organisation. This of course put a very real barrier on any development freethought organisations could undertake. Very soon after its foundation, the PPC had donated the not inconsiderable sum of £30 to the Liberty of Bequest Committee. This group, composed largely of freethinkers, was committed to ending this discrimination.

It is an amusing irony that it was G W Foote who was responsible for providing the impetus for the creation of the RPA. It was the person whose style of freethought advocacy the founders of the Propagandist Press Committee most wanted to distance themselves from who provided them with the style of freethought organisation they most wanted to emulate. Foote led the way by forming the Secular Society Limited in May 1898, which would allow legacies to be left to his organisation without fear of legal challenge. Inevitably, one legacy was challenged (not surprisingly; it was for £10,000) and Foote guided the case through every step of its protracted battle. It wasn't until 1915, the year of Foote's death, that the Court of Appeal decided for the Secular Society Limited. Even then the case continued, going on to the House of Lords, which confirmed the decision in 1917. This victory was an important milestone in the legal history of the United Kingdom. Opponents of the estate argued for its invalidity on the grounds that the Secular Society Ltd was constituted for illegal purposes, namely the subversion of Christianity, which was the acknowledged religion of the country. Many of the Lords were sympathetic to this argument, but it was decided, in the words of Lord Sumner, that England being a Christian country was a rhetorical rather than a legal commitment.

> '"Thou shalt not steal" was part of our law: "Thou shalt not commit adultery" was part of our law. But another part, "Thou shalt love they neighbour as thyself," was not part of our law at all. Christianity had tolerated chattel slavery; not so the present law of England.' (64)

It is far from clear that the implications of this decision have been explored as thoroughly as they might.

Inspired by Foote's discovery, the Rationalist Press Committee began investigating the transformation of the Committee into an Association and, more significantly, incorporation under the Companies Act. This process occupied much of the year from May 1898. The committee, aided by four sympathetic lawyers, helped draft the memorandum and articles for the association. They were particularly concerned with protecting any bequests from legal challenges from disaffected or unsympathetic family members. That there has been no successful challenge to any RPA bequest suggests their labour was not in vain. With regard to the aims and objects of the Association, it was apparent early on that Gould's influence was significant. In the first draft, which appeared in the *Literary Guide* in February 1899, emphasis was given to the task of producing books on moral instruction, secular education, humanist ethics and all the other areas of Gould's principal interests. But in March 1899 Gould left London to take up the post of Secretary and Organiser of the Leicester Secular Society, and quite a lot of that material was dropped from the final draft which was put to the members.

Notwithstanding the differences of emphasis, the contrasting loyalties and other issues which served to divide them, Charles Albert Watts never forgot the debt he, and hence the RPA, owed to G W Foote. Four decades later Watts can be found reminding readers of their collective debt to Foote. Underneath the differences there existed a recognition of broader and more important areas of common interest. This remains the case.

The certificate of registration for the Rationalist Press Association was issued on May 26 1899. The signatories of the memorandum that day were Charles Albert Watts, George Jacob Holyoake, Clair James Grece, Charles Gorham, Charles Hooper, Adam Gowans Whyte, R B Anderson and John Dryden. Gorham and Hooper had both joined the RPC in 1896, Adam Gowans Whyte two years later, having come south from Scotland. Clair James Grece, a solicitor and self-made man based at Redhill, had provided the bulk of the legal advice over the past year.

The memorandum of the Rationalist Press Association, to which these men put their names, read:

(a) to stimulate freedom of thought and inquiry in reference to ethics, theology, philosophy, and kindred subjects.
(b) to promote a secular system of education the main object of which shall be to cultivate in the young moral and intellectual fitness for social life.
(c) to maintain and assert the same right of propaganda for opinions and ideas which conflict with existing or traditional creeds and beliefs as is now legally exercisable in favour of such creeds and beliefs.
(d) to publish and distribute, either gratuitously or otherwise, books, pamphlets, and periodicals designed to promote the above objects, or any other of them, and generally to assist in the spread of Rationalist principles, especially in their bearing on human conduct. *Rationalism may be defined as the mental attitude which unreservedly accepts the supremacy of reason and aims at establishing a system of philosophy and ethics verifiable by experience and independent of all arbitrary assumptions of authority.*
(e) to originate and watch over, and, if necessary, petition Parliament in relation to measures affecting education in relation to ethics, theology, philosophy, and kindred subjects.

The memorandum had been a joint effort. Today, more than a century later, these aims still look good. They form the bedrock of what Karl Popper called the open society and what Ernest Gellner later on called civil society. They presuppose a society of conscientious people with a sense of duty to one another and a desire for justice. They belie the hoary old jibe that a secular education system operates in a moral vacuum. The early rationalists recognised, correctly, that an open society can only operate in a secular one.

The only section which looks problematic a century later is the definition of rationalism, which I have put in italics. The wording of the definition was mostly the work of Sir Leslie Stephen (1832-1904) one of the country's most prominent men of letters. (65) Stephen had given up his fellowship at Cambridge shortly after *Essays and Reviews* came out because he no longer believed that Christianity was true. Unlike many others who left the church in the second half of the nineteenth century, Stephen publicly criticised Christianity and declared his unbelief. As well as having written several influential works of his own, in particular his *History of English Thought in the Eighteenth Century* (2 volumes, 1876), *The Science of Ethics* (1882) and *The English Utilitarians* (3 volumes, 1900), Stephen served as editor of the *Dictionary of National Biography*. It was a tribute to Stephen's prestige that successive rationalists avoided the temptation to amend the definition – a process which would have been never-ending. Especially as it attracted criticism almost from the moment of its formulation. But it is important to recognise that the creators of the term were well aware of its shortcomings. We will return to this question in Chapter Six.

The inaugural meeting of the RPA took place on September 18 1899 with about a dozen people attending. One of those at the meeting commented on the small turnout and was reminded by Holyoake, who had the chair, that the Anti-Corn Law League had begun with only four men. And so had the Propagandist Press Committee. The Anti-Corn Law League went on to achieve great changes, and so would the RPA. It was left to F J Gould to ring in the new:

> We have worked only in a little corner of the estate. We now want to farm on a large scale. We want to publish more books, on more subjects, by more authors, and for more circles of readers. We want to rank in influence with the strongest publishers of Christian literature. (66)

Suitably galvanised, the rationalists turned their minds toward the twentieth century.

Chapter 2

The Blasphemy Depot

'In my opinion, the RPA is one of the most beneficent and philanthropic institutions in the country.'
Sir E Ray Lankester, 1912

The Edwardian years are about the least understood of any period in English history. It often depends on what axe one wants to grind as to how these years are portrayed. For those with a bias against rationalism, the Edwardian years are often dismissed as shallow and superficial because of their supposed confidence in progress and reason, both of which, the story goes, were cruelly disabused in the trenches of World War One. By contrast, those with a more wistful temperament warm to the supposed calm-before-the-storm innocence of the period. An undervalued popular historian of the period is J B Priestley, who saw the years between Victoria and Sarajevo in these terms:

> a time when a lot of people are trying to cling to the past while many others are trying to hurry themselves and everybody else into a future of their own devising. Most of the adjectives tacked on to this age – spacious, leisurely, and the rest – seem to me quite wrong. It was an era of tensions between extremes. (1)

Priestley's point is well made, but things were more complicated than that, because there was not a simple gulf between a conservative establishment and radical outsiders. Samuel Hynes is closer to the truth when he adds that the forces were not divided along simply demarcated lines. Neither side of the opposition 'was homogeneous enough to make the usual easy metaphors appropriate – they were not camps, or armies, or even wings, but simply two large categories of people, both composed of heterogeneous elements that were quite distinct and often incompatible with each other.' (2) Hynes also notes the sense of melancholy, or anxiety that pervaded the period, among both radicals and conservatives.

On the face of it the Rationalist Press Association was plainly on the side of the progressives, the outsiders, the people Priestley accuses of wanting to hurry everybody along to a future of their own devising. But this is not the case by any means. The RPA was a heterogeneous gathering of liberals, radicals, laissez faire individualists, socialists, and conservatives. Attitudes to education, sexuality, religion, imperialism, suffrage and many other issues varied sharply. Some people saw themselves as straightforward opponents of religion in all its forms, others saw themselves as guardians of what is true in religion, having rejected only the inessential dross. What united them was the conviction that the unfettered use of reason was the only sure way to arrive at any worthwhile conclusion.

Those wanting to see the Edwardian period as one of rationalist triumphalist pride before the fall in the trenches are likely to be disappointed when making a thorough study of the period. Some rationalists, it is true, thought that history was on their side and that rationalism was on the threshold of a definitive victory. This was especially true of those who remained at the more teleological extreme of the rationalist movement, Positivists in particular. Few rationalists, however, were so sanguine as to suppose that the secular age would simply fall into their lap. There was, in fact, a pervading sense of anxiety among them that the age of giants was over and the age of pygmies was beginning. They felt themselves to be in the fading shadow of Huxley, Mill, Tyndall, Bradlaugh, Spencer and Holyoake, and saw no figures of similar stature rising to take their place. They also saw themselves as in a period of reaction; they called it the 'flight from reason'.

One work, which can be taken as representative of the RPA's literature of the period, was a book called *The Religion of the Open Mind*, by Adam Gowans Whyte, a director since 1899. Whyte began his book with a sustained lament about the uncertainties of the age. The first sentence of his book read, 'Life is a great deal more complex than it used to be.' He then went on to outline the many changes over the preceding century: the dramatic broadening of intellectual horizons; the inability any more to speak of a single horizon; the fatigue caused by constant innovations and discoveries; the fracturing of the moral and religious consensus. (3) A century later, postmodernists write of these things as if they had discovered them. Not only is this not true, the very rationalists they despise so much were making the same observations a century before them.

So the small grouping of people who formed the Rationalist Press Association in 1899 brought with them a variety of hopes and fears, ambitions and dreams. Charles Albert Watts had quietly been gathering friends and supporters throughout the 1890s and many of these people actively helped in the creation of the RPA. Nonetheless, few people would have predicted the steady ascent in the Association's fortunes. Three main types of assistance were offered. First there were the activists who gave time and energy to the daily tasks of building the RPA up. Then there were the people whose assistance was principally financial or social. And then there were the people who lent their name to the association as Honorary Associates. These we will discuss in Chapter Eight. The RPA would not have grown in the way that it did if any of these three forms of support had been absent.

First, the activists. We have already seen that the Rationalist Press Committee had attracted two new workers, both of whom were destined to devote very considerable energy to the RPA. Charles E Hooper (1864-1932) had been born a Quaker but quickly passed through Unitarianism to agnosticism. He began contributing to the *Literary Guide* in 1896 and became active on the Rationalist Press Committee. The year before, when the *Guide* was ready to expand but lacked the funds to do so, Hooper promised half the £500 needed for the expansion if Watts could come up the other half. Watts mentioned the offer in the *Guide* and soon received the £250 from a man he had never met, an invalid, who had read the *Guide* for many years. The *Guide* retained this generous size until 1942. This is but one example of Watts's extraordinary ability to inspire confidence in other people. Even more impressive is that, over his long career, he never let any of them down.

When the RPA was formed in 1899, Hooper took on the crucial job as secretary, a post he was to hold until ill health forced him to retire in 1912. In an effort to be complimentary, the ever-amiable F J Gould described Hooper as the 'writer of many a grave philosophic page'. (4) Hooper was a minor philosopher of the then significant 'common sense' school, inspired by G E Moore (1873-1958). His two main works were *The Anatomy of Knowledge* (1906) and *Common Sense and the Rudiments of Philosophy* (1913). He also had articles published in *Mind*, the most academically prestigious journal of philosophy in Britain. In *The Anatomy of Knowledge*, Hooper attempted a synthetic philosophy after the manner of Herbert Spencer (1820-1903). It was Hooper's ambition to provide rationalism with a solid epistemological foundation. By means of a series of laws of objective logic and an exhaustive compartmentalisation of the sciences, Hooper hoped to establish definitively the uniting principles, as he called them, which would lead to a final and comprehensive understanding of reality. He retained, albeit in a somewhat modified form, Spencer's agnosticism. As with so many people active in the RPA, then and now, Hooper was also active in the South Place Ethical Society (SPES). This organisation was founded originally in 1793 and had only recently completed an intellectual odyssey away from Unitarianism to a position not unlike contemporary religious humanism. Hooper advocated a fusion of rationalism and ethicism into what he called humanism.

If Hooper aspired to become court sage, the second significant recruit from the class of 1896, Charles T Gorham had a lighter touch. Like Hooper, Gorham (1856-1933) had been educated privately. His religious education was amiable and undemanding, to which the young Gorham responded with an adolescence of evangelical zeal. After a time at the feet of Rev. Edward White, who preached the doctrine of conditional immortality, Gorham moved on to a more tolerant Universalism. While working as a solicitor's clerk in London in the 1890s he became active on the Rationalist Press Committee. Some notes he had compiled for an ongoing debate with a pious relative were seen by a friend, who recommended Gorham to Charles Watts. The notes were published as *Is the Bible a Revelation from God?* in 1894 and two years later Gorham became active on the RPC. Gorham was to succeed Hooper as secretary of the RPA in 1913, and retained the post until his retirement in 1928. Gorham was to become one of the movement's more prolific writers, supplying a large number of articles for the *Literary Guide* and several books, all designed for the non-specialist.

The third of the 1896 recruits was Joseph McCabe (1867-1955). Unlike virtually all his colleagues in the RPA, McCabe came from a Catholic background. He was also from considerably more modest circumstances than most of his newly-found colleagues. And McCabe was a rebel and a firebrand. For decades to come McCabe would be the joker in the pack. In 1896 McCabe had just walked away from twelve years as a priest in the Franciscan Order of the Church. Whereas men like Hooper and Gorham had made easy transitions from a genial non-dogmatic faith to an equally genial agnosticism, McCabe had been immersed for years in the cauldron of total belief. McCabe's path to rationalism had been infinitely more demanding and had required years of struggle, pain and sacrifice. In leaving the church, McCabe left the only world he really knew. Soon after his secession, he had to buy a book of etiquette to learn the ways of the world. Not surprisingly McCabe had higher expectations of the freethought movement than was really wise. He had assumed, he wrote in his autobiography many years later, that 'anti-clerical movements would be entirely honest and courageous. I found at once that my expectation had the enthusiasm of youth and inexperience.' (5)

Soon after his secession, and in need of assistance, McCabe approached F J Gould, who introduced him to the Rationalist Press Committee. The committee funded a pamphlet McCabe wrote about his experiences. It was called *From Rome to Rationalism* and appeared in 1897. McCabe soon expanded the pamphlet into a book-length autobiography, which became one of his most enduring books: *Twelve Years in a Monastery*. And in the same year McCabe wrote a summary of the current intellectual climate called *Modern Rationalism*. In 1898 he followed up his successful *Twelve Years* with *Life in a Modern Monastery*, which was published by Grant Richards. McCabe was to retain a work-rate at this level for another 58 years. McCabe had attracted the patronage of the influential agnostic and man of letters, Sir Leslie Stephen, whose support was sufficient to have reputable London publishing houses take on the young man's work. So when McCabe took his seat on the RPA's board of directors in 1899, at the age of 32, he was already a successful author and thinker in his own right.

As this book will show, Joseph McCabe's contribution to the success of the Rationalist Press Association was second only to Watts himself. What darkens this otherwise fulsome tribute is that McCabe also became progressively more difficult to work with. He loathed Hooper and Gorham (among others) whose paths to rationalism had been strewn with flowers where his had been covered in jagged stones. Hooper and Gorham loathed McCabe in return. They resented his arrogance, were infuriated by his prickliness, and were jealous of his greater ability.

The second group of people who were instrumental to the growth of the RPA was a small number of wealthy supporters, the most prominent of whom was George Anderson (1824-1915). Anderson was a self-made man and philanthropist who had made a fortune as an engineer in the gas industry. As well as extended periods of time in Leyden and Constantinople helping establish gas heating and lighting in those cities, Anderson built and owned several gasworks around the British Isles. Once the RPA was up and running, Anderson made a donation of £1000 to the Association and promised a further donation if others did the same. Over the next two years another £2000 was donated, half of that again from Anderson.

It is an obvious enough point to make that this money was terribly important for the young Association. The only other sources of revenue were subscriptions from members and earning from books and other material sold. But neither of these sources was anywhere near able to match the donations of George Anderson and his friends. The minimum subscription was five shillings but members were encouraged to contribute more if they were able. The five shillings subscription earned the member one vote at General Meetings, whereas a subscriber of £5 was deemed to be worth two votes, with a further vote for each extra £5 subscribed.

But the important point, and what most people joined the RPA for, was to get the books. Each subscriber would receive all titles published by the Association for the year to the value of their subscription.

The dream start

While the early contributions from people like Anderson were invaluable to its survival, it was clear that what the RPA really needed was a successful publishing career. None of the stock inherited from the RPC was moving in the numbers needed. The stock consisted mostly of works by Holyoake, Gould, Bithell, Samuel Laing (who had sold very well in the 1880s) and some compilations from various authors. All these titles were worthy contributions by worthy men, but they were not going to set the Thames on fire, as Gould had so memorably hoped would happen.

The first title published by the RPA was by Joseph McCabe. *The Religion of the Twentieth Century* was both a primer on rationalism and an optimistic prophecy of its victory in the century to come. 'With no hesitating voice,' wrote the unnamed reviewer, 'Mr McCabe declares that the phantoms of supernaturalism must, in time, cease to haunt the mind of man, that God and immortality must be torn from the real soul-life of man and relegated to the land of dreams.' (6) McCabe's book predates several of the better-known examples of this genre by H G Wells. Books like *Anticipations, The Discovery of the Future* (both 1902) and *Mankind in the Making* (1903) are all in the style of McCabe's first book written for the RPA. The most noticeable difference is that McCabe's work was free of the social darwinism and racism that marred aspects of Wells's work.

But for all this, neither McCabe's book, nor any of the other material published in the first year of the association was going to alter things in any dramatic way. Then came along a book that was destined to transform the future of the Rationalist Press Association, of publishing and even of science itself. The book, by Ernst Haeckel (1834-1919), was *The Riddle of the Universe*. Haeckel's book has been described as 'one of the most incredible publishing successes of all times.' (7) The rationalists were quick to note the book's importance and potential. The review of the book in its German original in the March 1900 issue of the *Literary Guide* would have to be among the first notices of this book in England.

> Dr Haeckel's work could not have arrived at a more opportune moment, and there could not have been a better work for the purpose. We have fallen upon a period of reaction, in these closing days of the nineteenth century, such as may well sadden the older thinkers who grew up in the splendid promise of the middle of the century. The great Rationalist thinkers are dead or dying, and there are none to "lift the mighty lance of the fallen."

The reviewer urged that

> Such a work is needed here in England as sorely as in Germany. It is a splendid response to those who talk of the "bankruptcy of science." We fear there is no one left among us to treat the subject with the vast

knowledge and the philosophic comprehensiveness of Dr Haeckel; so we trust the Rationalist Press Association will soon be in a position to publish a translation of this magnificent work. (8)

I suspect the reviewer was Dr Bithell, who would have been one of the few people left in the RPA who had grown up in the middle of the century, who could read German, and who could see that their day had passed. Either way, things moved fast. By April the RPA had secured the exclusive rights for *Die Welträtsel*, which was then in its ninth thousand and with French and Italian translations being arranged. This was a high-risk venture for the fledgling association. The whole exercise required an outlay of £250 – an enormous percentage of the RPA's funds given that the entire subscriptions for the 1899-1900 year, plus the balance remaining from the RPC came to £257.8s.6d.

The job of translating *Die Welträtsel* was given to Joseph McCabe. As well as translating the book in four months, he wrote a brilliant 5,500-word synopsis which appeared as a Supplement for the April issue of the *Guide*. The RPA board must have had an inkling of a groundswell of interest in Haeckel's book. The April issue with its Supplement quickly sold out, and the Supplement was hastily reprinted as a penny leaflet. In July an agreement was made with the American publisher Harper and Brothers for the American rights to the book and in October 1900 the book was launched on the world.

One of the interesting problems was how to translate the title into English. Literally translated, *Die Welträtsel* means 'the world riddle' and the first suggestions for the title were 'The World Problem' or 'The World Enigma'. Later in the year it had developed to 'The Problem of Life', but by August, the title settled on 'The Riddle of the Universe'. This was McCabe's idea, although the phrase had been in use for a while. I have speculated elsewhere that McCabe may well have come across the phrase in the writings of Sir Leslie Stephen, one of his mentors. (9) Either way, the title was brilliant, and helped in no small way to generate interest in the book, which was growing rapidly. The first print run of 2000 copies was in heavy demand even before it was published on October 1. Three weeks after publication the first thousand copies had gone. Before the year was out the decision was made to do another print run. The book had to be entirely reset as the first edition had not been stereotyped. Nobody had thought it would sell as quickly as it did.

Edward Royle, one of the most important historians of British freethought, described the response to *The Riddle* as 'the kind of success of which publishers dream.' He also ascribed this breakthrough into the mass market as illustrative of Watts's genius. (10) This is quite true, but, as the *Guide* itself acknowledged, the praise needed to be shared. 'It is only fair to acknowledge that the success which has attended this almost initial undertaking of the Rationalist Press Association is due in no inconsiderable degree to the admirable translation for which Mr Joseph McCabe is responsible.' (11)

By 1905, the RPA had sold 100,000 copies of *The Riddle*. It was to sell in the region of a quarter of a million copies (not including the half million which sold in Germany alone) and remain in print for over half a century. It also became the book most frequently mentioned by members of the RPA as a book that influenced their path to rationalism. It was translated into 25 languages and attracted more than a hundred reviews and a dozen printed responses. Thirty-one years after translating *The Riddle of the Universe*, McCabe declared that 'no book in my lifetime has had a wider influence in liberating the modern mind from superstition.' (12) Even in 1985, *The Riddle* was acknowledged as Watts & Co's 'most important single publication'. (13) Watts continued reprinting *The Riddle* until 1946, and its most recent reprint was by Prometheus Books in their Great Minds series in 1992. In the Introduction to this reprint, H James Birx, himself an important thinker on evolution, acknowledged Haeckel's errors, but was equally clear about the book's strengths.

> Haeckel's ideas in ecology and biogeography have won wide acceptance in modern biology; of special historical significance is his uncompromising support of organic evolution and its ramifications in science, philosophy, and theology. Haeckel's ideas and discoveries have continued to stimulate research science and to inspire naturalist philosophy. (14)

The huge success of *The Riddle of the Universe* gave the RPA the two things a new, vulnerable organisation needs the most: revenue and respectability. Not too much elaboration is necessary to underscore the importance of a generous capital base for a publishing firm. Publishing is an expensive business, the risks are high, most titles will only sell in modest numbers and there is always the chance that a title will not sell enough to cover costs. This is especially true of a firm committed to publishing for a cause. And just as important as the revenue is the respectability that comes with it. This was particularly important in late Victorian and Edwardian Britain. Following on from the success of *The Riddle*, the RPA could approach its fellow publishers not as a poor cousin with peculiar views about religion, but as an equal. This proved very important indeed when Watts launched his next blitzkrieg on the publishing world.

What was it about *The Riddle of the Universe* that made it such a success? Sixty years after it appeared the American naturalist philosopher Marvin Farber recommended *The Riddle* as an 'effective statement about the various stages of evolution of the earth and man, and it remains decidedly pertinent for philosophy.' (15) In today's language, *The Riddle* was attempting to provide a theory of everything. It has been lamented that, in the wake of the decline of religion, we have been left without a general picture of the universe and our place in it. We are without a teleological map (Mary Midgley's phrase) or sacred narrative (E O Wilson's phrase). What many people overlook are the outstanding contributions made by rationalist thinkers in providing just such an account. Haeckel's book was an ambitious and uplifting naturalistic vision of the universe. It stands as the model for later popular naturalistic accounts of the universe and our place in it, the most successful of which was Carl Sagan's book and television series *Cosmos*, but the works of Joseph McCabe, Isaac Asimov, Jacob Bronowski, Richard Dawkins and E O Wilson come to mind as other important figures in this tradition. This ability to write well and clearly for the general reader is one of the most valuable aspects of the humanist tradition.

The Cheap Reprints

The success of *The Riddle of the Universe* and the generosity of George Anderson allowed Watts to launch his most ambitious project. It was Watts's belief that modest means and little leisure did not necessarily mean a lack of intellectual curiosity. This was, and remains, a cornerstone of humanist thought. Watts didn't have to reason this out abstractly; he only had to think of his own experience. It was Watts's idea to make the great works of rationalist thought available to people like him, of modest means and limited leisure. Fortunately, George Anderson's generosity showed no signs of abating. In 1901 he had offered no less than £15,000 toward the cost of a Freethought Institute if a similar sum could be found from elsewhere. The Freethought Institute was modelled on the Secular Hall in Leicester, which had given life and continuity to the secular society in that city when many most other secular societies had withered or died. The proposed Institute would serve as headquarters of the RPA, and be a centre of learning and socialising for rationalists around the country and around the world. No alcohol, card-playing or gambling of any sort was to be permitted, although there would be a smoking room, billiards room and place for 'light refreshments of good quality'. (16)

But the other money could not be raised and the scheme came to nothing. The collection stalled at £4000 and the scheme was abandoned in August 1901. It is not clear whether that money was returned to the donors or re-routed to the Cheap Reprints project. Either way, the RPA was in sufficient funds the following year to begin its audacious publishing scheme. An unnamed benefactor (almost certainly George Anderson) donated £1000 in August 1902 and, in 1904, Anderson set up a regular donation of £200 a year for five years to help finance the Cheap Reprints. Empowered by this new ability to act, senior representatives of the RPA approached the publishing houses that owned the copyright of various freethought and rationalist classics and sought their permission to reprint them at what one competitor dismissed as a 'waste paper price'. It was Watts's plan to reprint these titles in paperback at the cost of only sixpence! Nobody believed Watts's scheme would work. Nobody believed Watts could produce the works cheaply enough to sell at that price or that there was a market for such material among sixpenny buyers. Watts recalled later, 'I was warned by leading publishers that I was inviting bankruptcy; and under ordinary conditions that fate might have overtaken me.' (17) But the conditions were not ordinary. The extraordinary factor in this situation was Watts himself, and in particular his ability to inspire confidence in other people; often people with the money and connections that Watts himself lacked.

A prime example of the sort of person Watts could gather around him is Edward Clodd (1840-1930). Born into a Baptist family of modest means, Clodd found his way to London, rising to become Secretary of the London Joint Stock Bank from 1872 until his retirement in 1915. In his spare time Clodd was a successful populariser of science and biblical criticism. He was an active member of the then influential Folklore Society. Clodd was the ideal person to succeed Holyoake as Chairman of the RPA in 1906, a post he held until 1913. He was the first of three RPA chairmen whose principal strength was their ability to network through their extensive contacts in the London clubs.

Clodd's rationalism was not dissimilar to Watts's close friend F J Gould in that it was opposed primarily to Christian doctrine, rather than to religious practice generally. He was strongly opposed to any direct criticism of religion in general, or Christianity in particular. For example, in 1902 he wrote:

> No religion, however repellent it may be to refined natures, has taken root which did not adjust itself to, and answer, some need of the human heart. And the measure of our knowledge of the various faiths of mankind will be the measure of our sympathy. (18)

Despite having rejected the Christian religion, Clodd retained a strong respect for the Bible. Clodd was entirely with Huxley and Bithell in his condemnation of militant criticism of Christianity, such as he saw in *The Freethinker*. He felt that the rote learning of much of the Bible during his childhood was a valuable lesson, for which he declared 'I cannot be too thankful.' Like many rationalists, Clodd was saddened by the widespread neglect of the Bible, this being a 'matter for grave concern.' (19) Predictably, Clodd was particularly unhappy about Joseph McCabe's writing, which he complained was like 'a pistol firing in his ears'. (20) It is a tribute to Clodd that despite holding unpopular opinions regarding religion, he was best known for the wide circle of friends he had acquired over the years. Clodd was a determinedly genial man. In his role as ambassador-at-large for the RPA, he performed the valuable service of approaching the various publishers for permission to reprint the various titles. Few could refuse him.

At the top of Watts's wishlist of titles to reprint was Thomas Henry Huxley's *Lectures and Essays*. Few senior rationalists would have disagreed, certainly not Clodd, who wrote a very positive, verging on hagiographical, account of Huxley for Blackwood's 'Modern English Writers' series in 1902, the same year the Cheap Reprints began. Clodd clearly felt he was not exaggerating when he declared Huxley to be 'an example and an inspiration to all men for all time.' (21) The rights to Huxley's *Lectures and Essays* were owned by the established firm of Macmillan. Its owner, Sir Frederick Macmillan, a staunch churchman and father of the future prime minister, shared the general suspicion of Watts's venture and of the RPA generally. It was not until he was approached by the Hon. John Collier and Leonard Huxley (1860-1933), Thomas Henry's son, that Macmillan relented. Collier (1850-1934), an old Etonian and son of Lord Monkswell, was able to put Macmillan at ease about the project. Collier's credentials as a Huxleian were also impeccable, having married both of Thomas Henry's daughters, Marian and, after her death, Ethel. And, incidentally, Leonard Huxley's willingness to ensure his father's work was reprinted by the RPA is further evidence that his father had relented of his early low opinion of Watts.

By 1902 the programme of Cheap Reprints was ready. What this involved was a collection of freethought and rationalist classics to be reprinted, either in hardcover for one shilling, or entirely in paper and to retail at no more than sixpence. The world was familiar with pamphlets and had recently been introduced to the popular press, but few people were ready for an entire book, and non-fiction to boot, to be made of paper, with no hard cover at all. Still less could people envision enough people buying such modestly priced and produced works. F J Gould, put it with characteristic whimsicality:

> It rained reprints at Johnson's Court, railway bookstalls, provincial towns, vicarages, and manses. The refreshing showers have continued in Britain, India, the Dominions, and the United States; and at the close of 1928 the output ...amounted to over 4,000,000. (22)

And buy them they did. The first five titles that came off the press in 1902 sold 155,000 copies in that year alone, three of them going into a second edition. Gould's point about the influence of the Cheap Reprints is valid. Thomas Hardy, one of Edward Clodd's more influential friends, congratulated the RPA on the Cheap Reprints in 1904, but with a characteristic proviso:

> I think the cheap publications are a powerful means of spreading scientific knowledge among those who would not otherwise get at it. One must, of course, always hope that, in destroying superstition, emotional fancy - which may be called make-believe superstition - will not be destroyed along with it, adding, as it does, so largely to the interest in life. (23)

Hardy need not have worried on that score, as there were a variety of emphases and approaches in the Cheap Reprints to appeal to most tastes. Looking further afield, the example of New Zealand can illustrate their influence. In 1907, William Whitehouse Collins (1853-1923) established a monthly paper called *The Examiner*, which soon became the official paper of the New Zealand Rationalist Association. In the ten years of *The Examiner's* life, the back page (or most of it, depending on the fortunes of the local piano dealer) was devoted to advertising RPA Cheap Reprints. One New Zealander, Mr R Thompson of Christchurch, returned to New Zealand in 1903 taking 1,200 Cheap Reprints with him. Thompson was the president of the Canterbury Freethought Association, which soon became the NZ Rationalist Association. This organisation, now called the NZ Association of Rationalists & Humanists, still flourishes today.

Of particular interest is to look at the people the RPA board considered worthy to reprint. Apart from the twenty-eighth reprint (*Hume's Essays*), most of the works had originally been printed between 1850 and 1904. Among the authors chosen, there were agnostics like T H Huxley, Herbert Spencer, Edward Clodd, Samuel Laing and Sir Leslie Stephen. But there were also theists of various stripes such as Matthew Arnold, Francis William Newman, W R Greg, Andrew Lang, and Ernest Renan. Also represented were positivists and pantheists. Conspicuous by their absence were the works of atheists. Not one Cheap Reprint was from the pen of an avowed atheist, Haeckel and McCabe coming closest to that description. Certainly the most notable absentee was Charles Bradlaugh. The practical reason for this is that the copyright for Bradlaugh's works was with G W Foote, and relations between Foote and the RPA were by now very cool. Foote had fallen out with George Anderson who, in 1902 forced him into bankruptcy over a debt. This finally estranged Charles Watts senior and Foote; Watts having retained his National Secular Society membership until this time. Foote had also argued with Joseph McCabe, who had worked for him on *The Freethinker* for a while in 1899. These disagreements were symptomatic of the deeper rift between them. The RPA was sure its most significant point of difference with the NSS was that it was not an atheist organisation.

We will return to this question later in the chapter, and again in Chapter Seven.

Theologically speaking, the most radical of the Cheap Reprints would perhaps have been Haeckel's *Riddle of the Universe* (the fifth in the series) while the most conservative was perhaps Greg's *The Creed of Christendom* (the twentieth in the series and published originally in 1851). But against this commendable eclecticism is a passage from Arnold Bennett in his journal. Bennett recalled Watts intimating to H G Wells in 1904 that they would have reprinted Wells's *Anticipations* but that the word 'God' is used and this would upset the RPA subscribers. It is hard to reconcile this claim with the observed breadth of the Cheap Reprints, several of which are far more overtly theistic than Wells's book. Bennett's remark attracted belated attention in the *Literary Guide*. Watts commented that this was unlikely to be a correct description of the conversation. 'If our memory serves us rightly, Mr Wells was at that time averse to identifying himself too closely with the RPA for reasons which were satisfactory to him, but not understandable by his guest.' (24) *Anticipations* was announced as a forthcoming Cheap Reprint in the March 1904 issue of the *Guide*, but nothing further was heard of it.

The series lasted for a decade, in effect drawing to a close in 1912 with the fifty-first number, a reprint of Joseph McCabe's *Twelve Years in a Monastery*. Formally, the last in the series was a compilation of W K Clifford's lectures and essays which was tacked on to the series in 1918. But changes to the law in 1912 which extended the life of copyright material, along with the silent censorship favoured by the churchmen, combined to scupper the Cheap Reprints. Although, as we will see, this was not to be the sole reason for the demise of the Cheap Reprints.

Thinking of the series in terms of twenty-first century opinion, it is interesting to draw parallels with contemporary authors. On religious matters, authors such as John Shelby Spong and Duncan Howlett from the United States, Anthony Freeman, Don Cupitt and Richard Holloway from the United Kingdom and Lloyd Geering from New Zealand would all have found a place in the list. Indeed these liberal theologians are all in the direct line of descent from their predecessors who were published by the RPA. While there is no direct parallel in scientific matters, one can't help feeling that preference would have been given to the evolutionary thinking of Stephen Jay Gould, Niles Eldridge, even Mary Midgley, over the more rigorous atheistic evolutionists such as Richard Dawkins, Daniel C Dennett or Susan Blackmore.

The most common features of the disparate philosophies and approaches which found new life in the Cheap Reprints were a confidence in reason and a meliorist progressionism. This requires some elaboration, as both confidence in reason and progressionism have fallen into disrepute. By these terms I certainly do not mean the specious cheerfulness of Dr Pangloss, who insisted, almost as a matter of dogma, that this was the best of all possible worlds. This has been the image of rationalism that its opponents have preferred to peddle. Perhaps the person who came closest to that image was Herbert Spencer. By confidence I mean the conviction, expressed with varying shades of diffidence, that humanity has the resources and will to effect necessary changes. For some of the authors included in the Cheap Reprints series, progress was a cosmological given, but for most, progress was thought of in meliorist terms. In other words, progress was possible, but improvement in the lot of humanity was something that had to be worked for, and opponents to various changes had to be taken seriously and engaged in dialogue, in the hope they may change their minds. It is important to note that the cosmological progressionism now thought to be untenable was held as much by the theists as by the agnostics and the more restrained meliorism was more characteristic of the agnostics. Far from being a quaint Victorian delusion, as many commentators, postmodernists in particular, like to believe, this sort of confidence in the possibility of progress is an essential component of any civilised, public-spirited ethic.

Notions of progress were, in many ways, central to what the Edwardians were about. But this has led many to dismiss the period airily as somehow shallow or superficial, given what has become of many of those dreams. We saw at the beginning of this chapter J B Priestley's division of society into the conservatives and the hurriers. By and large, the Rationalist Press Association was in the hurry camp, but what marks them off was the generosity of their vision of the future, and the degree to which, through the Cheap Reprints especially, they gave new voice to several, competing visions of the future. This diversity of opinions is one of the more remarkable points about the Cheap Reprints. Notwithstanding the common thread of confidence in reason and meliorism, the authors represented quite different outlooks on important philosophical, religious, scientific, political and social issues. The reason they were reprinted was that the RPA held dear another fundamental tenet of our Enlightenment heritage: a high regard for open and informed dialogue. It was less important to the RPA that they disagreed with many of the people whose works they published. It was more important to them that the works were thought constructive and conducive to peaceful development toward a secular, tolerant and pluralistic future. This point has been consistently misunderstood by the RPA's opponents. These detractors have tended to see the RPA as simply a secular version of a denominational publishing business, which will only print works that are doctrinally sound. Nothing could be further from the truth, and this error illustrates an important difference between the expectations of many religionists and those who are without religion.

Two examples can illustrate this point. In his otherwise excellent study of the development of social anthropology in Britain between the 1880s and the 1950s, G W Stocking noted that the 'evolutionary faithful' regarded Andrew Lang (1844-1912) as an 'apostate' after his about-face with regard to the origins of religion. No evidence is provided for this observation, which has the look of a throwaway quip. The point is that it isn't correct. Originally a supporter of the animist theories of E B Tylor (1832-1917), Lang moved toward a position critical of his former mentor in the 1890s, a position more favourable to conventional Christianity. Lang was one of Edward Clodd's many contacts and the two remained friends after Lang's retreat. Indeed, rather than regarding Lang as an apostate, the RPA compiled an original collection of Lang's works, for which Lang himself contributed an Introduction. The book, which came out as Number 34 of the Cheap Reprints, was published in 1908 when Lang's change of heart was more than apparent to his rationalist publishers. Watts had been aware of Lang's views for a while, Lang having rejected the term agnostic and declined an invitation to write for the *Agnostic Annual* in the 1890s. (25) But this did not prevent them from publishing his work. The book, called *The Origins of Religion*, included sections from Lang's early work, *Custom and Myth* (1884) and more recent work illustrative of his new views. The last essay in *The Origins of Religion* included this passage:

> On the whole, I am a rationalist about the rationalism of most of my masters and teachers, and deserve to be an outcast from the church anthropological of Mr Tylor, Mr Huxley, Mr Herbert Spencer, Sir Alfred Lyall, and Mr Grant Allen. But I have summarised the facts on which my opinion is based, and, for the rest, have gone where the *logos* leads me. (26)

Were the RPA to only print congenial material or to have regarded Lang as an apostate, it seems peculiar that they would have sullied their prized Cheap Reprints series with such a work. It also seems odd of Lang to supply an Introduction to an organisation he was making a showy stand against. The truth is more simple, the RPA was genuinely interested in presenting credible works to the non-specialist reader, and did so whether their cherished beliefs were vindicated or not. And Lang's position looks like little more than a pose. Stocking's throwaway line does a disservice to rationalism in general and the RPA in particular.

The openness of the rationalism of the RPA is no less evident in the case of Francis William Newman's *Phases of Faith*, which it reprinted in 1905. Francis William Newman (1805-1897) was the brother of the better-known, and infinitely more bigoted, John Henry Newman (1801-1890), who made a name for himself by becoming a Roman Catholic in 1845 and eventually becoming a cardinal. Francis William found the evangelicalism he was brought up with no more satisfactory than his brother, but his religious development took him in the opposite direction, towards a variety of eclectic, undoctrinal theism that would not be out of place among today's religious humanists. *Phases of Faith* is the awkward story of his religious journey. In his Introduction to the Cheap Reprint of the book, A W Benn praised *Phases of Faith* as an important milestone in the development of a more open attitude toward religious inquiry in England. Benn was also sure that 'it will be found that his Rationalism has borne the test of later inquiry.' (27) The fact that Newman remained a theist until his dying day was less important than that he had used his reason honestly to come to a position that squared with his intellect. That was good enough for the RPA. Newman expressed his position admirably, toward the end of his book.

> Having discovered that not all that is within the canon of the Scripture is infallibly correct, and that the human understanding is competent to arraign and convict at least some kinds of error therein contained, where was I to stop? And if I am guilty, where did my guilt begin? The further I inquired the more errors crowded upon me – in history, in chronology, in geography, in physiology, in geology. Did it then at last become a duty to close my eyes to the painful light? (28)

This dilemma, characterised by Duncan Howlett as the fatal flaw of religious liberalism, is just as alive today as it was then, and the position of the contemporary religious liberal no less equivocal and unsatisfactory.

On a more practical plane, the Cheap Reprints also worked as a commercial proposition. Watts's confidence that working people, people like him, wanted access to works of intellectual significance proved to be sound. A couple of publishers had sold a few carefully selected bestselling novels as sixpenny paperbacks, but nobody had thought there was a market for serious nonfiction in this form. Charles Albert Watts, self-taught printer's devil, proved them wrong. The first Cheap Reprint, T H Huxley's *Lectures and Essays*, sold out its first edition of 30,000 copies and a second edition of 15,000 in its first year alone. Not even the success of the first edition had reconciled Macmillan to the project entirely, and it required the intervention of T H Huxley's widow for the second edition to go ahead. Once more, this is evidence that Huxley acquiesced to Watts's interpretation of events during their dispute in 1884 that we referred to in the previous chapter. Watts faced considerably more obstinate opposition from Sir Herbert Longman, the publisher of the physicist and rationalist Professor John Tyndall (1820-1893). In his day Tyndall was as well known and respected as Huxley, and Watts was keen to reprint a collection of his lectures and essays. Longman made it clear that under no circumstances would he permit the reprint to go ahead, and refused to divulge who actually owned the copyright to the relevant essays. Having been rebuffed by Longman, Watts approached Tyndall's widow, with immediate results. It transpired that she, and not Longman, owned the copyright for the works Watts wanted to reprint, and was more than happy that her late husband's works be reprinted by the RPA. A few days after Watts's approach, Mrs Tyndall visited Johnson's Court and personally authorised the cheap reprint to go ahead. (29). *Tyndall's Lectures and Essays: A Selection* was duly published as Cheap Reprint number 10, in the middle of 1903. Thirty thousand copies of the first impression were printed.

The Cheap Reprints sold in the region of 4,000,000 copies. Doubtless with the Cheap Reprints in mind, Keir Hardie, the devout leader of the Labour Party, called Watts's printery 'the blasphemy depot'. (30) What were the secrets of the success of the Cheap Reprints? Watts himself understood the reasons well enough. 'I was successful through a combination of facts – the generous assistance of personal friends, the sympathetic support of well-known authors, and a willingness on my part to be content with a nominal profit on the printing and publishing.' (31)

The spectacular success of the Cheap Reprints had some interesting effects, not all of which had been expected. One of the main reasons for establishing the RPA in the first place was to provide a means by which heterodox works could find a publisher and an audience. It is one of the least attractive facets of the authoritarian mindset to gang together when possible and exercise a silent but none the less deadly censorship of heterodox opinions, particularly if those opinions are thought dangerous when heard by working men and women. In the days when open physical persecution of unbelievers is no longer tolerated, this more subtle form of control has been widely favoured by religious oligarchies and elites around the world. The RPA and its predecessors experienced this silent censorship in the form of a refusal by many booksellers to stock their work. And of those booksellers who *did* stock these works, their copies were in more expensive hardback form, and therefore out of the reach of many working people. But whatever reluctance there was to stock the Cheap Reprints evaporated rapidly once it was apparent that there was a considerable demand for these titles in reprint form. Pretty soon the Cheap Reprints were widely available and the more enterprising publishers soon saw value in seizing the initiative by approaching writers with proposals to publish heterodox works.

The irony of this change in attitude was that things actually became harder for the RPA, rather than easier. Where once the unbelieving author would have had little choice but to publish through the RPA or its predecessors, it now became realistic to expect one's work could secure publication with a reputable firm. And with this trend now underway, there was now less need for many people to join the RPA as the sole vehicle whereby one could procure heterodox publications. Adam Gowans Whyte summed the situation up in his 1949 study of the RPA.

> The guardians of conventional thought are still in control of most newspapers and periodicals, and they are still firmly entrenched in the field of broadcasting, but the fear of novel ideas and of the conflict of opinion no longer haunts the majority of publishers, and for this advance the experiment in publishing made fifty years ago by the RPA is largely responsible. (32)

This is a point which has never been appreciated by many historians who have ignored rationalist and humanist history, or dismissed the value of rationalist and humanist publications as marginal to the process of secularisation. An example of this type of thinking is Alan D Gilbert's work, *The Making of Post-Christian Britain*. After the briefest mention of the Cheap Reprints and the later Thinker's Library, Gilbert was nevertheless sure that:

> In terms of its overall importance in the development of modern culture, however, this kind of secularist campaign has been of only marginal significance. An index of its attraction as a cause in which people have sought active involvement is the fact that the combined membership of the Rationalist Press Association, the Ethical Union and the British Humanist Association (founded in 1963) has never grown beyond a few thousand. (33)

Gilbert gives no reason why the RPA's contribution to the process of secularisation should not be measured in terms of the four million Cheap Reprints which flooded the country. And, as we have seen, the very success of the Cheap Reprints was one of the principal reasons the RPA never became a mass membership organisation. The RPA's signal contribution toward making the conditions for an open, secular and pluralistic society militated against its own chances of being counted as successful in terms of membership. Surely, it is on these terms that the RPA should be judged, not on a mere body count. By this standard, even if the RPA's achievement is limited to the Cheap Reprints, its contribution to secularisation has been noteworthy, and, to my mind, admirable.

It is also worthwhile to put the record straight on a priority dispute. Many people have laid claim to being the first to come out with the serious non-fiction paperback. Penguin is usually thought of as the inventors of the mass circulation paperback but their own history recognises that not to be the case, although it wrongly attributed Ernest Benn as the pioneer of the sixpenny paperback. (34) In fact Benn's series did not begin until the middle twenties, more than two decades after the Cheap Reprints. The other series sometimes mentioned is J M Dent's Everyman's Library but this began in 1906, four years after the Cheap Reprints, and while designed for the general reader, was not originally produced in paperback, thus putting it out of reach for most working people. It is also worth noting that Dent's original fifty volumes were a lot safer than Watts's list. Dent's reprints included Boswell's *Life of Johnson* (numbers 1 and 2), Jane Austen, Carlyle, Macaulay, Sir Walter Scott, Robert Browning and Samuel Pepys. The only controversial publication was T H Huxley's *Man's Place in Nature*. It is not unreasonable to speculate that Dent was emboldened to reprint Huxley's book because of the success he could see Watts & Co had already enjoyed with similar titles. The place of honour, then, as the first systematic venture to publish affordable non-fiction in paperback goes to the Rationalist Press Association. This alone is sufficient reason to accord the RPA an honourable place in modern cultural history.

We have seen that the Cheap Reprints performed a notable service in the creation of post-Christian Britain. We also know that many people at the time thought in the same terms. We have already noted that the Cheap Reprints finished in 1912 because of changes in copyright laws, but this is not the end of the story. A campaign of silent censorship also played its part. The Annual Report of 1912 opened with an account of clerical attempts to freeze out the Cheap Reprints.

> It is within the knowledge of the Publishing Agents of the Association that the renters of certain bookstalls have been warned that the continued exposure of RPA publications would endanger the renewal of their tenancy; managers of large wholesale houses have declined to circulate our books except when ordered, on the ground that it would be inconsistent with their religious convictions; and numerous retail firms, which have hitherto included RPA books in their lists, have now withdrawn them. Pressure from clerical and other orthodox clients has been brought to bear on the booksellers in every direction, sometimes ineffectually, but in most cases successfully. (35)

Pressure for greater censorship and control of written material had been growing in Britain since at least 1908. A series of morals campaigns, usually dominated by churchmen, had been in operation since the turn of the century, but the largest of them had taken the initiative in 1911. The National Council of Public Morals issued a manifesto which attracted a fair number of highly public names (including Beatrice Webb). The manifesto began:

> We, the undersigned, desire to express our alarm at the low and degrading views of the racial instinct which are becoming widely circulated at the present time, not only because they offend against the highest ideals of morality and religion, but also because they therefore imperil our very life as a nation. (36)

The wave of hysteria over censorship had become a nationwide issue after the publication of H G Wells's novel *Ann Veronica* in 1909, and novels continued to be the main focus of this manifesto and other morals campaigns. But this didn't stop the Bishop of Hereford, for example, advocating the extension of the censorship to include 'the firms that supplied books and periodicals to railway bookstalls', or for the Archdeacon of London to ascribe literary impurity to 'clever reviewers and Agnostics'. (37) The vagueness of censorship laws in England at the time meant that the most effective form of censorship was an unofficial word in someone's ear. In this way, churchmen could bring pressure to bear on landlords and businessmen, for example, and expect the shutters to come down, almost imperceptibly. This was what happened to the Cheap Reprints.

It was a sign of the distinctly English nature of this censorship that it was not directed toward the works themselves, but to their form in Cheap Reprints, thus making them accessible to the less well off. When the National Council of Public Morals lamented the threat to the 'very life of the nation', it was the intellectual emancipation of the lower orders that most excited their fear. In this sense as well, then, the RPA can take credit for a significant contribution to the secularisation of society, but one which is difficult to measure, and one that, by measuring by membership, will give an altogether false picture of the RPA's effectiveness.

Other RPA publications

While the Cheap Reprints was the most spectacular initiative undertaken by the RPA, in its first decade, it by no means exhausted their programme of activities. There was, of course, the regular programme of publishing, which became more ambitious as each year passed. In 1902, for example, the RPA spent more than £500 reprinting a revised edition of Walter Cassels's (1826-1907) classic of Victorian rationalism, *Supernatural Religion*. Originally published anonymously in three volumes between 1874 and 1876, *Supernatural Religion* attracted a considerable reputation as a learned work. Many thought it must have come from a senior scholar of religion, such was the quality of scholarship the book revealed. It came as something of a shock to religious sensibilities that such a learned critique could have been written by an entirely self-taught merchant based in India. The significant expenditure on this book was eased by Cassels's refusal to accept any payment for his extensively revised edition.

Supernatural Religion was the sort of book the RPA existed for. The RPA had three categories into which books would be placed. These categories had important consequences for the way a work was published. First, there were works thought to be accessible to a large market and which could therefore be issued cheaply; works like *The Riddle of the Universe*. Second, there were sound rationalist works which would be attractive to a smaller market, such as McCabe's *Life and Letters of George Jacob Holyoake* (1908). And finally there were works whose merits were such that there was a responsibility to issue the work without undue regard to its covering publication costs. Books like *Supernatural Religion*. These decisions were usually left to Watts who, from the lifetime he had spent in the trade had 'a paranormal sense of the prospects of a book and also of the form and price that would achieve the best results.' (38). Watts demonstrated this ability even with a book like *Supernatural Religion*. Despite the revised and abridged version still covering nine hundred pages of close type, the 5000 copies were sold within three years.

The success of the Cheap Reprints was an obvious encouragement to the RPA to try other series as well. In 1903, the year after the Cheap Reprints began, the RPA began a series given the rather unhelpful title of 'RPA Extra Series'. This was a more eclectic series ranging from reprints of Victorian works indistinguishable from the Cheap Reprints, to paperback versions of current RPA publications. The reprints included the Prolegomena to George Lewes's (1817-1878) *History of Philosophy* (renamed *Science and Speculation*) and what was essentially a reader of Auguste Comte's philosophy, given the title *The Fundamental Principles of the Positive Philosophy*. Why these titles were not included in the Cheap Reprints, I have no idea. It was not a matter of being wary of positivism, as *The Service of Man*, by John Cotter Morison, was an early Cheap Reprint and was a popular exposition of positivism. And one or two rationalists, most notably F J Gould and Charles E Hooper, were very sympathetic to positivism. It is possible that it was a condition of permission to reprint the works that they not be included in the Cheap Reprints series, although the Extra Series was indistinguishable from its sister series. Another possible explanation is that most of the authors of titles in the Extra Series were RPA insiders: Charles Gorham, Joseph McCabe, J Allanson Picton and F H Hayward. Watts may well have wanted to retain the Cheap Reprints for better-known names. But on the other hand, Joseph McCabe had titles in both the Cheap Reprints and the Extra Series. We will probably never know.

As with the Cheap Reprints, the basic character of the Extra Series was to publish sixpenny paperbacks simultaneously with hardbacks costing a shilling. One person included in the series was who was not an RPA regular was Charlotte Perkins Gilman (1860-1935) who has come to be recognised as one of the most influential feminists of the early twentieth century and whose thought is most consistent with contemporary feminism. Gilman had experienced a considerable degree of harassment for being a divorced woman and a mother who had abandoned the care of her children to others while she lectured on feminist causes. Rationalists were overwhelmingly to be counted among the progressives on gender issues, as they are now called, and Gilman's past would not have been a barrier to her works being considered worthy of reprinting. The work reprinted was *Concerning Children*, published originally in 1900, which advocated a radical programme of co-operative care and socialisation of children.

More thematically unified was the History of Science Series, which, as the title suggests, was devoted to providing outline histories of various disciplines for the general reader. As well as what we would normally classify as sciences, this series included histories of Old and New Testament criticism. These histories were excellent introductions, written by people with expertise in the field. It began with a survey of astronomy by Professor George Forbes in 1909 and finished three years later with Alfred William Benn surveying modern philosophy. Several of the contributors, prominent men in their fields, were persuaded to write for the series by Edward Clodd. (39) This series, however, was not a financial success. It was repackaged in the 1920s as Story of the Sciences. Titles were given new dust jackets with catchier titles; for instance A W Benn's *History of Modern Philosophy* became *All About Modern Philosophy*.

In 1913, a new series began called The Inquirer's Library which had a slightly different focus. The series, under the supervision of Joseph McCabe, was intended to be an aid in religious controversy. It smacks strongly of McCabe's own priorities.

> The new "Library" will deal concisely with various leading issues (Theism, Immortality, the Bible, Morality, etc), and form a brief cyclopaedia of research on these most important subjects. It will contain historical sketches of the development of religions and sects, and will reply to all current arguments of supernaturalists. (40)

McCabe was always a strong advocate of direct and militant propaganda and this series was almost certainly a concession to him. It was the fate of the Inquirer's Library to be launched in 1913. It was cut short by the onset of the First World War, only five works being published in the series. The first was by McCabe himself and was a straightforward discussion on *The Existence of God*. This little book, only 150 pages long (it would be lucky to make half that in a modern paperback) is a masterpiece of intelligent popularisation of complex issues. It is a scandal that it is not regularly reprinted and anthologised.

Moving to the single-volume works published by Watts & Co for the RPA, one of the more controversial titles during these years was a well researched survey of contemporary Christianity from the viewpoint of a Chinese writer. Lin Shao-Yang wrote a work called *A Chinese Appeal to Christendom Concerning Christian Missions*. This work, published in 1911, drew attention to the paradox of missionaries presenting a simplistic series of truth-claims about Christianity to supposedly heathen Orientals while those very truth-claims were all under very severe challenge by theologians and thinkers in Europe. In the writer's words, a 'garrisoned city does not send away the flower of its troops when a powerful enemy is thundering at its gates.' (41) Not surprisingly, this book created a storm of controversy, and became the most successful book the RPA published that year.

Lin Shao-Yang showed himself remarkably familiar with contemporary western thought. So much so that it didn't take long for enemies of the RPA to accuse it of dishonesty. It was alleged that 'Lin Shao-Yang' was a pen-name for someone else, presumably an Englishman. In a letter sent to the *Spectator* and the *Daily News* and printed in both journals, Watts more or less admitted the work was pseudonymous.

> Dear Sir, - It seems to us unimportant whether Mr Lin Shao-Yang, the author of *A Chinese Appeal to Christendom concerning Christian Missions*, is a Chinese or an Englishman; but, were we in a position to disclose the authorship, we should have no objection to gratifying the curiosity of Mr Hodgkin and yourself...And the fundamental question is not who wrote the book, but the accuracy or otherwise of the statements on which the "appeal" is based. (42)

Watts suggested some precedents for using a non de plume, citing Sir Alfred Lyall's *Criticisms of Mr Balfour's Foundations of Belief* under the Hindu name of Vamadeo Shastri, and Lowes Dickinson's *Letters from John Chinaman*. Attention soon focused on Sir Hiram Maxim (1840-1916), an ebullient engineer and inventor of, among other things, the maxim gun. Maxim had spent a considerable time in China and had developed a huge admiration for Chinese culture and a proportionate dislike of European missionaries, who seemed to him arrogant, uncouth, and racist by comparison. At an RPA Annual Dinner and later in an article in the 1911 *RPA Annual*, Maxim called for the creation of an anti-missionary society. Missionaries, Maxim maintained are 'the greatest liars on the face of the earth'. (43) He followed this up with an article in the *Literary Guide* on his first experiences with the bigoted missionary mind-set. By the time *A Chinese Appeal to Christendom* was reviewed (by Hypatia Bradlaugh Bonner) in the May edition of the *Guide*, a fair old controversy had been worked up.

Before long the Spectator received a pseudonymous letter (quickly reprinted in the *Literary Guide*) in which 'Lin Shao-Yang' admitted that he was in fact a European. Many assumed this was Maxim admitting authorship, and the matter faded away. In fact, the book was written by Sir Reginald Fleming Johnston (1874-1938), one-time tutor to the last Manchu emperor P'u Yi, later a British diplomat in China and later still Professor of Oriental Languages at the School of Oriental Studies in London. Two years after this furore, in 1913, Johnston wrote a book called *Buddhist China* which contrasted Buddhism favourably with the Christianity of the missionaries and in 1919 Watts & Co published a work called *Letters to a Missionary*. Both these books were published under Johnston's own name. His authorship of *A Chinese Appeal to Christendom*, however, remained uncertain until after his death.

The controversy over the authorship notwithstanding, *A Chinese Appeal to Christendom* was a telling work. Johnston had many stories of missionaries setting up altars without permission in Chinese temples, only then to scorn the hardness of heart of the locals who ignored their blandishments. Not a word of praise, Johnston observed, of the forbearance of the Chinese in the face of such arrogance. He speculated as to the reception a group of Chinese visitors would receive were they to walk into an English church 'to join in a hymn of praise to Confucius or to Buddha. It might even happen that the Chinese visitors would be bundled unceremoniously out of the building.' (44) It might indeed. Johnston was deeply angered by the blustering attitude of westerners in China and foretold its inevitable failure.

> The gunboat policy – the policy that holds a pistol to China's head and says, "Admit Christianity freely into your Empire or we fire!" – can never be forgotten by the Chinese, and it can never be explained away. Christianity is now, and perhaps always will be, associated in the Chinese mind with the political humiliation of their country. (45)

This book also stands as a rebuke to the easy prejudice peddled by postmodernists that rationalism is a dominant discourse of the west at the expense of other peoples and cultures. This has never been true and here, once more, is some evidence for that.

For all this, it has to be acknowledged that few of the stand-alone volumes published by Watts & Co for the RPA in the years before the First World War qualify as works of exceptional literary or scholarly merit. Most of the works published then are of interest only to the specialist, or would be, if only more specialists would take notice of this valuable but under-utilised resource.

Central to the mission of the RPA at the time was its conviction that the churches were out of touch with contemporary thought, so it is not surprising that some books should have been devoted to that theme. The best example of this type of book was *The Churches and Modern Thought* by Vivian Phelps (1860-1938), who wrote under the pseudonym of Philip Vivian. Like many of his contemporaries, Phelps lost his faith while working in the colonial administration in India. Phelps was genuinely distressed at losing his faith, and he was genuinely interested to itemise the various points at which the churches were indeed at odds with the scholarship of the day. *The Churches and Modern Thought* was solidly researched, well-written and transparently honest. It went into two editions, selling 42,000 copies before it was re-released as No. 20 in the Thinker's Library in 1931, when it went on selling. Phelps cited seven main shocks suffered by Christianity in the modern era:

- myriads of worlds in the process of birth and death
- the vast antiquity of the earth
- the long history of man and his animal origin
- the reign of natural law and the consequent discredit of the supernatural
- the suspicions aroused by the study of comparative mythology
- the difficulties thrown up by biblical literalism
- the doubt thrown by the Higher Criticism on many cherished beliefs

Phelps concluded that these disturbances 'have shaken the very foundations of our faith, and are the cause of agnosticism among the vast majority of our leaders of thought and science.' (46) When Paul Tillich said the same things half a century later, he was credited with courage and wisdom, but for Vivian Phelps to say these things – why, that is shallow rationalism. Joseph McCabe's rewritten version of *Modern Rationalism*, published in 1909, covered similar ground to Phelps, although in less detail.

The surveys of Phelps and McCabe were designed for the general reader and disclaimed to be works of original scholarship, although the manner in which they brought the material together was impressive. Among the titles that *do* qualify as outstanding works of scholarship published by the RPA at this time are those of Frederick Cornwallis Conybeare (1856-1926). From a very distinguished family of scholars, Conybeare was a Fellow of University College, Oxford from 1881, and, from 1903, a Fellow of the British Academy. An unbeliever from his youth, Conybeare recalled protesting against attending chapel as an undergraduate, saying he hated it. He was told "You don't hate it more than I do, but you have to go." (47) His specialism was Armenian religious history and he wrote three excellent works for the RPA. In the History of Science series Conybeare contributed the volume on *History of New Testament Criticism* (1910), and his two stand-alone works were *Myth, Magic and Morals* (1909) and *The Historical Christ* (1914). Conybeare received an honorary doctorate of theology from Giessen for his works of biblical research.

Myth, Magic and Morals was a study of Christian origins and the historical Jesus, and it owed a debt to the work of Harnack, Wellhausen and Loisy. What made Conybeare's work original was his willingness to extend the conclusions of this sort of research to Christianity. This sort of study, when undertaken by theologians, very frequently ended up in circumlocutions and sophistry to avoid applying the conclusions of the study to Christian truth-claims. In Conybeare's words, the theologians 'lack thoroughness and sincerity, and they are forever pulling up their horses just as they seem about to leap.' (48) This tendency continues to this day. In 1996, James Veitch, a prominent liberal Christian theologian in New Zealand and member of the Jesus Seminar, complained of a 'deep, but disguised scholarly reluctance to fully apply the historical method to a study of the Gospels, because the impact the outcome might have for the figure of Jesus and the faith of the Church.' (49) Rationalists like Conybeare were aware of this a hundred years ago and received only scorn for being, in effect, ahead of their time. When theologians finally catch up and say the same thing, they are widely hailed as brave pioneers of a realistic new kind of faith.

Conybeare's conclusions were just as sophisticated as his method. Jesus, Conybeare concluded, came to the public with no cut and dried creeds, but with the single, all-encompassing conviction 'that a mighty upheaval was at hand, that the divine father, in his omnipotence, was about to bring his age to an end and inaugurate a new era of salvation.' (50) Jesus did not believe he was going to die at Jerusalem, but to consummate the Kingdom of God upon earth. And his message was directed solely at the Jews, although only those who hearkened to his own message and to John the Baptist's summons to repentance were to be part of the new dispensation. It was Jesus's singular misfortune to be followed by Paul, who was not interested in his life and mission, but only in his death. Paul's Christ 'is an *a priori* construction of his own, owing to the historical man of Nazareth and to those who knew that man and cherished his memory little except the bare name Jesus.' (51) Conybeare's portrayal of Jesus would not be out of place on the shelves of any reputable bookshop today. His conclusions are widely shared, including by people who call themselves Christian theologians. He placed in the hands of the general reader an approachable and yet deeply learned summary of all the best research on the New Testament and applied those conclusions with candour and honesty. It stands, therefore, as a valuable example of rationalist scholarship at its best.

Conybeare's work also counts as evidence against one of the more persistent prejudices held about the rationalist movement, which was its apparent insistence on a mythical Jesus. This idea had been around for more than a century, but it was J M Robertson who developed this thesis most thoroughly, although Arthur Drews in Germany and William Benjamin Smith in the United States (both of whom were theists) also pursued the theme. Robertson's two main books on the subject were *Christianity and Mythology* (1900) and *Pagan Christs* (1903), both published by Watts & Co. Both works were exhaustive collections of facts and inferences but what made life difficult was the imprecision and dogmatism of Robertson's writings. On the one hand, his work was a useful contribution to the literature on Jesus because he was not shackled with a theological charge to defend supernaturalism, and he brought together an impressive quantity of mythical parallels to the Jesus story which churchmen of the time shrank from doing. But on the other hand, Robertson's pet theory was not supported by much more evidence than the standard Christologies he was deriding. It was Robertson's belief that the Jesus story was not a narrative but a transcript of an older mystical drama, which was itself a later adaptation of an original rite of human sacrifice. Sometimes he seemed to acknowledge that there had been an actual person called Jesus whose real message had well and truly been lost; other times he seemed to be saying that the actual person had never lived at all. Robertson never appreciated the significance of the dating of the Gospels. As late as 1926, Robertson was insisting that the priority of the 'Mark' was of little more than 'a matter of literary history'. (52) Conybeare's grasp of the intricacies of biblical history and textual criticism was far more sophisticated than Robertson's, and *Myth, Magic and Morals* reads very well a century later, unlike Robertson's more ponderous tomes.

Soon after *Myth, Magic and Morals* appeared a senior theologian and biblical scholar, Professor Sanday, wrote a pamphlet called *A New Marcion* in which he urged Conybeare 'not to meddle in future with things with which I am hopelessly out of sympathy.' (53) This has been a common charge made by churchmen, who feel nonetheless entitled to write material hostile to unbelief. Sanday had himself written about the Bible in a spirit of shedding it of mythical accretions, but seemed offended when a non-Christian scholar did the same thing. In common with many religious attacks on rationalists, Sanday found it difficult to credit Conybeare with autonomous moral decency. 'Of course Mr Conybeare is better than his creed. This is what constantly happens: a Christian upbringing tells, and the effects of it survive, after it has been given up as theoretically untenable.' (54)

Sanday was not to be Conybeare's main antagonist, however. For the rest of his life, and indeed after his death, Conybeare was criticised by J M Robertson, sometimes quite fiercely. It was in the face of this criticism that Conybeare's next book, and his last for the RPA, was published in 1914. *The Historical Christ* was a full-frontal attack on the myth theory of Robertson, Drews and Smith, whose works were described as 'blundering extravaganzas.' (55) It was this book's task to 'provide an account of the historical Jesus that was a middle way between traditionalism on the one hand and absurdity on the other.' (56)

A point which has not been commented upon is that *The Historical Christ* was published by Watts & Co. This should help us appreciate once more the openness of rationalism. Religious opponents have often scoffed at the RPA as just another dogmatic publishing house, but if this were true, it would seem odd that it should publish works supporting *and* opposing a thesis then held to be significant. This is even more relevant when one looks at how *The Historical Christ* has been used. Again, New Zealand can serve as an illustration. From the 1900s to the 1930s public debates about the historicity of Jesus were relatively frequent and well attended. During one such debate a churchman could use *The Historical Christ* for support against the mythical Jesus and in so doing claim that he had vanquished rationalism! (57) While rationalism was open to different ideas, it has to be said that certain rationalists were less so. The ferocity of Robertson's criticisms led to Conybeare's resignation from the RPA in 1914. In 1915, Robertson even stooped to accusing Conybeare of being pro-German. Before long Conybeare would be hounded out of Oxford for holding relatively mild anti-war opinions. Having written for the rationalist press would not have helped his case one bit.

Another of the outstanding works published by Watts & Co before the First World War was Joseph McCabe's *The Sources of the Morality of the Gospels*, published in 1914. As with most of his work, McCabe had a non-specialist reader in mind. Like Conybeare, McCabe had little time for the mythical Jesus argument. In the Preface to this book he wrote, 'whether or no we can explain Christianity without Christ, we can assuredly explain the teaching attributed to him without assuming either that he existed or that an authentic word of his Gospel has reached us.' (58) And with reference to his experience debating with Christians, McCabe lamented that apologists 'are too apt to appraise the "uniqueness" of Christ's teaching without any close study of those other moralities which they thus assume to be inferior to that of Christ.' (59) This is a claim one can still hear being made. What McCabe then went on to do was to show the parallel (and precursor) to each supposedly unique pearl of New Testament wisdom in the literature of the Greeks, Romans and Jews. McCabe was unambiguous:

> There is no shade of originality in the Gospel ethic. There is no shade of moral idealism in the discourses attributed to Christ that had not found expression in the Old Testament centuries before, was not familiar among the Jewish teachers who spent their lives in meditation on the Old Testament, and was not put forward by some, if not all, of the great non-Christian and non-Jewish moralities of the time. (60)

Few people would have doubted McCabe's claim at this point, as the previous 88 pages had been a simple comparison, divided over four columns, of the New Testament maxims anticipated by a Jewish, Greek or Roman parallel. *The Sources of the Morality of the Gospels* is an unjustly forgotten rationalist classic.

And finally, one of the other more enterprising RPA initiatives was its decision in 1909 to issue a cheap reprint of the imposing *Encyclopaedia Biblica*, which had originally appeared between 1899 and 1903 in four volumes and was published by Adam & Charles Black. The Watts & Co reprints appeared in 58 instalments at 7d each. George Wilson, principal of A & C Black, though not himself a rationalist, was happy for his encyclopaedia to be distributed in this enterprising way. *The Encyclopaedia Biblica* was in its day a controversial publication. The contributing scholars were overwhelmingly either churchmen or sympathetic to the church. But the encyclopaedia brought together the combined conclusions of the nineteenth century Higher Criticism and revealed the Bible to be a document written by many different people over many centuries with many different aims and motives in mind. This is old hat to all but the most intransigent fundamentalist now, but in the Edwardian era, this was highly controversial.

Other RPA activities

One of the RPA's main initiatives outside the arena of publishing was to fund a small group of lecturers to address audiences on topics of importance to rationalism. This began in 1903, the year the Extra Series began and a year after the launching of the Cheap Reprints. The principal lecturers were Charles Watts senior, Hypatia Bradlaugh Bonner, Dennis Hird and Joseph McCabe. Watts remained a popular platform speaker until shortly before his death in 1906. One of the busier speakers was Dennis Hird (1850-1920), once a prominent Anglican churchman. While vicar at Eastnor in Herefordshire, Hird slowly lost his faith in revealed religion and was eventually forced out of his post by the Bishop of Hereford. After curacies in Battersea and Bournemouth, he had served as secretary of the Church of England Temperance Society and as the London Police Court Missionary. But increasing problems reconciling Darwinism and religion led him to lose his faith entirely. From 1899 to 1909 Hird was Principal of Ruskin College. His most important books were *An Easy Outline of Evolution*, which appeared as Cheap Reprint number 30 in 1907, and *A Picture Book of Evolution*. Both books had long lives, going through several editions. Not surprisingly, Hird spoke mainly on evolution and was a successful speaker on this topic.

But quite in any way the most prolific speaker was Joseph McCabe, whose energy for public speaking was almost limitless. Year in and year out, each RPA Annual Report would do what it could to praise McCabe's contribution sufficiently. The report for 1905, for instance, spoke of Hird and McCabe's lantern lectures on evolution as 'successful beyond all expectation' with audiences 'exceedingly large'. (61) Illness soon put an end to Hird's lecturing career, and parliamentary duties cut back the availability of J M Robertson. But for years to come, McCabe was one of the most indefatigable lecturers in Britain. The RPA Annual Report for 1907 began its section of platform activities with McCabe's work. 'Joseph McCabe, whose energies are apparently inexhaustible, has been addressing crowded audiences most week-nights during the season as well as twice on Sundays.' (62) Thirteen years later the RPA Annual Report of 1920 was struggling to say something new about McCabe's efforts. 'Mr McCabe's energy is untiring, and it is gratifying to record his invariable success. A complete list of his engagements for the RPA alone would occupy more than a page of this Report.' (63) The RPA's platform programme would have amounted to little without McCabe's extraordinary energy and dedication. He was a gifted lecturer and helped tens of thousands of people learn about the beauty and complexity of the real world of science and ideas.

The last initiative undertaken by the RPA in its early years which deserves mention was the decision in 1906 (though acted on the following year) to appoint Honorary Local Secretaries in points distant from London. Not surprisingly, the RPA's membership was drawn mainly from London, but there was a significant membership in the provinces and abroad. It was felt that voluntary secretaries could serve as local foci for RPA meetings and agents to encourage people to join the Association. The 1908 Annual Report listed 21 Honorary Local Secretaries around the United Kingdom and a further 19 in various parts of the world. By 1916 the number in the United Kingdom had dropped to 17 but the number of overseas Secretaries had risen to thirty. It soon transpired that there were several strong points of overseas interest in the RPA. The three best-represented foreign parts were Australia, New Zealand and India, with respectable showings in Canada, South Africa and Japan. One Local Secretary, William John Miles of Sydney, Australia, was mentioned in several Annual Reports as a particularly successful representative of the RPA. Miles (1871-1942), an accountant, was so successful in gathering members for the RPA in Sydney that, by 1910, it was thought to be the largest RPA grouping outside London. This gathering later formed the Rationalist Association of New South Wales. Other RPA groups formed in Melbourne in 1906, Brisbane in 1909 and Perth and Adelaide in 1918. (64) Another Local Secretary was Charles Lionel d'Avoine (1875-1945) a medical practitioner in Bombay. Originally a Catholic, d'Avoine became a rationalist after reading *The Riddle of the Universe* and John William Draper's classic *The History of the Conflict between Religion and Science*. In 1930 d'Avoine joined the newly-formed Anti-Priestcraft Association, which became the Rationalist Association of India, and which in 1950 merged with the Indian Rationalist Association, which remains active to this day.

For other people, this link with the RPA was a matter of considerable personal significance, as their holding rationalist opinions not infrequently resulted in a degree of ostracism or isolation. For William Brabant, the Local Secretary in Fiji, as an example, the RPA was his lifeline to the outside world. A member since 1904 and one of the first Life Members, Brabant served as a customs official in Fiji and must have looked forward to each new consignment of RPA material from 'home', as England was usually called by English-speaking people in Australasia. His large collection of rationalist works later became the core of the library now held by the New Zealand Association of Rationalists and Humanists in Auckland, New Zealand. Each book is lovingly stamped with 'The Brabant Library'. After retiring from his work in Fiji, Brabant was instrumental in re-forming the Rationalist Association in New Zealand, which had broken up in 1923. Brabant died in Fiji in 1951.

Religious reactions to the secularist snake

The success of the RPA's endeavours, the Cheap Reprints in particular, took just about everybody by surprise. The publishing community was taken unawares that a substantial market existed for inexpensive works of non-fiction. And the religious establishment had convinced itself that the hey-day of secularism was over with the passing of the great Victorian rationalists. The *Guardian* captured this mood in an article late in 1903 called 'The Recrudescence of Rationalism'. It remarked that there had been a lull in secularist propaganda since the demise of Charles Bradlaugh but that this lull was now well and truly over. There is, the *Guardian* went on:

> at present an organised movement for the spread of rationalistic and materialistic opinions which demands the serious attention of all Christian teachers and workers, and which gives clear evidence that, if the secularist snake was scotched, it has not been killed. (65)

The religious establishment was unprepared for a major initiative from a freethought organisation. As a result the reactions to the Cheap Reprints varied. From the less sophisticated clergy and religious journalists came complaints about the decay of reverence. This was grist to the mill for Joseph McCabe. In a lead article in the *Literary Guide* at the beginning of 1903 McCabe mocked this sort of complaint:

> For a few moments the pen of the critic dug deep into the ecclesiastical vocabulary. From a "decay of reverence" it flew to "monumental insolence" and various degrees (always superlative) of "conceit," "folly," and finally – by this time we must charitably suppose the writer's eye was dimmed with tears – "ignorance." (66)

This perception that criticism of religion is tantamount to insolence was (and remains) widespread among many religious believers. It was presumably shared by the stockists at Hull's municipal library, who refused to accept any Cheap Reprints, even though they were offered free of charge. Among significant sections of the religious press the reaction was close to panic, examples of which the *Literary Guide* delighted in reprinting for its readers. One rather breathless Methodist wrote to the *Methodist Times* that the sixpenny reprint of *The Riddle of the Universe* was

> circulating in the North in amazing numbers. It is being read in country villages where we have never known serious reading find entry before – at least, not to such an extent. Farm labourers are reading it, and young miners and factory hands. It is poisoning the minds and clouding the faith of a class from which we procure some of our best workers and most devout worshippers. The facts are beyond doubt, and they are becoming more plain every day. (67)

This person begged for a reply to Haeckel to be published before it was too late. More august periodicals such as the *London Quarterly Review* were just as alarmed. One of the most frequently-voiced concerns was that this literature was reaching the untutored masses, who, without proper Christian guidance, were all too liable to lapse into error, or worse.

> The point of interest, however, is that these books, breathing an intensely hostile spirit to Christianity, are published, are circulating in their tens of thousands (a sale of 250,000 was claimed some time since), are found in piles on the shelves of the most respectable booksellers, who, a few years ago, would have rigidly excluded avowedly secularist publications, are eagerly read by multitudes whose minds are utterly unformed in the study of such questions, and who greedily drink in the new teaching as gospel. (68)

It is hard to decide whether it is the patronising tone or the hostility to the idea of working people reading things for themselves that is the most offensive aspect of this passage. And it is simply untrue to describe the general content of the Cheap Reprints as 'breathing an intensely hostile spirit to Christianity'. A significant proportion of the authors were theists, several of them were specifically Christian. Another response frequently resorted to, one which also remains popular among religious apologists to this day, is to deny the sincerity of the unbeliever. In our more pluralistic twenty-first century this process is often referred to as demonising the opposition. There gathered in 1905 a symposium of churchmen to discuss reactions to the RPA initiatives. Rev T Allison, in a talk entitled 'The Evangelist in Contact with Aggressive Rationalism' reassured the audience that unbelievers 'of all sorts of conditions have the consciousness of their own experience, and deep down in their hearts there is always a response to the appeal of the Cross.' But only the paragraph earlier, Allison had intimated what may have been his real fear when he speculated that a 'tired, jaded, half-hearted, unbelieving, badly read clergy may lie at the root of the present distress.' (69).

Others preferred to resort to bluster. At a conference of diocesan clergy at Lambeth Palace which convened to discuss the Cheap Reprints, the Rev. W

Blissard was quoted in the *Daily Chronicle* as declaring to the infidel '"Do your worst; spend your money; but remember that we have got the last word." There were in the land 20,000 pulpits, and every Sunday a "son of Thunder" got into one of those pulpits, and had full scope to declare the truth and the whole truth.' (70) But, unbeknownst to Rev Blissard, many of his fellow sons of Thunder were succumbing to the pressure of the rationalist critique.

Quite the most outrageous of the Christian responses to rationalism came in the form of a work by Canon Henry Lewis. *Modern Rationalism as seen at work in its biographies*, published by SPCK in 1913, was an extended *ad hominem* attack, with the RPA identified on the first page as the target of Lewis's attack. Lewis quotes Joseph McCabe's claim in *The Religion of Woman* that the world grows more humane as it discards Christianity. 'It is to see whether humanity is now being made "greater than ever" by Modern Rationalism, or whether its effects upon human life are disastrous, that the present volume is written.' (71) Gathering together an eclectic ensemble of people, ranging from Voltaire to Nietzsche, Schopenhauer to Charles Bradlaugh, Lewis declared that they 'were meant for something truer to the possibilities which were manifestly in them. The Christian Religion could have made nobler men and women of them, had it been allowed to have the making of them.' Anticipating the query about the less than ideal lives of many professed Christians, Lewis assured us that such people 'are distinctly contrary to Religion. Moreover, the Religion was working out its nature in them in spite of their failures.' Having secured his flanks, Lewis then went on to drag up every possible error, folly, or unpleasantness from the life-stories of these men and declare his case proven.

A piece of scandal-mongering such as this deserved, and attracted, a fiery response. Joseph McCabe condemned Lewis's account as 'the silliest, sorriest, and pettiest contribution to clerical literature which I have seen for a long time.' Rationalists, McCabe said

> do not claim a monopoly of virtue; indeed, many of us decline to accept a Dean's standards…But we hold that sound character has nothing to do with theology, and this pitiful result of a survey of the careers of the innumerable prominent Rationalists of the nineteenth century confirms us. (72)

Churchmen are wont to burst with indignation when an attack is made on their religion which they feel to be undignified or churlish. But, sadly, this does not prevent some of their number from feeling justified in making precisely that sort of attack on non-believers while surrounding themselves in a halo of sanctity. It is amusing to then watch other apologists snatch the same halo to make a contrary claim. Late in the twenties, as part of another imbroglio, a prominent apologist claimed that 'Thoughtful Christians would never dream of asserting either that it is very wrong to criticise religion or that religion always makes men virtuous.' (73) This is clearly not true, as the experience of Canon Lewis attests.

Alongside Lewis's extended slander came more considered criticisms. The Edwardian period was the first period to my knowledge which felt the need to produce compendiums of heresy, so many were there to choose from. One of the more comprehensive attacks on rationalism from established religion at this time came from Rev. C L Drawbridge, MA, Organising Honorary Secretary of the Christian Evidence Society. Drawbridge noted that:

> if one may judge by the literature which it has carefully selected in the name of "Modern Thought," according to the Rationalist Press Association, it appears to be the negative theological opinions of past generations of atheists, agnostics, and other sceptics, such as Tom Paine.

Drawbridge concluded that while the RPA has 'the Huxleys and Herbert Spencers of the past, we have the Bergsons and Euckens of the present, as leaders of modern thought.' (74) Drawbridge made a valid point when he noted that the people selected by the RPA as examples of modern thought were carefully selected. But he was quite wrong to include the word atheist to describe any of them. Religious apologists often used the word 'atheist' as a scare tactic. But as we have already observed, one of the noticeable features of the authors chosen to be reprinted by the RPA was the absence of atheist thinkers. Drawbridge was also unfair in his point that the material being reprinted was old. After all, the series was called the Cheap Reprints. Reprints are reprinted versions of material now released from copyright or otherwise released for further publication. To criticise a reprint for being a reprint seems a little unfair. And Drawbridge must have been aware that the Society for the Promotion of Christian Knowledge had decided to copy the RPA when, in 1903, it released two works of Christian apologetic as sixpenny reprints. They were Dr Wace's *On Agnosticism: A Reply to Professor Huxley* and Drummond's *Natural Law in the Spiritual World*. Evidently, the Society for the Promotion of Christian Knowledge still saw the works of Huxley as a sufficient danger to warrant reprinting a rebuttal to them. A correspondent to the *Literary Guide*, W R Standage, probably captured the mood of the RPA when he declared confidently that 'Rationalists need have no fear of Christian efforts…The past with its bloodshed and crime belongs to the Church, the future with all its wonderful discoveries belongs to Rationalism.' (75)

Another point of Drawbridge's that is worth commenting on is his holding up Bergson and Eucken as exemplars of modern thought. Henri Bergson (1859-1941) who enjoyed tremendous popularity in France, particularly in the years before the First World War, was principally an 'apologist for the values of sentiment and of the spirit'. (76) Despite not making his religious views clear (he was a non-practising Jew) Bergson was taken up enthusiastically in France by right-wing anti-rationalist reactionaries. He is best remembered for positing the notion of the *élan vital*, or vital spark, which he held to be the motive force underlying evolution. This was his principal attraction to Protestant apologists such as Drawbridge. Bergson offered them hope that the materialist implications of evolution could somehow be mitigated, or even turned around. But Drawbridge should have been aware that Bergson's philosophy had been subjected to a scorching critique by Bertrand Russell in *The Monist* in 1912. And outside of a few non-philosophical champions, most notably George Bernard Shaw, Bergson's influence in Britain never fully recovered from Russell's attack.

Rudolf Eucken (1846-1926) was an even more unfortunate choice for Drawbridge to choose as an exemplar of the modern theism. Eucken was a neo-

Hegelian theist, in that he stressed the centrality of the 'Absolute Spiritual Life' in all things, even inanimate things. Eucken was not an apologist for a personal God but for 'the Godhead'. The same year Drawbridge was extolling Eucken as a bulwark against rationalism, the Idealist philosopher Bernard Bosanquet was dismissing the German's work as 'no really precise contribution to philosophical science. Free cognition has been submerged by moralistic rhetoric.'(77)

Drawbridge would doubtless also regret Eucken's nationalism. At precisely the same time as Drawbridge's eulogy of him was being published, Eucken was declaring that the German people alone were capable of the cultivation of the soul that comes with philosophy. Eucken was equally convinced that 'possession of a primordial world-encompassing inwardness gives us inexhaustible strength.' (78) To have chosen Bergson and Eucken as the best examples of modern theism, Drawbridge revealed just how bankrupt personal-God theology had become. The criticisms of Drawbridge and others was contradictory. On the one hand they feared 'modern thought' and so attempted to snare some moderns for themselves as well. But on the other hand they felt the need to question the status of the modern thinkers reprinted by the RPA by deriding them as nineteenth-century left-overs. When all else failed, the scare tactics of simply labelling the works as atheist, anti-Christian, or immoral was resorted to.

The worthy tomes of Drawbridge and his allies were never likely to secure a wide readership. Quite in any way the most widely-read opponent of rationalism before the First World War was the polemical journalist, G K Chesterton (1874-1936). His first important clash with rationalists took place in the pages of the *Clarion*, an influential socialist paper edited by Robert Blatchford (1851-1943). Blatchford's championing in the *Clarion* of the Cheap Reprint of Haeckel's *Riddle of the Universe* in 1903 was a significant reason for that book's success. Later that year, and under the influence of Haeckel's book, Blatchford published his own thoughts on religion. *God and My Neighbour* became one of the most successful works of popular rationalism ever produced, remaining in print for many decades. There followed a lengthy and inconclusive dialogue between Chesterton and Blatchford in the pages of the *Clarion* over 1903 and 1904. Eventually, Blatchford called in Joseph McCabe, as the most effective defender of rationalism. Nine decades later, McCabe's reply was described by David Dooley, a strong supporter of Chesterton, as a 'devastating attack on Chesterton's methods of argumentation.' (79)

McCabe began by unravelling the factual errors underlying Chesterton's notorious paradoxes. The real point was that Chesterton's paradoxes not only obscured from view these inaccuracies but paralysed serious study of problems.

> The ballets of the Alhambra and the fireworks of the Crystal Palace, and Mr Chesterton's *Daily News* articles, have their place in life. But how a serious social student can think of curing the thoughtlessness of our generation by strained paradoxes; of giving people a sane grasp of social problems by literary sleight-of-hand; of settling important questions by a reckless shower of rocket-metaphors and inaccurate "facts" and the substitution of imagination for judgment, I cannot see. (80)

Chesterton's reply was eventually included as the sixteenth chapter of his 1908 work, *Heretics*, in which he took swipes at most of the leading thinkers of Edwardian England. Beneath all the paradoxes, all Chesterton really said was that funny is not the opposite of serious, a point McCabe fully acknowledged in his original article.

Another way to gauge the impact of the RPA is to look at the effect it had within the churches themselves. Nowhere can its impact be more clearly seen than in the established church. The Church of England experienced a crisis of confidence in the Edwardian years from which it has not entirely recovered. Where most theological controversies in the nineteenth century involved the Old Testament, those of the new century moved into the heartland of Christianity, the New Testament. (81) Controversies were usually between those who were impressed by the need for a reinterpretation of traditional religious formulae in the light of modern knowledge and those who thought any such reinterpretation would involve a betrayal of ancient verities.

The Edwardian church was rent by just such a controversy when R J Campbell (1867-1956), minister of the Congregationalist City Temple in London, caused a storm in the religious world with what he called the New Theology. Campbell's theology would be unremarkable now; he emphasised the immanence of God, in the sense of God and the world being so intimate as to be pretty much indistinguishable. Campbell questioned the Virgin Birth while other, more radical thinkers who jumped on the New Theology bandwagon even veered toward the mythical Jesus position. When critics accused the New Theology of being little more than pantheism, the New Theologians insisted on the term 'monism'. It is difficult to imagine that Campbell had not been influenced by Haeckel's use of the term monism in *The Riddle of the Universe*. All the more so as Campbell had become enamoured of Christian Socialism prior to his heretical outburst.

The pained odyssey of R J Campbell was repeated by many of his contemporaries. Kingsley Martin (1897-1969), an influential journalist and editor, wrote movingly about the travails of his father, a Congregationalist minister. Under pressure of rationalist criticism of the foundations of Christianity, Rev. Basil Martin lost faith in much of the Christian creed. Immortality, the divinity of Jesus, and most other Christian dogmas were abandoned in favour of a simple creedless religious humanism involving 'loving your neighbour, paying good wages, and putting yourself out to help people who might not be successful or even respectable.' (82) In return, Martin was hounded by succeeding congregations, and even by his own church.

That the Established Church realised it had a crisis on its hands is plain from the series of essays several prominent theologians had published in 1912. The book was called *Foundations: A Statement of Christian Belief in Terms of Modern Thought* and was thought by its contributors ('seven Oxford men') to be the next major restatement of the advanced Christian thought since *Essays and Reviews* (1860) and *Lux Mundi* (1889). B H Streeter (1874-1937), who wrote the introduction, put the book in perspective:

> The world is calling for religion; but it cannot accept a religion if its theology is out of harmony with science, philosophy, and scholarship. Religion, if it is to dominate life, must satisfy both the head and the heart, a thing which neither obscurantism nor rationalism can do. (83)

Streeter called for a restatement of the foundations of belief 'in the light of the knowledge and thought of the day.' His own contribution to the work was a study of attitudes toward Christ. Streeter was in no doubt about the gravity of the problem. Ever since the Enlightenment, he acknowledged, orthodox theology had been on the defensive; giving way on x while holding on desperately to y.

> A more hopeless position can hardly be imagined for a religion of which the very life and essence consists in its being an attack and a challenge to the world. A Christ whom apologists have first to "save" is little likely to save mankind. (84)

The publication of *Foundations* unleashed another bitter debate among churchmen between those who saw open inquiry as crucial to the church's survival and those who wanted to hold fast to dogma. It was a similar battle to that conducted over *Essays and Reviews* half a century before, although unlike the earlier controversy, few people outside church circles took any notice. It is a debate that ended up engaging most branches of Christendom in the twentieth century, and one that few have resolved successfully. In an attempt to bring the conflict to a close Archbishop Davidson created a commission in 1923 to look into Anglican doctrine. But the commission didn't meet until 1938, by which time even fewer people were interested in the results. Only the RPA took much notice, in the form of a short critique of the commission's report, published within weeks of the report being released. The author, Joseph McCabe, had little difficulty seeing the strained attempts of the report to mollify liberals and conservatives with a series of carefully worded sophistries. One example should suffice:

> Statements affirming particular facts may be found to have value as pictorial expressions of spiritual truths, even though the supposed facts themselves did not actually happen…It is not therefore of necessity illegitimate to accept and affirm particular clauses of the Creeds while understanding them in this symbolic sense. (85)

McCabe also suggested that the real priority of the church was as much to stem the flow of people leaving the church as it was to reconcile irreconcilable differences among its theologians. It would have come as no surprise to him that such legal contortions did not succeed in doing this. The decade of turmoil the Church of England suffered after the publication of *Foundations* and the unsatisfying compromise that ensued from it fifteen years later are the result of a section of senior Church thinkers recognising that it was badly out of touch with modern thought. And Streeter left no doubts that when he spoke of modern thought, he had rationalism in mind. It is not unreasonable to infer from this that when he had rationalism in mind, he also had the RPA in mind. The Cheap Reprints were at their height of influence and circulation at the time he was writing and rationalism had become associated with the RPA. In conceding that the Church of England was out of touch with modern science, philosophy and scholarship, Streeter was conceding that the main complaint of the RPA against Christianity in general and the Church of England in particular, was valid. Other churchmen were not prepared to make that concession and the conflict for the soul of the church began; a conflict continuing to this day. This intellectual disabling of the Church of England is one of the RPA's most significant legacies.

While many theologians were in full retreat in the face of the rationalist onslaught, the highest-profile attack on rationalism from these years came from Arthur Balfour (1848-1930), Conservative politician, prime minister between 1902 and 1905, and amateur theologian. In retrospect, it is extraordinary that these works should have attracted any serious attention from rationalists at all. Maynard Keynes said of Balfour, "He never did anything but wonder whether Christianity was true and prove it wasn't and hope it was." (86) More recently, Piers Brendon has dismissed Balfour's writings as 'ambiguous at best and at worst contradictory.' (87) Nevertheless, Balfour's writings were influential at the time and the rationalists felt the need to respond to his challenge. The key to the threat Balfour posed was not so much from the quality of his arguments as from his privileged social standing. Balfour was a member of a small but very well-connected aristocratic discussion group called The Synthetics, which included people influential in politics, the universities and of course the Church. The Synthetics soon came to be known as The Souls – their own in particular being their favourite topic of conversation.

Balfour's two main books that are relevant here are *A Defence of Philosophic Doubt* (1879) and *The Foundations of Belief* (1894). Typical of Balfour's style of argument was the following comparison of Kant with beetles. 'Kant, as we all know, compared the Moral Law to the starry heavens, and found them both sublime. It would, on the naturalistic hypothesis, be more appropriate to compare it to the protective blotches on the beetle's back, and to find them both ingenious.' (88) So limited was Balfour's thought that it did not occur to him that what for him was a casual dismissal of something obviously absurd could in fact be a far more useful and beautiful point of reference than his own. Balfour was from a long line of religious apologists who could not bring themselves to acknowledge the moral integrity of the unbeliever. Such people, in Balfour's mind, are 'parasites on the society around them.' (89)

Balfour's arguments in defence of Christian theism were no more sound than those of his contemporaries. He endorsed the argument to design as that which 'gives a unity and a coherence to our apprehension of the natural world which it would not otherwise possess.' (90) In keeping with a trend among liberal divines of the day who claimed to have reconciled the conflict between religion and science, Balfour declared evolution to be 'the instrument for carrying out a Divine purpose…'(91) Indeed, without a belief in a supernatural basis for the universe, 'the scientific view of the world would not be less, but more, beset with difficulties than it is at present.' (92) When faced with the argument from evil, Balfour could do little more than retreat into rhetoric. 'What is needed [when faced with the reality of the problem of evil] is such a living faith in God's relation to Man as shall leave no place for that helpless resentment against the appointed Order so apt to rise within us at the sight of undeserved pain.' (93)

The RPA published an anonymous reply in 1903 called *Mr Balfour's Apologetics Critically Examined*. The work was written by William Brailsford Columbine (1859-1937) a self-made businessman based in Nottingham and long-time RPA supporter. J M Robertson also criticised Balfour in his short study of rationalism, published by Constable in 1912. While the rationalists' replies to Balfour were seen as important at the time – after all, he was the prime minister – we can skip them now, mainly because the replies to the next critic were of a similar order. It was Balfour's social eminence that gave weight to his defence of religion rather than his intellectual eminence. Of considerably greater intellectual power, but whose line of attack was not dissimilar, was William James (1842-1910), who presented the Gifford Lectures in Edinburgh over 1901 and 1902, and which were later published as *The Varieties of Religious Experience*. James made it quite clear that he had no more time for the conventional religious explanation than the materialist critic. The days were long gone, James insisted, when 'it could be said that for Science herself the heavens declare the glory of God and the firmament showeth his handiwork.' (94) In his memorable phrase, the only god that science could now recognise would be one who 'does a wholesale, not a retail business.' (95) James's god is the forerunner of the pallid mathematical equations that constitute the god of the more theistically-inclined physicists of today.

Where James was revolutionary was in his bracketing of religious truth-claims and ascribing a suitably emasculated religiousness an important place in human nature. It was the first in a line of study of religion which characterised the twentieth century. So long, James said, 'as men can use their God, they care very little who he is, or even, whether he is at all.' (96) What mattered for William James was the value of the religious experience. Whether it was true, and James was inclined to believe that most of it wasn't, was less important. James went on to postulate what he called spiritual truths as opposed to mere existential truths. The Higher Criticism of the Bible, with all its disastrous consequences for uncritical faith, was merely the product of existential truth-seeking. But this left the higher, spiritual truths of the book untouched. Inquiry on lines such as this tended to call into question the usefulness and relevance of the rationalist critique of religion. After all, the most distinguishing mark of the rationalist critique is the seriousness with which it has taken religious truth claims.

James came under close scrutiny from J M Robertson on two occasions; once in 1897 when he responded to *The Will to Believe* and then a few years later when he responded to the *Varieties of Religious Experience*. These are good examples of Robertson's intellectual firepower. Robertson couldn't help noticing that James's will to believe was very selective. If your will to believe led down theistic pathways, all to the good, and James would be there to help, but if your will to believe was toward atheism and humanism, 'why, that is the very thing that Professor James is bent on discrediting.' (97) James saw the unwillingness to believe as timidity or an unwillingness to expose oneself to the risk of being duped. Even more extraordinarily, James returned to the infamous wager first mooted by Pascal. After all, it might be true, James added helpfully, so why 'forfeit my sole chance in life of getting upon the winning side…'? Robertson's reaction was, as only it could be – volcanic. 'Shall we not here say once more, with Mill, that we had much rather be damned by such a deity as that than share in his despicable triumph?' (98)

Before finishing with this examination of the RPA's disputes with religionists, it is worth noting that it did not confine its attention to Christianity. Other forms of rampant irrationalism also attracted criticism. One of the more picturesque examples was Captain J F C Fuller's baroque hymn of praise to the poetry and spiritual prowess of the occultist Aleister Crowley (1875-1947). Fuller was nothing if not effusive:

> It has taken 100,000,000 years to produce Aleister Crowley. The world has indeed laboured, and has at last brought forth a man...He stands on the virgin rock of Pyrrhonic Zoroastrianism, which, unlike the Hindu world-conception, stands on neither Elephant nor Tortoise, but on the Absolute Zero of the metaphysical Qabalists...And he shall be called "Immanuel" – that is, "God" is with us, or, being interpreted, Aleister Crowley, the spiritual son of the Immanuel whose surname was Cant. (99)

The *Guide* reviewer noted dryly that Fuller 'must have felt a good deal better after writing that.' The man who liked to be known as 'The Beast 666' was praised for his philosophical system, which was, of course, to be known as 'Crowleyanity.' The reviewer's warning was as relevant today as it was then. If the reader accepts the teachings of Crowleanity 'he had better do so on an intelligent understanding of the message for at this he will have difficulty in arriving.' Rationalism is often mocked for taking the role of killjoy or humourless fault-finding. But the slightest glance at rationalist work shows that this is not true, and never has been true. The rationalist advice here is eminently sensible: make sure you know what you're getting yourself into.

Tensions inside the RPA

While the RPA was involved with a variety of controversies with religious apologists in the Edwardian years, it also became increasingly involved with tensions brewing within its ranks. There was an ongoing dialogue within the movement about where it stood on significant issues. The progressionist and agnostic flavour of most of the Cheap Reprints disguised an ongoing controversy among members as to what sort of works the RPA should be publishing. And this debate, in turn, revolved around the ongoing ideas of what rationalism is, and its relations to atheism and agnosticism. Charles Hooper referred to the problem in an otherwise contented review of the origins and growth of the RPA. Not only had the RPA to contend with clerical opposition, Hooper wrote, but it also needed to 'mediate between two opposed tendencies on the part of Rationalists themselves. I refer to the militant iconoclasm which is more concerned to expose the falsity of current opinions than to put anything positive in their place, and the academic apathy which, while harbouring advanced views, refrains from any attempt to enlighten the masses or to refute clerical and evangelical dogmatism.' (100)

We noted in the last chapter that, particularly for the older campaigners like Dr Bithell, it was important that the RPA avoid the more pointed, militant, criticism favoured by G W Foote and *The Freethinker*. And men like Bithell were more radical than some of his contemporaries, who had abandoned Christianity, but were even less keen than he to be seen publicly to be critical. The following review in the *Literary Guide* of Foote's *Bible Romances* in October 1900 illustrates this attitude well. Early on the reviewer notes Foote's favoured methods of 'banter, anecdote and scorn'.

> Nobody can beat him in this particular style of satire and scathing bluntness. He handles the heavy cudgel with all the refined cleverness of the fencing master, and his strong, biting English is softened and polished by the facility and graces of the scholar. Sometimes, it may be, he uses the knuckle-duster when a scourge of small cords would suffice.

But, in an effort at reasonableness and balance, the reviewer ended with this tribute.

> We lay stress on this characteristic of Mr Foote's writing, because it is only a superficial judgment which regards him as nothing but a mocker. His sarcasm is well backed by erudition, and, if he had elected to exercise his wit on less popular ground, he would have made a brilliant academic. (101)

The gentleness of the rebuke and warmth of the tribute, not to mention the style of metaphor, suggests the hand of F J Gould. It illustrates well the ambivalence of most RPA activists to Foote's style and personality, and to the views he was held to represent. In few cases was there any serious personal animosity – Joseph McCabe being a predictable exception. But the difference was more serious than merely one of style. As we saw in the previous chapter, this difference goes to the heart of the freethought movement, in Britain and around the world. This division between moderates and militants has remained an important component of the freethought movement around the world. The only significant difference between the various countries where there is a significant freethought presence is where the dividing line between the militants and moderates is drawn.

It is yet another irony that the moderate position, here illustrated by Gould, claims to be the more polite toward the religionist, and yet his attitude is in fact more inclined to trivialise his opponents' point of view. In another article from 1900, entitled 'Rationalist Politeness', Gould continued this theme. 'Do not let us set them [Christians] down straight-way [sic] as enemies and frauds. On the contrary, a Christian is a Rationalist who has not yet understood himself. The application of a cudgel or a hay-fork is not likely to convert him, or to extend the Brotherhood of Man.' (102) In other words, Gould's humanism was underpinned by a sanguine progressionist confidence that Christianity would wither away in the face of reason. Ironically, it is the militants – Gould's opponents – who have treated their religious adversaries with sufficient respect to take their point of view seriously. As such, it is the militants who could be seen to be more polite to the religionist than the moderate. In an article, also from 1900, W B Columbine articulated the more militant position.

> It is a sorrowful fact that there are many Rationalists who appear to think that supernaturalism may be destroyed without a blow being struck from the Rationalist camp. Time, they say, and the laws of nature are on our side, and we need do no more than calmly await the triumph of Rationalism which will follow in the wake of evolution. (103)

It was the more militant rationalists who did their opponents the greater courtesy of taking their views seriously, and who were less sanguine about the prospects of their views prevailing. And as the Edwardian years progressed, the militant approach became the more influential within the RPA, indeed, more influential than its founders would have expected, or wished.

Holyoake or Bradlaugh? The first major internal dispute.

Things are never simple, for rationalists or for anybody else. It is in fact one of the more remarkable features of the organisation in its first decade of existence that it was able to attract people who were devoted to Bradlaugh's memory, to the point of being relatively indifferent, or even hostile, to George Jacob Holyoake, Bradlaugh's principal rival for the leadership of nineteenth-century freethought, and the preferred chairman of the RPA and its predecessors. Two of the most important supporters of Bradlaugh who became active in the RPA early were Hypatia Bradlaugh Bonner (1858-1935) his surviving daughter, and J M Robertson, his most accomplished follower. These two were bound to Bradlaugh by ties of personal loyalty as well as ideological commitment. What brought them into the RPA was a combination of their dislike of G W Foote and their recognition that the RPA was making an impression in the way the National Secular Society was not. (104) *The Literary Guide* was by now the most prominent freethought journal in the country; *The Freethinker* was in Foote's hands and Bradlaugh's paper, the *National Reformer* a distant memory. Robertson had established a magazine called *The Free Review* in 1893, but it lasted only four years. Robertson and Bonner needed an outlet.

Neither wrote very much on atheism or agnosticism, but both shared a deep hostility to religion in general and Christianity in particular, not least because of the disgraceful way many self-proclaimed defenders of Christianity had treated Bradlaugh. Certainly in Bonner's case, anti-Christianity was the guiding *leit motif*. A quick perusal of her main published works will demonstrate this. Apart from the biography of her father she co-wrote with Robertson, Bonner's titles include *Penalties Upon Opinion* (1912), a survey of Christian persecution of dissidents in England; *The Christian Hell* (1913), a history of the more lurid Christian representations of that awful abode; *Christianity and Conduct* (1919), a study of the divergence between preaching and practice among many Christians; and *Christianizing the Heathen* (1922), a critique of missionary techniques. Hypatia Bradlaugh Bonner knew what she was against.

Coinciding with Bradlaugh Bonner and Robertson coming in, the last of the great Victorian agnostics were dying off. Richard Bithell died in 1902, Herbert Spencer in 1903, Sir Leslie Stephen in 1904, Charles Watts senior and George Jacob Holyoake in 1906. The passing of these men meant the passing of the attitude towards Christianity that motivated them. Instead of merely wanting to reform true religion by purging it of dogma and cant, the newer members were more critical of religion in any form. The RPA felt the need of, but did not find, a successor with the prestige of Stephen, Spencer or Holyoake. Those who followed, such as Edward Clodd, were in the stamp of the departed founders, but lacked important aspects of their charisma. The person best qualified in this respect was Joseph McCabe, but he never really succeeded in becoming one of the boys, as we shall see.

In the light of these changes, the struggle for the heart of the RPA took on the form of shadow-boxing, where the disputants remained outwardly civil. At the centre of the dispute, not surprisingly, was Joseph McCabe. It is also where we can begin to trace his slow estrangement from the RPA. It is one of the many paradoxes about Joseph McCabe that this aggressive man should have been such a staunch admirer of the genial Holyoake rather than of the more abrasive Bradlaugh. And it is no less odd that the admirers of Bradlaugh did, by and large, loathe the similarly-inclined McCabe.

I have written of this progressive estrangement at length elsewhere, but must go over this ground again here, because of its importance for the development of the RPA. (105) The shadow-boxing began in 1908 when McCabe wrote an article for the *Literary Guide* about a recent prosecution of a soap-box atheist for blasphemy. Harry Boulter had been bound over and was to receive a month's imprisonment for speeches at Highbury Corner in London. McCabe supported the prosecution, declaring he had 'not the faintest interest in securing for myself, or any other man, the liberty to attack Christianity in coarse, vulgar, or scurrilous terms.' (106) Now this wasn't problematic, but McCabe went on to make a far more controversial statement when he declared that the last genuine prosecution for atheism was that of his mentor George Jacob Holyoake, who had served six months for blasphemy in 1842. All prosecutions for blasphemy since Holyoake, McCabe concluded, had involved an element of scurrility and thus were to some extent justifiable. McCabe had just completed a two-volume biography of Holyoake, having been commissioned for the job by the RPA. This biography, a significant venture by the RPA, was due to be published in March, the same month as McCabe's article appeared. Many of these points were aired in greater detail in his work.

McCabe's article caused considerable offence, both to Foote and to supporters of Bradlaugh who were active within the RPA. It was hardly surprising that Foote would have been angered by McCabe's article. He had, after all, been prosecuted for blasphemy since Holyoake. Foote served a year in prison for publishing an article in *The Freethinker* in the first half of 1882. The case had attracted national prominence at the time, and Foote's subsequent reputation was built on the whole episode. By dismissing Foote's prosecution as a genuine case, McCabe had imputed a degree of scurrility to the Foote case and called into question the value of Foote's entire career. McCabe didn't stop there, also accusing Foote of unnecessary coarseness in his propaganda and exercising poor judgment in his handling of the controversy with Hugh Price Hughes, to which we referred in the previous chapter. (107) McCabe could have weathered the fallout from this, but what complicated matters was that it had a flow-on effect of insulting the supporters of Bradlaugh within the RPA, their own diffidence to Foote notwithstanding.

Things moved very quickly after this. McCabe's article appeared in the March 1908 issue of the *Guide*, and in the April issue came a rejoinder from Hypatia Bradlaugh Bonner and a reply from McCabe to Bonner and to criticisms Foote had made in *The Freethinker*. After an unconvincing protestation of admiration for McCabe's abilities, Hypatia Bradlaugh Bonner came to her real point. McCabe's article about blasphemy represented 'the position of the younger generation, and those who have come into the Rationalist Movement since the worst of the fight was over and the way was smoothed for their feet.' (108) Such condescension could only have made McCabe's blood boil, given how difficult his path to rationalism had in fact been. Things began to escalate after this. G W Foote had also attacked McCabe in *The Freethinker* and McCabe demanded the right of reply in the *Guide*. Watts's clearly hoped for calm, but to no avail. His view was evident in a short notice in the April issue.

> We publish with considerable reluctance the reply to Mr Foote which Mr McCabe contributes to this issue of the *Guide*. Personal controversy among Rationalists seldom disfigures our columns, and we on this occasion depart from our almost invariable rule only because of the exceptional circumstances of the case. (109)

McCabe replied with barely-concealed rage to Foote's tirade and responded point-by-point to his objections. That there was no love lost between Foote and McCabe was clear, but McCabe could have weathered that. What was making the issue more complicated was the dual nature of the dispute. On the one hand there was a dispute, conducted in the *Guide*, about what constitutes blasphemy and who had been convicted of it. The general view among Bradlaugh supporters was that Holyoake had been lukewarm in the advocacy of freethought and treacherous in his relations with Bradlaugh. McCabe's view was that relations between the two men were usually pleasant, if not warm, and generally improved 'as Bradlaugh's character matured…'. (110) But at a deeper level was the old point of contention about who (Bradlaugh or Holyoake) should be considered the real inspiration of the movement, and, more important still, what sort of movement it was. This dispute had become, in effect, a struggle for the heart of the RPA.

In this way, the disputes over McCabe's views on blasphemy were merely the cover for the larger struggle going on behind the scenes. The real battle was being fought behind the scenes about similar claims McCabe had made in his two-volume biography of Holyoake, due to be published in March 1908. In his autobiography McCabe recounted the series of events:

> My book was printed and bound, and copies were sent to special members. Sir E Brabrook, who got one, at once wrote Bradlaugh's daughter and J M Robertson that certain letters of Ingersoll to Holyoake which I included were damaging to Bradlaugh, Foote, and other leading members of the Freethought movement in Britain, and they presented the Rationalist publishers with an ultimatum: unless these letters and some remarks in my work were struck out, though it meant breaking up hundreds of copies of the bound two-volume work and reprinting many pages, Brabrook, Robertson, Mrs Bradlaugh-Bonner, and other Bradlaughites would quit the Association. (111)

There is no way that the historian will ever resolve this episode entirely satisfactorily after all this time, particularly in the absence of RPA minutes. But on the information available to us it seems that McCabe's claim was right, and that the changes to the Holyoake biography were made. The *Literary Guide* of January 1908 gave notice that the *Life and Letters of George Jacob Holyoake* is almost complete and parts of it are already going through the press. A loose flyer and order form for the book which accompanied that issue announced the publication date to be April 25. But the May issue advises readers that publication 'has been deferred until the end of May.' (112) No reason is given for the deferral. Only with the June issue does the review of the work appear. The review is duly appreciative, but concentrates more on Holyoake's life than McCabe's treatment of it. (113) It is definite, then, that publication of the Holyoake biography was deferred. What is not definite is the reason why this deferral took place. There are any number of reasons why the publication of a book can be delayed, but I suspect McCabe's account of events is accurate in this instance. McCabe's account helps explain why Watts should have felt moved to break his invariable rule and allow McCabe's rejoinder in the April issue of the *Guide*. Readers could interpret the 'exceptional circumstances of the case' as showing respect for McCabe, a tireless worker for the cause. But Watts knew the exceptional circumstances also referred to the difficulties he was having with Brabrook, Bonner and Robertson regarding their ultimatum over the offending passages in *Life and Letters of George Jacob Holyoake*. It might also explain why McCabe was made an Honorary Associate of the RPA later that year. It was a consolation for not rocking the boat unduly about the breaking up of the first print-run of the Holyoake biography.

This episode had several important consequences; for McCabe, for the RPA, and for the freethought movement generally. For McCabe, it marked the beginning, as we can now see with the advantage of hindsight, of his estrangement from the RPA. For the RPA, this incident spelled victory for the followers of Bradlaugh over those of Holyoake. And the victory of Bradlaugh's legacy in the RPA was to have important repercussions for the broader freethought movement, which we will trace as we proceed through this book. It is in this light that we can interpret the significance of the first Bradlaugh titles being reprinted by Watts & Co, which happened in 1911. There is also a discernible trend in the Cheap Reprints toward more openly naturalist and agnostic authors after 1908.

The Edwardian years really were the golden age of the Rationalist Press Association. Beginning from nothing and still a relatively small organisation at the end of this period, it had nonetheless succeeded in exerting an influence far beyond its numbers. The influence had been exerted not in parliamentary terms of altering legislation, although several moderate steps toward an open society had been made in Edwardian England. Rather, the RPA articulated the hopes and dreams of a significant, and growing, section of society. This grouping of people, usually of comfortable, though modest, means, shared the confidence in reason and the sense of a future that could be grand and noble, if only people of good will would come together to work for it. The people who bought the Cheap Reprints from the railway bookstands were not prepared to be brow-beaten by churchmen, morals campaigners and others who were deeply anxious for the moral rectitude of the lower orders. They had confidence in their own ability to read works by educated people and make up their mind accordingly. And the RPA deserves credit for being the first organisation to show the potential of the non-fiction paperback to the world.

It has become fashionable to see rationalism as arrogant, sterile or 'Promethean' (as if this is a rebuke), but the rationalism of the early RPA was tolerant, multi-faceted and humane. Works by theists, pantheists and agnostics vied for the readers' attention. Arguments in favour of and opposed to women's suffrage, the historicity of Jesus, and imperialism were aired. Supporters and opponents of a range of important issues of the day found a platform in the *Literary Guide* and its wide range of publications. And, free from the patronising pressure of churchmen and peddlers of conventional morals, people made up their own minds. So absorbing were these debates that few people would have had the least suspicion that they were soon to be consigned to history.

Chapter 3

War and Change

'Religion today is not so much a matter of ideas as of organisation.'
Joseph McCabe, 1921

The First World War changed everything, although it took until the end of the twenties for this to become apparent. The war which initially many people had welcomed turned quickly into a seemingly pointless slaughter of millions of young men. For millions of bereaved or distraught people, assumptions of continual progress toward better things seemed laughable – at best. Had there been even a marginal correlation between the promise of a war to end war and the reality, things might have been different. But it quickly transpired that the peace had been lost as completely as the dreams and fancies which inspired people at the war's beginning.

The war had consequences across virtually the entire field of human endeavour. In science, Einstein's theory of relativity, following its verification by Sir Arthur Eddington in 1919, rapidly became hot news. Einstein toured the United States and Britain in 1921 and was in Japan in 1922, when he heard he had received the Nobel Prize in Physics. Evolution was no longer the 'in' science of popular imagination as it had been before the war. Similarly in philosophy, the publication of Wittgenstein's *Tractatus Logico-Philosophicus* in 1919 spelt the beginning of the end to what were soon to be thought of as fusty debates about whether A or B was true. Once more, though, it was many years before the consequences of Wittgenstein's thought were to be felt beyond the confines of Cambridge. Both Einstein and Wittgenstein's new ideas had the added feature of being incomprehensible to the average person. This rendered them vulnerable to foolish and esoteric interpretations which had greater appeal than the dictates of reason.

Another new area of thought to gain popular attention in the years immediately after the First World War was psychoanalysis. It was no longer necessarily a reproach to be irrational, but it was to be repressed. In Britain, the publication in 1918 of Lytton Strachey's *Eminent Victorians* introduced the idea that people previously held up as paragons of selflessness and civic duty were in fact self-centred, troubled and most definitely repressed. 'Victorian' quickly became a term of derision. This social and intellectual upheaval was just as marked in literature, the arts and music. The cultural historian Modris Eksteins summed up the postwar crisis well. In the face of such an apparently meaningless slaughter, the war's meaning 'began to be enveloped in a fog of existential questioning' and the integrity of the so-called real world could be questioned. 'And as the external world collapsed in ruins, the only redoubt of integrity became the individual personality. (1)

This search for personal integrity took many people down strange paths, providing rich pickings for a variety of irrationalist cults, notably Theosophy, spiritualism, and anthroposophy. For those more politically inclined, movements like fascism and communism arose which called for the subsumption of the individual into the cause.

One thing was clear from all this; things had changed for the worse for rationalism. Whereas rationalism had looked suitably rebellious to the workers and suitably respectable to the middle class before the war, it now became more difficult to look suitable to anyone. Tens of thousands of the people who had read the Cheap Reprints were dead. And many of the bereaved left behind had resorted to spiritualism in an attempt to contact them from beyond the grave. In a few short years, rationalism had slipped from being the eventual home of all intelligent and honest people to being a refuge for Victorians. With the First World War rationalism lost the intellectual initiative.

Having said all this, it took twenty years or more for these trends to fully work their way through. The Britain of the 1920s was obsessed with returning to a pre-war state of prosperity and assurance. A J P Taylor, in his classic history of the period, *English History 1914-1945*, thought that reconstruction, restoration and recovery were the key words of the twenties, words, as he says, of return. 'Nineteen-fourteen was the standard by which everything was judged.' (2) If the country should be experiencing this sort of impulse, it is not surprising that the RPA should have done so as well.

Rationalists were aware that conditions had changed. To take one example, Edward Clodd spoke to the Royal Institution in May 1921 and expressed this new diffidence about notions of progress and reason. Clodd, who was 61 when Queen Victoria died, was particularly reluctant to see much fault in the beliefs of that era. Normally a genial man, Clodd was incensed by the tone of Strachey's *Eminent Victorians*. However, he recognised that things had changed. Citing the recent outbursts of irrationalism (spiritualism, the return of astrology to prominence, the Angel of Mons stories) Clodd concluded that the Victorians had been too confident in the triumph of reason, but the war had shown that there had been 'no far-reaching or progressive modification of instincts and emotions.' (3) Times changed in more ways than Clodd would have thought appropriate as well. Six years after Clodd's death the RPA approached James Strachey, Lytton's executor, for permission to reprint *Eminent Victorians* in the Thinker's Library. Strachey refused.

The First World War

Having begun this chapter with an outline of the changes brought about by the war, it is worth noting that the changes only began to become apparent after 1918. While war conditions necessarily reduced RPA activities and opportunities, it did not change the manner in which it operated, or the style of response it got from the churches. The RPA carried on much as it had done before the war.

The first problem the RPA faced with regard to the war was the sort of attitude it should take. This was a crisis faced by all campaigning organisations, whether political, intellectual or religious, although those on the left of the political spectrum felt the problem the most. The RPA emerged from this particular problem very well, generally. Independently of the RPA, Hypatia Bradlaugh Bonner had established in 1910 the Rationalist Peace Society. The leading members of its committee were all personalities from the various rationalist, secularist, ethical and positivist organisations around the country, including G W Foote, F J Gould and others. Bonner acted as chairperson throughout the eleven years the group operated and her friend J M Robertson was the group's president.

While the Rationalist Peace Society was opposed to militarism, it was not necessarily a pacifist organisation. On the outbreak of war in August 1914, it issued a statement which deplored the outbreak of war which it saw as 'the natural outcome of a long period of persistent arming' and made protests against both the German invasion of Belgium and mining of neutral waters. But as the war progressed, the group drifted more openly to supporting the Allied cause, recognising the distinction between just and unjust wars. Just wars were held to be wars of independence and wars of defence. While all war was condemned, this war was held to be the lesser evil than that of submitting to force. This trend to support the Allied cause was not undertaken without criticism or discord within the ranks of the Rationalist Peace Society, and by December 1917 it suspended activity for the duration of the war. It reconvened after the war but disbanded in 1921.

The existence of the Rationalist Peace Society meant that much of the discord within rationalist ranks about the war was played out there rather than within the RPA. Every now and then a comment in the *Literary Guide* aroused protest from either the pacifist or militarist wings of the movement, but the RPA steered its way through these disagreements successfully. It also suffered relatively few resignations: the most prominent being those of Ernst Haeckel and Paul Carus, both of whom were pro-German and resigned as Honorary Associates in 1915.

The first issue of the *Literary Guide* after the hostilities began ran a lead article by Joseph McCabe. Like many others, McCabe thought that the war would be over by the springtime, but he was by no means sanguine on this account. Neither was he jingoistic. His article, entitled 'Armageddon,' made it quite clear that a disaster had taken place. 'A stone was dislodged on the hills of Servia, and such an avalanche as the world has never known before is gathering strength for a murderous precipitation.' (4) Four years later, Charles Watts himself gave one of the most sustained statements of the RPA's view of the war. Watts began with the official declaration that the various views expressed in the *Guide* do not bind the RPA, which is a separate organisation with no editorial control over the *Guide*. 'On the other hand' Watts then admitted, 'it is only fair to say the principal writers are some of the leading representatives of the Rationalist Movement.' Having got this out of the way, Watts gave what was pretty much the agreed line:

> The writers who each month, in these columns, endeavour to interpret and apply the teachings of Rationalism have been primarily concerned with the ethical aspect of the great European struggle. Having

> carefully studied most of the evidence available, they have been forced to the conclusion that the Allied countries are fighting for Right as against Might, for Freedom as against Oppression, for a World Peace as against Militarist Domination.

However, Watts wasn't satisfied with a jingoistic hurrah.

> Only history will be able finally to adjudicate as to the responsibility for the War…It may, however, be granted that secret diplomacy played a not inconsiderable part in producing the necessary atmosphere for the outbreak, and England no doubt erred with other countries in encouraging the militarist spirit. (5)

Four years into the war, with no end in sight, this is a pretty commendable and dispassionate assessment. It certainly compares very favourably indeed with the lapses into fervent militarism of the Theosophical movement, or Rudolf Steiner's newly-created Anthroposophy. Senior Theosophists spoke in portentous terms about dark forces and the cosmic favour our lads would be doing in killing Huns, as it would only speed up their rise through the supernatural pecking order. Rudolf Steiner, by contrast, was equally sure that while each nationality was here on earth to represent one aspect of humanity, only the Germans were capable of representing them all at the same time. (6) This illustrates one of the many disadvantages of rationalism: being sensible is not news.

The more loopy claims were not confined to the fringes of the theistic community. For example, rationalism came under fairly regular attack from the clergy for being in some way responsible for the war. The *Literary Guide* spent a great deal of time responding to accusations that the war was somehow the consequence either of the British neglecting their religious duties or the Germans having abandoned Christianity for rationalism. A good example of the first style of accusation came from Australia, where the Roman Catholic Archbishop Carr of Melbourne lamented in the *Age* at the end of 1914 that:

> The reason that God was using the present war for the punishment of the nations was that for a very considerable time there had been not merely neglect of the worship and service of God, which had always existed to a greater or less extent, but a regular upraising of human light and human understanding and human will against the providence of God. (7)

The war, Archbishop Carr intoned, was for the humbling of such men. Joseph McCabe responded passionately to this idea. Archbishop Carr

> believes that God sent on Europe a war that will cost £10,000,000,000, that is blasting the homes and embittering the hearts of millions, that mingles the innocent and guilty in one common and fearful desolation, that sends millions to a premature death amidst circumstances which do not lend themselves to a devout preparation, that is raising storms of hatred and perverting the souls of millions, because a few other millions refuse to go to church. It would be difficult to conceive a cruder and more barbarous idea. (8)

One representative of the second variety of attack against rationalism was the Rev. Dugald Macfadyen, who declared that 'the Germans have for a quarter of a century been carrying on a thought war against Christianity.' These and various other attempts at scapegoating nonbelievers were relatively commonplace among some religious leaders. These attacks provoked several rationalist rebuttals. For instance, in April 1916 Charles Gorham devoted a lengthy article to demonstrating the strength of German Christian opinion in favour of the war, from the Kaiser down. He also drew attention to the incoherence of the clerical attacks. 'It will not do,' he wrote, 'for the orthodox to claim that the aggression of Germany is the result of a thought-war against Christianity, while the Allies are defending it, yet in doing so are being punished for their sins.' (9) Gorham's defences of rationalism were later released as pamphlets entitled *Religion and the War* and *God and the War*, both from 1916.

The *Guide* could not help noticing that, once victory seemed assured, talk of the war being a salutary lesson from God was replaced by more triumphalist declarations. Towards the end of the conflict, H Pike Pease, MP, told an intercession meeting at the Mansion House that the Germans had failed to reach Paris because 'God did not require that they should get there.' Watts, in his 'Random Jottings' column, noted caustically that 'it is to be regretted that he was not equally vigilant when the *Lusitania* was sunk, when the Belgian people were outraged and decimated, when more than a third of France was ruined and made desolate – not to speak of other well nigh indescribable horrors.' (10) It is often said that rationalists waste their, and everyone else's, time by bothering even to respond to such nonsense. But this is to miss the point that the people making these statements genuinely believe them to be true and want moral lessons to be drawn from their observations. It is central to rationalism, as has been noted already, that morality is undermined when based on unstable foundations. Any belief in God based on claims of his interventions in human affairs as posited by Mr Pike Pease has to be fallacious, and it is entirely reasonable to point this out.

The most telling statement of the rationalist view of the new situation was made by Joseph McCabe. He wrote *The Bankruptcy of Religion* in 1917 to show not merely the intellectual bankruptcy of religion, which had been known before the war, but its moral bankruptcy, which the war had revealed. McCabe noted that 'Archbishops tell us the war is punishment for unbelief and yet it is the poor, simple believers in places like Serbia or Belgium or Russia who have suffered the most.' (11) McCabe's argument was that, after every possible social, political and coercive advantage in their hands, Christianity had failed monumentally to change conditions for the better. This was because Christianity was 'dogmatic and authoritative; because it was mingled with impracticable and mischievous counsels; because it was shaped by conditions of life which have gone forever, and is entirely unsuited to the present conditions.' (12) Many decades later, religious radicals like John Shelby Spong, Don Cupitt and Richard Holloway would say the same things and retain religious respectability in all but fundamentalist circles.

At one point in this work, after a lament at the intellectual poverty of the age, McCabe asked his readers to take the hundred most distinguished thinkers in England and see if there were even six who accepted the Christian dogmas of the

Incarnation, Atonement, and Resurrection. Several months later, a Church of England clergyman took up McCabe's challenge and named his six candidates and the field in which he considered they excelled. They were Baron Friedrich von Hügel and the [unnamed, but referring to Dean Inge] Dean of St Paul's (philosophy), Baron Anatole von Hügel (art), Hastings Rashdall (philosophy and history), Ernest W Barnes (science), and T R Glover (history and letters). The *Literary Guide* could not help responding.

> Would it be possible to prove Mr McCabe's point more convincingly? Not one of these is among the hundred most eminent Englishmen, two are not Englishmen (except by a legal fiction), three of the others are clergymen, and it is doubtful if one of them accepts the above dogmas "as taught by Christian leaders and Churches from St Paul onward," as Mr McCabe stipulated. (13)

It is true that none of those names is one to conjure with. McCabe concluded that Christianity was now comprehensively discredited. 'The truth is that Christian Scholarship is drifting more and more toward an entire surrender of all that is distinctive of Christianity; and is merging into a cosmopolitan higher religion.' (14) McCabe's observation was, and is, valid, not least when we recall that the most capable of the six men mentioned, E W Barnes, went on to become a pronounced heretic while remaining in the church.

While the Churches were scoring own goals in their anguished attempts to escape the argument from evil, more down to earth problems beset the RPA. Loss of young members, rising costs, enemy action, and shortages of material all curtailed the RPA's activities. By 1917 the pinch of war was beginning to affect RPA activities. Joseph McCabe, who had been touring the United States, found himself stranded there as that country entered the war. In April £50 worth of RPA material was destroyed in a ship sunk by submarines, and remittances by overseas members were not infrequently ending up at the bottom of the Atlantic rather than at Johnson's Court. At this time the *Guide* was reduced from 16 to 12 pages and the price rose by a halfpenny. As late as September 1918, two ships carrying the *RPA Annual for 1918* and other rationalist material were sunk by German submarines.

More significant was the reduced publishing output during these years. There was no shortage of ideas or orders. For instance, an order towards the end of 1915 for 50,000 copies of the 'Pamphlets for the Million' series had to be turned down for lack of paper to print them on. Other ideas, such as reprinting Adam Gowans Whyte's popular *The Religion of the Open Mind* as a paperback reprint, foundered for the same reason. But other projects went ahead. Ten thousand more copies of *The Churches and Modern Thought* were reprinted in 1915 as it was held that 'Mr Phelips's work is so essential to the continuance of our propaganda that its withdrawal even temporarily cannot be entertained under any circumstances'. (15) Paper was not found to reprint Whyte's book until late in 1917.

Occasionally, projects could continue thanks to the largesse of wealthy supporters, although the incidence of this declined after about 1908 when George Anderson became senile. Every now and then, Clodd's successor as Chairman of the RPA, Sir Herbert Leon, Bt, would arrange for the RPA to send at his expense bundles of the Cheap Reprints to the troops. Watts recalled that many soldiers called on Johnson's Court during visits home to thank them for the books or to order more. There was also the occasional report of interference in soldiers' attempts to procure rationalist material. One Canadian soldier's letter fell foul of the military censors, who feared that a rationalist 'was a person who carried a revolver in one hand and a red flag in the other'. No explanation could persuade this censor otherwise, and the letter was referred to the Intelligence Branch for more information. The soldier eventually got the RPA material he wanted via a friend returning from leave. (16)

Then there was the problem of rationalist recruits being coerced to take a religious oath, in violation of the 1888 Oaths Act, and to attend religious services. One young rationalist, R R Towler, was actually turned down for military service for declining to take the oath, and then arrested as a deserter! Towler's appeal was upheld by the Divisional Court, which found that the military authorities were in violation of the law. Another young rationalist, upon being asked for his religion when enlisting, described himself as a Nothingarian. The *Guide* noted acidly that he 'was registered (perhaps appropriately) as belonging to the Church of England.' (17) The problem of compulsory attendances at church parades was never resolved satisfactorily, and remained a problem in the next war as well. But, like most efforts at coercion, the enforced Christianity was the surest breeding ground for unbelief. Many men either became unbelievers or met unbelievers during their military service. A man serving in the navy wrote to the RPA observing that he had met more freethinkers in the forces than ever in his life. 'I am glad to say I have found them always the straightest, cleanest, and knowledge-thirstiest (to coin a word) fellows. They get far, far more of the real happiness and wonderfulness of life than the average "CE".' (18) Another young soldier, born and raised in a fervently evangelical household, described his loss of faith at the front. Within less than a year at the front E Royston Pike realised that he was no longer a believer.

> How could one continue to believe in a Deity who, omnipotent, yet permitted the slaughter of ten million innocents; who looked on unmoved and unmoving at the doomed humans caught on the wire at Loos, stumbling through the awful valleys on the Somme, struggling up the beaches at Gallipoli, plunging to death at Coronel and Jutland? The vilest of men would exert every nerve to staunch the stream of blood: is God, then, less than man? (19)

Pike recalled reading Lecky 'in the front line before Armentières'. It is a common assertion of a particular class of believer that there are no atheists in foxholes. Few more insulting and offensive slanders have ever been made. On the contrary, many brave men become atheists in foxholes. Men like E Royston Pike. And more than that, they became atheists from a spirit of indignation and anger at the mocking hollowness which declarations of God's love would engender in those circumstances.

But while the front line was responsible for turning many people into atheists, it was also destroying many as well. From the earliest days of the war, notices appeared in the *Guide* to announce the death of a member, or the son of a member. As with the material damage, the human damage seemed to reach its peak in 1917. Julian Gould, son of F J Gould, was killed by a German shell near Arras on May 31 1917 and Percy Vaughan was decapitated on September 26 1917. Vaughan had edited two small reprints of prose works of Shelley and had served as a Director since 1904. Like so many other younger members, he had been introduced to rationalism by purchasing some Cheap Reprints at a railway bookstall. A lawyer, Vaughan had enlisted within weeks of the declaration of war. He had already been severely wounded in 1915 having been thrown by an explosion off an armoured vehicle. Arnold Bennett, an Honorary Associate, wrote a moving tribute to Vaughan, concluding that he was 'quite sure that no hero and martyr had a more biting, a more sardonic, a more passionate sense of the gigantic and incredible sheer idiocy of war than Percy Vaughan had. And I am quite sure that none combined with that sentiment a more winning, practical, human loving-kindness than his.' (20) The same issue featured Vaughan's last contribution to the *Guide*: a review of Anatole France's *The Revolt of the Angels*.

Combating the new irrationalisms

The First World War changed forever the generation of people who fought in it. The war also gave rise to the conditions which favoured many different strains of irrationalism and supernaturalism. Early on in the conflict, for example, came a public fuss about the appearance of the Angel of Mons. As with most allegedly supernatural events, this story had feet of clay. It began as a fictional short story written by Arthur Machen for a London paper in September 1914, only a few days after the skirmish at Mons took place. The story involved St George leading a company of English angels armed with longbows intervening at a crucial stage in the engagement, thus allowing the British forces to retire under cover of the angelic fire. The story took on a life of its own and before long people were confusing fact with fiction. Late in 1915, the *Guide* reprinted an extract from the *Occult Review*, which quoted a soldier who claimed he had seen a 'tall man with yellow hair and his mouth open as if he was saying: "Come on boys, I'll put the kybosh on the devils."' The *Guide* noted that if the Bible were to be rewritten in such popular language, it may well return to favour. (21). A Justice of the Peace from Birkenhead had even elicited a sworn affidavit from a Private Cleaver who had been at Mons. The JP told of Cleaver's experiences. 'He described it as "a flash." I asked him if the angels were mounted or winged. He could say no more than that it appeared as "a flash."' Sadly for the JP, his bubble well and truly burst when it transpired that Cleaver's sworn affidavit attesting to the Angel of Mons was worthless. Cleaver had not landed in France until September 6 1914, the battle of Mons having come to its inglorious conclusion on August 26. But as sceptics the world over know, destroying the credibility of a supernatural tale has little effect on its circulation.

Other examples of hysterical irrationalism only needed be shown; comment seemed superfluous. For instance, the hardy perennial of the number of the beast was given a regular airing. The obvious candidate among British Christians was of course the Kaiser. An ingenious correspondent told *The Scotsman* that 'Kaiser' equals 666, the number of the beast. This is done by taking the numerical ranking of each letter of the word, appending six to that number, then adding those six totals. (22) Thus:

```
K (11) + 6  =  116
A (1)  + 6  =   16
I (9)  + 6  =   96
S (19) + 6  =  196
E (5)  + 6  =   56
R (18) + 6  =  186

       Total =  666
```

So, Kaiser Wilhelm joined the not very select gathering of leaders who have been identified as The Beast. It is inconceivable that a German newspaper at some point during the war did not reveal the same ghastly reality with the name of Asquith, Lloyd George, Clemenceau or Wilson.

More mainstream manifestations of supernaturalism came from the Established church. The Church of England urged all its worshippers to pray to God on January 3 1915 for the war to end, with predictable results. Later the same year Joseph McCabe wrote: 'I will not indulge in any cheap sarcasm as to the result, though one would probably be right in saying that, if the end be deferred to the year 1917, they will still believe that their prayers had effect.' (23) A year later the increasingly desperate church leaders again called for a prayer-fest, but with a slightly different focus. At the beginning of 1916 the clergy held a 'Day of Intercession' in which they asked God to tell them the meaning of the war. Charles Gorham's reply was terse.

> No definite reply has yet been received. Do they really expect one, and how is it to come? By a startling manifestation of Almighty Power? Or by the still, small, voice? If the former, the absence of precedents makes one feel sceptical. If the latter, will the benefit of a sudden and sorely-needed increase of wisdom be confined to the clergy? And, as God must have listened to millions of similar petitions from individuals and congregations which have failed to receive attention, are we to assume that a special gathering of clerics stands a better chance of success? How many times does God need to be asked before he will do an act of mercy? If importunity is the secret of success in prayer, does it place the character of God in an attractive light? (24)

Religious apologists like to affect a superior attitude to questions such as these that have been posed by rationalists over many centuries. Not infrequently they resort to *ad hominem* attacks on the questioners, calling them shallow, mocking, irrelevant or irreverent. The one thing most apologists avoid is to try answering these questions.

But the main outburst of irrationalism at this time came in the form of spiritualism. Before the war spiritualism and other styles of esoteric thought enjoyed intermittent popularity. Spiritualists saw themselves as the first to recognise a noble new science, one that would reconcile the conflict between science and religion. But the horrors of the First World War opened up a whole new opportunity for purveyors of the supernatural as a new system of belief. So many people had lost loved ones in the conflict and found their lives difficult to bear without them. The traditional Christian consolations were no longer credible, and in their more primitive forms were supremely offensive. As one spiritualist proclaimed, rather than filling asylums 'the consolations of spiritualistic belief are saving from insanity many who otherwise would have lost their reason through grief.' (25) Even among those who had not lost loved ones, spiritualism provided reassurances to people that they did indeed matter to the universe. As is so often the case, the problem was stated most eloquently by H G Wells (1866-1946). His novel *Christina Alberta's Father*, published in 1925, was a study of the spiritualist craze. The main character of the novel is Albert Edward Preemby, a retired laundryman who, late in life, attends a séance and discovers he is in fact a reincarnation of Sargon the First, King of Kings. Preemby is searching, however improbably, for some meaning to his life. His flight from reality costs him dear but eventually he comes to his senses and realises that we can all be kings if only we act in a kingly way. The real challenge is simply to be a kingly person and work with other kingly people to make a world fit for kings to live in.

The main works of spiritualist apologetics from this time were *Raymond, or Life and Death* by Sir Oliver Lodge (1916), *Spiritualism: Its History, Phenomena and Doctrine*, by J Arthur Hill, and *The New Revelation* by Sir Arthur Conan Doyle, both from 1918. Hill's is the most coherent of the three, Conan Doyle's the most evangelical in tone, and Lodge's is, without question, the most tragic. It was also by far the most remunerative of the three titles, going through six editions in the first month of publication and two a year after that until 1922, when he published a revised version. Lodge (1851-1940) had made a successful career for himself as a scientist and was knighted in 1902. Like his close friend Arthur Balfour, Lodge was a member of the exclusive gathering known as The Souls. As he grew older, Lodge's interest in spiritualism became less a mark of curiosity and more an intense personal commitment. Lodge's eminence as a scientist helped the spiritualist cause a great deal. In a series of popular works of science, Lodge argued that ether combined elements of the material and spiritual worlds, which also had the effect of reconciling the conflict between science and religion. After the death of his son, Raymond, in the fighting in 1915, Lodge claimed to have experienced communications from him. Lodge's grief at his loss was so understandable and so human, but the 400-page miscellany of memoir, scrapbook and spiritualist apologetic that he produced in his son's name was simply an embarrassment – even to other spiritualists. Lodge recognised that much of the material the various mediums told him came from his deceased son could just as easily have been gleaned from the press. But for reasons known only to him, he chose to publish them as communications from his dead son nonetheless. (26) Out of respect for Lodge's loss, rationalists generally avoided quarrelling with Lodge over *Raymond*.

The brief flurry of spiritualism also provided the backdrop for another, unnoticed, milestone. Edward Clodd published one of the first of a series of criticisms of the new outburst of spiritualism in the wake of *Raymond*. That Clodd chose to publish his work with Grant Richards rather than Watts & Co is symptomatic of the times. There is no question Watts & Co would have published a criticism of spiritualism by a prominent and respected former RPA chairman. That Clodd elected to use a commercial publisher, and that a commercial publisher saw profit for himself in publishing the title, indicates that times had indeed changed. Heterodox titles were no longer to be feared or shunned by publishers and heterodox writers could reasonably expect publishers to consider their works as they would consider any other work.

If it didn't publish Clodd's work, the RPA was not idle in the face of the resurgent spiritualism. It had experience from before the war in controverting spiritualistic claims. The main champion of the rationalist position was Joseph McCabe, whose 1914 work, *The Religion of Sir Oliver Lodge*, was a bruising polemic. Lodge and McCabe had been at war for a decade on the relative merits of Ernst Haeckel's monism. As the decade went on the battle changed to the broader issue of science versus spirituality. Lodge, for all his scientific eminence, proved himself to be a remarkably credulous man, and an indifferent thinker outside his area of specialism. For instance, he drew the fallacious conclusion, one that remains popular today, that if a scientific explanation for some phenomenon is not entirely adequate, then this must mean some spiritual agency is at work. McCabe replied: 'Even granting the obscurities - even granting that science may never explain some phenomena - the conclusion does not follow in the least.' (27)

The case of Sir Oliver Lodge raises another important issue. W P Jolly wrote a biography of Lodge which was published in 1974. As happens so often, one searches in vain for a single reference to Edward Clodd, Joseph McCabe, *The Religion of Sir Oliver Lodge*, the *Literary Guide* or even the RPA. The closest one gets is an oblique dismissal of the 'superficial criticism' which questioned Lodge's whole concept of survival of personality (28) No names are given, even in footnotes, and no suggestion is made why this sort of criticism should be superficial. The least that can be said of such omissions is that it reflects sloppy scholarship. Not only is the significant role of the RPA, and in this case McCabe, obscured from the historical record, the account of Lodge's own life is no less impoverished. Nor is this negligence unusual. Much of the literature on Sir Arthur Conan Doyle and Hilaire Belloc is similarly weak. It is part of the job of this book to set the record straight.

Once the war was over and paper became easier to get hold of, the RPA looked to producing some refutations of spiritualism. In 1919 it produced two works designed for non-specialist readers. F J Gould wrote a short tract called *Common-Sense Thoughts on a Life Beyond* which tried hard not to fissure down a natural/supernatural divide. Being at heart sympathetic with the motives behind spiritualism, Gould sought to ease his readers into a naturalistic acceptance of life's limitations, but put in the flowery, almost sentimental manner that Gould made his own. Much more indignant was Walter Mann's *The Follies and Frauds of Spiritualism*, which combined a short history of the spiritualist movement with a comprehensive demolition of its claims. But when the RPA challenged Sir Arthur Conan Doyle (1859-1930) to a debate on spiritualism in 1920, there was only one person who could effectively champion the rationalist case. Joseph McCabe's preparations for the debate were so thorough that his research produced two books: *Spiritualism: A Popular History from 1847*, published jointly by T Fisher Unwin and Dodd Mead, and *Is Spiritualism Based on Fraud?*, published by Watts & Co.

The spiritualist bubble burst after it became known that some photographs of fairies, which Conan Doyle had championed as authentic, were the fakes everyone else knew them to be. The RPA didn't dwell unduly on spiritualism after that. In 1925 the prominent anatomist and evolutionist, Sir Arthur Keith (1866-1955) participated in a controversy with Conan Doyle over various claims of spiritualism, but the affair did not grab the public's attention as similar controversies did a few years previously. Keith recalled in his autobiography that the fees paid him by the newspapers were sufficient for him to buy a brand new Austin 12, which was dubbed 'Spooks'. The last serious engagement with spiritualism came in the form of the reprint of Ivor Tuckett's 1911 work, *The Evidence for the Supernatural*, published as No. 27 of the Thinker's Library in 1932.

Other wartime activities

While the RPA lost the initiative during the First World War, it would be wrong to see its activities as entirely reactive. As with most RPA activists, Charles Gorham was also involved in other freethought societies. In the second half of 1916 he was appointed editor of an ethical journal called *The Humanist*. It was the intention of *The Humanist* to 'produce a journal which will be acceptable to all sections of the Ethical Movement, and at the same time succeed in popularising the constructive principles of rational ethics.' (29) The *Guide* displayed no misgivings about another magazine entering an already tight market at a difficult time, but some must have been felt nonetheless. As a result of the regular supportive commentary the *Guide* gave to *The Humanist*, an anonymous benefactor donated £10 to its cause. The *Guide* loyally advertised the contents of each copy of *The Humanist* until it finally folded in 1920. Gorham had remained co-editor until 1919 and was replaced for its final year by Mrs M I Joad. The *Guide* had been similarly magnanimous with an earlier ethical journal; the first issue of the *Ethical World* was included in the posting to all readers of the *Guide* at the beginning of 1907. The *Ethical World* was edited by Stanton Coit and ran until 1916.

It is also characteristic of the RPA that its most ambitious single publishing venture during the First World War was a book for children. *The World's Wonder Stories*, by Adam Gowans Whyte was an expensively produced book of 272 pages with lots of plates and other illustrations. Whyte's book was less overtly didactic than Gould's moral lesson books. In fact, he began and ended the book with eulogies to the examined life. Many adults, Whyte lamented, don't like to confess they are still learning, but the wisest are those who never stop learning. '*Their* education is never finished. They are not too proud to go on asking questions even if they are a hundred years old.' (30) His first two examples of people who value the examined life were Charles Darwin and Socrates. *The World's Wonder Stories* is an admirable example of what Bertrand Russell, and later still Peter Singer, would recommend as the broad view required by fully aware human beings. After its opening eulogy to the examined life, the book proceeded to place the young reader in context of the universe, of nature (plants before humans) and of society, in that order. Having finished the book the young reader would have had a clear and inspiring overview of the complexity and interdependence of the universe, and of humanity's place in it. The reader would have a cosmological framework for a useful and active life. Anticipating the contemporary awareness of patterns of reciprocity among animals, Whyte exhorted his readers to learn from the animals.

82

> What I would like you to remember most of all is that, if animals had not shown kindness and heroism, they would not have been able to survive. If they had not been able to work together faithfully, and to help each other in times of danger, they would have been killed off by their enemies. In the animal world, then, there is a reason for "right" and "wrong." And when we turn from animals to men we find that there is still a reason for "right" and "wrong." (31)

Contrary to so many accusations of the arrogance of humanism, Whyte's book for children, published in 1916, shows an admirable awareness of nature, a gentleness in describing it, and a plea for us to learn from it.

Pressures caused by shortages of paper necessarily limited the RPA's publishing programme through the war years. Not surprisingly then, it remained committed to the lecturing circuit. Hypatia Bradlaugh Bonner was active through these years and Chapman Cohen maintained a busy lecturing programme on behalf of the National Secular Society. But Joseph McCabe remained by far the busiest and most popular rationalist lecturer in Britain. When John Settle, a Lancashire miner who had made some money buying property, died in February 1915, he left an estate which was to be dedicated to providing rationalist lectures in his home town of Wigan. It was Joseph McCabe who went to Wigan to give these lectures. In 1916, for example, McCabe spoke on evolution. The lectures went like this:

October 22, 'The Preparation of the Earth for Life'
October 29, 'The Early Development of Life'
November 5, 'The Rise of the Higher Animals'
November 12, 'The Evolution of Humanity'

Attendances at these lectures averaged 350, which the RPA report described as 'fairly large'. The next year McCabe was back, this time lecturing on the evolution of beauty, mind, morality and religion, and in 1918 he focussed mainly on the churches and the war. McCabe returned to Wigan until at least 1920.

Despite the difficult conditions of the war, the RPA was committed to increasing its membership and range of influence. In April 1918 the *Guide* announced 'The Rationalist "Great Advance"' as a counter to a plea by Cardinal Bourne's recent plea for a religious revival in Britain. The RPA chose four titles to spearhead the advance: *The Age of Reason* by Thomas Paine; *The Christian Hell* by Hypatia Bradlaugh Bonner; *The Churches and Modern Thought* by Vivian Phelips; and *The Religion of the Open Mind* by Adam Gowans Whyte. Any member, for the donation of 2s9d, could pay for one set of these titles to be sent to servicemen. Three months later, as another part of its campaign, Watts & Co spent £250 distributing a large consignment of the latter two books to the servicemen through the Camps Library network.

The war put paid to many other promising ideas and ventures, perhaps the most important being a second attempt to raise funds for a larger headquarters for the RPA. In 1903 the lease of 5 and 6 Johnson's Court was secured, and ten years later on a fundraising campaign was launched to purchase a headquarters. The driving force behind this was Sir Herbert Leon (1850-1926), Edward Clodd's successor as

Chairman of the RPA and George Anderson's principal successor as chief benefactor. Leon had been introduced to the RPA by Dennis Hird in 1901 and soon afterwards was invited onto the Board of Directors. The appeal, announced in the *Guide* at the beginning of 1913, grew unspectacularly from the initial £500 donated by the RPA itself. By October 1914 the Headquarters Fund had amassed £1123, including a generous donation of £17 from the Japan Rationalist Association. But in June the following year, the exigencies of war had seen the total drop by £77. The appeal dropped from public view after that, to be revived after the war.

Little more was done about the move to purchase headquarters until an opportunity arose in 1924 to purchase number 4 Johnson's Court. This four-storey building (including the basement) was between number 17, which the RPA already owned, and 5 and 6 Johnson's Court, on which the RPA had acquired a 54 year lease on in 1903 for £2400. Number 4 Johnson's Court cost the RPA £4500 and it launched an appeal at the beginning of 1924 for £10,000 for the ambitious plans it had for the buildings. Between them, 4, 5 and 6 Johnson's Court were to become a worldwide centre for rationalism. The buildings would house a shop, library and reading room, social facilities, boardroom, offices and storage space, although the library proved too small to accommodate J M Robertson's collection of 20,000 books, which he bequeathed to the RPA. Only a few titles were kept, the rest being sold. (32) The appeal was put to members optimistically:

> They will be headquarters that our London, provincial and overseas members will not be ashamed of, and which they will find adequate for our work. Within two hundred yards of the central traffic artery of the Metropolis, they yet preserve quiet for work, for study, or for social intercourse. The Directors have long desired space in which some of the activities pressed upon them could be conducted, and they believe that this scheme will secure them, not only for this generation, but also for the future. (33)

It is clear that many people shared this vision, although it is equally clear that the people who shared the vision were not those with large disposable incomes. As with the appeal before the war, the flow of funds after the initial rush was slow but steady. In the month following the appeal being sounded in January 1924 £2300 came in to add to the £1400 that had been retained from the pre-war appeal. By the end of the year the total had risen to £4292 and by 1927, when the fund was wound up, a total of £6219 had been collected. While some donations were in the £100 to £200 mark, most were between ten shillings and five pounds. For the first few years the majority of the building had to be let out, so as to bring in the revenue to pay for the building. The consolidation process was completed in 1929 when the RPA acquired the freehold of 5 and 6 Johnson's Court, thus completing its impressive property portfolio. That same year the South Place Ethical Society opened its imposing new building linking Red Lion Square and Theobald's Road in London. The building was named Conway Hall, after Moncure Conway (1832-1907), one of the most visionary of the South Place lecturers. Unlike so many churches, which can rely on generous endowments, rates relief, or tax incentives, these achievements of the RPA and the South Place Ethical Society were made possible by the devotion of ordinary men and women, in most cases people of modest means.

The acquisition of the headquarters was Leon's greatest legacy to the RPA. He had long provided sound financial advice and no-nonsense chairing of the Board of Directors. Leon was succeeded as Chairman in 1922 by George Whale (1849-1925), a man very much in his two predecessors' stamp. Leon had thought himself at 72 too old to continue as chairman, so he was replaced by someone who was 73. A solicitor by occupation, Whale was a brilliant raconteur and much-loved epicurean. He had been active in local politics, serving as Mayor of Woolwich and Chairman of Woolwich Polytechnic. He had written an account of London's government system in 1888 but was not a regular author, as his friend Clodd had managed to become. As befits his reputation as a socialite, Whale had helped form two London clubs, the Omar Khayyam Club and the Pepys Club. And, reminiscent of Clodd, Whale was familiar with an impressive range of literary and other prominent figures. He owned a major collection of 6000 works of English literature and history. One of his friends was H G Wells who was thought to have used Whale as the model for the kindly benefactor Oswald Sydenham who appeared in his 1918 novel *Joan and Peter*. Another novelist, Frank Swinnerton, whom Whale introduced into the Omar Khayyam, remembered him fondly. 'Bald, wise, and full of fun, he pinkly and benevolently shone upon the rest of the world with the warmth of an unwearyingly kind heart.' (34) Whale's other signal contribution to the RPA did not materialise until some years after his death. He persuaded an old friend of his, W C Johnson, that the RPA was a suitable recipient of a substantial legacy. True to his word, Johnson left the association £46,541 after his death, one of the largest bequests the RPA attracted.

Whale had caused a minor stir in 1917 when, at the Annual General Meeting of that year, he suggested that the *Literary Guide* could do with a facelift. Nobody had any doubts that Whale was 'sound', so offence was not taken. Indeed, he was asked to serve as a Director of the RPA, an invitation he accepted. Whale's main suggestions were that the *Guide* should be made more attractive to the general reader by making the articles shorter, including more reviews of material not strictly related to rationalism, more comment on passing matters and adopting a less aggressive approach. Little change followed this suggestion, mainly because too large a percentage of the correspondents who wrote in on the matter were opposed to the changes. The main person to take offence at Whale's suggestions would have been Joseph McCabe, the person responsible for most of the combative material in the *Guide*.

Whale's term as Chairman was the shortest of any so far, lasting only three years. He rather dampened the 1925 RPA Annual Dinner by collapsing dead straight after presenting his speech. It soon became part of RPA lore that Whale's last toast had been "Let us eat, drink and be merry for tomorrow we die." In fact he was quoting W K Clifford (1845-1879), the brilliant mathematician, who said "Let us take hands and work, for this day we are alive together." In the stunned silence after Whale's collapse, J B S Haldane whispered loudly enough to ensure being heard, "The Whale's been harpooned." (35)

Once the story got out, the RPA found itself the centre of some malevolent press attention. Quite the most bizarre treatment of the incident came from the New York based *American Standard*, which was keen to use the incident to snare as many foes as possible. This paper's heading went 'Atheist falls lifeless in chair after attacking Bible – His Fate seen as Warning to Romanists and Jews who fight Bible in Schools.' (36) Closer to home, the hostile Beaverbrook press used the incident to mock the RPA and rationalism. The *Daily Express* ran an article entitled 'Death after Denouncing Religion' while the *Sunday Express* ran a similar piece under the heading 'The Irrational Rationalists'. The gist of the articles was to imply that Whale had been struck down by God and to mock rationalists' alleged querying of God's purpose when clergymen are struck down while in church. *The Sunday Express's* tasteless article attracted a splenetic reply from J M Robertson. To take one item of abuse as representative, Robertson wrote:

> To point out that your "argument" is a tissue of imbecility, too crass to be appended to "Noodle's Oration," would be to risk obscuring the case. Observe that, though I have said you never were very wise, I am now suggesting that you are a fool. (37)

Thanks to Robertson's bad mannered reply, which went on in this vein for two full columns, the journalist in question, James Douglas, was able to escape taking responsibility for his article that a more balanced censure might have forced upon him. Robertson's unpleasant personality (I am distinguishing here between his personality and his intellect, which was an asset) was a liability for rationalism in general and the RPA in particular, especially as the RPA had been formed ostensibly to avoid what it saw as the vulgar and combative freethought advocacy of the National Secular Society. Having lost his seat in parliament in 1918, Robertson was active once more in the RPA. However, it remains true that had rationalists made the sort of comments about the circumstances of a churchman's demise that Douglas made about Whale, the heavens would have rung with righteous indignation.

RPA books

What sort of books was the RPA producing during these difficult times? It will come as no surprise that the RPA books published in the twenties addressed the issues that had been live before the war. This can be seen as another aspect of the organisation's fervent wish – one which the country as a whole shared – to return to the world of 1914. No better example of this wish can be found than a series begun in 1920 called Life Stories of Famous Men. It probably wouldn't take much thought to guess which men's stories were retold. The list went, in order of publication: Thomas Henry Huxley, Auguste Comte, Robert Owen, Charles Bradlaugh, Charles Darwin, Robert Ingersoll, Voltaire, George Jacob Holyoake and Ernest Renan. It would take as little effort to match the authors to the subject, but we can leave that to Appendix One. It quickly transpired that this series was not selling well, but I don't think the RPA could quite see why. The world had changed, and stories of extraordinary men overcoming great odds and establishment obscurantism by virtue of their greater courage and virtue weren't the stories that resonated with a postwar readership. These stories rested on a fundamental sense of justice and order, in which right would eventually prevail. After the First World War many people did not share this sense. Four works in this series were produced in 1920, two in 1921 and 1922 and Renan followed up in 1924. And that was that. A series of pamphlets called The People's Forum, also begun in 1920 and on themes familiar to the Edwardian world, didn't last the year.

A considerably better idea was launched in 1926. Joseph McCabe had suggested in 1924 that the RPA produce a series of cheap, accessible works of popular science. As ever, McCabe had led the way, having already produced a few works of popular science, notably *The ABC of Evolution* (1920) and its successor volume, *The Evolution of Civilisation* (1921) as well as a survey of the ice ages in 1922 and *The Wonders of the Stars* the following year. He also had in mind the small pamphlets produced in the United States by Emanuel Haldeman-Julius (1889-1951), then called the People's Pocket Series and soon to be renamed the Little Blue Books. McCabe's proposal was not proceeded with immediately, not least because of the increasing tensions between him and the RPA, but the following year plans for a series of this sort began. It was called The Forum Series and was a great success. Each Forum Series book was hardcovered, 56 pages long and sold for a shilling. It was the same basic formula that had made the Cheap Reprints a success: good quality and cheap.

The first book in the series was an adaptation of a series of science talks on radio by Julian Huxley (1887-1975). The book was called *The Stream of Life*, and the first impression of 10,000 copies was exhausted in six months. It went on selling for ten years and sold in the region of 26,000 copies. This was the beginning of what proved to be a long relationship between this great evolutionist and the RPA. Just as successful, and a lot more controversial, was the third book in the series, written by H G Wells. *Mr Belloc Objects to "The Outline of History"* would have to reckon on any list of outstanding controversial literature of the twentieth century. Hilaire Belloc (1870-1953) was a pugnacious Catholic apologist and anti-semite who had taken grave offence at Wells' *Outline of History*, which was published in 1920. Belloc wrote a *Companion to Mr Wells's "Outline of History"* in 1926, which urged items of Catholic dogma at every point in Wells's narrative where he felt this to be necessary. Belloc took special umbrage at Wells's evolutionary account and argued vehemently for the fixity of species and 'Design', suitably ennobled by capital letters. Belloc had no doubts about the gravity of the cause he was defending. 'Europe – the Soul of the World – is hesitating whether it will not return to the Faith: without which it cannot live.' (38) Even Michael Coren, in his otherwise jaundiced biography of Wells, admits that Belloc's *Companion* was 'severe, strident, even vicious'. (39) The *Companion* was brought together from a series of articles in the Catholic paper *The Universe*. Wells offered *The Universe* a series of articles to answer some of Belloc's objections free of charge. Most editors in the western world would have hardly dared dream of such an opportunity, but *The Universe*, anxious to deny its readers a second opinion, turned the offer down.

Mr Belloc Objects to "The Outline of History" could not compete with Belloc's work in terms of personal spite, but was an effective riposte. It is difficult, and perhaps irrelevant, to say whether either side emerged victorious from the battle. Belloc had ensured a level of viciousness that sullied what would otherwise have been a worthwhile exchange of views. One biographer of Wells noted that 'most people read Belloc for style, not content, and so the *Outline* continued to sell.' (40) Michael Foot was less sanguine, noting that 'Roman Catholic apologists had never been shiningly successful when they chose to fight on the battlefield of free speech and free printing, and Hilaire Belloc was no more successful than his predecessors.' (41) Interestingly, this constitutes the only significant intellectual contest between rationalists and Christians in the decade after the Great War.

While Huxley and Wells are perhaps the names most remembered now, another of the contributors to the Forum Series was, in his day, just as eminent. Sir Arthur Keith was for many years the Hunterian Professor and Conservator of the museum attached to the Royal College of Surgeons. The study of human anatomy had led Keith away from the faith of his childhood to rationalism. He became an Honorary Associate in 1923 and retained a close association with the RPA until his death in 1955. He was a capable controversialist, having taken on Sir Arthur Conan Doyle, as we mentioned earlier, over spiritualism, and later on Hilaire Belloc over his claims of 'Design' in nature. Keith came into his own in the Forum Series, contributing four titles: *Concerning Man's Origin* (1927), *Darwinism and What it Implies* (1928), *The Construction of Man's Family Tree* (1934), and *Darwinism and Its Critics* (1935). Most of these titles had originally been addresses given by Keith to a variety of respected institutions. Keith was a graceful writer and skilful populariser, so these titles were all to the credit of the Forum Series and the RPA generally.

The Forum Series traversed an admirable range of topics. Psychology, anthropology, economics, two books looking at aspects of the relationship between art and science, eugenics, microbiology and ornithology. But it was evolution which remained the most discussed subject, with 15 of the 21 titles having evolution as a point of reference. True to form, the RPA sought out a wide range of opinions for the series. Keith's books were Darwinian in orientation whereas Cyril Joad's book, *The Meaning of Life*, was Bergsonian and vitalist. Grafton Elliot Smith advanced his beloved diffusionist theory of human evolution while Leonard Darwin gave an introduction to eugenics. Interestingly, after the furore over *Mr Belloc Objects*, Watts & Co inserted a disclaimer: 'It should be clearly understood that each writer in this series of little books is alone responsible for the opinions expressed.' Other titles were contributed by J A Hobson and Professors Westermarck, Patten and Poulton, all very well known names at the time.

The noticeable gap in the Forum Series was a popular work on physics, definitely the 'in' science of the 1920s in the wake of Eddington's vindication of Einstein's theory of relativity. Part of the explanation of this is that a year before the series began Watts & Co published Joseph McCabe's book *The Marvels of Modern Physics* which covered this subject satisfactorily. But that wouldn't have stopped them producing another work had a suitable author been available. Bertrand Russell had already produced for other publishers his *ABC of Atoms* and *ABC of Relativity* in 1923 and 1925 respectively. But I can't help suspecting that the real reason the Forum Series had nothing on physics is that the RPA was uncertain what consequences relativity had for rationalism. Some rather extravagant claims were being made that relativity spelt the end of materialism and presaged the final reconciliation of religion and science. Most RPA people felt these claims to be untrue, correctly as it turned out, but there was nobody on hand to articulate the new situation effectively. It was put in the 'too hard' basket.

The next major initiative focused on younger readers. The 1929 Annual General Meeting resolved to give some practical application to the article in its Memorandum promoting secular education and cultivating the moral life. With this in mind the World of Youth Series was begun in 1930. The World of Youth series was a better idea than the Life-Stories of Famous Men series, but it was no more successful. In its four-year life, it produced fifteen titles, four of them by F J Gould, whose idea the series was. Gould introduced his readers to noble thoughts of the past while Adam Gowans Whyte wrote three short introductions to the world around us. Naomi Mitchison and Royston Pike wrote excellent primers on the world's religions and others wrote short histories of architecture, wild flowers and prehistory. The books were given sturdy hard covers and were all illustrated. The series was a good idea and the books were attractive, but they were too expensive to sell well as the world entered the years of the Depression. Well into the 1930s the whole series was being advertised for sale at bargain rates.

It is among the stand-alone titles published by Watts & Co for the RPA at this time that an awkward, backward-looking feel is apparent. Looking at these titles, one could be forgiven for thinking the First World War had not taken place. The continued focus was the criticism of Christian truth-claims and of the Bible as the carrier of those truth-claims. For instance, Keighley Snowdon wrote *Myth and Legend in the Bible* (1915), which outlined the strands of mythology in the Old Testament. After the war Macleod Yearsley wrote *The Story of the Bible*, which examined the social and intellectual contexts of the Old and New Testaments. This book was published originally in 1922 and reappeared as Number 35 of the Thinker's Library in 1933, with a revised edition in 1936. And the same year as Yearsley's book Watts & Co published *Shaken Creeds: The Virgin Birth Doctrine* by Major W J R Wingfield, who wrote under the pseudonym 'Jocelyn Rhys'. This was followed up two years later by *Shaken Creeds: The Resurrection Doctrines*. Wingfield's works were scholarly studies of the non-Christian parallels to these doctrines. His books, and the drive that underlay them, illustrate very well the attitude of many in the RPA at the time. In the *RPA Annual for 1925* Wingfield ended an article called 'A Challenge to the Churches' like this:

> Those of us who retain a sentimental attachment to the Churches of our childhood, and who realise most clearly the value of their ancient prestige, would like to know that the Churches were making some effort to clear themselves of the charge that they think more of retaining their vested interests than of teaching their flocks the truth. We would gladly cease from criticising the clergy if we found that they were doing their best to grow out of a discredited theology and to evolve a reformed organisation for teaching men, women, and children all that is best in human knowledge and humane ideals. (42)

This is classic rationalism, not the hostile harangue against religion as is so often claimed; more a pained sense of disappointment at the inability of the churches to act honestly. Wingfield had been raised in an atmosphere of, in his words, 'unadulterated orthodoxy', but the famous controversy between Gladstone and Huxley in the *Nineteenth Century* magazine in the 1880s introduced the first doubts. He finally lost his faith in 1912 when a nurse gave him a copy of the *Literary Guide* during a severe illness. His *Shaken Creeds* series were the result of the decade of study he had devoted to the origins of and pagan parallels to Christianity.

It is not that the RPA wasn't publishing other types of books at this time. Far from it. Neither is it to say that these sorts of books are unnecessary. It has long been fashionable among more sophisticated unbelievers to despise this sort of rationalist writing. But the continued prevalence of naïve beliefs about the origin of the Bible and the uniqueness of its historical and moral claims make the sort of critiques undertaken by Yearsley, Snowdon and Wingfield necessary and valuable. But it is fair to say that the focus of the RPA leadership remained relatively untouched by the war, at a time when fewer people were troubled by these issues than had been the case before the war. Worse still, the RPA was not reaching these newly secularised people.

There is no surer measure of the passage of time for an institution than the publication of its own history. The RPA decided this milestone had arrived in 1929. And why not? The RPA was thirty years old, or 39 if its predecessors were counted, and the *Literary Guide* and *Rationalist Annual* were 44 years old. The acquisition of the freeholds of 5 and 6 Johnson's Court must have been the occasion for real joy among rationalists. They were entitled to feel pride in their achievements. Perhaps inevitably the job was given to Watts' old friend, F J Gould. He did a fair job of it, certainly this centenary history would be poorer without it. But Gould's flowery style and understandable difficulty in achieving any critical distance from his subject limits the book's value. When Gould handed over the manuscript Charles Watts studied it quietly for a while, then looked up and said "This is my life." (43) And indeed it was.

It is significant that even the outstanding works published from this period were historical in flavour. Among them would have to be counted Joseph McCabe's *Biographical Dictionary of Modern Rationalists* and J M Robertson's two massive histories of freethought. McCabe's biographical dictionary, published in 1920, featured about 2200 people of diverse backgrounds and beliefs and was described by the RPA's annual report for that year as the 'Association's magnum opus'. The main problem in compiling a work such as this is the conditions of entry. Who qualifies as a rationalist? McCabe was well aware of the problem and acknowledged the difficulty in his opening essay. On the one hand he included Alfred Russel Wallace (1823-1913) and Cesare Lombroso (1836-1909), both of whom ended their lives convinced spiritualists, while Thomas Hardy, far more of an atheist, was not included. Wallace and Lombroso had both been members of the RPA and were included because, in view of their contributions to their respective branches of science, it would have been ungrateful not to. Hardy, by contrast, while sympathetic, was not a member of the RPA and, more to the point, had indicated his unwillingness to be included in the work. He had said the same when invited to become an Honorary Associate of the RPA in 1899. It was not, he said on both occasions, that he was not sympathetic, it was that he was not prepared to take on any label. (44) The crucial tests for McCabe were the candidate's view on personal immortality and whether they were members of a church. (45) McCabe recognised fully that many of the people included were not rationalists in the narrower sense of the term. But in the broader sense of rejecting orthodox creeds and honestly and carefully working out for themselves a comprehensive view of the world, all of them were rationalists. Once more this shows a greater ability to live with ambiguity and difference than rationalists have been given credit for. McCabe's *Biographical Dictionary of Modern Rationalists* remains one of the single most valuable reference works published by the RPA and as recently as 1998 was reprinted by Thoemmes Press.

The other outstanding works of this period are the two large histories written by J M Robertson. His first work in this field, *A Short History of Freethought: Ancient and Modern*, was published by Swan Sonnenschein in 1899 but as he read more and his thought developed, he published new and larger editions. A second, enlarged edition was published by Watts & Co in 1906 and a third, revised and expanded once more, in 1915. Upon retirement from politics and with time on his hands, Robertson expanded this work once again, to the point where the sheer bulk of material meant it could not longer stay under one title. So what in 1899 had been one short history had become two long histories. *A History of Freethought in the Nineteenth Century* was published in 1929 and the fourth edition of *A History of Freethought: Ancient and Modern*, now stopping at the French Revolution, appeared in 1936, three years after Robertson's death. Included in this edition were several appreciations of Robertson by a variety of intellectuals, from within and without the rationalist movement.

It is with these histories that Robertson's finest legacy lies. His works on the historical Jesus were ponderously written and supported an eccentric thesis, in support of which unscholarly leaps and jumps and unpleasant aspersions against opponents were made. These histories, by contrast, are a lot more readable, free from rancour and reveal Robertson's scholarship at its best. We noted in Chapter One that, in his 1975 work, Owen Chadwick was dismissive of Robertson as an historian. But more recent scholarship has vindicated his work in this area. In 1989 J C A Gaskin, editor of an excellent anthology of varieties of unbelief called Robertson's histories 'invaluable mines of information'. (46) The most comprehensive study of Robertson as an historian comes from David Berman. It was included in a collection of essays about all aspects of Robertson's career and published by the RPA in 1987. Berman agrees that Robertson's histories are mines of information, but also praises the theoretical and sociological thought which underlies the information. 'No one,' he wrote, 'has seen so much, so coherently, and in so much detail.' (47) Berman puts even the faults in Robertson's work down to his excessive commitment to truthfulness. Most recently, Odin Dekkers describes these histories as Robertson's greatest claim to fame outside his work in literary criticism. (48)

The challenge of new technologies

The advent of radio was one of the most significant developments of the 1920s. It is difficult in the twenty-first century to appreciate the significance of radio in its early days. Radio, writes the historian Eric Hobsbawm, 'transformed the life of the poor, and especially of housebound women, as nothing else had ever done. It brought the world into their room.' (49) Where once there had been silence and isolation, now even ordinary people could listen to the great and the wise in their own house. Radio meant that the age of the public lecture was now all but over. People still went to them, but in smaller numbers, and it became more difficult to reach the uncommitted. Radio, however, could reach everyone. This meant that the views of those in charge of radio was very important indeed. The churches realised this full well, and in 1923 an interdenominational advisory body was established which quickly enjoyed the strong support of Sir John Reith (1889-1971), who in the same year had become general manager of the newly-formed British Broadcasting Corporation. Before all this censorious machinery was in place, the BBC had allowed the RPA to give a short address over the air. It was called 'The Gospel of Reason' and was read by Charles Gorham. But by the end of 1923, things had been so arranged that no views on religion that established Christian opinion would disapprove of stood any chance of getting airtime. The churches, however, were permitted a generous allowance of airtime with little or no regard to the quality of the material broadcast. Most religious broadcasts were produced by the Religious Broadcasting Department of the BBC, which faced no requirement for objectivity, quality, or to produce material that was not mere propaganda.

Early in 1928 the BBC announced that it was going to expand its service to supply two programmes a day to most of its listeners. The only exception was the Sunday evening religious programmes – the notorious God-slot. The RPA organised a campaign of protest against this, claiming that, alongside the religious programmes, there should be something else for people to listen to, just as there was to be at all other times of the week. But it might as well not have bothered. The *Guide* quoted the BBC's Director-General Sir John Reith as saying; 'It has been against the policy of the BBC from the outset to have an alternative to a Christian Religious Service on Sunday evenings, and the Corporation does not see any justification for a change in this policy.' (50) And that was that.

That the BBC recognised the merit of the RPA's complaints is illustrated in the degree to which they sidestepped the issue. At one stage, for instance, they staged a 'debate' between a bishop and an atheist. Only later did it transpire that the bishop had written his argument *and that of the atheist*, the part of which was read by an actor! (51) Not surprisingly, the atheist's argument appeared shallow and unconvincing when compared to the profundity and depth of the bishop. The privileged access to the media by churchmen and their allies has remained a live issue for rationalists and humanists ever since.

The RPA soon learned that the most effective way of having its voice heard on the air was through its Honorary Associates, several of whom came into their own with this new medium. Julian Huxley, Bertrand Russell and H G Wells, in particular, succeeded in securing radio time in the interests of science or political liberalism. Their contributions were therefore rationalist, without being Rationalist. Their airtime was minimal, however, in contrast with that of the legions of churchmen, most of whom had far less that was original or even topical to say.

Chairman to President

Following the death of George Whale, the Board of Directors thought that the organisation needed a different structure at the top. Up until this time, the Chairman was the official face of the Association as well as its administrative heart. So far this combination had worked well with the likes of Holyoake, Clodd, Leon and Whale. But the time had come, the Directors decided, to create the position of President, which would take from the Chairman the formal leadership role. This was a good idea, as the position of President would not be unduly arduous, but hopefully the holder of the office would bring prestige to the RPA. In the meantime, the Association would continue to operate at the hands of an efficient Chairman of the Board of Directors. It also would lessen the disruption to the Association when one office-holder died or otherwise vacated the position.

The first person to take the position of President was Graham Wallas (1858-1932). Forgotten now, Wallas was well known in his day. He became an active rationalist after the school he taught at in Highgate dismissed him for refusing to go to communion. Along with Sidney Webb, Bernard Shaw, Annie Besant and others, Wallas was one of the contributors to the hugely influential *Fabian Essays in Socialism*, which came out in 1888. His contribution was on 'Property under Socialism'. Wallas was no ideologue about socialism. 'The system of property holding which we call Socialism is not in itself such a life any more than a good system of drainage is health, or the invention of printing is knowledge. Nor indeed is Socialism the only condition necessary to produce complete human happiness.' (52) Socialism and liberalism were not opposites in Wallas's mind. Wallas left the Fabians in 1904 when he became concerned at its antiliberal drift. So in many ways, Wallas was an inspired choice to act as the RPA's first President. The tall, genial, gifted teacher was the embodiment of a civilised human being. Kingsley Martin, who studied under him at Cambridge, remembered him as 'the most kindly of human beings, immensely stimulating and encouraging to the young.' (53) Also, his record of service with the Ethical Union was a useful link. At sixty-eight, Wallas was relatively youthful by the standards of the time.

Wallas's two best-known books were written before the First World War, and they serve as a warning to those who prefer stereotyped formulae about rationalists. In *Human Nature and Politics* (1908), Wallas attacked the notion of political action being the result of rational calculation. On the contrary, he stressed the contingency and messiness of much political decision-making. And in 1914, in his book *The Great Society*, Wallas warned that the ever-growing complexity of modern society posed a danger to individual development. And in 1926, the year he became the first RPA President, Wallas's last important book was published. In *The Art of Thought*, Wallas continued his life-long project of emphasising the value of the rational individual.

> The majority of the inhabitants of Europe now live under constitutions invented by Lenin, Mussolini, Rivera, or by the founders of the German Republic and of the Austrian and Russian successor states; but no one except a few partisans believes that stable forms of relation between the citizen and the state, or between the state and other political and social organisations, have yet been invented...Thought, therefore, whether as the concentrated mental activity of the professed thinker, or as penetrating and guiding other activities, is now required more urgently than ever before in the history of mankind. (54)

The RPA published an abridgement of *The Art of Thought* in 1945, when yet again the need for clear and rational thought was dire.

Despite his excellent credentials, Wallas was something of a disappointment as president. He failed to make much of a splash for the RPA. He was no longer young and probably lacked the drive at this stage in his life to really make a difference for the RPA. Few RPA insiders were unduly disappointed when Wallas retired as president in 1929. Wallas was succeeded as president by Harold Laski (1893-1950). The first remarkable thing about Laski was his youth. At a mere 36 years old, he was half the age of any of the previous chairmen or presidents. Where Wallas had made his contributions to society in the 1890s and 1900s, Laski was a man of the moment. Here was someone who could be the public face of the RPA for the 1930s. At last, the RPA was looking to the future, not to the past. We will follow his story in the next chapter.

The need for a breath of fresh air that Laski promised was becoming obvious to everyone. This was because relations among the veterans of the movement were becoming more strained. Or, to be more exact, relations between Joseph McCabe and everyone else were becoming more strained. Things had been set on this course after the events of 1908, as we related in the previous chapter, although relations did not deteriorate seriously until the beginning of the twenties. As the twenties progressed, McCabe became more and more aware of the expanding gulf between the RPA and the swelling numbers of unchurched people. McCabe attempted to address this need with his own paper, *The Tribune*, early in 1924, but he lacked the financial clout for such a venture to succeed, and the magazine folded after only three months. After returning to the *Literary Guide* in the middle of 1924, McCabe continued to press his point.

> Indeed, four-fifths of the people who do not go to church have no idea of the intellectual case against religion. So we do not want less Rationalism "of the old type," but more. We want it cheap and humorous and superficial. We want to put sound reasons in the minds of the twenty million who do not go to church. (55)

McCabe was scornful of the various plans to put before their readers some rival system of ritual or belief. Positivism he dismissed as 'one of the most dismal failures of the last half-century' and any sort of alliance with any political, social, aesthetic or social creed as a 'not very protracted form of euthanasia.' True to form, McCabe managed to offend both the reverent agnostics and the political progressives at the same time. He was good at this.

It appears that McCabe was presented with some sort of ultimatum late in 1925 or early in 1926. The ultimatum required that he make more effort to co-operate with the Directors and with Charles Watts in his capacity as *Literary Guide* editor, or move on. Such an approach was doomed to fail against a man like McCabe. The last article he ever wrote for the *Guide* was printed in March 1926, and was posted from Canada, where he was lecturing at the time. Two years later a group of McCabe's supporters called an Extraordinary General Meeting of the RPA, ostensibly to engineer a rapprochement, but really, if their tone is any guide, simply to castigate Directors and demand either their resignation or some sort of restitution for McCabe. The RPA brought out their heavy artillery in the form of J M Robertson and the result was an unattractive war of attrition from which nobody emerged honourably. The occasion brought out the pig-headed worst in both Robertson and McCabe. In the short-run McCabe was the loser, as he should have realised he would be, but in the longer term the RPA and rationalism generally were the losers.

The failure of the Extraordinary General Meeting to heal the rift was written up by McCabe in his autobiography in apocalyptic terms as the end of an era and the final betrayal of the movement's greatest son. But it was not nearly as simple as that. Many of the issues he cited as bringing on the rift were not nearly as straightforward as McCabe made out. McCabe was a very difficult man indeed. He *was* thin-skinned, intolerant of criticism and openly contemptuous of those he disagreed with. After a few years in the wilderness, McCabe was prepared to admit this. In 1932 he acknowledged that he was inclined to be too blunt on occasions and to 'make more fuss than the occasion required.' (56) It is difficult not to agree.

McCabe's dramatic self-immolation took place the same year another of the veterans of 1899 retired. Charles Gorham had filled the post since 1913, and had been an RPA stalwart since 1896. Gorham's replacement came from the next generation and must have been a source of hope to the aging Directors. When he became secretary of the RPA, E Royston Pike was still a young man, in his early thirties. Pike, as we saw earlier, had lost his faith while on active service during the First World War. He came from a long line of committed Nonconformists, mainly Baptists. His great-grandfather had written a couple of works reminiscent of that sect. One of them was entitled *Consolations of Gospel Truth, as exhibited in various interesting anecdotes respecting the Dying Hours of Persons who gloried in the Cross of Christ, to which are added some Affecting Narratives describing the horrors of unpardoned sin, in the prospect of Death and Eternity*. The memory of these works made Pike shudder; '…terrible books these, reeking of hell and punishment, deeply tinged with the flames of the everlasting fires.' (57)

Back on Civvy Street, and having read a lot of rationalist material in the trenches, Pike tracked down the RPA. This was in 1922. There he met Charles Watts and Charles Gorham. Watts responded warmly to the young man and recommended he read Vivian Phelips's *Churches and Modern Thought* and Samuel Laing's *Modern Science and Modern Thought*. Pike eagerly took the material away. Watts's suggestions for reading go a long way to explaining the problems the RPA was experiencing in the early twenties. Phelips' book was only 16 years old when Watts recommended it to the earnest young man, but it was a sixteen years that had seen a terrible war, one which had changed the intellectual scene forever. More problematic still, Laing's book was by this time 37 years old, older than Pike himself. Book titles which feature the word 'modern', not once but twice, are particularly susceptible to premature aging, and Laing's work was no exception. Watts and Gorham, in other words, were still operating in a Victorian/Edwardian mindset in the twenties, which was a very different time altogether. And as they grew older, Watts had fewer opportunities to exercise his appeal over wealthy acquaintances. This made the infusion of new blood by people like Pike even more important. Pike, like Harold Laski, was the first generation of RPA office holders and activists not to have been brought in by the influence of Charles Watts and his friends.

While many soldiers read and appreciated rationalist material, relatively few of them joined the RPA after the war, as Pike had done. Pike remained a rationalist for the rest of his life, but his career as secretary of the RPA was brief, lasting from 1928 until 1931. Ironically, it was not Charles Watts whom Pike had problems with, Rather, it was Fred Watts, Charles's son and a man Pike's own age. Until 1930 Charles Watts had been the ruling titan of the combined operations of the RPA and Watts & Co. He was Managing Director of Watts & Co and Chairman of its Board of Directors. He was also Vice-Chairman of the RPA's Board of Directors and editor of the *Literary Guide* and *Rationalist Annual*. So when the ailing Watts decided to retire in 1930, he was anxious to retain some indirect influence on what had been his life's work. With this in mind, he decided to retain his editorships but retire from his official positions in Watts & Co. So long as his son would take over from him and the right people were there to support him, all would be well. Accordingly he wrote to the Watts & Co board on March 23 1930. 'I have no desire to dictate to my fellow Directors' Watts wrote, knowing he was doing just that, 'but I shall be highly gratified if they decide to elect my son as my successor.' (58)

That Fred Watts (1896-1953) should have succeeded his father would have surprised nobody at all. And neither was it a bad move. Following in his father's footsteps, Fred began work with Watts & Co in 1912 aged sixteen (or seventeen, depending on the account you read). Over the next sixteen years, broken only by his war service, Fred gradually assumed more and more real decision-making power as his father ailed and gradually relinquished his last positions of responsibility. Fred Watts also ran his own small publishing concern, by the name of Chaterson. Fred's full name was Frederick Charles Chater Watts, and as he was Charles's son, thus the name. Chaterson specialised in easy reading works about the English counties, but also published the occasional humanist work. Fred inherited from his father the ability to inspire loyalty in those working around him, although Charles Watts' hard edge was closer to the surface in his son. When Constance Dowman retired from her forty-three year career with the RPA in 1975, it was Fred Watts she expressed her debt to. 'Without Fred Watts's confidence in my ability I would never have attempted to tackle the Secretaryship when I was offered the post in 1941, and he was always ready to help and advise me.' (59) And like his father, Fred Watts' instinct about people was usually correct; certainly his confidence in Dowman was well placed. The only exception to this, or at least the only exception that has attracted the attention of the historian, is Fred Watts's inability to work with the newly-appointed secretary, E Royston Pike. As his close friend Charles Bradlaugh Bonner put it after Fred's death

> Fred was brought up in the school of long hours for modest pay, and he expected his staff to give as good, or nearly, as he gave himself. Everyone had to be up to his job, and managing-director Fred could be a real tartar. (60)

As we noted above, Pike succeeded Charles Gorham in this position in 1928, and was a good find for the Association. But where Charles Watts and Charles Gorham had understood each other's position exactly, Pike tended to confuse his position as secretary with that of general secretary. It was with this confusion in mind that the post of RPA Managing Director was created in 1930 and given to

Fred Watts. Not even this cleared things up sufficiently, and the conflict between the two younger men soon became intolerable and in 1931, having ignored hints that he should resign, Pike was sacked. (61) Interestingly enough, Pike returned to an active role in the RPA (although not an employed one) after the Second World War. As well as a large number of articles for the *Literary Guide* and its successor, Watts & Co published several of Pike's titles after the war.

Having secured Fred's position as his successor, Charles Watts also took steps to ensure his approach to rationalism was continued. F J Gould had long since gone his own way, concentrating on his main interest of moral education, although Watts & Co still published his books. Watts' chosen guardian of his style of rationalism within the RPA fell on Adam Gowans Whyte (1875-1950). Whyte was one of the last original Directors from 1899 still living, and Watts felt the need for a steadying influence, especially when the time would come when he would have to relinquish the *Guide* to his son. Watts was almost a second father to Whyte, whose own father had died when he was twelve years old. One of Whyte's books, published in 1938, when he was 63, was dedicated to Charles Watts 'with filial affection'. Whyte was the seventh of nine children; his father was a dentist in Glasgow and by all accounts a genial epicurean. Young Adam had not shown the artistic talent his father wished of him, but inherited a certain facility with words. Whyte came south to London in 1898 where he earned a living as a journalist. He had already contributed to the *Literary Guide* while still a rookie journalist at the *Glasgow Weekly Citizen* and quickly sought out the rationalists on his arrival in the capital. From 1901 until his retirement Whyte was editor of the *Electrical Industries* journal. For thirty years Whyte had been a reliable lieutenant to Watts, Gorham, Hooper and the others who were senior to him. Whyte's staunch loyalty to Watts made his relationship with McCabe a difficult one, but in this Whyte was not alone. As the first echelon of Watts's friends began to retire or die, Whyte's turn arrived. For the last twenty years of his life, Whyte was at the heart of the RPA, performing the role of guardian of Charles Watts' memory and staunch ally to his son Fred.

At the beginning of 1930, Watts gave Whyte a generous allocation of space at the beginning of each issue of the *Literary Guide* called 'The Open Window', which he wrote under the pseudonym 'Protonius'. In his guise as Protonius and with the many articles under his own name, Whyte became the bulwark of the *Guide* for the next twenty years. Watts knew that he could trust Whyte to retain the standards of earnestness and courtesy in rationalist journalism that both men valued so much. Nine years later, Watts & Co appointed Whyte as 'Literary Advisor' with a salary of £4000 a year. He retained a significant role in selection of titles for the Thinker's Library and other Watts titles until his death.

What Charles Watts was trying to do was to solidify the outlook and attitude of the RPA of before the First World War. For the older leaders of the RPA, the standard was always to return to pre-1914 conditions. It is not unreasonable that they should do this – the whole country was doing the same thing. Neither is it surprising, although the coincidence is interesting, that the RPA should go through its period of change around the middle of 1931. A J P Taylor noted that Britain left the twenties in September 1931; well, so did the RPA. For the country, the change was manifested in the growing financial and political crisis as

MacDonald's Labour Government collapsed under the pressure of the spiralling Depression. A new National Coalition Government was created to deal with the crisis. For the RPA, the problem was basically the same. It was becoming evermore manifest that the old ways were no longer sufficient. The battle for the heart of the RPA was set to begin.

Chapter 4

Change and War

'Since religion is not true, what then? That is the question to which thinking people now are expecting an answer.'
Archibald Robertson, 1931

The world in the 1930s seemed to many people to have become a darker and more brutal place where the choices were fewer and more stark. The apparent recovery of the twenties was broken by the collapse of democracy in successive European nations and the Wall Street Crash in 1929. For many people, particularly in the West, the choice came down to one between fascism and communism. The new situation made it clear that the yearning to return to the conditions of 1914 was no longer credible. This presented rationalists with a new and particularly difficult set of choices to make. For the first time the battle was not simply between forces that valued the processes of reason and progress and those that did not. There were now people coming up who valued reason, or claimed to, just as much as rationalists, and who saw what rationalists were doing as outmoded.

The struggle began, as most do, from an unexpected quarter and proceeded in an unexpected direction. One of the younger members of the RPA, J B Coates, wrote a letter to the *Literary Guide* advocating change. The RPA had done a splendid job, Coates acknowledged, in combating superstition, religious obscurantism and intolerance and had thus made a commendable contribution to contemporary England. Few readers would have been unaware that a large 'but' lay in waiting and it was not long in coming. But, Coates wrote, has the time not come 'when the RPA and kindred societies, without abandoning their fundamental scepticism, should throw in their lot more definitely with the cause of Scientific Humanism?' Coates didn't make it clear what he meant by 'Scientific Humanism' beyond mentioning the authors he associated with the term: H G Wells, Julian Huxley and, later on, Bertrand Russell.

> The great work of the modern period, these eminent thinkers argue, is the framing of constructive moral and social policies. The special work of the modern Rationalist should be, therefore, to direct the modern world conscience so as to bring about that scientific world reconstruction which is the goal of the hopes of the scientific humanist.

Coates saw the work of the RPA as 'out of harmony with the modern spirit'.

> It must abandon its perhaps excessive pre-occupation with Christian evidences and Christian theology; it must abandon also a certain tendency which I think it shows to a type of individualism which it has inherited from nineteenth-century liberalism, and accept the proposition, which is axiomatic to the modern humanist, that the higher moral possibilities of mankind cannot be realised without the scientific control of the political and economic mechanism of the world. (1)

This was a very serious charge against the RPA, as it had made its reputation before the Great War precisely for being in harmony with the modern spirit. The influence of H G Wells, in particular, is evident in Coates's article. Wells was indeed one of the principal sources of inspiration for progressively minded people born between the 1890s and 1914. Coates was of that generation, having served on the Western Front during the Great War. He spent the last year of the war as a prisoner in Germany, and on his return to England became a schoolteacher. Until the end of the twenties, Coates' interests had been mainly literary, but the deteriorating world situation turned his attention to broader issues and led him inevitably to H G Wells.

From the large body of Wells's writings we could look to for evidence of this influence, we need only go back to 1928, and the short manifesto-like call to arms Wells wrote called *The Open Conspiracy: Blueprints for a World Revolution*. 'The old faiths have become unconvincing, unsubstantial and insincere, and though there are clear intimations of a new faith in the world, it still awaits embodiment in formulas and organisations that will bring it into effective reaction upon human affairs as a whole.' (2) Wells called for an 'open conspiracy' – a popular front led by motivated, socially concerned young men and women to sweep aside the self-serving obscurantism of the vested interests and reactionaries, and work together to build a new world of rational, compassionate, humanistic planning and building.

> It is impossible for any clear-headed person to suppose that the ever more destructive stupidities of war can be eliminated from human affairs until some common political control dominates the earth, and unless certain pressures due to the growth of population, due to the enlarging scope of human operations or due to conflicting standards and traditions of life, are disposed of. (3)

Wells wrote as an evangelist of a new order of planning and world government and he saw the work of creating this new order as fundamentally a religious quest. 'The first sentence in the modern creed must be, not "I believe" but "I give myself."' (4) The open conspiracy was to be an 'intellect rebirth'. The same year as Coates wrote his article for the *Literary Guide*, Wells had returned to the open conspiracy theme in another short work intended as a manifesto for action, called *What are we to do with our lives?* Coates' letter to the *Guide* is strongly suggestive of Wells's influence.

It is also likely that Coates had read, or was familiar with, Julian Huxley's work *What Dare I Think?* published by Chatto & Windus earlier in 1931. Huxley explained in his preface that he had wanted to call the book 'Essays in Scientific

Humanism' but had found an American work had already used that title. As well as expounding what he saw as scientific humanism, Huxley was directly critical of the rationalism hitherto championed by the RPA.

It is not surprising, then, that Coates's article touched a nerve. The following issue of the *Literary Guide* featured a large number of responses, and the controversy went on in various forms for several months. F J Gould contributed with characteristic whimsicality, but was basically backing change. He warmly endorsed the recent emergence of the notion of humanism in the United States, mainly by Unitarians and people who would now be called religious humanists. This was the movement which published the first *Humanist Manifesto* two years later, in 1933. It was essentially a theistic movement. More relevant comment came from Archibald Robertson (1886-1961), another of the newcomers. The son of the Bishop of Exeter, Robertson had been introduced to the RPA by the pioneering socialist and atheist, Belfort Bax (1854-1926). (5) A member since 1920, Robertson had served on the Board of Directors since 1925. While his father was alive and in order to spare him the embarrassment of a heretical son, Robertson wrote, and even took his seat on the RPA board, under the pseudonym 'Robert Arch'. Robertson supported Coates:

> I agree with him that the RPA is living too much on its past reputation, and that it is time we heard a little less about the excellent work done by the cheap reprints of a generation ago – even a little less, dare I say it? about Darwin and Bradlaugh – and a little more about the issues that interest 1931…Today no thinking person worries about the bearing of Darwinism on religion. It is all settled. (6)

Robertson was too young to have taken part in the heroic struggles of the RPA during the years of Cheap Reprints. And yet his path to rationalism had more in common with his seniors than with those younger than him. Reading a work on the French Revolution had shattered his youthful piety. 'You cannot suddenly discover that those whom you thought to be the enemies of God and man are human beings, and rather fine fellows at that, without a considerable shock to your fundamental beliefs.' (7) A chance overhearing of a schoolfellow mocking Shelley's *Queen Mab* led Robertson to his next appointment with heresy. From Shelley, he read Draper's *Conflict between Religion and Science*. By the time he went up to Oxford (where he took a First in 'Greats') Robertson was a secret unbeliever and socialist. In 1938 his political evolution came to an end when he joined the Communist Party.

Robertson was 45 years old in 1931 when he wrote his plea for a new direction for the RPA. His criticism goes to the heart of the divide that has bedevilled the freethought movement since its inception and which we have followed in this history. What are the proper priorities of the non-believer? Should the emphasis be upon the criticism of religion, so that people may make this important choice intelligently, or should the emphasis be on the construction of a credible alternative system of belief to religion? To return to the categories of Colin Campbell, who is to determine the agenda of the RPA – the abolitionists, or the substitutionists? Robertson articulated the problem:

> Since religion is not true, what then? That is the question to which thinking people now are expecting an answer. It is this which makes the position of a body like the RPA so difficult. For we are not ready with an answer. (8)

This was too much for J M Robertson (no relation to Archibald), since the departure of Joseph McCabe the last of the RPA's front-line titans. The irascible Robertson liked nothing about Coates's idea, the support he had received, or scientific humanism in general, and he was not reticent in expressing his dislike.

> If you believe that you can get a membership of hundreds of thousands of freethinkers or others by talking New or Scientific Humanism, why, in the name of practical reason (which surely you profess to respect), do you not establish such a society on your own account? (9)

In all probability, Robertson knew the answer. In April 1929 a journal had been launched amid much fanfare called *The Realist, A Journal of Scientific Humanism*. The editorial board included Wells, Julian and Aldous Huxley, Rebecca West, Arnold Bennett and Harold Laski. Originally it was thought that the lavish magazine was to be funded by Lord Melchett (Alfred Moritz Mond), then Chairman of ICI. It soon became apparent that this was not the case and *The Realist* ceased publication at the beginning of 1930 after ten issues.

Robertson had little difficulty showing that behind the rhetoric about the RPA 'doing something constructive' lay a potential minefield of divisive issues. Birth control, proportional representation, free trade, 'socialism' – any one of these issues could result in similar numbers leaving the RPA as would be attracted to it. But the heart of Robertson's objection was the notion that criticism of religion is a 'mere negation.'

> The answer is that any such process is one of intellectual construction, inasmuch as the "negative" proposition can be made good only by the establishment of a series of true propositions. The cliché "mere negation" is one of the grossest falsisms in common dialectic currency. Mere negation would consist in saying merely "No," or "I do not believe what is asserted." That would convince nobody, and would discredit no creed whatever. It is only by a rational construction that any belief is discredited. (10)

Here, again, we come to the heart of the fissure which divided, and still divides the freethought movement, in Britain and around the world. Robertson's declaration would have to be the epitome of the abolitionist position: there is no point in 'offering something new' until people are clear in their minds why the old is unsatisfactory. As against this, the substitutionists, in this case the 'scientific humanists', were equally convinced that nothing is to be gained by continual negative criticism. What people want is something else to function as a fulcrum for their belief system, and the scientific humanists thought that this was what they were doing.

Things came to a head in 1931 when nine reformers, principally C E M Joad (1891-1953), Archibald Robertson, J B Coates and J A Hobson (1858-1940) put themselves up for election to the Board of Directors on a platform of change. The absence of minutes for this time and the coyness of the Annual Reports make it infuriatingly difficult to build up a comprehensive picture of this episode. Either way, the plotters were comprehensively defeated and early the following year came together to form what they called a Federation of Progressive Societies and Individuals. This Federation was intended to become what they had sought to transform the RPA into, an umbrella grouping for progressive organisations. Archibald Robertson told Charles Watts that the Federation's aims were to 'advocate a platform far in advance of anything the RPA could approve, and with which it would probably not wish any of its Directors to identify themselves.' (11)

In March the following year, Archibald Robertson, the only RPA Director participating in the plot, resigned from his post on the Board as well, in order to devote his energies to the Federation. Watts urged Robertson to come and talk it over but the younger man decided their differences were unbridgeable. Watts had already said to him that he would consider it a breach of trust with past benefactors were the RPA to enlarge its objects so as to concern itself with social and political issues outside the explicit aims of the Association. This argument was to get a generous airing over the next several decades. Responding to Robertson's letter of resignation, Watts wrote:

> You seemingly do not disagree with what the RPA does. Your complaint, so far as I can judge, is that it does not do more. I suggest that other organisations can grapple with the urgent social and political problems which now face the world. Perhaps the Union of Societies of which you speak may supply what is wanted. (12)

Robertson's reply got to the crux of the issue.

> I think that the present activities of the RPA, though all very well in their way, are ineffectual, because they don't appeal to the present generation of people under 40. This is not my fancy. People I have tried to influence, to whom I have sent publications, or whom I have brought to the annual dinner as guests, all tell me the same tale. The younger generation are not interested in the criticism of religion except so far as it bears on social questions. They are interested in peace, economics, and sex questions. And the RPA doesn't help them. Unless we enlist and enthuse the young, we shall die of inanition, and not any amount of legacies will save us. (13)

Watts' reply showed the iron in his backbone.

> All right: I must bow to your decision, respectfully and regrettably. You evidently - and from your point of view perhaps rightly - elect to work for the converted, unfortunately an insignificant minority. I shall continue to work for the unconverted, still numbered by the millions. It was for this latter purpose that the RPA was founded, and its primary object is likely to appeal to the majority of Freethinkers for many generations. (14)

This exchange of letters is a fascinating illustration of the conflicts and stresses that have existed within the RPA, and the wider freethought community generally, throughout its existence.

The reformers went off and founded the Federation of Progressive Societies and Individuals (FPSI). The FPSI was intended to act as an umbrella grouping, a popular front for all left-leaning tendencies. Its platform can be taken as representing fairly closely what its founders had in mind when they spoke of scientific humanism. The new organisation released a grand manifesto outlining its vision of the future, but the clearest enunciation of the FPSI's programme can be found in Joad's autobiography, originally published in 1932. In it he set out what he called a Charter for Rationalists. The twelve points of the charter included, in this order:

- repeal of the divorce laws
- repeal of discriminatory laws against homosexuality
- diffusion of knowledge on birth control
- legalisation of abortion
- sterilisation of the feeble-minded
- abolition of censorship on plays, films and books
- abolition of all Sabbath restrictions
- disendowment and disestablishment of the Church of England
- conservation of the countryside, curbing urban development, creation of national parks
- prohibition of exhibitions of performing animals
- abolition of licensing restrictions
- unilateral and complete disarmament. (15)

The debt to H G Wells is enormous. The Federation's programme was essentially Wells's open conspiracy. Aware of the reputation of some of the founders of the Federation, critics joked that FPSI actually stood for the 'Federation for the Promotion of Sexual Intercourse'. (16) After little more than two years, it was clear to most founders of the FPSI that its aim to become an umbrella group for the left had not been realised. It later became the Progressive League and lingered on until the end of the century. Most of the Conway Hall plotters drifted back to the RPA and continued where they had left off. Archibald Robertson, in particular, remained active in the RPA for the rest of his life. He wrote a long account of his intellectual development for the *Guide* in 1944 and made no mention of the Great Conway Hall Plot.

Having seen the plotters off, the RPA made some effort to address their concerns. The RPA had always sat uncomfortably between being a mass membership organisation and a business. To some extent the problem was eased after it secured 5 and 6 Johnson's Court soon after the war, and had space to offer recreational, library and meeting facilities to members. But clearly more was felt to be needed. For one thing, the facilities could only be of benefit to those members living in London. Accordingly, it set up a Rationalist Council with the aims taken from the 1899 definition of rationalism:

- to stimulate freedom of thought and inquiry in regard to ethics, theology, and kindred subjects

- to defend freedom of speech, and to agitate against restrictions of all kinds imposed upon rational liberty by religious creeds and dogmas. (17)

The Rationalist Council had a shorter life than the FPSI and little more was heard of it. This was destined to be a problem that would not go away. The need for the RPA to provide some sort of social outlet for its members was a real one, and had not adequately been addressed. It had not been an issue for the generation of 1899, who had no intention to replace or compete with the National Secular Society or the various ethical societies then thriving. Outside of London, the Local Secretaries could take care of meetings as they saw fit. Consequently, some towns had flourishing rationalist networks while in others nothing ever got off the ground. The same was true overseas. In India, Australia and New Zealand, for example, these people formed the core of a series of rationalist societies after the Great War. But the simple expedient of forming a rationalist society in Britain was strangely problematic. The issue remained unresolved, not to be addressed again until after the Second World War.

The failure of the Great Conway Hall Plot had other consequences for the RPA. Not the least of them was that it spelt the end of Harold Laski's tenure as president of the RPA. Laski had been a great source of hope for the RPA, and an equally large source of disappointment. Laski taught political science at the London School of Economics and had also been active in the Fabians as a reformist intellectual. Laski was an even better choice for president than Wallas, not so much because he was different, as because he was much the same, only a lot younger. Many members must have been heartened by his article in the 1931 *Rationalist Annual* entitled 'On the Need for a Militant Rationalism'. Laski paid ritual obeisance to the nineteenth century titans, extolled the contribution rationalism had made over the years to the cause of advancing freedom, and lamented the number of rationalists outside the movement. 'They have profited from the effort of the dead pioneers without making any effort at a return.' (18) These people constituted the movement's greatest weakness, and Laski advocated greater effort in attracting these people into the movement, and a more aggressive propaganda generally. Joseph McCabe, now estranged from the RPA, had been arguing in this way for years.

Laski, however, was on the turn. As economic depression and events in Europe worsened, Laski became more impatient with what he saw as rationalist quietude to the darkening horizon. In the face of these grave challenges, no rationalist 'has the right to turn aside from the battle and cultivate his own garden.' (19) He described the new Hitler regime's mass dismissal of ideologically unsound academics as the most wholesale repudiation of toleration since the Revocation of the Edict of Nantes. In the space of 1933 and 1934, Laski's drift to the left gathered pace. In his contribution to the *Rationalist Annual* of 1935 he was more critical of the basis of traditional rationalist criticism.

> We need to exhibit Luther not merely as the enemy of Roman malpractice, but also as the enemy of peasant and industrial worker (sic); we need to reveal Calvin not only as the social autocrat of Geneva, but also as the author of doctrines essential to the needs of the rising business class of the sixteenth century, if the true significance of their work is to be understood. (20)

Pretty soon Laski found a more congenial ally in Victor Gollancz (1893-1967) and the Left Book Club, which rocketed into prominence in the second half of the thirties, quite eclipsing the growth of the RPA which had so astonished rationalists before the Great War. The Left Book Club was formed by Victor Gollancz in 1936 and grew rapidly, reaching, it is said, 60,000 members. It operated on lines similar to the Rationalist Press Association, though this debt has not been recognised. Members were kept in touch with forthcoming Book Club publications through its journal, the *Left Book Club News*. Alongside Gollancz and John Strachey, Laski became one of the leading influences in the Left Book Club, helping choose and commission its publications. Typical of Left Book Club publications was *Forward from Liberalism* by Stephen Spender (1909-1995), which was published in 1937. Spender combined relevant and perceptive observations of the follies and failures of capitalism with extraordinarily credulous assertions that all this would be solved under socialism. In his biography of A J Ayer, Ben Rogers noted that Spender was originally to have collaborated with Ayer on this book but the project did not proceed. (21) One cannot help feeling it would have been a far stronger book had the collaboration taken place. At the time, however, Spender's combination of analysis and dreaming found a ready market. A lot of people who had supported the general aims of the Great Conway Hall Plot must have felt vindicated, because here at last was an organisation devoted to scientific humanism. Or, more accurately, what they thought was scientific humanism.

Equally, of course, many people who had been just as zealous in the cause of scientific humanism, notably H G Wells, were strongly critical of the drift to Marxism in the thirties. In a radio broadcast given in July 1931 and later published by Watts & Co in *After Democracy*, Wells was at his most aggressive.

> Communism is the most narrow-minded cult that exists. Its devotees are convinced that the little bunch of Communist writers, beginning with Marx and Engels, provided the only intellectual activity of any importance in the past eighty years. They will not learn from, they will not listen to, anyone outside the party. (22)

Laski stopped writing for the *Rationalist Annual* in 1936, the year the Left Book Club began. He only ever wrote for the *Annual* once again when he criticised a recent work by a Catholic apologist in the 1944 Annual. There is no reason to suppose there was any animosity between Laski and the RPA. It was simply that Laski thought the RPA was out of touch with contemporary trends. Many in the RPA itself must have wondered about this as well.

Events were to vindicate the RPA. Laski's drift into an uncritical support for all things Soviet could hardly be more blatant than in a short work published by the Left Book Club called *Faith, Reason and Civilisation*. Here Laski declared that 'the spectacle of Russian heroism in the two years of the struggle against Hitlerism has convinced the common man, all over the world, that there was a magic in the Revolution of 1917 somehow adaptable to his own concerns.' (23) This was never true, and was soon to become significantly less true than when Laski had written it. While admiration of the Soviet war effort was genuine and deserved, few people then leapt to the conclusion that this implied some inherent superiority of the Soviet system. Laski's rationalism suffered in due proportion as his uncritical Sovietism took hold. Underpinning his uncritical Sovietism was an equally uncritical historicism. Laski endorsed the line adopted in many Left Book Club publications that communism was the logical and dialectical successor to Christianity.

> The power of any supernatural religion to build that [ie, civilised] tradition has gone; the deposit of scientific enquiry since Descartes has been fatal to its authority. It is therefore difficult to see upon what basis the civilised tradition can be rebuilt save that upon which the idea of the Russian Revolution is founded. It corresponds, its supernatural basis apart, pretty exactly to the mental climate in which Christianity became the official religion of the West. (24)

This is historicism run riot, and has done the rationalist movement a lot of damage. Many of the postwar critics had Left Book Club tracts such as this in mind when they criticised rationalism and scientism. But the RPA, which largely avoided most of these excesses, was caught up in the fallout. Laski's departure was thus both a lost opportunity and a relief. It was a lost opportunity because here was a dynamic, intelligent and capable young man who could have led the RPA to a leading role in a broad coalition of progressive forces. But given that Laski became increasingly mesmerised by communism and his conception of what constituted progressive forces became proportionately narrower, it was for the best that Laski departed.

Against the facile optimism of Spender or the grandiloquent triumphalism of Laski, the rationalist had little that could compete. John Rowland put the rationalist case in January 1939:

> No Rationalist as such can possibly believe that any particular political creed has achieved complete finality and uttered the last word on any question. That human ideals are fluid things, changing to meet the varying needs of different ages, must be admitted by all open-minded men and women; and even the most fervent supporter of any of the great political parties must perceive, if his mind has not become hermetically sealed, that the "party line" may on occasion be in error. (25)

Being seen to be right many decades on is, of course, little compensation for the problems the RPA was facing at the time. If the RPA was not going to take its part as a junior player in a communist-led popular front, what role was it to play? The failure of the Great Conway Hall Plot had left the RPA in an intellectual quandary. The word 'crisis' is badly over used by historians. This was not a crisis for the RPA or for rationalism generally. But it was an important phase in the RPA's history, and the decisions it made and the conditions it found itself making decisions in, influenced its future in significant ways. The first problem was to replace Laski. Here the RPA Board of Directors decided to go for a 'safety first' style of president, and so chose Harry Snell (1865-1944). Like Graham Wallas, Snell was 68 when he assumed the position of president in 1933. Snell had forty years of service to the broader freethought movement behind him in 1933 and worked his way up from modest circumstances to serve as a Labour MP.

But even this apparently straightforward decision became problematic. Snell was far too busy with the Labour Party to devote any time to the RPA, even the modest duties required of the president. About the time he became president of the RPA, Snell also became chairman of the London County Council. Later he became Baron Snell of Plumstead and served as Deputy-Leader of the Labour Party in the House of Lords. After little more than three years as president, Snell began to pressure the RPA to find a successor. Snell's obvious inability to find the time to perform his duties aroused dissatisfaction within the RPA. From 1936, the Board was actively looking for a replacement. Several people were mentioned as possible successors: J B S Haldane, Lord Horder, Sir Arthur Keith, but for one reason or another (too busy or too old usually) none of them accepted the position. It wasn't until 1940 that a replacement could be found. One of the Directors of the RPA, Surgeon Rear Admiral Charles M Beadnell (1872-1947) agreed to take the position. As if to confirm a pattern, Beadnell was 68 when he took up the position.

If the Directors thought they could forget about the presidency for a while, they were to be disappointed. Within months of accepting the position Beadnell got himself into trouble with a short pamphlet he wrote called *Fallacies of Conscientious Objection*. This led to complaints from some of the pacifist wing of the movement and queries to Beadnell from the Board. Beadnell, in turn, felt he had been misinterpreted by the Board and wrote to resign from the Board and as President, but added that he would be willing to remain as President if the Board saw fit. It fell to Fred Watts to sort out this spat. Eventually he persuaded Beadnell to remain a Director and President. (26)

The more difficult problem the RPA faced was to find the next cadre of rationalist opinion leaders. The early thirties saw the demise of many of the original generation of leaders. Edward Clodd died in 1930, Charles Hooper died in 1932, Charles Gorham and J M Robertson in 1933, Thomas Whittaker and Hypatia Bradlaugh Bonner in 1935. And to Charles Watts's dismay, his lifelong friend F J Gould died in 1938, aged 83. Watts dutifully recalled his deceased comrades on anniversaries of their deaths with small 'In Memoriam' notices in the *Guide*. But for his lifelong friend Gould, he recounted the last time they saw each other.

> We were shocked by his appearance, but said nothing. After tea he moved to his favourite easy chair, and there he sat, with my hand enclosed in his, for more than half an hour, during which he pointed to his lean body and his shrunken fingers, he recalled incidents in our long and happy friendship, always in gratitude and never breathing an ill word concerning anybody. Talk being ended, he rose from his chair in preparation for a majestic goodbye, and, escorted on one side by my wife and on the other by myself, he slowly passed to his waiting car, wrapped his tired body in a comfortable rug, waved his hand, and glided towards the everlasting silence. He survived only a brief period. (27)

Watts himself had many health scares in the last years of his life, and seemed close to death on several occasions, but in fact lived on until 1946, retaining a significant presence in the running of the organisation until about 1943.

Unlike the last significant changing of the guard, between 1903 and 1905, it was less clear who the next generation of leaders were. There was, and little could disguise it, an intellectual brittleness in the RPA. The more prominent people writing for the *Literary Guide* were not personalities of the same type as their predecessors. John Rowland was a writer of detective fiction and William Kent wrote guides to London. Rowland was employed by the RPA and Kent was a frequent contributor to the *Guide* in the thirties and forties. Both wrote reasonable stuff, but neither had the ability to inspire. And those who were undoubtedly inspirational, like Bertrand Russell, H G Wells and Julian Huxley, were able to conduct a publishing career independent of the RPA. Some of the new faces working with the RPA, such as Hyman Levy, were heavily involved in other ventures as well. Levy wrote for the Left Book Club as well as for the RPA. Others, such as Ernest Thurtle (1884-1954) divided their time between the RPA and the Labour Party. Thurtle, the MP for Shoreditch, succeeded Royston Pike as RPA secretary in 1932 and held the position until 1941, when he took over the chairmanship of the RPA from J P Gilmour, who had died. But within a few months Thurtle resigned his position to rejoin the army. Thurtle had served during the First World War, having been wounded at Cambrai. Thurtle's move was in effect a political promotion, as he now became Parliamentary Secretary to the Ministry of Information. Thurtle's resignation added significantly to the load borne by Fred Watts during the war years.

It was in the context of this felt need that the RPA initiated a limited rapprochement with Joseph McCabe. We followed the dismal story of his progressive estrangement from the RPA in the previous chapter. Reading McCabe's autobiography, written in 1947, one could be forgiven for thinking that he had been cast into the wilderness without a care, but this was not the case. Had McCabe become *persona non grata* as he made out, it is unlikely that within two years of the Extraordinary Meeting, *Twelve Years in a Monastery* would have appeared as the ninth title in the Thinker's Library and two years later again a rewritten *The Existence of God* as Number 34. And then, in 1934, a completely new McCabe title, *The Riddle of the Universe Today*, was published.

So, despite McCabe's difficult nature, the RPA decided to initiate a thaw in relations. The directors can't have been under any illusions about how uncomfortable this decision might prove. After all, only in 1931, McCabe had described the RPA as 'flabby, prosperous and "respectable".' (28) But the Great Conway Hall Plot had shown them that, for all his faults, McCabe was one of them. He was one of the last of the 1899 veterans left, and certainly the most capable of them. If anyone could produce works consonant with the rationalism they had in mind, it was McCabe. The approach was coordinated by Admiral Beadnell, who reported back to the Board in February 1935 that McCabe was prepared to work with the RPA again. The Board then wrote to Charles Watts to see whether he was willing to work alongside McCabe again. Watts indicated he was willing, although he was far from ecstatic about the prospect. (29)

The original idea was that McCabe would again contribute to the *Literary Guide*, although this never in fact happened. I suspect this is because McCabe refused to submit to the conditions imposed upon him as part of the deal. The old wounds were still raw, on both sides. However, things almost returned to normal on the book and pamphlet front, with McCabe titles again flowing from Watts & Co's machines. Three in 1935, and then one in 1937 and 1938, two in 1939, three in 1940, one in 1941, two in 1942 and 1943 and one in 1944, 1946, 1948 and 1951. But there was still the occasional hiccup. In 1937 McCabe wanted the RPA to publish a tract on the vice trials of Catholic priests then taking place in Germany, but the RPA rejected the proposal, deciding (rightly, as it turned out) that there was insufficient evidence upon which to base such an account. (30)

The guarded return of Joseph McCabe to the fold was not going to solve problems on its own. The serious problem of competing with the Left Book Club remained. The RPA was used to being scorned by its religious opponents, but it was an unpleasant development that it should be similarly treated by fellow atheists. The RPA's defensive reaction can easily be seen in this advertisement which the *Literary Guide* ran through part of 1938.

> The Rationalist Press Association has recently been referred to as "Victorian." If by this term is meant that men and women should be guided by reason, should seek to free themselves from beliefs which will not stand the test of reason, and should stand by the free play of human intelligence on current problems, then the RPA is quite content to be called "Victorian."
>
> If it is old-fashioned to dislike dictatorships of any kind, or to see people living under the domination of superstitions, which cannot be rationally defended and can do great harm, then we prefer to be old-fashioned. (31)

Needless to say, with campaigns such as this, the RPA was not swamped with new applicants. It was from this time that the RPA had more or less reconciled itself with having lost its appeal to the young.

That the RPA realised there was a problem is shown by their launching a major membership campaign in 1938, reminiscent of their 'Great Advance' twenty years before. But it is just as clear they were uncertain quite what the problem was. In an ambitious move, the RPA purchased five thousand copies of the abridged version of Sir James George Frazer's classic *The Golden Bough*. A book that would normally have cost 18s was sold to new members for five. It was a good idea but choosing Frazer's work would have done little to refute the impression of the RPA as a Victorian survival. *The Golden Bough* was not the book to bring in a new generation of members in the year of the Munich crisis. The campaign had little effect on membership, but it did have an effect, a negative one, on RPA funds.

The Thinker's Library

If the RPA as a membership organisation was struggling in the 1930s, the same was not true for its publishing wing. This was to be the second golden age of the

RPA. The Thinker's Library is the best-known legacy of the Rationalist Press Association. This is all the more remarkable, given that it was not a new idea when the series began in 1929. And its greater legacy is somewhat unfair to the memory of the Cheap Reprints, which was just as remarkable an achievement. The Thinker's Library ran for 22 years and produced 140 titles including works by some of the most profound thinkers of the nineteenth and twentieth century. And these thinkers were published for the general reader in an attractive, hardback format costing, to begin with at least, no more than one shilling. Throughout the life of the series, its new titles were widely and, usually, well reviewed.

Like most successful enterprises, the Thinker's Library was the product of several minds. The idea for the series came from Fred Watts, Charles' loyal son, while the title was suggested by Archibald Robertson, still at this time on the Board of Directors. Later on the sales were helped considerably by Percy R Chappell, Publicity Manager of W H Smith, who also became a Director of the RPA. It is noteworthy that as late as 1945, Chappell felt sufficiently concerned for his career in W H Smith to ask for all RPA printed material to refer to him as Dudley Grant. The Board agreed. (32) For many people around the world, the profession of any variety of freethought is still a risky exercise.

Even as they launched the Thinker's Library, the Directors knew they were embarking on a large project. In announcing the Library to the readers of the *Guide*, Charles Watts began by recalling the success of the Cheap Reprints and saw the Thinker's Library as a successor series. Like the Forum Series, the Thinker's Library would be hardback and cost a shilling. But the new series would be even better value, however, because they were longer books. The first volume in the series, a reprint of H G Wells's 1909 work *First and Last Things*, ran to 150 pages. This was incredibly good value.

The Thinker's Library was an amalgamation of the thought behind the Cheap Reprints and the Forum Series. A few Cheap Reprint titles were repeated in the Thinker's Library. Since the success of the Cheap Reprints several other publishing houses had begun similar types of series. Dent's Everyman's Library and Williams & Norgate's Home University Library were established in the field when the RPA launched the Thinker's Library at the beginning of 1929. And Ernest Benn had begun a series of sixpenny pamphlets on topical issues a couple of years before.

So, the RPA Directors clearly felt it was time to re-enter the field. The first point, as already observed, is that several of the classic titles from the Cheap Reprints were reissued as Thinker's Library titles. Twelve Thinker's Library titles had in a former life been a Cheap Reprint, and of those twelve, five were reprinted in 1929, the first year of the Thinker's Library. They were, in order: Herbert Spencer, *Education*; Ernst Haeckel, *The Riddle of the Universe*; J S Mill, *On Liberty*; Charles Darwin, *Origin of Species*; and Joseph McCabe, *Twelve Years in a Monastery*. Of the three other titles from the first year of the Thinker's Library, two were by H G Wells; *First and Last Things* and *A Short History of the World*. The other was Charles Darwin's *Autobiography*, which appeared as a stand-alone publication for the first time in this guise. The Thinker's Library version of *First and Last Things*, written originally in 1909, was called 'The Definitive Edition' and Wells used it to expunge several theistic additions he had inserted in intervening editions. The Thinker's Library version of *A Short History of the World* sold over a quarter of a million copies and went through several impressions. Revisions and additions were added in 1934, 1938, 1941, 1945 and 1946, ensuring this book remained the best-selling title of the Thinker's Library.

The Thinker's Library has been remembered by people in the way the Cheap Reprints have not, despite the greater impact of the earlier series. The Thinker's Library is one of the first things people mention when the Rationalist Press Association is mentioned. It is its best-known legacy to the world. This has not spared it from some disparagement. A N Wilson described the series as 'a vanished list of Agnostic Golden Oldies' (33) He says this in the context of expressing his astonishment that anyone could take Herbert Spencer seriously. While the second query may well be fair – we will examine the question in Chapter Seven – his swipe at the Thinker's Library is not. If we take 'agnostic golden oldies' to refer to what others have disparaged as 'Victorian rationalists', the comment certainly isn't fair. Of the 140 Thinker's Library titles 94 of them were titles published in the twentieth century, 78 of them since the First World War. And of the 46 other titles, six were reprints of material from before the nineteenth century; ranging from Euripides to Voltaire. So, are 40 titles from the nineteenth century in a library of 140, which ran from 1929 to 1950, too many? I don't think so. There is also the point that not by any means were all the contributors to the Thinker's Library agnostics. As with the Cheap Reprints, the Thinker's Library include a wide range of thinker from the transcendentalism of Emerson and the deism of Thomas Paine, through the agnostics to atheists like Charles Bradlaugh and communists like John Cohen. Many of the titles were introductions to various branches of science (such as *Geology in the Life of Man*, *Medicine and Mankind*, *The Distressed Mind*, *Astronomy for Beginners*, *The Science of Heredity*) where cosmological questions were less of an issue.

The other significant feature of the Thinker's Library series was that it slowly moved on to publish original titles, some of them by very reputable thinkers. Every title in the series between 1929 and 1932 was a reprint of some description. They were either repeats of Cheap Reprint titles (Huxley, Grant Allen, Spencer, Darwin and so on), or from more recent authors (H G Wells, A W Benn, Anatole France, J M Robertson) or they were original compilations, such as the fifteenth and sixteenth chapters of Gibbon's *Decline and Fall of the Roman Empire* being repackaged as *Gibbon on Christianity*. By no means were all the reprinted titles in the Thinker's Library from the nineteenth century. Fifty-two reprints were from titles originally published in the twentieth century, 19 from fewer than ten years previously. Contemporary authors reprinted in the series include Llewelyn Powys, H A L Fisher, H G Wells, Lord Raglan and L Susan Stebbing.

More significant still was the trend, which accelerated after 1935 to attract entirely new titles. Arguably the first new title was Joseph McCabe's rewritten *The Existence of God*. This appeared originally in the Inquirer's Library series in 1913 and McCabe rewrote the book twenty years later to include new material relating to claims made by the physicists Sir Arthur Eddington and Sir James Jeans. The first entirely new title was from an unlikely source. Some time in 1934 Watts & Co received unsolicited a manuscript on psychology from an unknown rationalist educator, based at the time in New Zealand. The manuscript went through the usual vetting process and was published in April 1935 as *Psychology for Everyman (and Woman)*. The Directors were uncertain about how this would sell and a lower than usual print run of 6500 was agreed to. This proved to be a very conservative estimate and within weeks a new impression was rushed through. This introduction to psychology by A E Mander sold more than 40,000 copies and went through fourteen impressions over the next fourteen years. By the time Mander's second title for the Thinker's Library was published the following year (a primer on logic) sales for the series reached its first million. Sadly, very little is known about this interesting man.

Another interesting feature of the Thinker's Library is the ten titles that are not non-fiction. The earliest of these is a translation of Euripides's *Iphigenia in Aulis* and *Iphigenia in Taulis*. The translation was by longtime RPA Director Charles Bradlaugh Bonner, son of Hypatia. The only novelist to have more than one work in the series was Anatole France, whose works, *Penguin Island* and *The Revolt of the Angels* were reprinted. The other titles reprinted were minor works. Winwood Reade achieved posthumous fame for his magisterial *Martyrdom of Man* (1872) but had actually wanted to be noticed as a novelist. The Thinker's Library reprinted his last work, *The Outcast* (1874), which told of the harsh experiences many nonbelievers faced in the nineteenth century. Other titles included *Act of God*, by F Tennyson Jesse, great-niece of the poet, and *The Mystery of Anna Berger* by George Godwin, which problematised the whole issue of peasant girls and religious visions. Interestingly, the only poetry included in the Thinker's Library series was a collection of the works of James Thomson, whose best-known poem was 'The City of Dreadful Night,' one of the blackest, most pessimistic works of great poetry in the modern age.

One of the changes we would expect to find from the days of the Cheap Reprints is a broadening of the focus of criticism from Christianity. And indeed this is what we find. To take one example, *Flight From Conflict* (1944), written by Laurence Collier (son of John Collier, artist, author and husband to successive Huxley daughters), was an extended critique of the quietism of his cousin Aldous Huxley and of Gerald Heard. There is, argued Collier, an awful narcissism and snobbery in the endless quest for personal salvation when the world needs people to engage with its problems and work co-operatively toward their solution. Collier accused Huxley of feeling disgust 'when his fellow men take pleasure in anything normal: eating, drinking, play, sex, even the pleasures of the intellect.' (34) This accusation remains valid today with regard to Huxley's new age descendants.

Another prejudice-buster from the Thinker's Library is L T Hobhouse's work *The Rational Good*. Hobhouse (1864-1929) was the first permanent professor of sociology in Britain, a post created at the London School of Economics in 1907. Hobhouse espoused a mature liberalism, and was an opponent of Spencerian progressionism and of eugenics. Opponents of rationalism have accused it of every sort of excess with regard to its understanding of reason. Originally published by George Allen & Unwin in 1921, Hobhouse argued for a reason rooted in, and thus constrained by, nature. We are not moved by reason, but by what he called impulse-feeling and rationality is the method by which we articulate an impulse into a purpose. Anticipating the contemporary evolutionary psychology, Hobhouse insisted on the evolutionary importance of altruistic behaviour. Hobhouse anticipated E O Wilson when he spoke about the ideal of knowledge, which is not some idealist self-evidence of isolated truths 'but that of the consilience of a system of partial truths completing each other.' (35) Once more, rationalism can be seen as having a far greater toleration of ambiguity than it has been credited with.

Turning our attention to the sciences, we see similar evidence of a broad-mindedness that rationalism is rarely acknowledged to possess. In the interests of space, let's focus on one branch of science. The field of anthropology has been particularly vulnerable to changes in intellectual fashion and many of the anthropologists from the first half of the twentieth century would now come across as racist, whether in a triumphalist or in a condescending manner. Alfred C Haddon (1855-1940) would, as far as is possible, break this stereotype. Unlike most of his contemporaries, Haddon displayed 'unusual sensitivity, for an anthropologist of his day, to certain aspects of what today would be called the "colonial situation" of his ethnography.' (36) He was alive to the arrogance and hypocrisy of the white man's burden myth beloved by Social Darwinists and missionaries alike, and was an outspoken opponent of the use of the word 'nigger', which was then commonplace. Haddon put the discipline of anthropology on a new footing following an influential, multi-discipline trip he led to Australia and Papua New Guinea in 1898. On the strength of his fieldwork, Haddon became the first recognised anthropologist at Cambridge. Haddon was a lifelong rationalist and a member of the RPA, becoming an Honorary Associate in 1927. The Thinker's Library reprinted two of Haddon's works, *Head-Hunters: Black, White and Brown*, published originally in 1901 and *A History of Anthropology*, published originally by Watts & Co in its History of Science series in 1910.

Another anthropologist published in the Thinker's Library series was A M Hocart (1883-1939). Hocart has been described as 'the most complete anthropologist of his generation.' (36) Like Haddon, Hocart was unusually sensitive to the difficulties of intercultural analysis, and in particular to the complications surrounding his position as colonial overlord and anthropologist. From 1934 until shortly before his early death, Hocart was Professor of Sociology at the University of Cairo. Unlike previous generations of armchair anthropologists, Hocart's studies were based on lengthy periods living with the peoples he would write about. He had less need of interpreters than most of his predecessors, as he was fluent in thirteen languages. The Thinker's Library reprinted his 1927 book *Kingship*, a study of the uncertain boundary line between kings and gods in primal societies.

Kingship was seen through to press in 1941 by Lord Raglan (1885-1964), himself a respected anthropologist and author of two further Thinker's Library titles, which appeared late in the series; *The Hero*, originally published in 1936, and *The Origins of Religion*, first published in the Thinker's Library. Haddon, Hocart and Raglan were only some of a number of distinguished anthropologists associated with the RPA, most notable among them being Bronislaw Malinowski (1884-1942), A R Radcliffe-Brown (1881-1955), Raymond Firth (1901-2002) and C D Forde (1902-1973).

Among the anthropologists whose reputation has not survived the most prominent would certainly be James George Frazer (1854-1941). Like Thomas Hardy, Frazer was a rationalist and atheist but with no wish to associate himself too closely with the RPA. The RPA, however, was very keen to associate itself with Frazer. As early as 1898, Frazer's work was summarised for readers in one of the *Guide's* Supplements and as we have seen, his work was used as an inducement in a membership campaign in 1938. Correspondence exists between Frazer and Charles Watts in 1919 with Frazer affirming his general support of the RPA, but indicating his strong disapproval of the militant tone of some rationalist work. Clodd later wrote to Watts suggesting that it was J M Robertson and Joseph McCabe's work at which Frazer took offence. On this occasion Frazer said that he would not agree to any of his work being published by the RPA. (37) Watts didn't give up and in 1924 succeeded in getting Frazer to write a Foreword for a work on the mythical Jesus by the French scholar Paul Couchoud. By this time most of Watts's dealings were with Lady Frazer, who managed her husband's activities with daunting thoroughness. Through 1935 and 1936 the RPA had a protracted correspondence with Lady Frazer about an ambitious plan to reprint large tracts of Frazer's main work in an anthology to be called *Leaves from the Golden Bough*, which would go over five Thinker's Library volumes. Lady Frazer was not hostile to the project, it was just that things took an awfully long time when she was involved. This scheme was shelved, but two Frazer titles were published in the Thinker's Library. *Adonis: A Study in the History of Oriental Religion* appeared as Number 30 in the series in 1932. It consisted of the first part of Frazer's *Adonis, Attis, Osiris*, which in turn had been detached from Part IV of *The Golden Bough*. Eventually G M Trevelyan oversaw a useful little synopsis of *The Golden Bough* called *Magic and Religion*, which appeared in 1944 as Number 100 of the Thinker's Library. Trevelyan turned down his fee for the project, saying he was happy to help.

Frazer's work, and that of Lord Raglan, crossed over into another topic rationalists are not usually given credit for taking an interest in: mythology. Contrary to long-standing prejudices, many rationalist scholars have been sympathetically interested in mythology. As well as this work, the series included two studies by the Scottish myth scholar Lewis Spence, one a short introduction to the principles of mythology and the other a survey of the religious and mythological beliefs of the ancient Mexicans.

It is also interesting to record some of the titles that did not become a Thinker's Library book. Lady Frazer was not the only person the RPA found it difficult to pin down. Heinemann twice refused permission for Edmund Gosse's classic autobiography *Father and Son*; in 1935 and again two years later, while Routledge refused permission in 1935 for Lancelot Hogben's *The Nature and Origin of Living Matter* to be reprinted. James Strachey refused permission for *Eminent Victorians* while Chapman Cohen refused permission for *Religion and Sex* but allowed *The Other Side of Death* to be included. Neither title was used in the end. Hogarth Press refused permission for Freud's *The Future of an Illusion*. And Thorton Butterworth refused permission for J B Bury's *History of Freedom of Thought* in 1936. After that title moved to Oxford University Press negotiations were resumed only to founder late in 1941 when Mrs Bury-Bagnall, the trustee of Bury's works, refused any changes being made to bring the work up to date.

115

Jonathan Cape declined permission for Julian Huxley's *We Europeans* and wanted too much for Graham Wallas' *The Art of Thought* in 1935, but things obviously changed because, as we have seen, this work was reprinted in 1945. George Bernard Shaw wrote saying his hands were tied with regard to having the Preface to *Androcles and the Lion* reprinted in the series. He advised writing direct to Odhams and Phoenix Press to see what could be done.

Some titles were rejected on the ground of being too scholarly to permit the editing required to fit into the series format. They included *The Five Stages of Greek Religion* by Gilbert Murray (1866-1957), *Myth, Magic and Morals* by F C Conybeare and *The Meaning of Meaning* by Ogden and Richards. Gilbert Murray's book was later published in the series, as Number 52 in 1935, only a year after it was originally rejected. That same year Julian Huxley's *Religion Without Revelation* was turned down as unsuitable on the recommendation of Adam Gowans Whyte, but the book was later published as Number 83 of the series in 1941. Other titles rejected for the Thinker's Library with no reason being left for the historian include Henry George's *Progress and Poverty*, James Cotter Morison's *The Service of Man*, Nietzsche's *Zarathustra*, Zola's *Lourdes, Rome and Paris*, Engels' *Anti-Dühring* and *The Origin of the Family* and McCabe's *The End of the World* and *Sources of the Morality of the Gospels*. A version of Ludwig Büchner's *Force and Matter* never got to press because the revisions and editings being undertaken by the president C M Beadnell got caught up in his quarrel with the Board in 1941. A selection of Lord Acton's essays went to an advanced stage of planning through 1942 and 1943 but never reached completion.

Looking through the titles of the Thinker's Library helps dispel the many prejudices about rationalists that have slowly accumulated over the century. Where prejudice sees 'Victorian rationalism' and agnosticism we find a hundred years' worth of varied ideas and outlooks. Where prejudice sees only superficial optimism, we find optimism and deep melancholy. Where prejudice sees dull didacticism we find novels, poetry and light relief. Where prejudice sees uncritical scientism we find science valued and questioned, as we find mythology valued and questioned. Where prejudice sees stifling conformity to a brutalising reason, we find conflict, pluralism, variety and choice.

Other RPA works

Another point worth mentioning about the Thinker's Library is the trend it took from, roughly, 1937 toward publishing more works about science. It wasn't so much a clear numerical increase, rather the proportion of scientific works increased. Even when restricting a scientific book to mean only the hard sciences and excluding works by scientists about non-scientific matters, the trend is noticeable. Roughly, where one title in five could be classed a scientific work before 1937, that proportion rose to two in five after that year.

Credit for this change must be given to Hyman Levy (1889-1975), whose first book *The Universe of Science*, was published by Watts & Co in 1932, with a revised edition appearing as No. 67 of the Thinker's Library in 1938. This book can be seen as the dividing point between the publishing priorities of the 1920s and those of the 1930s. Levy was a major catch for the RPA. After succeeding A

N Whitehead as Professor of Mathematics at Imperial College in London in 1924, Levy had made a national name for himself in a series of BBC talks on 'Science in a Changing World'. These broadcasts were later published as *The Web of Thought and Action* by Watts & Co in 1934. Levy, born into a very poor family of Jewish emigrants from Russia, had risen to the top in his field on sheer merit. As was the case for many of the brilliant men of his generation, Levy was, politically speaking, on a sharp leftward trajectory. In his case, this leftward drift had been fuelled by personal experience of class snobbery and anti-semitism.

The Universe of Science was the most significant single work of popular science published by Watts & Co since *The Riddle of the Universe*, thirty-two years previously. But unlike *The Riddle*, and most of the works in the Forum series, *The Universe of Science* scarcely mentioned evolution. Levy's world was the world of mathematics and theoretical physics, and his work sought to explain the universe in the terms of those disciplines. And as we have already had cause to mention with regard to other titles, most of the crimes commonly attributed to rationalist works of popular science do not appear in this book. There is no triumphalist march of science rhetoric, no uncritical progressionism, no anthropocentric arrogance. On the contrary, Levy continually reminds his readers that science is a social venture and the findings of science are liable to change. Levy's sharpest criticism was directed at scientists such as Sir Arthur Eddington (1882-1944) and Sir James Jeans (1877-1946), two theistically-inclined scientists who were gaining much publicity at the time inserting their religious nostrums into the pattern of the universe. Levy was able to fill the gap that existed, largely unperceived in the 1920s, of providing a rationalist perspective on the post-relativity world.

At a time when most academics still looked down their noses at the populariser, Levy was very successful as a writer and speaker. The common retort of establishment scientists, said only half in jest, was that to write science which can be read painlessly involves the neglect of one's students, one's laboratory and one's golf. (38) One of Levy's childhood mentors was a man from an earlier generation still, a pioneer in this area: Joseph McCabe. After the success of *The Universe of Science*, Levy and the RPA co-operated to create two new series of titles designed to make science approachable to the general reader. The Library of Science and Culture began in 1934, and the Changing World Library in 1936. The Library of Science and Culture was intended to be the vehicle for higher-brow publications than were appropriate for the Thinker's Library. The title of the series was deliberate. The most entrenched idea of what constituted 'culture' was familiarity with classical Greek and Latin, the sort of education against which H G Wells raged. Levy hoped that the title of the series would help signal the passing 'from one concept of culture to a new outgrowth of culture, a new development of cultural understanding.' (39) Levy was important to the RPA because he represented the type of new man their earlier concentrations on biblical criticism had failed to inspire or retain. Levy divided his time between the RPA and the Left Book Club, for which he also published.

The first title in the Library of Science and Culture was the ubiquitous Julian Huxley's *Scientific Research and Social Needs* and the series ended four years and seven titles later with *Galileo and Freedom of Thought* by F Sherwood Taylor.

Huxley's title, like Levy's, had originally been a radio series. But as so often happens, the most successful title in the series was from a completely unexpected quarter. The title that sold best and made the most lasting impression on the intellectual scene was a primer on anthropology, *Man Makes Himself* by a hitherto little-known Australian scholar, V Gordon Childe (1892-1957). Childe has been described as the most influential thinker on European prehistory of the twentieth century. (40) An Honorary Associate of the RPA from 1941 until his death, Childe later on contributed a work written specifically for the Thinker's Library (No. 102, *Progress and Archaeology*) and gave the Josiah Mason Lectures for 1947-8, which Watts & Co published as *Social Evolution*.

It is also worth considering briefly the sixth title in the series, as it can help answer yet another of the abiding prejudices about rationalism. Such people, the prejudice goes, hold science up uncritically as the only model for salvation and in doing so show how little they have really moved from religious ways of thinking and demonstrate their having missed the point about science. This prejudice is one of the few that is shared by religious and postmodernist opponents of rationalism. While rationalists certainly do value science and the scientific method, it has rarely been done in the uncritical way they have been accused of. Significantly, the most uncritical scientism was usually found among the works of Marxists, not infrequently in the same breath as they were criticising rationalism for being out of date.

The sixth title in the Library of Science and Culture series was from Dr David Watson, an American scholar, and was called *Scientists are Human*. John Dewey endorsed the book in a Foreword. Scientists, Watson wrote, are as susceptible to human temptations and error as anyone else. Watson argued that the psychological constitution and social origins of scientists are important clues to understanding the claims being made. It follows that scientific truth is more complicated than merely enunciating fixed and impersonal laws. The whole process is more dynamic than that. So much scientific knowledge is still incomplete and obscure that caution is required before declaring scientific findings to be scientific laws. Many critics of rationalism have stated these things with great solemnity, totally unaware that such warnings are not new to them and not new to rationalists. 'We do not need to esteem science less,' writes Mary Midgley in 1994, what we need 'is to esteem it in the right way. Especially we need to stop isolating it artificially from the rest of our mental life.' (41) Absolutely correct, but this hardly constitutes a rebuke to rationalists; it is not even news to them.

The other series run by the RPA at the time was called the Changing World library. These were more general titles than the Science and Culture series, and with more of a focus on technology. Subjects written about include weather science, air warfare, the mass media, noise, hygiene, nutrition and mental deficiency. Both series ended in 1938, owing in all probability to the worsening situation Watts & Co found itself in. The Changing World library had four more titles in the pipeline when the plug was pulled.

Moving from the various series to the stand-alone titles, we find once again that some of the best works were produced by Joseph McCabe. In 1934, newly reconciled with the RPA, McCabe had a golden opportunity to re-enter the world of popular science he had done so much to create. 1934 was the centenary of the birth of his old mentor, Ernst Haeckel, and McCabe recalled Haeckel's best-known book in the title of his 1934 survey of the sciences, *The Riddle of the Universe Today*. As McCabe proceeds through his survey of the sciences, he reminds his readers of all the confident predictions of the demise of materialism. Contrary to all these predictions, the materialist basis of the sciences is, McCabe argued, stronger than ever. Following on the work of Hyman Levy, McCabe was critical of the mystical obfuscations of Sir James Jeans and Sir Arthur Eddington. McCabe also exposed emergent evolution to some equally telling criticism. This was a short-lived fad in evolutionary thinking much beloved by churchmen, who saw it as signalling the death of materialism. McCabe's book compares well with Levy's. Whereas Levy was far more conversant with the Theory of Relativity and its consequences than McCabe, it was McCabe who was better able to express the spirit and findings of science in terms the layman could understand.

The year after *The Riddle of the Universe Today*, McCabe demonstrated his extraordinary versatility by producing an engaging history of Moorish Spain. *The Splendour of Moorish Spain* was an appreciation of Moorish culture and achievements. As with most of McCabe's books, this was not, and did not pretend to be, original research. But it was a clearly written summary and evaluation of what all the authorities had said on the subject, along with McCabe's own pithy observations from his travels in the region.

Another work worth recalling was the centenary tribute to Charles Bradlaugh which appeared in 1933. This excellent anthology of Bradlaugh's writings was put together under the watchful eye of J P Gilmour (1860-1941), George Whale's successor as chairman of the RPA Board of Directors, and a staunch disciple of Bradlaugh. The book even secured the co-operation of Chapman Cohen (1868-1954), successor to G W Foote as president of the National Secular Society and editor of *The Freethinker*. Cohen generally had little to do with the RPA, and nursed something of a grievance against its ambivalence to Foote. At one stage, the RPA considered inviting Cohen to become an Honorary Associate, but it decided that he would probably refuse anyway. (42) At about the same time as the centenary tribute was being prepared Charles Watts was corresponding with the literary critic Gerald Bullett who was embarking on a biography of Bradlaugh, but the project never proceeded. And ironically, Watts lamented on several occasions that no biography of Foote had yet appeared. For a while it looked as if Archibald Robertson would take the project on, but this never came to anything either. One thing the Bradlaugh centenary volume *did* resolve was the old controversy between the defenders of his memory as against those of Holyoake. Aside from McCabe's short study of Holyoake in the Life Stories of Famous Men series, published in 1922, Holyoake disappeared from history, even in the RPA.

The last of the single volumes from this period that we should mention is the genial anthology called *The Wisdom of Life*. Designed as a bedside companion, this work was compiled by Charles Watts and Somerset Maugham. Maugham, an Honorary Associate of the RPA from 1935 until his death thirty years later, told Watts that any fee he was due for his work should go to the Society for the Aid of Discharged Prisoners. Watts had the ten-guinea fee written out to that organisation and sent to Maugham, so that he might send it in person to the Society. (43)

Christian reactions to the army of the godless

As we noted in the previous chapter, the Church took on a more sophisticated attitude towards rationalism after the First World War. On the one hand it was involved in serious domestic strife itself and had little time or energy to combat the enemy. But on the other hand, the general attitude was to ignore rationalism or to resort to ridicule. Only occasionally was the extent of the RPA achievement recognised for the formidable threat it was. And each time this recognition was made it was carefully recorded in the *Literary Guide*. For instance, in the expanded edition of his history of the RPA F J Gould included this lengthy passage from the *Record*, a Christian journal.

> This matter in question is increasingly serious, and the object of these brief remarks is to fasten the attention of all religious teachers, clerical or lay, on what the RPA is doing - and, from its point of view, doing with considerable success. The present writer would suggest that every competent clergyman should carefully read, each month, the *Literary Guide*, and acquaint himself with its careful and systematic propaganda. In no other way will the menace to Christianity - at any rate, on its intellectual side - be adequately countered. (44)

Gould was not normally given to sarcasm but it is hard not to detect a note of it in his reply. 'We bow courteously to this sincere opponent and we await the onslaught of the "competent" bishops. We feel the tenseness of the crisis.'

Three years later, in 1938, the New Church Missionary and Tract Society, the Swedenborgian publishing house, put out a work aimed at rationalists. The specific target was Vivian Phelips's 1906 work *The Churches and Modern Thought*. Phelips, and by extension rationalism, was accused of failure to recognise that humanity had in fact declined from a blissful golden age, failure to place the Principle of Correspondence over the theory of evolution, and failure to give credence to the argument to design. Flushed with victory, the author concluded that rationalism 'is serving the present age by helping to liberate it from the errors of a dead past, also by demonstrating its inability, of itself, to give men a satisfying doctrine of life.' (45) The failure of rationalism, in other words, was its failure to be Swedenborgianism. The book attracted a polite response by Ernest Carr, who praised the author's sincerity and made some gentle criticisms of Swedenborgianism. (46) Carr (1868-1950), the son of a Baptist minister, was a long-standing RPA member, joining the Board of Directors in 1939.

Considerably more acute criticism was made by H G Wood, whom we have already come across in a dispute with Bertrand Russell in 1928. Wood wrote a pamphlet called *Christianity and Civilisation* for a series published by Cambridge University Press in 1943. Unlike most other apologists, Wood was not satisfied with knocking down a caricature. His criticism was based on a sound reading of H G Wells, Julian Huxley and C H Waddington (1905-1975), a respected geneticist who had written a book *The Scientific Attitude*, published by Penguin in 1941. Significantly, Wood spoke of scientific humanism, rather than rationalism. While Wood's construction of scientific humanism was not a caricature, it was not an accurate one either, as he claimed that scientific humanists wished to base their ethical views solely upon science. Having outlined, quite plausibly, the problems of a materialist view of human motivation and behaviour, he then closed his case, assuming that the considerably more problematic dualism required by orthodox Christianity could claim victory by default. This is a very common ploy among Christian apologists. (47)

One of the more illustrative of the popular criticisms of the RPA comes from an Australian evangelical. David Simpson's *The March of the Godless* (1937) was suitably apocalyptic about the growing menace to Christian civilisation posed by the forces of materialism and atheism. The fault for the rise of modern atheism was rather unfairly placed at the feet of Voltaire and Thomas Paine, both of whom specifically argued against atheism. There follows a glorious conspiracy in which Karl Marx, Darwin, Huxley and Lenin all play significant roles. And then comes the RPA which is accorded the honour of being 'a formidable battalion in the army of the godless…' (48) Simpson then goes on to portray the RPA as a sort of fifth column hiding safely behind the Christian front-line troops doing the actual fighting against 'the benighted races of the heathen and savagedom.'

Interestingly, a similar approach was taken up by the Catholic journalist Thomas Neill during the Second World War. In an article in *The Catholic World*, Neil denied that materialists, atheists 'and their ilk' can be consistent supporters of democracy because of the brutalising tendencies in their philosophy. The title of Neill's article was 'Democracy's Intellectual Fifth Column.' Jacques Maritain, an influential Catholic apologist of the time, argued the same way. For Maritain, 'rationalistic Humanism' inevitably ends up in ferocious irrationalism and slavery. (49) It is difficult to credit how such arguments can be stated with a straight face. More recently, reputable Catholic historians like Eamon Duffy and John Cornwell have written of the betrayal by Pius XI and Pius XII of the Catholic political parties in Italy and Germany, which helped undermine democratic resistance to fascism in those countries. Neither pope lamented the demise of those parties because, both historians admit, neither of these popes was a democrat. Joseph McCabe was saying these things as the events were unfolding, but few people took any notice. (50)

The holding of the World Union of Freethinkers International Congress in London in September 1938 also proved a challenge to notions of pluralism and democracy for a cross-section of Catholic opinion. This international body was founded in 1880, inspired largely by Charles Bradlaugh. Staging the 1938 Congress in England was the combined responsibility of the National Secular Society, the RPA, South Place Ethical Society and the Ethical Union. Most of the Protestant churches confined themselves to pious tut-tutting, but the Catholic Church and its right-wing fringe were spurred into action. The RPA was a relatively frequent target for the *Weekly Review*, the successor journal to Chesterton's *G K's Weekly*. After the Great War, Chesterton and Belloc (usually conflated to Chesterbelloc) became increasingly shrill and extreme, losing along the way most of the influence they enjoyed before 1914. Both men's anti-semitism, Belloc's in particular, became more blatant in their last years, fuelled by their drift towards fascism. One of Belloc's allies responsible for this drift was Captain A H M Ramsey, president of the pro-fascist Right Club and an outspoken anti-semite. Ramsey was also a Conservative MP, and he drafted the Alien

Restriction Bill which was designed to prevent foreigners from participating in any organisation in Britain which opposed organised religion. Ramsey's Bill failed, as it had to, but not without attracting 170 votes in support. Through much of 1938 the *Weekly Review* conducted a campaign to have what it called the Anti-God Congress prohibited. Fascists attacked Bradlaugh's tomb, stealing the bust and daubing offensive slogans all over it. The Home Secretary replied to their demands, deploring that the Congress was going ahead on British soil, but made it clear that it was beyond his powers to stop it.

Opposition to the Congress was not limited to the Catholic-fascist fringe. Cardinal Hinsley (1865-1943), Archbishop of Westminster, started the campaign seven months before the Congress met, accusing it of coming together to 'assail the Church as the enemy of capitalism and the enemy of social reform and to defend the Bolshevist persecution in Russia.' (51) Hinsley assailed the press with misinformation about the Congress being a Soviet puppet organisation, and claimed that sinister Soviet agents were entering the country loaded up with roubles and propaganda. Sadly, the repeated denials of these claims by the organising committee of the Congress were ignored by most newspapers. After failing to secure the prohibition of the Congress, Cardinal Hinsley even felt justified in inciting unruly elements to create disturbances at the Congress. As it happened, the Congress passed without incident. Most Protestant Churches had not involved themselves in the hysterical opposition. They were content to stage a 'March of Reparation to God' on the Sunday following the opening of the Congress, convinced that God would be assuaged by their public display of repentance that others should think freely.

These controversies were all part of the recognised order of things for rationalists and humanists. The reactions of Catholic and Protestant had little real influence except among those already susceptible to that sort of appeal. While Cardinal Hinsley and others were labelling rationalism as a running dog of Bolshevism, the growing communist movement was increasingly willing to portray rationalism as a bourgeois irrelevance. From the first weeks of the Bolshevik revolution in Russia, the RPA had been ambivalent about what was going on there, and about communism generally. This is not surprising as rationalism is liberal at its core and is suspicious of both collectivism and historicism. Bertrand Russell was one of the first people to warn the general reader of the realities behind the promise the Soviet Union was widely held to offer working people. In his *The Practice and Theory of Bolshevism*, published in 1920, Russell described Lenin's Russia as the closest parallel he had ever seen to Plato's Republic. Twenty-five years later Karl Popper would spell out just how ghastly such a parallel would be in *The Open Society and Its Enemies*. Russell's book was sneered at by Wittgenstein, who had come to the conclusion that writing books designed to inform the general reader was somehow vile. But among those who take democracy seriously, *The Practice and Theory of Bolshevism* has been praised as thirty years ahead of its time. (52)

There are few rewards for being ahead of one's time, as Russell and the RPA were to find out to their cost. As the 1930s progressed the RPA was increasingly overshadowed by the Left Book Club, the attitude of which to the Soviet Union was more in keeping with progressive opinion of the time. In 1935 the Left Book

Club published an extraordinary collection of essays called *Christianity and the Social Revolution*. Its eclectic range of contributors included W H Auden, Joseph Needham, Reinhold Niebuhr and Canon Raven. Marxists from Moscow and vicars from Yorkshire joined with scholars, Christian and non-Christian, to formulate a common front against the rising threat of fascism. Where the Roman Catholic Church had made it pretty clear that it regarded communism as the greater enemy, all the contributors to this volume regarded fascism as the greater threat. Communism was portrayed as the historical successor to Christianity. And they all agreed that the ongoing arguments between rationalism and Christianity were, at best, irrelevant to the crisis of the time. Rationalism was now portrayed as bourgeois.

> Communist atheism must not be confused with the rationalist and atheist movements of Liberalism. From Voltaire to Bradlaugh there persisted a radical criticism of the supernaturalism which buttressed feudal privilege which was of assistance to the rising capitalist class. It was of limited influence because too much atheism might have weakened the authority of the capitalists over the masses, and because a chilly rationalism affords these no comfort in their sufferings. (53)

Despite the bewildering incoherence of this critique, this new attitude of the left towards rationalism was influential. The house of cards built by the Left Book Club collapsed rapidly after Nazi Germany and Soviet Russia signed their non-aggression pact on August 23 1939. The *Literary Guide* reported, not entirely disinterestedly, the subsequent discord. The Soviet invasion of Finland occasioned great discord among the Club, with opinion sharply divided as to the proper policy toward the conflict. The *Guide* felt no need to comment further when Gollancz suggested that Mill's *On Liberty* 'would be worth all the recent Choices [ie books chosen for publication by the club] put together.' (54) One of the more important contributors to *Christianity and the Social Revolution* was Joseph Needham (1900-1995), an Anglo-Catholic, Marxist (later Maoist) biochemist at Cambridge University. Needham accepted an Honorary Associateship of the RPA in 1941 and retained the title until his death in 1995.

The Second World War

Under pressure from the Left Book Club and the Penguin paperbacks, Watts & Co became more concerned about the decline in its sales. The impact of the Penguin paperbacks had been noticed within weeks of their arrival on the market in 1935. Priced originally at only sixpence, the Penguins outdid even the RPA books for value, if not in binding and quality; something few in the industry thought possible. By 1939, the decline in sales was taking on serious proportions. Watts & Co wrote to the RPA in July of that year, advising it of the 'uneconomical basis upon which production and distribution of the Thinker's Library was carried on by them.' Watts & Co asked for 'sympathetic consideration to the question of making good the loss incurred by Messrs Watts & Co on the Thinker's Library during 1939, when this had been ascertained by the Auditors at the end of the year.' (55) The auditors advised that a loss of £1000 had been sustained for the year and a programme of staff cutbacks and other economies was recommended. Early the following year the RPA responded by increasing its annual fee to Watts & Co for publisher's services from £150 to £1200. At the same time the price of the Thinker's Library rose to 1s3d.

It is worth recording that, despite these financial difficulties, the RPA remained generous to overseas rationalist organisations going through hardship. Early in 1932 it donated £50 to the struggling rationalists in New Zealand, who had recently been fined for showing films on a Sunday. Other groups were doing the same thing, but it was only the rationalists who were faced with punitive fines. Seven years later the New Zealand group received another £25 which went towards an improvement in the presentation of its journal, the *NZ Rationalist*. Without the gift made in 1932 it is unlikely that the New Zealand rationalists would have survived the Depression. As a token of their gratitude, the New Zealand representative at the RPA's centenary conference in 1999 presented a cheque for £50. Rationalists from Czechoslovakia also benefited from the RPA, but there was nobody left after the war to acknowledge that debt. In 1936, largely at the prompting of Charles Bradlaugh Bonner, two Czech activists, Captain E V Voska, president of the Volna Myslenka, the Czech freethought organisation, and Dr L Milde became Honorary Associates of the RPA. Both of them attended the Freethought Congress in London in October 1938, only shortly after Czechoslovakia had lost the Sudetenland. There was a Sudeten delegate at the conference as well. Herr Sacher was anxious to dispel malicious rumours about his territory. Voska returned to his country with a donation of £50 for the relief of destitute and homeless rationalists, displaced by the Sudeten agreement. Captain Voska survived the war and was active in freethought activity at least until the World Union of Freethinkers meeting held in Rome in September 1949, but he disappears from view after that. They both remained listed as Honorary Associates until the early 1960s.

Support for the World Union of Freethinkers was sometimes controversial among RPA Directors, as some were concerned not to be seen supporting political activities. Closer to home, the economic worries were becoming even more pressing, and just as controversial. The problem was that some of its better-selling titles were works not related to the promotion of rationalism, and in some senses were antithetical to it. This is an ongoing issue for any publishing firm whose aims are not solely commercial. For instance, one of Watts & Co's most successful titles of the time was a work of popular psychoanalysis called *How to Psycho-Analyse Yourself* by Joseph Ralph, an American doctor. While this rather crass, populist (in the worst sense of the word) title was doing well, rationalist material was selling poorly. But when general material was taken on which sold poorly, then the issue became more urgent again, as this was diverting funds from works of rationalist interest. Accordingly, in April 1939 Watts & Co's finance committee adopted a policy of limiting general works to no more than one third of the annual list and maintaining a strict check on their price so as to minimise the risk of loss on titles which sell poorly. It is clear that the tough decisions made in 1939 were not made without dissension. Two Directors, G J Finch and G R Wormald, resigned between March and July citing substantial differences in opinion over policy.

It wasn't all doom and gloom, though; there were plans for dealing with the worsening situation as well. It was proposed to meet the competition from Penguin with a new series of publications which would not cost more than sixpence. The proposed new series was to include subjects like ideologies at war, curing the criminal, anti-semitism, the history of philosophy, industrial relations, the illusion of race, the human machine, modern psychical research, the future of party politics and other subjects. This and several other ideas were in the pipeline when war was declared on Sunday September 3 1939. A reduced version of this series began in 1940 called the Thinker's Forum. These publications were little more than pamphlets, starting at 48 pages in 1940 but down to 28 at the end of the war. There were 45 titles in this series, which finally ended in 1949.

The Thinker's Forum was the only important idea to reverse Watts & Co's decline that was not put on hold by the onset of war. In fact, the Thinker's Forum never sold in great numbers and did little to swell the coffers. Within the first year of the series print-runs were reduced from 7000 to 3000. But if the Thinker's Forum was proving not to be the solution, the original problem was also in retreat. Throughout the war years sales of the *Literary Guide* and Watts & Co titles expanded and the concerns of 1938 and 1939 were forgotten. Sales of Thinker's Library titles, in particular, revived. Most titles were positively reviewed, and received attention in the provincial press and the *Times Literary Supplement*.

The mood of the RPA when war was announced was, like the rest of the country, sombre. The first war article was written by Ernest Thurtle, MP, who noted the absence of jingoist noise and flag waving.

> It is not that we are less emotional than we were in 1914, but rather that we are more understanding. We are under no illusions as to the "glory" of war; we know how uncertain are its consequences and how depressing can be its aftermath. Above all, perhaps, we realise that because of the large-scale nature of modern war, and of the development of the bombing aeroplane, we are all involved in the struggle in a much more complete manner than in previous wars, and inevitably that fact has a sobering influence. (56)

Sombre mood notwithstanding, Thurtle expressed total support for the war now that it had been declared. In the same issue Charles Watts was clear that peace could only come 'by overthrowing beyond all doubt the military and unscrupulous despotism for which Herr Hitler is primarily if not wholly responsible, and in the pursuit of which he has sacrificed every honourable obligation.' (57)

The RPA's first action was to move its operations from Johnson's Court out to Elstree in Hertfordshire. There was a widely held fear that a modern war would include systematic bombing of cities, using both incendiaries and gases, and that the bomber would always get through. The government shared this fear, and encouraged the evacuation of children to the countryside. Towards the end of 1940, when many of these fears had been shown to be reasonable ones, an air-raid shelter underneath the building was constructed, at a cost of £250. Within a couple of months of the war, the RPA had donated a thousand copies of Thinker's Library titles to the armed forces and established a Troops Book Fund to finance future donations. It also loaned £5000 interest free to the government for the duration of the war.

The war rapidly embroiled Fred Watts in an enormous amount of extra work. Throughout the war there were problems with storage of books and damage from bombing. In November 1940, two warehouses rented by the RPA and full of equipment and books were destroyed in the bombing. In January 1941 the area around Johnson's Court was subjected to heavy bombing. The RPA headquarters escaped serious damage but Dr Johnson's house was damaged when a burning tin of paint fell onto its roof from a neighbouring building. However, later that month the RPA suffered a considerable loss of stock when the Ship Binding Works was completely destroyed by bombing and on May 10 1941 the RPA lost 45,000 Thinker's Library titles, destroyed in a warehouse in St Bride Street. (58) Even after the worst of the bombing was over, the problems created by war continued. In October 1942 all of the RPA's printer's storage space in Bungay, Suffolk was requisitioned by the government for military purposes and the RPA had to find new accommodation for a quarter of a million books. Space was at a premium and Fred Watts had considerable difficulty finding any suitable property. The bulk of the stock was moved to Highgate in London but before long it had to be moved once more because the property in Highgate was not zoned for this type of storage.

The other big problem was the strict rationing of paper. Many plans for future development had to be put on hold for the duration of the war for lack of paper. This was to have a drastic effect on the *Literary Guide*. At the beginning of the war the *Guide* was twenty pages long and a generous foolscap size. In July 1940 it was reduced to 16 pages and in December 1941 to twelve pages. None of these economies was sufficient, however, and in March 1942 the *Guide* went through an unprecedented diminution, being halved in size to a digest format, the number of pages increasing to 22 as some form of compensation. Further rationing cut that page number back to 16 and then twelve. The *Guide* and its readers put on a brave face. H Sykes of St Albans wrote in that he couldn't in all honesty say he liked the new format 'but I expect it is the best you can do under the circumstances.'(59) The paper situation meant the RPA had a constant juggling act to perform. 'With paper rationed as it is we are continually faced with the problem of deciding whether to use our limited supply for the issue of new books or for reprints of standard works.' (60) Occasionally things were made a little easier. Late in 1943 a government committee approved of eight Watts & Co titles for its Army Post War Education Scheme and allowed paper restrictions to be eased to allow these books to be printed. Sadly the minutes do not record what those titles were.

There are two notable points of comparison between the experience of the RPA in the Second World War and that in First. There was significantly less difficulty with the military and other authorities about discrimination toward rationalist servicemen, but there were also fewer reports of rationalist servicemen. There were the occasional reports of servicemen losing their faith after coming across rationalist material. Those with the most fervent belief in the goodness of God and of God's interest in the wishes and needs of his believers had the hardest time adjusting to the horrors, stupidities and futilities of war. One such man, a Lance Corporal in the Eighth Army wrote to the RPA, telling of his progressive loss of faith.

> I cannot really explain how it happened, but I gradually realised that the message I was preaching was too narrow and old-fashioned and to be true to my conscience I had to find something new to give me

purpose and guidance in life. I doubt if you can imagine the perplexed state of mind in which I found myself. Here I was, a young man who, to be true to his convictions, had to turn his back on a faith he had held and practised in the extreme for a number of years. Then came a lucky break. While on a few days' leave I searched among bookshops for some lead which would give me help for my search for Truth. Fortunately I came across four volumes of the Thinker's Library series. They were: *Liberty of Man, Religion of the Open Mind, Fact and Faith*, and *A Short History of the World*. I found it extremely difficult to clear my mind of my former dogmatic religious faith; but after many days of deliberate question and answer, with your publications as my excellent help, I found myself gaining confidence in my growing natural outlook on life. (61)

The war also brought another interesting development for the RPA. The mounting losses experienced in 1938 and 1939 were replaced by mounting profits as subscriptions to the *Literary Guide* and sales of RPA books took a dramatic turn upwards. This took place despite the disruption and delays in subscriptions and orders from overseas members reaching London. The RPA foresaw these problems this time, and in countries where there were enterprising Local Secretaries to manage them, bank accounts to handle RPA subscriptions were opened and remained active until the end of the war. Mr W G Gould, the RPA Local Secretary in New Zealand, advised readers of this in the *NZ Rationalist* at the end of 1941.

There were also fewer cases of excitable churchmen calling for God to intervene in the war or to otherwise show his hand. At the end of 1939 the Bishop of Exeter intoned darkly that 'the greatest disaster that can happen to a man or a nation is to lose the sense of God'. Adam Gowans Whyte noted how consoling the Poles must find such a thought. (62) Many churchmen tried to make capital out of the particularly fine weather which aided the evacuation of the British and French forces from the beaches of Dunkirk. But they were silent during all the catastrophes that befell the Allied war effort until the end of 1942. The 'miracle of Dunkirk' rhetoric was recalled in June 1944 when particularly foul weather prevented the Air Force from providing air cover to the Allied forces struggling to gain a foothold on the Normandy coast and to counter the new threat from Flying Bombs. John Rowland wrote in the *Guide*:

> We cannot be too careful to point the moral of these happenings, to show that the Churches are very much inclined to select such facts as appear to fit their theories and to omit those which are difficult or impossible to explain along orthodox lines. (63)

The Broadcasting Battle

As radio quickly became a hugely influential medium in the thirties, the BBC's exclusivism started to matter more and more to the RPA, and the campaign to have the BBC relax its policies became ever more urgent. There is little need here to prove once again the exclusionary policy of the BBC in its first decades, although there most certainly is a need to make known the battle the RPA conducted in challenging this state of affairs. One notorious example of the BBC's attitude at the time was its refusal to play the *Internationale*, even after the Soviet Union had been invaded by Germany in June 1941, and despite Soviet radio playing *God Save the King* at every available opportunity. The ban was on the instruction of Churchill himself and quickly became an embarrassment. Churchill grudgingly lifted the ban in January 1942. Less well known was the proposed series to be called 'The World Looks at the Christian'. Soon after an article on the series appeared in the *Guide*, the BBC asked the RPA to provide names of those willing to participate in the series. The RPA responded promptly, only to be told the following month that the whole series had been postponed.

Not surprisingly, resentment about this exclusivism reached its height during the war as each side was able to couch its wants in terms of 'what we are fighting for'. A very indignant RPA participated, along with most other freethought organisations, in the Radio Freedom League, which was founded in 1941. The League made little headway. In 1942 the BBC tightened its grip even further by changing its policy with regard to the popular and influential programme, the Brains Trust. This programme featured three speakers, Julian Huxley, C E M Joad and Commodore Campbell, who answered questions from listeners on all sorts of questions. But in 1942 the BBC decided that no question of any kind relating to religion would be accepted from then on.

The campaign to persuade the BBC to relax its stranglehold on debate of substantive issues continued, and achieved a measure of success. In 1942 the RPA took out a series of advertisements in *The Times*, *The Spectator*, *The Manchester Guardian*, *The Birmingham Post* and some other regional papers which asked people to respond to three questions:

1. Do you consider the BBC policy of propaganda for a particular form of religion consistent with the democratic principle?
2. Are you in favour of a reversal of this policy which will secure the freedom of discussion embodied in the Atlantic Charter?
3. In view of our alliances with non-Christian nations, and of the worldwide range of the BBC broadcasts, do you consider that international harmony is fostered by a State-controlled organisation that recognises only one religious system?

Given the way the questions were framed it is probably not surprising that the replies which came back to the RPA ran four to one opposed to the BBC's policies of restriction. Adam Gowans Whyte acknowledged this point but went on to add that 'if the BBC disputes the verdict, the power of appeal lies in its hands.' (64) In the meantime Fred Watts was writing to Kenneth Adam, Director of Publicity for the BBC. In a letter to *The Times*, Adam had unwisely claimed that the BBC kept in mind the tastes of minorities. When challenged on this by Fred Watts, Adam replied that he had been thinking of artistic and cultural as opposed to religious or non-religious minorities. He then changed tack slightly by claiming that time was given every now and then to ethical and philosophical questions from various points of view. When Watts wrote back asking for a single instance when a rationalist had been permitted airtime, Adam decided that not replying was the easiest recourse.

By the middle of 1943 it was becoming apparent even to the directors of the BBC that things had to change, if only slightly. There had been a debate in the first half of 1943 in the House of Commons about the BBC's policies. Mr McGovern led a motion criticising the BBC as an instrument of propaganda in the interest of the government in general and of Mr Churchill in particular. While most people recognised this was true, it could never pass in such an antagonistic form as that. McGovern's motion was lost by 143 votes to 3. But the debate revealed a degree of unease at the BBC policies. Reginald Sorenson, MP for Leyton West, though a religious man himself, was critical of what he described as the BBC's 'prejudice in favour of the careful, the cautious, and the orthodox.' Sorenson specifically mentioned Rationalists among the groups he thought had been unreasonably denied their rightful access to the airwaves. Brendan Bracken, the Minister of Information, had the thankless job of giving the official line when he declared that the BBC has 'no political partisanships and no religious bias.' (65)

The Commons debate was only the most visible sign that some thaw in broadcasting policy by the BBC was long overdue. By the middle of 1943 a series of small concessions were made. With what the *Guide* described as an air of 'pious patronage', the BBC ran a series of programmes on non-Christian religions and even permitted three broadcasts on aspects of humanism. Julian Huxley spoke on December 5 on 'Scientific Humanism', Gilbert Murray spoke on December 12 on 'Classical Humanism' and the series was completed on December 19 with a Dr Oldham on 'Christian Humanism'. Inevitably, a Christian was permitted the last word, but it was still a step forward. Early in 1944 the RPA had the three talks on humanism published as a threepenny pamphlet. But there were very definite limits to the BBC's climate of *perestroika*. Hamilton Fyfe (1869-1951), a prominent journalist (and later to become an RPA Honorary Associate) submitted a talk entitled 'Why I do not Believe in a Personal God', but it was rejected by Robert Foot, Reith's successor as Director-General, on the grounds that it 'ran counter to the State religion of this country'. (66)

Foot was succeeded as Director-General in 1944 by Sir William Haley, who opened the door to alternative views a little wider. This was signalled by running a series later in the year called 'What I Believe'. The series featured seven Christians, one spiritualist, one Jew and three unbelievers of various stripes. But these concessions were not allowed to escalate into genuine pluralism; the Christian stranglehold on the airwaves was never seriously threatened. When, at the end of the war, the RPA wrote again to the BBC suggesting a broader coverage of philosophic and religious discussion, the same answer was received. M G Farquharson repeated that the BBC 'is not opposed to broadcasts dealing with the fundamental problems of religion and philosophy so long as they do not directly attack the fundamental bases of Christian theology.' (67)

The Education Act

The other major area of activity was that of religious education. For several years prior to the passing of the 1944 Education Act, religious instruction in schools was a political hot potato. While technically the RPA had no policy on education, in deference to its non-political stance, in fact many of its members were active in the Secular Education League and the League was given favourable mention when education issues came to the fore. To all intents and purposes, the RPA's view was that it favoured what was known as the Secular Solution. Ernest Thurtle, soon after his election as MP for Shoreditch, advocated the maintenance of this principle as the fairest. The problem was a simple one: either the state should pay for all religious education, or it should pay for no religious education. As the first option would be both prohibitively expensive and probably impossible, the second option was the safer and more democratic one. Thurtle noted that this had been the case in New Zealand for half a century, with no notable collapse in the moral condition of New Zealanders as a result. The situation in Britain was iniquitous in that it favoured one strand of one faith and ignored the rest. Like so many other rationalist viewpoints, this remains a valid opinion today.

So, when education surfaced once more as a political issue during the war, the *Literary Guide* followed the argument closely. The various commentators in the *Guide* had little difficulty discerning two quite contradictory arguments in favour of compulsory Christian instruction in the schools. One of the arguments stressed that as Britain was a Christian country it was only right that Christian instruction should take place in Britain's schools. But the other argument, not infrequently expressed by the same person, was that Christian belief was so lamentably in decline that Christian instruction was urgently needed to undo the damage caused by the resultant moral decay.

Lord Elton was one such prophet. In a debate in the House of Lords in July 1942 on the future of education, Elton expressed the widely held view that Christianity and the British Empire were pretty much the same thing. 'I feel bound to say' began Lord Elton

> that in a sense we cannot claim to be spiritually preparing for victory as long as we tolerate an educational system which ignores the British Empire and which treats the teaching of religion as of less importance than the teaching of arithmetic…We are fighting this war to defend Christendom without having really taught our children fully what Christendom really is; and we are fighting to defend the British Empire without having allowed them to know what the British Empire means.

Lord Elton climaxed with a warning not to listen to groups like the RPA.

> Let the Minister bear such facts as this in mind when he receives a resolution from some well-organised minority to the effect that it is undemocratic for a Christian country to teach the elements of the Christian faith. (68)

It was the RPA's policy to point out that the Atlantic Charter, for the ideals of which the Allies were at war, insisted on religious freedom. But as is so often the case, then and now, religious freedom is frequently interpreted to mean the right to impose the dominant religion on everyone. Then and now, the RPA, indeed all humanist organisations, has interpreted freedom of religion to mean the freedom to be religious or non-religious according to one's conscience, with the state having no formal interest in that decision. This remains a live ethical issue.

To Lord Elton's attack Adam Gowans Whyte replied that what rationalists object to is the preaching of Christianity in schools.

> Knowledge of the elements of Christian religion is an ingredient in a liberal education; so also is knowledge of Hinduism, Buddhism, Mohammedanism, Confucianism, and other great religions; also of primitive religions and the evolution of religions. (69)

The Minister of Education to whom Lord Elton was directing his warning was R A Butler, who had surprised Churchill by taking on the unglamorous education ministry in preference to a foreign or war-related appointment. As chairman of the Conservative Party's Central Committee on Post-War Reconstruction, Butler set up a subcommittee on education, which in due course published a discussion paper. This paper admitted frankly the very widespread indifference to religion in general and Christianity in particular. And as Butler's committee included Anglicans, Catholics, Nonconformists and Jews, agreement on doctrinal matters could not be expected. Instead, they focused on the 'emotional awareness' of a divine purpose as 'an essential condition of all social excellence and the general character of all active religious belief.' (70) It was as if all the philosophical and social learning and discussion of the previous half century had not taken place.

In April 1943 the RPA appointed an Education Officer, J W H Brown, a past president of the National Union of Teachers, whose job it was to co-ordinate the RPA campaign on education questions. (71) Brown did a pretty good job. The campaign began with a letter to *The Times*, published August 8 1943 and signed by eight of the RPA's Honorary Associates (C D Darlington, Richard Gregory, Lord Horder, S I Hsiung, Julian Huxley, Sir Arthur Keith, Eden Phillpotts, Henry J Wood). A pamphlet outlining the RPA argument was sent to every member of the House of Commons and another was circulated on demand to teachers around the country. Use was also made of a Gallup Poll, commissioned in 1944 to ascertain the views of teachers regarding religious education. The majority favoured the retention of religious education, but wanted it to include elements from all the major faiths of the world. They were generally opposed to clerical influence in schools, religious instruction as opposed to education, and a Christian monopoly of the process.

The RPA's campaign was not, however, a success. The Education Act, which became law in August 1944, included a clause specifying a compulsory daily act of non-denominational worship in all state-funded schools. Fred Watts understood the situation well enough. 'Owing to the bargains made between the Ministry and the various great interests concerned, we are unable to claim much success, but our point of view was expressed at various stages in the passage of the Bill through the House.' (72) Twenty years later, A J P Taylor noted that the religious compulsion in the Education Act was tribute to the weakness of established religion, rather than to its strength. Those framing earlier education legislation had taken for granted that schools would allow for Christian worship. But now they had to shelter behind legislative fiat. This clause, Taylor wrote, 'could hardly spring from stronger Christian conviction. The explanation was surely the reverse. The Christian devotion of teachers, or of parents, could no longer be relied on. Christianity had to be propped up by legislative enactment.' (73) While this judgment is almost certainly true, the clear inequity of the clause has remained a legitimate source of discontent among rationalists and humanists to this day.

The RPA could be forgiven a little bitterness when, in the wake of all these declarations that 'Britain is a Christian country' being used as the stock slogan to justify religious privileges on the radio and in education, there came further evidence that this was not in fact the case. A report commissioned in 1943 by the Church of England admitted the fact graphically in its title: *Towards the Conversion of England*. It showed that only 10% to 15% of the population was closely linked to a Christian church, with a further 25% to 30% attending only for rites of passage.

So while the RPA was still banging its head against the brick wall of the BBC's exclusivism and its campaign for secular education had been outflanked by the established, though discredited, Church of England, the end of the war brought renewed hope. Membership had grown steadily through the war and book sales had been consistently satisfactory. Charles Watts felt able to note in June 1945 that the RPA and *Literary Guide* had not only survived the war, but were 'now stronger and better equipped in every way than they were before the war.' (74) He looked forward to further growth.

Chapter 5

The Humanist Labyrinth

'The new generation is much more interested in finding jobs and homes and stopping a third world war; and rightly so.'
Archibald Robertson, 1954

A tragically prominent feature of the years following the defeat of the Axis powers was how quickly the promised peace unravelled and a ghastly new tension between the victors tarnished almost overnight the hopes of a better world. On a smaller scale the same can be said of the RPA at this time. The most immediate danger to be faced was the passing of the old guard. When Charles Watts died on May 15 1946, the whole RPA grieved. There is virtually no organisation that does not go through a difficult adjustment after the death of the founder, and many fail to make this transition. Much depends on the dynamics between the last of the old guard and the new leaders coming on, in most cases a problematic relationship. The only veterans of 1899 still alive in 1946 were Adam Gowans Whyte and Joseph McCabe, who could not abide each other. For the most part this did not matter, as McCabe had nothing to do with the running of the RPA or the *Literary Guide*.

Unlike McCabe, Adam Gowans Whyte remained very much an insider. At 71 years of age when Charles Watts died, Whyte was the last of the original RPA Directors from 1899. His 51-year term on the Board remains the record for service in that office. After Watts's death Whyte recalled his considerable personal and intellectual debt to the founder of the RPA. Unlike McCabe, Whyte freely conceded to Watts the right to edit his work. 'Proofs marked with his corrections were a liberal education for the authors concerned, and I never wrote anything for *The Literary Guide*, or indeed for any other publication, without the consciousness of a salutary mentor.' (1) It is for this reason that, in 1930, Watts gifted to Whyte the influential first page and a half of the *Guide* for his column, called 'The Open Window'. Watts granted Whyte full freedom because he knew that Whyte's full freedom was difficult to distinguish from Watts's full freedom. This is also why Whyte was appointed as 'Literary Advisor' to the RPA.

But there was never any doubt who would replace Charles Watts. His son, Fred Watts had long been groomed for office. Already holding the specially created position of Managing Director, Fred became chairman of the Board of Directors in 1942, following the death of J P Gilmour. Even Charles Watts had never held the top offices in Watts & Co *and* the RPA. He hadn't needed to, of course, because it was Charles Watts's genius to be able to appoint others to important positions, knowing they would do his work faithfully, which they did. When

133

announcing Fred Watts's appointment as Board chairman, the *Guide* noted rather apologetically that it was customary for someone with personal standing outside the rationalist movement to be offered this position, but that wartime conditions made this difficult and Fred Watts would hold the post in the meantime. (2) In 1943 Fred succeeded his father as editor of the *Rationalist Annual* and immediately after his father's death assumed formal editorial control of the *Literary Guide*. He had been the de facto editor of the *Guide* for the better part of fifteen years. In the two years between the death of his father and the breakdown of his own health, Fred Watts held more formal power over the RPA and Watts & Co than anyone else, before or since. As with his father before him, the RPA was Fred Watts's life.

During the hectic war years, Fred Watts had been thinking about the future. Early in 1944 he wrote a report for his fellow directors outlining his ideas for developing the RPA once the war was over. His initial axioms were all positive. 'Activities in several directions must be planned on a scale hitherto not contemplated if we are to take advantage of present opportunities. With these facts in mind, and with the knowledge that our funds are now greater than they have ever been, I put forward the following proposals for consideration…' Among Watts's proposals were the appointment of a full-time press officer and a full-time organising secretary. There were already plans afoot to establish a Rationalist League after the war to cater for the social side of the movement that the RPA, as a publishing house, was not geared to do. This organising secretary would coordinate RPA and Rationalist League activities. Watts also suggested clerical assistance for himself and Constance Kerr, as her job would inevitably grow after the war. Watts estimated these expansions would cost around £5000 a year. And finally, Watts speculated on the future. 'In another twenty years or so (when I shall be approaching seventy) the spirit of the Watts family will have ceased to have any active control of the two concerns; I think, therefore, that this is the time to plan a staff as young as possible who can be trained and guided to take over all the most important parts of the routine, and especially the publishing side.' (3)

Watts was quite right to be thinking ahead, and also quite right to see that the next awkward transition for the RPA would be when the influence of the Watts family no longer prevails. But he didn't foresee two important things. First, Watts didn't consider the possibility that the postwar conditions might not permit a continual expansion on the scale seen during the war. And neither did Watts see that the transition to the post-Watts RPA would happen a lot sooner than he thought.

Postwar plans

In the light of Watts's report and all the other talking and thinking that had been going on, a committee for planning the RPA's postwar growth was established in January 1945. Over that year a series of initiatives were decided upon. In March came the first set of decisions. They included:-

- The creation of a monthly periodical called *The Thinker's Digest*, which was designed to appeal to the general public with neither the leisure nor inclination to read whole books. The *Digest* had originally been mooted in 1939 but had been shelved for the duration of the war.

- The appointment of a National Organiser at a salary of £750 per annum.
- £500 per annum be put aside for advertising campaigns, particularly on buses, in tube stations and similar places.
- The establishment of a draft curriculum of studies in rationalism and a lecture programme on rationalism that prominent scholars could be invited to give.
- The establishment of a chair of comparative religion to be staffed by a rationalist. (4)

The following month it was also proposed to formalise a publishing policy for the Thinker's Library and to appoint a general editor or editorial board to put that policy into effect. This was thought necessary because of inroads being made by the Penguin paperbacks. The board was eventually decided upon.

In October it was agreed that a Rationalist Society was to be created and the following month Hector Hawton was appointed to tour the regional rationalist groups. Hawton (1901-1975) was one of the younger members of the RPA, just released from his wartime duties in Bomber Command's Group 4 HQ at Heslington Hall in York. As well as lecturing, it was also Hawton's job to report back to London on the strength of the various groups and provide information for the proposed Rationalist Society. He was also put in charge of editing the *Thinker's Digest*. Hawton came on the warm recommendation of Adam Gowans Whyte, who, as literary adviser, had appreciated Hawton's intellectual ability and writing skill. Not everyone was enamoured of the new recruit. Fred Watts and Constance Kerr, in particular, were unconvinced by the newcomer.

What is remarkable is how quickly all these plans came unstuck. The first plan to unravel was the Rationalist Society, which lasted no longer than its predecessor in the 1930s. The problem this time was that the proposed society became entangled in a complex legal web: if the RPA Limited was going to remain in formal control of the Rationalist Society, it too would need to become a limited liability company. Conversely, if the Rationalist Society was to be free of this restraint, then the RPA would also have to relinquish its status as a business. This, clearly, was out of the question, so the RPA tried to persuade Sir Stafford Cripps's ministry to permit it to remain a limited liability company while dropping the word 'Limited' from its title. Understandably, Cripps turned this request down. The RPA's choices were now either to create a Rationalist Society Limited, which would in effect be a clone of the RPA, or form the society and relinquish all formal control over it, or drop the whole idea. They chose the third option.

This quickly meant that Hawton's work was unnecessary, so he was released. The demise of the Rationalist Society also lessened the need for a National Organiser and extra clerical assistance for Fred Watts and Constance Kerr, although their workloads continued to be demanding. Other plans did get off the ground, but ran into unexpected difficulties. Hawton wasn't lost to the movement, though, because in 1948 he took up the position of secretary of the South Place Ethical Society and retained the job of editing The *Thinker's Digest*. This publication began as a monthly but soon became a quarterly digest of contemporary writing with a slight slant to humanism. To take one issue at random, that of Spring 1949 (it was no longer a monthly by this time), there were short extracts from several topical works such as Arnold Toynbee's *Civilisation on Trial*, Jean-Paul Sartre's

Existentialism and Humanism and Wing-tsit Chan's contribution to *Twentieth Century Philosophy*. There were also summaries of talks by Jacob Bronowski, Viscount Samuel and Raymond Firth, several short book reviews, science trivia items, travel pieces, poems, nostalgia, and a good range of advertisements from publishing houses and magazines covering a range of disciplines and beliefs. As the names in the Spring 1949 issue attest, *The Thinker's Digests* carried a good range of material, not all rationalist by any means. But, good or not, *The Thinker's Digest* simply did not sell well enough to succeed. In June 1950 it ceased publication. It was probably too good, intellectually speaking, to succeed as a digest.

Problems with minor titles like *The Thinker's Digest* and projects like the Rationalist Society could be coped with. But the scale of the postwar challenge the RPA was confronted with took time to sink in. Things had looked pretty good during the war. The demand for books had grown steadily, readership of the *Literary Guide* had trebled and funds were at an all time high, when Fred Watts wrote his report to the Board at the beginning of 1944. RPA membership rose to a peak of 5000 in 1947. But the slide that began in 1946 was to escalate into what was later described as a 'devastating drain on our membership and finances.' (5) Watts & Co was beginning to lose money, and in quite serious quantities. Each year until the middle 1950s its losses ran into thousands of pounds. The demand for books, all sorts of books, not just Watts & Co titles, began to slacken almost immediately the war was over. Even the Thinker's Library was no longer holding its own. It began to stagger in 1949, stumbled in 1950, and fell the following year. The series had for a while been looking tired and out of joint with the times. In 1949, for example, the world worried about an imminent third world war as the Soviet Union exploded its first atomic bomb, the Berlin airlift was in full swing and China fell to the communists. The Thinker's Library titles for that year could scarcely have been less relevant to the crisis unfolding each day. There were two anthropological studies by Lord Raglan (*The Origins of Religion* and *The Hero*), a study of John Knox by Marjorie Bowen, a history of the French Revolution by Archibald Robertson and an abridged reprint of Graham Wallas's *The Art of Thought*. Noble titles all, but of little direct relevance to the concerns of the day. It is interesting that Wallas's book had been considered for reprinting in 1935 and rejected. Things got worse the following year. The year the Korean War began was the year the RPA reprinted a miscellaneous compilation of Herbert Spencer's lesser-known works under the title *Literary Style and Music*. It is difficult to imagine who the Directors thought would be energized by these 98-year-old essays at such a critical time. Following Spencer's essays it was thought to reprint another edition of *The Origin of Species*, despite having released it as Number 8 of the series in 1929. The 1950 edition was printed but never actually published. The final Thinker's Library title was a study published in 1951 of religious revivalists by George Godwin. The series was not officially put to rest until March 1954, when the Directors recognised that it was no longer capable of resurrection. (6)

Even when the decisions being made were sounder than those involving the Thinker's Library, the effects were little better. The same year as the Thinker's Library died, a new series was launched called Thrift Books. Advertised as a companion series to the Thinker's Library, the Thrift Books appeared in paperback only and were more cheaply produced than their predecessor. Thrift Books were to sell at a shilling each and be Watts & Co's answer to Penguin paperbacks. E Royston Pike was put in charge of the series, largely to attract a new generation of authors. The only veteran to publish in the Thrift series was Adam Gowans Whyte, who died before his work (*The Ladder of Life: From Molecule to Mind*) was published. Albert Einstein and Bertrand Russell were both approached to write for the series, but neither did. The author of the first book in the series was the most impressive. T Neville George was Professor of Geology at the University of Glasgow and at the time of writing was Chairman of the Mineral Resources Panel of the Scottish Council and the Extra-mural Education Committee at his university. And at 46, he was a relatively young man. He wrote a general overview of evolution, much in the tradition of Joseph McCabe's popular accounts forty years previously. Other subjects broached in the Thrift Books series included genetics, atomic energy, world history between the wars, our glands, and primers on English literature, the theatre, mathematics, medicine, music and family law. Thrift Books was a good idea; the price was low, and the topics written about had a contemporary appeal. But Watts & Co was caught in a bind: the price was low so as to compete, but it was too low to allow for the marketing the series required in order to compete effectively. The series was a failure and was canned at the end of 1952, after 22 titles.

One innovation from 1945 that *did* prosper was the idea to have an annual conference devoted to some particular theme. The first of these conference was entitled 'Rationalism in Education and Life' and was held at Wadham College, Oxford. Speakers included Professor P Sargent Florence on 'Rationalism in University Education', Dr Kenneth Urwin on 'Ethics and the Child', Professor V Gordon Childe on 'The Birth of God in the Brain of a Social Animal' and Professor A E Heath on 'Science and Cultural Values'. It was natural that this subject should have been chosen in the year after the Education Act and in a climate of anxiety about creating a postwar world that was an improvement on the interwar world. It is possible that Wadham was chosen because it was the college of A J Ayer, who had made a name for himself as an outspoken atheist in the 1930s. It is equally true that Ayer was still on active service in France when the conference took place, and did not himself address a conference until 1948 when he spoke on existentialism. The full list of speakers and themes for these conferences is given in Appendix Three. It is worth looking through the names of those who spoke at these conferences and at the range of issues discussed. They reveal a staggering range of thinkers bringing light to a wide range of topics over two decades. The conferences add up to an admirable contribution by the RPA toward the promotion of rational thinking on complex issues. Some of the addresses must have been memorable. One wonders if Karl Popper and Gilbert Ryle were in the same room during the conference on 'Reason and Unreason in Society' in 1948, for example. In the years to come, Ryle did his best to keep Popper out of Oxford, despite recognising his extraordinary ability. (7) Even Joseph McCabe, in his eighty-fifth year, addressed the 1952 conference on issues of Roman Catholicism. This was the last time the RPA and McCabe worked together, bringing to an end a tempestuous relationship spanning 56 years. Alongside McCabe was Dr Marie Stopes, who spoke on Catholic attitudes toward birth control. These conferences were held each year under the auspices of the RPA until 1962 when, as a preliminary to closer co-operation, that year's conference ('Youth in Revolt: The Conflict Between the Older and Younger Generation') was co-hosted with the Ethical Union. And from 1963 until 1967 the conferences were officially British Humanist Association conferences.

137

One of the speakers at the first RPA conference, P Sargant Florence (1890-1982), a respected economist and RPA Honorary Associate, was instrumental in setting up the Josiah Mason Lectures, which the RPA had a hand in financing. The first lectures of the series, in the winter of 1946-47, were given by Raymond Firth (1901- 2002), the New Zealand-born anthropologist. The lectures were later published by Watts & Co as *Elements of Social Organisation*, one of the most highly regarded works of anthropology of the twentieth century. Firth was followed by V Gordon Childe, another RPA Honorary Associate, and one who had already written for the RPA. Those lectures were published under the title *Social Evolution*.

It is evident that the RPA was under no intellectual disadvantage in the postwar years, quite the contrary. But conferences and sponsored lectures cost money rather than bring money in. And having this support of intellectual heavyweights does not necessarily translate into a successful publishing programme. In fact, the quality of Watts & Co publications during the immediate postwar years varied considerably. It is remarkable that, in these difficult years, Watts continued to publish as much good material as it did. For example, it was thought appropriate for a mid-century assessment of the condition of the various sciences. So, A E Heath (1887-1961), Professor of Philosophy at University College, Swansea and an Honorary Associate since 1944, was asked to edit the work. The result was *Scientific Thought in the Twentieth Century*, published in 1951. A simple list of some of the contributors should be enough to attest to its quality: philosophy of science, A J Ayer; statistics, R A Fisher; zoology, Peter Medawar; astronomy, Sir Harold Spencer Jones; sociology, Donald MacRae; psychology, Sir Cyril Burt. This was a quality work from distinguished specialists. *Scientific Thought in the Twentieth Century* was in the direct line of descent from the History of Science series Watts had published before the First World War. Albert Einstein, an Honorary Associate of the RPA, wrote congratulating the Board of Directors on this volume, especially the chapter written by Ayer on the development of philosophy. (8) It is astonishing to a person at the beginning of the twenty-first century to look back and see that no advantage was taken by Watts & Co of this endorsement.

In the field of classical rationalism, some excellent material was still being produced as well. Incredibly, Joseph McCabe still had energy to publish, producing *The Testament of Christian Civilisation* in 1946, *A Rationalist Encyclopaedia* in 1948 and his rewritten third edition of *The Papacy in Politics Today* in 1951. The premature death of Emanuel Haldeman-Julius at his home in Kansas in the same year effectively ended McCabe's career on both sides of the Atlantic. McCabe had quarrelled with the RPA incessantly about what he saw as interference by underqualified people with his work on the *Rationalist Encyclopaedia*. One of the people on the editorial board, Professor G W Keeton, left the board in 1944 and made it clear he did not want his name associated with the *Encyclopaedia*. Other advisors came and went, and McCabe argued every step of the way. The whole project had begun with McCabe's original suggestion in February 1940, eight long years previously. Everyone must have been very glad to have the whole project finished with after such a long time. The third edition of *The Papacy in Politics Today* was the last publishing collaboration between the RPA and McCabe. A few months before his death McCabe wrote to the RPA advising them he was severing links with them owing to the RPA's 'virtual abandonment of the policy for which it was founded'. (9) The RPA offered to send some Directors to his house to talk the matter over with him, but they did not change the old man's mind.

Among the younger writers, quite the most outstanding was Hector Hawton. By the time he took over the *Guide* from Frederick Watts, about which more later, Hawton had written three good books on aspects of rationalism. *Flight from Reality* (1941), *Men Without Gods* (1948), and *The Thinker's Handbook* (1950) were intelligent and well-written overviews of the rationalist/Christian encounter designed for the non-specialist. *The Thinker's Handbook* was one of the books most frequently mentioned by younger members as important to their becoming humanists. Unlike the veteran rationalists, Hawton had a sure grasp of intellectual developments that had taken place since the Great War such as psychoanalysis and existentialism. We shall examine this more closely in Chapter Seven. And following a surprisingly well-trodden path among rationalists, Hawton also wrote detective who-dunits as a leisure activity. As befits a former Fleet Street journalist, Hawton had built up a prodigious capacity for drink. This excited the suspicion of those with a more sober disposition but those who knew him better enjoyed his company. Hawton worked according to Voltaire's maxim; Sparta in the morning, Athens in the afternoon.

But while Hawton and others were responsible for some very good work coming out of Watts & Co, some problematic or downright poor material was also being produced, and at a time when this could not be afforded. For instance, considerable resources were devoted in 1950 to a substantial autobiography by Sir Arthur Keith, but Keith's hour in the sun was long gone and the book did not sell well, despite being finely written and unusually candid. Keith had built his substantial reputation by defending and analysing the Piltdown skull. He lamented in his biography that he was fated to 'espouse causes and theories which fail to carry conviction.' (10) This proved to be more true than even he knew at the time; this was written before the Piltdown fraud was exposed. It was Keith's tragedy to see his life's work unravel in the final two years of his long life.

As we noted in the previous chapter, Keith was a successful and prolific science writer and populariser, and in 1948 Watts & Co published his *A New Theory of Human Evolution*. This work got mixed reviews even from within the rationalist and humanist movement. Maurice Burton, himself a distinguished biologist, did his best to be positive about the book, but noted that 'as can so easily happen to those who proceed by giant strides, they are prone to step over difficulties as though they did not exist.' (11) A prominent feature of Keith's book was his 'amity-enmity principle' of race competition, another of Keith's lost causes. Burton noted that Keith had greatly over-simplified the situation to one of co-operation within racial groups and competition between them. Keith's advocacy of racialism as a natural method by which people protect their own ensured that his most favourable reviews came from South African papers. The sad irony was that Keith was not a racist in the sense of seeing race conflict as between superior and inferior peoples. He dismissed white supremacism in his autobiography as 'self-flattery'. (12) Whatever the merits of *A New Theory*, Keith was delighted with the look of it and with the publicity it was receiving in the *Literary Guide*. He wrote:

139

My dear Watts

What I saw when I opened the cover of the last issue of the *Literary Guide* made me hold my breath. If this new book does not succeed it will not be the fault of the publishers. You and Mr Chappell have given it a splendid start. If it fails it will be the fault of the author. With thanks and good wishes.

Believe me, yours sincerely

Arthur Keith. (13)

The same year as Keith's *New Theory of Human Evolution* hit the press, Watts also published the memoir of another central character of the Piltdown scandal, Sir Arthur Smith-Woodward. *The Earliest Englishman* was released as Number 127 of the Thinker's Library and remains the most accessible introduction to and defence of the Piltdown skull. Of course, it is only now that we realise that publishing this work was an embarrassing mistake. Even in 1948, there was absolutely no reason why this work should not have been considered a worthwhile addition to the series.

But the surest sign of trouble was the RPA's fiftieth anniversary history. 1949 was the fiftieth anniversary of the RPA and it was natural to want to commemorate the event with an historical account. Who is given such a sensitive job is always a test of an organisation's confidence and intellectual health. Sadly, the RPA made the wrong choice by opting for safety. Giving the job to Adam Gowans Whyte made sense on the one hand. He was, after all, the last of the 1899 veterans. But that is a double-edged sword, for he was too much of an insider to write an effective history. Whyte had no track record in writing history, and he was old and tired. The result was a tired and uncritical chronology. The finished work was given hardback treatment, with illustrations, but was little more than 90 pages long, with fully 20 of those pages outlining the development of freethought before the RPA was formed. Of the 70 pages left, 50 were devoted to the first fifteen years of the organisation's existence. In modern layout, Whyte's history would be little more than a pamphlet. The book had more the feel of an old man's reminiscences than an ordered, critical historical account. Virtually every possible disadvantage of entrusting anniversary accounts to a reliable veteran was displayed in this book. Wiser choices would have been Hector Hawton, or perhaps Donald MacRae, a prominent sociologist who was contributing regularly to the *Guide* at the time. An even braver choice (a lot braver, admittedly) would have been Joseph McCabe. The fiftieth anniversary history was a lost opportunity to reinvent rationalism in a very different world from that it was born into.

Defections

The other demoralising feature of the years immediately following the war was an apparent loss of confidence in rationalism and humanism and, in a couple of cases, outright defections to religion. To anybody convinced that secularism was a superior stage in development from religious adherence, this required some explaining. Gabrielle Long, a minor but prolific writer (pseudonym: Marjorie

Bowen) and RPA Director since 1948 resigned her chair in 1950 after a misunderstanding over whether she had been commissioned to write a book for the Thrift Series. Two years later, and only a few weeks before her death, Long resigned her Honorary Associateship, having become a member of the Church of Scotland. At about the same time John Rowland, who had written regularly for the *Guide* before the war, left the movement to become a Unitarian minister. But it was the big names that caused the real worry. The most significant instance was the much-publicised (and misunderstood) apparent collapse into despair of H G Wells. An Honorary Associate since 1929, Wells had inspired a whole generation of young idealists to work for a better world. But in 1945 his *Mind at the End of its Tether* seemed to call all that into question.

By way of background, it is interesting to note that at the very end of 1944 Wells wrote to Watts & Co offering them *Mind at the End of its Tether*. Some bits of it had already seen print in an essay appended to a revised edition of *A Short History of the World*, which Watts published in 1945. Watts replied that they could not undertake to publish *Mind* owing to the shortage of paper. (14) We will never know, but it is not unreasonable to speculate that Watts did not want to publish the work. While it is true there was a shortage of paper, this did not stop Watts & Co publishing nine other titles plus the *Literary Guide* and some pamphlets that year. Wells then approached Heinemann and the work was published in November 1945.

The *Mind at the End of its Tether* episode has become famous, having taken on a life of its own. Religious apologists constantly refer to it as evidence of the bankruptcy of the humanist worldview. A representative example is Michael Coren's bitterly hostile biography of H G Wells, published in 1993. Rather than make the condemnation himself, Coren hides behind those of *The Times Literary Supplement* and Malcolm Muggeridge. In the fifties, Colin Wilson gave *Mind at the End of its Tether* a brief vogue as a proto-existentialist work which awakens the outsider to the reality of chaos. The mistake these various commentators have made is to ignore the strand of pessimism that can be found in Wells's work from the very beginning of his career. His science fiction cannot be understood without recognising this. Bearing the pessimistic strain that was apparent throughout Wells's career, *Mind at the End of its Tether* is not a dramatic about face, but rather a strengthening of his pessimism as he approached his death. To see Wells's last work as a dramatic realisation of the futility of science, reason and humanism is to misunderstand science, reason and humanism and his understanding of these things.

Opponents of humanism have always seen fit to ignore the recognition most humanists have that progress is not a given and can come about only by constant hard work and the application of reason to human problems. These people also ignore the other book Wells published in 1945 called *The Happy Turning*. It is only an historical accident that *The Happy Turning* was not Wells's last book rather than *Mind at the End of its Tether*. Many of these points were brought up when Michael Foot, another Honorary Associate of the RPA, wrote *HG: The History of Mr Wells* in 1995, partly in order to answer the attacks of apologists like Coren.

At no time during the debate about Wells's last books has anyone seen fit to examine what humanists themselves have said about it all. In fact, A E Heath addressed the issue in the *Literary Guide* at the beginning of 1946. 'It has long

141

been known that the trim and tidy character of the Newtonian world has gone for ever.' Half a century later we see postmodernists and others saying the same thing to humanists in the fond belief that they are engaging in some sort of original reproach. Heath went on:

> I can understand the sense of uneasiness which all thoughtful minds must feel at the fact that vast extensions of power have fallen into the hands of men before they have achieved what Mr Wells has so long hoped for – that is, some sense of citizenship in a united world. But it is a very different thing from prophesying that our uncertainties mean that mind is at the end of its tether. So long as man can examine, criticise, and know, he stands to some extent above the forces which affect his life. (15)

There is no superficial optimism or scientism here. Heath recognised full well that things are not going to be easy, but reaffirmed the importance of making what effort we can to improve the world nonetheless.

If Wells was thought to have lapsed into despair as a result of the war, other prominent rationalists were finding solace by converting (or returning) to the church. The most significant of the defections was that of Cyril Joad. As with the last days of H G Wells, the story of Joad's conversion is not well understood. When Joad is referred to at all now, he is usually dismissed as a bumptious disciple of Bertrand Russell. While Joad was certainly bumptious, he was never a straight disciple of Russell. What is more, Russell could not abide the man. John Passmore is considerably more accurate in his description of Joad. 'Within a seam-bursting eclecticism, Russell, Bergson and Plato had somehow all to make room for themselves, as the representatives, respectively, of matter, life and value. The result was a conglomeration of considerable popular appeal but little philosophical consequence.' (16) Even today, Joad's 'return to faith' is occasionally trumpeted in the fundamentalist press. The truth, of course, is more complicated. John Passmore is correct to point out that Joad's philosophy was a highly unstable mix. Under the pressure of the war, and his having quarrelled with most of his friends and family, Joad's unstable philosophy broke up, with the vitalist core of his thinking making the small transition into full theism.

In the last year of his life Charles Watts invited Joad to give an account of his drift to Christianity in the *Rationalist Annual*. It is a feature of rationalism that it accords its opponents space in its journal for them to criticise rationalism. This commendable practice is rarely commented on by its detractors and even more rarely reciprocated. Anyway, Joad took the offer up and the 1946 *Rationalist Annual* carried his article 'On Being no Longer a Rationalist'. In this article Joad admitted that it was the instability of his philosophy that led to his conversion.

> From the first I had made provision in my scheme for certain immaterial values which I conceived, after the model of Plato's Forms, as changeless, eternal and perfect. (It will be seen that I was trying to find accommodation for three different sorts of reality within the bounds of my universe – namely, matter, the creative activity of life, and immaterial values. It was in recognition of this trinity that I called my most substantial philosophical book *Matter, Life and Value*. (17)

Not surprisingly, when Joad's life hit hard times and the pressures of war tested his philosophy, things fell apart. 'Then came the war, and for the first time in my life the existence of evil in the world made its impact upon me as a positive and obtrusive fact. All my life it had been staring me in the face; now it hit me in the face.' What Joad was actually rejecting is important to note. Reject Christianity, Joad warned 'and you fall victim, as so many of us whose minds developed in an atmosphere of Left-Wing politics and Rationalist philosophy have fallen victim, to a shallow optimism in regard to human nature which causes you to think that the millennium is just around the corner waiting to be introduced by a society of perfectly psycho-analysed, prosperous Communists.' (18)

Joad's warning against the follies of historicism is well stated and entirely just. But one can hardly fail to notice that he was criticising the Marxist historicism as championed by the Left Book Club rather than the more tolerant and sophisticated liberal individualism that has always been the core principle of the RPA. As the RPA knew before the war, psychoanalysis and humanism make uneasy bedfellows. Joad's conversion was not a straightforward jump from materialist atheism to Christian belief. Joad had never been a straightforward materialist or an atheist. It was a transition from an unstable vitalist progressionism to a more cocooning assurance of personal destiny. And Joad's value as a convert fell away dramatically in 1948 when he was caught cheating the railways by travelling on a false ticket. After that he was quickly dropped from the influential BBC Brains Trust programme and became something of a pariah.

The other person we should consider here is J W Poynter, who in 1948 returned to the Roman Catholic Church he had already left twice previously. Poynter had converted to Roman Catholicism in 1907, left it in 1926, rejoined in 1934 and left again the following year. While a rationalist Poynter had performed a useful service of scouring the regional press for relevant news items and sending them on to the RPA, for which he received a retainer. He wrote quite regularly for the *Guide*, almost exclusively on the situation in the Roman Catholic Church. His general approach was to criticise the obscurantism and oppressiveness of the Papacy. Only a few months previously, Watts & Co had published a very useful little work by Poynter looking at a long line of Papal Encyclicals and criticising their social attitudes. But, in an article in the *Guide* of August 1948, Poynter referred to a period of illness which had given him the time to ponder things more closely than he had previously been able to do. Five years previously, the RPA had provided financial assistance for Poynter to receive hospital attention for acute rheumatism. Poynter also expressed concern at the rise of 'secular State totalitarianism', which had forced on him a review of his thinking. 'Not only have I concluded that such a strong religious force as the Roman Church is needed, but on re-examining its philosophy, theology, and historic credentials, I have formed the renewed belief that Catholicism is indeed the vehicle of divine Revelation.' (19) And that was that. The following month Poynter wrote again, and was even more frank. 'The fact seems to be that the dreadful ordeal of illness and domestic distress through which I have passed since 1946, and which is not yet ended, has thrown me back on old consolations.' (20)

Retrenchment and readjustment

The various public crises of confidence suffered by Joad and Poynter all served to shake the confidence of rationalists. It lent weight to the fear that rationalism was past its prime and contributed towards a gloomy feel in the *Literary Guide*. The decline in membership continued steadily each year, loyally tracking the evermore unhealthy condition of Watts & Co. Clearly some drastic changes were needed, and needed soon, if disaster was to be averted.

Disaster was averted, but only just. The one thing Fred Watts did not inherit from his father was a sturdy constitution. When he finally succeeded his father in 1946 at the age of 50, Fred Watts was already an ill man. Right through the war years Fred Watts had been working a punishing six and a half day week at twelve hours a day. In 1948 he suffered a major stroke, described in the *Guide* as 'a complete breakdown, due to continued overstrain' and was out of action for several months. (21) The death of his daughter, Doreen, on Boxing Day in 1948, considerably aggravated his condition and, more important, his enthusiasm. Adam Gowans Whyte occupied the chair of the Board of Directors, first in his capacity as vice-chairman and later, once it was apparent that Watts would not be back for a while, as Acting Chairman. But this could not be a lasting solution as Whyte was himself an old man, twenty-one years older than Fred Watts, in fact. The real power was devolved onto Constance Kerr (1915-1982), in whom Watts had considerable confidence. From his sickbed, Watts urged the Board to appoint her Deputy Managing Director. Steps were taken to provide Kerr with the hundred shares required by any member of the Board. Watts's confidence in Kerr was amply reciprocated; in fact she loved him. When she retired in 1975, Constance Dowman, as she was then, made formal acknowledgement of only two people, Fred Watts and George Dowman, in that order. Kerr married George Dowman, another RPA member, a year after Watts' death. (22)

Ensuring Kerr's position was not going to solve the problems of the succession. Watts had not sired a son and his daughter was not inclined to follow him. The last thing the RPA needed was a sick and elderly man hanging on grimly to the bitter end. In 1952 he relinquished the Chair to Joseph Reeves MP, who, while only having come on the Board the year before, was nonetheless the best choice. In the middle of 1953 Watts relinquished the editorship of the *Guide* and *Rationalist Annual* to Hector Hawton. A couple of months later, on October 21 1953, Fred Watts died at the age of only 57. Watts was not keen on Hawton, and neither were his close friends and allies, Constance Kerr and Charles Bradlaugh Bonner. They would have preferred someone else to have succeeded him, but there was no one else with Hawton's ability, and they knew it. Watts had never really recovered from the stroke he suffered in 1948 and his last years were a constant battle against weakness and pain. He had literally worked himself to death for the RPA. Nonetheless, his contribution to an effective transfer of power was invaluable. The Watts era of the RPA was over.

Fred Watts had laid down bold plans for the postwar years, but it was his fate to see few of them come to fruition. Little did Watts know how much further the retrenchment would have to go. If there was anyone still doubting the need for change, it must have been dispelled by a precocious young man by the name of

David Stewart. Shortly before his death Fred Watts had inaugurated an annual essay contest designed for people under thirty years of age. Each year a question was set and in 1956 the question was simply entitled 'The Future of the RPA'. Stewart wasted no time. He was critical of the quality of the average RPA member, employing a term originally used by R C Churchill and later employed by Antony Flew. The average RPA member, Stewart wrote, could be likened to Darwin's Witnesses.

> When Darwin's Witnesses come together their programme too often consists of stories of the latest embarrassments of the Churches, particularly that of Rome, and suitably pre-digested titbits of Biblical criticism, theology, and some of the natural sciences, just detailed enough to be useful ammunition but not so much as to require any effort to assimilate…The RPA has a small membership, not because the country is predominantly hostile, but because only a few of the existing rationalists have ever heard of it, and even fewer are sufficiently attracted to want to join. The very toleration and lack of fanaticism which makes them sympathetic with rationalism also renders them very difficult to get as members of such a group as the RPA. Because of this, the RPA may go out of existence fairly soon. (23)

Stewart's solution was to transform the RPA into a sort of open university, so that members might truly appreciate the world of science and the scientific attitude. Stewart's solutions attracted little attention, but his diagnosis did. Hawton referred to it on several occasions during critical periods of change within the RPA.

But it was one thing for a young student to articulate the problem. It was another thing altogether to implement necessary changes. The RPA was very fortunate that Hawton had come along. He deserves to counted among the top handful of significant, intelligent and effective leaders the movement has produced. Hawton's path to rationalism was slightly unusual in that he converted to Roman Catholicism while at school after being brought up in a strongly anti-Catholic Calvinist household. Hawton was raised on the Bible, Bunyan's *Pilgrim's Progress* and *Foxe's Book of Martyrs* but, as a teenager, was bewitched by the sumptuousness of Catholic worship. He remained in the Catholic Church for about fifteen years, studying theology and philosophy along the way. These studies proved the undoing of his Catholicism and the young Hawton worked as a journalist and author in the years leading up to the Second World War. His first disillusionment with Catholicism came when he read Cardinal Newman proposing that it would be better for the entire universe to be destroyed than for one inconsequential sin to be committed. After that his passage out of the Catholic Church was relatively quick. He was introduced to the RPA by Hyman Levy, an important early influence on him. The two first met after the publication of Levy's *The Universe of Science* in 1932. Levy further influenced the young Hawton through his introduction to Marxism, written for the Left Book Club, called *A Philosophy for a Modern Man*. Having rejected Catholicism, Hawton was not likely to stay for long in its secular equivalent, and he soon drifted away from Marxism.

Hawton saw himself as an amateur. It was always a bit of a sore point for him that he had not been to university. In an appreciation of H G Wells on the centenary of his birth, Hawton described Wells as the 'last of the really great amateurs'. Hawton continued:

> As an amateur myself, albeit a very ordinary one, I can't rejoice at the extinction of the species to which I belong. Obviously science has become so complex that there is nothing much for an amateur to do outside natural history. One-man encyclopaedias are as dead as the dinosaurs... Today, nobody who is not at least an assistant lecturer in a university would dare express an opinion in public on a philosophical problem – if, indeed, it is still believed that any remain. (24)

Hawton was correct about the threat of extinction of the generally educated polymath. So far this genus has survived, although the ecosystems in which they can flourish are being destroyed at an alarming rate. Humanism has traditionally been one of the most welcoming environments for such people. Hawton was an endangered species in another sense as well. He was a rationalist in the traditional sense of seeing an important link between truth and morality. 'The question is not whether the traditional doctrines are useful, either socially or morally, but whether they are true. Once we find ourselves doubting their truth it is beneath human dignity to take refuge in evasions and subterfuges.' (25) Hawton had found himself in this position, like Joseph McCabe before him. And, also like McCabe, Hawton took what to both of them seemed the only honourable step: he followed the dictates of his conscience and left the church.

The other remarkable man who worked hard at this crucial time in the RPA's history was Joseph Reeves (1888-1969). When the dying Fred Watts relinquished the Chair of the Board of Directors in 1952, he must have been consoled that it went to a man like Reeves. As with many life-long rationalists, Reeves was born and raised in relative poverty. His background was with the Ethical movement and the Independent Labour Party, which he joined in 1914. A life-long pacifist and co-operator, Reeves was of the school of Robert Owen and George Jacob Holyoake. He contributed articles fairly regularly to the *Literary Guide* through the thirties before being elected as a Labour and Co-operative MP for Reigate in 1945 and remained in parliament until 1959. Reeves has the distinction of having introduced in 1953 the first Bill on abortion in the House of Commons. It was successfully scuppered by opposition led by Catholic MPs. Reeves joined the RPA Board in February 1951 and Hawton only in April 1953.

Between them, Reeves and Hawton saved the RPA. Overseeing retrenchment is a thankless task at the best of times, but Reeves and Hawton saw that there was no other way. Whereas the founders of a successful organisation undertake the heroic tasks of building new structures, it is left to the next generation of leaders to dismantle structures that grow unwieldy. Most operations of the RPA desperately needed this sort of attention. One of the first reforms overseen by the newcomers involved the voting system on the Board of Directors. Ever since 1899, the number of votes Directors could cast depended on the amount they paid in subscription. Hawton and Reeves brought in a simple one person, one vote system. More fraught was the first round of economies; they began before Fred Watts formally relinquished control. *The Free Mind* was axed in 1949 and *The Thinker's Digest* the following year. 1953 saw the demise of the short-lived Thrift

Books series and the following year the Thinker's Library was formally put to rest. But these were all relatively minor economies, amounting to little more than one or two loss-making adjuncts being extinguished and some expensive projects not being undertaken. The problems were considerably more deep-seated than these trimmings could solve by themselves. If the continual haemorrhaging was to be stopped, then much more drastic changes were needed.

Obviously the main source of the haemorrhaging was Watts & Co itself, its staff and its capacious headquarters. Not only were the company's publications not making a profit, but the 32 staff at the large headquarters at 5 and 6 Johnson's Court were becoming a significant drain on funds. Among the staff was a full-time artist, something larger firms like Allen & Unwin did not have. (26) In 1952 the deficit on operating costs reached £22,000. So significant were the losses becoming that drastic action was required very soon, or there would be nothing left to save. Between 1946 and 1953 Watts & Co lost £89,510 and investments of £118,000 had shrunk to £56,000, with a corresponding drop in income from those investments. (27) There are some pitiless economic laws that conspire against small publishing ventures, and Watts & Co was beginning to feel the full force of these laws.

Hawton and Reeves made the brave decision that the RPA should take over the running of Watts & Co directly and that it should be downsized. This allowed the headquarters at 5 and 6 Johnson's Court and another piece of property at Pemberton Row to be sold. This cannot have been an easy decision. The Johnson's Court properties had been acquired between 1903 and 1929 and were the most tangible symbol of the RPA's triumph against the odds. It must have been a dreadful wrench for the RPA Directors to sell these properties, but they really had no choice. Located as they were just off Fleet Street, and during a building boom in the area, the buildings were not difficult to sell. The sale was agreed in October 1954. The RPA did reasonably well, both properties going for £50,000, although the nett profit from the transaction was only £20,462. Just as important was the saving on wages, as only eight of the 32 staff survived the transition from Johnson's Court, and this figure soon reduced still further. In March 1955 the move to the new, leased, premises at 40 Drury Lane was made. The rent was £850 a year and £250 in rates. The building had room for the library, a shop on the ground floor, and Board Room. The RPA remained there until 1967.

But it was not long before it was apparent that even these difficult decisions had not been enough to reverse the RPA's financial difficulties. Taking over the direct management of Watts & Co had at least ensured an unbroken chain of command and put an end to the artificial division between it and the RPA. Hawton had moved decisively on this, beginning the process within days of Fred Watts's death, and in full knowledge of his opposition to the plan. But Hawton was convinced that only if Watts & Co was directly in the hands of the RPA Board could its future be assured, either by turning its losses into profits, or by being able to sell the company if it should come to that. That Hawton had the second option in mind is suggested by his being primarily responsible for creating a new publishing company while still owning Watts & Co. The story goes that, when searching for a name for the new firm, Hawton looked out of the window of its office at Pemberton Row, just around the corner from Johnson's Court, and saw the street sign. The new firm was called Pemberton Publishing Company. This was in 1954.

147

In its eight years of direct ownership the RPA failed to turn the losses of Watts & Co around. Indeed, they had continued to mount. Book sales had slumped generally since the war, and no exception had been made for material from Watts & Co. In April 1954, to take one example, Watts & Co's overdraft was £3,300 and was expected to reach £4000. It wasn't that Watts & Co was publishing poor works, although, as we have seen, the quality was uneven. The problem was simply one of scale. Watts & Co was not big enough to advertise sufficiently to justify a large print run. Two examples, taken at random, will suffice to illustrate the problem. *The English Sunday*, a non-specialist study of restrictive legislation and custom regarding Sunday trading and entertainment, by R C Churchill, was published in 1954. Two thousand copies of this work were printed, involving the total capital outlay of £399. But for costs of production to be met, let alone a profit to be realised, 2210 copies needed to be printed. From the same year came *Rationalism in Theory and Practice* by Archibald Robertson. Five thousand copies of this booklet were printed, total capital outlay being £351. But for that outlay to be recovered, more than seven thousand copies would have to be printed.

Reeves and Hawton co-wrote a series of plain-speaking reports on the state of the RPA's finances to the Directors at the end of 1954 and beginning of 1955. After speaking with some respected publishing executives sympathetic to rationalism, notably Michael Joseph, Hawton and Reeves approached Tavistock Publications with a view to their taking over the work of Watts & Co. However, this partnership was not a success, and ended acrimoniously in March 1958. The RPA felt that Tavistock had marketed its books poorly, but Tavistock was angered by the RPA continuing to operate independent of them through Pemberton Publishing. It also transpired that Tavistock was in considerable financial difficulty and withheld a payment of over £4000 to the RPA. The RPA was then obliged to reduce this debt by £1500 because of its dealings with Pemberton Publishing. There was fault on both sides, and nobody emerged a winner. In a report to the Board of Pemberton Publishing in the middle of 1957 Hawton concluded pessimistically that it 'is now obvious that for us to regard the publication of general books as a source of income is a delusion' (28) He recommended that for a period of three years publishing activity be restricted to humanist propaganda.

So it was with a mixture of sadness and relief that Watts & Co, with all its associated debts, was sold to Sir Isaac Pitman & Sons in 1960. Negotiations with Pitman & Sons began soon after the relationship with Tavistock ended in 1958. The Directors were anxious to assure members that this did not mean the end of rationalist publishing. Having faced opposition from some of the older members while the earlier economies were being made, the Directors were somewhat defensive. 'Obviously', went the Annual Report for 1960, 'it is not necessary to own a publishing company in order to finance the publication of books. The number of titles we shall make available in future will be determined both by our circumstances and the response of our members.' (29) And neither were the Directors of Sir Isaac Pitman & Sons unaware of the goodwill attached to the Watts & Co name, especially the Thinker's Library. In 1962 they began a series under the editorship of Raymond Williams called The New Thinker's Library, which included a fulsome tribute to the Thinker's Library. This series included some works destined to become classics of scholarship, such as Bryan

Wilson's *Religion in Secular Society*, Tom Bottomore's *Elites and Society*, Geoffrey Barraclough's *An Introduction to Contemporary History* and A Boyce Gibson's *Muse and Thinker*.

Even after the sale of Watts & Co, Pemberton was not brought into use. It was decided in 1961 that it would be more economical to enter into arrangements with existing publishing firms for the publication of rationalist and humanist material. This arrangement had worked well with *The Humanist*, which was published by H I Thompson Press Ltd. So, a similar sort of agreement was made for the publication of books with the small firm of Barrie & Rockliff. The outstanding success of this liaison was *The Humanist Anthology*, edited by Margaret Knight.

The End of the *Literary Guide*

What to do with the *Literary Guide* was just as difficult a question as the problems of accommodation and publishing. The *Guide* had gone through a drastic downsizing forced upon it in 1942, but enjoyed nonetheless a significant rise in readership throughout the war. But once the membership started falling away after 1947, it had few answers. In 1949 the *Guide* had a minor facelift, but its general range of articles did not change significantly. In 1951 Fred Watts sent out a questionnaire to readers in an attempt to gauge the new mood. He confessed to feeling uneasy that 'his assumptions about his readers' tastes are becoming a trifle arbitrary; his postbag sometimes confirms this view, for freethinkers tend to be free speakers.' (30) As anyone who has edited a journal will know, this exercise provided few clues to the road ahead. There was a general trend of comment in favour of the book reviews, but no clear preferences in most other areas. Those worried the *Guide* was soft on religion evenly matched the numbers thinking the *Guide* spent too much time criticising religion.

Joseph Reeves expanded on this general malaise in an article called 'Our Future' in the *Rationalist Review* of March 1955.

> The Directors became convinced that a certain traditional rigidity of attitude to publishing and to propaganda generally was failing to arouse the interest even of those outsiders whose views were in tune with our own, leave alone those who were apathetic to freethought. We knew that in the field of propaganda a much more scientific and, in many cases, a more subtle method of influencing the minds of people was being employed by agencies and institutions desirous of obtaining support. (31)

Once the retrenchment bug is caught, it can often become quite intoxicating, as anyone who has lived through the 1980s will testify. Reeves and Hawton would have been excused if they had extended their downsizing to take in the *Guide*. But they thought differently. Under Hawton's leadership, the *Guide* was transformed and money was put into it. It was consciously transformed into the principal organ of rationalist thought. (32) And Hawton had been brought onto the Board in 1953 specifically to take over the editorship of the *Guide*. Yet again Fred Watts deserves credit for his forbearance. It is not common that people should willingly recognise their incapacity to respond to new challenges and see in a younger person the ability one lacks. Watts, to his great credit, did have this ability. The old-style *Guide* had not been an attractive prospect for a wider circulation and he knew it. And each issue was produced at a loss and he knew that too.

The new-look *Guide*, however, was a different proposition. It rose from 16 to 32 pages, acquired a coloured cover and widespread use of photographs and illustrations. But without doubt the most significant change was the broadening of the journal's outlook. The *Guide* was now much more likely in its new format to appeal to the curious buyer at the newsstand. After the sounding out of some contacts of Reeves at the publishing firm of Odhams, Iain Thompson of H I Thompson Press was approached to take over the printing and distribution of the magazine. Thompson (1900-1970) later joined the Board of Directors and contributed relevant knowledge to help arrest the constant drain on finances. While Fred Watts was able to support many of the changes being made, he was opposed to the severing of Watts & Co from the distribution of the *Guide*. This change had to wait until his death to be implemented. Watts feared that the distribution system was going to run away with money without producing the desired results. He wrote a memorandum to that effect to the RPA board, dated October 20 1953, the day before his death. Charles Bradlaugh Bonner agreed with him and resigned from the Board in December 1953, having circulated to members his misgivings over the matter.

Watts and Bonner were both right and wrong. They were right, as it turned out, about the distribution exercise being a lot more expensive than Thompson had calculated. It required printing significantly larger stocks of each issue as well as a generous advertising budget over a reasonable period of time to build up a readership of 10,000, the number thought necessary to sustain this level of investment. (33) This expenditure placed heavy demands on depleted funds. After a year the attempt to distribute the *Guide* commercially was dropped. But the failure of this experiment does not totally vindicate the conservatism of Watts and Bonner. It was worth trying. Ironically, one of the reasons for the failure of the distribution scheme was one not foreseen by anybody. Despite these improvements the experiment to secure newsstand distribution of the *Guide* was not successful. More important than that, though, was the problem of the journal's name. The dilemma of the *Literary Guide* was discussed intelligently in the February 1956 issue of its instalment, the *Rationalist Review*. Though untitled, the piece was almost certainly by Hawton. 'We learned, for example, that many people who bought the *Guide* casually from the bookstalls found that it was not at all what the title had led them to expect. It was not a literary Baedeker, but a commentary from a somewhat unpopular point of view.' This meant that the *Guide* could go in one of two directions: 'either to dilute the 'rationalism' so that the *Guide* could be read contentedly in a country vicarage or increase the strength of the mixture in the hope of attracting the interest of those already in sympathy with our point of view.'

> Clearly the first direction was out of the question, but the second direction was not without difficulties either. To begin with, the traditional questions which brought rationalists together in the nineteenth century were no longer live issues. The criticism of religion, in other words, was no longer enough. The Britain of the

> 1950s included many millions of people for whom religion played no significant part in their lives. The issues that concerned them revolved around hydrogen bombs and the paradox of scientific progress being both a curse and a blessing. They are exasperated with antiquated laws which hold up common-sense reforms in regard to divorce, euthanasia, abortion, and so on. A rational approach to the modern world should throw new light on such problems as capital punishment and the treatment of criminals, sexual offenders and juvenile delinquents generally. (34)

Hawton was aware that to discuss these topics would inevitably mean entering the political arena, and this the *Guide* resolved to do, although it promised to remain strictly neutral with regard to party politics. This, very broadly, has been the policy of the RPA's journal ever since.

Strangely enough, these substantial changes were made with relatively little fuss. The most emotionally charged issue Hawton had to face was the change of name. As he observed, the title *Literary Guide* served only to confuse the general browser at the magazine stalls. What was need was a title which would be a successful branding exercise without appearing unnecessarily dogmatic or old-fashioned. Quite obviously the only feasible alternative was 'Humanist'. It was the label freethought was being given by Christian and media commentators and it was the title new freethought groups around Britain were using. All this notwithstanding, many people found this transition very difficult to come to terms with. For a significant minority of members, especially the older veterans, humanism meant an anaemic sort of compromise. No less a person than A E Heath, President of the RPA until the end of 1954, then Vice-president (having stood down to allow Bertrand Russell to take the presidency), expressed his concern about 'humanism' in these terms. Heath had a regular column in the *Rationalist Review* insert to the *Guide*. In October 1955 Heath expressed his misgivings.

> I am not entirely happy about the current fashion of substituting the word 'humanism' for 'rationalism'…My hesitancy comes from an uneasy feeling that there are forms of pietistic humanism which provides an excuse for wavering rationalist wills – an escape from refreshing cold showers of reason by those who need it (and who know they need it) but shrink from straying outside the Religious Umbrella. (35)

Here is the same fault line of discord that became noticeable between Charles Bradlaugh and George Jacob Holyoake a century earlier and which we have followed throughout this book. It is the fundamental abolitionist-substitutionist divide rearing its head again. The irony is that Hawton was no more enamoured of 'humanism' than Heath was. The difference was that Hawton could read what was needed more acutely. In the final issue of the *Literary Guide*, Hawton (the piece is unsigned, but it is highly suggestive of Hawton) saluted the old name.

> When the *Literary Guide* was founded it served the valuable purpose of calling attention to unorthodox books which, in those days, were usually kept out of shop windows…But as far as books are concerned,

> it is not necessary to ask inside for information about freethought publications nowadays. Few publishers would hesitate to bring out a book dealing with religion from a secularist point of view if they thought it would sell. There is no under-the-counter trading, and no need to resort to brown paper wrappings. (36)

The following month, October 1956, Hawton rang in the new.

> Humanists, rationalists, freethinkers, do not differ because they wear different labels. They are members of a movement that is influencing society in a certain way. As individuals, of course, they do not always come to the same conclusions. Yet, despite this diversity, the general effect of combining is to create a current of opinion in a very definite direction. The direction is away from otherworldly goals and towards the maximum realisation of human problems here and now. Wishful thinking is exchanged – as far as we are able to do so – for reality thinking, not because we are opposed to pleasures, but because no lasting satisfaction can be obtained by make-believe. (37)

As if to illustrate the symbolic nature of the dispute over the change of name, the last cover illustration of the *Literary Guide* was a painting of Thomas Paine and the illustration on the first cover of *The Humanist* was a photograph of the Museum of the History of Religion and Atheism in Kazan Cathedral in Leningrad.

The struggle to change the name was an important symbolic struggle for the RPA and for the freethought movement generally. But it was only one feature of a magazine which Hawton had successfully transformed in his three years' editorship. For one shilling, the reader was introduced to a remarkable range of intelligent material. The inaugural issue of *The Humanist* made no other significant alterations or additions, and can be taken as representative of the magazine at this stage. The first point to note was the range of articles. After Hawton's editorial and regular commentary called 'Personally Speaking', the lead article went to Margaret Knight, who reviewed current Christian apologetics, followed by Joseph Reeves surveying the inequity of the laws relating to abortion. Then came articles on the relationship between socialism and the British Labour Party, a review article on V Gordon Childe's latest work on archaeology, and a piece on Norbert Weiner, the founder of cybernetics. Following that A D Cohen reviewed a series of radio programmes on George Bernard Shaw, the RPA Annual Conference of the year was covered, and an intelligent summary of contemporary Chinese thought came next. Donald MacRae, a sociologist from the London School of Economics, examined the changing English village while Archibald Robertson translated some poems of Catullus, Hyman Levy remembered his world in 1900 and Antony Flew discussed Hobbes' *Leviathan*. There followed a page of letters to the editor, news of humanist activities around Britain and the regular crossword and advertisements for lectures and discussions held by various humanist bodies. Advertisements were carried for books by publishers Lawrence & Wishart and Rider, Collet's Bookshops and, of course, Watts & Co. All for one shilling.

In the years to come Hawton maintained this standard of *The Humanist*. Over his period as editor a very impressive range of intellectuals, covering a wide range of interests and disciplines, wrote for his journal: Antony Flew, Ernest Gellner, A J Ayer, Donald MacRae, Iris Murdoch, Kingsley Amis, E H Hutten, Ninian Smart, Herbert Dingle, Robin Odell, Colin Wilson. During Hawton's editorship *The Humanist* was the premier humanist magazine in the world. But not only did Hawton have the qualities to find and retain talented writers, he wrote an extraordinary amount of quality material himself. He used no fewer than six pseudonyms: 'Humphrey Skelton' focused on matters philosophical and historical, while 'George Robinson' was more concerned with social issues. 'James Plender' commented on questions of humanist thinking and kept an eye on Rome while 'Jonathan Yeo' had occasional forays into literature. 'W B Pengelly' was the odd-job man. But it was 'R J Mostyn' who was given the biggest assignments. 'Mostyn's' career began in 1953 and ended in 1969. He was the only Hawton pseudonym to feature regularly as a cover teaser and to appear in the *Rationalist Annual*. It was 'Mostyn', for example, who ran some sceptical articles about Julian Huxley's evolutionary humanism and who gave the first response from *The Humanist* to J A T Robinson's *Honest to God*, which was released to a blaze of publicity in 1963. One can't help but imagine that on at least one occasion someone must have lamented to Hawton Mostyn's continual absence from RPA gatherings.

Christian reaction to the age-old lie

Following, as we have in this chapter, the readjustment of the RPA to difficult new circumstances, it would be tempting to assume that the prospects of the churches were improving. This, of course, was not the case. If the conditions for rationalism were unfavourable in the post-war years, those of the churches were no better. In his survey of Anglicanism, written for Penguin and published in 1958, Stephen Neill concluded that when looking honestly at the state of the Churches one 'cannot help escape the temptation to anxiety, discouragement, or even despair.' (38) The churches themselves recognised this point in their alarmist report, issued in 1945, entitled *Towards the Conversion of England*. This is a remarkable document. Among its findings and chief claims are:

- Only 10% to 15% of Britons are regular churchgoers
- even among the converted, an improvement in their spiritual condition is needed
- the standard of preaching throughout the Church is 'deplorably low'
- the Church is irrelevant to much of society
- the Church's message is confused and uncertain
- a whole generation has been 'suckled on agnosticism'

It is important to note, once again, that this is what the RPA was saying in 1899, and that the same Church of England, which later produced *Towards the Conversion of England*, was scornful of it for making such outrageous claims. The dismal situation the churches found themselves in encouraged a bitter tone in their apologetics. *Towards the Conversion of England* denounced humanism as an 'age-old lie' and the commission recommended a £1m publicity campaign to arrest the decline in the Church's public standing. The commission called for a series of textbooks on the entire range of secular subjects written from an openly Christian perspective. The report quoted C S Lewis's lament that 'no evangelism can have wide success against the continual glut of cheap scientific books written on atheistic principles.' Adam Gowans Whyte was compelled to reply

> Why not? The Thinker's Library consists of little more than a hundred volumes, and if we add the more or less similar volumes included in other excellent series of cheap publications the total number is still only a fraction of the output of religious works. (39)

Towards the Conversion of England both annoyed and delighted the rationalists. They were annoyed by the duplicity of the Church, which only the year before had noisily agreed with Conservative politicians that the country was indeed a Christian one, thus legitimising the imposition of Christian indoctrination in schools. While campaigning in this way, the church leaders knew perfectly well that this was not the case and that in only a few months' time, they would be admitting as much. Religious instruction in schools was not just a recognition of the strength of Christianity in Britain; it was a desperate gambit by the religious establishment to halt any further decay in its already weak hold on the minds of the people. On the other hand, the report was a source of pride to rationalists. In a pamphlet as part of the Thinker's Forum, Archibald Robertson concluded that the 'brute fact remains that in spite of its position of social, political, economic, and educational privilege, the Church has lost its hold on the people.' (40)

It was in the spirit of *Towards the Conversion of England* that two series of apologetic works were launched, both in 1948. One of them, published by Paternoster and called the Second Thoughts Library, was heavily influenced by the Thinker's Library. There was no doubting whom the reader was being encouraged to have second thoughts about. Despite several changes in design layout over its career, Rodin's Thinker remained the icon for the Thinker's Library. It is due to the influence of the Thinker's Library that Rodin's Thinker has become one of the enduring images of rationalism and humanism. The Second Thoughts Library knew this perfectly well when it press-ganged Rodin's Thinker into service. Not one, in fact, but two. Their logo featured a blurry Thinker being replaced by a second, identical, Thinker in front of it and in sharp relief. Underneath this image was the slogan 'second thoughts are best'. The back cover of volume one announced itself in these terms.

> Under the capable editorship of Dr Clark, THE SECOND THOUGHTS LIBRARY provides in handy, inexpensive and well-produced volumes the results of fresh investigations into the many aspects of knowledge that bear upon faith, conducted and presented in that spirit of reverence that always characterises true scholarship.

The series editor, Dr Robert E D Clark, contributed the first and fifth volumes on evolution and cosmology respectively, while F F Bruce wrote three books for the series on the origins of Christianity. The arguments of these apologists had not moved ahead from those of Frank Ballard and Charles Loring Brace half a century before them. Clark was content to write off natural selection as a specious attempt by Charles Darwin to avoid the argument to design (41) and Bruce stuck with the nineteenth-century story of Christianity as bringing light to a benighted heathen world.

The Second Thoughts Library petered out in 1952 after eight titles. Another series, also launched in 1948, fared no better. It was called Viewpoints and was from the Student Christian Movement (SCM). The people who wrote for Viewpoints were more prepared than their Second Thoughts colleagues to make concessions on issues like evolution, bible criticism, the argument to design and so on. They preferred the experiential approach: one cannot really discover whether religion is true except by becoming religious, claimed the Bishop of Bristol, Dr F A Cockin in *Does Christianity Make Sense?* But Viewpoints lasted no longer than the Second Thoughts Library.

While Viewpoints had a short life, SCM emerged as a publishing operation to rival the RPA. Some of the most noteworthy and intellectually respectable discussions and criticisms of religion in the 1950s came from SCM. Amid all the works of Karl Barth, John Macquarrie and Martin Heidegger, SCM also published *New Essays in Philosophical Theology* (1955) edited by Antony Flew and Alasdair MacIntyre, three essays by MacIntyre, Stephen Toulmin and Ronald Hepburn under the title *Metaphysical Beliefs* (1957) and *Problems of Religious Knowledge* (1959) by Peter Munz. By far the most academically respectable work from Watts & Co at this time was a work called *Christianity and Paradox* (1958) by Ronald Hepburn, which sought to criticise Christian theology in the light of analytical philosophy. The newly-found ability of SCM to publish works critical of aspects of Christian thinking had two effects. On the one hand it helped take the role of criticising Christianity away from the rationalists, who up until then had largely been responsible for this thankless task. But on the other, SCM also helped to galvanise the more reactionary Christians, who found any accommodation to new realities upsetting. This hardening of attitudes helped contribute to the quite distinct liberal and fundamentalist Christianities that exist at the beginning of the twenty-first century, and which have increasingly little to say to each other.

While much of this sort of controversy would have been familiar to the veterans of 1899, the 1950s brought on a new and soon-to-become explosively influential mood. Its most eloquent spokesman of the time was Aldous Huxley (1894-1963). As would be expected of the brother of Julian, Aldous was not unfamiliar with the RPA. His series of essays, *Do What You Will*, was reprinted by Watts & Co as No. 56 of the Thinker's Library in 1936. But both brothers veered off on an eccentric trajectory after that, Aldous more especially. This became apparent to all when *The Doors of Perception* was published by Chatto & Windus in 1954, in which Huxley wrote of his mystical experiences while under the influence of mescalin. In his review of the book, Antony Flew noted the incongruity of Huxley advocating the need for a 'chemical vacation from intolerable selfhood and repulsive surroundings' when the same man had warned us in *Brave New World* of the dulling effects of the drug soma on the populace. While not opposed in principle to mind-expanding drugs, Flew was strongly critical of Huxley's narcissism.

> No doubt it did all seem desperately important and significant at the time: and that is one more clinical fact about mescalin. But why should any of this be taken as a revelation of anything at all except the possibility of unfamiliar varieties of experience and the effects of taking four-tenths of a gramme of mescalin? Huxley offers no reasons whatsoever. (42)

After Huxley's death in November 1963, Hector Hawton paid tribute to his prodigious ability but lamented his later drift to mysticism in books like *The Perennial Philosophy* and *The Doors of Perception*. This provoked Julian Huxley to write in defence, claiming his brother to be have been 'perhaps the greatest Humanist of our age, certainly the one with the most comprehensively illuminating vision.' (43) This exchange can, in retrospect, be seen as a graphic illustration of the problems the notion of humanism was to bring the movement.

The formation of the British Humanist Association

As we all know, solving one problem usually creates a new series of problems that quickly seem just as or even more intractable. If the *Literary Guide* had given way to *The Humanist* on the grounds of relevance, reaching a wider audience and maintaining academic quality, then could the same need not be felt for the RPA itself? It didn't take long for that question to assert itself. On a more practical level, it was becoming obvious to most freethought organisations in Britain at the time that there was a wasteful competition between them for members. With these issues in mind, the RPA and Ethical Union began tentative negotiations with a view to finding a way around the impasse. It has to be said that the Ethical Union took the initiative in this, leaving the RPA to shamble along in its wake. Harold Blackham (1903-), secretary of the Union, invited the RPA to send a delegate to a conference on the future of humanism to be held in Worcestershire in July of 1950, but no Director was interested in going. Only a month after receiving the invitation did A D Howell Smith agree to attend.

At the same time as the conference, Hector Hawton, in his capacity as secretary of the South Place Ethical Society, invited the RPA to take part in a coordinating body called the Humanist Council. The Council was Hawton's idea. It was to meet quarterly and consist of representatives of the RPA, Ethical Union and SPES. It met for the first time on September 18 1950. The RPA committed itself rather grudgingly to covering some secretarial costs the Council would incur but advised the Council it 'could not give any further material help such as office facilities and clerical assistance.' (44) Disagreements soon arose over whether the Council was merely a vehicle for finding new members for the constituent bodies or out to pursue objectives of its own. The Directors decided, without much enthusiasm, to persevere with the Council for a while. Despite this discouraging start the Council worked effectively as a coordinating body for seven years before it was wound up. In 1953 the National Secular Society joined the Council.

In the meantime the RPA and Ethical Union established in 1955 a Joint Development Committee to examine the possibility of closer collaboration between the two groups, particularly in light of the forthcoming Second International Humanist and Ethical Union Congress (IHEU), due in 1957. This gathering was the occasion for the next vehicle of co-operation: the Humanist Association. The Humanist Association, made up of the RPA and the Ethical Union was to last a year, during which time further investigation into amalgamation would be undertaken. The RPA was as lukewarm to the Humanist Association as it had been to its predecessor. For instance, the Board decided not to extend RPA membership privileges to members of the Humanist Association. Nevertheless, the constituent bodies of the Humanist Association agreed on support for political action in favour of unilateral abolition of nuclear tests, condemnation of racial discrimination and support for the United Nations and 'rationally planned policy for raising the level of production and of social life in underdeveloped areas.' (45)

The next two years were spent discovering the significant obstacles to full amalgamation. For a start, the two organisations had different approaches and emphases. These were even outlined in a report of representatives of the three bodies of a reconstituted Humanist Council.

> The RPA, the NSS and the EU are independent organisations with separate aims. These special purposes might be described in a few words as follows:
>
> - The RPA: to produce and disseminate rationalist propaganda and to advocate a rational approach to current problems.
> - The NSS: to conduct militant and popular propaganda for secularism.
> - The EU: to build up a movement which offers a humanist alternative to the churches. (46)

There weren't simply different emphases to contend with. Many RPA members remembered the many legal problems which scuppered the proposed Rationalist Society just after the war. And then there was the problem of money. As Hector Hawton explained it to members in 1964, even 'if it were possible to transfer present assets to a new organisation, serious difficulties might arise when future legacies became due if the RPA no longer had a separate existence.' (47) From the earliest days, the RPA had been the beneficiary of substantial legacies and it had no reason to see this trend slowing down in the future. Were the RPA to lose its legal existence by merging with another organisation, these bequests could be challenged. There were also the moral problems of abandoning the organisation which all those people had donated money to and requiring life members to join a new organisation, which might have aims and objectives which they did not share. Yet another problem was that, in contrast to the RPA, the Ethical Union was a registered charity, a legacy from its beginnings as a religious organisation. This had important legal implications.

Notwithstanding the difficulties associated with full amalgamation, co-operation continued, albeit in fits and starts. The Humanist Association had not been a great success and in April 1959 it was replaced by a reconstituted Humanist Council. This new Council was expanded to include the National Secular Society, which remained suspicious of any suggestions of unnecessary accommodation with religious styles or idioms and was soon to withdraw from the process. Negotiations were slow and at one point the Ethical Union came close to sidelining the whole process by simply changing its name to the Humanist Union. They didn't go through with this in the end because they were satisfied the RPA was in the mood to make some accommodation with them. In particular, any closer union would require the RPA to gain the charitable status already enjoyed by the Ethical Union. This was not an easy process and charitable status was only acquired at the beginning of 1963 on the grounds of being a charity for the advancement of education. The question of having, or not having, charitable status has cast a shadow over the whole humanist movement since the war. One of the last vestiges of religious exclusivism is a belief that only religious organisations could possibly be charitable. For the RPA the rub has been between its role as a charity (whether of an educational or any other type) on the one hand and its commercial role as a publisher on the other. This was not a problem for similarly constituted religious bodies, of course. Charitable status conveys significant privileges, not least relief on local and other taxes and, after the Budget of 1965, charities were able to change their investments without incurring a Capital Gains Tax liability. 'Having finally acquired charitable status, the way was now clear,' Hawton noted in *The Humanist*, 'to join with the Ethical Union in forming a united front by sponsoring the British Humanist Association.' (48) The two organisations had already formed a Joint Standing Committee, and this now stepped up a gear by becoming a provisional committee for the proposed British Humanist Association.

The RPA and the Ethical Union had taken great care to map out in advance their respective spheres of influence. The RPA, sensibly enough, was to direct the BHA's publishing activities and secretarial work, while the Ethical Union was to oversee the formation of branches, organising of conferences, study courses and other educational activities. Financial obligations were carefully shared and an agreement was made to review the whole operation at the end of five years. The inaugural committee of the BHA included four members drafted from the RPA and four from the Ethical Union. But the public face of the movement was to be the BHA, through which all advertising, publicity, conferences, campaigns and membership activity was to be done.

Finally, the day arrived. On May 17 1963 about 200 people gathered at the House of Commons for the inaugural dinner of the BHA. The venue came as a result of Laurie Pavitt, MP acting as Parliamentary host. Sir Julian Huxley, A J Ayer, Baroness Wootton and Kingsley Martin addressed the gathering and an executive was appointed. Huxley became its president, Ayer the vice-president. Joseph Reeves became the chairman, Constance Dowman the secretary, with Hector Hawton and H J Blackham taking other positions. The first conference was arranged to be held at Nottingham University on the appropriate topic of 'The Meaning of Co-existence in East-West Relations'. A new era was dawning.

Honest to Whom?

Early in the 1960s, the irrelevance of virtually all Christian apologetic that had preceded it was revealed in a startling new work, not from a rationalist, but from a senior churchman. *Honest to God*, by J A T Robinson (1919-1983), Bishop of Woolwich at the time of writing, changed the religious debate in Britain forever. Significantly, *Honest to God* was published by SCM. Robinson was by no means an out-and-out radical. He reiterated constantly his reluctance to explore religion in the way that he was, but felt the situation demanded it. At the beginning of his book, Robinson acknowledged that, when listening to radio discussions between Christians and humanists, his sympathies often lay with the humanist. Given how rarely such debates had actually been permitted to take place in the media, Robinson must have been an assiduous listener.

Robinson went on to formulate a radical gospel influenced very heavily by Dietrich Bonhoeffer and Paul Tillich in particular. Robinson wanted us to abandon a notion of god 'out there' and embrace the god within. Once more, Robinson expressed sympathy for atheists, but went on to say that 'the God they honestly feel they cannot believe in, is so often an image of God instead of a God, a way of conceiving him which has become an idol.'(49) Whereas Huxley was calling for a religion without revelation, Robinson following Bonhoeffer, called for a Christianity without religion.

Reactions from the rationalist and humanist thinkers was muted. While it was gratifying to have support for their position expressed by a bishop, his solutions were hardly new. Was this not, pretty much, what Francis William Newman or Stanton Coit had been saying upwards of half a century before? The existentialist jargon was new, but the thoughts behind it were not. As Hector Hawton noted, Robinson's new version of God was as old as the Upanishads. Hawton brought out his most heavy-duty pseudonym, 'R J Mostyn', to illustrate the problems in *Honest to God* in the form of a mock dialogue between 'Smith' (theist) and 'Brown' (atheist). Hawton has Brown say:

> it seems to me that these new theologians have merely worked out a highly ingenious explanation of their reluctance to leave a Church in whose straightforward doctrines they can't quite believe. What I would call debunking they call demythologising. It sounds more polite, but in any case it is half-hearted. Modern secular man, as you call him, won't be able to make head nor tail of it. (50)

Hawton was proved right. The vast majority of the religious public rejected Robinson's deified humanism. Most of his colleagues distanced themselves from him as well, including the Archbishop of Canterbury. And indeed the Church of England has retreated more and more into reaction since then. Those embracing Robinson's views are little more than a liberal fringe at the edges of the church. Religious liberals have always been in the difficult position of recognising the force of the rationalist critique of religion while wanting to preserve some increasingly hollow religious essence.

Nowhere was this more clear than in another work of this period, *The Secular Meaning of the Gospel* by Paul van Buren, another title published by SCM. This work was given close examination by Antony Flew in *The Humanist* early in 1964, contrasting it favourably with the 'utterly muddled' *Honest to God*. But Flew could not help but comment on the thinness of van Buren's humanist Jesus, shorn of supernaturalist pretensions.

> One is tempted to comment that had this been all they had to say, and had they said it only in this way, they would not have succeeded in laying the foundations for a worldwide society; nor perhaps would they have been inclined to try. (51)

Several years after Robinson's book Margaret Knight wrote *Honest to Man*, a straightforward restatement of the rationalist critique of Christianity. After noting the tendency among liberal theologians to render as symbolic everything nonsensical or contradictory, Knight also observed that they 'employ the device known as 're-thinking', which involves, roughly speaking, re-stating traditional doctrines in such a way that they cease to be obviously false by becoming meaningless.' (52)

The criticisms of Flew and Knight were echoed, although with a greater level of bitterness, by the increasingly isolated defenders of Christian orthodoxy. C S Lewis had championed what *The Humanist* dubbed 'the new obscurantism' in the 1950s and lived just long enough to see all his work come crashing down in the wake of *Honest to God*. Lewis's main successors were Sir Arnold Lunn (1888-1974) and Garth Lean, who co-wrote a series of books at this time which criticised in equal measure religious liberals and humanists for their part in contributing to what they saw as a moral decline. In an interesting development, the traditional unwillingness to recognise the intellectual or moral integrity of the unbeliever was now extended to the religious liberal. Speaking of the liberals, Lunn and Lean noted acidly that they 'have, of course, rejected the infallibility of the Church and the infallibility of the Bible, and seem in many cases to have adopted instead the infallibility of their personal intuition.' (53)

What Robinson and van Buren's books did from the humanist perspective was to complicate the religious scene. On the one hand religious conservatives and fundamentalists continued to brandish the traditional biblical literalism, while on the other hand the liberals sought to accommodate Christianity to the post-Copernican world. Humanists have tended to sympathise with the fundamentalists to a certain extent, because at least they are continuing to take the Christian creed at face value, with all the absurdities that this involves. The division between religious and non-religious worldviews reflects the fundamentally divergent views of the world implied by the naturalist and the supernaturalist philosophies. The conservative is accepting the full implications of the supernaturalist view, the liberal is wanting to have both the fuzziness and sentimentality of the supernaturalist worldview and the intellectual realism of the naturalist worldview. Religious conservatives and humanists generally agree that this position is untenable. But at the same time, the humanists are far more closely allied with the religious liberal's greater tolerance of diversity and respect for freedom of expression than religious conservatives have shown themselves to be. These tensions within organised Christianity have developed to such an extent that religious liberals and fundamentalists now operate largely independent of each other.

Towards freedom of the airwaves

In keeping with the slow opening up of Christian opinion-leaders to new ways of thinking, it is not surprising that a similar process should have taken place in the BBC. No real change was possible while Sir John Reith (dubbed 'that wuthering height' by Churchill) remained in charge; indeed, it took almost ten more years before any meaningful progress was made. The liberalisation process was given a boost in 1947 when a parliamentary deputation, organised by the RPA, submitted a memorandum to the BBC urging it to allow the same measure of controversy with regard to religious matters as permitted in most other areas. The BBC could clearly see the writing on the wall, and duly made the concession that 'affirmations of widely different beliefs and of unbelief can be made constructively'. (54) This was what rationalists had been saying and Reith had been denying for years. While this acknowledgement did not bring about a significant improvement in the access to the airwaves enjoyed by humanists, there was nonetheless a liberalising of attitudes to what was considered acceptable material for debate. In 1946, for instance, the BBC ran a series of 'lay sermons' on 'The Challenge of Our Time'. The assumption was that a growing chasm existed between the sciences and humanities and the talks were to analyse the differences. Of the ten who spoke, half were, or were to become, Honorary Associates of the RPA. (55) In May the following year, a similar series was run, this time with the title 'What I Believe'. Among the contributions was 'The Faith of a Rationalist' by Bertrand Russell, which quickly became a classic of rationalist literature. But by far the most significant breakthrough came about as a result of the persistence and courage of a woman from Aberdeen, and this story must wait until Chapter 8.

The new turn of events was fuelled largely by the newly formed Humanist Council/Humanist Association, which was involved in a lot more than attempts at merger. The Council also participated in forming the Humanist Broadcasting Council and promoted a well attended meeting at Caxton Hall condemning the BBC for its sectarian exclusion of humanist opinion or right of reply on radio and television. Joseph Reeves recalled in 1963 that the fairly regular deputations to the BBC about access received the same response: Britain is a constitutional monarchy and a Christian country and these are non-negotiable taboos. One such delegation approached the BBC in 1958, taking with it a memorandum calling for more openness and was signed by thirty prominent people, including Bertrand Russell, J B Priestley, E M Forster, Jacob Bronowski, Julian Huxley, even the Bishop of Sheffield. Among the delegation was Francis Williams, an ex-Governor of the BBC, who put forcefully the need for the BBC to represent all its constituents.

When the BBC eventually replied it rejected the proposal of a standing Humanist Advisory Committee but agreed to co-operate with a consultative body to be established with the Humanist Association. The BBC would not consider itself obliged to consult it 'but in so far as it was in their view broadly representative, they would be glad to avail themselves of it.' (56) The consultative group, which became known as the Humanist Broadcasting Council, was an impressive body, consisting of Julian Huxley, Lord Chorley, Morris Ginsberg, Cyril Bibby, Francis Williams, Norman Routledge and Robin Morris. It soon expanded to include A J Ayer, E M Forster, Margaret Knight, Bertrand Russell, Lionel Elvin and others. The Humanist Broadcasting Council went on to do some good work opening up the BBC to the realities of a pluralist society, but its impact was limited by the continued willingness of the Pilkington Report of 1962 to reiterate that the Christian churches 'have a special claim' to their privileged position.

Thanks largely to the Humanist Broadcasting Council humanists appeared on television occasionally in the early 1960s, albeit chaperoned by a bevy of Christians. One of the more successful of the council's ideas was a centenary re-enactment of the 1860 Huxley-Wilberforce debate, which placed the reality of the science-versus-religion debates before a much wider audience. This idea bore fruit in the form of the television programme *The Battle for Oxford*. But by this time society was moving faster than either the BBC or the humanists appreciated. It soon became apparent that earnest debates between knowledgeable disputants about this or that were far from riveting television. The attempted prosecution of Penguin Books in 1960 under the new Obscene Publications Act backfired on the reactionaries and created a climate for an easing of restrictions, rather than a hardening of them. More interesting still, in an era that spawned the delightful satires of *Beyond the Fringe*, earnest debates looked passé. So, the opening up of the airwaves resulted in something the humanists had not foreseen, namely that the new situation would also create a demand for entirely new styles of material for broadcast. This was even more pronounced once television replaced radio as the dominant mass communication medium.

The unravelling of the three-headed monster

In line with the positive developments towards freedom of the airwaves, the slow, even tortuous steps toward the creation of the British Humanist Association came to fruition in May 1963. But while the establishment of the BHA was a milestone in the history of freethought in Britain, it did not usher in a new age of humanism as some had hoped would happen. In fact, it didn't take long for the first set of problems to arise. The sponsorship of the BHA by the RPA and Ethical Union was hailed at the time as 'an eminently common-sense solution to a practical problem.' (57) But it very soon became an eminently messy addition to an existing problem. The problem was that people making enquiries about the BHA were also given the option to join either the RPA or the Ethical Union. Unfamiliar with the intricate ins and outs of freethought history, most general enquirers were bemused by the whole situation. If the RPA and Ethical Union still want members, some of them asked, why bother to set up the BHA at all? Where once a problem was acknowledged to exist with these two organisations, there were now three.

Criticism of the RPA soon arose from a new generation of younger, tertiary-educated activists who were increasingly impatient with what they saw as the stick-in-the-mud conservatism of the RPA. In April 1964, less than a year after the formation of the BHA, David Pollock (1942-) of the Oxford Humanist Group and one of the RPA's strongest critics criticised 'the present three-headed monster of the BHA, the RPA, and the EU...' (58) The article this comment appeared in had only gone ahead after a protracted and at times heated correspondence between its authors and Hawton, in his role as editor of *The Humanist*. The original version was clear in its advocacy of full merger between the RPA and Ethical Union into the BHA. In reply, Hawton seems weary.

> Although I am very willing to open the columns of *The Humanist* to a discussion of the formation of general policy and criticisms of our publications and activities, I am not willing to start a controversy about the 'merger' between the RPA and EU. If this passage is deleted I will use the rest of the article. I think that to reopen this old controversy about a merger would gravely damage the prospects of harmonious co-operation between the EU and the RPA and the successful operation of the five-year agreement into which the two bodies have entered. (59)

Hawton went on to add that either members of the BHA 'accept the existence (as well as the substantial contribution) of the RPA and agree to co-operate on the only terms that are possible, or the project will collapse.'

Pollock and his young allies were not prepared to accept this state of affairs. They put forward a radical motion at the RPA's 1964 Annual General Meeting in an attempt to hurry things along. Having outlined all the faults with the existing set-up, the motion called for the RPA to 'adopt as their object the legal and financial union of the RPA and EU under the title British Humanist Association'. (60) The RPA was in a no-win situation here. The Directors decided not to allow the motion to go to the meeting. They had good legal and procedural reasons for so doing, but such a gambit never wins hearts and minds. The RPA Directors had several objections to full merger. First there was the moral obligation to past benefactors of the RPA, and the threat of losing bequests from members in the future if the RPA lost its formal existence. Next there was the problem of life members, many of who were members of long standing (and likely benefactors) whose commitment was to rationalism and the RPA, not to humanism and the BHA. Related to this was the question of the substantial minority of RPA members who lived outside the United Kingdom. What to do with them? Clearly the BHA didn't hold the same attractions for members from Australia or South Africa as for members from Aldershot or South Shields.

But at heart, all these objections were window dressing. The real objection to merger among the RPA Directors was that they simply didn't want to. All the rational arguments were given regular airings, and were credible enough arguments. But the real objection was not a rational one. The ties were sentimental and emotional. They were deeply committed to the RPA and didn't want it to die. The best way to illustrate this attitude is to look briefly at two of the Directors of the time. Dr Ernest H Hutten (1908-1996) was a naturalised British citizen, having been born in Berlin to a Jewish family. His father was killed in action in the First World War. After active work as a young man in anti-fascist activities, Hutten was arrested and interned at Spandau. It was only thanks to some brave friends who provided forged papers that Hutten used to escape imprisonment and get to Britain. As a PhD in physics, he soon found gainful employment under the direction of Ernest Rutherford, but on his death Hutten moved to the United States. He returned to Britain after the war, having turned down lucrative employment in the American nuclear weapons programme. So it is not surprising that Hutten believed very strongly that the best safeguard against rigid orthodoxy is the existence of a variety of organisations with a variety of opinions and approaches. Hutten was a strong-minded, even difficult man, but one who had been through enough to make his intransigence more than understandable.

Another Director at the time was Frank Farr (1907-1979). Born to a militant working class London family, Farr saw active service as a volunteer with the British Battalion of the International Brigade during the Spanish Civil War. During that conflict he was powerfully impressed by the crucial support given to the fascists by the Catholic Church. Farr saw the criticism of religion as a central role for the RPA and was firmly of the belief that it should remain independent in order to do so unhindered. 'There can be no compromise with unreason' was Farr's view. (61) Men like Hutten and Farr were hard-boiled and not at all interested in pussy-footing around with talk of ultimate concern, Christian atheism and religious humanism. They were steeped in the history of the organisation and couldn't bring themselves to oversee its demise. Most of the Directors during this time had thirty years or more active service in the rationalist movement, much of it in the RPA. Many people will smile at this, seeing in it an admission that the rationalists weren't so rational after all. This is to misunderstand rationalism. No rationalist has ever said that all decisions, all thoughts, all commitments should be exclusively rational ones. Such a claim would be absurd. Charles Watts senior acknowledged fully that reason is not infallible as a guide, it is merely 'the best one known to us'. (62)

At the 1965 Annual General Meeting of the RPA, three young turks, Dr Peter Draper, Madeleine Simms and Graham Kingsley challenged Hyman Levy, Joseph Reeves and Lord Chorley respectively for their seats on the RPA Board. They were defeated decisively, mainly by proxy votes coming in from overseas and the provinces. This challenge is reminiscent of the Great Conway Hall Plot over three decades before. Both sets of reformers, those of the 1930s and the 1960s, championed a new understanding of freethought and were impatient with what they saw as the conservatism and intransigence of the older generation of office holders. Both sets of reformers were defeated and in both cases most of them stayed on and worked for the RPA for years to come.

As it happened, events conspired against both the RPA Directors and the young turks. The five-year agreement to co-sponsor the BHA came to a premature dissolution after only two years when the Ethical Union lost its charitable status in 1966. This forced the RPA to move quickly. If it lingered in sponsoring the BHA alongside an organisation which was no longer a registered charity, its own charitable status would be placed in jeopardy. It was not keen on exposing itself to this risk, and so had little choice but to withdraw its sponsorship of the BHA. This said, the RPA's tears had a crocodilian flavour about them. Withdrawing from this arrangement would put an end to the three-headed monster and cut off a source of criticism of its policies. Nevertheless, BHA members continued to receive the *Humanist* and *Rationalist Annual* free of charge. Over 1968 this situation was overhauled, but at the cost of members to the RPA as many members elected to remain with the BHA. Between September 1966 and September 1968 the RPA lost just under a thousand members, going down to 4681 members. RPA membership had reached its highest point in 1965 when it stood at 6500.

Into this gap stepped the ever-resourceful Ethical Union. At an Extraordinary General Meeting held on January 14 1967 it voted to change its name to the British Humanist Association. The new organisation resolved not to re-seek charitable status as it wished to campaign for law reform. The three-headed monster was dead, but all this meant was that the situation the RPA and Ethical Union found themselves in at the beginning of the fifties was no further ahead. And the problem was now beginning to escalate for all parties concerned, as membership of humanist bodies, the RPA included, began to fall alarmingly. The secular organisations were now about to pay the second instalment on the price of secularisation. The first instalment was paid before the First World War when the RPA introduced the publishing world to the reality of the market in serious non-fiction, which, as we saw, resulted in the diminution of its own role. The second instalment was even more costly, as it involved the ongoing relevance of humanist organisations in an increasingly secular society.

Chapter 6

A Voice in the Wilderness

'Our very success has turned against us...'
Nicolas Walter, 1975

The RPA was free again, to its evident relief. But, as the existentialists liked to say, with freedom comes loneliness and total responsibility, and the RPA was to feel both these forces in full measure. From 1968, its problems were to escalate dramatically. In the year of the massive student protests it was evident to all that change was underway, but there was uncertainty about the nature of the changes and of the direction the students wanted society to move. Hector Hawton was under no illusions at the time that a major reorientation of outlook was underway. He began an editorial in August 1968 on this very theme. 'The most disquieting explanation offered of student unrest is that basically it is a revolt against the liberal values of the great Rationalist tradition derived from John Stuart Mill.' Hawton ended the editorial with the same sense of unease.

> They believe that the whole of modern society has been so corrupted that it must be rejected. What would take its place is not clear – which distinguishes this view very sharply from Marxism. It is plain what the rebels want to destroy, and we cannot deny they have legitimate grievances. But it is folly to burn down your house in order to roast the pig. (1)

Up until 1968 the humanist movement had been a natural home for critics of the established order of society, but this was no longer the case. After 1968, humanism was liable to be seen, when it was seen at all, as just another of the fuddy-duddy old movements whose time had passed. Rationality was no longer the rebel's choice of weapon; choices now multiplied, the least constructive of them being dionysianism, miscellaneous spiritualities, nihilism and narcissism.

The RPA had been down this road before of course. As we saw in Chapter Four, many people in the 1930s thought that communism had replaced rationalism as the constructive, rational force of the future. This dream had slowly turned to dust through the 1950s and 1960s. The invasions of Hungary in 1956 and Czechoslovakia in 1968 shattered the Soviet dream for all but the die-hard true believers. For a while the New Left prospered and Maoism enjoyed a vogue, but they too, soon imploded from their own inconsistencies and contradictions. In the ashes of these discredited programmes arose postmodernism, which revelled in the whole idea of defeat and disintegration and delighted in its own inability to offer anything at all. The RPA now had to adjust to a considerably more complicated intellectual environment.

Faced with what it knew to be a new situation and invigorated by the annulment of its loveless marriage, 1968 had all the look of being a good year for the RPA. After a lean year in 1967, Pemberton Publishing, in association with Barrie & Rockliff, published a major statement on humanism edited by A J Ayer. Among the other contributors to *The Humanist Outlook* were Karl Popper, Antony Flew, H J Eysenck and Raymond Firth. We shall discuss this work in the next chapter. The RPA was also free to run its own annual conference and dinner again, and both resumed in 1968, tickets for the dinner soon selling out. The Conference was on the theme of 'The Knowledge Explosion'. Despite the drop in membership, the mood of the Annual Dinner was upbeat. The four principal speakers, Baroness Wootton, Dr Roger Manvell, David Kerr, MP and Lord Ritchie-Calder (1906-1981), all outlined various programmes for the RPA to pursue in the future, but all were proud of the RPA's record of achievement and ability to contribute constructively in their respective areas in the future. (2)

As part of the RPA's reinvention of itself, it was also decided to replace the *Rationalist Annual* with a new periodical called *Question*. The intention behind it was optimistic. As Hawton explained in the Introduction to the first volume, it was hoped that *Question* could be brought out more than once a year, which of course precluded any title with 'Annual' in it. But the more important reason for changing the name was that it would get rid of the word 'Rationalist', which had become something of a sticking point among various factions in the humanist movement. But there was little to be gained by simply replacing 'Rationalist' with 'Humanist'.

> After very careful consideration, it was decided that in the conditions of today a title that suggested the search rather than the answer would be the most appropriate. Commitment to rational inquiry means that at the outset nothing is taken for granted, everything is in question. (3)

Question was, in fact, pretty much like the *Rationalist Annual*, except the new name and layout gave it the look of an academic journal. And *Question 1* was a very impressive academic document. Ronald Fletcher attempted to define humanism, Bernard Williams and J A T Robinson discussed the meaning of God, D M Armstrong wrote on the nature of mind, and Rupert Crawshay-Williams, Kathleen Nott, Theodore Besterman, E H Hutten and H J McCloskey covered several different and interesting topics. With the advantage of hindsight, it is fairly clear that *Question* was not likely to sell in the numbers that would justify more than one issue a year. Its very academic quality conspired to reduce its appeal. By 1974 *Question* was being described as the RPA's annual collection of essays.

These bold new ventures took place against a backdrop of mounting financial difficulties. The RPA's general deficit for 1968 was £5217, down on the previous year, but still a cause for concern. And Pemberton Books went from a profit of £199 in 1967 to a loss of £2314 in 1968. Nevertheless, the general attitude of the Directors was calm, even bullish.

That the loss on *Humanist* is justified to the extent that it is the most important part of the Association's activities. That we should broaden the scope and interest of the magazine with a view to increasing its circulation among the unconverted. The publication of books is not so important, but it is within the scope of our activities to utilise our finances in this way, and, in view of the size of the Association's resources, the loss is not crippling. Accordingly, on purely financial grounds no drastic change in publishing policy is called for at the present time. (4)

With a view to those outside the movement, the *Humanist* actually underwent an enlargement at the beginning of 1969, adding a further eight pages and using a heavier grade of paper. This optimism looks unduly complacent with the comfort of hindsight, but at the time the Directors were justified in remaining generally optimistic. They also undertook a comprehensive reorganisation of the committee structure of the RPA in an attempt to improve efficiency and maximise people's skills. This was largely the work of the Chairman, Dr D J Stewart. Authority was devolved into a series of subcommittees with a certain power to operate independently but which needed to refer important decisions and those with financial implications to the Board. While the names and functions of the various committees have changed over the years, this structure has remained in place to the present day.

There was also a slight resurgence in publishing activity. After a lull in 1969, three titles were published in 1970 and seven the following year. Academically, the most impressive of the works was *The Jesus of the Early Christians*, by G[eorge] A[lbert] Wells (1926-), Professor of German at Birkbeck College in London. This was to be the first in a long line of intelligent, and, by and large, undervalued, works by this distinguished academic. Based on an extensive familiarity with biblical criticism, Wells argued that so many difficulties arise when the gospels are read as historical documents that Christianity could have developed just as easily without an historical Jesus. Some of the more reputable theologians acknowledged that Wells had raised serious difficulties, while others preferred to dismiss his views as those of an amateur and outsider. Yet more theologians criticised that attitude, and expressed concern that the bulk of the scholarly work on Jesus is by Christians who, inevitably, are going to bring their faith-based beliefs about a risen Christ with them. That reputable and skilled academics outside the Christian fold should devote their time to the study of Jesus should be welcomed. Instead, it is usually ridiculed or ignored.

A year later, in 1971, Pemberton published what was to be Hector Hawton's last book. Called *Controversy: The Humanist/Christian Encounter*, the work was primarily an up-date of his successful *Thinker's Handbook* of 21 years previously. But *Controversy* was Hawton's weakest book. He told his readers early on in the book that humanism is not simply a negative attitude towards religion. Quite rightly, Hawton saw humanism as a 'positive contribution to make as an alternative way of life. In a phrase, it is 'morality without religion'.' (5) Sadly, though, he ignored his own advice and wrote a book that dutifully went through all the traditional objections to religious, mainly Christian, belief. Only the last twenty pages were devoted to a brief survey of what humanism actually is.

Hawton's objections were intelligent and lucid, but we were left with good reasons for not being Christian rather than with good reasons for being a humanist. In an age that had very largely made the transition from Christian belief, *Controversy* had missed the mark. Hawton found the world after 1968 harder to understand.

Parallel with this mini-resurgence in quality publishing, a new ray of hope came from the United States in the form of Professor Paul Kurtz (1925-), a professor of philosophy at the State University of New York at Buffalo, who had created a publishing firm by the name of Prometheus Books. Kurtz proposed this firm act as the American wing to Pemberton. The identical initials of Prometheus and Pemberton allowed the American firm to use a very similar logo to the British firm. Kurtz met with Hawton in July 1969 and the two agreed on an ambitious programme of co-operation. A programme of publishing three or four books a year under the joint imprint of Pemberton and Prometheus was arranged, with Prometheus undertaking to purchase at least a thousand copies of each title. When the RPA Board accepted these proposals in October 1969, they must have been pretty excited. The Annual Report for 1971 expressed quiet satisfaction that this should help Pemberton's publishing viability in the future. (6)

While things were looking up on the publishing side, a series of threats to the credibility of the RPA took shape. The first of them was the challenge to the RPA's hard-won charitable status. Some time in 1969 it attracted the hostile attention of the Department of Education and Science, and this status was challenged. The challenge hinged on what constituted an educational charity. The department was not convinced that the RPA's educational aims were charitable. It is not unreasonable to suppose a degree of animus in the objection. The RPA's solicitors, in defending the status, dealt with this issue at some length.

> You apparently take issue with the content of the education which it is the object of our claims to promote on the ground that the "dominant purpose" is the spreading of rationalist principles and influencing the climate of educated opinion. This, we may be forgiven for remarking, amounts to no more than a forceful statement of the fact that you do not like the content of our clients' educational programme. But the question of content is, with the greatest possible respect to the Department, so long as the content is (as will obviously be conceded) not *contra bonos mores* and may result in the mental or moral improvement of those exposed to that content, wholly irrelevant. (7)

The Department of Education and Science was also anxious to stress that the RPA was principally involved in propagating a cause rather than education itself and, worse still, that the cause was rationalism, which, the Department said, was the opposite of religion and therefore not charitable. The solicitors' response was uncomprehending.

> We regret that we entirely fail to understand this. If read literally, since the principles of rationalism are only those of reason, what you appear to be stating is that Reason is the opposite of Religion. Even if this were the case, and our clients were advocating "the opposite of religion", upon what basis do you contend that education in such

principles (subject always to the qualifications which we have set out above which certainly do not apply to our clients' principles) is not charitable?...Roman Catholicism, Protestantism, and the Jewish Religion are all mutually incompatible, yet gifts for the advancement of each of these religions have been held charitable. (8)

It seems clear that the Department of Education and Science had already come to a decision and nothing was going to reverse it. The RPA was removed from the Register of Charities on March 23 1971. This immediately involved the RPA in a payment of £4,800 in taxation with the threat of a further £20,000. The Directors, in particular D J Stewart, the Chairman, struggled on for more than two years trying to regain charitable status before changing their tactics. After a great deal of legal to-ing and fro-ing, it became apparent that the RPA would need to alter its existing aims and objects in order to conform with the Department of Education and Science's requirements. But it wasn't as easy as that, because were they to go down this road, it was feared the RPA would become liable for substantial Capital Gains taxes it had not had to pay while it had enjoyed charitable status under the old aims and objects! The RPA was now in tricky legal territory. While it was no longer a charity, legally speaking, it was unclear whether this meant automatically that the RPA was now specifically *not* a charity. It slowly emerged that the RPA would escape the retrospective capital gains taxes because its aims and objects were exactly the same the day after as they had been the day before being struck off the charitable register. In May 1973, on the advice of their solicitors, it was decided to alter the stated aims and objects of the RPA in order to satisfy the requirement of the Department.

It was only partly with an eye to the charitable status dispute that the RPA decided in 1971 to involve itself with the *Journal of Moral Education* under the editorship of Derek Wright of Leicester University. The journal was a BHA initiative, largely the work of Harold Blackham, although D J Stewart participated in the journal on behalf of the RPA. Pemberton was involved as well, publishing *Let's Teach Them Right* in 1970 and the following year co-publishing *Moral Education: An Annotated List*, which was compiled by Blackham. RPA involvement in this exercise was in a direct line of descent from the work of F J Gould and Adam Gowans Whyte earlier on in the RPA's history.

Christopher Macy and the bold experiment

Overshadowing these developments was the prospect of Hector Hawton's retirement in March 1971. It is one of the dynamics of voluntary organisations that, with depressing frequency, the moment someone becomes irreplaceable, they also become insufferable. It is a tribute to the RPA that this otherwise iron law was often broken. Charles and Fred Watts, Hector Hawton and Constance Dowman all managed to be irreplaceable and yet collegial. And all of them took steps to ensure they could be replaced without difficulties. Therein lies true irreplaceability. The main problem was to find a successor to Hawton as editor of the *Humanist*. When Hawton retired, he had been only the third editor of the *Guide/Humanist* in its 86 years of continuous publication. Well aware that an era was ending, the Directors agreed in November 1969 (by a vote of six to three) that this position should be advertised. By the middle of 1970 Hawton's replacement had been found. The successful applicant was Christopher Macy (1939-), a young – only 31 – intelligent and educated humanist, with a particular interest in psychology and the arts. Macy was the first RPA editor with a degree, a BSc (Hons) from Brunel in Psychology. Since his graduation he had worked for Pemberton Publishing, first as publicity manager, then as general editor. In April 1971, he came on the Board. Macy was a technocrat, impatient for change, and saw the RPA as a vehicle for his version of applied humanism. He was a humanist more in the style of C P Snow than of any of the earlier rationalists.

Macy had ambitious plans for the *Humanist*. Ambitious and expensive. The *Humanist* was going to be relaunched as *New Humanist*, it was going to increase in size, length and circulation. An expensive advertising campaign - £300 per month - would be undertaken to increase the readership to 10,000 copies. Macy, along with Carmel Ross, a public relations consultant, approached W H Smith, the large book and stationery chain, to handle the magazine. They agreed to take 20,000 copies for a period of four months. Macy's plans were backed, but with a degree of unease. The proposal to relaunch the journal with the new name was passed with nine Directors in favour, but with three abstentions. More significantly, they added the following caveat. 'There was also a decision to record in the Minutes the Board's opinion that a criterion of success of not less than 10,000 copies per month and a no worse financial position than at present, but that we hope to achieve a circulation of up to 20,000 copies.' (9) This tidy note in the minutes betrays considerable disagreement at the meeting which passed it. Constance Dowman was very good at this sort of tidying up.

Pretty soon the big day arrived and in May 1972 Macy renamed the *Humanist* the *New Humanist*. The editorial he devoted to justifying this change ranged eclectically from the Soviet Union and the condition of Zhores Medvedev, to the situation in Northern Ireland, and Roy Jenkins' preference for the term 'civilised society' to 'permissive society'. But at no point did he address the issue of why the journal he edited was now called the *New Humanist*. Hector Hawton was not keen on the change, and that may well have been sufficient reason for Macy to seek the change. Hawton could be forgiven for feeling protective of the *Humanist*. After all, he had edited it for nineteen years and had rescued it from oblivion. But by the same token, Macy was also in a difficult position. The journal had been running for 87 years and he was only its fourth editor. He was stepping into large shoes, and probably felt some need to stamp his authority on the journal.

Macy's plans were never going to succeed. The first problems were the rising costs and the competence of Carmel Ross, the public relations consultant. Ross had made herself thoroughly unpopular by breezily knowing what was best and how best to market the RPA, without taking the trouble to consult the Directors unduly. By July her contract as publicity adviser was terminated and she was retained as space salesperson for the *New Humanist* only on the condition that her own business interests were not allowed to be advertised in the journal. Much more difficult was an increasing unease about Macy's use of the *New Humanist*. One of the subcommittees established in David Stewart's reorganisation was devoted to publications and publicity. At this subcommittee 'there was a lengthy discussion on the responsibilities of the Editor of "New Humanist" and the desirability of instituting some mechanism of accountability of the Editor to the

171

Board. It was finally proposed by Mr Blackham that the Publications and Publicity Committee be delegated the Board's power to examine each issue of "New Humanist" and give guide-lines to the Editor.' (10)

Even more disconcerting was that the journal under Macy was not helping the RPA's bid to regain charitable status. Among the questions the Department of Education and Science was posing was the extent to which rationalism is a cause, and, if it is, can it therefore be charitable? It also objected to the political nature of some of the articles.

> The issue of *The Humanist* relating to Northern Ireland is plainly in the nature of a political journal, dealing with a situation and advocating political measures. Its publication was not therefore a charitable activity and could not properly have been undertaken by a body established for charitable purposes only. (11)

The department acknowledged the work of the *Journal of Moral Education* but added that it 'appears to have no connexion with the Association'. Macy was frankly sceptical about the value of charitable status on the current terms. He suggested a bold new approach. In a memorandum to the Board late in 1971 Macy urged Directors to

> investigate the possibility of our setting up an entirely new charitable body to which the RPA could give most of its money, the object being that this body finances most of the background work at present carried out by the RPA. The RPA would then be free to give cut price subscriptions, to do members' editions of its own and perhaps more importantly now other publishers' books, to give reduced rate to members at conferences etc. (12)

The ongoing problems with the *New Humanist*, charitable status, and the financial situation were then exacerbated by dissension on the Board at a level not seen since the Great Conway Hall Plot four decades previously. At the Board meeting in October 1972 there was actually a contest for the position of vice-chairman between two Directors, Antony Chapman and Ivor Russell. Chapman was elected by five votes to three. There were also no fewer than four nominations for a vacancy on the Board following the death from leukaemia at only 46 of one of the Directors, Sydney Ruback. Two nominees, both friends of Christopher Macy, were ineligible because they were not members of the RPA. A series of other people were nominated or suggested and it was not until January 1973 that Maurice Temple-Smith (another nominee of Christopher Macy) was voted on to the Board, following discussion as to his suitability and on a vote of five for and two against. The next month, February, more voting was required. It was customary practice to re-elect the chairman and vice-chairman each year, but it was never more than a formality. But this year, there was a contest and, more significant still, an upset. David Stewart had been chairman since 1964, but was ousted by Antony Chapman on a vote of six votes to five. Chapman was the first person to take the chair of the RPA Board by a vote, let alone one with such a slender margin. There was also a vote for the position of vice-chairman, with Dr Colin Campbell beating Ivor Russell, again by six votes to five. These votes would normally suggest a Board firmly divided along factional lines, but this was not the case. There was no further voting along those lines after Dr Stewart was replaced. He was to remain on the Board for years to come and, while there were disputes, there was no established factionalism.

This was just as well because the Board had a mounting financial crisis to face. Macy's ambitious programme for the *New Humanist* was disintegrating. The net deficit of the journal at February 1973 was put at £15,773, *Question* at £2,329, the *Journal of Moral Education* at £3,177 and the book publishing programme at £11,088. On top of this were mounting difficulties with the relationship between Macy and other Directors. This reached a point in July 1973 when Professor E H Hutten, a Board member since 1966 and regular contributor to the *Humanist*, submitted a memorandum on the future policy of the *New Humanist*. Hutten pulled no punches.

> The basic formula of the *New Humanist* has been proved to be wrong. The basic assumption that we could have a mass appeal has been shown to be wrong. The trendy, commercial journalism of the 'exhilarating, young' editor who, however, is very inexperienced, has not been a recipe for success. The feeble imitation of the *New Statesman* or the *New Society* cannot possibly be any good when the originals are having a struggle to survive. (13)

Hutten acknowledged his clear dislike for Macy, but called nonetheless for his resignation on the grounds of his being 'unable and unwilling to carry out the wishes of the Board.' While there must have been some sympathy for Hutten's analysis of the problem, his proposed solutions were simply not credible. He wanted the *New Humanist* to fold and be replaced by 'The Rationalist Press Association News'. 'I would like to see a heading for the journal in which 'The Rationalist' would figure in large print followed by the rest of the name in smaller print. Thus, we would be known by our proper name.' Hutten was not supported and resigned from the Board at that meeting and, shortly after, from the Association.

Yet again we have an interesting illustration of the principal fault line which runs through the freethought movement. Christopher Macy sought to create a magazine which looked at the world in a broadly humanistic way. Hutten, by contrast, was wanting a magazine which presented the Humanist vision of the world. This is the divide between the mental attitude and the system of philosophy, both of which lived uneasily together in the original definition of rationalism devised by Sir Leslie Stephen in 1899. Normally these two approaches can rub along together reasonably well, but every now and then they clash. This was such an occasion.

The Board was in a very difficult position. On the one hand the *New Humanist* had got nowhere near the target of 10,000 copies sold, the average sale through 1973 being 3,200 to 3,500 and the monthly deficit usually around £1,750 per issue. This would have been more than enough justification to finish the experiment. But on the other hand, Hutten's comments notwithstanding, the general feedback on the *New Humanist* was fairly positive.

Hawton in particular must have felt in two minds about Macy's bold experiment. After all, he had gone down a similar path twenty years earlier. It had been his work that the *Humanist/New Humanist* was to be considered the central focus of the RPA. It was what the RPA existed for. He too had broadened the outlook of the magazine to conform with what he saw as existing realities, and had succeeded. He too had attempted to market a revamped magazine to a wider audience through the bookstalls, and had failed. But as older people perennially discover, the next generation comes along and makes the same mistakes as they did, but will not listen because they know better. What was the Board to do? It would have been churlish of the RPA to shut Macy down with the cry of having tried it all before. So they decided to continue with the *New Humanist* in its current form (and, though it wasn't stated, current editor as well) but to limit the financial and other damage being caused. And it was not as if the loss on the *New Humanist* was new. The *Humanist* under Hawton was losing £1,200 on each issue. In short, the RPA had tried the bolder of the options available to it. They failed, but they cannot be blamed for trying.

Courageous or not, the experiment was unravelling fast. W H Smith had already withdrawn from handling the *New Humanist* owing to low sales, and the other distribution firm, Hachette, must have been thinking along the same lines. So the Working Committee, which met in September 1973, agreed to pull out of the distribution system altogether and revert to concentrating on postal subscriptions. As its report said, 'If in the end we cannot please a wider public, at least let us please our members, without whose support the RPA would be nothing more than a bank account.' More importantly, an editorial policy was set down.

> The policy of *New Humanist* is to propagate Rationalism and Humanism to members of the Rationalist Press Association and to the general public. Since an important aspect of Rationalism and Humanism is their rejection of religion and certain forms of philosophical and political systems, the magazines should mount an on-going critique of such religions and systems. The magazine should also continually explore and develop the Humanist alternative to those systems.
>
> It is not only the philosophy of Rationalism and Humanism and their rivals which is to be explored; the practical application and embodiment of Rationalism and Humanism in everyday private and social life should also be examined and advocated. The magazine should seek to develop systematically a unified school of thought for the benefit, not only of already committed Rationalists and Humanists, but for the benefit of those many persons who sympathise with what we think and owe their position to the same historical roots. The magazine should show what Rationalists and Humanists think and what they do and establish, as far as possible, a single constituency embracing like-minded persons. (14)

The report made it clear that the editor was personally responsible for everything published in the magazine. It then put things as bluntly as possible. 'Consequently, the editor is free to disregard any directive on what he publishes,

Frederick Watts, the reliable son who worked himself to an early death for the RPA

Charles Albert Watts, the unassuming genius

J. M. Robertson, intelligent, hugely productive, and dauntingly authoritarian

Joseph McCabe, brilliant, mercurial and thin-skinned

Margaret Knight - Broadcast 'Morals without Religion' in 1955

Hector Hawton - Editor, author and director for the RPA

*Barbara Wootton - RPA Honorary Associate,
Leading criminologist and well-known broadcaster*

R.P.A. Headquarters

but his employer is equally free to sack him if he breaks the terms of his contract, or fails to observe the editorial policy laid down.' (15) Things shambled on for another twelve months before Macy resigned his position as editor in September 1974. Hector Hawton was appointed Acting Editor in the interim. The Board was quick to set a firm new editorial policy.

(i) That the first aim of the Association's journal should be to reinforce current members' Rationalism and to encourage their support of, and participation in, the RPA. It can then be used as a means of attracting new members who will share the aims and objects of the Association.

(ii) That editorial policy should be directed towards a more specifically Rationalist content. That is: the journal should contain house news of the RPA (but less of other organisations); articles and book reviews should be in the main by writers in sympathy with Rationalism and prepared to take a reasoned approach to their subject; the appropriate normal fee for articles would be £10 per thousand words. (16)

It was even agreed that the journal should be renamed *Reason*, although this never went ahead. Nicolas Walter was appointed editor.

Of Anarchism and Nicolas Walter

Nicolas Walter (1934-2000) was one of the most knowledgeable people to come along for the RPA since Hector Hawton (the other being G A Wells) and the most mercurial since Joseph McCabe. But while all these men promised much, Walter's actual achievement was the least permanent. Walter, appointed Managing Editor at the beginning of 1975, had spent a long career in the protest movement. He was a founding member of the anti-nuclear Committee of 100 and of Spies for Peace, a group dedicated to publicising the locations of the nuclear bunkers built for government members so that they at least might survive a nuclear attack. Walter was by nature and conviction an anarchist. His 1969 work *About Anarchism* remains one of the more intelligent and philosophically sound summaries of anarchism yet written. During the Vietnam War, Harold Wilson, a strong supporter of the United States' war effort, read the lesson in a Brighton church about beating swords into ploughshares. Many people must have thought it, but Nicolas Walter and a friend, Jim Radford, actually said it. They stood up in the church and shouted "Hypocrite!". For this exercise in truth telling both men were imprisoned for two months under the 1860 Ecclesiastical Jurisdiction Act for 'indecency in church'. A decade later Walter was involved in high-profile prosecution for blasphemy. A gay magazine published a poem by James Kirkup called 'The Love that Dares to Speak its Name', which featured a homosexual fantasy by the soldier who pierced the side of Jesus with a lance. Reminiscent of the infamous Scopes 'Monkey Trial' in 1925, the prosecution won the battle but lost the war. Denis Lemon, editor of the *Gay News* magazine, was sentenced to nine months imprisonment (suspended) and the magazine was faced with prohibitive fines and costs, but the cause of religious censorship and purity was hardly advanced by this victory. It also revealed the utter uselessness of blasphemy as a charge. This is a point rationalists have been making for a century and a half. While Walter was unmoved by the saccharined religiosity inherent in the poem, he republished and distributed it as widely as he could. (17) He also gave the whole affair extensive publicity in the *New Humanist*, providing some excellent background material.

Following in Hawton's footsteps, Walter had a long and successful career in journalism behind him. He had been deputy editor of *Which?* between 1963 and 1965 and chief sub editor of the *Times Literary Supplement* between 1968 and 1974. So, when the RPA took on Nicolas Walter in 1975, they knew they had taken on someone who knew his own mind. During Walter's editorship, the bitter ideological disputes over the look and content of the *New Humanist* disappeared overnight. This was partly due to the greater editorial control the Board took over the *New Humanist* in the wake of the Macy debacle, but also because of Walter's closer identification with the essentials of rationalism. One of his grandfathers was S K Ratcliffe (1868-1958), a veteran rationalist journalist and author. And, of course, the grim financial situation meant that the journal Walter oversaw was on a much more modest scale than Macy's.

Walter was formidably well read and articulate and had little patience with humbug. One marvellous example of Walter's approach was in the *New Statesman* in 1979 when he tore an article by Paul Johnson to shreds. Johnson has made a reputation for himself as a popular convert to and apologist for Christianity and for conservatism, rather in the vein of Malcolm Muggeridge. In a characteristically eclectic article, Johnson claimed that Christianity continues to survive and prosper in the face of the many predictions of its inevitable demise. He attributed this to the many errors and weaknesses of the various forms of unbelief. To give one example, Johnson told of listening to a radio programme on the Big Bang, 'I was startled,' he gasps, 'by the familiarity: not so very different from the first chapter of Genesis.' (18) Walter's reply was an object lesson in concise literary brutality. In an article half the length of Johnson's, Walter subdivided his claims into eight sections. Each section began 'Johnson is wrong about...' and proceeded to expose his breezy generalisations. Walter finished by pouring scorn on Johnson's claim, made against the demythologisers as much as against humanists, that religion is a constant truth. 'Religion does change in practice, though it pretends not to. But science changes in principle. The ultimate truth of science – as of freethought – is that there is no ultimate truth: certainly not Christianity.' (19)

As with many other incidents retold in this book, many people would wonder why rationalists bother to engage in verbal tussles with these purveyors of the supernatural. Isn't it a waste of time in that you'll never convince them as they will never convince you? It is true that very rarely is a disputant ever convinced by the arguments of an opponent. But it is equally true that it is not the opponent alone who is being addressed. Disputes of this sort are read by lots of people and a point made may set off a chain of events that causes one of those readers to re-evaluate their beliefs. This is the warp and woof of dialogue. Rationalists and their various opponents have always shared this perception. The subject matter in dispute is important, which means holding valid opinions on that matter is important, which also has to mean that trying to persuade those who disagree with your views is a worthwhile task. Only those whose minds are closed to the importance of what is being disputed or who care little about their views or those of other people would see the whole exercise as pointless.

Clearly, Walter was a formidable character. He won the position of editor of the *New Humanist* ahead of Brian Ash, a science fiction writer and active member of the H G Wells Society. Ash went on to compile *Who's Who in H G Wells* (Elm Tree Books, 1979) Nicolas Walter's skills as a formidable controversialist and writer were obvious gains for the RPA. It didn't take long, though, for Walter's equally formidable faults to became apparent as well. As one might expect in a committed anarchist, Walter was not a born administrator, and pretty soon the *New Humanist* began to appear irregularly and with some eccentric numbering. As part of the retrenchments of the period, it was decided the *New Humanist* should now become bi-monthly. The April 1976 issue was the last monthly issue of the journal, but the plan for it to appear on a bi-monthly basis never happened. Only five issues appeared in 1977, 1978 and 1979 while only three were produced in 1980 and 1981, two in 1982 and one in 1983. Then there was a year's gap before another issue appeared. This decline mirrors Walter's increasingly disordered personal situation, as well as his deteriorating health. He had been diagnosed with testicular cancer in 1973 and underwent a series of debilitating operations over the next fifteen years as he struggled with the disease. He was eventually confined to a wheelchair as a result of his treatment. On top of that his marriage broke up in 1981, resulting in the usual domestic disharmony. In a memorandum at the end of 1981, Walter asked the Board to 'bear with my infuriating muddles and mistakes' and promised to sort things out. (20) This, however, didn't happen, Things got worse instead. What complicated matters was Walter's obstinate resistance to being replaced in any of his roles, despite his manifest inability to perform them all adequately

Incredibly, Walter remained editor until July 1984, and even then he was replaced on what was thought to be a temporary basis while he recovered from the latest series of operations. His replacement was Jim Herrick (1944-), who was at the time completing an historical survey of rationalist thought which was published by Glover and Blair in Britain and Prometheus Books in the United States. In one of those interesting tricks history can play, between 1977 and 1981 Herrick had been editor of *The Freethinker*, the magazine whose style the founders of the *Literary Guide* did not want to emulate. Now, a hundred years later, Herrick moved from *The Freethinker* to the *Guide's* successor, the *New Humanist*. Thus, Herrick had the unusual distinction of overseeing the centenary issues of both *The Freethinker* and *New Humanist*. Since then, the RPA's journal has appeared regularly and with rational numbering.

The Bleak, and Expensive, Seventies

As life got tougher for the *New Humanist* and its personnel, so too did things deteriorate elsewhere. We noted earlier the optimism surrounding a venture with Prometheus Books, the new American publishing concern founded by Paul Kurtz. But things didn't go as well as either party hoped, principally because Pemberton titles did not sell well enough on the other side of the Atlantic. Among the first books Prometheus imported were Hawton's *Controversy*, F H George's *Computers, Science and Society* and *Let's Teach Them Right*, edited by Christopher Macy. Links between Prometheus and Pemberton continued, but not at the levels initially hoped for.

Hawton started to look around for another partner, and before long he found one. In March 1974 an agreement was signed with Paul Elek Ltd whereby Elek was granted exclusive rights to all Pemberton and RPA works. Elek was sympathetic to humanism, having published two books by David Tribe (1931-), at the time president of the National Secular Society; *A Hundred Years of Freethought* (1967) and *President Charles Bradlaugh*, MP (1971). The RPA undertook to provide Elek with quality material and Elek was not bound to accept all offerings. The first titles Elek handled were *Crime, Rape and Gin* by Bernard Crick, *Honest to Man* by Margaret Knight and *Did Jesus Exist?* by G A Wells. But in October 1976 Paul Elek died suddenly. Nicolas Walter expressed concern in a memo to Directors that 'I suspect that he was the leading open freethinker in the firm, and his absence may eventually lead to a lack of interest in our kind of book.' (21) Walter was correct. Within months of Elek's death, the agreement with Pemberton Books was terminated. The company cited insufficient interest in the titles. As if to justify Elek's claims, the last joint Elek/Pemberton publication was a collective memoir of the Cambridge philosopher C K Ogden (1889-1957). Ogden was clearly an engaging man and a philosophical insider, but this was not the sort of title that would arrest the trend of declining sales. Once the deal with Elek was over, the RPA was in no position to maintain Pemberton on its own resources. It would be five years before any more works appeared from the RPA – quite the longest lean spell to date. Paradoxically, one of the Elek/Pemberton titles, *Did Jesus Exist?* by G A Wells, was relatively popular in the United States and sold in respectable numbers there, contributing in no small way to the continued respectability of the mythical theory of Jesus in that country.

By 1975 the crisis was becoming evident to all. This bleak year was punctuated by deaths of significant people, the most prominent of them being Hyman Levy, Julian Huxley and Hector Hawton. It was also the year Constance Dowman finally retired as secretary of the RPA, having served with dogged loyalty since 1932. And, of course, it was the year Nicolas Walter became editor of the *New Humanist*. As with 1904-5, 1932-3 and 1952-3, 1975 can be seen as a pivotal year from which the RPA emerged a different organisation. At none of those other turning points, however, did the prospects look so grim. The October 1975 *New Humanist* editorial was pessimistic. 'Our very success has turned against us, since the kind of material which we used to handle and which conventional publishers wouldn't touch has become the common coin of the media – people who used to buy the Sixpenny Reprints and the Thinker's Library now buy Penguin Books or watch television.' (22) The editorial acknowledged continuing losses on the RPA's publishing activities and announced a price rise for the *New Humanist* from £3.25 to £4.50 a year. It was estimated that each member was receiving in the region of £10 worth of goods and services more than was covered by their subscription. This is a dilemma familiar to many voluntary organisations. There were warnings of drastic retrenchment across the entire range of RPA activities. Everything was up for consideration: the *New Humanist*, *Question*, the *Journal of Moral Education*, the Annual Dinner and Annual Conference. Dr D J Stewart, recently deposed Chairman of the Board of Directors though still on the Board, was only one of several people who warned at the Annual Dinner of 1975 that the situation could not continue. The shortfall each year was being met only through the generosity of a steady flow of bequests, but it was clear that this could not continue. Stewart put the problem graphically when he observed that 'each member can only die once, and we are running out of members.' (23)

Stewart's estrangement was not limited to matters of financial management. He had for some time been warning of impending doom. In all probability he likened his role to that of Cassandra, while others saw a closer resemblance to Jeremiah. Stewart's doubts extended to the entire direction the RPA had taken over the previous twenty years. He expressed concern that the trend to the term 'humanism' had worked for a short while but that 'if 'we are all humanists now', there is no point in joining a humanist group or buying a humanist magazine.' Stewart noted that the British Humanist Association, despite a wealth of talent and money, had not achieved anything like the size and prosperity that had been expected of it. It is important, Stewart said, not to be swimming with the tide all the time: an organisation like the RPA should be prepared to swim against the tide as well. As an example of this, he mentioned the re-emergence of anti-rational and anti-scientific cults and fashions and saw a legitimate role for the RPA in combating these tendencies. Stewart's gloomy prognostications were quickly borne out. Less than a year later the *New Humanist* editorial reiterated most of his warnings, and, as if to underscore the reality behind the warnings, it was in the April 1976 issue, the last of the monthly magazine. The new bi-monthly (although, as we have seen, it never actually appeared bi-monthly) was to cost 60p, effectively the same as the 30p for the monthly magazine, but it was promised that the bi-monthly magazine would be bigger.

Other, more drastic economies were also announced. *The Journal of Moral Education* was soon to be sold to another publisher. Discussions with the Social Morality Council and National Foundation for Educational Research about the transfer or sale of the journal were inconclusive. (24) *Question*, the successor to the *Rationalist Annual*, was to be reduced in size and cost. The editorship of the new, slimmer edition of *Question* was taken over by G A Wells after the death of Hector Hawton on December 14 1975. Pemberton was also to be drastically downsized and no new projects taken on for the foreseeable future. The Annual Dinner was axed and the Annual Conference was reduced to occupy only one day. At headquarters, office staff was reduced by half and economies were made in correspondence, stationery and other areas. Most of Nicolas Walter's early reports to the Board in his capacity as Managing Director were deeply pessimistic. In January 1976 he began his report

> I have now been at the RPA for exactly a year, and I find it difficult to imagine that I shall be here after another year. I have done everything I can to reduce unnecessary expenditure, and yet - as the Chairman's Forecast shows - the position I inherited has not improved at all. My only consolation is that it could be even worse, but as things are that will not last long. I feel that we are now in a particularly uncomfortable position, not really a commercial organisation because we are losing so much money when we no longer make much money, nor really a voluntary organisation because we still rely on paid staff and well-produced publications. (25)

Four years later, things did not look much better. Walter noted in his report to Directors in February 1980 that the RPA was in 'such a critical position that we must now make more radical decisions about our future than anything we have done during the past five years.' What had brought this critical position on was the final defeat of the legal battles over the loss of charitable status seven years previously. At the beginning of 1980 this long and expensive legal struggle was over, charitable status had not been recovered, legal costs had accumulated and, worst of all, the RPA was faced with accumulated taxes of between £40,000 and £50,000 – taxes which earlier in the decade it had been led to believe it would not be liable for. This was on top of a deficit for the 1979-80 year of £16,000. (26) It was in this climate that *Question* was finally axed. Walter made three suggestions for change. The one he favoured the most was approaching the BHA or NSS with a view to close alliance or complete union. He had advocated this as early as 1976. Alternatively, the RPA could go through another, even more drastic retrenchment. 'This would mean closing down *Question* and cutting *New Humanist*, remaindering all our books, selling most of our library and relics, selling 88 and 86 Islington High Street, and either moving to a smaller suburban (or exurban) office or else working from home with just an editor and a bookkeeper.' (27)

The 1980s revival

While these drastic economies were being contemplated, things took an unexpected turn for the better. As ever, the loyal membership continued leaving bequests to the RPA in their wills, but in the early 1980s a series of particularly generous bequests came to the aid of the RPA. In stark contrast to the gloom of the late seventies, Walter was able to tell members at the end of 1982 that the RPA was now in surplus to the tune of £58,000. (28) While these donations were more than welcome, they came too late to save an innovative idea by the eminent sociologist Colin Campbell. What Campbell had in mind was a single-volume reference work that presented a rationalist and humanist viewpoint on a wide variety of issues, from traditional topics such as the divinity of Christ, to debates on UFOs or the Turin Shroud. The entries would be scholarly and reliable while also being accessible to the non-specialist. This was pretty much what Joseph McCabe had devoted his life to doing in the first half of the twentieth century, the best single example being his *Rationalist Encyclopaedia*, published by Watts & Co in 1948. Campbell had in mind that this reference work would be updated regularly. Unfortunately this proposal was discussed into submission and never recovered.

When the improved state of RPA finances permitted a return to publishing activity, in the mid eighties, Campbell's reference work was long deceased. And the spate of publishing that did take place turned out to be Pemberton's last hurrah. In 1986 it was decided that a second edition of G A Wells's *Did Jesus Exist?* should be published. The second edition was extensively rewritten to cover criticisms of his earlier works and include recent research. Two thousand copies were printed, with Prometheus Books ordering 40% of the entire edition. More ambitious still was a series of essays on the life and work of J M Robertson, which appeared in 1987. The decision to go ahead with this publication was a brave one as the book was most unlikely to make a profit. But, like Cassels's *Supernatural Religion* eighty-two years previously, this is the sort of the book the RPA was there to produce. Twelve hundred hardback and a thousand paperback copies were printed at a cost of £11,626. The fact the book was required at all was symptomatic of the neglect of freethought history and thought within academia. G A Wells edited the series, which included essays on Robertson's contribution in politics, sociology, literary criticism, philosophy and religious studies. The contributions were by respected scholars and did a lot to help put Robertson back on the intellectual map.

This was the last work published by the RPA in the twentieth century to receive substantial recognition from reputable reviewers. *The Times Literary Supplement*, *The Times* and the *Sunday Telegraph* all reviewed the book, and were positive. The fullest review came from Hugh Trevor-Roper in the *Sunday Telegraph*. Trevor-Roper was critical of many of Robertson's main areas of interest, principally his Shakespearean studies and mythical Jesus theories. This notwithstanding, Trevor-Roper recognised him as an independent scholar with important things to say.

> However that may be, it is very good for us to have our assumptions thus questioned and to be forced to reconsider them in the light of reason. That, after all, was the method of Socrates. It did him no good in the short run, but we remember him still. (29)

The last book published by Pemberton was a collection of poetry brought together by Bet Cherrington (1912-1998). Two thousand copies of this work were produced at a cost of £10,810. It did not sell well. Pemberton Publishing lingered on for another decade but this work turned out to be its swan song.

As well as increasing publishing activity, the RPA contributed towards the open society. Responding to a request from the British Pregnancy Advisory Service and Abortion Law Reform Association, the RPA agreed to contribute one third of the cost of a £1,800 opinion poll on abortion, on condition there was a question about religion in it. And early in 1988 the RPA joined the computer age.

While Pemberton returned to a respectable level of publishing, RPA publicity rose to levels not seen for twenty years. This was mainly due to the work of Nicolas Walter, who supplied a continual stream of letters to the editor in a variety of newspapers and periodicals. He was a frequent obituarist for the quality press and appeared in public impressively frequently, for someone as unwell as he really was. For example, in 1988 he spoke alongside James Hemming (an RPA Honorary Associate) against Jerry Adams at the Oxford Union debate on religion and violence. Around the same time, Walter spoke to humanist groups in Hampstead and Brighton, attended a luncheon held by Sir Hermann Bondi at Churchill College, Cambridge, and contributed a small item on spiritualism on Channel 4's *Comment on Easter*. He kept this up for many years.

As the 1980s drew to a close another issue flared up, seemingly out of nowhere, in which the RPA took a significant part. The furore over Salman Rushdie's novel *The Satanic Verses* was a shock to many people. It was a shock to those who thought the struggle for an open society to be a straightforward case of a battle between progressives and reactionaries, and it was a shock for many people to see just how diverse and pluralist Britain had become. Few people took much notice when *The Satanic Verses* was published in September 1988, but by the end of the year the book had been banned across the Indian Subcontinent and by the time Iran's Ayatollah Khomeini had issued his *fatwa* in February 1989, Britain had experienced major demonstrations including book-burnings and the firebombing of two large London bookshops for stocking the book. In other incidents, bookstore staff were threatened at knifepoint to remove copies of the book. A move was begun to expand the blasphemy laws to include religions other than Christianity. When the *New Humanist* directed its attentions to the crisis in May 1989, its counsel was characteristically even-handed.

> In Bradford Muslims have felt a deep sense of oppression in British society. Rushdie's book was the last straw. The more an immigrant community feels under threat, the harder it will hold on to traditional certainties. Racist attacks against Muslims give good reason to feel beleaguered. (30)

In a humanist tradition long practised but little commented upon, the *New Humanist* opened its pages to its opponents, so that their voice might also be heard. H S Karmi articulated Muslim outrage over the affair. Karmi made the rather desperate plea that one 'cannot equate Islam with the version of Islam found in Saudi Arabia, Egypt, Morocco, Pakistan or anywhere else in the Muslim world.' Freed from the responsibility of any earthly involvement, it was easy to present Islam as the pure ideal. More plausibly, Karmi noted that outrage over Khomeini's fatwa was hypocritical, given the various CIA plots to assassinate Nasser, Castro and Gadafi, and the successful murder of Lumumba. He evaded the question of whether this justified the fatwa against Rushdie or condemned it by association.

The secularist view was put most forcefully by Richard Dawkins, who had recently become an Honorary Associate of the RPA. Dawkins concentrated on the dishonesty implicit in claiming one's faith has been outraged. 'The assumption is remarkably widespread that *religious* sensitivities are somehow especially deserving of consideration – a consideration not accorded to ordinary prejudice.' Dawkins went on:

> I admit to being offended by Father Christmas, "Baby Jesus", and Rudolf the Red Nosed Reindeer, but if I tried to act on these prejudices I'd quite rightly be held accountable. I'd be challenged to justify myself. But let someone's *religion* be offended and it's another matter entirely. Not only do the affronted themselves kick up an almighty fuss; they are abetted and encouraged by influential figures from other religions and the liberal establishment. Far from being challenged to justify their beliefs like anybody else, the religious are granted sanctuary in a sort of intellectual no-go area. (31)

Dawkins was quite right; this form of intellectual cowardice continues to this day, and poses a standing threat to free speech and the secular society. The RPA's consistent policy throughout the *Satanic Verses* affair was that in an open society toleration means accepting a variety of different ideas, many of which will be offensive. And neither was this merely an intellectual pose; atheists are one of the last minorities which can be maligned with impunity.

The Committee Against Blasphemy Law, which had last been busy during the *Gay News* case, was revived, with Nicolas Walter as its press officer and William McIlroy (1928-), longtime National Secular Society activist and editor of *The*

Freethinker, as its secretary. The Committee saw little to be gained by expanding an already unjust and outmoded law, and called for the abolition of the law instead. It issued a *Statement Against Blasphemy Law* to this effect, and attracted the signatures of more than 200 distinguished public figures, including a very generous number of RPA Honorary Associates.

The rationalists soon came up against the business end of intolerance. On May 27 Walter and then NSS president, Barbara Smoker (1923-), were attacked by a mob of Muslims during a counter-demonstration to the first Muslim denunciations. Neither was seriously injured, and neither was intimidated. In July Walter was invited to attend a meeting of a newly formed International Committee for the Defence of Salman Rushdie and His Publishers. A pamphlet put out by this committee drew heavily on RPA material. Walter also convened a meeting of sympathetic peers at the House of Lords at the request of Lord Sefton of Garston, an Honorary Associate. Walter spoke against the blasphemy laws and in favour of Salman Rushdie to the media and at many meetings around the country. A lengthy interview for the *New Statesman*, given in August, was never published.

In April 1990 the High Court heard the case brought by Muslim groups to prosecute the *Satanic Verses* for blasphemy. The decision went against the Muslims on the grounds that the blasphemy laws applied to Christianity alone. Not surprisingly, this fuelled two reactions: one to abolish the law of blasphemy altogether and another to extend it to include all religions. Bills to do both of those things were prepared for the Commons to consider. Walter kept busy by penning a short tract called *Blasphemy Ancient and Modern*, which discussed the Rushdie case in the context of earlier blasphemy scandals in Britain. It was published by the RPA. The following year a Muslim account of the episode was published. The book, *Sacrilege versus Civility*, stated that *Blasphemy Ancient and Modern* is written 'from "a blatantly psuedo [sic]-rationalist viewpoint" and...contains an item describing the RPA as "a main bulwark of the secular establishment"!' (32) This accusation encapsulates the silliness of many religious criticisms of rationalism. On the one hand comes the jibe that rationalism is a marginal irrelevance, but on the other hand it is also said to wield disproportionate influence in the corridors of power. Both gambits help the accuser evade the task of actually responding to the opponent's claims. And whether Walter's book is blatantly pseudo-rationalist – whatever that might mean – or whether the RPA is intimately linked to the corridors of power is not directly relevant to whether the points made are valid. *Sacrilege versus Civility* is in fact an extraordinary document. In true conspiracy-theory style, it begins with the claim that *The Satanic Verses* was used as 'a pretext to launch an attack against Islam and the Muslim community in the West.' (33) Islam is defended on the strength of a string of long-discredited theses: the cosmological argument, the argument to design and even Pascal's infamous wager. While claiming to defend civility, in just the first few pages of this book, Rushdie is described as ingenious but malicious (p 29), deranged and perverted (p 30), obscene, vulgar and intensely hateful (p 32).

The *Satanic Verses* affair led Daniel Easterman, a one-time Islamic scholar at Durham University with a long record of defending Islam from western prejudices, to state publicly his support for openness and toleration. His book on the affair, *New Jerusalems: Reflections on Islam, Fundamentalism and the Rushdie Affair* (Grafton, 1992) featured a series of articles on aspects of the Rushdie affair, several of them having originally appeared in the *New Humanist*. Later on, when the debate widened to the possible state funding of Muslim schools, the *New Humanist* line was consistent. In contrast to Cardinal Basil Hume, who opposed the extension of the state funding already enjoyed by Christian schools to Muslim ones, Jim Herrick argued that the most balanced solution, given the pluralist nature of British society, was that no religious schools should receive this sort of funding. (34)

The activities of Nicolas Walter and the RPA during the *Satanic Verses* affair represent well the humanist belief in the open society. The RPA had little directly to gain and quite a lot to lose by involving itself in this messy issue. Indeed, its spokespeople were exposed to physical intimidation. And it has certainly received no recognition for its activities on behalf of free speech. But its role was admirable and the RPA can be accounted among the progressive forces in society which put their ideals into practice.

Ten Years of Shadow Boxing (Part One)

The RPA did good work during the *Satanic Verses* imbroglio. It was able to defend the open society without demonising its opponents, while being demonised by them. This is humanism in action. The RPA had also published useful and intelligent books, participated in important public debate on a range of issues, returned the *New Humanist* to normalcy, and modernised its administrative procedures. But the ongoing problems had not gone away and in the 1990s they returned with a vengeance.

The most pressing problem of the 1990s was the future of the RPA itself. It had long been clear that it no longer had the resources to publish material in any serious quantity. And it had also long been apparent that heterodox works coming from mainstream publishers had a better chance of public notice and adequate sales than those emanating from heterodox publishing houses. And some of the more telling criticisms of Christian theology were coming from Christian publishing houses like SCM. Society truly had changed since the days of Charles Watts's youth. These and other facts came home to roost in the 1990s, but the RPA was unable to deal with them decisively.

The question of the future of the RPA became an issue in 1988 following an initiative from the BHA, which opened negotiations with the RPA about a possible merger. The BHA initiative was also directed to the National Secular Society and the South Place Ethical Society. In a BHA memorandum, David Williams, at the time serving as BHA chairman, wrote that some of the reasons for trying to bring humanists together in the 1960s were still valid. On the face of it, the case against the existing duplication of resources in four main organisations, all devoted to the criticism of religion and propagation of humanism, differing only in emphasis, was obvious. Office space, equipment and staff, magazine production and other resources, all being duplicated unnecessarily. (35)

However, it is one thing to state the obvious, and quite another for the obvious to be actioned. A meeting of the Humanist Liaison Committee was convened on October 24 1988 to discuss the BHA initiative. Jim Herrick, one of the RPA representatives, was reported as commenting that 'as someone who had worked for all the organisations, he was uncertain which one he was speaking for, and that he saw this as symbolic of the situation.' (36) Indeed it was, but despite that, none of the three RPA delegates thought the merger would go ahead. Most people suspected that the organisations were all too entrenched in their respective ways and were still prone to nurture old grievances and disputes for effective change to be possible. At the next RPA Board meeting, Directors were generally sceptical about the merits of complete merger but 'expressed approval for much more serious co-operation' (37) The question was discussed again at a special Board meeting on January 7 1989. Debate was wide ranging at this meeting, with concerns from D J Stewart about the term 'humanism' being fairly influential. 'It was agreed that Mr Walter should produce for the next Board meeting a draft motion welcoming the current tendency with appropriate reservations about actual merger.' (38) This did not happen and things drifted.

Co-operation with other humanist organisations again raised itself as an issue in 1990 when the possibility of Conway Hall becoming a centre for all British humanist organisations began. It was noted that 'at times in the past there have been personal problems and mutual suspicions that have stood in the way of such co-operation but they are absent today.' (39) It was first thought that the co-operation would involve the BHA moving into the RPA's buildings in Islington High Street. This possibility was thoroughly explored in the first half of 1990 but came to nothing. Instead, the BHA took on a tenancy of a property in Lamb's Conduit Passage, owned by the South Place Ethical Society and adjacent to Conway Hall, and the RPA partially moved its office to the same address (the administrative offices were retained in Islington, where Nicolas worked). The RPA had a long-term hope of freeing up its properties in Islington to earn much-needed rental income. Most participants in the move were realistic. Announcing the move in a rather terse editorial, Jim Herrick said that 'the dream (or nightmare) of any of the organisations merging is a long way off.' (40)

The next step in this ghostly dance came in the middle of 1992 when the building next door to the property owned by the South Place Ethical Society became available. 'A potentially major opportunity for the whole humanist movement has arisen at Conway Hall. A lease property next to the north entrance has become vacant, either for unexpired lease, for a new lease, or for freehold sale. Staff members of all four national humanist organisations inspected it on 15 April, all reporting back to their respective organisations.' (41) For a while it appeared nothing was going to happen until, late in 1993 the National Secular Society purchased the building. Early the following year it extended an invitation to the RPA and other humanist organisations to share the premises. The RPA attended a joint gathering of humanist organisations on January 27 1994 and agreed to move in. The building, named Bradlaugh House, was formally opened on June 21 with Michael Foot and Sir Hermann Bondi speaking.

The move of all four humanist organisations to Bradlaugh House was widely hailed as a significant event in the history of British freethought. On top of this,

185

the move came at the same time as two other initiatives were being launched. In May 1994 Lord Dormand, formerly Labour MP for Easington, convened a meeting at the House of Lords to revive the Humanist Parliamentary Group. This group had originally been set up at the initiative of the BHA in the 1960s and had been quite active for a few years. Of equal potential significance was an approach to the RPA by a freelance television and radio producer. Chris Templeton had the idea of being pro-active regarding the media world. Rather than waiting passively for invitations to present the humanist viewpoint on other people's programmes, Templeton proposed making humanist programmes which commissioning editors could choose from in the way they choose from any other list. He was already preparing a programme called 'Living Without Religion'. Not surprisingly, the *New Humanist* was upbeat. Each of these three ventures is a step forward for humanism, wrote Jim Herrick. 'Together they provide a very optimistic moment for the humanist movement.' (42)

The Decline of Nicolas Walter

The *Satanic Verses* affair had been Nicolas Walter's finest hour. He had worked unceasingly for a cause from which he had little to gain. His contribution had been splendid in both the administrative and intellectual facets of the dispute. Even allowing for the erratic publication of the *New Humanist*, it could be said that his faults had been outweighed by his strengths, but in the 1990s the balance was to swing the other way. It had been recognised in 1984 that the *New Humanist* needed to be put in hands other than his. For a while Walter nursed the dream of the editorship being returned to him, but Jim Herrick was confirmed as editor in August 1985. Walter was bitter and resentful for a while, but before long was reconciled to his position as Managing Director and his unofficial position as correspondent-at-large. Then came the *Satanic Verses* episode and his excellent contribution. After that, Walter ran out of puff.

From the beginning of the 1990s, the Directors became more and more frustrated with Walter's attitude. And justifiably so. On the one hand, his ability was recognised and the RPA was keen for him to devote most of his time to writing, but, apart from the journalistic work, little was produced. Walter had agreed to produce a work on the history of religion in education, but despite regular and positive progress reports, this book never appeared. At the same time, Walter became increasingly defensive about suggestions that some of his administrative burden should be taken from him. Walter produced reports on a regular basis for the Directors to this effect. This one, from August 1993 is representative:

> I am 58 years old, and in reasonable health apart from increasing disability. I have worked for the RPA for eighteen years - half my working life - and I consider that I still have much to contribute, in administrative and liaison as well as in publicity and editorial activity. I think that this view is held by most of the people I work with in the humanist movement. I have already suggested that I should work (and be paid) for fewer hours, partly in order to make way (and pay) for more administrative assistance, and partly to be able to concentrate on writing. But I don't feel I am yet ready to be removed from administrative responsibilities or deprived of employment...I know

that some of the criticisms of my work are justified, but I doubt whether I deserve what amounts to constructive dismissal, and I regret the tone of some of the things said and the manner of some of the things done in this affair. (43)

This battle dragged on, becoming particularly heated at the annual general meeting of 1993. But the RPA was caught in a trap. It wanted to be reasonable to Walter, it recognised his many strengths, but it was no less aware of his equally lengthy list of failings. Eventually, in the beginning of 1996, Walter was replaced as Company Secretary by John Metcalf, who had joined the staff in the previous year. Walter was unhappy with his position. In a report to the Board in December 1995 he complained:

> In general, going by your latest communications, I get the impression that the RPA is to pay me as little as possible to do as much as possible, to reduce my hours and my responsibilities to the minimum, until I have an interesting position as the person who has worked the longest for one of the humanist organisations, and has worked as hard and achieved as much as anyone in the humanist movement to advance its cause, yet is treated worse and paid less than any other employee in it.' (44)

This was followed by another lengthy memorandum on the terms of Walter's employment from David Pollock early in 1996. Pollock reiterated that the Board preferred Walter to focus on writing the books, articles and letters rather than concentrate on administration, particularly as the RPA had found in John Metcalf an efficient administrator. Pollock wrote

> I must emphasise that I have never proposed - and do not now - that anything should be imposed on Nicolas without his agreement. However, the history of the last many years has seen many failures to achieve planned and agreed changes, and I do not wish to see the occasion of John Metcalf assuming the administrative role (at extra expense to the Association) fail to achieve the corollary (even, major) objective of allowing us to take full advantage of Nicolas's huge knowledge of the field and talent for writing. If we do so fail, I venture that we shall be blamed by future generations. (45)

The war continued, with Walter reporting his objections to the changes in ever more menacing tones. 'In conclusion, it seems to me that the proposals for changes in my terms of employment are so radical and objectionable that they would amount to a breach of contract which would normally involve substantial compensation.' (46) The RPA Directors may well have felt the same way, as they were kept waiting for book-length publications that Walter repeatedly promised to write, and never did. He had a long track record of this sort of thing. He had originally been deputed to write the centenary history of *The Freethinker* for the National Secular Society in 1981. As the deadline came and went, it became apparent that Walter had not started the book. The project was passed on to Jim Herrick, whose work *Vision and Realism: A Hundred Years of The Freethinker* was published in 1982, a year after the magazine's centenary celebrations. Ten years later Walter was asked to write the history of the South Place Ethical Society for bi-centenary celebrations in 1993. This book never appeared, and no one was found to take the project over. And as we have already seen, the RPA waited patiently through the 1990s for the proposed book on religion and education in Britain. Despite all this, the Board asked Walter to write the centenary history of the RPA. When it became apparent that this history was not going to be ready for the centenary conference which had been scheduled for June 1999, the Board were 'dismayed' and passed a strongly worded motion relaying to Walter that they felt 'very let down by his failure to keep his promised deadline.' (47)

Why did Walter accomplish so little of permanent value? Barbara Smoker, who campaigned, and argued, with Walter for four decades, suggests that the reasons lay in his 'professional journalism and the tightness of his prose style; but more so, perhaps, was his perfectionism, and the fact that there were always more urgent projects in hand...' (48) Walter's journalistic style was indeed tight. Unlike the other proposed publications, we know that Walter had made some preparatory research for the centenary history. It resulted in two articles for the *New Humanist* outlining in clear detail the entire history of the RPA. He felt little need to dilate unnecessarily, as he would have seen it, beyond the bare outline of facts which always formed the core of his writing. Another reason is that he took on too much. At the same time as Walter was juggling his various book projects, editing or writing for the *New Humanist* and contributing articles, letters and obituaries to newspapers, he was also writing regularly for *The Freethinker*, and the anarchist journal *Freedom*, and serving as company secretary of G W Foote & Co Ltd and Secular Society Ltd.

The other point that must always be remembered was that, by the middle of 1999, Walter was once again a tired and sick man. Rightly or wrongly, he felt aggrieved at his treatment by the RPA and towards the end of 1999 wrote a caustic farewell to the movement in the *New Humanist* and retired to Leighton Buzzard. But within weeks of his retirement there it was discovered that his cancer had returned and was by this time terminal. He died on March 7 2000.

Without doubt, Walter's main contribution was the constant outpouring of articles, obituary notices and letters to the editor in most British newspapers. He frequently wrote letters under pseudonyms and was delighted on the occasions when he managed to get two of his on the same letters page of a newspaper. He also left an impressive collection of articles on a broad range of topics in the *New Humanist*. He gave rationalism and the RPA a higher public profile than it had enjoyed for a long time. His legacy within the RPA was more troubled. No one could doubt his courage in the face of his increasing disability. When it was apparent that he was dying, Walter had the opportunity to write on the subject of dying without the comforts of religion to the *Guardian*. He wrote:

> Raging against the dying of the light may be good art, but it is bad advice. 'Why me?' may be a natural question, but it prompts a natural answer, 'Why not?' Religion may promise life everlasting, but we should grow up, and accept that life has an end as well as a beginning...Mortality is inevitable, but morbidity is not. (49)

Other RPA activities

Amid all this uncertainty and conflict, the RPA continued to produce material, although on a very modest scale. The most successful were two works published in September 1990 by Carl Lofmark (1936-1991). These books, *Does God Exist?* and *What is the Bible?* were intended for British school-age children who were being faced with renewed levels of religious indoctrination in the wake of the Conservative government's education bill in 1988. Lofmark was a brilliant linguist, being fluent in German, Swedish and Welsh. His academic reputation was based on his works on the twelfth century renaissance in Germany, but he had also introduced English readers to the poetry of the Swedish freethinker Hjalmar Söderberg, and to Welsh poetry. Lofmark's two books follow in the tradition begun by F J Gould and Adam Gowans Whyte of writing approachable works for younger readers. Along with Gould and Whyte, Lofmark asked the rationalist's question, 'yes, but is it *true*?' It is not enough for any tradition making truth-claims to fall back on appeals to sentiment or tradition once those claims no longer have the ring of truth about them. For any movement, whether religious or secular, once the foundational truth-claims made for it have been shown to be false, then the movement is false. Few more positive contributions to moral development can be made, and yet rationalists are constantly accused of being negative.

Lofmark's books were reviewed intelligently by one of his target audience, a student then studying for her A-levels. The student appreciated the tone and humour of the works but thought that Lofmark had underestimated the power of faith. 'Maybe,' she suggested, 'people cannot accept the truth, and religion offers a shelter.' (50) Quite likely. Either way, Lofmark was now too ill to respond. Only days before his death, he gave a BBC World Service talk on 'The Problem of Evil'. The notion of an all-powerful God who is also all-loving, he, with some reason, denounced as preposterous.

> A contradiction in terms, because if he were good and had the power to impose his good, the world would be good and I wouldn't be dying here of cancer. The greatest minds in the world for the past two thousand years have been trying to explain how it is possible that there could be evil in a world created by a good God and after two thousand years they have still not found an answer to that question. I suggest there is not an answer. (51)

Two of the three other publications put out by the RPA in the 1990s also came from a single hand. Fresh from the struggles over the *Satanic Verses* affair, Nicolas Walter wrote a short summary of the blasphemy disputes and in 1997 he attempted an overview of the changing meanings of the word 'humanism'. These two works illustrated the strengths and weaknesses of Walter's scholarship. Both works were well researched but they lacked the levels of analysis that the quality of the research would have justified. The other work to appear was a new edition of Margaret Knight's *Humanist Anthology*, extensively revised by Jim Herrick, from the original edition, which appeared in 1961.

These publications notwithstanding, it was clear the RPA needed to be putting its energies somewhere else in order to justify its existence. With this in mind, the

RPA found itself looking abroad, with attention soon focusing on the International Humanist and Ethical Union and the Indian subcontinent. The RPA had affiliated with the IHEU in January 1961, although informal links had existed from the beginning of the IHEU in 1952, thanks mainly to Hector Hawton, who had attended the first congress in Amsterdam. The Second Congress of the IHEU was held in 1957 at Conway Hall, in favour of which the RPA dropped its annual conference. The next IHEU Congress was held at Oslo in 1962, and Hector Hawton and Joseph Reeves were the official RPA representatives at that meeting. Hawton was enthusiastic.

> There are no simple solutions to these menacing problems, but here at Oslo we had the encouraging spectacle of men and women from many nations united in their refusal to be defeatist and in their determination to find a rational answer. (52)

Contact with the IHEU was maintained through the 1970s and 1980s although more pressing problems at home tended to dominate the RPA through these decades. The return of focus on international affairs gathered pace after 1992 when Jim Herrick took on the role as editor of the IHEU's magazine, the *International Humanist News*. This meant the activities of humanist organisations and individuals around the world also received greater attention in the *New Humanist* than had previously been the case.

All this came together between 1995 and 1998, when a succession of conferences in India focused attention on the robust state of humanism in the Subcontinent. Rationalism and humanism have long been represented strongly in this region, particularly in India. Many Indians recalled the representations made on Indian affairs by Charles Bradlaugh in the 1880s. So conscientious was Bradlaugh about Indian matters that he was dubbed 'the Member for India' by his opponents, imagining this to be a rebuke. The interest of the RPA in Indian affairs was revived when F J Gould's moral lessons books received wide support and sales in India. The encouraging response to his books and the existence of a vigorous RPA Local Secretary in the person of Charles Lionel d'Avoine, whom we met in Chapter 2, prompted Gould to make a tour of India in 1913. While on tour, Gould met a leading mathematician, educator, politician and RPA member, Raghunath P (later Sir) Paranjpye (1876-1966). In 1931, probably at Gould's urging, Paranjpye became an Honorary Associate of the RPA. Paranjpye was at that time Vice-Chancellor of Lucknow University. The same year Watts & Co published his book, *The Crux of the Indian Problem*, which argued for a secular future for the Subcontinent if it was to achieve independence and then build on it constructively. Paranjpye went on to devote the rest of his life to that ideal. Another Indian humanist to become an Honorary Associate of the RPA was Dr V M Tarkunde (1909-), a former judge of the Mumbai Court and longtime Chairman of the Indian Radical Humanist Association. Like Paranjpye, Tarkunde worked across a broad section of areas over a long life: scholar, educator, civil rights activist. Tarkunde became an Honorary Associate of the RPA in 1976 and received the Humanist Award at the IHEU Congress in London in 1978.

As well as providing a platform for people like Tarkunde, the RPA has taken part in various schemes to help finance humanism in the Subcontinent. In 1974 the

RPA helped establish the South Asia Humanist Foundation with the aim of maintaining worthwhile projects run by Indian organisations themselves undergoing financial difficulties. Sadly, the RPA was in no position in 1974 to be rescuing other organisations in financial difficulties. After a relatively short time, the fund was closed down and distributed among several Indian organisations. At the beginning of its Fourteenth Congress, being held at Mumbai, the IHEU's new president, Levi Fragell declared that the future of humanism lay in India. As well as the greater levels of co-operation, the RPA committed to financial assistance to the development of an ambitious humanist centre being built in Mumbai. This co-operation was helped along after 1997 when Babu Gogineni, the IHEU's new executive director joined the other humanist leaders at Bradlaugh House. In 2000 and 2001, the RPA, along with most other humanist organisations around the world, was active in generating publicity about and seeking the release of Dr Younis Shaikh, a Pakistani physician and lecturer charged with blasphemy. Dr Shaikh had made in the course of a lecture the perfectly reasonable observation that the parents of the Prophet Muhammad could not themselves have been Muslims as Allah had only revealed his perfect truth to their son after their own deaths. The original complainant, a student, later retracted his accusation, but by this time it was too late and hysteria had been whipped up by fundamentalist zealots. It was then Dr Shaikh's tragedy to be caught up in the new situation the world found itself in after the terrorist attacks on the World Trade Center and the Pentagon on September 11 2001. After the attacks, Pakistan overnight became a crucial ally of the West in its war on the Taleban regime in Afghanistan. In the new climate, few people were willing to badger the Pakistani government to secure Dr Shaikh's release. At the time of writing, he remains condemned of blasphemy, which carries the death penalty.

Ten Years of Shadow Boxing (Part Two)

Having made the move to Bradlaugh House, along with the British Humanist Association, National Secular Society and South Place Ethical Society, to be joined later by the International Humanist & Ethical Union, the RPA had time to take stock of its future role. The initiative was taken by David Pollock, chairman of the Board since 1989, who in the second half of 1995 put before his colleagues the most innovative proposal for the future of the RPA so far seen. Pollock's initiative was launched against the background of an unpleasant but inconsequential dispute at that year's Annual General Meeting regarding a nomination for the Board which had been rejected on technical grounds. The nomination of Terry Mullins was ruled out of order on the grounds of it being past the notified deadline for nominations and including an incorrect address. These objections were all quite valid but members at the Annual Meeting complained, with equal validity, of the unnecessary formalism of the rules and difficulty in getting onto the Board. This dispute had little to do with Pollock's initiative, but it helped charge the atmosphere in which it was undertaken.

Pollock's report outlined what he saw as the role of the RPA. This included the promotion of rationalism as a distinct philosophy; the continued publication of *New Humanist* with an editor to whom a great deal of editorial independence is granted; and the continued production of relevant books whenever possible. There was nothing remarkable in this - this is how the RPA had seen its role for four decades. But where Pollock was innovative was to make the obvious point that none of these minimum requirements necessarily entails the continued existence of the RPA as an independent body. 'The question' Pollock wrote,

> is whether they can be provided for *better* by other means. I believe they can, and that the attractions of such a way forward - in terms both of economy of administration and of closer and more productive co-operation within the humanist movement - are such that the Board should regard themselves as under an obligation to explore the possibilities.' (53)

Pollock's idea was to remodel the RPA as a trust, modelled on the Rationalist Trust, working within the general framework of the BHA. Existing RPA Directors would serve as trustees and future trustees would be appointed from within. Trust funds would go toward the *New Humanist* and such other publications as could be afforded. The editor of the *New Humanist* would be appointed by and responsible to the trustees. The *New Humanist* would go to all members of the BHA and RPA members would be offered the choice of switching to the BHA or remaining as subscription-only readers of the *New Humanist*. Pollock was realistic.

> Although we are not confident of the possibility of all the RPA's activities fitting within the charitable Rationalist Trust, it seems much more likely that they could fit within a trust structured within the BHA's overall activities, since the proportion of 'purely' publishing activities would be much less within the wider organisation than in a stand-alone Rationalist Trust. This would need exploring with lawyers. (54)

Pollock's opponents were not opposed to consultations and closer co-operation, it was only actual amalgamation at which they baulked. Nicolas Walter submitted a memorandum agreeing that changes in the direction of the Trust could be made but, contrary to his earlier views, saw no reason why the Trust should operate under the aegis of the BHA or any other organisation. 'I propose', concluded Walter, 'that rather than trying to make changes in the RPA (and also the BHA), we should concentrate on making the best of all the organisations as they are, and build on the fact that we are physically and personally closer than ever before to develop practical co-operation without actual coalition.' Walter went further still when he questioned whether the Directors who were also active in the BHA did not have a conflict of interest. (55) At the Board meeting of October 16 1995 Pollock's memorandum was discussed and revealed the deep division over the future of the RPA. In the end Pollock's motion 'That the RPA should approach the BHA with a view to holding discussion on a possible integration of the RPA and BHA' attracted five votes whereas an alternative motion 'That the RPA should approach the BHA with a view to holding discussions on closer co-operation over publicity and publications' attracted only three votes. (56)

Two months after the vote, a deputation met representatives of the BHA for talks. But as the talks began, so did opposition to the whole process harden. Early the following year Antony Chapman led the attack against the trend toward negotiations led by Pollock. A series of delaying actions took place, and the desirability of one of the RPA delegates, Jane Wynne Willson, representing the RPA was questioned. Wynne Willson had previously served for a long time on the BHA executive and maintained close contacts within that organisation. By April a grim stalemate had been reached. At the Board meeting of that month it was agreed:

a) that the constitutional position of the RPA was not for discussion and, in particular, that any proposals for a joint Trust should not be pursued;
b) that staff should pursue sensible options for administrative collaboration wherever possible
c) that attempts should be made to reactivate the joint publications committee
d) that a preliminary meeting with the BHA should be sought as a possible prelude to regular liaison meetings at Board level (RPA representatives to be the Chairman, Jane Wynne Willson, Jim Herrick, Daniel O'Hara and Nicolas Walter). (57)

Towards the end of 1996 the suggestion was made that the RPA and BHA should look toward co-operating on the magazine. This idea didn't find favour, with concern expressed about the effects this would have on membership. This decision was taken from the RPA when, in the middle of 1997, the BHA decided to develop its magazine on its own. The BHA was expressing a great deal of dissatisfaction with the accommodation at Bradlaugh House and was at this time looking to leaving the building, with all the symbolic harm this would have done to the optimism of 1994 when all the freethought organisations agreed to work in the same building. The RPA Board agreed that Bradlaugh House was not perfect but they regretted the BHA decision to move. The RPA felt that no decision was required of it at this stage. In the end the BHA did not leave Bradlaugh House and a nervous calm descended on the building. David Pollock, the prime mover of the changes, stood down as Chairman of the Board of Directors at the annual meeting of 1997 and was replaced by Ivor Russell, a long-standing RPA stalwart, and a strong opponent of amalgamation.

The RPA spent the last couple of years of the twentieth century in a state of anxious paralysis. One faction of directors was in favour of closer co-operation and possible amalgamation with the BHA, another, slightly larger, group was opposed. Neither side had the power to administer the telling blow. It was becoming plain to most Directors that something had to be done, but there was no clear idea what. The last real proposal, that of David Pollock, had not proceeded, but nobody had any viable alternative. Early in 1999 all Directors were invited to submit individual memoranda on their views as to the RPA's continued viability. Questions raised included how to propagate rationalism in the era of television and the internet; the independence of the RPA; the impression that the RPA was moribund and the BHA was alive and dynamic; and the changing attitudes toward the criticism of religion and the existence of four separate humanist organisations.

The other humanist organisations were all seen to have a clear role, but that of the RPA seemed less clear. It was recognised that the RPA's original role as publisher of rationalist material was no longer tenable; commercial publishers were so much better equipped to perform this task. The other humanist organisations all had their particular niche. Most Directors seemed to agree that the RPA had a future through the occasional publication of books too specialist in nature for commercial publication, and in producing the *New Humanist*, although it was agreed it needed improvement. In an interesting replication of the thinking of the RPA founders in 1899, the directors of 1999 saw the RPA and its publications as charting a middle ground between the stridency of *The Freethinker* and the ethicism of the humanists. The consensus was that the *New Humanist* needed to present intellectually credible viewpoints on a wide range of contemporary issues and disputes.

This was all well and good, but the question remained; was it necessary that the RPA remain a stand-alone body in order to achieve these aims? In this way the challenge David Pollock had laid down in 1995 had not been addressed. Understanding this, Pollock returned to the plan he suggested in 1995. He saw no reason why those aims could not be pursued with the RPA operating as an autonomous trust within the orbit of the BHA. In the absence of any better plan, Pollock's proposal was acceded to, but with certain provisos. The BHA was to be approached but the RPA's independence was not to be sacrificed. Characteristically, Nicolas Walter tabled a lengthy memorandum on the history of the RPA, the special role it has played, and the need to retain its independence, only then to move and vote for the motion to look toward closer collaboration! Jim Herrick, who had worked closely with Walter over many years, had seen this all before: "That's Nicolas" he shrugged.

While at the time of writing the long-term future of the RPA remains unsettled, what is clear is the new climate of close co-operation with the BHA. The *New Humanist* has undergone a significant expansion (the sixteenth since its inception in 1885) in an attempt to attract a wider range of readers. In order to accommodate this, the BHA has reduced emphasis on its own publication. The *New Humanist* now goes to all members of the BHA as well as of the RPA. But while the organisational vehicles have changed over the century of existence, the basic message of humanism has remained fundamentally the same. In welcoming the new-look *New Humanist*, Sir Hermann Bondi wrote:

> The Humanist is by nature ready to applaud the diversity of human attitudes and cultures and must recognise that many individuals have a personal faith that helps them through the trials and tribulations of life. We can no more quarrel with such a choice than with a taste for the music of one particular composer. What does appal us is the pernicious claim that one's own faith *is the Truth* and that everybody who does not share it (whether through belief in a different revelation or none) is bereft of the Truth. (58)

It is significant that Charles Watts, F J Gould, George Jacob Holyoake or any other founder of the RPA could have written exactly the same thing.

There was also a slight increase in publishing activity in 2000. The range of publications at the end of our historical survey reinforces this important point about the continuity of the humanist message. *Rationalism in the Twenty-First Century* was the proceedings of the centenary RPA conference held at Westfield

College, Birmingham. It included papers by Honorary Associates and other prominent thinkers on several aspects of science and culture. The principal address was given by Professor Sir Colin Blakemore, who required a police presence as he had been threatened with physical harm by animal rights activists. Blakemore, and most of the other principal speakers, expressed concern about the future. The growing irrationality, the spread of cults, the nihilism of postmodernism and wanton ignorance and hostility to science, were all areas of concern. While the list of concerns was a bit different from those in 1899, the sense of the magnitude of the task ahead would have been quite familiar to the pioneers of 1899. If anything, the leading rationalists of 1999 were less confident than their predecessors a century before.

The other two publications reflected other long-held priorities of the RPA. *Seasons of Life* is a collection of prose and poems suitable for secular ceremonies or as a bedside companion while *The Thinker's Guide to Life* is a short work of quotations on various themes of living. *Seasons of Life* is the latest in a long line going back to F J Gould's *Funeral Services without Theology*, published originally in 1906, and the various books of quotations which are earlier still. This long tradition of rationalist publishing runs counter to the stereotype of rationalism as overly intellectual. These books are short, easy-reference guides to the thoughts of others, so that we might survive a personal crisis or simply learn how to live better.

And, mindful that we no longer need paper to read on, the RPA's website was created in 1999. In 2002 sections of five Thinker's Library titles and Carl Lofmark's *What is the Bible?* were re-released as e-publications on this site.(59) For those with less free time, clicking on to the Rationalist Eye serves up a pithy summary of a current issue. For instance, in October of 2001 the visitor to the website could read about the reaction of a Generation Xer to the September 11 events. This was written by Dr Shirley Dent, newly appointed assistant editor and self-confessed Generation Xer. Unlike most Generation Xers, Shirley Dent has a doctorate in the work of William Blake and has contributed to a broadening of approach in the *New Humanist* and the RPA. And, reminiscent of the articles in *The Humanist* of the 1950s which gave summaries and evaluations of what was on the radio, the *New Humanist* ran a series of articles providing the same sort of information and analysis of the many humanist websites around the world.

So, the RPA begins its second century as it began its first; trying new ways, and against formidable odds, to propagate the principles of rationalism and humanism. We must turn now to examine what exactly these principles are, and how they have changed.

Chapter 7

Rationalism, Humanism and the retreat from Spencer

Rationalism 'cannot give us the glittering prizes of final certitude which resplendent dogmatisms hold out for our attraction.'
A E Heath, 1947

Having come to the end of our historical survey of the RPA, we need now to look at the achievement and legacy of this organisation from the standpoint of the ideas it has championed. To do this we need to be clear what those ideas were. Looking first at rationalism and philosophy, we can borrow a heading used by Bertrand Russell to illustrate this relationship. Writing of his philosophical development, Russell described the process as the retreat from Pythagoras. His early philosophy had embraced the quasi-mystical idea of mathematics as somehow capturing essential facts about the universe. Gradually each of these certainties had to be let go and a new attitude of toleration of ambiguities had to be come to terms with. Decades later postmodernists would reinvent this particular wheel and use it to criticise people like Bertrand Russell.

For rationalists the retreat was not from Pythagoras but from Herbert Spencer. It is more or less mandatory now to dismiss Spencer in the most scathing terms that can be brought to bear, but in his day Spencer was widely considered not only the outstanding thinker of the day, but of all history. In an exhaustive and, it has to be said, exhausting collection of writings known as the Synthetic Philosophy, Spencer sought to apply the central fact of evolution to all other fields of knowledge. The central fact of evolution was that everything - organisms, ideas, and societies - progresses from the simple to the complex. Each of his books was an attempt to demonstrate that fact and its consequences in the various fields of knowledge. Spencer sidelined God by renaming him the Unknowable and rendering him redundant in the evolutionary process. Spencer was happy to adopt Huxley's term 'agnostic' to describe his position, once it became available in 1869.

While most of Spencer's evolutionary thinking is now of interest only to specialists in the history of ideas, his contributions to sociology, in particular the way he employed his notions of structure and function, remain an important legacy and have become part of the intellectual equipment of that discipline. In politics and economics, Spencer was an advocate of laissez-faire, as he thought nothing should interfere with the natural evolutionary processes.

Spencer's attraction to rationalists is obvious. God as an active agent is factored out of the equation without resorting to what they would have feared to be a dogmatic atheism. And in God's place is a thoroughly deterministic cosmic principle of evolution. This principle becomes the central fact of the universe. But Spencer appealed not only to rationalists. He was no less significant to many religious believers who were anxious to reconcile the conflict between science and religion. Spencer's thought allowed them to do that because God was not entirely dismissed in the Synthetic Philosophy, but was merely a Prime Mover now at rest. Until he was replaced by Bergson, Spencer was highly valued by a great many theistically inclined scientists.

So, believer and unbeliever, determinist and laissez faire enthusiast all had something to gain from Herbert Spencer. As these were among the principal intellectual fissures of the nineteenth century in much of the English-speaking world, his appeal is understandable. W[illiam] H[enry] Hudson (1862-1918), an academic and one time secretary to Spencer (not to be confused with W[illiam] H[enry] Hudson [1841-1924], minor novelist and travel writer), wrote an introduction to his philosophy in 1894, which in 1904 was reprinted as a Cheap Reprint. Hudson declared Spencer to be 'a man whose writings have marked an epoch in the development of the world's thought...'. (1) Charles Watts noted Spencer's death with special pessimism:

> Intellectually the world is getting poorer every year. The passing of Herbert Spencer may be a mere incident in the lives of the democracy, who vegetate but seldom live; yet with his demise the small band of great masters which illumined the nineteenth century have nearly all departed, with practically no successors to fill their place. Posterity will acclaim the well-nigh incomparable eminence of the author of the Synthetic Philosophy, ranking him in learning and genius with the greatest thinkers of the ages. (2)

This is an excellent illustration of the Edwardian anxiety I made mention of in Chapter Two. The determination of some of the first generation of RPA leaders, Charles Watts in particular, to preserve Spencer's memory was as much a tribute to their pessimism as to their triumphalist optimism, of which rationalists are frequently accused. Watts devoted the back cover of the *Rationalist Annual* to a full-page advertisement for the works of Spencer. The advertisement ran without a break from 1911 to 1940. And until the 1937 issue of the *Annual*, this was to the benefit of Williams & Norgate, who owned the copyright until Watts & Co took it over. Spencer was also well represented in the Cheap Reprints. Number Six in the series was his 1861 work *Education: Intellectual, Moral and Physical*, Number 18 was the outline of his philosophy by W H Hudson, from which we have quoted, and Number 29 was a collection of Spencer's essays. Another Spencer essay, 'Degrees of Utility in Knowledge', appeared as an RPA Tract in 1906.

All this was quite reasonable before the First World War. Spencer remained a credible authority until then, although his reputation suffered a sharp decline around the time of his death, not least because of G E Moore's work *Principia Ethica*, which introduced the notion of the naturalistic fallacy, using Spencer as his prime example. The naturalistic fallacy is still thoroughly contested, but Moore saw problems with deducing conclusions about what *ought* to be the case from observations about what *is* the case. Happily, this problem need not detain us here. Suffice it to say that rationalists were no less aware of this problem. In a lengthy appreciation of Spencer written for *The Times* in 1904, J M Robertson was critical of elements of Spencer's racism. Speaking of Spencer's opposition to inter-racial marriages, Robertson retorted 'Never was the fatality of resolving sociological into biological problems more flagrant.'(3)

It was after the First World War that the defence of Spencer began to look problematic. Progressionist liberalism had fractured under the pressure of war and was now facing competition from a variety of philosophies, movements and cults. By this time many theistic scientists had abandoned Spencer for Bergson and rationalists were left with Spencer for themselves. By the middle of the thirties even Spencer's own trustees were willing to move on. In January 1936 the RPA purchased the complete stock of Spencer's titles, plates and copyrights from the Spencer Trustees for £605. It began at once to prepare *First Principles* for the Thinker's Library, which it duly published the following year as Number 62 in the series, the bulkiest of all the Thinker's Library titles. *Education* had already been reprinted as Number 2 of the series, having appeared already as a Cheap Reprint. And the rationalists still weren't finished with Spencer; as we saw in Chapter Four, a collection of his essays on aesthetics was reprinted in 1950. Ironically, the RPA derived little benefit from its newly acquired stock of Spencer publications; most of it was destroyed in the bombing of November 1940.

Few people expressed what Spencer meant to them more clearly than Adam Gowans Whyte, who declared in 1938 that 'Spencer was, and remains, the only fundamentally sound philosopher.' Whyte then went on to provide an apology for his inability to 'get anything' from the long line of metaphysicians from Plato onwards. His apology was, of course, tongue-in-cheek, because 'metaphysics' for many rationalists of Whyte's ilk meant what 'meaningless gobbledygook' means to us. Whyte then got to the real point:

> Compared with Hegel, Herbert Spencer was, of course, a poor fish. He never attained the level of writing so that people, wondering what the devil he could mean, would conclude that he must have meant something too profound for words. Spencer merely ranged over the whole field of knowledge, collecting and collating, building out of his orderly material a coherent structure of thought about the cosmos. It was a colossal task for one man to undertake, and nothing could be easier than for specialists to pick holes in this or that part of the structure. Nevertheless his method seems to me the only one that can produce a philosophy worthwhile. A philosophy that is not a synthesis of all knowledge is not, to my mind at least, a philosophy at all. (4)

Three important points are apparent from Whyte's summary. Whyte is here expressing the long and justly held suspicion among empirically minded people that pretentious verbiage does not necessarily imply profound thought. In making a choice between the Spencerian vision of the universe and the Hegelian, the rationalists felt they had made the right choice. Robertson said much the same in his 1904 appreciation. He noted that Hegelians 'are apt to suppose that Hegelian dialectic is the true and final measure of mental power; but as that test would rule out nearly everybody but Hegel and the particular Hegelian who applies it...'. (5)

Spencer's works were at least presented in an approachable (if inelegant) prose, and the difficulties in the system were plain to see. This preference for plain language is a constant feature among rationalists. In our time, John Passmore, Richard Dawkins and Alan Sokal have given voice to this same suspicion with regard to the current range of mystagogues. The second point Whyte is making is that it is Spencer's *method* as much as the content of his philosophy that he prizes. Whyte takes Spencer's method to be patient observation of the facts and reasoning on that basis. This is what was once praised as the scientific method and is now sometimes referred to as informed scepticism. Whatever the label, rationalists have not altered their preference for this approach to knowledge. The third point Whyte was making is that he values Spencer's attempt at a broad picture. He (as was Robertson) was quite prepared to acknowledge errors on Spencer's part; but the value of his work is the general view of the world Spencer's thought provided him. Whyte and Robertson appreciated the attempted synthesis of knowledge in Spencer.

Aspects of this more interesting relationship between rationalists and Spencer were discernible before the First World War. Even then, when acceptance of Spencer's conclusions was a lot less problematic, we find not so much an acceptance, uncritical or otherwise, as admiration for what they perceive to be his method. This can be illustrated from as early as 1900, when the Cambridge philosopher and theologian James Ward criticised Spencer. Ward was an idealist and argued for the unity of 'Nature is Spirit', both suitably capitalised. The *Literary Guide* covered the controversy fully and quoted Spencer's reply to Ward: 'In saying 'Nature is Spirit' Professor Ward implies that he knows all about it, while I, on the other hand, am sure that I know nothing about it.' (6) The *Guide* recommended this as a clear exposition of the agnostic attitude. The *Guide* was equally clear that the Synthetic Philosophy was not a fixed revelation, quoting at length Spencer listing all the revisions the various works of the Synthetic Philosophy had undergone. Robertson was also clear about the weaknesses in Spencer's system.

As late as 1950, Spencer was still being praised in the *Literary Guide*. In an article devoted to Spencer, Royston Pike told of his debt. Speaking of *The Study of Sociology*, Pike said:

> It was the first book I had read about thinking, and after thirty years I still think that it is one of the best. It taught me that thinking is not something that "comes natural," like eating or falling in love; it is an art that has to be learnt. (7)

This was pretty much Spencer's last hurrah, and once again we see that this is praise for his method as much as for his conclusions.

The passion for Spencer was strongest among Charles Albert Watts and his generation. Among the post-Watts leadership, attitudes were less enthusiastic. This is illustrated by an incident in 1940 when the elderly Watts wrote to the Board suggesting a reprinting of *The Study of Sociology*, but the Directors thought it was not worth reprinting as it was out of date. They then wrote to the sociologist Morris Ginsberg (1889-1970) suggesting he write a modern version of Spencer's work. Ginsberg wasn't interested in that project, but indicated he would write something along other lines. (8) Nothing came of this project, but Ginsberg remained connected with the rationalist movement, becoming an Honorary Associate in 1962.

Even from the beginning, there was criticism of Spencer. In the very first issue of *Watts's Literary Guide*, in November 1885, notice was given on the front page of a forthcoming title which was intended to show that Spencer's philosophy was fallacious. In the first decades of the twentieth century H G Wells would have spoken for many in his recurring criticisms of Spencer. For example, in *Joan and Peter* (1918), Wells declared Spencer's supreme gift to a generation of hasty profiteers 'was the discovery that the blind scuffle of fate could be called "Evolution," and so given an air of intention altogether superior to our poor struggles to make a decent order out of a greedy scramble.' (9)

Towards the end of the century Antony Flew agreed that the Synthetic Philosophy is 'best left to moulder on the shelves of the libraries' but did recommend *The Man versus The State* and *The Study of Sociology*. For him, both books were plainly-written accounts of politics and social sciences, free from the temptation to misrepresent and falsify, which he saw as endemic among contemporary social theorists. (10) For those whose views incline more to the left, even these works would be of little interest.

Nor were the objections to Spencer solely in economic terms. Where Wells was criticising the laissez-faire implications of Spencer's thinking, evolutionists like Joseph McCabe protested the teleological flavour to his evolutionary thinking. In *The Principles of Evolution* (1913), McCabe was prepared to praise Spencer's overall vision while dissenting from some of his most important conclusions. He doubted, for instance, whether all evolution could be contained in the formula of simple-to-complex, noting that flowers and some flowering plants had not in fact evolved in this way. (11) McCabe's career as a populariser of evolution was spent combating some of the fallacies, like survival-of-the-fittest social darwinism and eugenics, which some historians of evolution have attributed in large part to Spencer's influence. McCabe specifically opposed grandiose conceptions of laws of nature and the inheritance of acquired characteristics, both of which Spencer championed. McCabe's evolutionary thinking was straightforwardly Darwinian. After the First World War, McCabe pretty much stopped referring to Spencer in his popular accounts of evolution.

Nor did Spencer's notorious peevishness escape mention. In 1937, only a year after taking over the work of the Spencer trustees, the *Guide* retold a story about an irate Spencer having been kept waiting for his shaving water while staying at a friend's house. As he was leaving he waved the sovereign in front of the servant and said "I should have given you this, Emily, had you not been five minutes late this morning." (12) There is even a delightful story from 1908 of three RPA members who made a trip to Derby – 'dull Derby', as Spencer called it – to find Spencer's birthplace. The article tells how the three collapsed in laughter after knocking on every house of the street only to discover that nobody had heard of him. "A what-er?" one resident asked upon being told that Spencer was a philosopher. The trio eventually found the house on another street, one which had 'reached the nadir of dinginess.' (13)

From the 1930s the nature of the criticism of Spencer changed in interesting ways. Spencer's crime, according to these people, was not that he advocated grand narratives, but that he advocated the *wrong* grand narrative. Most of the critics of the 1930s were Marxists, who made the same error as Spencer in seeing their grand narrative as normatively explanatory. These were the people who left the RPA to work for the Progressive League and write for the Left Book Club. Whereas Spencer saw evolution as pointing in the direction of laissez-faire capitalism, the Marxists posited a different terminus. H G Wells recognised this in his novel *The Brothers*, published in 1938, when he said 'Marx stinks of Herbert Spencer and Herbert Spencer stinks of Marx.' (14) It is worthwhile to note here Wells' incredulity toward metanarratives – something a later generation of postmodernists would presume they had invented and criticise rationalists for not having.

While Spencer's grandiose evolutionism was untenable, it did at least terminate in an open society; the Marxist train of history terminated in dictatorship and repression. It was no accident that Marxists were among the last to let go of Lamarckian notions of inheritance of acquired characteristics. Lysenko flourished in the Soviet Union because communist orthodoxy required him to. Put bluntly, the choice the rationalists made in the 1930s for Spencer over Marx was the right one. If one is going to persist in error, it might as well be a benign error.

After the Second World War, and particularly once Hector Hawton assumed the intellectual direction of the movement, Spencer's day was well and truly over. This was done not by means of a frontal assault on Spencer, but simply by ignoring him. Spencer was irrelevant to Hawton's worldview. But even Hawton would respect the manner in which the synoptic thinkers (Hawton's term) operate. Citing Marx, Comte, Spencer and Frazer, Hawton acknowledged that the age of the giants is over

> and instead we have an army of clever, industrious, niggling minds working – but unable to see. The price we have to pay for such over-specialisation is the absence of creative daring and imaginative leaps. No doubt the great creative minds of the past made bad mistakes, but at least they were men of vision and they were not afraid of being wrong. (15)

A similar point was made two years later in an intelligent summary of Spencer's career and legacy by the sociologist Donald MacRae. MacRae was under no illusions about Spencer's errors, eccentricities and confusions, all of which he enumerated clearly and even-handedly. But, like Hawton, MacRae was grateful for the good Spencer had done. 'He cared about freedom and truth. There is no one of similar breadth of vision among us today, and this is a genuine misfortune.'(16)

Hector Hawton and the new turn

The story of Spencer and the RPA is the story of the move away from simply replacing a theistic teleology with an agnostic one and toward adopting a genuinely rationalist and sceptical view of the world. Over the first half of the twentieth century, the rationalists gradually abandoned the Spencerian teleology while retaining their respect for the breadth of his vision and for his methodology. It was a small step to then detach that respect for Spencer's method from Spencer himself. Among those who were still unable to divest themselves of grand teleological schemes there was always the temptation of Marxism and its apparently scientific method. But for those who were unwilling to simply replace one teleological scheme with another, the path was more difficult.

The difficulty for humanist thinkers since the Second World War has been to recognise the flaws in grand-vision thinking while providing an inspiring vision of the world and of our place in it. Christianity and Marxism both presented their followers with a straightforward vision of the world and a comforting division of people into goodies and baddies. Even more brilliantly, they both were able to provide their followers with a sense of being important to the cosmos while believing themselves to be humble. Against such a heady brew, most alternatives will appear unsatisfying.

The RPA, and the humanist movement generally, were fortunate indeed that Hector Hawton was on the scene at this time. Hawton had a considerably more sophisticated grasp of philosophy than most of his predecessors in the RPA. Just as it was Hawton's job to rebuild a more streamlined RPA in the 1950s, so it was his job to help reorient rationalism to the postwar world. He did this himself in his books and articles in the *Literary Guide/Humanist* and with the help of the large number of able people he encouraged into the movement and to write for him. A good example of his work in this regard is the reaction to Francis Huxley's debunking of the theory of mythology built up by J G Frazer, who was enormously influential among earlier generations of rationalists. Anxious readers of *The Humanist* asked Hawton to comment on Huxley's book. Hawton told them the truth.

> It is a pity to spoil a good story, but truth will out. All attempts to trace mythology to a common source have been suspect for some time. There are, of course, divine kings, vegetation gods and magical rites of tantalizing similarity, but the unified tapestry which Frazer wove must be regarded as a patchwork quilt. (17)

In the area of philosophy, Hawton's ability was made abundantly clear in *Philosophy for Pleasure*, published by Watts & Co in 1949 and intended for the general reader. This book, forgotten like so much rationalist material, compares favourably with Bertrand Russell's *History of Western Philosophy*, which had appeared three years previously. Unlike Russell's work, Hawton emphasised the ongoing nature of philosophical discourse. And Hawton had a greater appreciation of philosophies he was not sympathetic with than Russell had demonstrated. Hawton lamented the confusion of philosophy with system building. There are still those, he wrote, '…who believe that the task of philosophy is to weave scientific knowledge into a pattern, patch up the holes with guesses and present the result as a finished picture of reality.' (18) With this in mind, noting the levels of scorn and derision of Hegel is a reliable and, at times, entertaining, litmus test for the rationality of rationalists. Russell, for instance, could rarely resist the temptation to excoriate Hegel. The chapter dealing with Hegel in *History of Western Philosophy*, for example, is brutal. Hawton was a lot fairer, although he was hardly less opposed to Hegel's ideas. 'I personally believe that Hegel failed in his central purpose; but it was something worth attempting. His failure was a bigger achievement than most people's successes, despite its extravagances and occasional absurdities.' (19) Hawton recognised the problems in grand-vision thinking. This is why he could not remain content with Marxism for long. And, unusually for rationalists at the time, Hawton had a profound admiration for the philosophy of A N Whitehead (1861-1947), of which he gave an admirable summary in *Philosophy for Pleasure* as well as in the *Literary Guide*. (20). *Philosophy for Pleasure* had a long career as a cheap paperback reprint in the United States.

It has long been the standard charge that humanists have turned to science to provide some sort of alternative to religion for a grand vision of the universe. So widespread has this prejudice become that it is rarely challenged now. The fact that this perception is confused and inaccurate has been lost amid the blare of accusation. I have shown elsewhere that this is untrue in the case of Joseph McCabe and can show also that it was untrue of Hector Hawton. In *Philosophy for Pleasure*, Hawton took his readers through the main problem David Hume has posed for the philosophy of science. Hume did not deny, Hawton wrote, 'that observations suggest causal uniformities. Hume asked what the connection was between one fact and another which could *compel* invariable consequence?' (21) Hawton concluded that Hume's question has still not been satisfactorily answered but that the contemporary discussion of the meaning of terms such as 'law' and 'probability' was certainly helping clarify the situation. Hawton's position here is more philosophically informed, but not fundamentally different from that of most humanists who have been involved in the RPA. Few humanists in the RPA or elsewhere have been as uncritically laudatory of science as their critics have claimed.

For Hawton, philosophy, like all other branches of learning, was to be pursued for its own sake, for the simple pleasure of it, but also in the pursuit of truth, which he firmly distinguished from certainty. He ended *Philosophy for Pleasure* with the words of the Buddha to his students:

> Do not believe what you have imagined, persuading yourself that a god inspires you. Believe nothing on the sole authority of your masters or priests. After examination, believe what you yourself have tested and found to be reasonable, and conform your conduct thereto. (22)

After *Philosophy for Pleasure* and *The Thinker's Handbook*, Hawton wrote what is, in my opinion, his finest work. *The Feast of Unreason*, published in 1952, was a brilliant and passionate attack on existentialism. As with so many works of rationalist philosophy, this book has been unjustly neglected, not least because it was written by a non-specialist. Focusing on Pascal, Kierkegaard, Nietzsche and Sartre, Hawton condemned existentialism as 'not a philosophy but a painful technique for obtaining certain experiences.' (23) Hawton complained that many rationalists were accustomed to thinking that atheists are necessarily more rational than theists, but the experience of existentialism showed this clearly was not the case. And Hawton was not unmindful of the existentialist contribution. He thanked them for pinpointing 'the anxiety of the man who has suddenly gained his individuality but lost the warmth and comfort of submergence in the mass.' (24) The real question now was not atheism versus theism so much as rationality versus irrationality. He finished his book in the manner many current critics of postmodernism have also finished theirs. 'Faced with the greatest crisis in his history' he wrote, 'it is an ill-chosen moment for man to scorn rational foresight.' (25) In criticising the irrationalism and narcissism of existentialism, Hawton contributed significantly to bringing rationalism up to date with a new set of problems and challenges. This was, intellectually speaking, his greatest legacy to the RPA.

It is worthwhile to note that in the same year as Hawton's *Feast of Unreason* was published, H J Blackham also published a work on existentialism. *Six Existentialist Thinkers* enjoyed considerably more critical acclaim than Hawton's work, not least because it was a lot more sympathetic, and therefore more in keeping with the times. Blackham criticised the tendency to seeing existentialism as 'an hysterical symptom of the irrationalism,' preferring instead to see it as the latest manifestation of a particular type of individualism that recurs in the history of ideas. (26) This is a feature of rationalism that has never been appreciated. Contrary to those who see it as little more than another creed, rationalism has taken seriously its respect for the truth and has frequently published works quite opposed to those of other rationalists. Unlike dogmatic systems of belief, where such disagreements would be a sign of discord, in rationalism it is a sign of strength.

And before we leave the subject of existentialism, it should also be noted just how high the quality of rationalist discussion of existentialism was. Donald MacRae wrote perceptively on Sartre in the *Guide* and the 1954 *Rationalist Annual*; and Ayer's 'Some Aspects of Existentialism', which appeared in the 1948 *Annual*, was praised by Ben Rogers, alongside his other material on existentialism, as 'a model of their kind; lucid, judicious and engaged, [and] make uncomfortable reading for those who say that the analytic philosophers of Ayer's generation were parochial.'(27) And this is not to forget Bertrand Russell's brilliant satire, 'The Existentialist's Nightmare', which had the existentialist seek greater and greater experiences of feeling, without regard to who was harmed along the way. (28) It is also salutary to notice how much of the rationalist critique of existentialism remains valid against the postmodernism of our own times.

As the fifties drew on and linguistic philosophy took hold, Hawton became impatient. Anticipating Bryan Magee four decades later, Hawton suspected that linguistic philosophers had no burning philosophical questions to ask. Their erudite specialism involved an abandonment of the inquiring general citizen. 'The professional philosopher's dignity is offended if he is regarded as running an advice bureau – like such amateurs as Socrates, for example.' (29) While Hawton could sympathise with the philosopher applying his new tools of linguistic analysis to determine real from pseudo questions, he also sympathised with the general citizen who found such a specialism thoroughly uninvolving. Existentialism and linguistic philosophy will do little for the average person in search of a meaningful way to live. In Hawton's words they 'may give him a few bricks to build with but he will look in vain for cement.' (30) Forty years later Bryan Magee would say the same thing, while also criticising humanism.

Hawton's vision was of a humanist philosophy which would replace the outmoded two-world model of natural and supernatural. 'The supernatural would be totally eliminated, and instead of a twofold division of theology and philosophy we would have a single body of provisional knowledge, science or natural philosophy.' (31) He made no apology for offering up such a philosophy because he had no illusions that it was some permanent contribution. He knew full well that it would be subject to drastic changes as knowledge advanced. For Hawton, the aim of humanist philosophy is to help those who have abandoned religion to find new bearings.

> It serves as a map to guide man on his journey through life. Part of the map covers territory that is known, but part of it is surmise of an unexplored region. In constructing this map and conjecturing the probable outlines of the unknown, the function of reason may be likened to a compass. There are many old maps based on guesswork which are worth consulting in spite of their mixture of fact and fancy; and there are many travellers' tales, alarmist rumours of haunted valleys and magic mountains, which can be disregarded. (32)

Hawton's breadth of vision gave leading academic thinkers the confidence to contribute to the *Literary Guide/Humanist* during his editorship. As we saw in Chapter Five, a succession of distinguished thinkers contributed to the RPA's journal through the fifties to the seventies, making it one of the least exploited intellectual treasure houses of postwar Britain.

Agnosticism and Atheism

It is important to follow the same transition of rationalist and humanist thought over the past century by looking at some of the main ideas championed by the movement. Few things would surprise and disappoint the founders of the RPA more than the decline of agnosticism among freethinkers. Nowhere was the divide between moderates and militants in the movement more clearly marked in the early years of the twentieth century than in their respective views on atheism. The importance of this divide was illustrated by no less a person than Charles Watts senior. In the lead article in the *Literary Guide* of August 1898, Watts went out of his way to distinguish atheism from agnosticism. The agnostic considers that any affirmation, either to assert or to deny, the existence of God

> is both unphilosophical and unwise, to say nothing of its being utterly useless. The dogmatism both of the Theist and the Atheist the Agnostic eschews, seeing that both are tacitly claiming to have some sort of a conception of the inconceivable and thoughts of the unthinkable. (33)

From the vantage point of a hundred years, we can see that the debate about the relative merits of agnosticism over atheism suffered from a high level of confusion as to the nature and purpose of both positions. It was only in a series of seminal works of atheist philosophy from the 1950s to the early 1990s that these confusions were laid to rest. This literature has established forever the intellectual respectability of atheism. (34) What was so helpful in these books was the distinction made between positive and negative atheism. This distinction had been implicitly recognised before the 1950s, and underlay the division between those who preferred the terms 'agnostic' to 'atheist'. Joseph McCabe was the first person to specifically allude to the distinction, but it was not until Antony Flew in the 1950s and 1960s that it was authoritatively articulated. Negative atheism is the weaker of the two claims, confining itself to saying that there is no conclusive evidence to justify belief in God. This is distinct from positive atheism, which is the stronger position of affirming that there is sufficient evidence to justify the claim that God does not exist. (35) Until relatively recently, atheism was generally held to mean positive atheism; this was certainly what Charles Watts had in mind. But, in the light of this recent work, we can see that the disputed territory was what we now know as negative atheism. But in the days before this muddle was cleared up, the dispute over this disputed territory was confused and patchy. We can now see that in their revolt against dogma, the early rationalists felt obliged to shy away from positive atheism, but because this distinction had not yet been drawn, were also uncomfortable with expressions of negative atheism.

The following little spat illustrates well the problem. In November of 1900, William Brailsford Columbine, a self-made businessman from Nottingham and regular contributor to the *Guide*, took issue with comments made by Foote in the previous month's *Freethinker*. There G W Foote chided Thomas Henry Huxley for adopting the term 'agnostic' 'because he had over a thousand pounds a year, and moved in the "upper circles", and filled "honourable" positions'. Now it has to be said that referring to Huxley in anything less than reverential terms was enough to outrage most of the pioneers of the RPA. But to call into question the integrity of agnosticism was to question the integrity of rationalism itself. Columbine saw it in these terms:

> He [Huxley] expressed the single indispensable principle of Agnosticism in the words: "It is wrong for a man to say that he is certain of the objective truth of any proposition unless he can produce evidence which logically justifies that certainty." It is at once evident that, although this far-reaching proposition would, in the opinion of Mr Foote, involve Atheism as expounded by himself, it includes much more than Atheism of that type. Agnosticism, as thus defined by Huxley, may be applied, and must be applied by consistent Agnostics, to problems of every kind, whether they belong to the realm of philosophy or religion, politics, ethics, or science. (36)

What Columbine was saying here is that agnosticism and rationalism were the same in that they both stressed the open, undogmatic approach toward any sort of claim or proposition. This attitude is still central to the rationalist view of the world, although it is no longer goes under the name of agnosticism. Atheism, Columbine implied, failed the test of rationality because of the inability of the atheist to provide a level of evidence requisite to the claim being made.

This is all clear enough. The confusion comes with the understanding of what atheism actually entails. In the light of the more recent work, it is evident that Columbine has what we call positive atheism in mind. Now Foote, who was not a fool, understood Columbine's point well. And so had Foote's mentor, Charles Bradlaugh, who, several decades earlier had given one of the classic descriptions of negative atheism.

The Atheist does not say "There is no God," but he says: "I know not what you mean by God; the word "God" is to me a sound conveying no clear or distinct affirmation. I do not deny God, because I cannot deny that of which I have no conception, and the conception of which, by its affirmer, is so imperfect that he is unable to define it to me." (37)

Followers of Bradlaugh for the next century were to use this formula for describing their atheism as being without a conception of God as opposed to denying any conception of God. It is a view that virtually no religious apologist has noticed or credited rationalists with, a neglect which has the effect of making much of their apologetics irrelevant and question begging.

Now there was virtually nobody in the RPA who did not have a tremendous respect for Charles Bradlaugh, but, equally, there were few who were comfortable with taking on the label atheist, even Bradlaugh's carefully worded negative atheism. But the agnosticism of most of the RPA stalwarts was virtually indistinguishable from negative atheism. So the dispute between Columbine and Foote – a dispute that has been replayed again and again over the RPA's history – was little more than shadowboxing between two virtually identical positions, but with different labels. So for many decades the atheists found Foote's National Secular Society a more congenial home, while agnostics found the RPA more agreeable. But, in practical terms, there were few meaningful differences between them.

Another ever-popular charge laid by religious apologists, invariably without citing an example, is that atheism involves a degree of arrogance or presumptuousness. Were these people to actually read rationalist material they would find expressions of atheism that point in a contrary direction. The problem was not the arrogance of the atheist, but the presumptuousness of religions to think their system of belief sufficiently grand to function as an explanation for the entire universe. This is how J M Robertson put it early in the twentieth century:

> To look into shoreless space, starred with unnumbered worlds, till the mind swoons with the sense of its unthinkableness, and then to turn to the histories of the religion and philosophy with which men seek to balance it, is to feel in the uttermost fibres of heart and brain that the God of Jerusalem or of Harvard, of Kant or James, is as vain a chimera as Moloch or Cotytto, as flagrantly subjective, man-made, contradictory, preposterous, puerile. (38)

A while later the author Llewelyn Powys (1884-1939) captured brilliantly the cosmic modesty which underlies the atheist position. In a powerful and under-appreciated criticism of Christianity called *The Pathetic Fallacy*, which was published in 1930 and reprinted in the Thinker's Library the following year, Powys wrote:

> The human race has suffered three grave humiliations: when Copernicus showed that the earth was not the centre of the universe; when Darwin proved that man's origin was not the result of a direct creation; when Freud explained that man was not the master of his

own thoughts and actions. It must endure an increment of ignominy before it will be prepared to temper its demands. (39)

Since the Second World War atheism has had what could only be called a golden age. Beginning with Antony Flew's brilliant essay 'Theology and Falsification' and through to Michael Martin's seminal work *Atheism: A Philosophical Justification* in 1990, atheism has been put very firmly on the intellectual map. Sadly, this story has not been told, and it is beyond the scope of this book to tell it. Accordingly, we will limit our comments to those who have had a role to play in the RPA. Antony Flew's essay, little more than a thousand words, was written originally for a long defunct university magazine but has since been reprinted many times, including by the RPA, in 1976. 'Theology and Falsification' began with a memorable parable about two travellers who stumble on a garden strewn with flowers and weeds. The presence of flowers provokes one of the travellers to declare that there must be a gardener, but when none appears, he supposes the gardener to be invisible. Rather like modern conceptions of god, the traveller shrouds the gardener in an evermore-absurd web of qualifications and provisos. Flew ends the essay with the challenge 'What would have to occur or to have occurred to constitute for you a disproof of the love of, or of the existence of, God?' (40)

Flew's next major contribution to the philosophy of atheism came in the form of his argument for the presumption of atheism. It was Flew's contention that the burden of proof lay with the theist. After all, it is the theist who is making the greater claim. This puts us in mind of the bright child at school who, when told God created the universe, retorts "Yes, but who created God?" This is a thoroughly reasonable question, and one which takes the presumption of atheism seriously. Flew's presumption of atheism also follows in the tradition of Robertson and Powys in being the opposite of presumptuous. Like his predecessors, Flew reminds his readers that the presumption of atheism in fact works in the direction of a 'modest teachability'. (41)

Pemberton Publishing complemented Antony Flew's important work in 1971 when it published *A Short History of Western Atheism*, by James Thrower, then only 35 years old and teaching at the University of Ghana. Designed for the non-specialist, Thrower's history traced atheistic thought from the presocratic philosophers to the modern syntheses. Thrower doesn't examine the differences between atheism and agnosticism but treats them as merely different expressions of the same conscious rejection of theism. *A Short History of Western Atheism* is still in print, a new impression having been published by Prometheus Books. Thrower went on to do useful work examining the atheistic thoughts of ancient world.

So, in the century since the RPA was founded, agnosticism has been outflanked and rendered redundant. Agnosticism has been outflanked in the sense of no longer being the only, or even the best, word to describe holding one's opinions in direct proportion to the available evidence. Contemporary rationalists and humanists still value this principle as much as the founders of the RPA, it is simply that it now goes under the name of scientific method, or informed scepticism. And agnosticism, in the sense of meaning that the question of God's existence cannot be decided upon with any confidence, has been rendered redundant by the philosophically more flexible and subtle distinctions of negative and positive atheism. There is no valid reason to use the term 'agnostic' any more.

Rationalism

Another concept that has changed significantly over the past century is that of rationalism. So many people claim to have administered the fatal stroke that felled the monster of rationalism that it is difficult to appreciate how flawed most of those attacks have been. Many of them have been little more than caricatures of straw men. Among Christian apologists, a representative sample comes from Canon Alan Richardson (1905-1975) in his work *Christian Apologetics*, published originally in 1947 and passing through several editions over the next quarter of a century. Richardson does little more than set up a circular argument of blanket assertions.

> Man comes to the knowledge of the truth, not by the untrammelled exercise of his reasoning powers, but by accepting or being given the faith which enables him to use his reason aright; reason cannot work until it first makes an act of faith, and it does not work correctly – that is, rationally – unless it makes the *right* act of faith, unless it has the faith in the Truth itself. Reason does not precede faith, as rationalism supposes, but faith precedes reason. (42)

The crucial action, Richardson urges, is not one's independent reasoning, but *accepting or being given the faith* which enables us to use our reason aright! Richardson then narrows the gate even more by insisting that it must be the *right* act of faith. By this argument, knowledge of truth comes by being told what the truth is by people whom Canon Richardson approves of. Is it any wonder that more popular works of apologetics skim over the issue of faith and reason by trying to have it both ways? To take one example from the 1980s, Roger Forster and Paul Marston insist that:

> Christian faith is a relationship of trust in God – not just a reasoned set of beliefs. God's kingdom is entered in a childlike way, through a response of the will to the message of the cross (Mt 18:3-4; Lk 18:17; Jn 1:12; I Cor 1:17). Neither reason, nor knowledge, nor intellectual belief in God can substitute for this kind of faith which involves response (I Cor 8:1; Jas 2: 18-23). Paul argues that worldly wisdom, if it actually begins by ruling out the message of the cross and Resurrection, is not true wisdom but folly, and is spiritually barren (I Cor 1:18-25). (43)

This approach is not dissimilar to Richardson's. It amounts to 'we will use reason when it suits us, childlike faith when it suits us, and anyone who disagrees with us is wrong and dishonest anyway.' Forster and Marston's account is more suggestive of the fundamentalist approach, peppered as it is with appeals to the authority of the New Testament.

Very rarely do calumniators of rationalism actually take the time to examine what rationalists themselves have said on the subject. This, then, is what we will do here. But first, let us return to the core definition of rationalism that the RPA devised when it was founded in 1899. As we saw in Chapter One, the definition read as follows:

> Rationalism may be defined as the mental attitude which unreservedly accepts the supremacy of reason and aims at establishing a system of philosophy and ethics verifiable by experience and independent of all arbitrary assumptions of authority.

It does not take long for this definition to become problematic, and neither did it take long for rationalists to appreciate the difficulties inherent in the definition. Adam Gowans Whyte is interesting on this question, and is worth quoting at some length. In his fiftieth anniversary history, Whyte noted that:

> Rarely does any definition meet with universal approval, and this one, in spite of its high authority, was, and is still, criticised on various grounds. It is held by some to be too scholastic in tone and too lengthy; something shorter, simpler, and more easily remembered is called for. Others maintain that it is inconsistent, as it proclaims a mental attitude and also aims at establishing a system. Others, again, feel that a movement so closely associated with the application of the scientific method to all questions should not omit the word "science" in its statement of principles. It has also been argued that science itself is based upon assumptions which philosophers regard as arbitrary. (44)

Given the rationalists were well aware of the problems raised by the definition, why did they persevere with it? Whyte is clear on this: 'Yet no alternative offered during half a century of Rationalist progress has shown any sign of being more acceptable.' And a quarter of a century later again, in an appreciation of the RPA on the occasion of its 75th anniversary, Hector Hawton said the same thing. 'Today the phraseology of the definition admittedly looks dated, but no-one has propounded an acceptable alternative.' (45) And a quarter of a century down the road after Hawton's comments, the RPA still uses this definition and, when it is discussed at all, the same objections to it are raised.

All this shows, to use contemporary jargon, that rationalists are more able to 'tolerate ambiguity' than they are given credit for. And this is just as well, as the definition is thoroughly ambiguous. On the one hand it admits rationalism to be a mental attitude while on the other it aims to establish a system of philosophy and ethics. And then it wants on the one hand to exclude all arbitrary assumptions of authority while also claiming to accept unreservedly the supremacy of reason. Most of the stresses and strains of the freethought movement over the past century can be found in this definition. Most notably, it accommodates both the substitutionist and abolitionist tendencies of the movement. And this breadth is, of course, precisely why it has lasted so long.

The other reason this definition has lasted so long is that it has not been subjected to the same sort of anxious scrutiny as religious thinkers have subjected their creeds to over the past century. The reason for this is simple: it is not a creed. This point is critical to the understanding of rationalism and of humanism. The 1899 definition of rationalism does not have the status of inerrant or gospel wisdom. It is not something which future generations are expected to go back to and measure themselves against. Reason, Charles Gorham wrote in 1899,

> develops, not always on one line, but in many diverse directions; the judgment is biased by numberless influences, derived from heredity, training, environment. Such influences are often strongest where unperceived by those whose opinions they mould; but the Rationalist should be the most alert to perceive and allow for them. (46)

So, rather than involving themselves in years of tortuous debate about its meaning and status, rationalists have happily continued on their way, using reason as a tool, like the many other tools homo sapiens has evolved in order to make sense of its world and to enhance its prospects in it.

Before the First World War rationalists had three understandings of rationalism, each one different in important ways from the others. Among the older generation, those born before 1850 let us say, rationalism was seen principally as a necessary corrective to an essentially sound and valuable religious (read: Christian) view of the world. Charles Watts senior illustrates this well. Watts insisted that rationalism does not seek to destroy the truths of religion, 'but rather to divest religion of traditional error, and to adapt what good it may contain to the requirements of modern life.' Charles Watts, Richard Bithell, George Jacob Holyoake and the men of their generation, all believed in a primary religious impulse which they held to be basically sound. All that was required was that this native religious impulse be shorn of the false accretions of dogmatic theism and restrictive creeds. This was rationalism's task. The degree of their hostility to conventional Christianity was the measure of how deeply they believed the false accretions had permeated. They all agreed that agnosticism was at the heart of rationalism. They were opposed to dogmatising about the existence of God or a future life, whether from a theist or an atheist point of view. Their opposition to atheism was scarcely less pronounced than their opposition to theism, rather more so in the case of Richard Bithell. These men looked forward to the day when they could co-operate with conventional Christians to solve social problems of the day in a spirit of fraternity.

This is not to say that they saw no differences between rationalism and religion. On the contrary, the *Literary Guide* in January 1898 outlined the four main areas where the two forces stood apart:

- the method of reaching convictions
- the mode of regarding nature
- the mode of interpreting history
- the ideals pursued and reverenced (47)

The men who held these opinions were dead by 1908 and were being replaced by the next cohort, those born in the 1850s and 1860s. The principal division between the older generation and this one was its greater hostility to religion. The new men were more of a mind to stress that a moral person does not need to be religious at all. It is not a matter of true religion. This harder line was frequently the result of harsh experiences with religion during formative years, followed by witnessing the unwillingness of conventionally religious thinkers to see the rationalists as allies. J M Robertson expressed the next cohort's thinking in a short monograph written for the publishing house Constable, which was producing a series of short works designed to acquaint the general reader with most of the isms on the market. Thirty years later, the RPA reprinted Robertson's monograph as Number 37 in the Thinker's Forum series. Rationalism had pretty well come to mean what 'freethinker' had meant in the nineteenth century, Robertson argued. So, to be significant today, rationalism

> should stand first and last for the habit and tendency to challenge the doctrines which claim 'religious' or sacrosanct authority – to seek by reflection a defensible theory of things rather accept enrolment under traditional creeds which demand allegiance on supernaturalist grounds. (48)

The rationalist is differentiated from other thinkers by carrying further the processes of doubt, analysis and judgement. Robertson acknowledged that rationalists have biases like anyone else, in their case a bias toward 'seeking coherence in a naturalistic sense, while the religionist seeks coherence in a supernaturalist sense.' (49) Joseph McCabe thought of rationalism in much the same way early on in his career.

> The Rationalistic spirit is, therefore, a critical action of reason on authoritative religious tradition, which leads to its partial or entire rejection, either from defect of satisfactory evidence to recommend it, or because it conflicts with known facts or evident moral or speculative principles. (50)

These understandings of rationalism are problematic at best, and McCabe's is especially unstable. Both set up a stark reason/unreason fissure and McCabe's notion even anticipates the outcome of the reasoning process, which of course, rather undermines the claim that rationalism is a method of inquiry. Both notions fail to recognise the tension in the 1899 definition between rationalism as a method of inquiry and rationalism as a system of philosophy. Furthermore, both confuse being independent of authority with being antagonistic to authority. And finally, a criticism which can only be made with the advantage of hindsight, these ideas of rationalism fail to allow for there being non-convergent, but equally rational, outlooks. It is probably these conceptions of rationalism that the apologists mentioned above had in mind. We cannot know of course, because they don't mention any. But for all these failures, the rationalists of Robertson and McCabe's generation appreciated better than their predecessors the essential dividing line between the naturalist and the supernaturalist views of the world.

We don't have to look far to find other senior rationalists of the day thinking about rationalism in quite different ways. The finest example comes from Adam Gowans Whyte's best-known book *The Religion of the Open Mind*. As a Director of the RPA of 14 years' standing when this book went to print, Whyte's book can be seen as equally representative of Edwardian rationalist opinion as that of Robertson and McCabe. Published originally in 1913 *The Religion of the Open Mind* went into a second edition in 1915 and was reprinted as Number 49 of the

Thinker's Library in 1935, with a revised edition of the Thinker's Library edition coming out in 1942. Whyte quotes the RPA's definition of rationalism toward the end of his book and doesn't worry too much about its ambiguities. In fact, he seems to like that element of rationalism. On the same page as he quotes the definition, Whyte notes that there is 'every variety of opinion among Rationalists; and it is certain that no two men or women among them would set forth their views on the great issues of religion in the same words.' (51) But Whyte is not content to extend to rationalists alone the benefits of variety.

> A direct principle of Rationalism is that every man must make his own religion. Saints and apostles have dreamed of the day when all men will profess the same faith, subscribe to the same creeds, worship the same God in the same way, and present the spectacle of a world-wide uniformity in affairs of the spirit. Missionaries have been sent to the ends of the earth in pursuit of that ideal. But it will, happily, never be realised. (52)

Adding to this pluralism, Whyte adds the other essential ingredient of his religion of the open mind. To those 'who have hugged the delusion of absolute and eternal truth, the religion of the open mind may seem nothing more than the apotheosis of uncertainty.' Whyte appears unperturbed by this. In any case, he writes:

> The limitations of the human intellect must be accepted, even in those speculations by which man hopes to transcend them. We may rebel against these limitations, just as we rebel against death; but such rebellion does not alter the facts of the case. And perhaps when we have made a survey of what has been attained within these limitations, and independently of the beliefs and hopes born of rebellion, we may be more content. (53)

Set against passages such as these, the lurid charges that humanism arrogantly replaces god as the centre of the universe with man, fearing genuine diversity, or parading an inflated confidence in human reason against the mystery of existence are revealed as little more than ill-informed rhetoric. What is more, the long-standing practice in the RPA of giving space in its journals to its detractors and publishing the works of those with whom they disagree stands as ample testimony to putting into practice this commitment to pluralism and the clash of ideas.

Since the First World War, the either/or conceptions of rationalism favoured by Robertson gave way to the pluralist and open notion favoured by Whyte. Charles Gorham, who shared Whyte's approach, warned readers in 1922 that rationalists should not see themselves as solitary sentinels of reason.

> We must not imagine that reason is confined to the operations of organised Rationalism. There is a vast fund of reason outside the Rationalist Press Association. From this fund humanity draws, and always has drawn, its creative energy. But creative energy is not to be "cabined, cribbed, confined" within a formal creed. Rationalism is not a dogmatic system, but a synthetic aspiration – a way of looking at the universe of which mankind is a part. (54)

But the finest example of the new understanding of rationalism comes from Joseph McCabe, who had moved considerably from his earlier understanding. In 1920, during his famous debate with Sir Arthur Conan Doyle, McCabe postulated what is, in my opinion, the finest vision of rationalism. He said:

> I represent Rationalism. That is to say, I want the whole world to use its reason, every man and woman in the world. I will respect any man or any woman, no matter what their conclusions may be, if they have used their own personality, their own mind, and their own judgment, rigorously and conscientiously. I do not care what conclusions they come to. (55)

McCabe never successfully achieved that goal, but then few people do. However, that does not make it an unworthy goal to strive for. No significant shift has happened in the RPA's conception of reason since McCabe's classic formulation of it in 1920. All that is necessary here is to give a few more examples of this open, tolerant, inquisitive and demanding vision of rationalism.

Towards the end of the Second World War, the RPA was faced with some stern questioning as to the nature of rationalism from younger members. So insistent did these challenges become that Miss James, the RPA's Public Relations Officer, sent out a memo for someone to provide some sort of answer. The job was taken up by Archibald Heath, lecturer in philosophy at the University of Swansea. The first thing he said about rationalism was this:

> Before we go any further I think we ought to make it quite clear that there are *two* things Rationalism cannot, and should not, offer. It cannot give us the glittering prizes of final certitude which resplendent dogmatisms hold out for our attraction. Nor can it provide us with the assurances and comfort of intellectual safety. That can be purchased only at the price of intellectual servitude. (56)

Elements of the either/or notion of rationalism remained influential, particularly among those who also happened to be Marxists. An example of this later and more dogmatic understanding of rationalism comes from 1954 in the form of a short work by Archibald Robertson. *Rationalism in Theory and Practice* argued that the supernaturalist and rationalist outlooks both acknowledge the dependence of humanity, but the crucial point is that they acknowledge very different forces. Rationalism not only does not acknowledge supernaturalism, it denies its validity as a legitimate explanation of the way the world works. The work of the rationalist movement is 'to break people of the opium habit, to wake them from their pipe dream, and to educate them in the scientific view of the world. For this reason, though unwedded to any social theory, it is nevertheless an agent of social progress.' (57) Robertson's short work was not a success. It was a sullen tract, the work of an old and tired man. The son of a bishop, Robertson's Marxism became more doctrinal and rigid as he grew older.

Robertson's tract was the last time rationalism was treated as an end rather than as a means. From this time on, rationalism has usually been discussed as a function rather than as a destination. In 1975, for instance, the lead article in that year's edition of *Question* was by Sheila Chown, a social psychologist, whose article asked 'What is a rationalist?' Chown attempted to understand the rationalist approach by means of a six-point model of behaviour. It is an unsatisfactory piece of work, but the relevant point here is that she was acknowledging the multifaceted nature of the reasoning process. Rationalists need to be able to live with ambiguity because areas of doubt and uncertainty cannot be resolved quickly and easily. (58) Years later, postmodernists would chide rationalists for an inability to live with ambiguity, as if this was some radical new insight.

At the same time as Sheila Chown's article, G A Wells was writing about rationalism in the *New Humanist*. We have already come across several instances where rationalists have warned against over-reliance on simple formulae, or what might today be called binary thinking. Here Wells argued that it is a misconception to suppose that there is some general rational method which qualifies one to tackle any problem rationally. There are, he went on to argue, three conditions for reasoning to take place: adequate knowledge of the subject, absence of bias and a motive for inquiry that is free from any tendency to favour one conclusion over another. It is evident from this, Wells said, that 'all of them are relative to and vary with, the question at issue.' In this way, Sir Isaac Newton, not a stupid man, could write uninteresting, even foolish things about scriptural interpretation. Wells also noted that increasing knowledge and education can also have the effect of increasing irrationalism, in that people understand less and less of the world around them and as a result are unable to see why they cannot attribute extraordinary powers to science or some anti-science nostrum. (59) This appreciation of the problems of modernity is not new of course, but it is worth noticing that rationalists were aware of the issues at hand, often well before their critics were.

Far from worshipping reason, as rationalists are frequently accused of doing, once the transition from rationalism to reasoning is made, rationalists have been ever more prepared to see rationality as bounded by biology. To take one example from a large number, Ronald Englefield discussed rationality in these terms in his article 'The Nature of Thinking', which appeared in the final issue of *Question*. It is not so much a battle between reason and the passions as between rival passions, into which 'reason' intercedes. However, reason in this context 'is merely the imagination which presents in turn the different memories of the consequences of the actions to which the opposed passions prompt.' (60)

So not only is reason simply a tool, it is a fragile tool, easily misused. But the point so often missed by anti-rationalists is that it is reason's very fragility that makes it all the more important for us to nurture and use it. As G A Wells wrote:

> What the rationalist says is that, for all reason's limitations, we have nothing else with which to understand the world, and that theologians suppose us capable of absolute truth either by simply alleging that this is so or by positing dubious and vague psychological faculties. (61)

Speaking to the RPA's Annual Dinner in 1971 H Gwynne Jones, Professor of Psychology at Leeds University, denied that rationalism was tantamount to a zero-sum heart versus head equation. 'For me to be rational is to adopt a non-dogmatic, sceptical essentially scientific approach to problems, knowing at the same time that I'm not going to reach any final answer. It follows, I believe, that the real enemy of rationalism is dogma.' (62) This, of course, was pretty much what the founders of the RPA had in mind.

In RPA publications since the 1950s that have spoken specifically of rationalism or featured the word 'rationalism' in the title, the term has been employed as Jones had in mind. *Rationalism in the 1970s* (1973) and *Rationalism in the Twenty-First Century* (2001) are good examples of this. Both publications are collections of addresses presented at RPA conferences. Neither work makes any attempt to enforce an ideological unity on the addresses. They are the results of intelligent people coming to grips with difficult issues by asking sensible questions and not being herded towards one type of answer by virtue of a prior-held commitment or prejudice. They are working examples of what Steven Lukes has called non-convergent ways of being reasonable. (63)

Before we leave the subject of rationalism, it is worth looking at what a non-specialist has described rationalism as. Ivor Russell, a member since 1948, long-standing RPA director, and chairman since 1997, spent his working life in business and wrote very little for any rationalist publication. But when the directors put their thoughts on paper about rationalism early in 1999, Russell itemised what rationalism was to him. For Russell, rationalism was made up of curiosity, the application of reasoning, learning from one's own experience and from the experience of others, and an unwillingness to accept the status quo. From these elements he deduced that rationalism involved no reliance on prejudice, superstition, dogma or fanaticism. Neither should there be distrust of the intellect or barriers of any kind to free inquiry. The positives to arise from this approach Russell put down as:

- the awareness that there are no eternal truths
- the awareness of the need for tolerance
- the awareness of the need for relaxation
- the awareness that the patient search for truth of any matter can have its own intellectual and emotional reward
- the awareness of the need of a way of life that conserves the diversity of nature now and for the future
- the awareness of humankind's responsibility for the future of the environment (64)

Now it would be gratifying to parade one's superiority by pointing out some inconsistencies in Russell's approach. Perhaps some level of scepticism toward the intellect would be more in keeping with his general approach, for example. But the point is that, contrary to the critics who declare it to be arid and dry, rationalism can and does provide a civilised, intellectually flexible and emotionally rewarding code by which ordinary men and women may live happy and fulfilled lives. And the RPA has been a reference point, a resource centre, for people wishing to live in this way for more than a century.

Humanism

The evolution of ideas about humanism through the twentieth century is more complicated than is the case for rationalism, agnosticism or atheism. It is also difficult to generalise about the charges made against humanism over the last century. Humanism has been held to account for practically every crime imaginable, from the Holocaust to muzak. Depending on the prejudices of the accuser, humanism has been held responsible for the decline in morals and for a moralistic priggishness. Humanism has been portrayed as a grave threat to society and a massive irrelevance to it, not infrequently by the same people. It has on the one hand been seen as shallow and foolishly optimistic while on the other hand humanism has been held to be a symptom of how grey and gloomy the human condition has become. Humanist leaders have been accused of being utopian muddleheads and of lacking a vision of the future.

While ill-informed assaults are to be expected from the fundamentalist fringe, some have come from reputable sources. Without doubt the most splenetic of recent attacks on humanism from a reputable source comes from John Carroll, at the time of his attack Reader in Sociology at the University of La Trobe in Melbourne, Australia. The title of his book, *Humanism: The Wreck of Western Culture*, says it all. Humanism, he says, has wrecked everything, and it was always bound to fail. Notwithstanding his drawing a salary from such an institution, Carroll is particularly severe on the universities, calling them mausoleums of dead ideas. He sees nothing good in humanism at all, which he divides into simple blocks of mockers and nihilists, the 'chief wreckers' being Darwin and Marx. The notion of equality, he holds, is rancorous, the Enlightenment was narrow-minded, Darwin was the greatest example of liberal vandalism, and humanists are, at heart, dishonest, because they fail to acknowledge the universal laws which their souls know to be true. The *New Humanist* review of Carroll's philippic also laments the decline in standards, although the standards are those Carroll doesn't mention: 'accuracy, fairness, balance and moderation.' (65)

The back cover of Carroll's book comes with a fulsome endorsement by Zygmunt Bauman, another of the most intemperate critics of humanism. But Bauman's antipathy is motivated not by Catholicism but by postmodernism. In Bauman's mind, the pretensions of modernity collapsed with the fall of communism. Instead, we are left with postmodernism, which seems to retain a similar helping of historical inevitability.

> Postmodernity is not a transitory departure from the 'normal state' of modernity, neither is it a diseased state of modernity, an ailment likely to be rectified, a case of 'modernity in crisis'. It is instead, a self-producing, pragmatically self-sustainable and logically self-contained social condition defined by distinctive features of its own.' (66)

This confident declaration is in the same book which gravely announces that the closer we come to portraying postmodernism as a balanced programme, the graver the faults that analysis has. At this end of the book, postmodernism is held to be a state of mind. 'This is a state of mind marked above all by its all-deriding, all-eroding, all-dissolving *destructiveness*.' (67) Just in case the reader missed the point, Bauman kindly puts the last word in italics. Other postmodernists have pronounced the end of any meaningful debate between naturalistic and supernaturalistic worldviews. For instance, John Milbank is pleased to announce that '...I find the issue validation versus non-validation of the sacred to be a more or less spurious and uninteresting one. What is more important is the mode of sacrality, the logic of a particular theological articulation.' (68)

It is difficult to respond systematically to these attacks. They seem to be motivated either by simple rancour or an unwillingness to take other arguments seriously. It is rare now to show humanism (or religion, for that matter) the courtesy of studying that which opponents seek to dismiss. In Bauman's case, the state of mind he characterises as postmodern compares miserably with the humanism he affects to despise.

Is Humanism a Religion?

Before we do what these critics have not done, which is to actually examine what humanists have said about their outlook, we need to embark upon a lengthy digression. One of the oddest and least helpful arguments within humanism in the twentieth century was over the degree to which it should be seen as a religion. The religious nature of humanism has long been expounded by its various advocates, and has, in equal measure, been decried by its opponents within the freethought movement. We have followed manifestations of this conflict throughout this book. The misplaced zeal of some in the United States to portray humanism in this way almost led to disastrous consequences, when fundamentalists led a legal challenge to having the humanist 'religion' excluded from public schools on that account. Had this gambit been successful, most of the advances in education built up over the past century would have been lost.

The debate in the United Kingdom has run along different lines, which themselves have taken on different forms at the different stages of the RPA's life. Before the First World War, it came in the form of debate between positivists and their opponents within the movement. Among the more prominent advocates of a substitutionist approach to rationalism were Charles Hooper and F J Gould. In an article in 1898 called 'The Parting of the Ways', Hooper made it clear that rationalism stood opposed to the arbitrary claims of revealed religion. The religionist, Hooper argued, 'has not really recovered from the still present effects of the old arbitrary division of history into sacred and profane; the latter half made to fit nature, the former to fit supernature.' Against this arbitrary division, Hooper looked forward to the emergence of the

> grand human ideals of freedom and self-completeness, sympathy and social completeness, truth and philosophic completeness – ideals between some of which there are passing antagonisms, yet which tend to be both theoretically and practically reconciled, as man faithfully follows the light of reason, into the deeper arcana of that Nature which culminates, for him, in an endless vista of progress. (69)

This was what Hooper understood by the religion of humanity. In a short, unsigned article from 1907, called 'First Principles of the RPA', the writer repeated the articles of the RPA and concluded that rationalism could be summed up under two connected principles: the supremacy of reason and the need to base the whole structure of rational opinion on experience. From this, it was inferred, no claim is made to formulate the opinions to which these foundational approaches could lead the inquirer. But the writer was also anxious to insist that rationalism as conceived here does have a faith, though not a creed:

> a faith that its objects are worth striving for – that the light of reason and its logical uses are needful for mankind; that "moral and intellectual fitness for social life" may be attained independently of belief in the supernatural and the blessings of ecclesiastical persons; that to bring the literature of reason and science within the reach of the multitude is to wield the greatest of intellectual forces for the good of our own and future generations. (70)

This sounds so much like Hooper. The positivist strand within organised rationalism flickered out well before the First World War and few lamented its departure. The torch of rational religion was not left untended, however, as it was a central motif of the ethical movement and therefore lies beyond the scope of this book. One of its main champions was Stanton Coit (1857-1944) who argued in the *Rationalist Annual* of 1927 for continued use of terms like 'God' and 'religion' free from their supernaturalistic accretions. Coit claimed that human life is holy and 'holy' is the greatest word in religion. (71)

The abolitionist view held among members of the RPA was best put in a *Guide* article from April 1936. J P Gilmour, at the time Chairman of the RPA Board of Directors wrote a lengthy article bringing together a great number of definitions of religion. Gilmour's conclusion was explicit. The attempts by 'neologians and some improvising Rationalists' to retain helpful elements in religion for unbelief was well-meant but sentimental.

> If terms such as "God" and "religion" are to be denuded of every shred of meaning hitherto denoted or implied by them, then surely it is an insult to our intelligence to retain them in contexts in which they are meaningless or mischievous…(72)

Gilmour's point could well have been written thirty years later, when the arguments espoused by Stanton Coit passed on to their strongest advocate. Julian Huxley had long stood in the substitutionist wing of the freethought movement. His most systematic working out of a substitutionist cosmology was in *Religion without Revelation*. This book appeared originally in 1927 and then again, in an abridged form, in the RPA's Thinker's Library in 1941, although not without opposition, as we saw in Chapter Three. The first suggestion to include it in the Thinker's Library in 1935 was turned down. In the middle 1950s Huxley felt the need to expand and revise *Religion without Revelation* but lacked the time to do it, so on Huxley's 'importunate request' H J Blackham took the task on. As Blackham later recalled, 'I did not tamper with the original thesis, with which I did not pretend to be in sympathy. In both revisions, I excised substantial parts and incorporated later and better statements of his Evolutionary Humanism.' (73)

Humanism as a term was already in the air but Huxley's book did a lot to build on that momentum. What the world needs, Huxley wrote, is 'an essentially religious idea system, unitary instead of dualistically split, and charged with the total dynamic of knowledge old and new, objective and subjective, of experience scientific and spiritual.' (74) Huxley then proceeded to offer up evolutionary humanism as that religious idea system. Huxley's evolutionary humanism was a strangely anthropocentric notion. Its claim to be scientifically sound notwithstanding, evolutionary humanism retained the distinctly pre-scientific notion of the great chain of being. Man is 'the highest product of the cosmic process of which we have any knowledge; accordingly, we can formulate the ultimate aim of the human species as the realisation of more possibilities by more, and more fully developed, individuals.' (75)

Huxley was anxious for evolutionary humanism to be seen as a religion. He saw the essence of religion as that which 'springs from man's capacity for awe and reverence, that the objects of religion, however much later rationalised by intellect or moralised by ethics...are in origin and essence those things, events, and ideas which arouse the feeling of sacredness.' (76) At the inauguration of the BHA, Huxley said the same thing, claiming that 'religion is a universal and inevitable function of human life.' (77)

Huxley's views met with a mixed reception inside the humanist movement; indeed, his influence was greater in the United States than in the United Kingdom. But he certainly had his supporters. One of them was Jean Mackay (1920-1986), who in 1963 wrote *What Humanism is About* under the name Kit Mouat. This book, published by Pemberton, was very much a popular recycling of Huxley's approach. Huxley was praised as 'perhaps the greatest living Humanist' and religion was divorced from supernaturalism and defined as 'the up-reaching and aspiring impulse in a human life.' Humanism, in that sense, was to be seen as a religion. (78)

Hector Hawton was strongly opposed to this line of thinking. Indeed, this was the fault line on which the rationalist-humanist tensions of the sixties rested. In the same year as Pemberton published *What Humanism is About*, it also published Hector Hawton's book, *The Humanist Revolution*. There, Hawton made his thoughts clear:

> What Humanism unquestionably rejects is religion in the narrow and more usual connotation. This is a form of dualism, a two-world theory. Behind the tangible, visible world of Nature there is said to be an intangible, invisible world.' (79)

A year later, in *The Humanist*, Hawton said the same thing, from a different point of view when he called for the retention of the rationalist element of humanism. (80) Hawton saw humanism and religion as quite different things. And yet he was by no means a consistent abolitionist. Hawton understood religion, having been genuinely and enthusiastically religious throughout the formative years of his life. His writings exhibit no personal animus against religion at all. Indeed, he retained a nostalgia for the picturesqueness of the symbolism and poetry of religion all his life. But to muddy the distinction between the two was folly.

> I suspect that the reason why some people complain that Humanism is vague is that they want it to provide the unequivocal rulings which the Church attempts, though quite often evades. In fact, they expect

Humanism to function in the same way as conventional religion. It cannot do so, which is one reason why I think some Humanists are unwise in claiming to offer a new religion. People who ask to be told how to behave have come to the wrong address. (81)

The soapy bubble of Huxleyism had well and truly popped by the later 1960s, not least because of Hawton's intelligent and persistent opposition. But toward the end of the 1970s the whole idea returned, although it was of interest to a significantly smaller audience. It was at this time that Peter Cadogan, then general secretary of the South Place Ethical Society, led a concerted attempt to reclothe humanism in religious garb. Following the distinction made by Huxley, Cadogan wanted to distinguish religion from supernaturalism, and then see religion as a basic attribute of *homo sapiens*. This was in line with an attempt he masterminded to have the South Place Ethical Society's charitable status returned to it. The opposition to Cadogan was led this time by Nicolas Walter, who subjected it to biting criticism. Under Walter's leadership, the *New Humanist* became the main organ for promoting the secularist argument against Cadogan and his allies. Walter wished South Place well in its attempt to regain charitable status, but then added:

> But I am sure it is true to say that in this country most Humanists see religion as being linked inextricably with supernaturalism and therefore reject it, and few Humanists are still impressed or even interested in the various attempts to establish a non-theistic form of religion – whether the 'Rational Religion' of the Owenite movement, or the 'Religion of Humanity' of the Positivist Churches, or the 'Religious Humanism' of the Ethical Societies. (82)

H J Blackham, who, as we have seen, shares part of the responsibility for religious humanism achieving what popularity it did, was even clearer. Of religious humanism, he said '"Tried and failed" is its epitaph, and its doom. It does not offer what people who want religion want from religion.' (83) The failure of liberal Christianity attests to the accuracy of that observation.

Paradoxically, Cadogan's attempt to recast humanism as religious was unsuccessful, but his efforts to regain charitable status for the South Place Ethical Society paid off. In June 1980 the Chancery Division of the High Court found that the society was not a religious organisation but that it was nonetheless eligible for charity status on the grounds of its educational role. (84)

More recently the tendencies toward religious humanism have become the preserve of the Sea of Faith movement, inspired largely by the heretical Anglican, Don Cupitt. This movement is mostly a phenomenon of the extremes of liberal Christianity, rather than that of the humanist movement, and so falls outside the view of this book. This said, the vast majority of Sea of Faith enthusiasts would have felt at home in the RPA of before the First World War. Their position is not that dissimilar to the non-doctrinal theism of F W Newman, whose *Phases of Faith* the RPA published in 1907. Their main problem is that they have not moved on from Newman's positions in any significant way.

The most recent foray into this area within the auspices of the RPA came in the middle of the 1990s when Harold Stopes-Roe devised an interesting way to solve the problem. Stopes-Roe's innovation was to portray humanism as a 'life-stance'. He argued that there are two meanings usually implied when people speak of 'religion'. On the one hand they are referring to the focus of what is most important in life. This was the sense in which the word was used by Huxley and Cadogan. But on the other hand, religion very often involves speaking of God. It was Stopes-Roe's idea to clarify this confusion which had bedevilled much humanist discourse for most of the twentieth century. He was content that religion should retain its supernaturalist implications, on the grounds of this being how most people understand the term. But Stopes-Roe was *not* content that religions should be permitted to retain their self-declared monopoly on the focus of what is most important in life. Non-religious people, from the classical Indian materialists, Confucian and other Chinese thinkers, and the pre-Socratic Greeks have been vitally interested in what really matters in life without being religious in the sense of positing some sort of God figure.

In light of this, Stopes-Roe offered the term 'life-stance' to refer to the concern with meaning and purpose without borrowing religious terminology. His formal definition of 'life-stance' was

> An individual's or a community's relationship with what they accept as of ultimate importance; the commitments and the presuppositions of this, and the theory and the practice of this relationship working itself out in living. (85)

Stopes-Roe was happy for religious people to see their worldview in terms of a life-stance as well, indeed one of the advantages of 'life-stance' was its sensitivity to their position *and* that of non-believers. As for humanism, Stopes-Roe was quite clear that the naturalistic view of the universe is fundamentally at odds with the religious worldview, which posits some sort of superpurposive agency. 'The definition of humanism excludes superpurposive realities and therefore the idea of a god; this must be a root element.' But one's life stance is not some philosophical exercise. He quoted the American athlete Mildred Didrikson as illustrating what he had in mind. "It's not enough just to swing at the ball. You've got to loosen your girdle and really let the ball have it." (86) As Britain gropes its way toward becoming a genuinely pluralist society, the idea of life stance has become quite popular and has found its way into legal and educational documents.

What humanism is

Having seen the caricatures of humanism put up and knocked down by its religious and postmodernist enemies, and then having established firmly that humanism is not a religion, we need now ask what humanism actually is. As we have done with rationalism, it is worthwhile to actually look at what humanists have said. The 1950s and 1960s were the golden decades in the development of humanism in Britain. Since the 1980s, however, the leadership has passed ever more surely to the United States. The RPA had a central role to play in the first of these phases and an important one in the second. In the 1960s and 1970s it provided significant intellectual leadership and took a leading role in formulating and propagating humanist principles. More recently it has been significant mainly in the propagating of developments taking place elsewhere. This said, Harry Stopes-Roe's contribution is significant because it makes clear humanism's value as a legitimate system of belief, without it being a pseudo-religion.

This was pretty much what Hector Hawton had in mind as well. Introducing a collection of essays in 1956, Hawton summarised humanism in this way:

> Humanism is not a single, comprehensive system of philosophy which you must take or leave. It is an attempt to deal with the situation in which no such system and no religious revelation are conveniently available to resolve all our perplexities. If we are thrown on our own human resources, compelled to create our own standards of conduct, unable to count on some future existences in which mistakes and injustices will be redressed – what then? (87)

Among many of the important contributions Hawton made to the contemporary understanding of humanism was that he gave it a rationalist backbone. It is precisely this rationalist backbone that distinguishes humanism from religions or other systems of belief. The rationalist backbone is provided not by 'whether the traditional doctrines are useful, either socially or morally, but whether they are *true*. Once we find ourselves doubting their truth it is beneath human dignity to take refuge in evasions and subterfuges.' (88) Working from this, Hawton went on to describe the aims of humanism in these terms:

> The aim of Humanism is to discover the true place of man in Nature, to find out what he may reasonably hope to achieve and what would be folly to attempt, in the light of purely secular knowledge. (89)

It was part of Hawton's genius that he then devised several series of articles in the *Literary Guide/Humanist* which sought to put these principles into action. The first of these series, which ran from March until November 1955, was entitled 'What can we believe?' As well as getting brief surveys of Christianity, Marxism and Scientific Humanism, readers were acquainted with current thoughts on how we should approach epistemological questions. Two months after this series began, Hawton launched 'In Search of Knowledge', where scholars wrote clear introductions to their various disciplines. Thus, readers were given a thumbnail sketch of the principles of physics, philosophy, social anthropology, literary criticism and so on. And as this series drew to a close, Hawton began his next series, called 'Amend This Law', where various reforms were advocated. They included abortion, divorce, euthanasia, Sunday restrictions, blasphemy, adoption, censorship and religious instruction in schools. It is interesting to note how similar this list is with Cyril Joad's so-called rationalist's charter that served as a focus for the Progressive League twenty years previously, and for the programme of reformers associated with the RPA from before the First World War. What was new about Hawton's vision of applied humanism was the vastly greater coverage given to art, literature, short stories and entertainment than had ever been seen in a rationalist magazine. But Hawton did not neglect the sciences. On the contrary, he ran more articles outlining elements of science than had previously been common in the *Guide*. He also broadened the range from the traditional focus on evolution. One of the shorter runs from this time was a four-part series called 'The Intelligence of Animals', by Maurice Burton.

One of the authorities Hawton relied on for these series was Antony Flew. In his article on scientific humanism written for the 'What can we believe?' series, Flew outlined a conception of humanism which was largely indistinguishable from earlier notions of rationalism. As was popular at the time, he spoke of scientific humanism:

> So I take my stand as a scientific humanist: 'scientific' primarily as regards matters of fact; 'humanist' concerning questions of value. Scientific humanism is not a system, even a sketchy system, of doctrine; but rather a cast of mind, a type of approach, a climate of opinion. (90)

What made Antony Flew's contribution so valuable to the humanist movement, apart from his ability to write clearly, was his willingness to use the same term as employed by many on the political left. For the Marxist and pro-Soviet elements in the movement tended to presume the 'scientific' part referred to their political beliefs. By the 1960s this group was calling itself socialist humanism. Eventually most prefixes were jettisoned, so by the 1960s most people spoke simply of humanism.

The longest lasting of Hawton's series in *The Humanist* was called 'The Humanist Tradition'. As the name suggests, this series was designed to acquaint readers with people and ideas from the history of humanism. The series began in February 1957 with an article by H J Blackham on the rise of secularism, followed by Benjamin Farrington on the legacy of Greece and Rome and D C Lau on the humanism of Confucius. Lau had a long academic career in London and Hong Kong and translated and wrote introductions to the *Tao Te Ching*, *Mencius* and Confucius' *Analects* for the Penguin Classics series. Aspects of Chinese and Indian thought were covered extensively and generously during Hawton's years at *The Humanist*.

As well as the ongoing work in *The Humanist*, the RPA was responsible for some good books devoted to outlining what humanism is. The first of them was from M Roshwald of the Hebrew University in Jerusalem, whose book *Humanism in Practice* (1955) was an approachable essay that gave a simple summary of humanism. Roshwald defined humanism as 'a philosophy demanding the fullest possible development of the faculties of every human being in order to secure to each and every one the conditions of happiness.' (91) Three years later, J B Coates, the man who had let the humanistic cat among the rationalist pigeons back in 1931, wrote *A Challenge to Christianity*. Coates's book was a lot longer and more academic than Roshwald's work, and spent more time comparing humanism favourably with Christianity. But the two books shared a common approach to humanism. And then, in 1963, came Hawton's book *The Humanist Revolution*, which we have examined elsewhere. So by the time the British Humanist Association was established, Hawton had done his very best to have the reading public ready for, and supportive of, the idea of humanism. It constitutes one of the RPA's greatest achievements.

The high point of British humanism was 1968 when H J Blackham's short introduction to humanism was published by Penguin, Pemberton published a collection of essays, edited by A J Ayer, called *The Humanist Outlook*, and Ronald Fletcher (1921-1992), Professor of Sociology at the University of York, wrote 'A Definition of Humanism' which appeared in the first volume of *Question* and later as a pamphlet. Strictly speaking, both books fall outside the range of this book as neither was an RPA initiative. All the contributors to *The Humanist Outlook* were members of the BHA's advisory council, and Blackham was the BHA's Director at the time his book was published. However, virtually every contributor to *The Humanist Outlook* was also an Honorary Associate of the RPA and the work was published by Pemberton, the RPA's publishing arm. The considerable cross-membership between the four freethought organisations in the United Kingdom and their shared common goals make too careful a differentiation among them seem pedantic.

While both *Humanism* and *The Humanist Outlook* were intellectually respectable, neither sparkled with life. Both works sought, rightly, to disentangle humanism from Marxism, with Blackham putting the case most strongly when he denied that Marxism-Leninism has made or even can make a lasting contribution to humanism. Both stressed the central role rationality plays in the humanist worldview, but also said that humanism is more than rationalism. Again, Blackham put it best when he said that there 'is more than reason in the life of reason or it is not reasonable.' (92) This is a point about rationalism and humanism that is consistently misunderstood and even misrepresented, not infrequently by the movement's friends as well as its enemies.

The essays which made up *The Humanist Outlook* succeeded in giving an impression of the values and priorities of the humanist view of things, but still left in the air the question of what humanism actually is. This is where Ronald Fletcher's article in *Question* was particularly useful. As is true for most definitions of humanism, Fletcher began by emphasising that humanism is not a creed but an approach. Human knowledge, he wrote, can 'never be final or dogmatic, but always be limited, uncertain, open to question. And this is a position adopted not on the basis of *arrogating* powers of truth to the human mind but on that of recognising its necessary limitations.' (93) Working from this initial position of intellectual modesty, Fletcher saw humanism as being active in the world. It's not enough to sympathise with suffering, to wring one's hands before sitting on them. The humanist must be socially active and make some actual contribution to the betterment of the world. He then went on to add that while humanists are human-centred, they are not human-confined. 'A sensitive vulnerability to all the dimensions of our entanglement in the world, and the desire to probe and to articulate the experience of some deeply sensed meaning in it all, are not exclusive to religions.' (94) He then emphasised the importance of toleration, self-responsibility, opposition to the arbitrary imposition of authority, and the development of character. Contrary to two of the most well worn caricatures of humanism, Fletcher's account was neither shallowly optimistic nor devoid of hope.

> Humanism, it seems to me, has to recognise an inescapable undertone of tragedy in the world. Ultimately, the situation of mankind in the world is a tragic one. Human life is transient...All that we are, all that we love,

all those things, people, and values to which and to whom we are attached by love, perish. Nothing of an individual nature seems permanent. Nothing is certain. Humanism can offer no consolation. (95)

What humanism can offer in the light of this reality is the awareness that we can value people, ideas, and things no less despite knowing they are transient. The recognition of the tragic undertone to human existence is what gives our love of it while we are alive a special poignancy and colour. Fletcher's vision of humanism remains one of the finest in the British humanist tradition.

The next person to outline the need for a broader picture of humanism was Colin Campbell, who wrote an excellent article for the *New Humanist* in 1977, outlining the need for a humanist vision. Sadly, Campbell's article, as with some other of his first-rate ideas, got lost in the daily blaze. Paul Kurtz, the leading humanist thinker in the United States, has taken up the task of actually articulating this vision. What Kurtz has been able to do that other humanist thinkers have not done is to provide humanism with an effective message without resorting to formulae or slogans. The RPA, to its credit, recognised this shift and reprinted Kurtz's articles regularly in the *New Humanist*. An article from *Free Inquiry* in 1983, which was reproduced in the *New Humanist* the following year, will serve to illustrate the message.

> I interpret the message of contemporary Humanism as having four major components: (1) it is a method of inquiry; (2) it presents a world view…; (3) it offers a set of moral values to provide meaning and direction for life; and (4) it provides a rich storehouse of artistic, poetic, and literary forms of expression. (96)

Kurtz then translated this programme into a set of principles and values. Humanism involves a commitment to free and open inquiry, a belief in the courage to live without fear and trembling, confidence in human creativity, constant effort to improve the human condition, respect for the rights of others, the cultivation of happiness and the full life, of love, shared experience and human joy, and the defence of the pluralistic, open society which can best allow these ideals to find fruit. These principles were a development of the *Secular Humanist Declaration*, which Kurtz had drafted in 1980 in response to some apoplectic attacks on humanism in the United States. In Britain, where the fundamentalist threat has never been remotely so serious as it has become in the United States, the reaction to the *Secular Humanist Declaration* was muted. The *Declaration* was reprinted in the January 1981 issue of the *New Humanist* along with comment on the local response. The irregular appearance of the *New Humanist* at the time worked against any systematic response to the *Declaration* in Britain. This provided the most graphic illustration of the initiative in world humanism having crossed the Atlantic.

Rationalism, humanism and the wider world

Having looked briefly at what the rationalists and humanists have said about their beliefs, how consistent have they been in advocating them? Wordy declarations of noble intention are one thing, putting them into practice is altogether another.

After all, one of the most nobly worded documents of the twentieth century was the Soviet constitution of 1936. Let us look, then, at the relationship between theory and practice in the RPA.

From the very beginning, the RPA has championed pluralism and diversity; what *has* expanded is the notion of what constitutes pluralism and diversity. For instance, Charles Watts's senior celebrated rationalism as a means by which people could think differently and work together. 'As all persons cannot think alike, Rationalism eschews persecution for heresy, and encourages co-operation for the general good, irrespective of differences of opinion.' (97) The diversity Watts had in mind was that of opinions about religion, morality and society. As the twentieth century developed, so did the diversity that rationalists sought to defend, and the RPA developed with it.

There are many examples that could be used to illustrate this commitment to pluralism and diversity. We have already covered the RPA's long-standing commitment to issues like moral education and the repeal of the blasphemy laws. So let us simply take racism as a case study. As with most Britons at the turn of the twentieth century, the early RPA members had little experience with racial diversity. Certainly there are examples of racism to be found, although they are remarkably few, given how uncontroversial racist views were, and were to remain for a long time. The most explicitly racist work published by Watts & Co was called *The Peace of the Anglo-Saxons* by Major Stewart L Murray and was published in 1905. Subtitled 'To the working men and their representatives', Murray's book was an attempt to unite capital and labour in the pressing task of imperial defence. It was frankly social-darwinist (he actually quotes the 'nature, red in tooth and claw' passage that has become the litmus test of social-darwinism) and imbued with the romance of the white man's burden. Murray did not speak of non-white people with rancour, in fact he hardly mentioned them at all. His book was a plea to the English working classes to join a common front of the Anglo-Saxon nations to take up the burden together. To the extent that the RPA had a considered view on the imperial question, it can be said to have been indifferent to the empire. Most of its leading thinkers of the time, J M Robertson and Joseph McCabe, were unmoved by, or actively opposed to, imperial rhetoric.

Among leading RPA activists, there has been little open racism. The clearest example is from Edward Clodd in a book on T H Huxley and published by Blackwood. Clodd took pains to acquit his hero of the charge of 'believing in the negro', his opposition to slavery notwithstanding. Huxley knew, wrote Clodd approvingly, 'how permanent are the natural inequalities of the races'. (98) About the only example of explicit racism in the pages of the *Literary Guide/Humanist/New Humanist* in its long life comes from 1928 when Macleod Yearsley (1867-1951), author of *The Story of the Bible* (1922) and at this time editor of a column in the *Guide* called 'Book Chat', aired his anti-semitism. Yearsley said 'I believe this cheating strain still exists in Abraham's descendants to-day, even to the extent of cozening one another; the "goy" is always fair game...'. (99) Yearsley's comments provoked a reaction two issues later when Charles Watts distanced himself from Yearsley's comments, reiterated that they were not the view of the RPA, and recalled the generous assistance of Jewish rationalists (most notably Sir Herbert Leon) to the development of the organisation. 'We trust that this explanation will convince Jewish members of the RPA that the organisation, so far as its officials are concerned, has no anti-semitic prejudices; on the contrary, the Directors place high value on the co-operation of Jews in humanist propaganda.' Yearsley's career with the *Guide* soon ended, although he remained a member of the RPA until his death.

Against these examples of racism, and contrary to the more recent accusation that rationalism and humanism are 'Eurocentric discourses', we find the opposite to be the case. I have written at length elsewhere on Joseph McCabe's generally enlightened view on race questions. His views were slightly in advance of most of his contemporaries, but can still be taken as broadly representative. We have also commented on the RPA's long record of friendship with Indian rationalists. Another interesting example is Sir R F Johnston – the notorious 'Lin Shao-Yang' of 1911. In his *Chinese Appeal to Christendom* he spoke in these terms:

> Where they [missionaries] think they are inculcating a higher morality it frequently happens that they are merely inculcating a different morality. In other words, one of the objects steadily kept before them is to persuade the Chinese that the western code of ethics is the standard to which the rest of the world ought to be required to conform.

But Johnston was not content to assign this fault exclusively to missionaries. He went on to acknowledge that genuine toleration of others' cultures is not an easy thing for anyone to manage.

> To a great extent this inability to see things from other people's points of view is common to nearly every one. Perhaps one of the rarest of human qualities (if indeed it is to be found at all) is complete freedom from racial, political, social, and religious prejudices. (100)

Changing tack slightly, it is also worth noting that the RPA published a work of poetry in 1912 by Claude McKay (1890-1948), a black man born in Jamaica who later emigrated to the United States and become one of black America's finest poets, novelists and political activists of the early twentieth century. In the same year as Watts & Co published *Constab Ballads*, the *Literary Guide* reviewed very positively McKay's previous work *Songs of Jamaica*. McKay was introduced to the RPA by Walter Jekyll, an Englishman and longtime RPA member, who had lived for many years in Jamaica. Jekyll had two books published by Watts & Co: an anthology called *The Wisdom of Schopenhauer* and a critique of the Bible called *The Bible Untrustworthy*. Jekyll also brought together a collection of Jamaican ballads and ensured they were published, thereby contributing towards their preservation. (101)

After the Second World War, the RPA demonstrated a more specific interest in and commitment to racial equality. Among books critical of racism was Hamilton Fyfe's book, *The Illusion of National Character*, originally published by Watts & Co in 1940 and reprinted in abridged form as No. 116 in the Thinker's Library six years later. Fyfe was one of the more effective smiters of humbug among his generation. He became an Honorary Associate of the RPA in 1948. *The Illusion of National Character* poured scorn on then commonly used stereotypes like 'the

German mind', 'the dour Scot' or the 'mysticism of the East'. There are, he said, all sorts of Americans, many kinds of Frenchmen. In the same year, Watts & Co published *Racial Pride and Prejudice* by Dr Eric Dingwall, an anthropologist and psychologist. This book covered a wider field than Fyfe's but was just as dismissive of racial pretensions. The significant thing about these books is that they were both directed toward the general reader.

At the beginning of the 1960s, attention turned to the newly independent countries of Africa. In 1961 the RPA devoted its Annual Conference to the theme of 'The African Revolution: A Challenge to Humanists'. The subtitle was deliberate. A high calibre of speaker was invited, although two of the speakers, Leopold Takawira of the National Democratic Party of Southern Rhodesia and Dennis Phombeah, Secretary General of the Committee of African Organisations, had to return to Africa on urgent business. Both speakers ensured that they sent capable replacements. The other African speaker was Joao Cabral, at the time wanted by the Portuguese government for his activities in the Portuguese colonies. His account of the brutality and inefficiency of Portuguese rule was a shock for some of the audience. In 1962 Hawton ran an article by Cabral praising Nehru for moving into Portuguese Goa, which was at the time collapsing into civil strife.

We saw that during the *Satanic Verses* affair, the *New Humanist* maintained a consistent line of defending freedom of speech and the open society while not demonising Muslim opponents, and, indeed, opening its pages to its opponents. The same level of even-handedness is evident in the treatment of the September 11 terrorist attacks.

It can fairly be said, then, that the RPA has an admirable record on the question of racism. Were we to have followed the RPA's attitudes and publications on gender issues, we would find a no less remarkable record of openness. That this should be so is testament to another commitment central to humanism. Humanists have championed more consistently than any other group, the notion of the open society. In all likelihood Henri Bergson was the first person to use the term, but it is now associated with Karl Popper, and in particular his two volume work, *The Open Society and Its Enemies*, which he wrote while in exile in New Zealand from the ravages of Nazism. Popper characterised a closed society as one in which the institutions are said to be fixed and unchangeable by virtue of some creed or a supposed historical dialectic. The open society, by contrast, is one where the institutions are not sacrosanct but are themselves able to be changed and redesigned as the need arises. Similarly, people may enter or leave any institution (think of a university, church, union or government department) without risk to their person or safety, as can be the case in closed societies. In this way, opportunity for quality education and employment is not based on differences of creed or social position, or indeed of any other contrived distinction.

But even a notion like the open society is vulnerable to criticism, and humanists have been among the first to recognise the problems. A J Ayer expressed his concern at a seminar on the open society organised by the BHA in 1969. An open society is one thing, but Ayer was worried about a society so fluid that no sense of positive identity was possible. He was worried that people in the affluent west are increasingly tending to define themselves in terms of the possessions they own or the football club they support, or, less helpfully, on their race, age or some other arbitrary division. Decades later, Ayer's fear has in no sense been assuaged. And from the other end of the freethought movement David Tribe, president of the National Secular Society between 1963 and 1971, complained that the term is too vague for practical application and in a literal sense is an oxymoron.

So, the commitment of rationalists and humanists to the open society is not an uncritical acceptance of a slogan, but a thoughtful commitment to a prescription bitter experience has shown will impinge on our freedoms the least. This puts humanism at odds almost by definition with religions, which have rarely been at their most convincing in conditions of diversity. Theistic religions like Christianity, and secular systems like Marxism, share a way of thinking about history, and about their opponents, which operates most effectively in a closed society. Responding to the September 11 attacks, Laurie Taylor wrote:

> [O]ur response to recent events in America must go beyond a resigned 'told you so' reaction to yet another example of the horrors that can be perpetrated in the name of religion. We must actively resist the facile link between secularism and materialism and continue to argue that the best hope for human happiness lies not with either the advocates of rampant here-and-now materialism or the prophets of eternal bliss but with those who treat their fellow human beings with respect and love for no other reason than a recognition of their common humanity. (102)

Chapter 8

Eupraxophy in Action

'What they have in common is a commitment to rational enquiry in matters of belief and an opposition to irrationalism in all its forms...'.
Hector Hawton, 1974

Does any organisation have a more impressive array of Honorary Associates than the Rationalist Press Association? I pose this question rhetorically as a measure of my confidence as to the answer. The staggering intellectual wealth of the many Honorary Associates is one of the features most commented upon about the RPA. One immediately apparent feature of the RPA Honorary Associates is their diversity. Hector Hawton noted this in an appreciation of the 75th anniversary of the RPA in May 1974. Among the Honorary Associates, he wrote

> you will see that some are agnostics, some atheists, others pragmatists or dialectical materialists or logical positivists. There are also representatives of different political parties – Liberal, Conservative, Socialist and Communist. What they have in common is a commitment to rational enquiry in matters of belief and an opposition to irrationalism in all its forms – to thinking with the blood, like Hitler, through the solar plexus with D H Lawrence, through blind faith with Kierkegaard. (1)

Appendix Two has the full list of RPA Honorary Associates, but in this final chapter it seems worthwhile to look at a few of them in an attempt to understand what rationalism and humanism mean in people's lives. There is no particular rationale for who has been examined and who not, apart from my having concentrated on the unjustly treated, the unjustly forgotten and the surprise packages.

Paul Kurtz, an Honorary Associate since 1979, coined the term eupraxophy, which means the dynamic fusion of wisdom and practice in making for a full life. It is all very well to be wise and it is all very well to be active; Kurtz wants humanists to be both, and to the fullest degree possible. Peter Singer has the same thing in mind when he writes about the ethical life. In this chapter it would be nice to wander among these names and see what we can learn about them as people, and what we can learn about the rationalism and the humanism that they, in their various ways, embraced. Finishing in this way also serves to remind us that rationalism and humanism, as with all systems of belief, are nothing without the people who devote time and energy to their propagation.

Many people are surprised, for instance, to be told that Albert Einstein (1879-1955) was an Honorary Associate. When in 1958 the New Zealand Rationalist Association was given permission to make a presentation on radio about rationalism, the only point the state broadcasting corporation queried was Einstein's status as an Honorary Associate of the RPA. Einstein accepted the title in 1934 and held it until his death in 1955. Now it would be misleading to claim that Einstein, and many of the other RPA Honorary Associates, was any more involved than in a strictly honorary capacity. The RPA was just one of a number of organisations which approached Einstein in the early thirties for his endorsement. But having said this, Einstein accepted the title and did so because he was in full agreement with the principles of rationalism and humanism. And, it appears, Einstein kept up to date with humanist thinking via the *Literary Guide*. The June 1955 issue of the *Guide* reprinted a photograph of Einstein's desk as it was at the time of his death a couple of months earlier. On the desk, amid pages of equations and Einstein's pipe sat the April issue of the *Literary Guide*, complete with Hawton's editorial 'The Challenge of the Bomb'. This photograph later appeared in Ronald W Clark's biography of Einstein.

It is important to make these things clear, particularly in the light of the many rather strained attempts by various groups to claim Einstein as one of their own. This has been particularly noticeable among advocates of mystical cults, or various branches of eastern philosophy. He has even been claimed by Theosophists. Hawton had to contest claims Einstein had made a late conversion to Christianity within weeks of his death. Then and now, these attempts to capture Einstein for some weird creed or another collapse under scrutiny. Albert Einstein was, in any meaningful sense of the word, an atheist. Einstein wrote

> I cannot conceive of a God who rewards and punishes his creatures, or has a will of the type of which we are conscious of ourselves. An individual who should survive his physical death is also beyond my comprehension; nor do I wish it otherwise. Such notions are the fears or absurd egoism of feeble souls. (2)

If Einstein did not believe in a personal God, neither was he a mystic, despite the many attempts to paint him in these colours. (3) Five years after his work *Mein Weltbild* was published in English as *The World As I See It*, the RPA had secured the rights to reprint it. Einstein's book was released as No. 79 of the Thinker's Library series. Here Einstein made his views clear. The origin of religion, Einstein wrote, lay in primitive humanity's fear of the power of nature, and to this day most people remain locked in notions of an anthropomorphic god. Einstein's cosmology was monistic in the same way as Ernst Haeckel's was monistic. Haeckel spoke of a law of substance which underlay the apparent opposites of mind and matter. Einstein's understanding of the universe was, of course, vastly more sophisticated than this, but it amounted to a similar thing; atheistic monism.

Einstein posited what he called cosmic religious feeling. Such feeling 'knows no dogma and no God conceived in man's image; so that there can be no Church whose central teachings are based on it.' (4) Einstein's conception of cosmic religious feeling revolved around the sense of wonder and loss of sense of self that scientific investigations of the workings of the universe can engender. In this

Einstein is at one with later eminent scientists who shared that sense of wonder and awe in the face of the universe. People like Carl Sagan, Richard Dawkins, James Trefil – all atheists.

In a speech he called 'My Credo', given in Berlin in 1932, Einstein spoke of the most beautiful and deep experience we can have in the sense of the mysterious.

> To sense that behind anything that can be experienced there is a something that our mind cannot grasp and whose beauty and sublimity reaches us only indirectly and as a feeble reflection, this is religiousness. In this sense I am religious. To me it suffices to wonder at these secrets and to attempt humbly to grasp with my mind a mere image of the lofty structure of all that there is. (5)

And in a speech entitled 'Science and Religion', given at a conference of Jewish intellectuals in New York toward the end of 1940, Einstein, made it quite clear that rationality had a central role to play in the any spiritual quest.

> The further the spiritual evolution of mankind advances, the more certain it seems to be that the path to genuine religion does not lie through the fear of life, or the fear of death, and blind faith, but through striving after rational knowledge. (6)

It is a conceit of mystagogues to suppose rationalists cannot express themselves in this way. Such people assume that references to deeper experience or underlying reality mean that their fanciful schema of the universe has been vindicated. They also fail to appreciate the significance of the last sentence here quoted. Rather than accept as revealed truth some miscellany of catchphrases, Einstein was content that the most coherent picture of the universe he could have would be a mere image of the lofty structure of all there is. Whereas mystics usually like to cover themselves in the shroud of humility, their claims to understand infinitely more than Einstein of the ultimate workings of the universe smack of cosmic presumption. The consequence of Einstein's cosmic religious feeling was a simple humanism. 'It is,' Einstein wrote, 'the duty of every man of good will to strive steadfastly in his own little world to make this teaching of pure humanity a living force, so far as he can.' (7)

Albert Einstein was not, of course, the only scientist who was an Honorary Associate of the RPA. From the best-known scientist of the twentieth-century, perhaps we could illustrate the scope of the RPA's reach by following the life of one of the least-known scientists of the century. Take for example Joseph Thomas Ward (1861-1927, Honorary Associate 1926-7). Ward was born into an old English Catholic family and was, as a child, a chorister in Cardinal Newman's church. But the settled life of a conservative Catholic family was not for him and he ran away to sea. He eventually arrived in New Zealand, where he originally worked as a shepherd on a farm in Marlborough, on the northeastern corner of the South Island. He eventually settled in Wanganui, on the southwest coast of the North Island, where he opened a bookshop. Ward's shop, which was on the main street, traumatised the local clergy because of the RPA titles displayed prominently in the front window. To make matters worse, he was the president of the thriving Wanganui Rationalist Society. This organisation formed in 1923 as a result of the visit of Joseph McCabe to that city.

But Ward was more than simply an iconoclast. He became one of the leading authorities on astronomy in the country. Ward's observations on a transit of Venus were accepted by the French Astronomical Society and published in their proceedings. And, because it was New Zealand, where skills had to be practical as well as theoretical, Ward also made telescopes. His own telescope was twenty inches in diameter. After Ward's death the city of Wanganui had a telescope built from his drawings. It remained the largest in Australasia for many years. Ward insisted on a secular funeral and a fellow-rationalist, Mr J S Barton, SM, conducted a service using F J Gould's *Funeral Services Without Theology*. (8) The Wanganui Rationalist Society never recovered from Ward's death, but it continued on for many years in a reduced capacity. The point of retelling the story of Ward's life is that here is one of the least-known names of RPA Honorary Associates and yet, in his corner of the world, his work for rationalism in general and the RPA in particular was ongoing and impressive. The local clergy could, and did, complain, but they lacked the intellectual firepower or personal appeal of the rationalist.

Among the scientists currently serving as Honorary Associates is Sir Hermann Bondi, who since 1981 has served as the President of the RPA. Born to a family of non-practising Jews in Vienna, Bondi, along with Karl Popper, Sigmund Freud, Thomas Gold and many others, fled the rise of National Socialism in his native country. Austria's loss was Britain's gain and in 1943 Bondi became a Fellow at Trinity College, Cambridge for work in theoretical astronomy. In 1954 he took the position of Professor of Applied Mathematics at King's College, London. Bondi's name is best associated with his development, along with Sir Fred Hoyle (another RPA Honorary Associate) and Thomas Gold, of the steady state theory of the universe. This theory has since been replaced by the Big Bang theory once the existence of residual radiation throughout the universe was discovered. Seeing a theory to which he had associated his name being discarded did not deter him. This is yet another point those who attack science and the scientific method fail to understand. Bondi's work contributed no less to the success of the Big Bang theory than those working directly from that hypothesis. This is how science works. We would be less than human not to be disappointed to see our own theory disproved, but it is the mark of the rationalist to then welcome the development and be thankful to have played a part in the development of knowledge.

More recently Bondi served as the Director-General of the European Space Research Organisation and Secretary of the Royal Astronomical Society, and helped assess the various proposals for the anti-flood barrage on the River Thames. Bondi has been an active humanist since the mid-fifties, becoming an Honorary Associate of the RPA in 1967 and President since 1981.

In his Conway Memorial Lecture in 1992, Bondi argued against the assumptions of superiority which religious belief permits its adherents. 'Can you imagine anything more immoral than to regard yourself, on the basis of your own belief, to be superior!' In contrast to supremacist notions of the chosen people, the Elect or the umma, Bondi said he could see nothing wrong with different people holding different views 'providing they can discuss them in a tolerant manner and without reference to anything absolute, because none of us have access to anything absolute.' This, Bondi said, was the basis of Humanism. (9)

We can do no more than mention some of the other prominent scientists on the list of RPA Honorary Associates. A noticeable feature of the scientists is the number of geneticists. Among them include Cyril Dean Darlington (1903-1981, Honorary Associate 1943-1981) who was briefly president of the RPA between 1948 and 1949, although he resigned over differences of opinion regarding what should be published in the *Free Mind*, a short-lived journal the RPA set up for students. Darlington was a pioneer in cytology, the study of cells. His work, *Recent Advances in Cytology*, published in 1932 imposed a new level of order in the discipline, establishing beyond doubt the central role played by chromosomes in heredity.

While in his short spell as RPA president, Darlington gave the Conway Memorial Lecture to the South Place Ethical Society. His address, titled 'The Conflict of Science and Society', revealed an iconoclast at work. He was strongly critical of the destruction of Soviet genetics going on at that time at the hands of Stalin's hack, Trofim Lysenko, whom he dismissed as a 'rustic prophet'. But Darlington was no less critical of the western academic system's ability to shut down change and stifle innovation. Only half in jest, he called for the creation of a 'Ministry of Disturbance, a regulated source of annoyance; a destroyer of routine, and underminer of complacency'. On a more serious note, he advocated greater co-operation among university departments, especially between the sciences and humanities, and greater weight given to the social sciences. (10)

Among the physicists Frédéric Joliot-Curie (1900-1958, Honorary Associate 1954-1958) won, with his wife Irène (Marie Curie's daughter), the Nobel prize in chemistry for their work in creating radioactive isotopes, which have since become very important in medicine and industry. Work undertaken jointly and published in 1932 led in the same year to the discovery of the neutron, thus completing our contemporary understanding of the atom. Joliot-Curie, a hero of the resistance and outspoken communist, signed the Russell-Einstein Manifesto in 1955, which called for nuclear disarmament. Outside of Einstein and Bondi, the best-known astrophysicist among the Honorary Associates of the RPA would be Subrahmanyan Chandrasekhar (1910-1995, Honorary Associate 1968-1995) who established some important early principles regarding the mass of dying stars, which led on to later theories of Black Holes. Significantly, Chandrasekhar's mentor, Sir Arthur Eddington, opposed his theories with a level of personal rancour which for a while led Chandrasekhar to leave England and abandon that field of study. Hermann Bondi has speculated, not unreasonably, that it was Eddington's religious beliefs which led him to reject the implications of Chandrasekhar's research. How could a universe imbued with purpose allow something like a Black Hole to form naturally? Events of course proved Chandrasekhar right and Eddington wrong, although there remain plenty of people ready to follow in Eddington's footsteps. Chandrasekhar went on to receive the Nobel Prize for physics in 1983. Shortly before his death, Chandrasekhar was asked about his religious beliefs. He replied "I am a Hindu atheist with no belief in God but following a rational way of life." (11) It is a credit to Chandrasekhar's integrity, but also the intellectual flexibility of Hinduism, which can allow an answer like that. Chandrasekhar wrote an article for the *Guide* in 1950 on Jawaharlal Nehru.

Philosophers

Moving from the world of scientists to that of philosophers, we find an equally compelling range of people among the list of Honorary Associates. Again, some have been more active than others. But all have upheld the process of reason as a significant part of their life and most have been sufficiently motivated to see value in sharing that awareness with the general public.

Clearly the best known philosopher on the list is Bertrand Russell (1872-1970). An Honorary Associate since 1927 and President of the RPA from 1955, Russell was an active rationalist. He was for many people the public face of rationalism. Russell relates his passage to unbelief in his autobiography. He recalled worrying that he would become deeply unhappy if he were to believe no longer in God, freedom and immortality. He found, though, that the arguments in favour of these dogmas were too unconvincing to offer any practical solace. Pretty soon, he had argued his way to atheism. 'Throughout the long period of religious doubt, I had been rendered very unhappy by the gradual loss of belief, but when the process was completed, I found to my surprise that I was quite glad to be done with the whole subject.' (12) After a while the emotional tensions involved in trying to believe something one knows not to be true becomes too much and the charade can be preserved no longer.

Russell retained a genuine respect for religiosity for many years. His early thoughts on the subject can be traced in his haunting *A Free Man's Worship* (1903), as well as *The Essence of Religion* (1913) and *Mysticism and Logic* (1917). Russell was quite clear that Christian dogma was untenable. What he tried to do in these years was place religious faith on a new footing. Ronald Jager described his endeavour as articulating 'a religious faith for man utterly independent of any beliefs about the universe'. This would involve a monistic oneness with the universe. (13)

Most writers on Russell deal with the hardening of his views on religion in the twenties with embarrassment, or else avoid the subject entirely. Russell's attitude towards religion after the twenties remains among the most poorly covered areas of his otherwise exhaustively documented and written-about life. The most comprehensive treatment of this subject comes from Ronald W Clark's 1975 study. Clark claims that the hardening of Russell's attitude came under the influence of his second wife, Dora Black. This is probably true: they both joined the RPA in March 1927, although Russell had contributed to the *RPA Annual* in 1923. But Russell had been aware of the RPA a long time before that, as is shown by his two reviews of the second edition of J M Robertson's *Short History of Freethought*, from 1906. At about the time he joined the RPA, Russell debated Bishop Gore on Christianity. The debate took place while Russell's son John was recovering from a life-threatening illness. The pious Bishop Gore intoned that suffering is sent as a purification from sin. As most fathers would be, Russell was furious. 'Poor little John never sinned in his life. I wanted to spit in their faces –

they were so cold and abstract, with a sadistic pleasure in the tortures their God inflicts.' (14) Nowadays it is Russell who is scorned as cold and abstract.

It was around the same time that Russell gave his lecture on 'Why I am Not a Christian' to the South London branch of National Secular Society at the Battersea Town Hall. The pamphlet, printed by Watts & Co, provoked a predictably splenetic reaction. Russell's former friend, T S Eliot, dismissed the lecture as curious and pathetic and added sniffily that any more complicated argument would have been beyond the comprehension of an audience at Battersea Town Hall. Despite, or possibly even because of this sort of highbrow condescension, *Why I am Not a Christian* has remained in print ever since. The RPA and National Secular Society reprinted it, along with *The Faith of a Rationalist*, in 1983. It is true that *Why I am Not a Christian* is polemical and adds little new to the body of denunciation against the Christian religion, but what of it? The more important question is: are the criticisms valid, or at least worth considering? Clearly H G Wood thought so, because he penned a short reply called *Why Mr Bertrand Russell is Not a Christian*. Wood, a Quaker, was a wide-ranging and humane scholar, at the time lecturing in New Testament studies at Selly Oak College. He later went on to become the first Professor of Theology at the University of Birmingham. Predictably, Wood's main line of attack was that Russell was not a Christian because he did not know what Christianity is. This is an evergreen apologetic gambit, one not limited to Christians. Rather more oddly, Wood also insisted that Darwin and Einstein had delivered mortal blows to secular materialism. Russell replied to Wood in the *Literary Guide* in March 1929 in an article entitled 'Why Mr Wood is Not a Freethinker'.

Russell's reply to Wood was not his first article for the *Guide*. In January 1927 the *Guide* reprinted sections of 'Behaviourism and Values', which had appeared in *The Century Magazine* the month before. This article reflected his current preoccupation with Watson and Behaviourism, to which he devoted some time in *An Outline of Philosophy*, which was published in the same year. 'Behaviourism and Values' appeared the following year in Russell's *Sceptical Essays*, but his reply to H G Wood has not been anthologised in any publication I am familiar with. Russell wrote quite regularly for the RPA after that. The titles included:

1923 - Can Men be Rational?
1927 - Is Science Superstitious?
1930 - Has Religion Made Useful Contributions to Civilisation?
1938 - My Religious Reminiscences
1946 - Mind and Matter in Modern Science
1954 - Are the World's Troubles Due to Decay of Faith?

In 1941 Watts & Co got permission from George Allen & Unwin to reprint a series of Russell's shorter essays in a collection called *Let the People Think*, which came out as Number 84 of the Thinker's Library. Along with his radio broadcast, *The Faith of a Rationalist*, *Let the People Think* was reprinted by the RPA in 1961.

Russell also spoke to rationalist audiences every now and then. For instance, Conway Hall was packed on October 1 1935 to hear him speak on 'Purpose in the Universe.' The presumptuousness of supposing humanity sufficiently grand to justify a universe created in its honour was guaranteed to provoke Russell's wrath, and this occasion was no exception. But Russell didn't merely feed rationalists what they wanted to hear. He raised some eyebrows at the RPA's Jubilee Dinner in 1949 when he lamented that it would be rather a pity if Christian education were to cease, 'because you would then get no more Rationalists.'

> They arise chiefly out of reaction to a system of education which considers it quite right that a father should decree that his son should be brought up as a Muggletonian, we will say, or brought up on any other kind of nonsense, but we must on no account be brought up to try to think rationally. When I was young that was considered to be illegal. (15)

From 1955 until his death, Russell also served as President of the RPA. These were his most radical years. The story is well known, but repeating it will do no harm. At the end of 1954 Russell returned to public life with a radio broadcast entitled 'Man's Peril', which outlined the appalling risks of a nuclear war. In the first half of 1955 he expanded this draft and sent it to Einstein in America, who signed it enthusiastically. Two days later Einstein died, making his signature on the manifesto his last public act, which only helped the media interest in the whole exercise. It soon became known as the Russell-Einstein Manifesto. It was later signed by several other very prominent scientists like Linus Pauling, Joseph Rotblat, Max Born, Frédéric Joliot-Curie, Hermann Müller and Leopold Infeld (the last three also Honorary Associates of the RPA). In July 1955 Russell launched the Manifesto at Caxton Hall in London.

The manifesto helped create a momentum for other citizens to make some contribution toward world peace. In 1957 Cyrus Eaton, a wealthy Canadian-born industrialist, offered to fund a series of high-profile peace conferences. These were called the Pugwash conferences, after Eaton's hometown in Nova Scotia where the first conference was held. Russell missed the first Pugwash conference owing to ill health but attended the 1958, 1959 and 1962 conferences. Joseph Rotblat himself later recalled that it 'was the great influence which Russell had on the scientific community, the magic of his name, the respect for his judgment, that made scientists heed his call and assemble at this conference.' (16)

Eaton was also instrumental in persuading Khrushchev to visit the United States and to extend an invitation to Eisenhower to visit the Soviet Union. Eisenhower's visit never happened, but that was not for lack of effort on Eaton's part. Later in his life, Eaton secured the Russell papers for his *alma mater*, McMaster University in Ontario. And yes, Cyrus Eaton was an Honorary Associate of the RPA, from 1966 to his death in 1979. Eaton was an active rationalist, having been a member prior to becoming an Honorary Associate. The Pugwash conferences broke new ground in that, for the first time, scientists from both sides of the Iron Curtain were able to speak about peace in the same room. The US Senate Internal Security Committee took this as evidence that the Americans involved must be either fools or traitors and insinuated that Russell must be senile. But this sort of paranoia couldn't last long in the face of the obvious sincerity and ability of the scientists involved in the Pugwash movement. Pugwash has been widely credited with being responsible for the partial Test-Ban Treaty of 1964. (17)

Russell soon moved on to more radical forms of protest against the nuclear madness. He worked successively with the Campaign for Nuclear Disarmament, the Committee of 100 and the Bertrand Russell Peace Foundation. Following an article in the *New Statesman* by J B Priestley advocating immediate unilateral nuclear disarmament, Russell, Priestley, Kingsley Martin (another RPA Honorary Associate) and others brought the CND into existence. Because of the contribution of Canon Collins, there has often been an impression of CND and the peace movement generally as an arm of radical Christianity. This is not true – the contributions of rationalists and humanists were every bit as significant. In 1960 Russell resigned as president of CND and helped establish the more radical Committee of 100 with the Rev. Michael Scott. The idea here was a simple one. One hundred very prominent people would declare their willingness to face arrest and imprisonment as part of their protest against nuclear weapons in general and British nuclear policy in particular. The high point in this campaign was in August 1961 when Russell took part in a large-scale sit-down protest in Trafalgar Square. He was arrested for incitement and spent a week in Brixton Prison. And finally, he moved on once more when he founded the Bertrand Russell Peace Foundation in September 1963. At the same time he wound up his association with the Committee of 100. The Peace Foundation became more concerned with American involvement in the Vietnam War than with nuclear disarmament.

Now, we could spend a great deal of time and energy finding fault with Russell's activities here; his political naivety, his tendency to quarrel with fellow committee members, his ever-spiralling radicalism. We could also notice, as has been done, the ideological and political muddles the peace movement got itself into. But all this is to ignore the very real fear people felt at the time that a nuclear war was just around the corner. A poll in the United States during the Berlin Wall crisis in 1961 showed that 71% of respondents were in favour of a nuclear strike against the Soviet Union. Russell concentrated people's minds on the question. Hector Hawton, who heard Russell speak at the Hiroshima Day protest in 1961, wrote in *The Humanist* afterwards 'Whichever side humanists take, I think nothing of a man who has not squarely faced this issue and made his choice.' (18) Russell certainly did that, and encouraged tens of thousands of others to do the same. He also spoke for a huge section of the world when he wrote to Kennedy and Khrushchev. Michael Foot was right when he said that Russell's real contribution with these letters 'was the way in which he voiced the opinion of millions of people all over the world, than in the arguments he put to the national leaders.' (19)

The other point ignored by the recent critics of Russell is that their criticisms are not new. Those who knew Russell and shared his concerns were no less sceptical about his weaknesses. For instance, Kingsley Martin said of Russell: 'As always throughout his life, I admired the swiftness of his intellect, his never-failing wit, his Voltairean iconoclasm, and his readiness, in accordance with the precepts of the Apostles, to change his mind. My doubt was always about his political judgment…' (20). Later on Alan Ryan in his excellent study of Russell's political life recognised that Russell was 'politically inept and absurdly optimistic about the possibility of changing the entire political climate by mere argument', but went on to say that his arguments enlivened the intellectual life of the day and that 'he deserves the gratitude of several generations for his career as gad-fly.' (21) More recently, Ryan has suggested that the sneering at Russell's concern about the gravity of the nuclear threat reveals a 'very weird world view'. What could Russell have done to avoid posthumous censure? It is easy to criticise those active in the political domain from behind an academic's desk. But to people committed to the humanist maxim of helping with the problems of the here and now, that is not good enough. Barbara Wootton, who succeeded Russell as president of the RPA in 1970, spoke of her debt to her predecessor:

> I myself owe him an enormous debt because I grew up in a generation to whom the *Principles of Social Reconstruction* was a gospel in a very dark time. And whenever I have set out to write anything more than a casual article I have made it a lifetime practice to read some passages from Bertrand Russell beforehand, in the hope that I might get something of the rhythm of his beautiful English. (22)

Working from Russell's example, Wootton went on to devote her life to social and intellectual improvement of British society. These assessments are so much more balanced and reasonable than the recent evaluations of Russell's career, which constitute little more than character assassination. It may have become fashionable to mock Russell and dismiss his work, but the clever things responsible for this attitude could not hold a candle to the real work Russell did to make the world a better place.

If Russell was one of the unjustly maligned philosophers of the twentieth century, L Susan Stebbing could be classed as one of the unjustly forgotten. Among the philosophers in the list of RPA Honorary Associates, few are more interesting than this powerful woman. Stebbing (1885-1943) developed a formidable reputation as someone who would not suffer fools gladly, or any other way for that matter. Archibald Heath acknowledged that 'she was no respecter of persons, eminent or otherwise, when they talked pretentious nonsense.' (23) It is a venerable rationalist tradition not to respect nonsense, but to call it by its real name. T H Huxley spoke of himself as a smiter of humbug. Joseph McCabe was Huxley's principal successor in that role. More recently, John Searle's work has been described as like that of the nonsense police and Ted Honderich described A J Ayer as a hussar against nonsense. An excellent example of Stebbing smiting humbug is her review in the *Literary Guide* of Cyril Joad's widely publicised book *God and Evil*, where he renounced his vitalism in favour of Christian belief. Joad's bewildering array of invalid assumptions, sweeping generalisations and personal anecdote was subjected to a withering examination. (24)

But like most smiters of humbug, Stebbing was a genial and loving person to those around her. Heath said of her that 'I know of no Professor of Philosophy or indeed of any other subject who was more beloved by students for the real reasons for loving; she gave them friendliness without sentimentality, and scrupulous regard for personal qualities without any tempering of that fierce intellectual criticism which individual quality deserves.' (25) In other words, Stebbing respected her students and took them seriously enough to subject their work to praise or criticism as she thought suitable.

Stebbing enjoyed as illustrious a career as was open to a woman of her time. Her areas of interest were mathematical logic, philosophy of science, and the theory of language. She was Director of Moral Science Studies at Girton and then at Newnham College, Cambridge. She also lectured in Symbolic Logic at Columbia University, New York through 1931 and 1932, and from 1933 was Professor of Philosophy at the University of London, the first woman to become a professor of philosophy in the United Kingdom. At the time of her death she was president of the Ethical Union, Britain's largest organisation devoted to the principles of Ethicism.

Under the influence of Wittgenstein's *Tractatus Logico-Philosophicus*, Stebbing was one of the founders of the journal *Analysis*, which sought to publish a new type of philosophical article. Articles in *Analysis* were short and devoted to 'limited and precisely defined philosophical questions about the elucidation of known facts, instead of long, very general and abstract metaphysical speculations about possible facts or about the world as a whole.' (26) True to the rationalist tradition, Stebbing did not forget the general reader. Her book *Thinking to Some Purpose* was published as a Penguin paperback in 1939 and served as a popular introduction to clear thinking for three decades. Stebbing's other important contribution was her book *Philosophy and the Physicists* (1937), which pricked the bubble of the more mystical physicists of her day, Sir James Jeans and Sir Arthur Eddington. Both these gentlemen were happy to theorise outside their area of expertise and find God in the workings of the universe. And Eddington, as we have seen, went on to give Chandrasekhar a hard time for not allowing a theistic reading of astrophysics. As we saw in Chapter 4, Stebbing's book followed Hyman Levy and Joseph McCabe, who had both subjected Eddington and Jeans to searching criticisms.

But while Stebbing made a name for herself as a smiter of humbug, it would be quite wrong to conclude she was therefore an arid rationalist, the usual retort of people whose fanciful speculations have been exposed. On the contrary, Stebbing wrote movingly of what mattered to her. She was even prepared to use the word 'spiritual' to describe them, although she was at pains to add that this had no supernatural connotation whatsoever.

> The excellences I call spiritual include love for human beings, delight in creative activities of all kinds, respect for truth, satisfaction in learning to know what is true about this world (which includes ourselves), loyalty to other human beings, generosity of thought and sympathy with those who suffer, hatred of cruelty and other evils, devotion to duty and steadfastness in seeking one's ideals, delight in the beauty of nature and in art – in short, the love and pursuit of what is worth while for its own sake. (27)

Stebbing died in her home at Tintagel, in Cornwall, aged only 57, her plans for a new book to be published by Watts & Co unrealised.

More recently it has become a fairly common complaint that professional philosophers are now too busy and remote to involve themselves in the thankless task of writing for the general reader. While religious fundamentalism and irrational pseudoscience wield a disproportionate influence in society, philosophers continue to read their refereed journals and live out their lives in splendid isolation. They know full well the fundamentalists and the paranormalists are wrong, but are too preoccupied with their careers to enter the public debate and say so. Those few among them who are postmodernist go a step further and decry such a process as elitist. Well, nobody can make this claim against Antony Flew (1923-), whose association with the RPA goes back to the early 1950s, when Hector Hawton was instrumental in having his first book published by Watts & Co. From that time on, Flew has written regularly for the *Humanist/New Humanist*. After twenty years of writing for the magazine, Flew became a vice-president of the RPA in 1973 and an Honorary Associate in 1976, the same year as Bernard Crick, V M Tarkunde and Karl Popper.

Fresh from editing the two highly successful collections of works under the heading *Logic and Language*, and still only thirty years old, Flew could have been forgiven for feeling himself superior to the world of organised humanism. Many must have feared that writing for the *Literary Guide* would not be good for his career or image. But within months of Hector Hawton assuming the editorship of the *Guide*, Flew was a regular contributor, and has remained so ever since. One of his first articles was a review essay on Wittgenstein's *Philosophical Investigations*, a work then hot off the press. In a short article, Flew gave his readers a brief account of the *Tractatus Logico-Philosophicus*, and of Wittgenstein's erratic career. Quite sensibly, Flew advised reading someone else about Wittgenstein before reading him directly. (28)

Antony Flew's contribution to the development of rationalism and humanism since the war is not confined to his willingness and skill in writing for the general reader. His strongly articulated support for political conservatism has provided an important extra dimension to a movement that otherwise would be tempted to see itself as an exclusively left-leaning one. In fine rationalist tradition, Flew has been a tireless smiter of humbug. But it has been his special contribution to recognise that humbug is not the special preserve of religionists, reactionaries and the political right. On a straightforward level, this can be illustrated well in an exchange in 1974. Following a challenge from the *New Humanist*, John Biggs-Davison, Conservative MP for Epping Forest and a devout Catholic, declared that no Tory can be a humanist. The Conservative Party had sensibly charted a course between laissez faire and collectivism and its social vision was centred around a belief in a personal god. (29). The following month Antony Flew replied with an article entitled 'Yet Humanists Should be Conservatives'. Flew skilfully exploited the gap which often exists between people's advocacy of an open society and what this should mean in practice. For instance, he had little difficulty highlighting the anti-humanist tendencies of censorious left-wing student bodies and the Institute of Marxism-Leninism in Moscow. His attacks on the Clause Four of the Labour Party, which spoke of the socialisation of the means of production, distribution and exchange, were probably less effective, if only because the clause had long since been abandoned by the real decision-makers within the party. Flew didn't speak of the open society, but set the humanist ideal as a property-owning democracy and argued that, however flawed the Conservative party may be in its pursuit of this ideal, it is nonetheless its ideal. (30) Flew has never been under any illusion that his views are strictly in the minority in the humanist movement, but that, of course, only serves to make his advocacy of them all the more important.

Antony Flew's consistent advocacy of a humanism informed by political conservatism tended to land him in trouble with sections of the RPA membership, much as Russell's anti-nuclear and anti-Vietnam protests had done in the 1950s and 1960s. For instance, trouble arose over a book called *Anti-racism: An Assault on Education and Value*, for which Flew had contributed an article. The RPA Board decided that 'even if Professor Flew's contribution were objectionable it did not affect his position as a Vice-president of the RPA, provided that he did not claim to speak in the name of the RPA. It was agreed that freedom of thought and speech for RPA members, Honorary Associates and officials must be maintained even in the sensitive area of racism.' (31) Problems with Flew's involvement in Conservative politics intensified in 1988 after he associated himself with the Unification Church and with protagonists of strengthening religious education in the Education Reform Act, due before parliament that year. 'It was agreed that there was no question of guilt by association or of political bias, but anxiety was voiced by several Directors about aspects of Professor Flew's activities which seemed to conflict with the basic principles of the RPA and which causes us embarrassment.' It was agreed to reaffirm his Vice-presidency for another year. (32) Following ongoing correspondence with him about the matter, he resigned as Vice-president. 'This outcome was welcomed by most Directors...' (33) In what must be a seen as a tribute to the ideals of humanism, Antony Flew has continued to take an active part in the RPA, contributing articles on a regular basis and speaking at conferences.

No greater contrast is possible, politically speaking, than that between Antony Flew on the right and Ted Honderich on the left. Like Flew, Honderich was active in the humanist movement before becoming an Honorary Associate, although not for anything like as long. He had joined the RPA of his own accord before he was approached to be an Honorary Associate in 1988. He was articulating the humanist viewpoint from the early sixties. It will come as no surprise to anyone remotely familiar with his work that Honderich is a committed atheist and rationalist. Replying to the invitation to become an Honorary Associate, Honderich's answer was characteristic.

> It seems to me important that the RPA should keep up its good work, partly because it must always be important in itself to assert the truth against emotionality and superstition, partly because of the effects of that emotionality and superstition, not least its political effects. (34)

He has contributed several items to the *New Humanist* and accepted the invitation to give the keynote address at the RPA conference in 2001 on the theme of 'Mind and Other Matter'. But, in the wake of his extraordinary autobiography, much of the interest in this remarkable man is focused on himself as much as on his philosophy. His autobiography, *Philosopher: A Kind of Life* (Routledge, 2001) is, as several reviewers have observed, is in fact a substantial work of philosophy. But for most of the readers of this book, it will be the greater degree of frank personal testimony that will attract attention.

Yet another of the many prejudices against rationalists is countered by reference to this book. The stock prejudice is that the account of the life of a rationalist would be an especially tendentious exercise. But Honderich has shown this is not the case. Speaking in the context of determinism, a cause he has devoted much time to, and of autobiography, as well as that of his own life, Honderich concludes that 'there seems no possibility of acquiring the one true understanding of a life in an ordinary sense.' (35) He even says that we need to 'become post-modern, if that means unsure about explanatory facts.' (36) Happily, we do not need to become postmodern in order to avoid certainty about explanatory facts. Bertrand Russell, among others, was warning us of this in the 1940s and 1950s. This said, the journey over the century, if measured by the autobiographies of rationalists, is an interesting one. The line from George Jacob Holyoake's autobiography, published originally in 1892, to *Philosopher: A Kind of Life* reveals the extraordinary changes in the way rationalists and humanists account for their lives. Sir Arthur Keith's autobiography, published in 1948, serves as an interesting middle point.

No survey of the philosophers among the ranks of RPA Honorary Associate would be complete without considering the work of Paul Kurtz, who has been an Honorary Associate since 1979 and its Vice-president since 1982. As a young soldier, Kurtz saw action from the Battle of the Bulge to VE day. He was among the first Allied troops to enter Buchenwald and Dachau camps. That experience, and those of speaking to displaced Russians terrified to return to their country, served as a philosophical wake-up call. Back in the United States, Kurtz associated himself with naturalism and humanism in philosophy from the start of his career, very much in the tradition of his mentor, Sidney Hook. Kurtz's academic career was mainly involved in developing and defending naturalism, particularly as it relates to ethics. In *Decision and the Condition of Man* (1964), Kurtz worked towards a reconciliation among naturalism, linguistic philosophy and existentialism in a reworking of decision theory.

As with most other RPA Honorary Associates, Kurtz was not satisfied in making a contribution that would be confined within the groves of academe. Through the sixties he was closely involved with the American Humanist Association and from 1967 edited its magazine, the *Humanist*. Nicolas Walter, not a man to give undeserved praise, described the *Humanist* under Kurtz's editorship as 'the best freethought paper certainly in the English-speaking world and probably in the whole world.' (37) In 1969 Kurtz founded Prometheus Books. Speaking to its centenary conference in Birmingham in 1999, Kurtz said that the RPA was the inspiration for his establishing Prometheus Books. It could well be that Prometheus Books is the RPA's most significant legacy because Prometheus has taken over the RPA's role as the principal publisher of rationalist and humanist material in the world. It is a relevant question why Prometheus Books has succeeded in the past thirty years at a level far outstripping that of the RPA. The quality and consistency of Kurtz's leadership during that time is surely a significant factor. In contrast to Charles Watts, Kurtz has taken on a leadership role in world humanism on his own account. The choices he faced among existing organisations in the United States was either a wavering, anaemic religious humanism or the unhelpfully extreme anti-Christianity of Madalyn Murray-O'Hair and the American Atheists. These being unappetising, Kurtz founded *Free Inquiry* magazine in 1980 and the Council for Democratic and Secular Humanism to run it. *Free Inquiry* has developed into the leading humanist magazine in the world, exercising the sort of influence that the *Literary Guide* did in its earlier days.

The launching of *Free Inquiry* coincided with the *Secular Humanist Declaration*, which was the first of several initiatives that helped redefine humanism and, incidentally, shift the powerhouse of humanist thinking from Britain to the United States. We followed the nature of humanism as outlined by Kurtz in the previous chapter. But, for all that, he has remained closely involved in the RPA since then. His articles dot the *New Humanist* over the past two decades. Few people have articulated more clearly than Kurtz the dilemma of contemporary humanism. 'Although people demand certainties, we can only offer them probabilities. When they seek absolutes, we say that they should examine situations and be aware of possible exceptions. When they hunger for easy solutions, we point to complexities. They thirst for spiritual bread and wine, and we serve them sceptical doubts.' He lamented the humanist movement's fluctuations in style and content between 'strident noise and warmed-over porridge, neither of which appeals to the educated world.' (38)

Most recently, Kurtz was instrumental in producing the *Humanist Manifesto 2000*, which sought to outline a new humanist programme for the twenty-first century. In the face of new challenges on a worldwide scale, nothing less than a planetary humanism could be an effective response. He noted the twin threats of traditional belief systems drawn from a premodern world view on the one hand and a sophistical and dishonest postmodernism on the other. 'We need', he wrote, 'to convince our fellow human beings about the imperative to work together in creating a new planetary consensus in which preserving and improving the lot of humanity as a whole is our supreme obligation.' (39) In the wake of the escalation of world tensions since the terrorist attacks in September 2001, this seems truer than ever.

As with the scientists, this quick perusal of a few of the philosophers from the ranks of RPA Honorary Associates by no means exhausts the list. The most prominent of those not mentioned are Karl Popper (1902-1994), John Dewey (1859-1952), Noam Chomsky (1928-), Paul Edwards (1923-) and A J Ayer (1910-1989), whose story is told well by Ben Rogers in his recent biography.

Sociologists

Looking now at the field of sociology, we find another impressive list of names. Colin Campbell, Ronald Fletcher and Morris Ginsberg have already been mentioned on several occasions. But among the other prominent sociologists who have been Honorary Associates of the RPA are Barbara Wootton and Richard Hoggart. Barbara Wootton (1897-1988) was not only a distinguished sociologist, she was deeply committed to public service for most of the life. She became an Honorary Associate of the RPA in 1950 and served as president following the death of Bertrand Russell in 1970 until the beginning of 1973. She was a frequent contributor to the *Humanist/New Humanist* and regular attender at RPA Annual Dinners and conferences. Sixteen years of her public career were spent as chairperson of the Juvenile Courts in London. It was from her experience here that her most important work *Social Science and Social Pathology* (1959) was born. It was on Wootton's initiative that the Community Service Order was instigated, which allowed a new option of sentencing for minor offences. Wootton served on four Royal Commissions and four Departmental Committees. One of them investigated the use of marijuana in 1968. She was also instrumental in the legislation which led to the abolition of the death penalty in Britain in 1967. On the recommendation of Hugh Gaitskell, Wootton was one of four women to be the first to become life peers, in 1958. She was later the first woman to serve as Deputy Speaker of the House of Lords. She was made a Companion of Honour in 1977.

But amid this glamorous public life, Barbara Wootton was a woman of great courage. Before her twenty-first birthday she had experienced the deaths of her father, brother, closest school friend and her husband of five weeks (in theory) and 48 hours (in practice). As she recalled in her autobiography, 'In ten years I had learned little about life, much about death.' Wootton married again, but this marriage did not bring her the children she yearned for so desperately. Indeed, her second husband died prematurely, as did others of her friends. It was terribly important for Wootton to encourage feelings of self-respect among the young, for she herself would not have survived her personal tragedies and disappointments without such self-belief. She wrote:

> To the young, particularly, it should be the future, not the past, that counts. For the young to brood upon the past is unnatural and unwholesome; and today when I see a lovely girl of sixteen with all her life before her, who excuses herself for some temporary mess by bursting into floods of self-pitying tears because she "never had a father" I find the spectacle incongruous, even almost ludicrous. We should do better, I think, to encourage children from the earliest possible age, however wretched their backgrounds, to believe that they are, or at least soon will be, masters of their fates. (40)

Wootton resigned as president of the RPA late in 1972, becoming active the following year, over her disagreement on abortion. The RPA was in favour of women's choice, Wootton preferred alternatives to abortion, especially adoption. As is the case with virtually all the other people who resigned from some position, Wootton retained close and friendly relations with the RPA until her death.

Psychologists

It is quite misleading to describe Margaret Knight solely as a psychologist. She was also a philosopher, historian and activist. Still, psychology was her chosen discipline, and so perhaps it is the least inaccurate pigeon-hole for her. In looking at the life and work of this remarkable woman, I couldn't help noticing how many parallels there are in her life to that of the RPA itself. Like Susan Stebbing, Margaret Knight (1903-1983) succeeded in a man's world. After leaving Cambridge she worked for ten years at the National Institute of Industrial Psychology and then followed her husband to Aberdeen, where he took a position lecturing on the subject at the university. While he was off on war service, Knight served as Acting Head of Department, only to step down and take on a part-time role once her husband returned home. Together they wrote *A Modern Introduction to Psychology*, which went through several editions, remaining in print for more than twenty years. In 1950 she was asked to edit the works of William James and provide an introductory essay for a Pelican series on psychology. This book went through six editions. Rex, her husband, died suddenly and unexpectedly in 1959, and she spent the rest of her life a widow.

Margaret Knight was an atheist and a rationalist, having shed her religious beliefs at Cambridge under the influence of Bertrand Russell, J M McTaggart and C D Broad. 'A fresh, cleansing wind swept through the stuffy room that contained the relics of my religious beliefs. I let them go with a profound sense of relief, and ever since I have lived happily without them.' (41) We have already noted how frequently people express *relief* at the shedding of their religious beliefs. The strain of trying to believe something inherently unbelievable is stressful to honest people. In middle age, having become more confident in her own beliefs and indignant over the continual barrage of religious propaganda on the air, Knight decided to approach the BBC with a proposal for a series of talks. Her first suggestions, made in November 1953, were, in her words, 'rather forcibly rejected', but she 'was prepared to make a nuisance of herself' and persisted. Finally, in July 1954, her third series of suggested talks was taken up. Knight had wanted to criticise a recent Ministry of Education brochure which advocated the moral education of children within the 'natural setting of religious instruction'. (42) To her surprise, the BBC not only agreed to this theme but suggested she even give advice to non-Christian parents on moral education. Knight's talks are, by contemporary standards, thoroughly sound and uncontroversial discussions on bringing up children to be moral and caring but without the fear of God being forced into them. They follow in the line from Gould's moral lessons through Whyte's wonder stories of the world and the World of Youth Series in the 1930s.

Reaction to the talks quickly escalated into an avalanche of bile. The *Daily Telegraph* described the first talk as 'one large slab of atheistical propaganda' and called on God and the BBC to prohibit the second broadcast. The *Sunday Graphic* went even further. Under a two-inch heading 'The Unholy Mrs Knight' readers were warned 'Don't let this woman fool you…She looks – doesn't she – just like the typical housewife; cool, comfortable, harmless. But Mrs Margaret Knight is a menace. A dangerous woman. Make no mistake about that.' In an extraordinary display of hypocrisy, many prominent churchmen expressed concern that Knight should have been allowed access to the microphone without a Christian to chaperone her. Figures as diverse as the Catholic Bishop of Liverpool and the Dean of Windsor lamented the talks had been permitted. The Bishop of Coventry dismissed her as a 'brusque, so-competent, bossy female' (43) Even Mervyn Stockwood, often hailed as a paragon of Christian liberalism said that 'such one-sided attacks make things difficult.' (44) The *Telegraph* returned to the fray accusing the BBC of 'coddling atheists'.

But hard on the heels of the calumniators came the second wave of reaction, either from those in favour of the broadcasts, or those in favour of the right to hear them. Following an acknowledgement from the Very Rev. W R Matthews, Dean of St Paul's, that Knight's broadcasts had in fact been moderate and courteous and reflected the actual state of thought in Britain at the time, the mood changed. Some of the most virulent clerical opponents actually made a public apology for their rudeness, although the Catholics baulked at this. *The Church of England Newspaper* put the case as honestly as anyone.

> If the Christian faith can only reply to such a person as Mrs Knight with personal abuse and can find no compelling answer, it deserves to fail and will, in fact, disappear. The suggestion that the BBC erred in

allowing Mrs Knight to broadcast only plays into the hands of Christianity's critics by implying that the Church is a vested interest with power of censorship. Big Brother is no less sinister for wearing a dog-collar...Those who share Mrs Knight's doubts about Christianity probably out-number those who do not in Britain at the present time, and included large numbers of our most respected and highly responsible citizens. (45)

After the radio talks, Knight mused on why the reaction had been so splenetic. On the one hand she observed that people reacted defensively because many of the beliefs challenged were not held rationally. But the real reason was that she had actually said – at last – what most people knew to be true, but few had said. This theme was evident in much of the correspondence she received on the matter. Knight paraphrased the theme: ' "Someone's said it at last!" For years there had been an elaborate pretence that we were, with negligible exceptions, a nation of Christian believers. Now I had "blown the gaff"' (46)

The morals without religion affair was a significant milestone in the secularisation of Britain. And it was brought about by one courageous woman. This episode demonstrated to Britain that it was in fact a nation of diverse beliefs. It had long been true, but now it was known to be true. It had just needed someone to stand up and say that the emperor had no clothes. While the church continued to enjoy a privileged level of access to radio and, shortly, television, never again would it be so presumptuous as to assume it deserved the privilege.

Less than two years after being publicly vilified for her radio talks on 'Morals Without Religion', Knight was featured on a television programme of the same title. True to form the BBC ensured she was well hedged in by a bevy of Christians. Two priests and a layman recently converted to Christianity were ranged against her. The men tried to bully and patronise Knight in turns, calling her an 'honest-to-God atheist'. When the Rev. Ian Pitt-Watson inferred that it follows that if we have outgrown belief in witches we must also have outgrown belief in the family, Knight patiently replied that we could not make such an inference. (47) After the programme, she reported to Hawton her fear that humanism must be becoming respectable.

Knight denied that Christianity and communism were the great alternatives of the day, suggesting instead that both are dogmatic systems and, as such, stood together against Scientific Humanism. Children, Knight said, should be taught Bible stories in the same way they are taught any other ancient myth. The essence of humanism was held to be disinterestedness, or not letting our own claims blind us to those of other people. True to the ideal of eupraxophy as outlined by Paul Kurtz, Knight's humanism was an active one. She was the first president of the Humanist Housing Association, serving from 1961 until 1965.

The furore over the Morals Without Religion broadcasts made Margaret Knight a popular speaker for a long time and contributed materially to spreading humanist views. She was to speak at most British universities on humanism during the remainder of her career. The year after the broadcasts she was invited to become an Honorary Associate of the RPA, and she remained an active humanist for the rest of her life. When, twenty years later, she returned to the air, there was not a murmur.

It was during her frequent talks to students and the general public on humanism that she saw the need for a single-volume anthology of humanist thought. This was her next important contribution. *Humanist Anthology: from Confucius to Bertrand Russell* was a great success. Beginning with Lao Tzu and Confucius, then going through the Greeks and Romans down to Albert Einstein and E M Forster, Knight brought together a marvellous variety of thinkers, disagreeing on many very significant issues but sharing a commitment to humanity and to reason. *Humanist Anthology* was the first book the RPA published after the sale of Watts & Co, which reflects the confidence they had in this work.

Margaret Knight remained an uncompromising atheist and secularist until her dying day. When called upon to give her opinions on a suggestion that radical Christians and religious humanists should unite with rationalists and humanists, her opinion was plain. There was no reason why all these groups could not make common cause in areas where they agree, but she opposed permanent union on the grounds of irreconcilable differences. As she put it, 'Secular Humanists set store by lucidity and precision; religious Humanists tend to favour an 'inspirational' approach with plenty of abstract nouns.'(48)

So what are the parallels between Margaret Knight and the RPA? Both succeeded in an environment, if not actively hostile to them, at least indifferent to their success. Margaret Knight and the RPA have both made a noteworthy, and undervalued, contribution to the secularisation of British society. Margaret Knight, like the RPA she belonged to, was animated by a dislike of humbug, a scrupulous honesty and a respect for reason without at any time wanting to displace or undervalue the non-rational facets of human existence. In return, the RPA and Margaret Knight have been patronised and ridiculed, but rarely answered. And Margaret Knight died unnoticed and forgotten. While the RPA shows no sign of dying, nobody is beating down the doors to thank it for a job well done.

Another point among the psychologists who are Honorary Associates of the RPA, one can see some of the greatest intellectual divides of the twentieth century. B F Skinner (1904-1990, Honorary Associate 1972-1990) was the world's leading behaviourist psychologist while Karl Popper (Honorary Associate 1976-1994) was one of the philosophers most hostile to behaviourism. Similarly, Sigmund Freud (1856-1939, Honorary Associate 1938-1939) and Ernest Jones (1879-1958, Honorary Associate 1943-1958) his greatest English-speaking disciple, were leading exponents of psychoanalysis, while Ernest Gellner (1925-1995, Honorary Associate 1979-1995) was one of the most vociferous critics of the pseudo-scientific nature of psychoanalysis.

Polymaths

One of the distinguishing features of rationalism and humanism is the high number of polymaths within the movement. Polymaths are people who are hard to bracket as a philosopher, historian, scientist or artist. They may be mixtures of all these, and more. Rationalism and humanism have, by definition, attracted the free thinker, the self-educated person. Joseph McCabe, J M Robertson and Hector Hawton were all polymaths, people who educated themselves, who were voracious readers, and who valued the process of inquiry for its own sake. For such people the biblical injunction to lean not on your own understanding but that the fear of God is the beginning of wisdom is an obscenity. Perhaps the best known of the twentieth-century polymaths was H G Wells, that dynamic and mercurial mixture of philosopher and scientist, novelist and journalist. 'To my generation' wrote Royston Pike, 'to the generation that was hung on the wire at Loos, gutted on the Somme, and bogged at Passchendaele – Wells was the teacher of teachers.' (49)

Wells's rationalism was always ambivalent. He went through a theistic phase between 1915 or so and 1919, but even having emerged from that spell was never, as he put it, an orthodox unbeliever. His treatment of the RPA illustrates this well. In 1915, in *The Research Magnificent*, Wells has a character in the book called White who is not given much description beyond being identified as a member of the Rationalist Press Association. White is a 'decent, self-respecting sceptic' who is a little shocked to read William Benham, his friend and the book's main character, theorising vaguely about God. Benham's thoughts anticipated the vein of *God the Invisible King*, published two years later. White's character does not develop, as his role is to be the reliable narrator of Benham's odyssey. White is mocked gently for his shock at Benham's god-talk, having assumed his friend to be an orthodox unbeliever. But it is Benham who fails and not White.

But in the same year as *The Research Magnificent*, Wells also wrote his extravagant ramble called *Boon, The Mind of the Race, The Wild Asses of the Devil, and The Last Trump*. Among the several people lampooned in *Boon* is Edward Clodd. Wells had known Clodd for a few years by then; Clodd had supported Wells's admission into the Omar Khayyam Club. In *Boon* Clodd, under the not impenetrable disguise of 'Dodd', is described as

> a leading member of the Rationalist Press Association, a militant agnostic, and a dear, compact man, one of those Middle Victorians who go about with a preoccupied, caulking air, as though, after having been at great cost and pains to banish God from the Universe, they were resolved not to permit Him back on any terms whatever. (50)

Boon and Dodd are in a conservatory talking, almost arguing, about Boon's notion of the mind of the race. Dodd, sitting on an upended flowerpot, becomes impatient with Boon's inability to define or characterise the mind of the race in any other than poetic or rhetorical terms.

> "Mysticism!" said Dodd. "Give me the Rock of Fact!" He shook his head so violently that suddenly his balance was disturbed; clap went his feet, and the flowerpot broke beneath him, and our talk was lost in the consequent solicitudes. (51)

Over the next few years Wells experimented with various theistic colourings to his notion of the mind of the race, most notably in *God the Invisible King*. In this work Wells criticises another leading rationalist, Joseph McCabe. Wells sent

McCabe a copy of the work wishing him 'a speedy conversion'. But Wells's Invisible King proved no easier to portray than the mind of the race; it was the same idea becoming ever more wrapped in mystical language. Rather unconvincingly, Wells insisted that none of it was his own invention or construction, rather the Invisible King was merely the findings of science put in religious language. Perhaps the least inaccurate renderings of the mind of the race/Invisible King are deified humanism or a Jungian collective unconscious.

Not surprisingly, *God the Invisible King* aroused quite a storm. William Archer, a prominent journalist and RPA Honorary Associate, penned a short reply called *God and Mr Wells*, published by Watts & Co, and the *Literary Guide* was animated by a series of letters between August and October 1917 on the matter. By and large the controversy was amicable, the conspicuous exception being Edward Clodd, who felt understandably aggrieved at being labelled a militant agnostic, given his entire career as a freethinker had been in the opposite direction. Clodd described Wells's work as 'jejune fatuous stuff into which no originality enters, only a mixture of pietistic jargon and Bible tags.' Clodd prophesied that 'the author will curse the day he wrote it.' (52) Wells's main criticism was what he saw as the RPA's fixation on the word 'God'. By the Invisible King, Wells claimed he meant the Moral Imperative or the Spirit of Man, both of which he put in capitals. 'I hold that this is what most modern religious people mean when they say "God." Thereupon arises all this Atheistical screaming and shouting. Demetrius the Silversmith is bawling in Johnson's Court. They won't have a "God" at any price. Anything but that!' (53)

Joseph McCabe, not always the politest man in the heat of public controversy, was on this occasion remarkably calm and wrote the shortest and least theatrical letters of the controversy. 'I don't quarrel about a name. I don't believe in the something in which he believes; and I really do not turn a single hair whether he calls it He, She, or It, God or Quob.' (54) Ironically, Clodd's prophecy proved correct. Wells came to regret not just *God the Invisible King*, but his entire theistic phase. 'God the Invisible King', he wrote in 1931, had been an error of expression. As he wrote in his autobiography:

> At no time did my deistic phrasing make any concessions to doctrinal Christianity. If my gestures were pious, my hands were clean. I never sold myself to organised orthodoxy. At its most artificial my religiosity was a flaming heresy and not a timeserving compromise. (55)

From the end of the twenties, the ideal which Wells had hitherto couched in mystical language was shorn of these pretensions. He now couched the same urge, but in entirely humanistic language. 'The alternative before man now is either magnificence of spirit and magnificence of achievement, or disaster.' (56) The mind of the race now became the need of people to think of themselves as citizens of the world, rather than as adherents to some miserable creed, nationality or race. And it was at this time (1929) that Wells became an Honorary Associate of the RPA. In the same year the Thinker's Library began and such was Wells's prestige that he upstaged even Huxley, Haeckel and Spencer to have the honour of providing the first volume for the series. The work was *First and Last Things*, which had originally been published in 1909. The first edition had been frankly agnostic but had been altered in a revised edition in 1917, the same year as *God the Invisible King*, to fit in with his theistic leanings at the time. The Thinker's Library edition reverted to the original line. While *First and Last Things* is in many ways a weak book, its faults can all be forgiven because he began with the classic rationalist caveat:

> This is *my* system that I place before you in order that you should make *your* system. You can no more think about the world according to another man's system than you can look at it with a dead man's eye. (57)

Three years after *First and Last Things* Watts & Co also published a series of Wells's papers and articles under the heading *After Democracy*. In 1942 Wells wrote *The Conquest of Time*, which was specifically intended to replace *First and Last Things*, which he now saw as 'mentally adolescent.' (58) *Conquest* appeared as No. 92 of the Thinker's Library. By this time Wells was less confident than he had been in 1909 of the peaceful progress of humanity. *The Conquest of Time* expressed his extreme meliorism most sharply. Here again, Wells spoke of religion.

> The creed of the new religion which is destined to bind a regenerate world together is clear and simple. It demands the subordination of the self, of the aggressive personality, to the common creative task, which is the conquest and animation of the universe by life. The new religion soothes the innate fears and restrains the natural egotism of the young. It repudiates the idea of Sin and the idea of Personal Immortality; which are both in their several ways begotten by Fear. It denies the existence of an anthropomorphic God, and it cannot afford to recognise any prevaricating use of the word "God." That word implies a personality or it implies nothing. (59)

Really, though, it wasn't so much *what* Wells said that inspired people. It was how he said it. Wells, wrote Royston Pike in his 1947 eulogy 'taught us that ideas were exciting things…Wells skipped and plodded, scattering seed of fecund potency. Much of it fell by the wayside. Some of it sprang up swiftly, and as swiftly withered and died. Some of it stuck.' (60)

One particularly interesting episode with regard to H G Wells is worth retelling. In the middle of 1942 he wrote to the RPA's Board advising it of a manuscript of a short work provisionally entitled *The Twilight of the Cross*. The Directors must have been delighted to have another Wells title coming their way. They were at the time getting *The Conquest of Time* through the press. But their delight quickly turned to ashes because, to the dismay of most of the Directors, Wells's manuscript was found to be 'libellous and objectionable' and Wells was asked to delete certain passages. (61) He duly agreed to do this and a contract was signed for the publication of the book. It soon transpired, however, that substantial parts of the work were still quite unsuitable for publication. At the meeting of October 1942, Fred Watts explained to the Board that there remained libellous and objectionable passages that would need to be deleted. Watts arranged for proofs to be sent to all Directors for their opinions. A majority of the Board agreed that *The Twilight of the Cross* was not fit for publication as it stood, but they were now tied by a contract to publish it. At the next Board meeting it was decided not to go ahead with the book, contract or no contract. They must have feared a volcanic reaction from Wells, but that was not how it went. Rather oddly, Wells said he would contemplate legal action and asked whether in the meantime the RPA would prefer he withdrew as an Honorary Associate! The RPA replied that there was no need for this. (62) In the meantime Wells sent the manuscript of *The Twilight of the Cross* to Secker and Warburg, but was beginning to have second thoughts about it himself. By late November, he had completely changed his view on the book. In a letter to Fred Watts he admitted that

> he considered that it bore all the marks of ill-health, haste and the unstable aim of a very troubled mind. He had therefore decided to scrap it, and if possible to destroy all memory of it. He sent his friendliest regards to the RPA and stated that he might incorporate some passages from the work in a subsequent booklet later on. All proofs had now been destroyed, and instructions had been given to the printers to distribute the type. (63)

How characteristic of Wells this is. A hasty polemic putting a case in highly memorable terms, only for the author of it to change his mind and apologise. I assume that this manuscript was in fact destroyed although it is possible certain passages were then transferred to *Crux Ansata: An Indictment of the Roman Catholic Church*, which was published by Penguin in 1943.

Like Russell, Wells has, largely, either been ignored or vilified since his death. Both men have attracted biographers who so dislike their subject they are unwilling to acknowledge any good in them at all. Others have used these two men as examples of everything they are determined to find wrong in the humanist worldview.

Once more, we can do no more than mention briefly some of the other polymaths who are Honorary Associates of the RPA. David Tribe was active in the National Secular Society in the 1960s, serving as its president from 1963 to 1971. During that time he wrote some important and long overdue works of freethought history. *One Hundred Years of Freethought*, published by Elek in 1967, was the first attempt at a global survey of the wider freethought movement. He then went on to write the most significant biography of Charles Bradlaugh in almost a century, and a bold restatement of ethical issues and needs in which rationalism and humanism were both criticised. He has contributed to rationalist and humanist journals around the world for four decades.

Novelists

One of the favourite jibes about rationalism is that it is dry, cold, chilly and doesn't allow for the artistic or literary sides of human experience. This, of course, is untrue, and a brief survey of the Honorary Associates can demonstrate that it is untrue. Looking at novelists, we can see that some of the most prominent English novelists of the early twentieth century were associated with the RPA. A good example is Arnold Bennett (1867-1931), a prolific author and journalist.

Bennett's adult life was a long reaction to and rebellion against the hypocrisy and mean-spiritedness of the Methodist upbringing he received in the Staffordshire potteries, where he grew up. The best of Bennett's novels are explorations of the joylessness of provincial life in England under the influence of this loveless Protestantism. Unlike many other youthful rebels against religion, Bennett remained a rationalist and materialist for the remainder of his life. He made his views clear to his friend H G Wells soon after the publication of *A Modern Utopia*. In this work, Wells postulated a new class of philosopher-guardians of society he called the samurai. Why, Bennett asked 'should the samurai have any religion? I hope you aren't going to defend that worn out platitude to the effect that religion is a necessity of man's nature. Because it isn't. Religion is done for – any sort of religion.' (64) Bennett's rationalism was a humane, natural affair – much as it is for most people. He wrote in his diary on May 23 1908:

> Always haunted by dissatisfaction at the discrepancy between reason and conduct! No reason why conduct should not conform to the ideas of the brain. This that I am always preaching, and with a success of popular interest too, I cannot perfectly practise. It is the clumsiness of my living that disgusts me. The rough carpentry instead of fine carpentry. (65)

Every now and then one sees passages such as this used to decry rationalism. But to use passages like this in such a way is to misunderstand it. Setting to one side his self-loathing, Bennett is articulating the essence of rationalism here. As becomes a feeling human being, Bennett was not always rational. But far from being a recognition of failure, Bennett's lament is a triumphant vindication of how well he used reason in his life. He recognised his faults, thought rationally about them, and did what he could to become a better person.

Bennett was not a systematic thinker, but was reasonably well read in philosophy. Like many people of his generation, he was deeply influenced by Herbert Spencer, particularly his *First Principles*, which first appeared in 1862. When reading Spencer's autobiography in 1910, Bennett had cause to recall the influence of *First Principles*. This book filled him 'with the sense of causation everywhere, has altered my whole view of life, and undoubtedly immensely improved it…You can see *First Principles* in nearly every line I write.' (66)

Bennett became an Honorary Associate of the RPA in 1916, along with William Archer and G M Trevelyan. Bennett was at the height of his fame in 1916 and had nothing to gain, but potentially quite a lot to lose, from being associated with the RPA. He accepted the position because he sympathised with its aims. Ironically, Bennett's rationalism became public knowledge at the same time as his friend Wells was descending into his short-lived theistic phase. Bennett noted in his journal that Wells was starting a new work, published the following year as *God the Invisible King*, which would speak of God. 'Apparently', Bennett noted rather bemusedly, 'he can be what you like.' (67) That same year Bennett wrote an article for the *Rationalist Annual*. He made his atheism quite unambiguous.

> I have no supernatural religion, and I never had one. I do not feel the need of a supernatural religion, and I have never felt such a need. And though it would be unphilosophical to be positive about the future, I do not think that I shall ever feel such a need, or that if I do

feel it I shall ever succeed in satisfying it. I was brought up in an atmosphere of dogma. I regularly attended all sorts of divine services, and some of my earliest recollected feelings are those of instinctive protest against their absolute futility. I never prayed sincerely or without a sharp sense of the ridiculous. The moment when I could cut myself free from any religious organisation was a moment of intense relief, and from that moment I have never entered a place of worship save in a spirit of sociological, historical, or artistic curiosity, or to take part in some quasi-legal ceremony at which my presence was imperative. (68)

Late in his life, Bennett wrote a short work called *The Religious Interregnum* in which religion was strongly criticised.

Bennett was persuaded to take up writing as his career largely by another man destined to become an Honorary Associate of the RPA: Eden Phillpotts (1862-1960, Honorary Associate 1904-1960). Like many other hypochondriacs, Phillpotts lived an extravagantly long life. He hailed from Devon and was to spend most of his life there, specialising in novels and plays set in his beloved home county. Phillpotts was more active in the RPA than Bennett. In 1908, for instance, the grandly titled RPA Social Meetings and Discussions Committee performed *The Prude's Progress*, a play he co-wrote with Jerome K Jerome. And the 1918 RPA Annual featured a Miltonesque poem by him called 'The Rationalists'. When he and Bennett first met, Phillpotts was in the process of having *Children of the Mist* published, one of his more successful works. He enjoyed huge success with the play *The Farmer's Wife*, which ran for years, clocking up a total of 1,320 performances. He was to write in the region of 250 works over his long career.

Perhaps the most gifted novelist among the RPA Honorary Associates was E M Forster (1879-1970, Honorary Associate, 1959-1970). Like Arnold Bennett's, Forster's humanism was simple without being simplistic and intelligent without being academic. In a tribute after his death, R C Churchill wrote that while Bertrand Russell had been the head of the humanist movement, E M Forster had been its heart. (69)

In a talk to the Cambridge University humanists in 1963 Forster gave an account of his humanism. 'Some Humanists are born enlightened' Forster said, 'others have striven toward the light, but in my case the gas got slowly turned up.' His upbringing had been unostentatiously Church of England. The odd prayer was said but otherwise few demands were made on his time or affections. It was not until university that the flimsy structure of Forster's faith collapsed. His early attempts to stabilise his faith in the Trinity 'kept falling apart like an unmanageable toy' and pretty soon he was completely free of his Christian upbringing. Like so many other non-believers, Forster expressed admiration for aspects of the New Testament, but he confessed also that the tendency 'towards preaching and threats, so much emphasis on followers, on an elite, so little intellectual power (as opposed to insight), such an absence of humour and fun that my blood's chilled.' He told his listeners that 'the fact that my rejection is not vehement does not save it from being tenacious.' (70)

Forster expressed his simple humanism in the phrase that has since become famous, his trademark aphorism 'only connect'.

> Only connect! That was the whole of her sermon. Only connect the prose and the passion, and both will be exalted, and human love will be seen at its highest. Live in fragments no longer. Only connect, and the beast and the monk, robbed of the isolation that is life to either, will die. (71)

And Forster did connect. He was President of the Cambridge Humanists from 1955 until his death, and publicly supported nuclear disarmament and the abolition of capital punishment. He saw humanism as the alternative to Christianity and Communism. He outlined his views in a letter to the *Twentieth Century*, which, six years later, Margaret Knight included in her *Humanist Anthology*. Programmes, Forster said, mean pogroms. It is in this sense that his humanism was simple. Decades later postmodernists would rediscover this point and then use it to attack humanism!

Then there is Brigid Brophy (1929-1995, Honorary Associate 1984-1995), novelist and biographer, friend of Iris Murdoch, feminist and hell-raiser. Brophy earned the lasting hatred of the die-hard defenders of traditional Christian morality in the 1960s. Reminiscent of the vilifying of Margaret Knight a decade previously, Brophy was denounced by two of the more humourless of the religious conservatives, Arnold Lunn and Garth Lean, as 'the high priestess of British humanism'. (72) A couple of incidents from her colourful life will help illustrate what Lunn and Lean had in mind.

In 1965 Brophy was invited to write an article for the *Sunday Times* on the subject of marriage. The same year she addressed the BHA conference (still at this time being co-hosted by the RPA) which was considering the theme of 'Revaluations of the Family'. Her address, and the title of her subsequent article in *The Humanist*, was 'The Immorality of Marriage'. Brophy argued that only with new legislation bringing equality to women could marriage become a true marriage of minds. One minor part of the article stated that, given the unjust divorce laws, there was an element of immorality in marrying under the laws of the state as it implied tacit consent to those unjust laws. In fact, married couples are party to a position of privilege as against unmarried couples and thus help prop up a spurious respectability. Brophy also made the point that it is the love between the two people, not the legal contract, that is the most important feature of the union. (73)

As Margaret Knight had experienced a decade previously, Brophy received an avalanche of threatening and malevolent letters from outraged Christians. She later appeared on a BBC debate about her article and was lined up against a parade of tut-tutting clerics. The whole affair was written up for the November issue of the *Humanist*.

At about the same time, Brophy defended a colleague on the Literature Panel of the Arts Council whose appointment had come under threat after his drug habit became public knowledge. Brophy enquired whether, were they to be in the eighteenth century and Samuel Taylor Coleridge was on the panel, he too would have been thrown off it. Her protest was to no avail. More successful was her campaign through the 1970s to secure payments to authors on a basis proportionate to their rate of being lent out by libraries. This finally passed into law in 1979. Brophy was also a determined campaigner for animal rights, as the National Secular Society found to its cost. When speaking at its Annual Dinner, she burned her NSS membership card in front of her astonished audience in protest against the society not withdrawing its affiliation to Amnesty International for its refusal to include animal experiments as a type of torture. Brophy was married to the respected art historian and critic Sir Michael Levey, also an Honorary Associate.

In 1979, the year she secured library fees for authors, Brophy learned she had multiple sclerosis. This illness crippled her and contributed to her relatively early death in 1995. Brophy described herself as a 'declared and indeed a proselytising atheist' and ensured her funeral was entirely without religious content. (74)

Once again, these few paragraphs by no means exhaust the list of novelists and authors among the RPA Honorary Associates, the most notable among them being Somerset Maugham (1874-1965, Honorary Associate 1935-1965), David Garnett (1892-1981, Honorary Associate, 1972-1981) and Brian Moore. Maugham is well known and has been much-discussed but Brian Moore (1921-1999, Honorary Associate 1995-1999) deserves more attention. A feature of Moore's writing often commented on was his unusual ability to write from a woman's perspective. His best-known book, *The Lonely Passion of Judith Hearne* (1955) told the story of the slow destruction by loneliness of Judith Hearne, whose personal resources had been so impoverished by the narrow Belfast Catholicism she was raised in. Moore wrote superbly and dealt with a wide range of subjects. The *New Humanist* noted in Moore's obituary that his writing career was dominated by the question 'what are we to believe and if we believe nothing, how are we to live?' (75) Another Honorary Associate, the poet Gavin Ewart, asked the same question. Not long before he died, Ewart wrote the Foreword to the last title published by Pemberton Books, an anthology of poems edited by Bet Cherrington called *Facing the World*. In it he wrote, 'The rationalist and the atheist must be stoical. There is no afterlife, and justice may never be done...If we want justice on this earth, we must get it for ourselves.'

As the RPA counts gifted novelists among its Honorary Associates, so has it included scholars of literature and critics. Chief among them from the early life of the RPA would be William Archer (1856-1924, Honorary Associate 1916-1924). While his own plays met with little acclaim, Archer became a very influential and sympathetic critic. It was Archer who, along with George Bernard Shaw, was chiefly responsible for introducing Ibsen's plays to Britain. And as we saw with his controversy with H G Wells in 1917, Archer was at all times an earnest and polite controversialist. He wrote many articles for the RPA, and his long-time friend J M Robertson brought them together in a memorial volume published by Watts & Co, called *William Archer as Rationalist* in 1925. Following Archer would be I A Richards (1893-1979), who accepted the role in the last year of his life. Richards was well versed in philosophy; one of his first books was a co-operative venture with C K Ogden called *The Meaning of Meaning*, published in 1923. All of Richards's subsequent work was more squarely within the field of literary criticism. His work *Practical Criticism* (1929) remained an influential study of poetry for many years.

Much more obscure now is Winifred Stephens Whale, who died in 1944, but whose year of birth has so far eluded me. Before marrying George Whale relatively late in her life, Winifred Stephens enjoyed a successful career as a translator and professional Francophile. A series of lectures she gave on 'French Novelists of Today' in 1907 was published by John Lane the following year. The success of this book led Lane to suggest she translate the works of Anatole France into English, which she did. Stephens edited *The Book of France* in 1915 and in 1918 wrote *The France I Know*. She enjoyed the friendship of H G Wells, Augustine Birrell, Edmund Gosse and others. This is not surprising as Winifred Stephens was exactly the sort of independent and intelligent woman Wells in particular celebrated in his writing. She was active on the fundraising committee of Bedford College for a while and was very interested in the League of Nations Union, speaking on its behalf around the country on many occasions. Stephens married George Whale in 1923 and became an Honorary Associate of the RPA in 1928. She translated *The Enigma of Jesus* by the French author Paul Louis Couchoud for Watts & Co in 1924 and *The Life of a Priest: My Own Experience, 1867-1912* by Albert Houtin in 1927. Couchoud's book had an Introduction written for it by James George Frazer. Winifred Whale died in 1944 after a long illness.

Another remarkable person from Winifred Whale's generation was Sir Henry Wood (1869-1944, Honorary Associate 1937-1944) who became the first professional conductor of 'The Proms' in August 1895. Wood had a background of interest in the sciences and in engineering and only had his first experience of conducting at the age of twenty. He devoted his life to popularising classical music. It was Wood who conducted the first English performance of Sibelius's First Symphony, in 1902. His book *About Conducting* remains one of the classic works on the subject. We saw in Chapter 4 that Wood signed, along with seven other RPA Honorary Associates, a letter to *The Times* protesting at the encroachments of religion in education.

It would exhaust the patience of the reader to troop dutifully through each discipline and note the RPA Honorary Associates along the way. And it is not strictly what this chapter is about. But as an historian, it would feel disrespectful not to at least name the distinguished historians among the RPA Honorary Associates. Sir Leslie Stephen, J M Robertson, G M Trevelyan, J B Bury, Jane Harrison, M I Finley, A J P Taylor, Eric Hobsbawm, Christopher Hill, Conrad Russell and David Starkey form an impressive list by any standards. Some of these scholars qualify as being household names *about* which extensive literatures exist, let alone what exists *by* them. But, sadly, we must name them and move on. The point of this chapter is to show how rationalism and humanism operate in different people with different aims, strengths and ideas. Each of these people has sought to combine thought and action in order make some sort of contribution toward making the world a better place. This is the essence of Paul Kurtz's ideal of eupraxophy. Most of these people disdained self-serving notions of an afterlife and so were doing good, not for some perceived future reward, but because doing good is good to do. This commitment is at the heart of humanism. And all these people disdained to follow creeds and the pronouncements of others, and so had to work out their solutions for themselves. This commitment is at the heart of rationalism.

The best way to finish a survey such as this is to look quickly at the most recent additions to this extraordinary list. They include an economist, an activist, a journalist, a philosopher, and a scientist. The journalist is Hazhir Teimourian, a refugee from the Iranian-dominated areas of Kurdistan, now living in London. A lot of Teimourian's journalism within the humanist movement has been focused on alerting the West to the fanatical strain within Islam. Since the terrorist attacks on New York and Washington on September 11 2001, these warnings have all of a sudden become commonplace. It would be quite wrong to caricature Teimourian as ignorantly hostile towards Islam. Having fled the theocratic dictatorship of Iran, he is more qualified than most to comment on the intolerances that the Islamic religion harbours. Whereas many Anglo-American Islam scholars have bent over backwards to portray Islam as essentially a religion of peace and toleration, people like Teimourian know better. If the Western Islam scholars are right, Teimourian wrote in the *New Humanist* after the September 11 attacks, why did the prominent, and apparently liberal, Egyptian newspaper *Al Ahrar* proclaim it 'our religious and national duty to rejoice'? And why did Syria's main literary weekly magazine, *Al Osbu Al Adabi* declare that our 'lungs filled with fresh air as they had never done before'? Teimourian was pessimistic about the prospects for world peace and for the preservation of civil liberties in the West. (76)

It is characteristic of the humanist to be able to see things from several contrasting angles. While Teimourian was writing about Islamic fanaticism in militant terms, in the very same issue of the *New Humanist* he showed himself to be alive to the grace and beauty that also exists in the Islamic tradition. At the time he became an Honorary Associate, he was working on a biography of the eleventh-century poet and mathematician Omar Khayyam. Teimourian translated a section of the famous *Rubaiyat*, one stanza of which reads

> Lord of the *fatwa*, what a rogue you are!
> Drinker, I may be, I prefer by far
> From the juice of grapes to secure a thrill
> Than to cheat orphans of their father's will!

It is interesting how inspirational Khayyam has been to generations of rationalists. Readers will recall Edward Clodd and George Whale founding the Omar Khayyam Club in London at the end of the nineteenth century.

The philosopher is A C Grayling, Reader in Philosophy at Birkbeck College, London, an institution with a long tradition of supporting humanist thinkers. Grayling is also a columnist on philosophical matters in *The Guardian*. It was from here that he defended the reputation of Bertrand Russell from one of his most recent detractors. Grayling has edited two comprehensive sets of readings covering virtually the entire spectrum of philosophy and has been impudent enough even to criticise Wittgenstein. This is regarded by many as a very great crime. Interestingly enough, some of the other most trenchant critics of

Wittgenstein – Bertrand Russell, A J Ayer, Ernest Gellner and Ted Honderich – were or are all active rationalists. In contrast to the runic mysticism of Wittgenstein, Grayling has consistently looked to making his academic speciality accessible to the non-specialist. This is one of the features of humanism that Wittgenstein most despised. Grayling's most recent book at the time he became an Honorary Associate exemplifies these priorities. *The Meaning of Things*, subtitled 'Applying Philosophy to Life', is a collection of his *Guardian* articles organised thematically and allowing the book to be read systematically or to be dipped into. As the title suggests, Grayling covers real-life questions and applies some clear thinking to them. The result is a fuller understanding of the issues at question, which leads to a more humane and thus compassionate approach to life's problems. These are the core values of rationalism and humanism.

The economist is Amartya Sen, Master of Trinity College, Cambridge, and winner of the 1998 Nobel Prize in Economics. Sen is an expert on issues of world poverty and his work has been devoted largely to its eradication. He is author of many works, although the best-known to the non-specialist is his 1999 book *Development as Freedom*, where he maps out a general theory of development that takes place in tandem with the classic humanist priorities of freedom and dignity. As the *Times of India* said, when speaking of Sen's Nobel Prize, 'Professor Sen deserves the accolade for giving the 'dismal science' of economics the humanist face of a universal moral philosophy.' (77). In the middle of 2001, the *New Humanist* ran as lead article Sen's talk to the Indian History Congress, in which he criticised the growing tendency in India to rewrite history in sectarian terms. Not only does this make for bad history, he argued, but it expressly works against the heterodoxy which is so essential to social and scientific development. 'The incursion of sectarian orthodoxy in Indian history involves two distinct problems, to wit, (1) narrow sectarianism, and (2) unreasoned orthodoxy. The enterprise of knowledge is threatened by both.' (78) How very true, and how true not just for India, but for the whole world.

The activist is Sanal Edamaruku, President of the Rationalist International and Secretary General of the Indian Rationalist Association and one of the leading advocates of rationalism in India. While in the west it has become fashionable to revel in irrationality, in India the malevolent consequences of irrationality are better understood. He has been instrumental in organising teachers to go into villages and show the villagers how the godmen do their simple tricks. India has tens of thousands of itinerant charlatans who go from village to village performing simple tricks and passing them off as proof of their divine status. Suitably rewarded with food, clothing and money, they then leave. Edamaruku's Indian Rationalist Association has helped organise people to show the villagers how the godmen's cheap tricks are done, in the hope they will not line their pockets the next time they come calling. He has also been taking a leading role in exposing the pretensions of Sai Baba.

Edamaruku was active during a bout of mass hysteria which hit New Delhi in the first half of 2000. Reports of a psychotic man-monkey arose seemingly out of nowhere and soon had the city in a grip of panic. Edamaruku later recalled that the monster was, depending on the source, an amalgam of anything from Hanuman to Batman. Irresponsible media companies gave credence to the rumours, with television crews asking leading questions of frightened people. The police put on a thousand additional policemen, later increased to 3000, with orders to shoot the creature on sight. But some judicious questioning by Edamaruku and timely media interviews helped to defuse the situation. Sensing the escalating dangers the rumours were exposing the city to, the police, the media and other authorities fell into line, mentioning specifically the rationalists' initiatives. Edamaruku later wrote that during 'these days of hard and hectic work around the clock we felt like fire fighters trying to stop an expanding area of conflagration.' (79)

The work of people like Sanal Edamaruku is one of the finest examples of practical rationalism in action. Contrary to the oft-repeated sneers that rationalism is intellectual – as if that should be a rebuke – the work undertaken by Edamaruku reveals just how central to a healthy body and body politic the proper application of rationality really is.

And finally, one of the most recent scientists to accept the title of Honorary Associate of the RPA is Baroness Greenfield CBE, Professor of Pharmacology at Oxford University, and since 1998 the first female director of the Royal Institution. In fact, the year after accepting an Honorary Associateship she deepened her commitment to the RPA by becoming Vice-president. Baroness Greenfield has come to the attention of the non-scientific public in a number of different ways. She has become a regular science commentator on television and radio on everything from in-depth documentaries to 'Desert Island Discs'. She has written a fortnightly column on aspects of science for *The Independent on Sunday* and features regularly in most other quality British newspapers. She has won a series of awards for her contribution to the public understanding of science. Her book *The Human Brain: A Guided Tour* is part of Weidenfeld & Nicolson's excellent 'Science Masters' series and made the bestseller list. And it has to be said that the confidence Weidenfeld & Nicolson showed in publishing this successful series of popular science titles is tribute to the pioneering work in this area by the Rationalist Press Association a century ago. Baroness Greenfield's willingness and proficiency in making science attractive and understandable to the general citizen is a guiding motif in what rationalism is about. Greenfield is particularly concerned to raise the profile of science among girls.

Epilogue

The Summing Up

In summarising the record of the papacy, Eamon Duffy, a very fine historian of that institution, was modest. 'For all its sins, and despite its recurring commitment to the repression of 'error', the papacy does seem to me to have been on balance a force for human freedom, and largeness of spirit.' (1) This is very far from being a ringing endorsement, particularly for an organisation claiming to enjoy divine favour. Happily, the task of evaluating the record of the RPA allows for a more generous assessment, its poorer supernatural authority notwithstanding. Towards the end of 1942 a correspondent to the *Literary Guide* outlined what he thought to be the achievements of the RPA. They are worth listing in full and in the same order:

(1) The publication of more than four million sixpenny books, comprising many of the principal heterodox works written in the nineteenth century.

(2) The delivery of hundreds of educational lectures on Evolution and cognate subjects in London and provincial centres.

(3) The sale of thousands of copies of *The Encyclopaedia Biblica*, containing acknowledgements that the cardinal doctrines of the Christian faith are simple beliefs and are not based on demonstrable facts.

(4) The purchase of over 5000 copies of *The Golden Bough* (abridged edition), published at 18s, for sale to RPA members at 5s.

(5) The publication of hundreds of original works by authors whose names are now familiar to advanced thinkers throughout the British Commonwealth of Nations.

(6) Being the chief factor in the establishment of kindred organisations in India, Australia, New Zealand and South Africa, which are exercising enormous influence in disintegrating orthodox beliefs in those countries.

(7) In missionary efforts, sending an official representative to one or two colonies to deliver lectures expository of the aims of the Association.

(8) Lastly, to crown all, launching of the Thinker's Library, which includes the ripest thought of both the past and present century. (2)

The attention to detail, as in the fourth item, suggests this letter was a plant for the historical record, probably penned by Fred Watts or Adam Gowans Whyte. Generally speaking, it is a fair assessment of the RPA's achievements in the first half-century of its existence. If this list exaggerates the influence of the overseas rationalist organisations, it probably underestimates the RPA's own influence in contributing to the making of a post-Christian Britain. It has been widely observed that it was during the 1960s that the post-Christian, pluralist Britain emerged. Why the new Britain emerged so quickly during that decade was because the post-war generation then coming of age, the so-called baby-boomers, were the first to realise that not only were they not Christians, their parents weren't either. By this time the RPA had been working on the minds of the baby-boomers' parents, grandparents, even great-grandparents. Slowly the various pockets of unbelief, confined to elements of the upper classes and working classes in the nineteenth century had spread until the new young middle class of the 1960s consummated the process. It seems to me quite reasonable to claim that the RPA can take a share of the credit for creating the conditions which led to the vaporisation of Christian belief after the sixties.

That the post-1960s generations have, by and large, been as unmoved by the RPA's message as they have by those of the churches is less a cause for congratulation. But the RPA is no more immune to this dilemma than any other humanist organisation. The founders of the RPA did not foresee the emergence of a post-Christian Britain where religious belief would decay but where non-religious organisations such as their own would languish in direct proportion to that decay. It is to be hoped that the closer ties with the BHA will go some way toward addressing that dilemma.

So, in conscious imitation of the 1942 list, I want to suggest my own eight-point report card for the RPA as it begins its second century. The main achievements and legacy of the RPA seem to me to include:

(1) Making a success of the Cheap Reprints, which altered forever the perceptions of publishers as to what readers of modest means wanted to read. This created the climate that Penguin later exploited so successfully. And, also by virtue of the Cheap Reprints, opening the market for heterodox books to become commercially and socially acceptable to publish. The RPA was the first publisher to democratise learning without dumbing down. These were significant contributions to the development of post-Christian Britain.

(2) Championing ideas and values at which the churches sneered in 1890 and now claim as their own. The simple fact is that the rationalist and humanist view of the world has been proved substantially correct, based as it is on a solid naturalism. The extent of the victory is shown by the prevalence of humanist, even atheist beliefs among churchmen.

(3) Publishing so many good books and for remaining committed to the *Literary Guide*, through to *The Humanist* and on to the *New Humanist*.

(4) For consistently encouraging free inquiry, the smiting of humbug and the advocacy of unpopular causes, such as opposition to the blasphemy laws and access to the broadcast media.

(5) By doing the above in such a way as to not alienate prominent supporters, many of whom have given yeoman service to rationalism and humanism as a result.

(6) Being the inspiration for the creation of Prometheus Books, which has carried on where the RPA left off.

(7) Providing a vehicle for unusual talents such as Joseph McCabe, Hector Hawton and Nicolas Walter to thrive.

(8) Supporting to the best of its ability the promotion of rationalism and humanism in Australia, New Zealand and India in particular.

Merely to have survived such a long time, and to have seen off the challenges from organised Christianity and Marxism is a major victory, given the resources the RPA has had at its command. It is to be hoped that the current challenges from fundamentalism, new-age flummery and postmodernism will be repelled as effectively as the earlier ones were.

Appendix 1

Works published by the RPA since 1890

This appendix attempts to provide as comprehensive a list as possible of publications from Watts & Co, its successor company, Pemberton Publishing, and the RPA itself. Accordingly, the list ignores Watts & Co titles from before the foundation of the Propagandist Press Committee in July 1890 and after the company was sold to Sir Isaac Pitman & Sons in 1960. The list includes all known Watts & Co commercial publishing ventures not related to the RPA. All known Pemberton titles, along with their respective co-publisher, have been listed. The last Pemberton title was in 1989, and since then all titles have been published directly by the RPA.

The books are listed in chronological order, under the headings of books, revised editions and reprints, and pamphlets. New or revised editions of pamphlets are included in the revised editions section. When known, the date of the first edition is placed in brackets. Titles published as part of a series are included in the list of that series, otherwise they are listed in chronological order. Occasionally a title was published as part of a series *and* as a stand-alone title, in which case they are listed with the series and in the general list.

Pseudonyms are in single quotation marks and, when known, the actual name in square brackets. The only exception is when an author is chiefly known by a pseudonym but has penned this particular title under his or her real name. And finally, a few titles were purchased from other publishers and rebound in Watts & Co covers. These have not been included in this list. An asterisk alerts the viewer to cases where some doubt exists.

SINGLE VOLUMES
Watts & Co, for the PPC/RPC

1890 (July onwards)

- *Finger-posts to Truth*, anonymous compilation
- *Pioneer Pith: The Gist of Lectures on Rationalism*, Robert C Adams
- *A Nirvana Trilogy*, William Maccall
- *The Bible and Evolution*, Arthur B Moss

Revised Editions and Reprints
- *The Curse of Conventionalism*, 'A Clergyman of the Church of England' [Rev John Bacon], [pamphlet]

Pamphlets
- *Origin of the Genesis Story of the Creation and Fall of Man*, Henry Day
- *Agnosticism and Immortality*, Samuel Laing
- *Myth of the Great Deluge*, James M McCann
- *Humanity and Dogma*, Amos Waters
- *The Christian Doctrine of Hell*, J M Wheeler

1891

Books
- *The Soul of Man: An Investigation of the Facts of Psychological and Experimental Psychology*, Paul Carus
- *The Liberty Annual, 1892* (eds) W S Crawshay and Frederick Millar
- *The Agnostic Island: A Novel*, F J Gould
- *Stepping-stones to Agnosticism*, F J Gould
- *From Alps to Orient*, H[erbert] J[unius] Hardwicke
- *A Song for My Son*, George Henry Martin
- *Antidotes to Superstition*, George Henry Martin
- *The Practical Value of Christianity*, Rev J Broadhurst Nichols & C W Dymond

Revised Editions and Reprints
- *Rambles Abroad*, Dr H J Hardwicke
- *Evolution and Creation*, Dr H J Hardwicke
- *My Lyrical Life: Poems Old and New*, Gerald Massey
- *The Secret Drama of Shakespeare's Sonnets*, Gerald Massey

Pamphlets
- *Satan: Two Lectures*, Rev John Page Hopps
- *Possibilities and Impossibilities*, Thomas Henry Huxley
- *The Four Gospels*, 'Julian' [Ebenezer Cobham Brewer]
- *The Subject of the Four Gospels*, 'Julian' [Ebenezer Cobham Brewer]
- *The Old and New Testament Examined*, 'Julian' [Ebenezer Cobham Brewer]
- *Darwinism and Religious Thought*, Frederick Millar
- *Lessons of Agnosticism*, Alfred Thompson
- *The Destiny of Man, from an Agnostic Viewpoint*, Charles Watts

1892

Books
- *Handbook of Scientific Agnosticism*, Richard Bithell
- *Richard Savage: A Play; and Bernicia*, Charles Colton
- *The Liberty Annual, 1893* (eds) W S Crawshay and Frederick Millar
- *Christianity and Evolution*, Arthur B Moss

Revised Editions and Reprints
- *The Religion of This Life*, Charles C Cattell [pamphlet] *
- *Christianity Incredible and Impracticable*, Charles C Cattell (1875?) *
- *Thoughts for Thinking, from the Literature of all Ages*, Charles C Cattell *
- *Collected Essays on Politics, Science and Freethought*, Charles C Cattell *
- *Bible Morality* (third, revised edition), Charles Watts

Pamphlets
- *Man of the Past: His Natural Origin and Great Antiquity*, Charles C Cattell
- *Is the Second Coming of Jesus Probable in this Generation?* Charles C Cattell
- *Recollections of Charles Bradlaugh MP*, Charles C Cattell
- *Man's Allegedly Spiritual Nature*, W M Knox
- *An Agnostic View of the Bible*, Samuel Laing

* uncertain whether these titles are reprints and, in the second and third case, whether they are book or pamphlet-length works.

1893

Books
- *Truth in Fiction: Twelve Tales with a Moral*, Paul Carus
- *The Liberty Annual for 1894*, W S Crawshay
- *A Concise History of Religion*, Volume One, F J Gould
- *Amy Clarefoot (A Romance of the Year 1900)*, 'Philosophicus'
- *The Religion of the Brain*, Henry Smith
- *The Dawn of Civilisation, or, England in the Nineteenth Century*, J C Spence

Revised Editions and Reprints
- *The Wandering Jew*, Robert Buchanan
- *Sixty Years of an Agitator's Life*, George Jacob Holyoake (1892)
- *Antiqua Mater: A Study of Christian Origins*, Edwin Johnson (1887)
- *The Rise of Christendom*, Edwin Johnson
- *The Science of Mechanics*, Ernst Mach (first English translation, with Open Court)

Pamphlets
- *The Construction of the Bible and the Koran*, anonymous
- *The Worship of the Unknowable*, Richard Bithell
- *Miss Naden's "World-Scheme"*, George M McCrie
- *A Rationalist Bibliography*, Frederick Millar
- *Marriage in Relation to the Sexes*, Marquis of Queensbury
- *Mind and Form*, Robert Park
- *Evolution and Special Creation*, Charles Watts
- *Happiness in Hell and Misery in Heaven*, Charles Watts
- *A Critical Essay in the Philosophy of History*, Thomas Whittaker

1894

Books
- *A Primer of Philosophy*, Paul Carus
- *Ghebers of Hebron*, Samuel Fales Dunlap
- *Is the Bible a Revelation from God?* Charles T Gorham
- *Songs of Love and Duty for the Young* (ed) Gustav Spiller

Revised Editions and Reprints
- *Agnostic Problems* (cheap edition) Richard Bithell (1887)
- *Orthodoxy: An Impeachment*, R G Ingersoll (1884) [pamphlet]
- *Antidote to Superstition* (cheap edition) George Martin (1891)

Pamphlets
- *The Pauline Epistles*, Edwin Johnson
- *Scripture Inspiration*, Otho George Medhurst
- *What Do I Believe?* Henry Smith
- *The Bible Up to Date*, Charles Watts
- *Education: True and False*, Charles Watts
- *Is There a Life Beyond the Grave?* Charles Watts
- *Secularism and Its Relations to Social Problems*, Charles Watts
- *Christianity and Civilisation*, Charles Watts
- *The Existence of God*, Charles Watts

1895

Books
- *Researches in Oriental History*, George W Brown
- *A Concise History of Religion*, Volume Two, F J Gould
- *Tales from the Bible, Told to My Daughter*, F J Gould

Revised Editions and Reprints
- *The Path I Took and Where it Led Me* (revised by G J Holyoake), 'A Monmouthshire Farmer' [pamphlet]
- *Possibilities and Impossibilities*, Thomas Henry Huxley (1891) [pamphlet]
- *Thoughts on Science, Theology, and Ethics* (cheap edition), John Wilson

Pamphlets
- *Shall Thought be Fettered in England?* E G Taylor
- *Was Jesus Christ a Social and Political Reformer?* Charles Watts
- *The Claims of Christianity Examined from a Rationalist Perspective*, Charles Watts

1896

Books
- *Social Evolution and the Evolution of Socialism: A Critical Essay*, George Schoobridge Carr *
- *The Origin and Nature of Secularism*, George Jacob Holyoake
- *The Christian's Looking Glass: A Mirror of Christ's Doctrines*, Henry Smith

Revised Editions and Reprints
- *The Dynamic Theory of Life and Mind*, Dr James B Alexander (1893)
- *The Foundations of Faith* (revised edition), R G Ingersoll (1896) [pamphlet]
- *An Inquiry into the Age of the Moabite Stone*, Samuel Sharpe
- *The Religion of the Brain* (second edition), Henry Smith
- *Songs of Love and Duty for the Young* (enlarged edition), Gustav Spiller (ed)
- *What Must I Do to Get Well, and How Can I Keep So?* Elma Stuart (1895) [pamphlet]

Pamphlets
- *The New Marriage in Ten Tableaux*, anon
- *The Secularist's Catechism*, Charles Watts

* this book could be a reprint.

1897

Books
- *Voices in the Twilight*, L Cranmer-King
- *A Concise History of Religion*, Volume Three, F J Gould
- *Irish Finance, an Unroyal Commission, and - a Lady*, Egmont Hake
- *A Rationalist's Manual*, 'Aletheia' [W W Hardwicke]
- *Modern Rationalism*, Joseph McCabe
- *The Non-Christian Cross*, John Denham Parsons
- *Our Sun-God; or, Christianity Before Christ*, John Denham Parsons
- *A Plea for the Unborn*, Henry Smith

Revised Editions and Reprints
- *Steps to the Temple of Happiness*, Henry Smith

Pamphlets
- *The Old Bible from a New Point of View*, 'Incognito'
- *The Triumph of Mammon; or, Christ Betrayed by the Clergy*, 'Stella Beatti'
- *The Story of the Prayer Book*, anonymous
- *The New Conversion*, F J Gould
- *A Rationalist's Catechism*, 'Aletheia' [W W Hardwicke]
- *From Rome to Rationalism*, Joseph McCabe
- *The Martyrdom of Percy Whitcomb: Socialist and Agnostic*, Erwin McCall
- *Mature Thought on Christianity*, F W Newman
- *Christian Rationalism*, Walter Sweetman

1898

Books
- *The Faith of a Physician*, anonymous
- *The Woman's Bible (The Pentateuch)*, anonymous
- *The Bible Inquirer: A Key to Bible Investigation*, anonymous
- *Some Account of Church-going; the Declining Belief in the Supernatural; and the Uselessness of Religious Worship as a Means of Purifying the Soul; together with Matters purely Secular*, 'Theophilus Binks'

- *The Process of Creation Discovered*, James Dunbar
- *The Ethics of the Great Religions*, Charles T Gorham
- *Chats With Pioneers of Modern Thought*, F J Gould
- *Tales From the New Testament*, F J Gould
- *Criminal or Irresponsible?* Henry Smith

Revised Editions and Reprints
- *The Ten Commandments*, Stanton Coit [pamphlet]
- *The Lord's Prayer*, Stanton Coit [pamphlet]
- *The Sermon on the Mount*, Stanton Coit [pamphlet]
- *The Sacrament of the Lord's Prayer*, Stanton Coit [pamphlet]
- *The Ethical Movement Defined*, Stanton Coit [pamphlet]
- *A Sketch of Morality Independent of Obligation or Sanction*, M Guyau (1885)
- *Why I am an Agnostic*, R G Ingersoll (1895)
- *Steps to the Temple of Happiness*, Henry Smith

Pamphlets
- *The New Trinity*, Auden Amyand
- *Do You Believe the Bible is the Inspired Word of God?* 'G B D'
- *The Building of the Bible*, F J Gould
- *Superstition*, R G Ingersoll

1899

Books
- *A Modern Omar Khayyam*, R Didden
- *The Children's Book of Moral Lessons* (First Series), F J Gould
- *The Metaphysic of Christianity and Buddhism*, M Dawsonne Strong

Revised Editions and Reprints
- *The Devil*, R G Ingersoll (1899) [pamphlet]

Pamphlets
- *Why I am a Secularist*, Charles Cattell
- *The Ethical Riches: A Lecture*, F J Gould
- *Christianity and Agnosticism: A Correspondence between a Clergyman of the Church of England and George Anderson, Agnostic, London* (ed) K E Watts

Watts & Co for the RPA

1899

Books
- *Present Immortality: The Modern Revelation of Truth*, A H Curror
- *The Evolution of Man: His Religious Beliefs and Social Systems*, W W Hardwicke
- *The Religion of the Twentieth Century*, Joseph McCabe
- *Modern Thought on Life and Conduct*, H W Smith

Revised Editions and Reprints
- *Charles Watts's Pamphlets* (two volumes), Charles Watts

Pamphlets
- *Will Women Help?* F J Gould

1900

Books
- *The Truthseeker Collection of Forms and Ceremonies*, anonymous compilation
- *Zoroaster: Philosopher, Teacher, Hermit*, 'Aristo'
- *Christ in London*, R C Fillingham
- *Scientific Theology: A Reply to Popular Evangelicalism*, C P Gasquoine
- *The Web Unwoven; or the Dolos Theory of the Book of Acts*, W Glanville
- *Ethics of the Great French Rationalists*, Charles T Gorham
- *Was Jesus Christ a Ritualist?* Dennis Hird
- *Gospel Christianity versus Dogma and Ritual*, James Stuart Laurie
- *Christianity and Mythology*, J M Robertson
- *Studies in Religious Fallacy*, J M Robertson
- *Religion and Reason*, 'Truthseeker'

Revised Editions and Reprints
- *The Riddle of the Universe*, Ernst Haeckel (1899)
- *A Vision of War*, R G Ingersoll (1899)
- *The Prophet of Nazareth*, Evan Powell Meredith (1864)

Pamphlets
- *England and Islam*, Henry Crossfield
- *The Marvellous Birth of the Buddhas*, Albert J Edmunds
- *Spiritualism a Delusion*, Charles Watts
- *The Christ Myth*, Elizabeth E Evans

1901

Books
- *The Melita of the Midlands*, 'An Ex-Rector'
- *The Moon of Leaves and Other Poems*, 'Aristo'
- *Last Words on Materialism*, Ludwig Büchner (translated by Joseph McCabe, original compilation)
- *The Religion of the First Christians*, F J Gould
- *The New Story of the Bible*, W A Leonard
- *What is Truth? Or, the Value of Comparison*, Alfred Dixon Lord
- *The Bible in School: A Question of Ethics*, J Allanson Picton

Revised Editions and Reprints
- *The Evolution of the Idea of God*, Grant Allen (1897)
- *Men, Women, and Gods*, Helen H Gardner
- *Parson Dash: A Rap at Ritualism in Hudibrastic Verse*, Erasmus Holiday

Pamphlets
- *Mr Chamberlain Against England*, 'A Free Briton'
- *The Dread Alternative: "Come to Jesus" or: -!* 'A Protestant Dissenter'
- *Christianity and Buddhism*, Ludwig Büchner
- *Robert Owen and His Life-Work*, Rev. John Glasse

1902

Books
- *Some Problems in Religion and Morals*, Arthur Collis
- *The Faith of an Agnostic*, 'George Forester' [George Greenwood]
- *Faith: Its Freaks and Follies*, Charles T Gorham
- *A New Catechism*, M M Mangasarian
- *The New Morality*, 'Geoffrey Mortimer' [Walter M Gallichan]
- *On the Progress of Liberty of Thought During Queen Victoria's Reign*, Constance Plumptre
- *Letters on Reasoning*, J M Robertson
- *A Short History of Christianity*, J M Robertson
- *Miracles of Christian Belief*, Charles Watts

Revised Editions and Reprints
- *The Logic of Death* (revised edition), George Jacob Holyoake (1850)
- *Supernatural Religion* (abridged version), W R Cassels (1874-6)

Pamphlets
- *The King Who Wouldn't be a Pagan*, 'Rashleigh Cumming Forward'

1903

Books
- *Mr Balfour's Apologetics Critically Examined*, anonymous [W B Columbine]
- *An Ethical Calendar*, anonymous
- *The Voice of One*, Henry Allsopp
- *Religion: A Short Homily from an Agnostic Point of View*, Max Henry Ferrars
- *The Children's Book of Moral Lessons*, (Second Series) F J Gould
- *An Easy Outline of Evolution*, Dennis Hird
- *Road-Makers and Other Poems*, Harrold Johnson
- *The Cosmos and the Creeds*, W Usborne Moore
- *Studies in Little-Known Subjects*, Constance Plumptre
- *Pagan Christs*, J M Robertson

Revised Editions and Reprints
- *Sunday: The People's Holiday*, W W Hardwicke (1898)
- *Twelve Years in a Monastery* (revised and enlarged), Joseph McCabe (1897)
- *The Martyrdom of Man*, Winwood Reade (1872)

Pamphlets
- *Feathered Enfranchisement: Why Should Blackbirds Wait?* anonymous
- *Towards Freedom: An Appeal to Thoughtful Men and Women*, Lady Florence Dixie
- *Theism Found Wanting*, W S Godfrey
- *Two Great Preachers: The Rev Hugh Price Hughes and the Rev Dr Joseph Parker*, George Jacob Holyoake
- *Every-day Songs*, E Josephine Troup

1904

Books
- *Christianity and Rationalism on Trial*, anonymous compilation
- *The Latest Hell (A Phantasy)*, anonymous
- *The Worthlessness of Christianity*, 'A Japanese'
- *Some Chapters in a Rationalist's Life*, George Anderson
- *The Hammurabi Code*, 'Chilperic Edwards' [Edward Pilcher]
- *New Stories for Children*, Mrs F K Gregory
- *The Children's Book of Moral Lessons* (Third Series), F J Gould
- *The Wonders of Life*, Ernst Haeckel
- *Do We Believe? A Brief Exposition of the Rationalist Faith*, 'JA Hedderwick' [Adam Gowans Whyte]
- *The Believing Bishop*, Dennis Hird
- *The Bible Untrustworthy*, Walter Jekyll
- *The Road-Makers and Other Poems*, Harrold Johnson
- *Matter and Life: What are They?* William Naismith
- *Some Reasons Against Church-going*, Max O'Rell
- *Courses of Study*, J M Robertson
- *Modern Thoughts on Life and Conduct*, H W Smith
- *Modern Thoughts on Religion and Culture*, H W Smith
- *The Origins of Christianity*, Thomas Whittaker

Revised Editions and Reprints
- *The Founders of Christianity*, Rev James Cranbrook
- *Towards Freedom: An Appeal to Thoughtful Men and Women*, Lady Florence Dixie [pamphlet]
- *The Wonders of Life*, Ernst Haeckel
- *Lectures and Essays* (First Series), R G Ingersoll, (original compilation from Collected Works 1900, with Introduction by Charles T Gorham)
- *The New Story of the Bible*, William A Leonard (1901)
- *Nature, The Utility of Religion, and Theism*, J S Mill (1874)
- *On the Nature of Knowledge*, Frances Wright [pamphlet]

Pamphlets
- *An Educational Concordat*, 'A Liberal Candidate'
- *The Transformation of Christianity*, Charles T Gorham
- *Idealism and Dogma*, Arthur H Harington
- *Haeckel's Contribution to Religion*, A S Mories
- *What to Read*, J M Robertson
- *The Ethics of Criticism*, Robert M Theobald
- *Reason and Emotion in Relation to Conduct*, Lucian de Zilwa

1905

Books
- *The Mind Birth: A Poem and a Philosophy*, 'by the author of "The Latest Hell"'
- *King David of Israel: A Study in the Evolution of Ethics*, Charles Callaway
- *Perils of Genius, being Brief Biographies of Persecuted Men*, Charles C Cattell
- *Last Words on Evolution*, Ernst Haeckel

- *Philosophy and Christianity: An Introduction to the Works of Schopenhauer. Part I, A Defence of Pessimism*, David Irvine
- *The Gospel of Humanity*, 'Ithuriel'
- *The Religion of Woman: An Historical Study*, Joseph McCabe
- *The Peace of the Anglo-Saxons*, Stewart L Murray
- *Edmund Burke: Apostle of Justice and Liberty*, T Dundas Pillans
- *An Idol of Four*, Hon Ernest Pomeroy
- *Did Shakespeare Write "Titus Andronicus"?* J M Robertson
- *Walt Whitman and Leaves of Grass*, W H Trimble
- *The Meaning of Rationalism, and Other Essays*, Charles Watts

Revised Editions and Reprints
- *Supernatural Religion* (reprint of 1902 edition), anon [Walter Cassels]
- *Bible Myths, and Their Parallels in Other Religions*, T W Doane
- *The Children's Book of Moral Lessons* (First Series), F J Gould (1899)
- *The Evolution of Man*, Ernst Haeckel (earlier editions entitled *Anthropogonie*)
- *Possibilities and Impossibilities* (cheap edition), T H Huxley (1891) [pamphlet]
- *Lectures and Essays* (Second Series), R G Ingersoll (original compilation from Collected Works 1900, with Introduction by Charles T Gorham)
- *Problems of the Future* Samuel Laing (1890)
- *From Rome to Rationalism* (cheap edition), Joseph McCabe (1897)
- *Letters on Reasoning* (second edition), J M Robertson (1902)
- *A Short History of Freethought* (expanded and revised edition), J M Robertson (1899)

Pamphlets
- *Faith and Fact: Credulity and Common Sense*, 'Inquirer'
- *The Religion That Fulfills: A Simple Account of Positivism*, F J Gould
- *On False Education*, Frederick Hovenden
- *Ritual in Ethical Services*, C J Melrose
- *Chamberlain: A Study*, J M Robertson
- *The Church and Education*, J M Robertson & Adam Gowans Whyte
- *Early Shelley Pamphlets*, Percy Vaughan

1906

Books
- *Christianity and Tradition*, P G Blyth
- *A Few Footprints*, J Passmore Edwards
- *New Scientific System of Morality*, G Gore
- *Funeral Services Without Theology*, F J Gould
- *The Children's Plutarch*, F J Gould
- *A Knight of the Holy Ghost*, E S Grossmann
- *A Picture Book of Evolution*, Volume One, Dennis Hird
- *The Anatomy of Knowledge: An Essay in Objective Logic*, Charles E Hooper
- *The Origin of Life: A Reply to Sir Oliver Lodge*, Joseph McCabe
- *The Churches and Modern Thought*, 'Philip Vivian' [Vivian Phelips]
- *The Cultivation of Man*, C A Witchell

Revised Editions and Reprints
- *The Building of the Bible* (third, revised edition), F J Gould [pamphlet]

- *A Short History of Freethought, Ancient and Modern* (second, revised edition), John M Robertson
- *What to Read: Suggestions for the Better Utilisation of Public Libraries* (revised edition), J M Robertson
- *The Necessity of Atheism*, Percy Bysshe Shelley, edited by Thomas Wise and Percy Vaughan (1811) [pamphlet]

Pamphlets
- *Sunday and the Sabbath Question*, W W Hardwicke
- *Sunday Observance: Its Origins and Meaning*, W W Hardwicke
- *The Truth About Secular Education: Its History and Results*, Joseph McCabe
- *Socialism: Its Fallacies and Dangers*, Frederick Millar
- *The Faith of Richard Jefferies*, Henry S Salt

1907

Books
- *Illustrations of Positivism*, John Henry Bridges
- *The Children's Book of Moral Lessons* (Fourth Series) F J Gould
- *A Picture Book of Evolution*, Volume Two, Dennis Hird
- *The Rise of Christianity*, Albert Kalthoff (translated by Joseph McCabe)
- *The Bible in Europe*, Joseph McCabe
- *Pioneer Humanists*, J M Robertson
- *Man: The Prodigy and Freak of Nature*, 'Keridon' [J C Thomas]
- *The Liberal State: A Speculation*, Thomas Whittaker

Revised Editions and Reprints
- *Lessons of the Day*, Moncure Conway (1882-3)
- *Lectures and Essays* (Third Series), R G Ingersoll (original compilation from Collected Works 1900, with Introduction by Charles T Gorham)

Pamphlets
- *Exeunt Mahatmas!* G A Gaskell
- *The Need of Nations: An International Parliament*, Charles E Hooper
- *The Evolution of Faith: An Essay*, Edmond John Hunt
- *The Independence of Ethics*, Joseph McCabe and Rev A J Waldren
- *The New Theology*, A S Mories
- *Sovereignty and the State: Their Nature and Relation*, Horace Samuel Seal

1908

Books
- *Modern England*, A W Benn
- *The First Easter Dawn: An Inquiry into the Evidence for the Resurrection of Jesus*, Charles T Gorham
- *The Positive Science of Morals*, Pierre Lafitte
- *Life and Letters of George Jacob Holyoake*, Joseph McCabe
- *Between Boy and Man*, 'Quilibet'

Revised Editions and Reprints
- *An Analysis of Religious Belief*, Viscount Amberley (1876)
- *Autobiography*, John Stuart Mill (1873)
- *The Conflict of Owen Prytherch*, 'Geoffrey Mortimer' [Walter M Gallichan] (1905)
- *Courses of Study* (revised, expanded edition), J M Robertson (1904)
- *The Churches and Modern Thought* (cheap edition), 'Philip Vivian' [Vivian Phelips] (1906)

Pamphlets
- *Songs o' the South*, W Blocksidge
- *The Religious Education of Children*, Rev James Cranbrook
- *A Catechism of Religion and the Social Life*, F J Gould
- *Heart Failure: How to Prevent It*, C Godfrey Gümpel
- *The Freedom of Women*, Ethel B Harrison
- *The RPA: Its Origin and Growth*, Charles E Hooper
- *On the Influence of the Natural Sciences*, Albert Ladenberg

1909

Books
- *Revaluations: Historical and Ideal*, A W Benn
- *Myth, Magic, and Morals*, F C Conybeare
- *Stories for Moral Instruction*, F J Gould
- *On the Threshold of Sex*, F J Gould
- *Education and the Heredity Spectre*, F H Hayward
- *The Unknown History of the Jews*, E E Jessel
- *Woman in Political Evolution*, Joseph McCabe
- *The Martyrdom of Ferrer*, Joseph McCabe
- *Report on Moral Instruction*, Gustav Spiller

Revised Editions and Reprints
- *Thomas Paine: Library Edition of his Writings: Political, Sociological, Religious, and Literary* (four volumes), (ed) Moncure Conway
- *The Life of Thomas Paine* (two volumes), Moncure Conway (1892)
- *Modern Rationalism* (enlarged, revised edition), Joseph McCabe (1897)
- *Paine's Political Writings* (original compilation), Thomas Paine
- *The Works of Thomas Paine* (original compilation), Thomas Paine
- *The Age of Reason*, Thomas Paine (1793-4)
- *Man: The Prodigy and Freak of Nature* (revised and enlarged edition), 'Keridon' [J C Thomas] (1907)
- *The Origins of Christianity* (second edition), Thomas Whittaker (1904)

Pamphlets
- *The Rise and Destiny of Man*, Edmond John Hunt
- *Science and the Purpose of Life*, Dr Fridtjof Nansen
- *The Near-Eastern Problem and the Pan-German Peril*, Vladimir Yovanovitch

1910

Books
- *The Confessions of Faith of a Man of Science*, Ernst Haeckel
- *Ritual, Faith, and Morals*, F H Perrycoste
- *The Tasks of Rationalism*, John Russell (Conway Memorial Lecture)
- *What is Man?* Mark Twain (first published edition)

Revised Editions and Reprints
- *The Unity of Comte's Life and Doctrine: A Reply to Strictures on Comte's Later Writings*, J H Bridges [pamphlet]
- *The Story of Creation* (revised edition), Edward Clodd (1888)
- *Myth, Magic, and Morals* (second, revised edition), F C Conybeare (1909)
- *The Evolution of Man* (new edition), Ernst Haeckel
- *The Confession of Faith of a Man of Science*, Ernst Haeckel (1895)
- *From Rome to Rationalism*, Joseph McCabe (1897)
- *Christianity and Mythology* (revised and enlarged edition), J M Robertson (1900)
- *Social Statics*, Herbert Spencer (1851)
- *First Principles*, Herbert Spencer (1862)
- *The Man versus The State*, Herbert Spencer (1884)

Pamphlets
- *The Later Gospel*, 'J S B'
- *The New Trend in Religion: Modernist, Ethical, Progressive* (ed) H J Bale
- *Friedrich Nietzsche: A Plain Account of the Fiery Philosopher*, Arthur W Knapp
- *"Dare to be Wise"*, John McTaggart Ellis McTaggart
- *Auguste Comte and Richard Congreve*, Philip Thomas
- *The Legend of Christ*, Ch Virolleaud

1911

Books
- *The Great Secret*, anonymous [Robert McMillan]
- *War and Pessimism; and other Studies*, George Chamier
- *Brave Citizens*, F J Gould
- *Captain Klek: A Romance of Marseilles*, 'W F H'
- *Things of Time: A Story*, W Nevill Heard
- *The Metaphysical Rudiments of Liberalism*, David Irvine
- *O, King, Live for Ever! Or, The Last Days of Babylon*, Richard Wade Jenkins
- *Ingersoll: A Biographical Appreciation*, Hermann Kittredge
- *A Chinese Appeal to Christendom Concerning Christian Missions*, 'Lin Shao-Yang' [Sir R F Johnston]
- *Glimpses of the Next State*, Vice-Admiral W Usborne Moore
- *Peace and War in the Balance*, Henry W Nevinson (Conway Memorial Lecture)

Revised Editions and Reprints
- *The Impeachment of the House of Brunswick*, Charles Bradlaugh (1871) [pamphlet]
- *Doubts in Dialogue*, Charles Bradlaugh (1891) [pamphlet]
- *Taxation: How it Originated, how it is Spent, and who Bears it*, Charles Bradlaugh (1878) [pamphlet]

- *The Civil List of Royal Grants*, Charles Bradlaugh (1901?) [pamphlet]
- *The Compulsory Cultivation of Waste Lands*, Charles Bradlaugh (1887) [pamphlet]
- *Did Charles Bradlaugh Die an Atheist?* Hypatia Bradlaugh Bonner (1898) [pamphlet]
- *The Encyclopedia Biblica*, four volume re-issue (eds) Rev T K Cheyne & J Sutherland Black (1899-1903)
- *The Source of the Christian Tradition*, Édouard Dujardin
- *The Wisdom of Schopenhauer as Revealed in Some of His Principal Writings*, (ed) Walter Jekyll
- *The Kingdom of Man*, E Ray Lankester (1907)
- *History of European Morals*, W E H Lecky (1869)
- *Pagan Christs* (second, expanded edition), J M Robertson (1903)
- *The Idea of a Free Church* (second edition), Henry Sturt (1909)
- *The Churches and Modern Thought* (third edition), 'Philip Vivian' [Vivian Phelips] (1906)

Pamphlets
- *Heresy and Humanity*, Jane Ellen Harrison
- *Christianity or Secularism: Which is Better for Mankind? Verbatim report of debate between Joseph McCabe and W T Lee*
- *Psychical Research as a Thought Transference*, M Eden Paul
- *The Collapse of Historical Christianity*, Rev R Roberts

1912

Books
- *Art and the Commonweal*, William Archer (Conway Memorial Lecture)
- *Penalties Upon Opinion*, Hypatia Bradlaugh Bonner
- *Witnesses to the Historicity of Jesus*, Arthur Drews
- *What Nature Is: An Outline of Scientific Naturalism*, C K Franklin
- *The Darkness, the Dawn, and the Day*, 'Keridon' [J C Thomas]
- *Constab Ballads*, Claude McKay
- *Vancouver to the Coronation*, J J Miller
- *The Evolution of States: An Introduction to English Politics*, J M Robertson
- *Ecce Deus: Studies in Primitive Christianity*, W B Smith
- *Practical Anthropology*, Thomas E Smurthwaite
- *Radical Views About the New Testament*, Dr D G A van den Bergh van Eysinga

Revised Editions and Reprints
- *Twelve Years in a Monastery* (third, revised edition), Joseph McCabe (1897)
- *Treasures of Lucretius* (new translation and compilation), H S Salt
- *The Life Worth Living*, (ed) H W Smith

Pamphlets
- *The Invention of a New Religion*, Prof B H Chamberlain
- *Modern Morality and Modern Toleration*, E S P Haynes
- *Can the Doctors Work the Insurance Act?* Ernest Ward Lowry
- *Natural Ethics in Theory and Practice*, Dr C W Saleeby

1913

Books
- *Character and Conduct Syllabus*, anonymous
- *War and the Essential Realities*, Norman Angell (Conway Memorial Lecture)
- *Facts and Fancies for Boys and Girls* (ed) Hypatia Bradlaugh Bonner
- *The Christian Hell*, Hypatia Bradlaugh Bonner
- *What Are We to Believe*, C R A
- *New Lamps for Old*, 'A S Ervant'
- *With Other Races*, Aaron Hoskin
- *In Memoriam: Richard Wagner*, David Irvine
- *Li Hung Chang's Scrap-book* (ed) Sir Hiram Stevens Maxim
- *The Voices: A Sequel to "Glimpses of the Next State"*, W Usborne Moore
- *The Influence of Religion Upon Truthfulness*, Frank Hill Perrycoste
- *Essays Towards Peace*, J M Robertson, Edward Westermarck, Norman Angell, S H Swinny
- *Percy Bysshe Shelley*, Henry S Salt
- *Songs of Love and Duty*, Gustav Spiller
- *In Quest of Truth*, Hubert Stansbury
- *A Religion of This World, Being a Selection of Positivist Addresses*, Philip Thomas
- *The Religion of the Open Mind*, Adam Gowans Whyte

Revised Editions and Reprints
- *Life and Destiny*, Felix Adler (1903)
- *The Origin of Life* (second edition), Charlton Bastian
- *The Origin and ideals of the Modern School*, Francisco Ferrer, translated by Joseph McCabe
- *Whither British?* F J Gould
- *The Riddle of the Universe*, Ernst Haeckel, translated by Joseph McCabe (1900)
- *Transcendent Speculations on Apparent Design in the Fate of the Individual*, Arthur Schopenhauer, translated by David Irvine
- *The Age of Reason*, Thomas Paine (1793-4)
- *A Short History of Christianity* (second edition, revised and expanded), J M Robertson (1902)

Pamphlets
- *Obscurantism in Modern Science*, Edward Clodd
- *Peace and War in the Balance*, H W Nevinson

1914

Books
- *The Historical Christ*, F C Conybeare
- *Common Sense: An Analysis and Interpretation*, Charles E Hooper
- *The Religion of a Naturalist*, Heber A Longman
- *The Religion of Sir Oliver Lodge*, Joseph McCabe
- *The Sources of the Morality of the Gospels*, Joseph McCabe
- *The Origin of the World*, Robert McMillan
- *The Life Pilgrimage of Moncure Daniel Conway*, J M Robertson (Conway Memorial Lecture)

- *The Life of James Thomson ("BV")*, Henry S Salt
- *The Meaning of Marriage*, Gustav Spiller

Revised Editions and Reprints
- *The Origins of Christianity* (new edition), Thomas Whittaker (1904)

Pamphlets
- *Do Miracles Happen?* report of debate with various contributors
- *The Celibate's Apology*, 'A Misogynist'
- *Correspondence on "In Quest of Truth"*, Sir Arthur Conan Doyle and Hubert Stansbury
- *The Family Chain: Marriage and Relationships of Native Australian Tribes*, J Hopkins
- *Some Religious Terms Simply Defined*, E L Marsden
- *Help for the Pleasure-Ethics*, Horace Seal

1915

Books
- *Letters on Love*, anonymous
- *Chronicles of Man*, C Fillingham Coxwell
- *The War and the Churches*, Joseph McCabe
- *The Stoic Philosophy*, Gilbert Murray (Conway Memorial Lecture)
- *Religion and Moral Civilisation*, Frank Hill Perrycoste
- *Selected Prose Works of Shelley*, H S Salt (ed)
- *Myth and Legend in the Bible*, Keighley Snowden
- *The Religious Revolution of To-day*, James T Shotwell

Revised Editions and Reprints
- *Illustrations of Positivism* (enlarged edition), John Henry Bridges (1907)
- *A Christian with Two Wives* (new edition), Dennis Hird
- *The Religion of the Open Mind* (enlarged edition), Adam Gowans Whyte (1913)

Pamphlets
- *The World War: Who is to Blame?* Charles T Gorham
- *Moral Teaching as Life-Revelation*, F J Gould
- *"Rain and Rivers"* George Greenwood
- *The British Currency Decimalised and Imperialised*, W W Hardwicke
- *War and Rational Politics*, Charles W Hayward
- *The Wider Outlook Beyond the World-War*, Charles E Hooper
- *Has Germany a Conscience?* J C Thomas ['Keridon']

1916

Books
- *Gibbon and Christianity*, Edward Clodd (Conway Memorial Lecture)
- *Worth While People*, F J Gould
- *The Influence of the Church on Marriage and Divorce*, Joseph McCabe
- *The Religion of Kindness*, 'Geoffrey Mortimer' [Walter M Gallichan]
- *The Historical Jesus: A Survey of Positions*, J M Robertson
- *A Generation of Religious Progress*, (ed) Gustav Spiller
- *The World's Wonder Stories*, Adam Gowans Whyte

Pamphlets
- *Religion and the War*, Charles T Gorham
- *God and the War*, Charles T Gorham

1917

Books
- *God and Mr Wells*, William Archer
- *Old Testament Legends for Young Readers*, F J Gould
- *British Education After the War*, F J Gould
- *The Bankruptcy of Religion*, Joseph McCabe
- *Freedom Songs*, Reddie Mallett
- *The Jesus Problem: A Restatement of the Myth Theory*, J M Robertson
- *The Principle of Nationalities*, Israel Zangwill (Conway Memorial Lecture)

Pamphlets
- *Christ's Secret Doctrine*, A S Mories

1918

Books
- *The Medieval Inquisition*, Charles T Gorham
- *New Testament Legends for Young Readers*, F J Gould
- *On the Urgent Need for Reform in our National and Class Education*, Sir Harry H Johnston (Conway Memorial Lecture)
- *The Growth of Religion*, Joseph McCabe
- *The Popes and Their Church: A Candid Account*, Joseph McCabe

Revised Editions and Reprints
- *Savage Survivals*, J Howard Moore (1916)

Pamphlets
- *The Problem of the Will*, Sir George Greenwood MP
- *How much do you care for your children?* F J Gould
- *The Credentials of Faith*, W R Patterson ['Benjamin Swift']

1919

Books
- *Christianity and Conduct; or, the Influence of Religious Beliefs on Morals*, Hypatia Bradlaugh Bonner
- *A Plain Man's Plea for Rationalism*, Charles T Gorham
- *Common-Sense Thoughts on a Life Beyond*, F J Gould
- *Rationalism and Religious Reaction*, Jane E Harrison (Conway Memorial Lecture)
- *Letters to a Missionary*, Sir R F Johnston
- *The Church and the People*, Joseph McCabe
- *Georges Clemenceau: France's Grand Old Man*, Joseph McCabe
- *Poems from Beyond*, Reddie Mallett
- *The Frauds and Follies of Spiritualism*, Walter Mann

- *Spiritualism and Sir Oliver Lodge*, Charles A Mercier

Revised Editions and Reprints
- *The Faith of an Agnostic* (enlarged edition), George Greenwood (1902)
- *Savage Survivals: The Story of the Race Told in Simple Language*, J Howard Moore (1916)

Pamphlets
- *Gibraltar: or, The Foreign Policy of England*, Richard Congreve
- *Health and Honour: Sex Light for Younger Readers*, F J Gould
- *Spirit Experiences*, Charles A Mercier
- *Does Man Survive Death?* T F Palmer

1920

Books
- *The Reality or Unreality of Spiritualistic Phenomena*, C M Beadnell
- *A Biographical Dictionary of Modern Rationalists*, Joseph McCabe
- *Verbatim Report of a Public Debate on "The Truth of Spiritualism"*, Joseph McCabe and Sir Arthur Conan Doyle
- *Is Spiritualism Based on Fraud?* Joseph McCabe
- *The ABC of Evolution*, Joseph McCabe
- *A Short History of Morals*, J M Robertson
- *The Solution of the Synoptic Problem*, Robinson Smith
- *The Voice of the Nineteenth Century: A Woman's Echo*, Jane M Style
- *Mysticism and the Way Out*, Ivor L Tuckett (Conway Memorial Lecture)
- *The Natural History of Evil*, Adam Gowans Whyte

Revised Editions and Reprints
- *Theism Found Wanting* (enlarged edition), W S Godfrey (1903)
- *A Picture Book of Evolution* (second, revised edition), Dennis Hird (1906)
- *Common Sense and the Rudiments of Philosophy* (revised edition), Charles E Hooper (1914)

Pamphlets
- *Towards a World at Peace*, F J Gould
- *The Twofold Aspect of Thought*, Nicolas Petrescu

1921

Books
- *Still Found Wanting*, W S Godfrey
- *Moss from the Mill-Wheel*, Miller Grey
- *Astronomy,* Prof George Forbes
- *My Lady's Garden*, 'Hackleplume'
- *The Practical Value of Ethnology*, Prof A C Haddon (Conway Memorial Lecture)
- *Life, Mind, and Knowledge, or, the Circuit of Sentient Existence*, 'Keridon' [J C Thomas]
- *The Evolution of Civilisation*, Joseph McCabe
- *Thoughts on War and Peace*, Nicolas Petrescu
- *A New System of Scientific Procedure*, Gustav Spiller

Revised Editions and Reprints
- *The Hammurabi Code and the Sinaitic Legislation* (third, revised edition), 'Chilperic Edwards' [Edward Pilcher] (1904)
- *Sunday and the Sabbath Question* (rewritten), W W Hardwicke
- *Man: The Prodigy and Freak of Nature, or, an Animal Run to Brain*, 'Keridon' [J C Thomas]
- *The Evolution of Mind* (second edition), Joseph McCabe
- *The Great Secret* (revised edition), Robert McMillan (1911)
- *On the Influence of Religion Upon Truthfulness* (cheap edition), F H Perrycoste (1913)
- *Ritual, Faith, and Morals* (cheap edition), F H Perrycoste (1910)

Pamphlets
- *The Ether Stream: An Explanation of the Cause of Gravitation*, J S Millar
- *Your Apprenticeship and What it Means to You*, John R Mungo
- *The State: True and False: With Further Considerations Concerning Sovereignty*, Horace S Seal

1922

Books
- *A Brief History of Education*, H M Beatty
- *Christianizing the Heathen: First-hand Evidence Concerning Overseas Missions*, Hypatia Bradlaugh Bonner
- *Occultism*, Edward Clodd
- *Ice Ages: The Story of the Earth's Revolutions*, Joseph McCabe
- *Shaken Creeds: The Virgin Birth Doctrine*, 'Jocelyn Rhys' [Major W J R Wingfield]
- *Freethought and Official Propaganda*, Bertrand Russell (Conway Memorial Lecture)
- *Quatrains of Omar Khayyam*, O A Shrubsole
- *Cardiac Arrhythmia and the Neocardiology*, Alfred Webster
- *The All Electric Age*, Adam Gowans Whyte
- *The Story of the Bible*, Macleod Yearsley

Revised Editions and Reprints
- *The Influence of the Church Upon Marriage and Divorce* (cheap edition), Joseph McCabe (1916)

Pamphlets
- *The Blasphemy Laws, what they are and why they should be abolished*, anonymous
- *Was Darwin a Christian?* Charles T Gorham
- *The Failure of Christianity*, Charles T Gorham
- *What is Christian Science?* M M Mangasarian

1923

Books
- *Ancient Times*, James Henry Breasted
- *The Poet and Communication*, John Drinkwater (Conway Memorial Lecture)
- *The Life Story of a Humanist*, F J Gould
- *The Ancient Temple at Avebury and Its Gods*, Christopher Harvey
- *The Wonders of the Stars*, Joseph McCabe

- *The Twilight of the Gods*, Joseph McCabe
- *The Design Argument Reconsidered*, Joseph McCabe & C J Shebbeare
- *Explorations*, J M Robertson

Pamphlets
- *The Dean's Apologia*, William Archer
- *A New Creed for a New World*, Joseph McCabe (Douglas Price Memorial Lecture)
- *The Case for Sunday Games*, Harry Snell

1924

Books
- *The Life Work of Lord Avebury (Sir John Lubbock) 1834-1913* (ed) Mrs Ursula Grant Duff
- *France Under Richelieu and Colbert*, J H Bridges
- *The Enigma of Jesus*, Paul Louis Couchoud
- *Why We Do Right: A Rational View of Conscience*, Charles T Gorham
- *300 Stories to Tell*, F J Gould
- *The Churches, Religion and Progress*, G M Irvine
- *The Great Physician, or Miracles of the Gospel Narrative*, 'Juridicus' [Walter Russell Donogh]
- *The Disaster*, Paul Victor Marguerita
- *The Principles of Comparative Sociology*, Nicolas Petrescu
- *Thoughts in Prose and Verse*, Eden Phillpotts
- *The Supremacy of Reason*, W Nicol Reid
- *Shaken Creeds: The Resurrection Doctrines*, 'Jocelyn Rhys' [Major W J R Wingfield]
- *The Religion of Shakespeare*, George Siebel
- *William Johnson Fox (1786-1864)*, Graham Wallas (Conway Memorial Lecture)
- *The Folklore of Fairytale*, Macleod Yearsley

Revised Editions and Reprints
- *Introduction to the History of Civilisation in England*, Thomas Henry Buckle (1856)
- *The Popes and Their Church* (revised edition), Joseph McCabe (1918)
- *The Martyrdom of Man* (cheap edition), Winwood Reade (1872)

Pamphlets
- *The Religion of Humanity, in Simple Outline*, F J Gould
- *Nature's Way: A Means of Health Without Medicine*, Reddie Mallett
- *Nature's Building Power*, Reddie Mallett
- *Constipation and Cancer*, Reddie Mallett
- *The Invincible Smile: The Autobiography of a Bottom Dog*, William Margrie
- *The Adolescent Problem*, Elsie White

1925

Books
- *The Religion of Tomorrow: A Friendly Correspondence*, William Archer & H H Powers
- *The Wisdom of Life: An Anthology of Noble Thoughts*, compiled by J Frederick Green
- *Shakespeare's Handwriting and the Northumberland Manuscript*, Sir George Greenwood

- *Relativity, Meaning, and Motion*, Claude G Henderson
- *The Religion of a Darwinist*, Sir Arthur Keith (Conway Memorial Lecture)
- *The Lourdes Miracles: A Candid Report*, Joseph McCabe
- *The Marvels of Modern Physics*, Joseph McCabe
- *1825-1925: A Century of Stupendous Progress*, Joseph McCabe
- *Is Evolution True?* Joseph McCabe and George McCready Price
- *The Mighty Heart*, William Margrie
- *Egyptian Religion and Ethics*, F W Read
- *Objective Reality*, George Leitch Roberts
- *Spoken Essays*, J M Robertson
- *William Archer as Rationalist* (ed) J M Robertson (original compilation)
- *Bernard Shaw Explained: A Critical Exposition of the Shavian Religion*, George Whitehead

Revised Editions and Reprints
- *Myth, Magic, and Morals* (third impression), F C Conybeare (1909)
- *The Origin of the World* (fifth impression), Robert McMillan (1911)
- *Priests, Philosophers, and Prophets* (second, revised edition), Thomas Whittaker (1911)

Pamphlets
- *Troasm: A Belief for Plain Men*, anonymous
- *Britain and Her Commonwealth*, F J Gould
- *The Triumph of Evolution*, Joseph McCabe
- *The Gospel of Feeding*, Reddie Mallett
- *Maggots and Men: A Boy's Opinion of the Universe*, William Margrie
- *Coal and Iron*, William Margrie
- *The Fighting Rationalist*, William Margrie
- *The Religions of India*, A L Saunders

1926

Books
- *"The Secret" and Other Plays*, 'Robot'
- *Whence, Whither and Why?* 'Robert Arch' [Archibald Robertson]
- *The Temple of Truth*, Arthur Craven
- *Light on the Bible for Young and Old*, F J Gould
- *Progress and the Unfit*, Leonard Huxley (Conway Memorial Lecture)
- *Healing by Manipulation*, J Henry Jones
- *Reflections on the Structure of the Atom*, Florence M Langworthy
- *Elysia: A New Philosophy of Happiness*, Albert Luc
- *Reddie Mallett's Book of Health*, Reddie Mallett
- *The Human Hive*, A H Mackmurdo
- *The Miniature*, Eden Phillpotts

Revised Editions and Reprints
- *Memories*, Edward Clodd (1916)
- *The Clergy Under Fire* (third impression), Marshall Gauvin [pamphlet]
- *Lectures and Essays* (first, second and third series in one volume), R G Ingersoll
- *How to Get Well* (second edition), Reddie Mallett [pamphlet]
- *A Camberwell Man*, William Margrie (first published as *Glorious Camberwell*)

- *The Dynamics of Religion* (second edition), J M Robertson (1897)
- *A Short History of Freethought: Ancient and Modern* (third, revised edition), J M Robertson (1899)
- *An Autobiography*, Herbert Spencer (1904)
- *The World's Wonder Stories* (new, revised edition), Adam Gowans Whyte (1916)

Pamphlets
- *The Road from Rome*, A Working Man
- *The Religion of an Artist*, John Collier
- *The Story of Dido and Aeneas*, Henry S Salt

1927

Books
- *A Visit to Bombay*, 'Ben Diqui'
- *Paul of Tarsus: His Life and Teaching*, C Clayton Dove
- *The Messianic Idea*, 'Chilperic Edwards' [Edward Pilcher]
- *The Life of a Priest: My Own Experience, 1867-1912*, Albert Houtin
- *Poems from Beyond, and Other Verses*, Reddie Mallett
- *The Story of a Great Experiment*, William Margrie
- *A Cockney's Pilgrimage: In Search of Truth*, William Margrie
- *The Story of the Crusades: A Popular Account*, E Royston Pike
- *The Far Hope*, Robert Prenton
- *Jesus and Judas: A Textual and Historical Investigation*, J M Robertson
- *Modern Humanists Reconsidered*, J M Robertson
- *The Evolution of Christianity*, L Gordon Rylands
- *Homo Rapiens, and Other Verses*, Henry S Salt
- *Human Nature*, Prof Grafton Elliot Smith (Conway Memorial Lecture)
- *World Religion: The Church, the Creeds, and Veracity*, G F Stutchbury

Revised Editions and Reprints
- *History of the Conflict Between Religion and Science*, J W Draper (1873)
- *The Building of the Bible* (fifth edition, rewritten and enlarged), F J Gould [pamphlet] (1898)
- *The Wonder World*, Adam Gowans Whyte (1916)

Pamphlets
- *Is Jesus the Christ?* 'A clergyman of the Church of England'
- *Did the Jews Kill Jesus?* W A Campbell
- *The Historical Reality of Jesus*, Edward Greenly
- *Why I am Not a Christian*, Bertrand Russell
- *Nature's Meal Times*, H K Whitehorn

1928

Books
- *Rational Religion: A Plea for Drastic Revaluation*, 'A Modernist Clergyman'
- *Materialism: Has it Been Exploded? Verbatim Report of Debate between Chapman Cohen and C E M Joad*
- *Science and Ethics*, J B S Haldane (Conway Memorial Lecture)

- *Questions for Catholics*, F H Hayward
- *Goodwill*, Eden Phillpotts
- *Moral Experience: An Outline of Ethics for Class Teaching*, Henry Sturt
- *The Sacred Fire*, (ed) Theodore Sydmont
- *What Existence Means*, Elystan Thomas
- *Spiritualism Explained*, George Whitehead
- *Thinker or Believer?* W H Williamson

Revised Editions and Reprints
- *The Liberal State*, Thomas Whittaker, with Foreword by J M Robertson (1907)

Pamphlets
- *The Truth About Mexico*, J W Brown
- *Free Thought, Advance!* F J Gould
- *The Human Purgatory*, F J Gould
- *The Earth: Its Nature and History*, E Greenly
- *Everybody's Trouble*, Reddie Mallett
- *Our Vanishing Wildflowers*, Henry S Salt
- *The Case for Secular Education*, anonymous [Harry Snell]
- *What Christianity Has Done For Abyssinia*, R Symons

1929

Books
- *The Pioneers of Johnson's Court: A History of the Rationalist Press Association From 1899 Onwards*, F J Gould
- *The Religious Advance Towards Rationalism*, Laurence Housman (Conway Memorial Lecture)
- *Nature First and Last*, C Law
- *The Decadence: An Excerpt from "A History of the Triumph and the Decay of England". Dateable 1949*, 'L Macauley' [J M Robertson]
- *The Interpretation of National Differentiations*, Nicolas Petrescu
- *Hilaire Belloc Keeps the Bridge*, J W Poynter
- *A History of Freethought in the Nineteenth Century*, J M Robertson
- *A Critical Analysis of the Four Chief Pauline Epistles*, L Gordon Rylands
- *Posterity in the Light of Science, Philanthropy and Population*, Frank W White

Revised Editions and Reprints
- *The Belief in Personal Immortality*, E S P Haynes (1913)

Pamphlets
- *A Note-Book for Christians*, Charles T Gorham
- *A Capitalist's Utopia*, W Margrie
- *Reflections*, G F Stutchbury

1930

Books
- *The Span of Education*, Sir John Adams *
- *The Evolution of the Mass*, 'Louis Coulange' [Abbé Turmel]
- *Marcus Aurelius Antoninus: His Life and Times*, C Clayton Dove

- *This England*, F J Gould
- *The Fallacies of Fatalism, or, The Real World and the Rational Will*, Charles E Hooper
- *Science, Religion and Human Nature*, Julian Huxley (Conway Memorial Lecture)
- *Dickens and Religion*, William Kent *
- *Roses and Kippers*, William Margrie
- *The Reliquary: A Collection of Relics*, 'Jocelyn Rhys' [Major W J R Wingfield]

Pamphlets
- *Natural Singing and Speaking*, Ernest Cameron
- *Has Religion Made Useful Contributions to Civilisation?* Bertrand Russell

* uncertain whether these titles were published by Watts & Co or simply advertised by them.

1931

Books
- *Three Things That Matter: Religion; Philosophy; Science*, W G Bond
- *The Life of the Devil*, 'Louis Coulange' [Abbé Turmel]
- *A Supper with the Borgias and Other Poems*, Charles T Gorham
- *Young People's Bible Book*, F J Gould
- *Cordis Flamma*, Charles Gower
- *Race as a Political Factor*, Prof J W Gregory (Conway Memorial Lecture)
- *A Crusade for Humanity: The History of Organised Positivism in England*, John Edwin A McGee
- *The Crux of the Indian Problem*, R P Paranjpye
- *Slayers of Superstition: A Popular Account of Some of the Leading Personalities of the Deist Movement*, E Royston Pike
- *The Case for Determinism*, J Raymond Solly

Pamphlets
- *Food the Physician*, Reddie Mallett
- *The Voice of Everyman*, W Margrie

1932

Books
- *The Maniac*, anonymous
- *A Book of Revelation: A Key to Christian Origins*, Paul Louis Couchoud
- *The Revenues of Religion*, Alan Handsacre
- *London for Heretics*, William Kent
- *Nationalism and the Future of Civilisation*, Harold J Laski (Conway Memorial Lecture)
- *The Universe of Science*, H Levy
- *Adventures in Religion*, H C Mason
- *After Democracy*, H G Wells

Revised Editions and Reprints
- *A Picture Book of Evolution* (third, revised edition), C M Beadnell (1906)
- *The Mystic Rose: A Study of Primitive Marriage and of Primitive Thought in its Bearing on Marriage* (revised and enlarged), Ernest Crawley (1902)
- *History of Sacerdotal Celibacy in the Christian Church* (fourth, revised edition), Henry C Lea (1867)
- *Courses of Study* (third edition, rewritten), J M Robertson (1904)

1933

Books
- *Charles Bradlaugh: Champion of Liberty*, anonymous compilation by Bradlaugh Centenary Committee
- *Bradlaugh and Today*, anonymous compilation by Bradlaugh Centenary Committee [with Pioneer Press]
- *Suivez Raison and IT; or, A Chap's Chequered Career*, Lindsay W Brown
- *A Short History of the Inquisition*, Sir Alexander Cardew
- *Rationalism and Humanism*, John A Hobson (Conway Memorial Lecture)
- *Old Age Deferred*, Bernard Hollander
- *Social Basis of the German Reformation: Martin Luther and His Times*, Roy Pascal
- *The Diffusion of Culture*, Sir Grafton Elliot Smith

Pamphlets
- *The Case for Sunday Cinemas*, Ernest Thurtle

1934

Books
- *The Twilight of Parenthood*, Enid Charles
- *Hints for Self Culture*, Har Dayal
- *Liberty Today*, C E M Joad
- *A Martian Examines Christianity*, Arthur Levett
- *Numerical Studies in Differential Equations*, H Levy & A E Baggott
- *Aspects of Dialectical Materialism*, H Levy *
- *Science in an Irrational Society*, H Levy (Conway Memorial Lecture)
- *The Riddle of the Universe Today*, Joseph McCabe
- *Diary of a London Explorer*, William Margrie
- *Modern Knowledge and Old Beliefs*, Vivian Phelips
- *The Fateful Diamonds*, 'Jocelyn Rhys' [Major W J R Wingfield]
- *The Diary of the Visits of John Yeoman to London in the Years 1774 and 1777*,
- Macleod Yearsley (ed)

Revised Editions and Reprints
- *A Picture Book of Evolution* (popular edition), C M Beadnell (1906)
- *Crime: Its Causes and Treatment*, Clarence Darrow (1922)
- *Theism Found Wanting*, W S Godfrey (1903)
- *Christabel's Fairyland*, Adam Gowans Whyte (1926) *

---

* uncertain whether these titles were published by Watts & Co or simply advertised by them.

1935

Books
- *Primitive Law*, A S Diamond
- *Dictatorship in Theory and Practice*, G P Gooch (Conway Memorial Lecture)
- *In Defence of Evolution*, Sir Arthur Keith
- *The Splendour of Moorish Spain*, Joseph McCabe
- *Sonnets from Nature*, Eden Phillpotts
- *Damnable Opinions*, Llewelyn Powys
- *Did Jesus Ever Live?* L Gordon Rylands

Revised Editions and Reprints
- *The Pioneers of Johnson's Court* (revised and enlarged edition), F J Gould (1929)
- *The Popes and Their Church* (cheap edition), Joseph McCabe (1918)
- *Philosophers on Holiday*, 'Robert Arch', Archibald Robertson *
- *What Christianity Has Done For Abyssinia*, R Symons [pamphlet]

Pamphlets
- *A History of Darwin's Parish*, O J R & Eleanor Howarth

* uncertain if this is Watts & Co reprint or whether they picked up remaindered copies.

1936

Books
- *The Science of Social Development: A Study in Anthropology*, F A Brooke
- *Signs of the Times in Religion*, H J Bridges
- *Religious Inventions and Frauds*, 'Louis Coulange' [Abbé Turmel]
- *The Heavens and Faith*, Martin Davidson
- *Are These Things So? or, the Triumph of Darwinism*, P J Dear
- *Nature-Cure Health and Beauty*, Elizabeth Louise Donnachie
- *Perplexes and Complexes: An Approach to True Happiness*, Raymond Henniker-Heaton
- *Mrs Eddy Purloins from Hegel: Newly Discovered Source Reveals Amazing Plagiarisms in Science and Health*, Walter M Haushalter
- *A New Earth and a New Heaven*, William Doyle Hill
- *The Retreat from Reason*, Lancelot Hogben (Conway Memorial Lecture)
- *A Glance at the Great Religions of the World*, Sir Willem van Hulsteijn
- *Science and Reality: A New Interpretation of the Universe and Its Evolution*, John M Lowson
- *English Grass: Signifying the Soul and Soil of England*, William Margrie
- *Concerning Progressive Revelation*, Vivian Phelips
- *Mechanistic Biology and Animal Behaviour*, Theodore H Savory
- *Gods Divide*, A D Howell Smith
- *A View of all Existence*, Elystan Thomas

Revised Editions and Reprints
- *Why I am an Agnostic*, R G Ingersoll (1895) [pamphlet]
- *The Illusion of Immortality*, Corliss Lamont (1935)
- *Thoughts in Prose and Verse* (second edition), Eden Phillpotts (1924)
- *A History of Freethought, Ancient and Modern*, (fourth, revised and enlarged edition of *A Short History of Freethought*), J M Robertson (1899)
- *Christianity and Mythology*, J M Robertson (1900)

Pamphlets
- *Rationalism Advances*, F J Gould
- *Roman Catholicism and Toleration*, J W Poynter
- *A Liberal Education in Problems of Today*, unknown

1937

Books
- *Life in a Nutshell*, 'A Realist'
- *The Emerging Faith: Answers to Questions on Ethical Religion*, Horace Bridges
- *Poems of the Past and Present*, Charles Stratford Catty
- *The One Sure Foundation for Democracy*, Stanton Coit (Conway Memorial Lecture)
- *Free Will or Determinism*, Martin Davidson
- *The Second Epistle to the Corinthians*, 'Henri Delafosse' [Joseph Turmel]
- *The Popular Divorce Guide*, Alfred Fellows
- *Nationalism and the Communal Mind*, E Hanbury Hankin
- *The Papacy in Politics Today*, Joseph McCabe
- *Streamline Your Mind*, James L Mursell
- *A Dartmoor Village*, Eden Phillpotts
- *Rats in the Sacristy*, Llewelyn Powys
- *How to Psycho-Analyse Yourself*, Joseph Ralph
- *Julian the Apostate and the Rise of Christianity*, F A Ridley
- *The Christian Tradition*, L Gordon Rylands
- *A Public Schooling for All*, Charles T Smith

Pamphlets
- *What I Believe*, Julian Huxley
- *The Spanish Church and Politics*, John Langdon-Davies

1938

Books
- *Dictionary of Scientific Terms*, C M Beadnell
- *Ancient History of the God Jesus*, Édouard Dujardin
- *Obscurantism*, Lord Horder (Conway Memorial Lecture)
- *The Passing of Heaven and Hell*, Joseph McCabe
- *Pickwicks of Peckham*, William Margrie
- *Personal Pie*, 'Protonius' [Adam Gowans Whyte]
- *Popular Psychological Fallacies*, James Taylor
- *Griselda's Friend, and other poems*, Millicent Wedmore

Revised Editions and Reprints
- *Why I am an Agnostic*, R G Ingersoll (1895) [pamphlet]
- *The Wisdom of Life: An Anthology* (expanded edition), Somerset Maugham & Charles Watts (eds) (1925)
- *The Nature of Man* (revised edition), Élie Metchnikoff (1903)
- *A Short History of the World* (revised and updated edition), H G Wells (1922)

Pamphlets
- *The Fellowship of Reason*, Ernest Thurtle

1939

Books
- *World Union of Freethinkers International Congress 1938*, anonymous compilation (with pioneer Press)
- *The Liberation of Germany*, 'Martin Abbotson' [Joseph McCabe]
- *Ethics in Modern Art*, 'Marjorie Bowen' [Gabrielle Long] (Conway Memorial Lecture)
- *The Creation of Christ* (two volumes), Paul Louis Couchoud
- *A History of the Popes*, Joseph McCabe

Revised Editions and Reprints
- *Funeral Services without Theology* (revised by E A Carr), F J Gould (1906)
- *Why I Left the Church* (reprint), Joseph McCabe (1897) [pamphlet]
- *The Papacy in Politics Today* (revised edition), Joseph McCabe (1937)
- *My Lyrical Life: Poems Old and New*, Gerald Massey (1889)
- *Why I am Not a Christian* (reprint), Bertrand Russell (1927) [pamphlet]
- *A View of all Existence* (cheap edition), Elystan Thomas

Pamphlets
- *Life Can be Worth Living*, Julian Huxley

1940

Books
- *Bureaucracy Run Mad*, 'Martin Abbotson' [Joseph McCabe]
- *A Short History of Sex Worship*, Herbert Cutner
- *James George Frazer: Portrait of a Scholar*, R Angus Downie
- *The Illusion of National Character*, Hamilton Fyfe
- *The Human Mind: The Key to Peace and War*, Alfred Hook
- *The Golden Ages of History*, Joseph McCabe
- *Man, Mind, and Psychology*, Malcolm Mactaggart
- *Stoic, Christian and Humanist*, Gilbert Murray (with George Allen & Unwin)
- *A Mixed Grill*, Eden Phillpotts
- *The Contempt of Freedom: The Russian Experiment and After*, Prof M Polanyi
- *Keep Fit in Wartime*, Dr Harry Roberts
- *The Beginnings of Gnostic Christianity*, L Gordon Rylands
- *Britain, America and World Leadership*, Lord Snell (Conway Memorial Lecture)
- *Secrets of the Mind*, C E Wager

Revised Editions and Reprints
- *Man Makes Himself* (cheap edition), V Gordon Childe (1936)
- *Funeral Services Without Theology* (third edition), F J Gould (1906)
- *The Papacy in Politics Today* (revised and expanded edition), Joseph McCabe (1937)

Pamphlets
- *Man in the Past, Present, and Future*, J E Nicholson
- *Abortion: Right or Wrong?* Dorothy Thurtle

1941

Books
- *Life Magnificent*, Henry Atkinson
- *The Bases of a World Commonwealth*, C B Fawcett
- *The Moral Paradox of Peace and War*, J C Flugel (Conway Memorial Lecture)
- *The Flight from Reality*, Hector Hawton
- *Invasion Today*, Joseph King
- *No Friend of Democracy*, Edith Moore
- *Ideals and Illusions*, L Susan Stebbing

Revised Editions and Reprints
- *History of Sacerdotal Celibacy*, Henry C Lea (1867)
- *War and Crime*, Hermann Mannheim

Pamphlets
- *What is Wrong with International Law?* W Friedmann
- *The Case for an International University*, G W Keeton

1942

Books
- *Why I Am a Rationalist*, anonymous compilation
- *Hypatia Bradlaugh Bonner*, Arthur Bonner & Charles Bradlaugh Bonner
- *Crisis in Christendom*, 'Andor Butt'
- *The Free Will Controversy*, Martin Davidson
- *I Wander*, Emil Davies
- *Jesus Not a Myth*, A D Howell Smith
- *Miniatures*, Eden Phillpotts
- *Ethical Ideas in India Today*, Edward Thompson (Conway Memorial Lecture)
- *What the Future Demands of Religion*, R F D Wellbye

Pamphlets
- *Science in Soviet Russia*, (ed) Joseph Needham
- *Ethical Ideas in India To-day*, Edward Thompson

1943

Books
- *An Encyclopædic Dictionary of Science and War*, C M Beadnell
- *Education in World Ethics and Science*, Richard Gregory (Conway Memorial Lecture)
- *Miniatures*, Eden Phillpotts
- *Secrets of Keeping Healthy and Living Long*, George Ryley Scott
- *Russia's Economic Front for War and Peace*, A Yugow

Revised Editions and Reprints
- *Can We Comprehend God?* William Ralph Hall Caine
- *The Bases of a World Commonwealth* (second, revised edition), C B Fawcett
- *The Papacy in Politics Today* (rewritten), Joseph McCabe (1937)

- *Man, Mind, and Psychology* (second edition), Malcolm Mactaggart
- *Streamline Your Mind* (second edition), James D Mursell
- *How to Psycho-Analyse Yourself*, Joseph Ralph (1937)•
- *Ideals and Illusions* (second edition), L Susan Stebbing (1941)

1944

Books
- *Myths and Ethics: or, Humanism and the World's Need*, Gilbert Murray (Conway Memorial Lecture)
- *In the Country: Poems*, J H B Peel

Revised Editions and Reprints
- *The Wisdom of Life* (reprint), Somerset Maugham & Charles Watts (eds) (1938)
- *Dictionary of Scientific Terms*, C M Beadnell (1938)
- *The Golden Ages of History* (second impression), Joseph McCabe (1940)
- *Why I Left the Church*, Joseph McCabe (1898) [pamphlet]
- *Time To Go: Poems* (second edition), J H B Peel

Pamphlets
- *Humanism: Three BBC Talks*, Julian Huxley, Gilbert Murray, Dr J H Oldham
- *The Teacher's Case for Religious Instruction*, C T Smith

1945

Books
- *Truth and the Public*, Kingsley Martin (Conway Memorial Lecture)
- *Faiths of Many Lands*, E Royston Pike
- *Death and Rebirth*, Lord Raglan
- *Morals in World History*, Archibald Robertson

Revised Editions and Reprints
- *Science and Nutrition* (second edition), Alfred Louis Bacharach (1938)
- *Lectures and Essays*, (reprint of 1926 collected edition), R G Ingersoll
- *The Art of Thought*, (abridgement of 1926 edition), Graham Wallas
- *The World's Wonder Stories for Boys and Girls* (revised edition), Adam Gowans Whyte (1916)

Pamphlets
- *Julian Huxley on T H Huxley*, Julian Huxley
- *The New World*, Lord Snell

1946

Books
- *Rationalism in Education and Life*, anonymous compilation
- *Four Dialogues of Plato*, (ed) Ruth Borchard
- *Women: An Analytical Study*, Richard Curle
- *Racial Pride and Prejudice*, Eric John Dingwall
- *Essays on Human Evolution*, Sir Arthur Keith

- *Dragon Doodles*, Howard Kelly
- *The Testament to Christian Civilisation*, Joseph McCabe
- *The Resurgence of Asia*, S K Ratcliffe (Conway Memorial Lecture)
- *British Fairy Origins*, Lewis Spence
- *Angels and Ministers of Grace*, Adam Gowans Whyte
- *Thy Will be Done?* Adam Gowans Whyte, adapted as a play by R Bowman

Revised Editions and Reprints
- *History of Rationalism in Europe*, W E H Lecky (1865)
- *History of European Morals*, W E H Lecky (1869)
- *How Life Goes On* (revised edition, second impression), Adam Gowans Whyte

Pamphlets
- *The Church of England: A Study in Industrial Depression*, 'Christopher Churchmouse'

1947

Books
- *The Stars and the Mind*, Martin Davidson
- *The Catholic Church Against the Twentieth Century*, Avro Manhattan
- *Science and Society in Ancient China*, Joseph Needham (Conway Memorial Lecture)
- *Is the Roman Catholic Church a Secret Society?* John V Simcox
- *Music and Reason*, Charles T Smith
- *Now, in This Time*, Leon de Sousa
- *Myth and Ritual in Dance, Game and Rhyme*, Lewis Spence

Revised Editions and Reprints
- *The Wisdom of Life* (reprint), Somerset Maugham & Charles Watts (eds) (1938)
- *Cobbett's Legacy to Parsons*, William Cobbett (1835)
- *Women: An Analytical Study* (second edition), Richard Curle (1946)
- *The World's Wonder Stories*, Adam Gowans Whyte
- *Our World and Us*, Adam Gowans Whyte (second edition)

Pamphlets
- *The Faith of a Rationalist*, Bertrand Russell

1948

Books
- *Nature's Own Zoo*, C M Beadnell
- *The Conflict of Science and Society*, C D Darlington (Conway Memorial Lecture)
- *Social Pragmatism*, Ian Freed
- *A Rationalist Encyclopedia*, Joseph McCabe
- *A New Theory of Human Evolution*, Sir Arthur Keith
- *The Enchanted Wood*, Eden Phillpotts
- *Ethics of the Great Religions*, E Royston Pike

Revised Editions and Reprints
- *A Picture Book of Evolution* (fourth, revised edition) C M Beadnell (1906)
- *Nature's Way: A Means to Health Without Medicine*, Reddie Mallett (new edition, revised by George Ryley Scott) [pamphlet]
- *Our World and Us*, Adam Gowans Whyte (second revised edition)

1949

Books
- *The Church Looks at Herself*, Martin Davidson
- *Traits of Divine Kingship in Africa*, Rev. P Hadfield
- *Philosophy for Pleasure*, Hector Hawton
- *The New Authoritarianism*, Lancelot Hogben (Conway Memorial Lecture)
- *What is Man? Evolution's Answer*, Alfred Machin
- *Round the Year with the Great Religions*, E Royston Pike
- *The Popes and Social Problems*, J W Poynter
- *Church and People in Britain*, Archibald Robertson
- *The Story of the RPA: 1899-1949*, Adam Gowans Whyte

Revised Editions and Reprints
- *The Cradle of God*, Llewelyn Powys (1929)

1950

Books
- *Finding the Missing Link*, Robert Broom
- *The Four Pillars of Wisdom: A Rational Approach to a Healthy Education*, Sir Sheldon F Dudley
- *The Thinker's Handbook: A Guide to Religious Controversy*, Hector Hawton
- *An Autobiography*, Sir Arthur Keith
- *Thou Art Peter: A History of the Roman Catholic Doctrine and Practice*, A D Howell Smith

Revised Editions and Reprints
- *A Short History of Sex-Worship*, Herbert Cutner (1940)
- *On the Origin of Species* (reprint of first edition with an Introduction by C D Darlington), Charles Darwin (1859)
- *Primitive Law* (second edition), A S Diamond (1935)
- *Hereditary Genius: An Inquiry into Its Laws and Consequences*, Francis Galton (1869)
- *The Catholic Church against the Twentieth Century* (revised edition), Avro Manhattan (1947)
- *Stoic, Christian, and Humanist*, Gilbert Murray (1940)

Pamphlets
- *The Task of Rationalism*, Adam Gowans Whyte

1951

Books
- *Road to Happiness: A New Ideology*, C Wicksteed Armstrong
- *Readings from World Religions*, (eds) Selwyn Gurney Champion and Dorothy Short
- *Social Evolution*, V Gordon Childe (Josiah Mason Lecture)
- *The Story of Prehistoric Civilisations*, Dorothy Davison
- *The Evolution of Law and Order*, A S Diamond
- *Elements of Social Organisation*, Raymond Firth (Josiah Mason Lecture)

- *Round the World with Willa Webfoot*, A J Harrop
- *Scientific Thought in the Twentieth Century*, (ed) A E Heath
- *The Anatomy of Man and Other Animals*, D Stark Murray & Grace Jeffree
- *Ex-Italian Somaliland*, E Sylvia Pankhurst
- *Your Children's Feet*, Charles A Pratt
- *The Single Woman of Today*, M B Smith
- *Life Has Kept me Young*, Harold M Watkins

Revised Editions and Reprints
- *Finding the Missing Link* (revised, expanded edition), Robert Broom (1950)
- *The Papacy in Politics Today* (rewritten), Joseph McCabe (1937)

1952

Books
- *Mind: A Social Phenomenon*, F S A Doran
- *The Feast of Unreason*, Hector Hawton
- *Your Brain and You*, G N Ridley
- *Catholic Imperialism and World Freedom*, Avro Manhattan
- *How to Read History*, Archibald Robertson
- *The Life and Letters of Robert G Ingersoll*, (eds) Eva Ingersoll Wakefield & E Royston Pike

Revised Editions and Reprints
- *Problems of Life: An Evaluation of Modern Biological Thought* (first English edition), Ludwig von Bertalanffy (1949)
- *Studies in Logic and Probability*, George Boole (1854)
- *Philosophy for Pleasure* (second impression), Hector Hawton (1949)
- *Humanism as a Philosophy*, Corliss Lamont (1949)
- *Man Answers Death* (second edition), Corliss Lamont (1936)
- *The Illusion of Immortality* (second edition), Corliss Lamont (1935)

1953

Books
- *A New Approach to Psychical Research*, Antony Flew
- *An Introduction to Malthus*, D V Glass
- *The Deaf and Their Problems: A Study in Special Education*, Kenneth Hodgson
- *Some Religious Illusions in Art, Literature and Experience*, Prof Sir Ernest Kennaway
- *Terror Yugoslavia: The Threat to Europe*, Avro Manhattan
- *Leaves of Life,* H N Robbins
- *Searchlight on Morals*, T A Ryder
- *Natural Therapy: An Exposition of the Scientific and Educational Aspects of Nature Cure,* E K Lederman

1954

Books
- *Science in History*, J D Bernal
- *Social Change in South West Wales*, T Brennan, E W Cooney & H Pollins
- *The English Sunday*, R C Churchill
- *Our National Ill Health Service*, Sir Sheldon F Dudley
- *Community and Social Environment*, E A Gutkind
- *The Uprooted: From the Old World to the New*, Oscar Handlin
- *Man's Place in the Universe*, I Harris
- *Social Origins*, A M Hocart
- *Introduction to Philosophy*, John Lewis
- *A Social History of the Jews in England 1850-1950*, V D Lipman
- *William Thompson (1775-1833)*, Richard E Pankhurst
- *Jehovah's Witnesses*, E Royston Pike
- *Science and Social Action*, W J H Sprott (Josiah Mason Lecture)
- *Inside Buchmanism*, Geoffrey Williamson

Pamphlets
- *Rationalism in Theory and Practice*, Archibald Robertson

1955

Books
- *The Mystique of Modern Monarchy*, Percy Black
- *Czeck Tragedy*, Glorney Bolton
- *African Glory: The Story of Vanished Negro Civilisations*, J C de Graft-Johnson
- *Olive Schreiner*, D L Hobman
- *Darwin Revalued*, Sir Arthur Keith
- *Humanism in Practice: A Blue-print for a Better World*, M Roshwald
- *Pools and the Punter*, Hubert Phillips
- *The Story of South Place*, S K Ratcliffe
- *Morality Fair*, Geoffrey Williamson

1956

Books
- *Karl Marx: Selected Writings in Sociology and Social Philosophy* (ed) Tom Bottomore
- *Eleven Plus and All That*, Flann Campbell
- *Reflections on Woman*, Richard Curle
- *Crime and Social Action*, George Godwin
- *Reason in Action*, edited by Hector Hawton
- *Government and Politics in Tribal Societies*, I Schapera (Josiah Mason Lecture)
- *Modern English and American Poetry*, Margaret Schlauch

Revised Editions and Reprints
- *Man Makes Himself*, V Gordon Childe (1936)
- *Lectures and Essays* (reprint of 1926 collected edition), R G Ingersoll

1957

Books
- *John Stuart Mill: the Man*, Ruth Borchard
- *The Atomic Age and Our Biological Future*, H V Brønsted
- *Science for the Underdeveloped Countries* (Charles Beard Lectures for 1957) Ritchie Calder
- *African Experiment: Co-operative Agriculture and Banking in British West Africa*, J C de Graft-Johnson
- *Go Spin You Jade: Studies in the Emancipation of Women*, D L Hobman
- *Seeds of Life*, John Langdon-Davies
- *The Background of Astronomy*, Henry C King
- *The Direction of Human Development*, M F Ashley Montagu
- *Search for Purpose*, Arthur E Morgan
- *The Problem of Divorce*, R S W Pollard

1958

Books
- *A Challenge to Christianity*, J B Coates
- *Christianity and Paradox: Critical Studies in Twentieth-Century Theology*, Ronald W Hepburn
- *Social Change*, H Ian Hogbin (Josiah Mason Lecture for 1958)

1959

Books
- *T H Huxley: Scientist, Humanist and Educator*, Cyril Bibby
- *Karl Marx: Economic and Philosophical Manuscripts* (ed) Tom Bottomore

Pamphlets
- *Religion and Your Child: A Symposium on Problems of Humanist Parents*, Margaret Knight et al

1960

Books
- *The Bitches' Brew, or, the Plot Against Bertrand Russell*, 'Myra Buttle' (Victor Purcell)
- *The Reformation*, Archibald Robertson

Pemberton Publishing

1961

Books
- *Humanist Anthology: From Confucius to Bertrand Russell*, (ed) Margaret Knight (Barrie & Rockliff/Pemberton)

Revised Editions and Reprints
- *Let the People Think*, Bertrand Russell (1942)
- *The Faith of a Rationalist*, Bertrand Russell (1947)

1963

Books
- *The Humanist Revolution*, Hector Hawton (Barrie & Rockliff/Pemberton)
- *The Science of Behaviour*, John McLeish (Barrie & Rockliff/Pemberton)
- *What Humanism is About*, 'Kit Mouat' [Jean Mackay] (Barrie & Rockliff/Pemberton)
- *Pioneers of Social Change*, E Royston Pike (Barrie & Rockliff/Pemberton)

1964

Books
- *The Loom of Life*, Rona Hurst

1966

Books
- *The Child's Attitude to Death*, Marjorie Mitchell

Revised Editions and Reprints
- *The Philosophy of Humanism*, Corliss Lamont (1961)

1967

Pamphlets
- *A Humanist Glossary*, Robin Odell & Tom Barfield

1968

Books
- *The Humanist Outlook*, A J Ayer (ed) (Barrie & Rockliff/Pemberton)
- *Verdicts on Vietnam*, James Cameron
- *Marriage and Divorce*, various contributors (ed) Christopher Macy

Revised Editions and Reprints
- *Science and Life: Essays of a Rationalist*, J B S Haldane, original compilation, edited by John Maynard Smith (Pemberton/Barrie & Rockliff)
- *The Martyrdom of Man*, Winwood Reade, with Introduction by Michael Foot (1872)

Pamphlets
- *A Definition of Humanism*, Ronald Fletcher

1970

Books
- *Planners versus People*, anonymous compilation
- *Computers, Science and Society*, F H George
- *The Theory and Practice of Regional Planning*, Peter Hall (Charles Beard Lecture for 1969)
- *Let's Teach them Right* (ed) Christopher Macy

1971

Books
- *Towards an Open Society*, anonymous compilation
- *Controversy: The Humanist/Christian Encounter*, Hector Hawton
- *The Arts in a Permissive Society*, Christopher Macy (ed)
- *Population versus Liberty*, Jack Parsons
- *To Seek a Humane World*, Howard B Radest
- *The Jesus of the Early Christians*, G A Wells

Revised Editions and Reprints
- *Freedom of Choice Affirmed*, Corliss Lamont (1967)
- *Humanism and Moral Theory: A Psychological and Social Inquiry*, Reuben Osborne

Pamphlets
- *Moral Education: An Annotated List*, H J Blackham (in conjunction with National Book League and Campaign for Moral Education)

1972

Books
- *A Catholic/Humanist Dialogue: Humanists and Roman Catholics in a Common World*, Paul Kurtz & Albert Dondeyne (Pemberton/Prometheus)
- *Why a National Health Service: The Part Played by the Socialist Medical Association*, D Stark Murray
- *A Short History of Western Atheism*, James Thrower

1973

Books
- *Rationalism in the 1970s*, anonymous compilation
- *Faces of the Future: The Lessons of Science Fiction*, Brian Ash (Elek/Pemberton)
- *Crime, Rape and Gin: Reflections on Contemporary Attitudes to Violence*, Bernard Crick (Elek/Pemberton)
- *Let There Be Love*, Gunnel Enby (translated by Irene D Morris) (Elek/Pemberton)
- *The Humanist Alternative: Some Definitions of Humanism*, Paul Kurtz (Pemberton/Prometheus)
- *Rationalism and Humanism in the New Europe*, Christopher Macy (1973)
- *Ethics Without God*, Kai Nielsen (Pemberton/Prometheus)
- *The Hot house Plant*, Yvonne Stevenson (Elek/Pemberton)
- *Humanistic Perspectives in Medical Ethics*, (ed) Maurice B Visscher

1974

Books
- *Humanism in the English Novel*, Peter Faulkner (Elek/Pemberton)
- *Honest to Man*, Margaret Knight (Elek/Pemberton)
- *The Making of the TVA*, Arthur E Morgan (Pemberton/Prometheus)

1975

Books
- *The Tamarisk Tree: My Quest for Liberty and Love*, Dora Russell (Elek/Pemberton)
- *Did Jesus exist?* G A Wells (Elek/Pemberton)

1976

Books
- *The Presumption of Atheism and Other Essays*, Antony Flew (Elek/Pemberton)
- *The Trial of Annie Besant and Charles Bradlaugh*, Roger Manvell (Elek/Pemberton)

1977

Books
- *Language: Its Origin and Its Relation to Thought*, F R H Englefield, edited by G A Wells & D R Oppenheimer (Elek/Pemberton)
- *C K Ogden: A Collective Memoir*, (eds) edited by P Sargant Florence & J R L Anderson (Elek/Pemberton)
- *Population Fallacies*, Jack Parsons (Elek/Pemberton)
- *Spit Once for Luck; Fostering Julie, a Disturbed Child*, John Swain (Elek/Pemberton)

1982

Books
- *The Historical Evidence for Jesus*, G A Wells

1983

Revised Editions and Reprints
- *Why I am Not a Christian and The Faith of a Rationalist*, Bertrand Russell (with the National Secular Society)

1986

Revised Editions and Reprints
- *Did Jesus exist?* G A Wells (revised edition)

1987

Books
- *J M Robertson (1856-1933): Liberal, Rationalist, and Scholar: An Assessment by Several Hands*, G A Wells (ed)

1989

Books
- *Facing the World: An Anthology of Poetry for Humanists*, Bet Cherrington (ed)

Published directly by the RPA

1990

Books
- *Does God Exist?* Carl Lofmark
- *What is the Bible?* Carl Lofmark
- *Blasphemy: Ancient and Modern*, Nicolas Walter

1995

Revised Editions and Reprints
- *A Humanist Anthology*, Margaret Knight, revised by Jim Herrick (RPA/Prometheus) (1961)

1997

Books
- *Humanism: What's in the Word*, Nicolas Walter (in association with the British Humanist Association and Secular Society (G W Foote) Ltd)

2000

Books
- *Seasons of Life: Prose and Poetry for Secular Ceremonies and Private Reflection*, compiled by Nigel Collins, co-edited by Jim Herrick and John Pearce
- *The Thinker's Guide to Life* (ed) Marilyn Mason

2001

Books
- *Rationalism in the Twenty-First Century* (ed) Jim Herrick

SERIES PUBLISHED BY WATTS & CO

The RPA Cheap Reprints

1902
1. *Lectures and Essays*, Thomas Henry Huxley
2. *The Pioneers of Evolution*, Edward Clodd (1897)
3. *Modern Science and Modern Thought*, Samuel Laing (1885)
4. *Literature and Dogma*, Matthew Arnold (1873)
5. *The Riddle of the Universe*, Ernst Haeckel (1899)

1903
6. *Education: Intellectual, Moral and Physical*, Herbert Spencer (1861)
7. *The Evolution of the Idea of God*, Grant Allen (1897)
8. *Human Origins*, Samuel Laing (1892)
9. *The Service of Man*, John Cotter Morison (1887)
10. *Tyndall's Lectures and Essays: A Selection*, John Tyndall (original compilation from *Fragments of Science*, 1871)
11. *The Origin of Species*, Charles Darwin (1859)
12. *Emerson's Addresses and Essays*, Ralph Waldo Emerson (original compilation)
13. *On Liberty*, John Stuart Mill (1859)

1904
14. *The Story of Creation*, Edward Clodd (1888)
15. *An Agnostic's Apology*, Sir Leslie Stephen (1876)
16. *Life of Jesus*, Ernest Renan (1863)
17. *A Modern Zoroastrian*, Samuel Laing (1887)
18. *An Introduction to the Philosophy of Herbert Spencer*, W H Hudson (1894)
19. *Three Essays on Religion*, John Stuart Mill (1874)

1905
20. *The Creed of Christendom*, William Rathbone Greg (1851)
21. *The Apostles*, Ernest Renan (1866)
22. *Problems of the Future*, Samuel Laing (1889)
23. *Wonders of Life*, Ernst Haeckel (1904)
24. *Jesus of Nazareth*, Edward Clodd (1879)

1906
25. *God and the Bible*, Matthew Arnold (1875)
26. *The Evolution of Man*, Volume One, Ernst Haeckel (1874)
27. *The Evolution of Man*, Volume Two, Ernst Haeckel (1874)
28. *Hume's Essays*, David Hume (1748 & 1752)

1907
29. *Herbert Spencer's Essays*, Herbert Spencer (original compilation)
30. *An Easy Outline of Evolution*, Dennis Hird (1903)
31. *Phases of Faith*, Frances William Newman (1850)
32. *Asiatic Studies*, Sir A C Lyall (1882)

1908

33. *Man's Place in Nature*, Thomas Henry Huxley (1863)
34. *The Origins of Religion, and Other Essays*, Andrew Lang. Original compilation, taken mostly from *Custom and Myth* (1884).
35. *Twelve Lectures and Essays*, Thomas Henry Huxley

1909

36. *Haeckel: His Life and Work*, Wilhelm Bölsche (1906)
37. *The Life of Thomas Paine, Volume One*, Moncure Conway (1892)
38. *The Life of Thomas Paine, Volume Two*, Moncure Conway (1892)
39. *The Life of Thomas Paine, Volume Three*, Moncure Conway (1892)
40. *The Hand of God*, Grant Allen (first edition)

1910

41. *The Nature and Origin of Living Matter*, H Charlton Bastian (1905)
42. *Last Words on Evolution*, Ernst Haeckel (1905)
43. *Paganism and Christianity*, J A Farrer
44. *The Rise and Influence of the Spirit of Rationalism in Europe*, Volume One, W E H Lecky (1865)
45. *The Rise and Influence of the Spirit of Rationalism in Europe*, Volume Two, W E H Lecky (1865)

1911

46. *Aphorisms and Reflections*, Thomas Henry Huxley (1908?)
47. *History of European Morals*, Volume One, W E H Lecky (1869)
48. *History of European Morals*, Volume Two, W E H Lecky (1869)
49. *Selected Works of Voltaire*, by Joseph McCabe

1912

50. *The Kingdom of Man*, Sir E Ray Lankester (1907)
51. *Twelve Years in a Monastery*, Joseph McCabe (1897)

1918

52. *Lectures and Essays*, W K Clifford (1902)

The RPA Extra Series

1903

1. *Jesus Christ: His Apostles and Disciples in the Twentieth Century*, Count De Renesse
2. *Haeckel's Critics Answered*, Joseph McCabe

1904

3. *Science and Speculation*, G H Lewes (being the Prolegomena to Lewes' *The History of Philosophy*)
4. *New Light on Old Problems*, John Wilson
5. *Ethics of the Great Religions*, Charles T Gorham
6. *A New Catechism*, M M Mangasarian (1902)

1905
7. *The Religion of Woman*, Joseph McCabe (first edition)
8. *The Fundamental Principles of the Positive Philosophy*, Auguste Comte
9. *Ethical Religion*, W M Salter (1889)

1906
10. *Religious Persecution*, E S P Haynes (1904)
11. *The Oldest Laws in the World*, 'Chilperic Edwards' [Edward Pilcher]

1907
12. *The Science of Education (The Secret of Herbart)*, F H Hayward
13. *Concerning Children*, Charlotte Perkins Gilman (1900)
14. *The Bible in School*, J Allanson Picton (1901)

RPA Tracts

1906
1. *Modern Science and Supernaturalism*, T H Huxley
2. *The Religion of Charles Darwin*, Edward Clodd
3. *How Miracles May be Explained*, Samuel Laing
4. *The Miracles of the Bible*, Matthew Arnold
5. *The Faith of Our Fathers*, Ernst Haeckel
6. *Degrees of Utility in Knowledge*, Herbert Spencer
7. *The World Before Christ*, Grant Allen
8. *The Historical Element in the Old Testament*, Samuel Laing

History of Science Series

1909
History of Chemistry (Volume One: 2000BC to 1850 AD), Sir Edward Thorpe
History of Astronomy, Professor George Forbes

1910
History of New Testament Criticism, F C Conybeare
History of Old Testament Criticism, Archibald Duff
History of Anthropology, A C Haddon
History of Chemistry (Volume Two: 1850 to Date), Sir Edward Thorpe

1911
History of Biology, Professor L C Miall
History of Geology, Horace B Woodward

1912
History of Ancient Philosophy, A W Benn
History of Modern Philosophy, A W Benn

1913
History of Psychology (Two Volumes) James Mark Baldwin
History of Geography, Dr John Scott Keltie

Pamphlets for the Million

1912
1. *Why I Left the Church*, Joseph McCabe
2. *Why I am an Agnostic*, R G Ingersoll
3. *Christianity's Debt to Earlier Religions*, 'Philip Vivian' [Vivian Phelips]
4. *How to Reform Mankind*, R G Ingersoll
5. *Myth or History in the Old Testament?* Samuel Laing
6. *Liberty of Man, Woman, and Child*, R G Ingersoll
7. *Age of Reason*, Thomas Paine (1793-4)
8. *Last Words on Evolution*, Ernst Haeckel
9. *Science and the Purpose of Life*, Fridtjof Nansen
10. *The Ghosts*, R G Ingersoll
11. *The Passing of Historical Christianity*, Rev R Roberts

The Inquirer's Library (edited by Joseph McCabe & Percy Vaughan)

1913
The Existence of God, Joseph McCabe
The Belief in Personal Immortality, E S P Haynes
The Old Testament, 'Chilperic Edwards' [Edward Pilcher]

1914
Christianity and Civilisation, Charles T Gorham
The New Testament, F J Gould

Life-Stories of Famous Men

1920
Thomas Henry Huxley, Leonard Huxley
Auguste Comte, F J Gould
Robert Owen, Joseph McCabe
Charles Bradlaugh, J M Robertson

1921
Charles Darwin, Leonard Huxley
Robert G Ingersoll, Charles T Gorham

1922
Voltaire, J M Robertson
George Jacob Holyoake, Joseph McCabe

1924
Ernest Renan, J M Robertson

The People's Platform

<u>1920</u>
1. *Belief, Make Belief, and Unbelief*, Hypatia Bradlaugh Bonner
2. *Does Democracy Need Religion?* Joseph McCabe
3. *The Great Ghost Illusion*, Adam Gowans Whyte
4. *The Truth About Christianity and the Bible*, Charles T Gorham

The Forum Series

<u>1926</u>
1. *The Stream of Life*, Julian Huxley
2. *The Religion of an Artist*, John Collier
3. *Mr Belloc Objects to "The Outline of History"*, H G Wells
4. *The Goodness of Gods*, Edward Westermarck

<u>1927</u>
5. *Concerning Man's Origin*, Sir Arthur Keith
6. *The Earth: Its Nature and History*, Edward Greenly

<u>1928</u>
7. *Craftsmanship and Science*, Sir William Bragg
8. *Darwinism and What it Implies*, Sir Arthur Keith
9. *What is Eugenics?* Leonard Darwin
10. *The Meaning of Life as Shown in the Process of Evolution*, C E M Joad

<u>1930</u>
11. *From Meteorite to Man: The Evolution of the Earth*, Prof J W Gregory, Sir Arthur Smith Woodward, Prof W W Watts, Prof A C Seward
12. *Religion as a Bar to Progress*, Charles T Gorham

<u>1931</u>
13. *God and Mammon: The Relations of Religion and Economics*, J A Hobson
14. *Triumphs in Bird-Life*, Prof C J Patten
15. *Seeing Ourselves in the Light of Modern Psychology*, Bernard Hollander
16. *The Search for Man's Ancestors*, Prof G Elliot Smith

<u>1932</u>
17. *Man's Microbic Enemies*, D Stark Murray

<u>1934</u>
18. *The Construction of Man's Family Tree*, Sir Arthur Keith
19. *Human Sterilisation Today*, Cora B Hodson

<u>1935</u>
20. *Darwinism and Its Critics*, Sir Arthur Keith

<u>1937</u>
21. *The History of Evolution*, Sir Edward B Poulton

The World of Youth Series

1930
1. *Great Sons of Greece*, F J Gould
2. *Temple Bells*, E Royston Pike
3. *The Origin of the World*, R McMillan
4. *HMS Beagle in South America*, Amabel Williams-Ellis
5. *Our World And Us*, Adam Gowans Whyte

1931
6. *Boys and Girls and Gods*, Naomi Mitchison
7. *From Pyramid to Skyscraper: A Little Book on Architecture*, H Bellis

1932
8. *Great Sons of Rome*, F J Gould
9. *Bright Lamps of History and Daily Life*, Volume One, F J Gould
10. *The Wonder World: A Simple Introduction to Biology*, Adam Gowans Whyte
11. *African Stories*, Alice Werner
12. *How Life Goes On*, Adam Gowans Whyte

1933
13. *In Search of Wild Flowers*, J F Rayner
14. *A Pre-History Reader*, T F G Dexter
15. *Bright Lamps of History and Daily Life*, Volume Two, F J Gould

The New Knowledge Series *

1930
Civilisation in Britain, 2000 BC, T F G Dexter
The Pagan Origin of Fairs, T F G Dexter
The Sacred Stone, T F G Dexter

1931
Fire Worship in Great Britain, T F G Dexter

* later in 1931 this series was repackaged as 'The Pre-History of Britain'

The Library of Science and Culture (edited by H Levy)

1934
1. *Scientific Research and Social Needs*, Julian Huxley
2. *The Web of Thought and Action*, H Levy

1935
3. *Problems of Destiny*, William Romaine Paterson
4. *Psychology and Religion*, David Forsyth

<u>1936</u>
5. *Man Makes Himself*, V Gordon Childe

<u>1938</u>
6. *Scientists are Human*, David Lindsay Watson
7. *Galileo and Freedom of Thought*, F Sherwood Taylor

Changing World Library (edited by H Levy)

<u>1936</u>
The Nation's Intelligence, Prof J L Gray
Weather Science for Everybody, Prof David Brunt
Press Parade, Hamilton Fyfe
Science Fights Death, D Stark Murray

<u>1937</u>
The Tongues of Men, J R Firth
Man Marches On: The New Patriotism, A E Mander
Noise, A H Davies
Psychology: the Changing Outlook, Francis Aveling
Radio Is Changing Us, D Cleghorn Thomson
Air War: Its Technical and Social Aspects, W O'D Pierce

<u>1938</u>
Science and Nutrition, A L Bacharach
Mental Deficiency, J Duncan

The Thinker's Library

<u>1929</u>
1. *First and Last Things*, H G Wells (1909)
2. *Education: Intellectual, Moral, and Physical*, Herbert Spencer (1861, Cheap Reprint No.6, 1903)
3. *The Riddle of the Universe*, Ernst Haeckel (1899, Cheap Reprint No. 5, 1902)
4. *Humanity's Gain from Unbelief*, Charles Bradlaugh (original compilation)
5. *On Liberty*, John Stuart Mill (1859, Cheap Reprint No. 13, 1903)
6. *A Short History of the World*, H G Wells (1922)
7. *Autobiography of Charles Darwin*, Charles Darwin (original compilation)
8. *The Origin of Species*, Charles Darwin (1859, Cheap Reprint No. 11, 1903)
9. *Twelve Years in a Monastery*, Joseph McCabe (1897, Cheap Reprint No. 51, 1912)

<u>1930</u>
10. *A History of Modern Philosophy*, A W Benn (1912)
11. *Gibbon on Christianity*, (original compilation)
12. *The Descent of Man*, Charles Darwin (1871)
13. *Civilization in England*, Thomas Henry Buckle (1856)
14. *Anthropology*, Volume One, E B Tylor (1881)

15. *Anthropology*, Volume Two, E B Tylor (1881)
16. *Iphigenia: Two Plays by Euripides*, translated by C B Bonner

1931
17. *Lectures and Essays*, Thomas Henry Huxley (??? Cheap Reprint No. 1, 1902)
18. *The Evolution of the Idea of God*, Grant Allen (1897, Cheap Reprint No. 7, 1903)
19. *An Agnostic's Apology*, Sir Leslie Stephen (1876, Cheap Reprint No. 15, 1904)
20. *The Churches and Modern Thought*, Vivian Phelips (1906)
21. *Penguin Island*, Anatole France (1908)
22. *The Pathetic Fallacy*, Llewelyn Powys (1930)
23. *Historical Trials (A Selection)*, Sir John MacDonell (1927)
24. *A Short History of Christianity*, J M Robertson (1902)

1932
25. *The Martyrdom of Man*, Winwood Reade (1872)
26. *Head-Hunters: Black, White, and Brown*, A C Haddon (1901)
27. *The Evidence for the Supernatural*, Ivor L L Tuckett (1911)
28. *The City of Dreadful Night*, James Thomson 'BV' (1874)
29. *In the Beginning: The Origin of Civilization*, G Elliot Smith
30. *Adonis: A Study in the History of Oriental Religion*, Sir J G Frazer (original compilation)

1933
31. *Our New Religion*, H A L Fisher (1929)
32. *On Compromise*, John Morley (1874)
33. *A History of the Taxes on Knowledge*, Collet Dobson Collet (1899)
34. *The Existence of God*, Joseph McCabe (rewritten from 1913 first edition)
35. *The Story of the Bible*, MacLeod Yearsley (1922)
36. *Savage Survivals: The Story of the Race Told in Simple Language*, J Howard Moore (1916)
37. *The Revolt of the Angels*, Anatole France
38. *The Outcast*, Winwood Reade (1875)

1934
39. *Penalties Upon Opinion*, Hypatia Bradlaugh Bonner (1912)
40. *Oath, Curse, and Blessing*, Ernest Crawley (original compilation)
41. *Fireside Science*, Sir E Ray Lankester (original compilation)
42. *History of Anthropology*, A C Haddon (revised edition of first edition written for the History of Science Series in 1910)
43. *The World's Earliest Laws*, 'Chilperic Edwards' [Edward Pilcher] (1904)
44. *Fact and Faith*, J B S Haldane (original compilation)
45. *Men of the Dawn*, Dorothy Davison (1927?)
46. *The Mind in the Making*, James Harvey Johnson (1921)
47. *The Expression of the Emotions in Man and Animals*, Charles Darwin (1872)

1935
48. *Psychology for Everyman (and Woman)*, A E Mander (first edition)
49. *The Religion of the Open Mind*, Adam Gowans Whyte (1913)
50. *Letters on Reasoning*, J M Robertson (1902)

51. *The Social Record of Christianity*, Joseph McCabe (first edition)
52. *The Five Stage of Greek Religion*, Gilbert Murray (1912)
53. *The Life of Jesus*, Ernest Renan (1863, Cheap Reprint No. 16, 1904)
54. *Selected Works of Voltaire*, Joseph McCabe (1911)
55. *What are we to do with our lives?* H G Wells (1931)

1936
56. *Do what you will*, Aldous Huxley (1929)
57. *Clearer Thinking (Logic for Everyman)*, A E Mander (first edition)
58. *History of Ancient Philosophy*, A W Benn (1912)
59. *Your Body: How it is built and how it works*, D Stark Murray (first edition)
60. *What is Man?* Mark Twain (1905)

1937
61. *Man and His Universe*, John Langdon-Davies (1930)
62. *First Principles*, Herbert Spencer (1862)
63. *Rights of Man*, Thomas Paine (1791)
64. *This Human Nature*, Charles Duff (1930)

1938
65. *Dictionary of Scientific Terms*, C M Beadnell (first edition)
66. *A Book of Good Faith*, Montaigne (original compilation)
67. *The Universe of Science*, H Levy (1932)
68. *Liberty To-day*, C E M Joad (1934)
69. *The Age of Reason*, Thomas Paine (1793-4)
70. *The Fair Haven*, Samuel Butler (1873)
71. *A Candidate for Truth*, Ralph Waldo Emerson (original compilation)
72. *A Short History of Women*, John Langdon-Davies (1928)

1939
73. *Natural Causes and Supernatural Seemings*, Henry Maudsley (1886)
74. *Morals, Manners, and Men*, Havelock Ellis (original compilation)
75. *Pages from a Lawyer's Notebooks*, E S P Haynes (original compilation)
76. *An Architect of Nature*, Luther Burbank (original compilation)

1940
77. *Act of God*, F Tennyson Jesse (1937)
78. *The Man versus the State*, Herbert Spencer (1884)
79. *The World as I See It*, Albert Einstein (1935)
80. *Jocasta's Crime: An Anthropological Study*, Lord Raglan (1933)
81. *The Twilight of the Gods and Other Tales*, Richard Garnett (1888)

1941
82. *Kingship*, A M Hocart (1927)
83. *Religion Without Revelation*, Julian Huxley (1927)
84. *Let the People Think*, Bertrand Russell (original compilation)
85. *The Myth of the Mind*, Frank Kenyon (first edition)
86. *The Liberty of Man and Other Essays*, R G Ingersoll (original compilation)
87. *Man Makes Himself*, V Gordon Childe (1936)

1942

88. *World Revolution and the Future of the West*, W Friedmann (1941)
89. *The Origin of the Kiss and Other Scientific Diversions*, C M Beadnell (original compilation)
90. *The Bible and Its Background, Volume One*, Archibald Robertson (first edition)
91. *The Bible and Its Background, Volume Two*, Archibald Robertson (first edition)
92. *The Conquest of Time*, H G Wells (first edition)
93. *The Gospel of Rationalism*, Charles T Gorham (original compilation)

1943

94. *Life's Unfolding*, Sir Charles Sherrington (1938)
95. *An Easy Outline of Astronomy*, M Davidson (first edition)
96. *The God of the Bible*, Evans Bell (first edition)
98. *In Search of the Real Bible*, A D Howell Smith (first edition)

1944

97. *Man Studies Life*, G N Ridley (first edition)
99. *The Outlines of Mythology*, Lewis Spence (first edition)
100. *Magic and Religion*, Sir J G Frazer (original compilation)
101. *Flight from Conflict*, Laurence Collier (first edition)
102. *Progress and Archaeology*, V Gordon Childe (first edition)
103. *The Chemistry of Life*, J S D Bacon (first edition)
104. *Medicine and Mankind*, Arnold Sorsby (1941)

1945

105. *The Church and Social Progress*, 'Marjorie Bowen' [Gabrielle Long] (first edition)
106. *The Great Mystics*, George Godwin (first edition)
107. *The Religion of Ancient Mexico*, Lewis Spence (1923)
108. *Geology in the Life of Man*, Duncan Leitch (first edition)

1946

109. *A Century of Freedom*, Kenneth Urwin (first edition)
110. *Jesus: Myth or History?* Archibald Robertson (first edition)
112. *Human Nature, War, and Society*, John Cohen (first edition)
114. *Man: The Verdict of Science*, G N Ridley (first edition)
115. *The Distressed Mind*, J A C Brown (first edition)
116. *The Illusion of National Character*, Hamilton Fyfe (1940)

1947

111. *The Ethics of Belief and Other Essays*, W K Clifford (1877)
113. *The Rational Good: A Study in the Logic of Practice*, L T Hobhouse (1921)
117. *Population, Psychology, and Peace*, J C Flugel (first edition)
120. *An Outline of the Development of Science*, M Mansel Davies
121. *Head and Hand in Ancient Greece*, Benjamin Farrington (original compilation)
122. *The Evolution of Society*, J A C Brown (first edition)
123. *Background to Modern Thought*, C D Hardie (first edition)

1948

118. *Friar's Lantern*, G G Coulton (1906)
119. *Ideals and Illusions*, L Susan Stebbing (1941)

124. *The Holy Heretics: The Story of the Albigensian Crusade*, Edmond Holmes
125. *Man His Own Master*, Archibald Robertson (first edition)
126. *Men Without Gods*, Hector Hawton (first edition)
127. *The Earliest Englishman*, Sir Arthur Smith-Woodward (first edition)
128. *Astronomy for Beginners*, Martin Davidson (first edition)
129. *The Search for Health*, D Stark Murray (first edition)
130. *The Mystery of Anna Berger*, George Godwin (1935)
131. *Wrestling Jacob*, 'Marjorie Bowen' [Gabrielle Long] (1937)

1949
132. *The Origins of Religion*, Lord Raglan (first edition)
133. *The Hero*, Lord Raglan (1936)
134. *The Life of John Knox*, 'Marjorie Bowen' [Gabrielle Long] (1940)
135. *The French Revolution*, Archibald Robertson (first edition)
136. *The Art of Thought*, Graham Wallas (1926)

1950
137. *Literary Style and Music*, Herbert Spencer (original compilation)
138. *The Origin of Species*, Charles Darwin (printed but never published)

1951
139. *The Science of Heredity*, J S D Bacon
140. *The Great Revivalists*, George Godwin (1950)

Thinker's Forum

1940
1. *The God of War*, Joseph McCabe
2. *The Danger of Being an Atheist*, Adam Gowans Whyte
3. *Turkey: The Modern Miracle*, E W F Tomlin
4. *Science: Curse or Blessing?* H Levy
5. *Make Your Own Religion*, Adam Gowans Whyte
6. *A Young Man's Morals*, Henry Ll Cribb
7. *Why Be Moral?* Hector Hawton
8. *The Giddy God of Luck*, Protonius

1941
9. *The Art of Astrology*, Gemini
10. *Priest or Physician?* George Godwin
11. *After War – Peace?* C Deslisle Burns
12. *The Crisis in the Church*, "Clericus"
13. *Do we want life after death?* Lord Ponsonby
14. *The Nazi Attack on International Science*, Joseph Needham
15. *The Body as a Guide to Politics*, Dr W B Cannon
16. *Russia and the Roman Church*, Joseph McCabe
17. *The Vatican and the Nazis*, Joseph McCabe
18. *The Pope and the Italian Jackal*, Joseph McCabe
19. *Science and Human Prospects*, Prof Eliot Blackwelder
20. *Wars of Ideas*, Muriel Jaeger

1942

21. *BBC Religion*, "Clericus"
22. *The Riddle of Religious Education and a New Solution*, Adam Gowans Whyte
23. *Japan's New Order*, George Godwin
24. *Will Religion Survive?* Hector Hawton

1943

25. *The New Orthodoxy*, F H Amphlett Micklewright
26. *The Papacy in France*, Joseph McCabe
27. *The Church and Education*, J M Robertson and Adam Gowans Whyte
28. *The Churches and the New World*, Archibald Robertson
29. *Religion and the Indian Problem*, Sir R P Paranjpye

1944

30. *Religion and the Rights of Man*, Joseph McCabe
31. *Chinese Ideals of Life*, Lin Yutang
32. *English Literature and the Agnostic*, R C Churchill
33. *Rationalism and Culture*, F H Amphlett Micklewright

1945

34. *Roman Catholic Schools and Democratic Rights*, F H Amphlett Micklewright
35. *Art and Christianity*, R C Churchill
36. *Anglican Shipwreck*, Archibald Robertson
37. *Rationalism*, J M Robertson

1946

38. *Religion as an Objective Problem*, Julian Huxley
39. *Make Your Own Religion*, Adam Gowans Whyte
40. *Spain and the Vatican*, Avro Manhattan
41. *The Vatican and the USA*, Avro Manhattan
42. *Latin America and the Vatican*, Avro Manhattan

1948 *

43. *The Vatican in Asia*, Avro Manhattan
44. *Religion in Russia*, Avro Manhattan

1949

45. *Man, Science, and Deity*, D H H Martin

* uncertain if this is correct.

Thrift Books (edited by E Royston Pike)

1951

1. *Evolution in Outline*, Prof. T Neville George
2. *Theatregoing*, Harold Downs
3. *What's all this about genetics?* Rona Hurst
4. *The Ladder of Life: From Molecule to Mind*, Adam Gowans Whyte
5. *Getting to Know English Literature*, T G Williams

6. *Finding Out About Atomic Energy*, D J L Michiels
7. *A Short History of Our Times (1919-1950)*, Esmond Wright
8. *A Signpost to Mathematics*, A H Read
9. *Secrets of an Author*, Peter Fontaine
10. *The Glands Inside Us*, John Ebling
11. *You Shall Have Music*, Sidney Harrison
12. *Browsing Among Words of Science*, T H Savory

1952
13. *Your Family and the Law*, R S W Pollard
14. *From Magic to Modern Medicine*, S G Blaxland Stubbs
15. *The Polished Ploughshare*, Syd Fox
16. *This Matter of Mind*, Dr Brian H Kirman
17. *Focus on Films*, J P Le Harivel
18. *Must Man Wage War?* F A E Crew
19. *What Goes on Beneath Big Ben?* C D Bateman
20. *Botany from the Beginning*, H L K Whitehouse *

1953
21. *Ballet in Britain Since the War*, Clive Barnes
22. *Your Child at School*, G F Lamb

* uncertain if published in 1952 or 1953.

Appendix 2

Honorary Associates of the Rationalist Press Association

Sir Leslie Stephen	1899-1904	thinker/author
Edward Clodd	1899-1930	banker/author
Emile Zola	1899-1902 (France)	novelist
Prof Ernst Haeckel	1899-1915 (Germany) resigned	zoologist
Prof Edward Westermarck	1899-1939 (Finland)	anthropologist
Dr Paul Carus	1899-1915 (United States) resigned	philosopher
John Stuart McKenzie	1899-1900 resigned	philosopher
Dr W C Coupland	1899-1904	physician
Dr Stanton Coit	1899-1944	ethicist
John Mackinnon Robertson	1899-1933	thinker/author
Dr W R Washington Sullivan	1899-1916	ethical lecturer
Frederick James Gould	1899-1938	ethicist
James George Roche Forlong	1899-1904	engineer
Leonard Huxley	1902-1933	author
Prof Pierre Marcellin Berthelot	1904-1907 (France)	chemist
Dr Frederick James Furnivall	1904-1910	lawyer/reformer
Prof Willem Christian van Manen	1904-1905 (Netherlands)	biblical scholar
Eden Phillpotts	1904-1960	author
Thomas Whittaker	1904-1935	philosopher
Prof Lester F Ward	1905-1913 (United States)	sociologist
Alfred William Benn	1906-1915	philosopher
Björnstjerne Björnson	1906-1910 (Norway)	novelist/dramatist
Georg Brandes	1906-1926 (Denmark)	author/critic
Prof Basil Hall Chamberlain	1906-1917	philologist
Prof Cesare Lombroso	1906-1909 (Italy)	psychologist
Dr Charles Callaway	1908-1915	geologist
Joseph McCabe	1908-1955	thinker/author
Sir Edward Brabrook	1909-1930	anthropologist
William Whitehouse Collins	1911-1923 (New Zealand)	politician
Hypatia Bradlaugh Bonner	1912-1935	author
Prof John Bagnell Bury	1913-1927	historian
Sir E Ray Lankester	1914-1929	zoologist
Prof Andrew D White	1915-1918 (United States)	historian
William Archer	1916-1924	journalist/critic

Arnold Bennett	1916-1931	novelist
George Macaulay Trevelyan, OM	1916-1925	historian
Sydney A Gimson	1918-1938	engineer
E Sidney Hartland	1918-1927	anthropologist
Prof Jacques Loeb	1918-1924 (United States)	physiologist
Viscount Morley	1919-1923	politician
Prof Sir Arthur Keith	1923-1955	anatomist
Sir Herbert Leon	1923-1926	businessman
Francis Sydney Marvin	1924-1946	author/teacher
Sir George Greenwood	1924-1928	politician/author
Prof C J Patten	1924-1948	physician
Hon John Collier	1925-1934	artist
Ferdinand Buisson	1925-1932 (France)	educationist
Ernest Newman	1925-1959	music critic
Prof Grafton Elliot Smith	1925-1936 (Australia)	anthropologist
Sir Robert Stout	1926-1930 (New Zealand)	politician
Joseph Thomas Ward	1926-1927 (New Zealand)	astronomer
Sir H Bryan Donkin	1927-1927	physician
Dr C Delisle Burns	1927-1942	polymath
Dr Alfred Cort Haddon	1927-1940	anthropologist
Earl Russell	1927-1931	author/lawyer
Bertrand Russell	1927-1970	philosopher
H S Tuke	1927-1929	artist
Prof Carveth Read	1927-1931	philosopher
John A Hobson	1927-1940	economist
Prof Sir Patrick Geddes	1927-1932	biologist/sociologist
Prof John Burdon Sanderson Haldane	1927-1964	biologist
Sir P Chalmers Mitchell	1927-1945	zoologist
Prof Carleton Stanley	1927-1931	
Dr Theodore Reinach	1927-1928 (France)	archaeologist
Dr Julian Huxley	1927-1975	biologist/author
Dr Jane Harrison	1927-1928	classicist
Winifred Stephens Whale	1928-1944	linguist
Georges Clemenceau	1929-1929 (France)	politician
Heber A Longman	1929-1954 (Australia)	palæontologist
Prof Harold Laski	1929-1950	political scientist
Dr Bernard Hollander	1929-1934	psychologist
Herbert George Wells	1929-1946	polymath
Dr James Henry Breasted	1930-1935 (United States)	archaeologist/historian
Dr Paul Luis Couchoud	1930-1959 (France)	Biblical scholar
Prof F A E Crew	1930-1973	geneticist
Prof John Dewey	1930-1952 (United States)	philosopher
Prof J W Gregory	1930-1932	geologist/explorer
Prof Bronislaw Malinowski	1930-1942 (Poland)	anthropologist
Prof Thomas Okey	1930-1935	Italian scholar
Henry Stephens Salt	1930-1939	reformer/author
Dr Griffith Evans	1930-1935	physician
Prof Graham Wallas	1930-1932	political scientist
Edward Tuck	1931-1938	activist

Sir Raghunath P Paranjpye	1931-1966 (India)	politician/thinker
W S Godfrey	1931-1936	author
Prof M C Bouglé	1931-1940 (France)	educationist/politician
Sir John Sumner	1932-1934	businessman/philanthropist
Sir J A Hammerton	1932-1949	author/editor
Prof Frank C Sharp	1933-1943	philosopher
George E Macdonald	1933-1944 (United States)	author/editor
Clarence Darrow	1934-1938 (United States)	lawyer
Albert Einstein	1934-1955 (United States)	physicist
Hyman Levy	1935-1975	mathematician
Prof Ivan Petrovich Pavlov	1935-1936 (Russia)	psychologist
Prof C Guignebert	1935-1939 (France)	Biblical scholar
Dr M Terwagne	1935-1945 (Belgium)	physician
W Somerset Maugham	1935-1965	novelist
Jan Hoving	1935-1939 (Netherlands)	activist
Sir Willem van Hulsteijn	1936-1939 (South Africa)	lawyer/politician
E V Voska	1936-1960s * (Czechoslovakia)	activist
Dr L Milde	1936-1960s * (Czechoslovakia)	activist
Prof G A F Molengraaf	1936-1950 * (Netherlands)	
Lord Horder	1936-1955	diagnostician
Hon Ursula Grant Duff	1936-1958	author
Sir Buckston Browne	1936-1945	physician
Sir Henry J Wood	1937-1944	conductor
Prof Sigmund Freud	1938-1939 (Austria)	psychoanalyst
Sir Richard Gregory	1938-1952	science writer/editor
Edouard Herriot	1938-1957 (France)	politician
Dr William King Gregory	1939-1970 (United States)	palæontologist
Prof Sir Thomas A Hunter	1939-1953 (New Zealand)	psychologist/administrator
Gabrielle Long 'Marjorie Bowen'	1940-1952 resigned	novelist
Prof V Gordon Childe	1941-1957 (Australia)	anthropologist
Prof James Vincent Duhig	1941-1963 (Australia)	physician
Prof P Sargant Florence	1941-1982	economist
Prof J C Flugel	1941-1955	psychologist
Judge Alfred William Foster	1941-1962 (Australia)	barrister
Dr Joseph Needham	1941-1995	biochemist/historian
Prof William Alexander Osborne	1941-1967 (Australia)	physiologist
Sir Charles Sherrington, OM	1941-1952	neurophysiologist
Prof L Susan Stebbing	1941-1943	philosopher
Prof F M Cornford	1942-1943	philosopher
Henry J Hayward	1942-1945 (New Zealand)	businessman
Frederick Archibald de la Mare	1942-1960 (New Zealand)	lawyer
Prof A Wolf	1942-1948	philosopher
Dr Geoffrey Bourne	1943-1988	physician
H N Brailsford	1943-1958	journalist
Osborne Henry Mavor 'James Bridie'	1943-1944 resigned	dramatist

Dr Cyril Dean Darlington	1943-1981	geneticist
Dr Raymond Firth	1943-2002	anthropologist
Prof C D Forde	1943-1973	anthropologist
Shih Hsiung	1943-1996 * (China)	author/translator
Dr Ernest Jones	1943-1958	psychoanalyst
Prof Kirsopp Lake	1943-1946	Biblical scholar
Kingsley Martin	1943-1969	journalist/author
Dr C S Myers	1943-1946	physician
Prof A E Heath	1944-1961	philosopher
Ivor Brown	1945-1974	journalist/critic
Sir John Boyd Orr	1945-1971	biologist
Prof John Brande Trend	1945-1958	Spanish scholar
Dr G Brock Chisholm	1946-1971 (Canada)	psychologist/ statesman
Prof Alfred Jules Ayer	1947-1989	philosopher
Prof John Desmond Bernal	1947-1971	physicist/writer
Richard Crossman	1947-1974	politician
Dr Meyer Fortes	1947-1982 (South Africa)	social anthropologist
Mlle P H Pardon	1947-1970s * (Belgium)	activist
Hamilton Fyfe	1948-1951	journalist/author
J W Robertson Scott	1948-1962	journalist/author
A L Bacharach	1949-1966	food technologist
Prof Edward Joseph Dent	1949-1957	music scholar
Prof Sir Ernest Laurence Kennaway	1949-1958	pathologist
Prof L J Russell	1949-1971	philosopher
Sir Fred Hoyle	1950-2001	cosmologist
Arnulf Overland	1950-1968 (Norway)	poet
Prof Barbara Wootton	1950-1988	sociologist/ politician
Sir Frank Macfarlane Burnet, OM	1951-1985 (Australia)	geneticist
Lord Chorley (R S T Chorley)	1951-1978	politician
Prof Prosper Alfaric	1952-1955 (France)	theologian
Senator Albert Buisseret	1952-1970s * (Belgium)	politician
Prof George Douglas Howard Cole	1952-1958	political scientist
Sir Sheldon Dudley	1952-1956	psychologist
Lord Haden Guest	1952-1960	physician
Prof A R Radcliffe-Brown	1952-1955	anthropologist
Professor John Zachary Young	1952-1997	neurologist
Ture Nerman	1953-1971 (Sweden)	
Marcel Boll	1954-1970s * (France)	philosopher
Prof A Heintz	1954-1975 (Norway)	
Prof Frédéric Joliot-Curie	1954-1958 (France)	physicist
Lord Raglan	1955-1964	anthropologist
Margaret Knight	1956-1983	psychologist
Dr Ernest Nagel	1956-1985 (United States)	philosopher
Alexander Sutherland Neill	1956-1973	educationist
Dr Jacob Bronowski	1958-1974	scientist/educator
Dr Hermann Joseph Müller	1958-1967 (United States)	geneticist
Prof Conrad Hal Waddington	1958-1975	geneticist

321

Edward Morgan Forster	1959-1970	novelist
Prof Sir Alexander Haddow	1959-1976	bacteriologist
A D Howell Smith	1959-1966	historian
Prof Francis Crick	1962-	biologist
Prof Morris Ginsberg	1962-1970	sociologist
Prof Leopold Infeld	1962-1968 (Poland)	physicist
Prof Margaret Schlauch	1962-1986 (Poland)	literature scholar
Lord Ritchie-Calder	1965-1982	science writer
Theodore Besterman	1966-1976	scholar
Cyrus S Eaton	1966-1979 (Canada)	businessman
Miles Malleson	1966-1969	playwright
Lord Willis (Edward Henry Willis)	1966-1992	playwright
Prof Sir Hermann Bondi	1967-	cosmologist
Prof G H Parikh	1967-1977 (India)	economist
Dr Subrahmanyan Chandrasekhar	1968-1995 (India)	physicist
Sir Gerald Barry	1968-1968	journalist
Leonard Woolf	1969-1969	author
Rupert Crawshay-Williams	1970-1977	philosopher
David Garnett	1972-1981	novelist
Prof Jacques Monod	1972-1976 (France)	biologist
Dr Conor Cruise O'Brien	1972-	historian/author
Prof A B Shah	1972-1981 (India)	Islam scholar
Burrhus Frederic Skinner	1972-1990 (United States)	psychologist
Dora Russell	1974-1986	author/activist
Prof Bernard Crick	1976-	political scientist
Dr E J Dingwall	1976-1986	polymath
Prof Antony Flew	1976-	philosopher
John Scott Lennox Gilmour	1976-1986	botanist
Prof Karl Popper	1976-1994	philosopher
Dr Vithal Mahadev Tarkunde	1976- (India)	lawyer and judge
Harold Blackham	1977-	polymath
Prof Sir William Empson	1979-1984	poet/critic
Ernest Gellner	1979-1995	philosopher
Prof Paul Kurtz	1979- (United States)	philosopher
Dr James Hemming	1979-	educational psychologist
Kathleen Nott	1979-1999	polymath/author
Prof Ivor Armstrong Richards	1979-1979	English literature scholar
Corliss Lamont	1982-1995 (United States)	thinker
Prof Paul Edwards	1983- (United States)	philosopher
Brigid Brophy	1984-1995	author
Naomi Mitchison	1984-1999	author
Colin Blakemore	1986-	neurologist
Lionel Elvin	1986-	educationalist
Prof Moses Finley	1986-1986	historian
Prof Ronald Fletcher	1986-1992	sociologist
Christopher Hill	1986-	historian
Ludovic Kennedy	1986-	author/broadcaster

Prof Sir Edmund Leach	1986-1989		social anthropologist
Carl Lofmark	1986-1991		linguist
Lord Houghton of Sowerby (Arthur Leslie Noel Douglas Houghton)			
	1986-1996		politician
John Maynard Smith	1986-		biologist
George Melly	1986-		humorist/entertainer
Sir John Royden Maddox	1986-		author/broadcaster
Prof Patrick Nowell-Smith	1986-		ethicist
Dr David Oppenheimer	1986-1991		physician
Renée Short	1986-		politician
Alan John Percivale Taylor	1986-1990		historian
Baron Young of Dartington	1986-2002		sociologist
Dr H Montgomery Hyde	1987-1989		author/barrister
Colin Campbell	1988-		sociologist
Ted Honderich	1988-		philosopher
Prof the Earl Russell (Conrad Russell)	1988-		historian
Prof Haydn Mason	1988-		linguist
Richard Dawkins	1989-		zoologist
Lord Dormand of Easington (John Dormand)			
	1989-		politician
Lord Sefton of Garston (William Henry Sefton)			
	1989-		politician
Baroness Turner of Camden (Muriel Winifred Turner)			
	1989-		politician
Prof George Albert Wells	1989-		polymath
Dr David J Stewart	1990-		psychologist
Michael Foot	1992-		politician/author
Peter Atkins	1993-		physicist
Lewis Wolpert	1993-		embryologist
Edward Blishen	1995-1996		author
Alan Brownjohn	1995-		poet/novelist
Noam Chomsky	1995-	(United States)	polymath
Gavin Ewart	1995-1995		poet
Lord Foot (Dingle Foot)	1995-2000		politician
Tony Harrison	1995-		poet
Eric Hobsbawm	1995-		historian
Richard Hoggart	1995-		sociologist/educationist
Arthur Jacobs	1995-1996		music scholar
Lord Jenkins of Putney (Hugh Jenkins)	1995-		politician/author
Richard Leakey	1995-	(Kenya)	anthropologist/conservationist
Sir Michael Levey	1995-		art historian
Brian Moore	1995-1999		novelist
Edwin Mullins	1995-		art critic
Jack Parsons	1995-		population scholar
Prof John Postgate	1995-		microbiologist
Clair Rayner	1995-		writer/broadcaster

Dr David Starkey	1995-		historian
David Tribe	1995-	(Australia)	polymath/author
Arnold Wesker	1995-		playwright
Sanal Edamaruku	2000-	(India)	activist
Prof Susan Greenfield	2000-		pharmacologist
Prof Amartya Sen	2000-	(India)	economist
Laurie Taylor	2000-		sociologist
Prof A C Grayling	2001-		philosopher
Hazhir Teimourian	2001-		journalist

* denotes uncertainty about year of death or country of residence.

Appendix 3

Office Holders of the Rationalist Press Association

Chairmen of the Board of Directors

George Jacob Holyoake	1899-1906
Edward Clodd	1906-1913
Sir Herbert Leon, Bt.	1913-1922
George Whale	1922-1925
J P Gilmour	1925-1941
Ernest Thurtle, MP	1941
Frederick Watts	1942-1952
Joseph Reeves, MP	1952-1964
Dr David Stewart	1964-1973
Antony Chapman	1973-1981
Prof G A Wells	1981-1989
David Pollock	1989-1997
Ivor Russell	1997-2002

Presidents

Prof Graham Wallas	1926-1929
Prof Harold Laski	1929-1933
Lord Snell of Plumstead (Harry Snell)	1933-1940
Surgeon Rear Admiral C M Beadnell	1940-1947
Dr C D Darlington	1948-1949
Prof A E Heath	1949-1954
Bertrand Russell	1955-1970
Baroness Wootton	1970-1973
Lord Ritchie Calder	1973-1981
Prof Hermann Bondi	1981-

Vice-presidents

Prof A E Heath	1955-1961
Sir Julian Huxley	1957-1975
Baroness Wootton	1962-1970

Joseph Reeves   1965-1969
Lord Ritchie-Calder   1972-1973
Prof Antony Flew   1973-1988
Prof Paul Kurtz   1982-
Baroness Greenfield   2001-
Laurie Taylor   2001-

Editors of the *Literary Guide/Humanist/New Humanist*

Charles Albert Watts   Nov 1885-May 1946
Frederick Watts   May 1946-1953
Hector Hawton   July 1953-March 1971
Christopher Macy   Aug 1971-Oct 1974
Hector Hawton (Acting Editor)   Nov 1974-Feb 1975
Nicolas Walter   Feb 1975-July 1984
Jim Herrick (Acting Editor)   July 1984-Aug 1985
Jim Herrick   Aug 1985-

Watts' Literary Guide began in November 1885
Became *Literary Guide* in October 1894
Took subtitle *and Rationalist Review* in July 1896
Became *The Humanist* in October 1956
Became *Humanist* in April 1966
Became *New Humanist* in May 1972

Editors of the Agnostic/Rationalist Annual/Question

Charles Albert Watts   1885-1943
Frederick Watts   1944-1952
Hector Hawton   1953-1975
G A Wells   1976-1980

Secretaries

Charles E Hooper   1899-1912
Charles T Gorham   1912-1928
E Royston Pike   1928-1931
Ernest Thurtle   1932-1941 General Secretary
Miss J M Bridge   1932-1937 Executive Secretary
Constance Kerr   1938-1941 Executive Secretary
Constance Kerr   1941-1954
Constance Dowman (nee Kerr)   1954-1975 General Secretary
F Cooke   1975-1981 Company Secretary
Nicolas Walter   1981-1996 Company Secretary
John Metcalf   1996-

Appendix 4

Books or Issues Featured as Supplements of the Literary Guide, 1893-1907

- June 1893, Leslie Stephen, *An Agnostic's Apology*, by F J Gould
- September 1893, W E H Lecky, *The Rise and Influence of the Spirit of Rationalism in Europe*, by Frederick Millar
- April 1894 on 'Religion in Board Schools' by 'Mirabeau Brown' [F J Gould]
- September 1894, Moncure Conway, *Life of Thomas Paine*, anon
- January 1895, on 'Who Wrote Genesis?' by F J Gould
- March 1895, William Graham, *The Creed of Science*, anon
- July 1895, 'Who Wrote the Four Gospels?' by F J Gould
- November 1895, Ernest Renan, *History of the Origins of Christianity*, by Thomas C Laws
- January 1896, Thomas Buckle, *History of Civilisation*, by C T Gorham
- April 1896, 'Did an Agnostic Write the Book of Job?' by F J Gould
- July 1896 W E H Lecky, *History of European Morals*, by C T Gorham
- October 1896, 'A Woman's Plea for Freedom of Thought', by F J Gould
- January 1897, J S Mill, *Autobiography*, by Richard Bithell
- March 1897, Herbert Spencer's *Data of Ethics*, by C T Gorham
- July 1897 'A Plan for Moral Instruction', by F J Gould
- July 1897, Godwin Smith, *Guesses at the Riddle of Existence*, by F J Gould
- October 1897, Dean Farrer, *The Bible: Its Meaning and Supremacy*, by F J Gould
- January 1898, J G Frazer, 'The Origins of Sacrifice' from *The Golden Bough*, by Amos Waters
- April 1898, Herbert Spencer, *Principles of Ethics*, by C T Gorham
- July 1898, J M Guyau, *Morality Independent of Obligation or Sanction*, by 'G K'
- October 1898, Herbert Spencer, *Principles of Ethics* (Part 4), by C T Gorham
- January 1899, Charles Darwin, *Descent of Man*, by Joseph McCabe
- April 1899, W K Clifford, *Lectures and Essays*, by C T Gorham
- July 1899, Theophila Carlile Campbell, *The Battle for the Press, as Told in the Story of the Life of Richard Carlile*, by C T Gorham
- October 1899, 'The Religion of Charles Darwin', by F J Gould
- January 1900, Dr J Martineau, *Types of Ethical Theory*, by anon
- July 1900, G F Stout, *A Manual of Psychology*, by C E Hooper
- October 1900, John Henry Kurtz, *Church History*, by F J Gould
- January 1901, Leonard Huxley, *Life and Letters of Thomas Henry Huxley*, by Joseph McCabe

- April 1901, Winwood Reade, *The Martyrdom of Man*, by C T Gorham
- July 1901, Clara Chamberlain McLean, *Ingersoll: Agnostic, Critic and Prophet*, by F J Gould
- October 1901, Ludwig Büchner, *Last Words on Materialism*, anonymous (almost certainly Joseph McCabe)
- January 1902, J W Cross, *George Eliot's Life, as Related in her Letters and Journals*, by F J Gould
- April 1902 'Sir Thomas More's "Utopia": A Retrospect and Forecast', by Constance Plumptre
- July 1902, 'A Treasury of Education' on George Coombe's writings on education, by C T Gorham
- October 1902, 'The Genius of "BV": A Sketch of the Life and Writings of James Thomson', by F J Gould
- January 1903, Ernst Haeckel, *The Riddle of the Universe*, anonymous (almost certainly Joseph McCabe)
- April 1903, Grant Allen, *The Evolution of the Idea of God*, by C T Gorham
- October 1903, Edward Carpenter, *Towards Democracy*, by F J Gould
- January 1904, S G Tallentyre, *Life of Voltaire*, by C T Gorham
- April 1904, 'Sir Leslie Stephen', by Joseph McCabe
- July 1904, 'The Transformation of Christianity' on the principal conclusions of the *Encyclopedia Biblica*, by
- C T Gorham, subsequently released as a pamphlet
- October 1904, 'The Awakening of Bruno', by F J Gould
- January 1905, Ernst Haeckel, *The Wonders of Life*, by Joseph McCabe
- April 1905, 'The Growth of a Mind' on Moncure's Conway's Autobiography, by Charles T Gorham
- July 1905, 'The Tragedy of a Soul: An Epitome of the Recent Biography of Dr Momerie, by his Widow' by C T Gorham
- October 1905, 'Freethinkers in Council: A Chat About the Paris Congress', by C T Gorham
- January 1906, What to Read: Suggestions for the Better Utilisation of Public Libraries', by J M Robertson
- April 1906, George Jacob Holyoake, *History of Co-operation*, by C T Gorham
- July 1906, J M Robertson, *Short History of Freethought*, by F J Gould
- October, 1906, 'The Evolution of Morals', by E W Lowry
- January 1907, Herbert Spencer, *Ecclesiastical Institutions*, by C T Gorham
- April 1907, AW Benn's *History of English Rationalism in the Nineteenth Century*, anonymous
- July 1907, 'Human Nature: The study of which should be pursued with the enthusiasm once devoted to theology', by F J Gould
- October 1907, 'On the Mental Qualities of Women, as viewed by some distinguished masculine thinkers of the later half of the nineteenth century', by Constance Plumptre

Appendix 5

Topics and Speakers at Rationalist Press Association conferences, 1945-2001

1945 **Rationalism in Education and Life**
Wadham College, Oxford, August 23-27
Speakers included Prof P Sargent Florence 'Rationalism in University Education'; Prof G R Owst 'The Case for the RPA Programme for Religious Instruction in Schools'; Dr Kenneth Urwin 'Ethics and the Child'; Prof V Gordon Childe 'The Birth of God in the Brain of a Social Animal'; Prof A E Heath 'Science and Cultural Values'.

1947 **Rationalism and Social Progress**
Wadham College, Oxford, July 31-August 4
Speakers included Prof A E Heath 'The Idea of Progress'; Rupert Crawshay-Williams 'The Emotional Resistance to Rationalism'; Gilbert Murray 'The Many Meanings of Rationalism'; Dr Maurice Burton 'Some Biological Aspects of Human Nature'; Prof P Sargant Florence 'Measures of Social Progress'.

1948 **Reason and Unreason in Society**
Magdalen College, Oxford, July 23-27
Speakers included Jacob Bronowski 'Is Science Really Destructive?'; Joan Malleson 'Is Rational Behaviour Possible in Sexual Matters?'; Karl Popper 'Towards a Rational Theory of Tradition'; Dr J A C Brown 'Rational and Irrational Behaviour in Industrial Groups'; Gilbert Ryle 'Talk About Talk'; Margery Fry 'Changing Ideas of Punishment'.

1950 **The Irrational in Modern Thought**
Magdalen College, Oxford, August 4-8
Speakers included Hamilton Fyfe 'Some Limitations of Rationalism'; A J Ayer 'Existentialism'; Hermann Bondi 'New Thoughts on the Nature of the Universe'; Archibald Robertson 'Karl Barth'; Stuart Hampshire 'Some Recent Forms of Irrationalism'.

1951 **A Clearer View of Man**
Beatrice Webb House, Dorking, September 7-11
Speakers included Dr W E Swinton 'Man the Animal'; Dr D Stark Murray 'Man Survives'; Prof A E Heath 'Man in the Round'; Donald MacRae 'Man Forms Societies' and J A C Brown 'Man the Social Unit'.

1952 **The Menace of Roman Catholicism**
Beaumont Hall, Leicester University College, Oadby, August 8-12
Speakers included Joseph McCabe 'Roman Catholicism and Crime'; Kingsley Martin 'The Roman Catholic Counter Revolution in the West'; Dr Marie Stopes 'Roman Catholicism and Birth Control'; A D Howell Smith 'Roman Catholic Dogma Today and Yesterday'.

1953 **The Impact of Religion on Daily Life**
Stephenson Hall, Sheffield University, July 10-14
Speakers included Sir Sheldon Dudley 'Religion and Medicine'; R S W Pollard on 'Religion and the Law'; Winnifred Taylor on 'Religion and Education'; Douglas Houghton on 'The Pressure brought by religious bodies regarding legislation'; Dr H S Ferns on 'Religion and the Press'.

1954 **Evolution, Progress and Ethics**
Somerville College, Oxford, July 23-7
Speakers included Dr W E Swinton on 'Man Among the Vertebrates'; Prof Morris Ginsberg on 'Evolution and Ethics'; Prof A E Heath on 'The Idea of Evolution'; J S L Gilmour on 'Evolutionary Progress and Ethical Progress'; Prof K Mather on 'The Evolution of Human Relations'; Prof C A Mace on 'Evolution of the Mind'.

1955 **The Arts in Society**
Lady Margaret Hall, Oxford, July 30 to August 3
Speakers included Adrian Brunel on 'The Film and the Community'; Prof Helen Rosenau on 'Art and Social Revolution'; C T Smith on 'Music and the Community and You'; Donald Fraser on 'The New Patronage'; and G S Fraser on 'The Writer as a Critic of Society'.

1956 **Rationalism in the Modern World**
Girton College, Cambridge, August 10-14
Speakers included Ronald Hepburn 'Scepticism and the Naturally Religious Mind?'; Donald MacRae 'Rational Investigation in an Irrational Society'; Dr John Lewis; Prof T H Pear 'Rationalism and Human Nature'; Joseph Reeves MP 'The International Scene: Viewpoint of a Rationalist'.

1957 no conference owing to proximity of the IHEU conference

1958 **Living with Reality**
Girton College, Cambridge, August 8-12
Speakers included H Levy, 'Science and the World Crisis'; Ronald Fletcher, 'Humanist Issues in Education'; H J Eysenck, 'Psychology and the Concept of Conscience'; O R McGregor, 'Broken Homes'.

1959 **Humanism in Everyday Life**
Girton College, Cambridge, August 7-11
Speakers included R W Sorenson MP, 'The Individual and the Community'; Kathleen Nott, 'The Life of the Imagination'; Dr Philip Bloom, 'Success in Marriage'.

1960 **Humanist and Christian Morality**
St Hilda's College, Oxford, July 22-26
Speakers included P H Nowell-Smith 'The Humanist Basis of Ethics'; Victor Purcell, 'Non-Christian Morality'; Olaf Drewitt 'Christianity and Sex'; Ritchie Calder 'Science and Morality'.

1961 **The African Revolution: A Challenge to Humanists**
Girton College, Cambridge, August 4-8
Speakers included Enoch Dumbutshena (replacing Leopold Takawira) 'The African Revolution'; Lionel Elvin 'Educational Problems in Africa'; Preston King (replacing Dennis Phombeah) 'African Unity'; Joao Cabral 'Portuguese Colonialism'.

Joint RPA/Ethical Union Conference

1962 **Youth in Revolt: The Conflict Between the Older and Younger Generation**
Florence Nightingale Hall, Nottingham University, September 7-11
Speakers included Dr Ronald Fletcher on 'The Adolescent and the Family'; Dr Howard Jones on 'Juvenile Delinquency'; D A Feasey on 'The Attitude of Young People to Religion'; J H Wallis on 'The Changing Pattern of Sexual Relationships'.

First Annual Conference of the BHA

1963 **The Meaning of Co-existence; East and West**
Hugh Stewart Hall, Nottingham University, July 26-30
Speakers included Dr F S Northedge 'Power Politics: Yesterday, Today and Tomorrow'; Reginald Paget MP 'A British View of Co-existence'; A I Romanov 'The Russian View of Peaceful Co-existence'; G R Barker 'Economic Aspects of Co-existence'.

Second Annual Conference of the BHA

1964 **Humanism and the Social Revolution**
Hugh Stewart Hall, Nottingham University, July 24-27
Speakers included Sir Julian Huxley 'Values in an Age of Scientific Integration'; David Stewart 'Technology's Challenge to Humanists'; Arthur Ling 'The Future of the City'; James Hemming 'Values in an Age of Technology'.

Third Annual Conference of the BHA

1965 **Revaluations of the Family**
University of Keele, August 27-30
Speakers included Professor Lester Kirkendall 'The Twentieth Century Context'; Michael Power 'The Family: Therapeutic or Pathogenic?'; Brigid Brophy 'The Immorality of Marriage'

Fourth Annual Conference of the BHA

1966 **Aggression**
Schaptoft College, Leicester, August 26-29
Speakers included Margaret Knight 'The Foundations of Aggression'; Michael Nicholson 'Aggression, Rationality and the Strategic Thinkers'; Joe Sanders 'Racial Conflict'; Richard Hauser 'Methods of Conciliation'.

Fifth Annual Conference of the BHA

1967 devoted to internal issues of BHA

Sixteenth Annual Conference of the RPA

1968 **The Knowledge Explosion**
Churchill College, Cambridge, September 6-8
Speakers included Dr L F Thomas 'Self Organisation in Learning'; Professor C H Longuet-Higgins 'The Human Significance of the Computer Revolution'; Rupert Crawshay-Williams 'Classification as the Basis of Knowledge'.

Seventeenth Annual Conference of the RPA

1969 **Planners versus People**
Goodricke College, University of York, September 5-7
Speakers included Jack Parsons 'Population versus Liberty'; Dr Peter Draper 'Democracy and Expertise: The Conflict in Medical Planning'; Ivor Russell 'Planning and Architecture: A Twentieth Century Failure?'; and Dr Douglas M C MacEwan 'Conservation: The Rational Control of the Human Environment'.

Eighteenth Annual Conference of the RPA

1970 **The Arts in a Permissive Society**
Sussex University, September 4-6
Speakers included Peter Faulkner 'The Historical Perspective'; John Calder 'The Novel'; Roger Manvell 'The Cinema and Television' Daniel Salem 'Is Social Theatre Possible?'.

1971 **Rationalism: an Answer to the Problems of the 1970s**
St Peter's College, Oxford, September 3-5
Speakers included David Stewart 'What is the Message?'; Professor E H Hutten 'Science in the 1970s'; Dr Christopher Evans 'Modern Superstitions'; Dr Colin Campbell 'The Rational Approach to Secularisation'.

1972 **Rationalism and Humanism in the New Europe**
Churchill College, Cambridge, August 11-13
Speakers included Ernst van Brakel 'Humanist and Freethought Organisation in Britain and Europe'; Erwin Fischer 'Humanism and the Churches in Europe'; Lucien de Connick 'The Environment in Europe'; Jaap van Praag 'Tasks for Humanists in the New Europe'.

1973 Manipulating Minds
Hulme Hall, Manchester University, August 17-19
Speakers included Dr James Wright on 'The Brain and Direct Action'; Judie Lannon on 'Psychological Techniques in Advertising'; Valerie Stone on 'Mind Control Behaviour Therapy and Psycho-Therapy'; Dr W Grey Walter on 'The Current State of Brain Research'.

1974 New Women in a New Society
St Peter's College, Oxford, September 13-15
Speakers included Dora Russell on 'The Long Campaign'; Eva Figes on 'Population and Motherhood'; Barbara Smoker on 'Women and Patriarchal God'; Patricia Hewitt on 'Women at Work'; Anna Raeburn on 'Women and Sexuality'.

1975 Science and the Paranormal
Churchill College, Cambridge, September 12-14
Speakers included Prof Antony Flew 'A Philosophical View of the Paranormal'; Prof John Taylor 'Current Research in Paranormal Phenomena: 1'; Dr Cristopher Evans Taylor 'Current Research in Paranormal Phenomena: 2'; Trevor Hall 'An Historical View of Psychical Research'; and David Berglas 'A Practical View of Paranormal Phenomena'.

1976 Threats to Freedom
Harkness Hall, Birkbeck College, London, September 11
Discussions led by Tony Smythe, Antony Flew and Dora Russell.

1999 Rationalism in the Twenty-first Century
Westhill Conference Centre, Birmingham, June 25-27
Speakers included Prof Colin Blakemore 'What hope for rationalism in the twenty-first century?'; Helena Cronin 'Natural-born Co-operators: Darwin for Policy Makers'; Hazhir Teimourian 'Fundamentalism in the Next Century'; Antony Flew 'Against the New Irrationalism'; Lewis Wolpert 'Belief and the Unbelievable'; Colin Campbell 'The Easternisation of the West: the Threat to Rationalism in the New Millennium'; Babu Gogineni 'Humanism and Ketchup'.

2001 Mind and Other Matter
Writtle College, Chelmsford, July 13-15
Speakers included Ted Honderich, 'Consciousness as Existence'; Dorothy Rowe 'The Mind Distressed'; Peter Faulkner 'The Mind of the Novelist'; Kenan Malik 'Mechanism, Humanism and the Human Mind'; David Marks 'The Psychology of the Psychic'; Linda Melvern 'The Mindset of Genocide'.

Endnotes

Chapter 1: The Gathering of the Infidels

1. Warren Sylvester Smith, *The London Heretics 1870-1914*, London: Constable, 1967, p 279.
2. J M Robertson, *A History of Freethought in the Nineteenth Century*, London: Watts, 1929, Volume 2, p 608.
3. Owen Chadwick, *The Secularisation of the European Mind in the 19th Century*, Cambridge: Canto, 1991, p 5.
4. J M Robertson, *A History of Freethought in the Nineteenth Century*, Volume 2, p 617.
5. Owen Chadwick, *The Secularisation of the European Mind in the 19th Century*, p 262.
6. Ibid, p 6.
7. John F Hurst, *History of Rationalism*, London: Trübner & Co, 1867, p 27.
8. Ibid, p 476.
9. Stephen Neill, *Anglicanism*, London: Penguin, 1958, p 245.
10. P T Marsh, *The Victorian Church in Decline*, London: Routledge & Kegan Paul, 1969, p 6.
11. Ibid, p 7.
12. *Essays and Reviews*, London: Longman, Green, Longman, and Roberts, 1861, note 'To the Reader'.
13. H G Wood, *Belief and Unbelief Since 1850*, London: Cambridge University Press, 1955, p 66.
14. G W Stocking, *After Tylor: British Social Anthropology 1888-1951*, Madison, Wisc: University of Wisconsin Press, 1995, p 66.
15. P T Marsh, *The Victorian Church in Decline*, pp 281-2.
16. J M Robertson, op.cit., Volume 2, p 393. F J Gould also knew Brewer to be the 'Julian' who contributed to the *Literary Guide*. See *Literary Guide*, January 1936, p 3. And finally, Charles Watts, revealed 'Julian' as Brewer in the September 1939 issue of the *Guide* (page 174). See, also, the obituary notice of Brewer in the *Literary Guide* of April 1897, p 153, although 'Julian' is not mentioned.
17. Walter Arnstein, *The Bradlaugh Case: Atheism, Sex, and Politics among the Late Victorians*, Columbia: University of Missouri Press, 1983, p 344.
18. Colin Campbell, *Towards a Sociology of Irreligion*, London: Macmillan, 1971, p 54.
19. *Watts's Literary Guide*, February 15 1887, p 3.
20. *New Humanist*, July 1975, p 62.
21. J M Robertson, *A History of Freethought in the Nineteenth Century*, Volume 2, p 439.
22. *Literary Guide*, January 1924, p 19.
23. *Watts's Literary Guide*, February 15 1891, p 3.
24. This constitutes quite the most significant research detail I inherited from Nicolas Walter. Walter wrote parts of this up as the article 'Travelling with the Huxleys from Agnosticism to Humanism', *New Humanist*, November 1997, pp 6-7.
25. Ibid.
26. Adrian Desmond, *Huxley*, London: Penguin, 1998, p 527. This error was also repeated in Cyril Bibby's earlier study *T H Huxley: Scientist, Humanist and Educator*, London: Watts, 1959, p 253, published, ironically, by Watts & Co.
27. Adrian Desmond, *Huxley*, p 726.
28. C A Watts, 'Introductory', *The Agnostic Annual 1884*, London: Watts & Co, p 4.
29. *Literary Guide*, January 1924, p 19.
30. *Literary Guide*, April 1895, p 3.

31. *Watts's Literary Guide*, November 15 1889, p 3.
32. Ibid, November 15 1889, p 3.
33. Ibid, December 15 1889, p 3.
34. Ibid, June 15 1890, p 3. See also Gould's *The Pioneers of Johnson's Court*, London: Watts, 1929, p 12.
35. Joseph McCabe, *Life and Letters of George Jacob Holyoake*, London: Watts, 1908, Volume 2, p 264.
36. Richard Bithell, *The Creed of a Modern Agnostic*, London: George Routledge, 1883, pp 151-2.
37. Ibid, p 12.
38. Richard Bithell, 'Hindrances to Rationalist Propagandism', *The Agnostic Annual, 1897*, London: Watts, p 43.
39. Charles Watts, 'The Meaning of Rationalism', in *The Meaning of Rationalism and Other Essays*, London, Watts, 1905, p 8.
40. F J Gould, *The Life-Story of a Humanist*, London: Watts, 1923, p 53.
41. Ibid, p 165.
42. Supplement to *Literary Guide*, July 1897 'A Plan of Moral Instruction', p 1.
43. F J Gould, *The Children's Book of Moral Lessons*: Third Series, London: Watts, 1909, p 35.
44. F J Gould, *The Children's Book of Moral Lessons*: Second Series, London: Watts, 1907, p 62.
45. *Watts's Literary Guide*, December 15 1891, p 3.
46. Edward Royle, *Radicals, Secularists and Republicans*, Manchester: Manchester University Press, 1980, p 48.
47. Adam Gowans Whyte, *The Story of the RPA*, London: Watts, 1949, p 14.
48. Noel Annan, *Leslie Stephen*, Macgibbon & Kee, London, 1951, p 159.
49. I am grateful to David Tribe for this observation, as I am for many others, which have helped in no small measure to tighten this history up.
50. *Literary Guide*, July 1896, p 1.
51. Ibid, October 1896, p 56.
52. Joseph McCabe, *Life and Letters of George Jacob Holyoake*, Volume 2, p 255.
53. Charles Watts, 'What is Agnosticism?', in *The Meaning of Rationalism and Other Essays*, p 84.
54. T H Huxley, 'Agnosticism', in *Science and Christian Tradition*, London & New York: Macmillan, 1902, pp 245-6.
55. Charles Watts, 'The Meaning of Rationalism', in *The Meaning of Rationalism and Other Essays*, p 5.
56. Ibid, p 1.
57. David Nash, *Secularism, Art and Freedom*, Leicester, Leicester University Press, 1992, p 18.
58. Charles Watts, 'The Meaning of Rationalism', in *The Meaning of Rationalism and Other Essays*, p 4.
59. For this claim, see Gould, *Pioneers of Johnson's Court*, p 8 and for the concession see Whyte, *The Story of the RPA*, p 24.
60. John F Hurst, *History of Rationalism*, p 476 & 478.
61. W E H Lecky, *History of the Rise and Influence of the Spirit of Rationalism in Europe*, London: Longmans, Green & Co, 1904, Volume 1, p 169.
62. Ibid, Volume 1, p vii.
63. *Watts's Literary Guide*, September 15 1890, p 3.
64. *Daily Telegraph*, May 16 1917.
65. George Jacob Holyoake, 'Introduction', in George Anderson, *Some Chapters in a Rationalist's Life*, London: Watts, 1904, p 5.
66. F J Gould, "To Stimulate Freedom of Thought", *Literary Guide*, May 1899, p 67.

Chapter 2: The Blasphemy Depot

1. J B Priestley, *The Edwardians*, London: Heinemann, 1970, p 84.
2. Samuel Hynes, *The Edwardian Turn of Mind*, Princeton, NJ: Princeton University Press, 1975 [1968], p 8.
3. Adam Gowans Whyte, *The Religion of the Open Mind*, London: Watts, 1913, pp 1-3.
4. F J Gould, *The Pioneers of Johnson's Court*, London: Watts, 1929, p 26.
5. Joseph McCabe, *Eighty Years a Rebel*, Girard, Kan: Haldeman-Julius, 1947, p 26.
6. *Literary Guide*, January 1900, p 5.
7. Richard Milner, *The Encyclopaedia of Evolution*, London & New York: Facts on File, 1990, p 206.
8. *Literary Guide*, March 1900, pp 35-6.
9. See my *A Rebel to His Last Breath: Joseph McCabe and Rationalism*, Amherst, NY: Prometheus Books, 2001, especially Chapter Three.
10. Edward Royle, *Radicals, Secularists and Republicans*, Manchester: Manchester University Press, 1980, p 166.
11. *Guide*, November 1900, p 168.
12. Joseph McCabe, *One Hundred Men Who Moved the World*, Girard, Kan: Haldeman-Julius, Volume 17, p 34.
13. *New Humanist*, Autumn 1985, p 4.
14. H James Birx, Introduction to Ernst Haeckel's *The Riddle of the Universe*, Amherst, NY: Prometheus Books, 1992, p xiii.
15. Marvin Farber, *Naturalism and Subjectivism*, Springfield, Ill: Charles C Thomas, 1959, p 262. I am grateful to Professor H James Birx for alerting me to this book.
16. *Literary Guide*, April 1901, p 64.
17. Ibid, June 1918, p 90.
18. Edward Clodd, *Thomas Henry Huxley*, Edinburgh: William Blackwood, 1902, p 150.
19. Edward Clodd, *Memories*, London: Watts, 1926, pp 5-6.
20. Joseph McCabe, *Edward Clodd: A Memoir*, London: John Lane The Bodley Head, 1932, p 128.
21. Edward Clodd, *Thomas Henry Huxley*, p 56.
22. F J Gould, *The Pioneers of Johnson's Court*, p 42.
23. *Literary Guide*, April 1904, p 58.
24. Arnold Bennett, *The Journals of Arnold Bennett*, selected and edited by Frank Swinnerton, London: Penguin, 1954, p 109. Watts' recollection is from the *Literary Guide*, July 1932, p 128.
25. Letter from Andrew Lang to C A Watts, dated June 1, no year, but in all likelihood in the later 1890s. RPA archive.
26. Andrew Lang, *The Origins of Religion*, London: Watts, 1908, p 127.
27. 'Introduction to the Present Reprint', Alfred W Benn, in Francis William Newman, *Phases of Faith*, London: Watts, 1907, p 13.
28. Francis William Newman, *Phases of Faith*, p 119.
29. This story is recounted by Watts in the *Literary Guide*, May 1940, p 88 and again in June 1942, p 82.
30. This comes from one of C A Watts's few articles, entitled 'Some Reminiscences of No. 17 Johnson's Court', *Literary Guide*, January 1924, p 20. It was repeated in Gould's, *The Pioneers of Johnson's Court*, p 4.
31. *Literary Guide*, June 1918, p 90.
32. Adam Gowans Whyte, *1899-1949: The Story of the RPA*, London: Watts, 1949, p 56.
33. Alan D Gilbert, *The Making of Post-Christian Britain*, London & New York: Longman, 1980, p 56.

34. See Steve Hare (ed) *Penguin Portrait: Allen Lane and the Penguin Editions 1935-1970*, London: Penguin, 1995, and Rosemary A Haile, 'The Paperback: A Threat to the Culture of the Publishing Industry'. http://www.brookes.ac.uk/schools/apm/publishing/culture/1997/haile.html.
35. *The Rationalist Press Association, Limited, Fourteenth Annual Report: 1912*, p 5.
36. Samuel Hynes, *The Edwardian Turn of Mind*, p 285.
37. Ibid, pp 301 & 289.
38. Whyte, *1899-1949: The Story of the RPA*, pp 59-60.
39. *Literary Guide*, October 1942, p 128.
40. Blurb inside the first volume in the series, McCabe's own work, *Existence of God*.
41. 'Lin Shao-Yang' [Sir R F Johnston], *A Chinese Appeal to Christendom concerning Christian Missions*, London: Watts, 1911, p 2.
42. *Literary Guide*, September 1911, p 136.
43. 'Wanted, an Anti-Missionary Society' Sir Hiram Maxim, *The RPA Annual 1911*, London: Watts & Co, p 60.
44. 'Lin Shao-Yang' [Sir R F Johnston], *A Chinese Appeal to Christendom concerning Christian Missions*, p 73.
45. Ibid, p 82.
46. 'Vivian, Philip' [Vivian Phelips], *The Churches and Modern Thought*, London: Watts, 1931 [1906], p 3.
47. *Literary Guide*, February 1924, p 34.
48. F C Conybeare, *Myth, Magic, and Morals*, London: Watts, 1910, p 361.
49. James Veitch, 'Searching for Jesus', *Stimulus*, Volume 4, No. 4, Nov 1996, p 5.
50. F C Conybeare, *Myth, Magic, and Morals*, p 349.
51. Ibid, p 6.
52. J M Robertson, 'The Problem of "Mark"', *The RPA Annual for 1926*, London: Watts, p 36.
53. F C Conybeare, *Myth, Magic, and Morals*, p xvii.
54. Professor Sanday, *The New Marcion*, p 16, quoted in 'Lin Shao-Yang' [Sir R F Johnston], *A Chinese Appeal to Christendom concerning Christian Missions*, p 25.
55. F C Conybeare, *The Historical Christ*, London: Watts, 1914, p 222.
56. Ibid, p vii.
57. Bill Cooke, *Heathen in Godzone: Seventy Years of Rationalism in New Zealand*, Auckland: NZARH, 1998, p 15.
58. Joseph McCabe, *The Sources of the Morality of the Gospels*, London: Watts, 1914, p viii.
59. Ibid, p vii.
60. Ibid, p 298.
61. *The Rationalist Press Association, Limited, Seventh Annual Report: 1905*, pp 6-7.
62. *The Rationalist Press Association, Limited, Tenth Annual Report: 1908*, p 8.
63. *The Rationalist Press Association, Limited, Twenty-Second Annual Report: 1920*, p 9.
64. This story has been told by Dr Ralph Biddington in his excellent work, *The Supremacy of Reason: Episodes in Victoria's Rationalist History, 1880-1972*, unpublished manuscript, Melbourne, 2001. Sadly this work reached me too late to be influential in this book.
65. *Literary Guide*, December 1903, p 177.
66. Ibid, January 1903, p 1.
67. Ibid, August 1903, p 120.
68. Ibid.
69. Rev. D Allison, 'The Evangelist in Contact with Aggressive Rationalism', in W Gordon (ed) *Rationalism and the Gospel*, London: The Record, 1905, p 65.
70. *Literary Guide*, July 1 1904, p 105.

71. Canon Henry Lewis, *Modern Rationalism as Seen in its Biographies*, London: SPCK, 1913, p vi.
72. *Literary Guide*, January 1914, pp 2-3.
73. H G Wood, *Why Mr Bertrand Russell is Not a Christian*, London: SCM, 1928, p 40.
74. C L Drawbridge, *Common Objections to Christianity*, London: Robert Scott, 1914, pp 14-5.
75. *Literary Guide*, February 1903, p 20.
76. H Stuart Hughes, *Consciousness and Society: The Reorientation of European Thought 1890-1930*, London: Macgibbon & Kee, 1959, p 115.
77. Bernard Bosanquet in the *Quarterly Review* in 1914, quoted from John Passmore, *A Hundred Years of Philosophy*, London: Penguin, 1978, p 85.
78. Hans Sluga, *Heidegger's Crisis: Philosophy and Politics in Nazi Germany*, Cambridge, Mass: Harvard University Press, 1993, pp 77-8.
79. David J Dooley, 'Chesterton in Debate with Blatchford: The Development of a Controversialist', pp 211-2, in Michael H Macdonald & Andrew A Tadie (eds), *G K Chesterton and C S Lewis: The Riddle of Joy*, Grand Rapids, Michigan, Eerdmans, 1989.
80. Joseph McCabe, 'Christianity Defended by Sleight of Hand', p 88, in *Christianity and Rationalism on Trial*, London: Watts, 1904.
81. Keith Clements, *Lovers of Discord: Twentieth Century Theological Controversies in England*, London: SCM, 1988, p 16.
82. Kingsley Martin, *Father Figures*, London: Penguin, 1969, p 38.
83. B H Streeter, 'Introduction', in B H Streeter (ed), *Foundations: A Statement of Christian Belief in Terms of Modern Thought*, London: Macmillan, 1922, p vii.
84. B H Streeter, 'The Historic Christ', in B H Streeter (ed), *Foundations: A Statement of Christian Belief in Terms of Modern Thought*, p 78.
85. Doctrine of the Church of England, quoted from Margaret Knight's *Honest to Man*, Amherst, NY: Prometheus Books, 1974, p 172.
86. Piers Brendon, *Eminent Edwardians*, London: Penguin, 1981, p 76.
87. Ibid, p 77.
88. Arthur James Balfour, *The Foundations of Belief*, London: Longmans, Green, 1895, p 18.
89. Ibid, pp 82-3.
90. Ibid, p 295.
91. Ibid, p 324.
92. Ibid, p 294.
93. Ibid, p 354.
94. William James, *The Varieties of Religious Experience*, London: Longmans, Green & Co, 1952, p 481.
95. Ibid, pp 483-4.
96. Ibid, p 497.
97. J M Robertson, 'Professor James's Plea for Theism', p 178, in *Explorations*, London: Watts, n.d [1923].
98. Robertson is quoting from James' *The Will To Believe*, in 'Professor James's Plea for Theism', p 185, in *Explorations*, London, Watts & Co, n.d [1923].
99. *Literary Guide*, November 1907, p 166.
100. Charles E Hooper, 'The RPA: Its Origin and Growth', in *The RPA Annual and Ethical Review, 1908*, London: Watts & Co, p 79.
101. *Literary Guide*, October 1900, p 150.
102. Ibid, August 1900, p 115.
103. Ibid, February 1900, p 19.
104. David Tribe, in *President Charles Bradlaugh, MP*, London: Elek, 1971, p 296 refers to Hypatia Bradlaugh Bonner's dislike of Foote and Odin Dekkers, in *J M Robertson:*

Rationalist and Literary Critic, Aldershot & Brookfield, Vermont: Ashgate, 1998, pp 26-7 mentions Robertson's dislike of Foote.
105. See Bill Cooke, *A Rebel to His Last Breath: Joseph McCabe and Rationalism*, Amherst, NY: Prometheus Books, 2001, pp 48-50.
106. *Literary Guide*, March 1908, pp 1-3.
107. Joseph McCabe, *The Life and Letters of George Jacob Holyoake*, London: Watts, 1908, Volume II, pp 148 & 258-60.
108. Hypatia Bradlaugh Bonner, 'Penalties on Opinion' *Literary Guide*, April 1908, pp 50-51.
109. Ibid, p 56.
110. Joseph McCabe, *The Life and Letters of George Jacob Holyoake*, Volume II, p 252.
111. Joseph McCabe, *Eighty Years a Rebel*, p 28.
112. *Literary Guide*, May 1908, p 72.
113. Ibid, June 1908, pp 85-6.

Chapter 3: War and Change

1. Modris Eksteins, *Rites of Spring*, London: Black Swan, 1990, pp 286-7.
2. A J P Taylor, *English History 1914-1945*, London: Oxford University Press, 1965, p 299.
3. Joseph McCabe, *Edward Clodd: A Memoir*, London: John Lane The Bodley Head, 1932, pp 155-6.
4. Joseph McCabe, 'Armageddon', *Literary Guide*, September 1914, p 129.
5. Ibid, August 1918, p 120.
6. This, and other no less peculiar manifestations of irrationality, are recounted amusingly in Peter Washington, *Madame Blavatsky's Baboon*, New York: Schocken Books, 1995.
7. *Melbourne Age*, December 28 1914, quoted in Joseph McCabe, *War and the Churches*, London: Watts, 1915, pp 53-4.
8. Joseph McCabe, *War and the Churches*, pp 53-4.
9. Charles T Gorham, 'Rationalism and the War', *Literary Guide*, April 1916, pp 49-51.
10. Ibid, September 1918, p 136.
11. Joseph McCabe, *The Bankruptcy of Religion*, London: Watts, 1917, pp 4-5.
12. Ibid, p 22.
13. *Literary Guide*, June 1918, p 88.
14. Joseph McCabe, *The Bankruptcy of Religion*, p 197.
15. *Literary Guide*, October 1915, p 152.
16. Ibid, April 1918, p 57.
17. Ibid, July 1918, p 110.
18. Ibid, September 1918, p 142.
19. Ibid, July 1929, p 130.
20. Ibid, November 1917, p 169.
21. Ibid, October 1915, p 151.
22. Ibid, December 1915, p 185.
23. Joseph McCabe, *The War and the Churches*, p 66.
24. *Literary Guide*, February 1916, pp 25-6.
25. J Arthur Hill, *Spiritualism: Its History, Phenomena and Doctrine*, London: Cassell, 1918, p 203.
26. W P Jolly, *Sir Oliver Lodge*, London: Constable, 1974, p 207.
27. Joseph McCabe, *The Religion of Sir Oliver Lodge*, London: Watts, 1914, pp 125-6.
28. W P Jolly, *Sir Oliver Lodge*, p 208.
29. *Literary Guide*, November 1916, p 168.

30. Adam Gowans Whyte, *The World's Wonder Stories*, London: Watts, 1916, p 4.
31. Ibid, p 221.
32. Odin Dekkers, *J M Robertson: Rationalist and Literary Critic*, Aldershot & Brookfield, Vermont: Ashgate, 1998, pp 45-6.
33. *Literary Guide*, January 1924, p 16.
34. Frank Swinnerton, *Swinnerton: An Autobiography*, London: Hutchinson, 1937, p 296.
35. Ronald Clark, *J.B.S: The Life and Work of J B S Haldane*, London: Hodder & Stoughton, 1968, pp 62-3.
36. *Literary Guide*, July 1925, p 131.
37. *Sunday Express*, late May 1925, the article is undated, in the RPA archive.
38. Hilaire Belloc, *A Companion to Mr Wells's "Outline of History"*, London: Sheed & Ward, 1929, p 230.
39. Michael Coren, *The Invisible Man: The Life and Liberties of H G Wells*, London: Bloomsbury, 1994, p 62.
40. David C Smith, *H G Wells: Desperately Mortal* (New Haven, Conn: Yale University Press, 1986, p 256.
41. Michael Foot, *H G: The History of Mr Wells*, London: Doubleday, 1995, p 210.
42. 'Jocelyn Rhys', [Major W J R Wingfield], 'A Challenge to the Churches', *The RPA Annual for 1925*, London: Watts & Co, p 54.
43. *Literary Guide*, July 1946, p 102.
44. Thomas Seymour-Smith, *Hardy*, London: Bloomsbury, 1994, pp 621 & 319-20. This book is an honourable exception to the usual run of works which fail to investigate thoroughly a prominent person's variety of atheism.
45. Joseph McCabe, *A Biographical Dictionary of Modern Rationalists*, London: Watts, 1920, p x.
46. J C A Gaskin (ed), *Varieties of Unbelief From Epicurus to Sartre*, New York: Macmillan, 1989, p 232.
47. David Berman, 'J M Robertson: Freethinker and historian of freethought', *New Humanist*, Summer 1984, p 12.
48. Odin Dekkers, *J M Robertson: Rationalist and Literary Critic*, p 73.
49. Eric Hobsbawm, *Age of Extremes: The Short Twentieth Century, 1914-1991*, London: Michael Joseph, 1995, p 195.
50. *Literary Guide*, May 1928, p 88.
51. *The Freethinker*, Volume 101, No. 5, p 69.
52. Graham Wallas, 'Property Under Socialism', in George Bernard Shaw (ed) *Fabian Essays in Socialism*, London: Walter Scott, 1889, p 148.
53. Kingsley Martin, *Father Figures*, London: Penguin, 1969, p 92.
54. Graham Wallas, *The Art of Thought*, London: Watts, 1945 [1926], p 2.
55. *Literary Guide*, June 1924, p 95.
56. Joseph McCabe, *Getting the Most Out of Life*, Girard, Kansas: Haldeman-Julius, 1941 [1932], p 55.
57. E Royston Pike, 'A Rationalist in the Making', *Literary Guide*, July 1929, p 130.
58. Letter from Charles Watts to RPA Board, March 23 1930, RPA archive.
59. *New Humanist*, July 1975, pp 62-3.
60. *Literary Guide*, December 1953, p 211.
61. The only place this episode is referred to is in the correspondence between Charles Watts and Archibald Robertson following the latter's resignation from the Board early in 1932. All this correspondence is in the RPA archive.

Chapter 4: Change and War

1. J B Coates, 'Scientific Humanism and the RPA', *Literary Guide*, August 1931, p 155.
2. H G Wells, *The Open Conspiracy: Blueprints for a World Revolution*, London: Victor Gollancz, 1928, p 15.
3. Ibid, pp 28-9.
4. Ibid, pp 24-5.
5. Archibald Robertson was no relation to J M Robertson, nor of the prominent American fundamentalist apologist of the same time, Archibald Thomas Robertson.
6. 'Robert Arch', 'The RPA and the Future', *Literary Guide*, September 1931, p 165.
7. Ibid, February 1947, p 27.
8. Ibid, September 1931, p 165.
9. J M Robertson, 'Notes and Queries about "Scientific Humanism"', *Literary Guide*, October 1931, p 180.
10. Ibid.
11. Letter from Archibald Robertson to Charles Watts, March 11 1932, RPA archive.
12. Letter from Charles Watts to Archibald Robertson, undated but between March 11 and 15 1932, RPA archive.
13. Letter from Archibald Robertson to Charles Watts, March 15 1932, RPA archive.
14. Letter from Charles Watts to Archibald Robertson, March 17 1932, RPA archive.
15. C E M Joad, *The Book of Joad*, London: Faber & Faber, 1945 [1932], p 68.
16. David Tribe, *100 Years of Freethought*, London: Elek, 1967, pp 49-50.
17. F J Gould, *The Pioneers of Johnson's Court*, London: Watts, 1935 [1929], p 164.
18. Harold Laski, 'On the Need for a Militant Rationalism', *The Rationalist Annual 1931*, London: Watts, p 14.
19. Harold Laski, 'On the Social Obligation of Rationalists', *The Rationalist Annual 1934*, London: Watts, p 4.
20. Harold Laski, 'The Next Phase of Rationalism', *The Rationalist Annual 1935*, London: Watts, p 15.
21. Ben Rogers, *A J Ayer: A Life*, New York: Grove Press, 1999, p 136.
22. H G Wells, *After Democracy*, London: Watts, 1932, pp 178-9.
23. Harold Laski, *Faith, Reason, and Civilisation*, London: Victor Gollancz, 1944, pp 45-6.
24. Ibid, p 54.
25. John Rowland, 'Youth Speaks', *Literary Guide*, January 1939, p 10.
26. RPA Minutes, September 5 1940, p 159.
27. *Literary Guide*, May 1942, p 70.
28. Joseph McCabe, *The Rise and Fall of the Gods*, Girard, Kansas: Haldeman-Julius, 1931, Volume 5, p 36.
29. RPA Minutes, March 28, 1935, p 33.
30. Ibid, June 24 1937, p 85.
31. *Literary Guide*, August 1938, p iv.
32. RPA Minutes, May 31 1945, p 112.
33. A N Wilson, *God's Funeral*, London: John Murray, 1999, pp 164-5.
34. Laurence Collier, *Flight from Conflict*, London: Watts, 1944, p 71.
35. L T Hobhouse, *The Rational Good*, London: George Allen & Unwin, 1921, p 61.
36. G W Stocking, *After Tylor: British Social Anthropology 1888-1951*, Madison, Wisc: University of Wisconsin Press, 1995, p 101.
36. Ibid, p 232.
37. Both these letters are in the RPA archive. Letter from J G Frazer to Charles Watts May 20 1919, and from Edward Clodd to Watts May 24 1919.

38. Gary Werskey, *The Visible College*, London: Penguin, 1978.
39. Interview of Hyman Levy by Gary Werskey, April 10 1968 and reproduced in *The Visible College*, p 171.
40. Alan Bullock & R B Woodings (eds) *The Fontana Biographical Companion to Modern Thought*, London: Fontana, 1983, p 145.
41. Mary Midgley, *Science as Salvation*, London & New York, Routledge, 1994, p 37.
42. RPA Minutes, February 24 1938, p 136.
43. Ibid, December 30 1937, p 113.
44. F J Gould, *The Pioneers of Johnson's Court*, 1935 edition, p 171.
45. Edward J Pulsford, *Rationalists Should be Christians!* London: New Church Missionary and Tract Society, 1938, p 204.
46. Ernest Carr, 'Swedenborgianism and Modern Thought', *Literary Guide*, June 1938, p 101.
47. H G Wood, 'Christianity and Scientific Humanism' in *Christianity and Civilisation*, London: Cambridge University Press, 1943.
48. David Simpson, *The March of the Godless*, Melbourne: Keswick Book Depot, 1937, p 96.
49. John Dewey, 'Antinaturalism in Extremis', in Yervant H Krikorian (ed) *Naturalism and the Human Spirit*, New York: Columbia University Press, 1944, pp 5-6.
50. For a fuller discussion of this see Chapter 8 of my *A Rebel to His Last Breath: Joseph McCabe and Rationalism*.
51. Chapman Cohen, 'Introduction', World Union of Freethinkers International Congress, London: Watts & Pioneer Press, 1939, p xi. It is interesting to note that the *Chambers Biographical Dictionary*, in its short entry on Hinsley, describes him as an outspoken opponent of fascism. This is, at the very least, a particularly generous assessment.
52. See Alan Ryan, *Bertrand Russell: A Political Life*, London, Allen Lane, 1988, p 92.
53. Ivan Levisky, 'Communism and Religion', in Lewis, John, Polanyi, Karl & Kitchin, Donald B (eds), *Christianity and the Social Revolution*, London: Victor Gollancz, 1937, p 273.
54. *Literary Guide*, March 1940, p 62.
55. RPA Minutes, July 27 1939, p 76.
56. Ernest Thurtle, 'The Guns Roar Again', *Literary Guide*, October 1939, p 179.
57. Ibid, p 184.
58. RPA Minutes, January 30 1941, p 4 & May 29 1941, p 37.
59. *Literary Guide*, March 1942, p 43.
60. Fred Watts, 'Chairman's Report', *Literary Guide*, August 1944, p 91.
61. *Literary Guide*, January 1944, p 12.
62. Ibid, January 1940, p 2.
63. John Rowland, 'The Weather and the War', *Literary Guide*, August 1944, p 88.
64. Ibid, July 1942, p 99.
65. Adam Gowans Whyte, '"No Religious Bias"', *Literary Guide*, June 1943, p 60.
66. Ibid, July 1944, p 79.
67. Ibid, August 1945, p 96. I am particularly grateful for David Tribe for assistance in getting this section right.
68. Adam Gowans Whyte, 'The "Well-organised Minority"', September 1942, p 113.
69. Ibid.
70. *Looking Ahead: Educational Aims*, published by Conservative and Unionist Party, London, 1942, quoted in *Literary Guide*, October 1942, p 125.
71. There has been a discrepancy of dates I have been unable to unravel here. The *Literary Guide* mentions this appointment in June 1942 but it is not mentioned in the RPA minutes until April 1943.
72. Fred Watts, 'Chairman's Report', *Literary Guide*, August 1944, pp 91-2.

73. A J P Taylor, *English History 1914-1945*, p 368.
74. *Literary Guide*, June 1945, p 74.

Chapter 5: The Humanist Labyrinth

1. *Literary Guide*, July 1946, p 99.
2. Ibid, May 1942, p iii.
3. Fred Watts, Report to RPA Board of Directors, February 21 1944.
4. RPA Minutes, March 1 1945, pp 84-5.
5. D J Stewart, Chairman's Report, RPA AGM, June 10 1965, *Humanist*, August 1965, p 252.
6. RPA Minutes March 11 1954, p 107.
7. This is commented upon, for instance, by Bryan Magee in *Confessions of a Philosopher*, London: Weidenfeld & Nicolson, 1997, pp 72-3.
8. RPA Minutes, June 7 1951, p 148.
9. Ibid, May 13 1954, p 110.
10. Sir Arthur Keith, *An Autobiography*, London: Watts, 1950, pp 406-7.
11. Maurice Burton, 'Keith on Evolution', *Literary Guide*, November 1948, p 171.
12. Sir Arthur Keith, *An Autobiography*, p 119.
13. Letter to Fred Watts, May 24 1948, RPA archive.
14. Wells, G P, *The Last Books of H G Wells*, London: H G Wells Society, 1982, p 84.
15. A E Heath, 'The Despair of Mr Wells', *Literary Guide*, February 1946, p 21.
16. John Passmore, *A Hundred Years of Philosophy*, London: Duckworth, 1962, pp 279-80.
17. C E M Joad, 'On Being No Longer a Rationalist', *The Rationalist Annual, 1946*, p 71.
18. Ibid, pp 73-4.
19. *Literary Guide*, August 1948, p 116.
20. Ibid, September 1948, p 152.
21. Ibid.
22. It is also noteworthy that Dowman made no mention of Hector Hawton, even though she had worked beside him for more than twenty years, *New Humanist*, July 1975, pp 62-3.
23. D J Stewart, 'The Future of the RPA', *Rationalist Review*, January 1956, p iii.
24. *Humanist*, November 1966, p 320.
25. Hector Hawton, *The Humanist Revolution*, London: Barrie & Rockliff/ Pemberton, 1963, p 40.
26. Letter to author from Mary Vidal (Hector Hawton's widow), May 23 2001
27. Report on Watts & Co's financial position by Hawton and Reeves, RPA Minutes, Dec 1 1954, p 175.
28. Report on Meeting of Pemberton Publishing Co Ltd Board of Directors, June 18 1957, Minutes, July 11 1957, p 9.
29. RPA Annual Report 1960, p 4.
30. Fred Watts, '"The Literary Guide"', *Literary Guide*, October 1951, p 192.
31. *Rationalist Review*, March 1955, p i.
32. RPA Annual Report 1959, p 5.
33. 'Report on the Prospects of "The Literary Guide"', RPA Minutes, September 22, 1953.
34. *Rationalist Review*, February 1956, pp 32-3.
35. Ibid, October 1955, p ix.
36. Unsigned article, 'Changing our Name', *Literary Guide*, September 1956, p 6.
37. *The Humanist*, October 1956, p 3.
38. Stephen Neill, *Anglicanism*, London: Penguin, 1958, pp 408-9.
39. Adam Gowans Whyte, 'The Twilight of the Church', *The Rationalist Annual, 1946*, p 11.

40. Archibald Robertson, *Anglican Shipwreck*, London: Watts, 1945, p 5.
41. R E D Clark, *Darwin: Before and After*, London: Paternoster Press, 1948, p 97.
42. Antony Flew, 'The Ephemeral Philosophy', *Literary Guide*, June 1954, p 28.
43. *The Humanist*, March 1964, p 92.
44. RPA Minutes, October 12 1950, p 70.
45. Humanist Association Minutes, February 6 1958, p 37.
46. Report of the Joint Committee of Representatives of the RPA, NSS and the Ethical Union, Humanist Association Minutes June 12 1958, p 49. The representatives were, for the RPA Reeves and Hawton; the NSS F A Ridley and Colin McCall, and Ethical Union A A Burall and H J Blackham.
47. Hector Hawton, 'The RPA and the BHA', *The Humanist*, August 1964, p 246.
48. *The Humanist*, March 1963, p 94.
49. J A T Robinson, *Honest to God*, London: SCM, 1963, p 126.
50. *The Humanist*, May 1963, p 141.
51. Ibid, March 1964, p 79.
52. Margaret Knight, *Honest to Man*, Amherst, NY: Prometheus Books, 1974, p 171.
53. Arnold Lunn, & Garth Lean, *The New Morality*, London: Blandford, 1964, p 53.
54. Margaret Knight, *Morals Without Religion*, London: Dennis Dobson, 1955, p 17 and see also Nicolas Walter 'Religious Broadcasting', *New Humanist*, May-June 1976, pp 17-18, and David Tribe, *Broadcasting, Brainwashing, Conditioning*, London: National Secular Society, 1972, pp 10-11.
55. They were J D Bernal, Benjamin Farrington, E M Forster, C H Waddington and J B S Haldane. The other five were E L Woodward, Lord Lindsay, A D Ritchie, Arthur Koestler, and Michael Polanyi.
56. Humanist Council Minutes, May 12 1959, p 79.
57. Hector Hawton, 'Common Front', *The Humanist*, June 1963, p 163.
58. Leonard Evans & David Pollock, 'What are we waiting for?' *The Humanist*, April 1964, p 116.
59. Hector Hawton to Evans & Pollock, January 31 1964, in possession of David Pollock. I am grateful to David Pollock for access to this, and a large amount of other relevant material.
60. Motion at RPA Annual General Meeting, September 24 1964. Wording taken from undated correspondence of David Pollock to RPA, in possession of David Pollock.
61. *Humanist*, October 1966, pp 308-9. I am very grateful to Mary Vidal for tracking down the date of Frank Farr's death despite at the time undergoing serious medical treatment.
62. Charles Watts, *The Meaning of Rationalism and Other Essays*, London: Watts, 1905, p 3.

Chapter 6: Going It Alone

1. Hector Hawton, 'Student revolt against Rationalism' *Humanist*, August 1968, p 227.
2. Ibid, September 1968, pp 262-7.
3. Hector Hawton, 'Introducing Question 1', *Question 1*, February 1968, London: Pemberton Publishing in association with Barrie & Rockliff, 1968, p 4.
4. RPA Minutes, 29 January 1969, p 4.
5. Hector Hawton, *Controversy: The Humanist/Christian Encounter*, London: Pemberton, 1971, p 5.
6. RPA Annual Report, 1971, p 4.
7. Letter from RPA solicitors Alexander Rubens, Weil & Co, to Dept of Education and Science, 8 Oct 1970, RPA Minutes December 9 1970, p 54.
8. Ibid, p 55.

9. RPA Minutes, March 4 1972, p 91.
10. Ibid, July 14 1972, p 106. Emphasis in the original.
11. Letter from Dept of Education and Science to RPA's solicitors, May 9 1972, RPA archive.
12. Memorandum to Board of Directors from Chris Macy, October 7 1971, RPA archive.
13. E H Hutten, 'Future Policy of the *New Humanist*', memorandum to the Board of Directors, March 23 1973. RPA Minutes July 26 1973, p 151.
14. 'Report of the Working Party on *New Humanist*', RPA Minutes, September 10 1973, p 153.
15. Ibid, p 156.
16. RPA Minutes September 25 1974, p 183.
17. Obituary notice on Nicolas Walter by Barbara Smoker, *Ethical Record*, Volume 105, No. 3, March 2000, p 4.
18. *New Statesman*, June 1 1979, p 787.
19. Ibid, August 10 1979, p 197.
20. Nicolas Walter, Memorandum to Board of Directors from Managing Director, November 1981, in the possession of David Pollock.
21. Nicolas Walter, Managing Director's Report to Board of Directors, November 1976, RPA archive.
22. Nicolas Walter, 'The Future of the RPA', *New Humanist*, October 1975, p 143.
23. Ibid, July 1975, p 63.
24. Nicolas Walter, Managing Director's Report to the Board of Directors, July 1976, RPA archive.
25. Nicolas Walter, Managing Editor's Report to the Board of Directors, Nicolas Walter, January 1976, RPA archive.
26. *New Humanist*, March 1980, p 128.
27. Nicolas Walter, Memorandum from Managing Director to Board of Directors, February 1980, RPA archive.
28. *New Humanist*, Winter 1982, p 4.
29. *Sunday Telegraph*, May 8 1988, p 18.
30. Jim Herrick, 'The Rushdie Affair', *New Humanist*, May 1989, p 3.
31. Ibid, May 1989, p 7. This article appeared originally in the *New Statesman & Society*.
32. RPA Minutes, November 4 1991, p 180.
33. M M Ahsan & A R Kidwai, *Sacrilege versus Civility: Muslim Perspectives on the Satanic Verses Affair*, Leicester: The Islamic Foundation, 1991, p 25.
34. Jim Herrick, 'Humanism and Islamic Schools', *New Humanist*, November 1993, pp 16-7.
35. David Williams, 'Towards a Humanist Merger: A Position Paper', October 17 1988, RPA archive.
36. Humanist Liaison Committee Minutes, October 24 1988, p 36.
37. RPA Minutes October 27 1988, p 40.
38. Ibid, January 7 1989, p 50.
39. David Pollock, Report of Finance Subcommittee to RPA Board of Directors, February 25 1990, p 108.
40. *New Humanist*, December 1990, p 1.
41. RPA Minutes, May 5 1992, pp 193-4.
42. Jim Herrick, 'Humanism Moves Forward', *New Humanist*, May 1994, p 1.
43. Nicolas Walter, Special Report to Board of Directors, August 27 1993, p 226.
44. Nicolas Walter, Memorandum to David Pollock, RPA Minutes, December 8 1995, p 313.
45. David Pollock, 'Terms of Nicolas Walter's Employment', RPA Minutes March 6 1996, p 318.
46. Nicolas Walter, Memorandum to Board of Directors, RPA Minutes, March 18 1996, p 320.
47. RPA Minutes, June 7 1999, p 386.

48. Barbara Smoker, Obituary notice, *Ethical Record*, Volume 195, No. 3, March 2000, p 4.
49. Ibid, p 3.
50. *New Humanist*, March 1991, p 23.
51. Ibid, March 1992, p 16.
52. *The Humanist*, October 1962, p 296.
53. David Pollock, Matters Arising from the AGM: The Future of the Association (Memorandum from the Chairman) RPA Minutes, Aug 29 1995, pp 282-5.
54. Ibid.
55. RPA Minutes, October 12 1995, p 298.
56. Ibid, October 16 1995, p 287.
57. Ibid, April 29 1996, p 324.
58. Sir Hermann Bondi, 'A Humanist Outlook', *New Humanist*, Spring 2001, p 4.
59. The Thinker's Library titles were *Let the People Think*, *A Short History of the World*, *Religion Without Revelation*, *Do What You Will* and *The Ethics of Belief*.

Chapter 7: Rationalism, Humanism and the retreat from Spencer

1. W H Hudson, *An Introduction to the Philosophy of Herbert Spencer*, London: Watts, 1911, p 9.
2. *Literary Guide*, January 1904, p 8.
3. J M Robertson, 'Herbert Spencer', in *Explorations*, London: Watts, n.d [1923], p 129.
4. 'Protonius' [Adam Gowans Whyte], *Personal Pie*, London: Watts, 1938, p 69.
5. J M Robertson, 'Herbert Spencer', in *Explorations*, p 114.
6. *Literary Guide*, January 1900, p 12.
7. E Royston Pike, 'What of Spencer After Fifty Years?' *Literary Guide*, January 1950, p 16.
8. RPA Minutes July 25 1940, p 157.
9. H G Wells, *Joan and Peter*, London: Cassell, 1918, p 486.
10. Antony Flew, 'Towards True Social Science', *New Humanist*, Autumn 1985, pp 21-2.
11. Joseph McCabe, *Principles of Evolution*, London & Glasgow: Collins, n.d [1913], p 257.
12. *Literary Guide*, January 1937, p 28.
13. Ibid, February 1908, p 27.
14. H G Wells, *The Brothers*, London: Chatto & Windus, 1938, p 121.
15. Hector Hawton, 'First and Last Things', in Hector Hawton (ed) *Reason in Action*, London: Watts, 1956, p 17.
16. Donald MacRae, 'Herbert Spencer Revalued', *The Humanist*, May 1958, p 15.
17. *The Humanist*, June 1960, p 165.
18. Hector Hawton, *Philosophy for Pleasure*, London: Watts & Co, 1952, p 137.
19. Ibid, p 105.
20. See, for example 'Dinner with the Whiteheads', *Literary Guide*, October 1954, pp 5-6.
21. Hector Hawton, *Philosophy for Pleasure*, p 145.
22. Ibid, p 200.
23. Hector Hawton, *The Feast of Unreason*, London: Watts, 1952, pp 10-11.
24. Hector Hawton, 'First and Last Things', in Hector Hawton (ed) *Reason in Action*, p 12.
25. Hector Hawton, *The Feast of Unreason*, p 223.
26. H J Blackham, *Six Existentialist Thinkers*, New York: Harper Torchbooks, 1959, p vi. First published by Routledge, Kegan Paul Ltd in 1951.
27. Ben Rogers, *A J Ayer: A Life*, New York: Grove Press, 1999, p 195.
28. Bertrand Russell, 'The Existentialist's Nightmare', in *Nightmares of Eminent Persons*, London: The Bodley Head, pp 36-9.

29. Hector Hawton, 'First and Last Things', in Hector Hawton (ed) *Reason in Action*, p 13.
30. Ibid, p 16.
31. Ibid, p 18.
32. Ibid, p 29.
33. *Literary Guide*, August 1898 p 113.
34. The best of these books include Wallace Matson, *The Existence of God* (Cornell University Press, 1965), Antony Flew, *God and Philosophy* (Hutchinson, 1966), and *The Presumption of Atheism* (Pemberton, 1976, later reissued as *God, Freedom and Immortality* by Prometheus Books, 1984), J L Mackie, *The Miracle of Theism* (Oxford University Press, 1982), George H Smith, *Atheism: The Case Against God* (Prometheus, 1989) and Michael Martin, *Atheism: A Philosophical Justification* (Temple University Press, 1990). Prometheus Books has also published some excellent shorter surveys. Among the best of the single-volume debates on the existence of God are *Does God Exist?* by Terry Miethe and Antony Flew (HarperSanFrancisco, 1991) and *Atheism and Theism* by J J C Smart and J Haldane (Blackwell, 1996).
35. See, for example Michael Martin, *Atheism: A Philosophical Justification*, p 77.
36. W B Columbine, 'The Origin and Meaning of Agnosticism', *Literary Guide*, November 1900, p 169.
37. Charles Bradlaugh, 'A Plea for Atheism', in *Humanity's Gain from Unbelief*, edited by Hypatia Bradlaugh Bonner, London: Watts, 1932, p 25.
38. J M Robertson, 'Professor James's Plea for Theism', in *Explorations*, p 207.
39. Llewelyn Powys, *The Pathetic Fallacy*, Watts, London, 1931, pp 113-4.
40. Antony Flew, *God, Freedom and Immortality*, p 74.
41. Ibid, p 13.
42. Alan Richardson, *Christian Apologetics*, London: SCM, 1960, p 77.
43. Roger Forster, & Paul Marston, *Reason and Faith*, Eastbourne, Monarch Publications, 1989, p 19.
44. Adam Gowans Whyte, *The Story of the RPA*, London: Watts, 1949, pp 36-7.
45. *New Humanist*, May 1974, p 16.
46. Charles Gorham, 'The New Forward Movement', *Literary Guide*, March 1899, p 33.
47. Charles E Hooper, 'The Parting of the Ways', *Literary Guide*, January 1898, p 2.
48. J M Robertson, *Rationalism*, London: Constable, 1912, p 8.
49. Ibid, pp 23-4.
50. Joseph McCabe, *Modern Rationalism*, London: Watts, 1909, p 8.
51. Adam Gowans Whyte, *The Religion of the Open Mind*, London: Watts, 1913, p 163.
52. Ibid, p 159.
53. Ibid, pp 39-40.
54. Charles Gorham 'Constructive Rationalism', *RPA Annual for 1922*, London: Watts, p 63.
55. Sir Arthur Conan Doyle & Joseph McCabe, *Verbatim Report of a Public Debate on "The Truth of Spiritualism"*, London: Watts, 1920, pp 47-8.
56. A E Heath, 'On Defining Rationalism', *Literary Guide*, June 1947, p 99.
57. Archibald Robertson, *Rationalism in Theory and Practice*, London: Watts, 1954, p 33.
58. Sheila Chown, 'What is a Rationalist?' *Question 9*, London, Pemberton, 1975, p 4.
59. G A Wells, 'Rationalism Today', *New Humanist*, July 1975, pp 64-5.
60. Ronald Englefield, 'The Nature of Thinking', *Question 13*, London: Pemberton, 1980, p 43.
61. Wells, G A, *Religious Postures: Essays on Modern Christian Apologists and Religious Problems*, La Salle, Ill: Open Court, 1988, p 197.
62. H Gwynne Jones, 'Rationalism: A Personal View', *Humanist*, July 1971, p 205.
63. Steven Lukes, *The Curious Enlightenment of Professor Caritat*, London: Verso, 1996, p 19.
64. 'The Future of the RPA', memorandum to Directors by Ivor Russell, April 1999, RPA archive.

65. *New Humanist*, August 1994, p 24.
66. Zygmunt Bauman, *Intimations of Postmodernity*, London & New York: Routledge, 1993, p 188.
67. Ibid, pp vii-viii.
68. John Milbank, 'Problematising the secular: the post-postmodern agenda', in Philippa Berry, & Andrew Wernick, (eds) *Shadow of Spirit: Postmodernism and Religion*, London & New York, Routledge, 1992, p 31.
69. Charles E Hooper, 'The Parting of the Ways', *Literary Guide*, January 1898, p 3.
70. 'First Principles of the RPA', *Literary Guide*, February 1907, p 25.
71. Stanton Coit, 'The Religion of a Rationalist', *The Rationalist Annual: 1927*, London: Watts, p 69.
72. J P Gilmour, 'The Misuse of the Term "Religion"', *Literary Guide*, April 1936, p 69.
73. H J Blackham, 'Is South Place Religious?' *New Humanist*, September/October 1980, p 38.
74. Julian Huxley, *Religion without Revelation*, London: Max Parrish, 1957, p ix.
75. Ibid, p 218.
76. Ibid, p 120.
77. *The Humanist*, July 1963, p 198.
78. 'Kit Mouat' [Jean Mackay], *What Humanism is About*, London: Barrie & Rockliff/Pemberton Publishing, 1963, p 13.
79. Hector Hawton, *The Humanist Revolution*, London: Barrie & Rockliff/Pemberton Publishing, 1963, p 18.
80. Hector Hawton, 'The RPA and the BHA', *The Humanist*, August 1964, p 248.
81. Hector Hawton, *The Humanist Revolution*, pp 234-5.
82. *New Humanist*, June 1979, p 38.
83. H J Blackham, 'Is South Place Religious?' *New Humanist*, September/October 1980, p 37.
84. Nicolas Walter 'A Century of the Ethical Movement', *Ethical Record*, Volume 93, No. 8, September 1988, p 9.
85. Harry Stopes-Roe, 'The Presuppositions of Dialogue: A Fair Vocabulary', *Journal for the Critical Study of Religion, Ethics and Society*, Volume 1, No. 2, Summer/Fall 1996, pp 9-15.
86. Ibid, p 13.
87. Hector Hawton, 'Preface', in Hector Hawton (ed) *Reason in Action*, p 5.
88. Hector Hawton, *The Humanist Revolution*, p 40.
89. Ibid, p 67.
90. Antony Flew, 'What I Mean by Scientific Humanism', *Literary Guide*, August 1955, p 13.
91. M Roshwald, *Humanism in Practice*, London: Watts, 1955, p 21.
92. H J Blackham, *Humanism*, London: Penguin, 1968, p 30.
93. Ronald Fletcher, 'A Definition of Humanism', *Question 1*, London: Pemberton Publishing, 1968, p 7.
94. Ibid, pp 9-10.
95. Ibid, p 15.
96. Paul Kurtz, 'The Future of Humanism', *New Humanist*, Summer 1984, p 10.
97. Charles Watts, 'The Meaning of Rationalism', in *The Meaning of Rationalism and Other Essays*, London, Watts, 1905, p 4.
98. Edward Clodd, *Thomas Henry Huxley*, Edinburgh: William Blackwood, 1902, p 23.
99. *Literary Guide*, October 1928, p 183.
100. 'Lin Shao-Yang' [Sir R F Johnston], *A Chinese Appeal to Christendom concerning Christian Missions*, London: Watts, 1911, p 214.
101. I owe this insight to Winston James, Associate Professor of History at Columbia University, who is undertaking extensive research on the works of Claude McKay.
102. *New Humanist*, Winter 2001, p 4.

Chapter 8 Eupraxophy in Action

1. *New Humanist*, May 1974, p 17.
2. *Literary Guide*, June 1955, p 5.
3. Michael White and John Gribbin lament this in their accessible work, *Einstein: A Life in Science*, London: Simon & Schuster, 1993, pp 153-4 & 160.
4. Albert Einstein, *The World as I See It*, London: Watts, 1935, p 26.
5. Michael White and John Gribbin, *Einstein: A Life in Science*, p 263.
6. Adam Gowans Whyte, 'Einstein the Peacemaker', *Literary Guide*, January 1941, p 4.
7. Albert Einstein, *The World as I See It*, pp 111-2.
8. *Wanganui Chronicle*, Jan 5 1927, p 5.
9. Sir Hermann Bondi, *Humanism – the only valid foundation of ethics*, 67th Conway Memorial Lecture, London: South Place Ethical Society, 1992, pp 5-9.
10. C D Darlington, *The Conflict of Science and Society*, 38th Conway Memorial Lecture, London: Watts, 1948, pp 49-50.
11. *The Atheist*, September 1995, p 2.
12. Bertrand Russell, *The Autobiography of Bertrand Russell, 1872-1914*, London: George Allen & Unwin, 1967, p 41.
13. Ronald Jager, *The Development of Bertrand Russell's Philosophy*, London & New York: George Allen & Unwin/Humanities Press, 1972, p 503.
14. Ronald W Clark, *The Life of Bertrand Russell*, London: Jonathan Cape & Weidenfeld & Nicolson, 1975. p 413.
15. *Literary Guide*, July 1949, p 115.
16. Joseph Rotblat, 'Russell Remembered', *New Humanist*, December 1972, p 325.
17. Even Ray Monk had to acknowledge this point. See his *Bertrand Russell, 1921-1970: The Ghost of Madness*, London: Jonathan Cape, 2000, p 380.
18. *The Humanist*, September 1961, p 261.
19. Michael Foot, 'Russell Remembered', *New Humanist*, December 1972, p 320.
20. Kingsley Martin, *Father Figures*, London: Penguin, 1969, p 100.
21. Alan Ryan, *Bertrand Russell: A Political Life*, London: Allen Lane The Penguin Press, 1988, p 163.
22. *Humanist*, August 1971, p 230.
23. A E Heath, 'Introduction to the Thinker's Library Edition', in L Susan Stebbing, *Ideals and Illusions*, London: Watts, 1948, p v.
24. *Literary Guide*, April 1943, pp 36-7.
25. A E Heath, 'Introduction to the Thinker's Library Edition', in L Susan Stebbing, *Ideals and Illusions*, p iii.
26. John Passmore, *A Hundred Years of Philosophy*, London: Duckworth, 1962, p 363.
27. L Susan Stebbing, *Ideals and Illusions*, pp 29-30
28. Antony Flew, 'Wittgenstein's Logical Investigations', *Literary Guide*, September 1953, pp 140-1.
29. John Biggs-Davison, 'No Tory can be a Humanist!' *New Humanist*, October 1974, pp 185-6. I don't how Biggs-Davison responded to the Thatcher years or to more non-religious understandings of conservatism as expounded by Roger Scruton.
30. Antony Flew, 'Yet Humanists should be Conservatives', *New Humanist*, November 1974, pp 221-2.
31. RPA Minutes February 19 1987, p 9.
32. Ibid, August 31 1988, p 31.
33. Ibid, October 27 1988, p 40.
34. *New Humanist*, May 1990, p 2.

35. Ted Honderich, *Philosopher: A Kind of Life*, London: Routledge, 2001, p 391.
36. Ibid, p 411.
37. *New Humanist*, June 1979, p 23. And this was during Walter's own term as editor of the *New Humanist*.
38. Paul Kurtz, 'The Future of Humanism', *New Humanist*, Summer 1984, pp 11-2.
39. Paul Kurtz, *Humanist Manifesto 2000: A Call for a New Planetary Humanism*, Amherst: Prometheus Books, 1999, p 39.
40. Barbara Wootton, *In a World I Never Made: Autobiographical Reflections*, London: George Allen & Unwin, 1967, p 51.
41. Margaret Knight, *Morals Without Religion*, London: Dennis Dobson, 1955, p 14.
42. Ibid, pp 17-8.
43. *The Humanist*, February 1955, p 4.
44. Margaret Knight, *Morals Without Religion*, p 55.
45. Ibid, pp 58-9.
46. Ibid, p 54.
47. A D Cohen, 'Mrs Knight scores again', *The Humanist*, December 1957, pp 23-4.
48. Margaret Knight, 'Religious Humanists?' *New Humanist*, July 1975, p 69.
49. E Royston Pike, 'What Wells Meant to My Generation', *The Rationalist Annual, 1947*, London: Watts, pp 73-4.
50. H G Wells, *Boon, The Mind of the Race, The Wild Asses of the Devil, and The Last Trump*, London: T Fisher Unwin, 1915, pp 44-5.
51. Ibid, pp 51-2.
52. *Literary Guide*, August 1917, p 128.
53. Ibid, p 121.
54. Ibid, p 122.
55. H G Wells, *Experiment in Autobiography*, London: Victor Gollancz/Cresset, 1934, Volume 2, p 674.
56. H G Wells, *What are we to do with our lives?* London: William Heinemann, 1931, p 35.
57. H G Wells, *First and Last Things*, London: Watts, 1929, p 6.
58. H G Wells, *The Conquest of Time*, London: Watts, 1942, p 1.
59. Ibid, p 62.
60. E Royston Pike, 'What Wells Meant to My Generation', *The Rationalist Annual, 1947*, pp 74-5.
61. RPA Minutes, June 25 1942, p 154.
62. Ibid, October 29 1942, p 189.
63. Ibid, November 26 1942, p 8.
64. Harris Wilson (ed) *Arnold Bennett & H G Wells: A Record of a Personal and Literary Friendship*, London: Rupert Hart-Davis, 1960, p 119.
65. Frank Swinnerton (ed), *The Journals of Arnold Bennett*, London: Penguin, 1954, p 173.
66. Ibid, pp 227-8.
67. Ibid, p 294.
68. Arnold Bennett, 'Religion After the War', *The RPA Annual and Ethical Review, 1917*, pp 8-9.
69. R C Churchill, 'Forster the Novelist: A Passage to Greatness', *Humanist*, August 1970, p 231.
70. E M Forster, 'How I Lost My Faith', *The Humanist*, September 1963, p 262.
71. E M Forster, *Howards End*, London: Penguin, 1983, p 188.
72. Arnold Lunn, & Garth Lean, *Christian Counter-Attack*, London: Blandford, 1969, p 23.
73. It is worth recording that Joseph McCabe had made the same arguments, in material published by Watts & Co before the First World War.
74. *New Humanist*, June 1996, p 18.
75. Ibid, March 1999, p 12.

76. Hazhir Teimourian, 'The World After Manhattan', *New Humanist*, Winter 2001, pp 12-3.
77. *Times of India*, October 15 1998, taken from www.nd.edu.
78. Amartya Sen, 'History and the Enterprise of Knowledge', *New Humanist*, Summer 2001, p 8.
79. Sanal Edamaruku, 'Monkey Mania', *New Humanist*, Autumn 2001, p 16.

Epilogue: The Summing Up

1. Eamon Duffy, *Saints and Sinners: A History of the Popes*, New Haven & London: Yale University Press, 1997, Preface.
2. *Literary Guide*, October 1942, p 128.

Index

Agnostic Annual, 8, 12-14, 41
Agnostic, The, 14
Agnosticism, 12, 13-15, 17-19, 24-25, 196-197, 205-209, 211
Anderson, George, 33-34, 37, 76, 84
Allen, Grant, 22, 42, 112
Annan, Noel, 22
'Arch, Robert', see Robertson, Archibald
Archer, William, 251, 257, 318
Arnold, Matthew, 22, 39
Asimov, Isaac, 36
Atheism, 10-11, 17-19, 24-25, 58, 63, 77, 121, 159, 203-205, 205-209, 211
Australia, 54, 74, 105, 262
Aveling, Edward, 9
Ayer A J, 106, 137, 138, 153, 158, 161, 167, 204, 225, 229-230, 240, 245, 260, 321, 329
Balfour, Arthur, 62-63, 80
Barnes, E W, 76
Barrie & Rockliff, 149, 167, 300-301
Bax, Ernest Belfort, 101
Beadnell, Surgeon Rear Admiral Charles M 108, 109, 116, 325
Belloc, Hilaire, 81, 87-88, 121
Benn, A W, 42, 47, 112, 318
Bennett, Arnold, 40, 78, 102, 253-255, 319
Bergson, Henri, 58, 197-198, 229
Besant, Annie, 9-10, 19, 21, 25, 93
Birx, H James, 36
Bithell, Richard, 17-18, 24, 26, 34, 35, 64, 66, 211
Blackham, Harold, 156-158, 170, 219, 224, 322
Blakemore, Sir Colin, 195, 333
Blasphemy, 16-17, 43, 67-69, 175, 181-184, 189, 191, 227, 263
Blatchford, Robert, 59
Bondi, Sir Hermann, 181, 185, 194, 234-235, 322, 325, 329
Bonner, Charles Bradlaugh, 96, 113, 124, 144, 150
Bonner, Hypatia Bradlaugh, 49, 53, 66-70, 73, 83, 108, 113, 318
'Bowen, Marjorie', see Long, Gabrielle
Brabrook, Sir E, 68-69, 318
Bradlaugh, Charles, 5, 8, 9-10, 12, 23, 31, 39, 66, 86, 101, 112, 121, 123
legacy of, 10, 12, 23, 66-69, 119, 190, 206-207
Bradlaugh House, 185-186, 191-194
Brains Trust, 128, 143
Brewer, Ebenezer Cobham, 8
British Humanist Association, 44, 156-158, 162-165, 170, 178, 180, 184-185, 191-194, 220, 225, 229, 256, 331-332
British Secular Union, 11, 21, 24
Bronowski, Jacob, 36, 136, 161, 321, 329
Brophy, Brigid, 256-257, 322, 331
Büchner, Ludwig, 9, 116
Buddha, the, 19, 49, 203
Bullett, Gerald, 119
Bury, J B, 115, 258, 318
Cadogan, Peter, 221
Campbell, Colin, 10, 101, 172, 180, 226, 245, 323, 332, 333
Carlile, Richard, 22
Carr, Ernest, 120

Cassels, Walter, 46, 180
Chadwick, Owen, 6-7, 91
Chandrasekhar, Subrahmanyan, 235-236, 241, 322
Chapman, Antony, 4, 172, 192-193, 325
Chesterton, G K, 59-60, 121
Childe, V Gordon, 118, 137, 138, 152, 320, 329
China, 48-49
Christianity
 anti-rationalist apologetics, 9, 26-27, 52, 55-64, 75-76, 79, 85-86, 142-143, 153-155, 209, 217
 liberal Christianity, 40, 42, 50, 51, 75, 158-160, 221-222, 247
 reactions to rationalism, 40, 43-45, 52, 55-64, 120-123, 130, 153-155, 237, 247-249, 256
 decline of, 5-6, 60-64, 155, 263
Churchill, R C, 145, 148, 255
Church of England, 79
 Foundations, 60-62
 reactions to rationalism, 21, 45-46, 55-64, 153-154, 158-160, 209, 247-249
 decline of, 7-8, 60-64, 131-132, 153, 263
 Towards the Conversion of England, 132, 153-154
Clifford, W K, 40, 85
Clodd, Edward, 37-38, 41, 47, 66, 72, 76, 80-81, 85, 92, 108, 227, 250-251, 259, 318, 325
Coates, J B, 99-101, 103, 224
Cohen, Chapman, 83, 115, 119
Cohen, John, 112
Coit, Stanton, 82, 219
Collier, John, 38, 113, 319
Collier, Laurence, 113
Collins, William Whitehouse, 39, 327
Columbine, William Brailsford, 62, 65, 206-207
Comte, August, 18, 86, 201
Confucianism, 20, 49, 222, 224, 249
Congreve, Richard, 18
Conybeare, Frederick Conwallis, 50-52, 116
Coren, Michael, 87, 141
Cornwell, John, 121
Crick, Bernard, 178, 242, 322
Crowley, Aleister, 64
Czeckoslovakia, 124, 166
Darlington, C D, 131, 235, 321, 325
Darwin, Charles, 82, 86, 101, 111, 112, 121, 154, 217
 Origin of Species, 7, 111, 136
d'Avoine, Charles Lionel, 54-55, 190
Dawkins, Richard, 36, 40, 182, 199, 233, 323
Desmond, Adrian, 13
Dewey, John, 118, 319
Dowman (nee Kerr), Constance, 11, 96, 134, 144, 158, 170, 178, 326
Doyle, Sir Arthur Conan, 80, 81-82, 88, 214
Draper, John William, 55, 101
Duffy, Eamon, 121, 262
Eaton, Cyrus, 238, 322
Edamaruku, Sanal, 260, 324
Eddington, Sir Arthur, 71, 88, 112, 117, 118, 235, 241
Einstein, Albert, 71, 88, 138, 232-233, 235, 238, 249, 320
Eliot, George, 22
Essays and Reviews, 7-8, 29, 60-61
Ethical Union, 82, 93, 121, 156-158, 162-165, 241
Eucken, Rudolf, 58-59

352

Eupraxophy, 231, 248, 258
Evolution, 36, 53-54, 58, 62, 71, 88, 137, 262, 330
  disputes over, 87-88, 139-140, 200
Farber, Marvin, 36
Farr, Frank, 163-164
Farrington, Benjamin, 224
Federation of Progressive Societies and Individuals / Progressive League, 103-105, 201, 223
Firth, Raymond, 114, 136, 138, 167, 321
Fisher, H A L, 112
Fletcher, Ronald, 167, 225-226, 245, 322, 330, 331
Flew, Antony, 145, 152, 153, 155-156, 159, 167, 200, 206, 208, 224, 242-243, 322, 326, 333
Florence, F Sargent, 137, 138, 320, 329
Foot, Michael, 141, 185, 239, 323
Foote, G W, 18, 21, 23, 24, 26, 27-29, 39, 64-69, 206-207
Forster, E M, 161, 249, 255-256, 322
France, Anatole, 78, 112, 113
Frazer, James George, 110, 115, 201, 202
Free Inquiry, 226, 244
Freethinker, The, 18, 23, 38, 39, 64-69, 119, 177, 182-183, 187-188, 194, 206
Freethought
  discrimination against, 15, 16, 21, 27-29
  divisions within, 10, 12, 17-18, 22-23, 24-25
  ignoring the history of, 5-6, 13
  misconceptions about, 21, 29
  publishing and, 11, 14, 21, 22, 28
Freethought Publishing Company, 9, 10
Fruits of Philosophy, The, 9-10
Fyfe, Hamilton, 129, 228-229, 321
Gay News, 175, 182-183
Gellner, Ernest, 29, 153, 248, 260, 322
George, F H, 177
George, T Neville, 137
Gilbert, Alan D, 44
Gilman, Charlotte Perkins, 47
Gilmour, J P, 109, 119, 133, 219, 325
Ginsberg, Morris, 199-200, 245, 322, 330
Gollancz, Victor, 106
Gorham, Charles T, 28, 32, 47, 75, 79, 82, 92, 94, 96, 211, 213, 326
Gosse, Edmund, 115, 258
Gould, F J, 5, 15, 18-21, 25, 26-27, 28, 29, 32, 33, 78, 89, 101, 108, 120, 170, 189, 190, 318
  beliefs, 19-21, 38, 47, 65, 194, 218
  character of, 18-20, 25
  importance to the RPA, 18-19, 25, 28, 89, 108-109
  publications of, 15, 19-21, 26, 34, 81, 89, 90, 190, 195, 234, 247
Grayling, A C, 259-260, 324
Grece, Clair James, 28
Greenfield, Baroness Susan, 261, 324, 326
Greg, William R, 39, 40
Haddon, A C, 114, 319
Haeckel, Ernst, 9, 12, 34-36, 39, 73, 232, 318
  The Riddle of the Universe, 34-36, 40, 46, 55-56, 59, 111, 117
Haldane, J B S, 85, 108, 319
Haldeman-Julius, Emanuel, 87, 138
Hardie, Keir, 43
Hardy, Thomas, 39, 90, 115
Hawton, Hector, 4, 135-136, 144, 162-163, 166, 170, 171-175, 177, 178, 190, 210, 223-224, 239
  character of, 139, 145-146, 149-150, 250, 264
  contribution to the RPA, 135-136, 139, 146-149, 149-153, 156-158, 170, 202, 326

publications of, 139, 159, 167-168, 177, 202-205, 220-221, 224
Heath, A E, 137, 138, 141-142, 151, 214, 240, 321, 325, 329, 330
Hegel, G W F, 59, 198, 202-203
Hemming, James, 181, 322, 331
Hepburn, Ronald W, 155, 330
Herrick, Jim, 3, 177, 184-186, 187, 189-190, 193-194, 326
Hird, Dennis, 53-54, 84
Hobhouse, L T, 113
Hobsbawm, Eric, 91, 258, 323
Hobson, J A, 88, 103, 319
Hocart, A M, 114
Holyoake, Austin, 9-10, 11
Holyoake, George Jacob, 5, 9, 10, 16-17, 23, 25, 28, 29, 31, 34, 66-69, 86, 92, 194, 325
  legacy of, 10, 12, 16-17, 22, 23, 66-69, 146, 211, 244
Honderich, Ted, 240, 243-244, 260, 323, 333
Hooper, Charles, 28, 31-32, 47, 64, 108, 218-219, 326
Horder, Lord, 108, 131, 320
House of Lords, 27-28
Hudson, W H, 197
Humanism, 32, 63, 83
  and philosophy, 202-205
  and rationalism, 99-104, 120, 146, 150-153, 156-158, 167, 173-174, 222-226, 231, 258-259
  and religion, 99-104, 120, 129, 153-156, 158-160, 167-168, 191, 217-222, 249, 255-256
  and science, 99-101, 104, 129
  definition of, 173-174, 222-226
  meaning of, 99-105, 141, 222, 229-230, 234-235, 248, 255-256
  misconceptions about, 83, 120-121, 203-204, 213, 216-217
  value of, 36, 189, 225-226, 229-230, 231, 241, 258-259, 260
Humanist Association, 156-158, 161
Humanist Council, 156-158, 161
Humanist Manifesto I, 101
Humanist Manifesto 2000, 245
Humanist, The, 149-153, 160, 162-163, 167, 170-171, 202, 223-224, 242, 263
Hurst, John F, 6, 8, 25
Hutten, E H, 153, 163-164, 167, 173
Huxley, Aldous, 102, 113, 155-156, 159
Huxley, Julian, 88, 92, 99, 102, 109, 117-118, 120, 128, 131, 156, 158, 161, 178, 222, 227, 319, 325, 331
  publications of, 87, 100-101, 219-220
Huxley, Leonard, 38, 318
Huxley, T H, 12-13, 22, 24, 25, 26, 38, 42, 45, 86, 112, 121, 196, 206, 240
Hynes, Samuel, 30
India, 20, 54-55, 105, 181-182, 190-191, 222, 224, 260-261, 262
International Humanist & Ethical Union, 156, 190-191
Islam, 181-184, 191, 229, 259
James, William, 63
Jeans, Sir James, 112, 117, 118
Jesus, 19, 25, 50-53, 60, 61, 91, 159, 168, 178, 180, 182
Joad, C E M, 88, 103, 128, 142-143
  publications of, 88, 142, 223, 240
Johnson, Paul, 176

353

Johnson's Court
  numbers 2, 3 & 4, 83-84, 90, 104, 125-126, 147
  number 15, 10, 11, 16, 19, 84-85, 125-126, 147
Johnston, Sir Reginald Fleming, 48-49, 228
Joliot-Curie, Frédéric, 235, 238, 321
Journal of Moral Education, 170, 172, 178-180
'Julian', see Brewer, Ebenezer Cobham
Keeton, G W, 138
Keith, Sir Arthur, 82, 88, 108, 131, 139-140, 244, 319
Knight, Margaret, 149, 152, 159-160, 161, 178, 189, 246-249, 256, 321, 331
Knowlton, Charles, 9-10
Kurtz, Paul, 169, 177, 226, 231, 244-245, 248, 258, 322, 326
Laing, Samuel, 34, 39, 95
Lang, Andrew, 39, 41-42
Lankester, Sir E Ray, 30, 318
Laski, Harold, 94, 102, 105-107, 325
Lecky, William Edward Hartpole, 25-26, 77
Left Book Club, 108-109, 109, 110, 117, 122-123, 143, 145, 200
Leicester Secular Society, 21, 28, 37
Leon, Sir Herbert, 76-77, 83-85, 92, 227, 319, 325
Levy, Hyman, 116-117, 145, 152, 164, 178, 241, 320
Lewis, C S, 153-154, 160
Liberty of Bequest Committee, 16, 27
'Lin Shao-Yang', see Johnston, Sir Reginald Fleming
Literary Guide, 23, 31-32, 55, 64, 68-69, 73-74, 76, 78, 82, 85, 94, 99-101, 109, 110, 120, 123, 125, 126, 133, 139-140, 143, 149-153, 170, 199, 202, 223-224, 227-228, 232, 237, 242, 263
Literary Guide Supplements, 15, 35, 115, 327-328
Lodge, Sir Oliver, 80-81
Lofmark, Carl, 189, 195
Lombroso, Cesare, 90, 318
Long, Gabrielle, 136, 140-141, 320
McCabe, Joseph, 3, 17, 23, 26, 32-33, 34-36, 38, 54, 59-60, 65, 66-70, 75-76, 83, 105, 115, 133, 137, 212, 318, 330
  character of, 32-33, 38, 66-70, 94-95, 109, 138-139, 250
  legacy of, 33, 47-48, 54, 87, 109-110, 117, 175, 180, 206, 241, 250-251, 264
  publications of, 33, 34, 39, 40, 46, 47-48, 50, 52-53, 57, 68-69, 75, 81, 87, 88, 90-91, 109, 110-112, 117, 138-139, 180, 200
McIlroy, William, 182-183
MacIntyre, Alasdair, 155
McKay, Claude, 228
Mackay, Jean, 220
Macmillan, Sir Frederick, 38, 43
MacRae, Donald, 138, 152, 153, 201, 204, 330
Macy, Christopher, 4, 171-175, 177, 326
Malinowski, Bronislaw, 114, 319
Mander, A E, 112-113
Manvell, Roger, 167, 332
Marsh, P T, 7
Martin, Kingsley, 60, 93, 158, 239, 321, 330
Martin, Michael, 208
Marx, Karl, 106, 121, 201, 217
Maugham, Somerset, 119, 257, 320
Maxim, Sir Hiram, 48-49
Metcalf, John, 187, 326
Midgley, Mary, 36, 40, 118
Mill, John Stuart, 22, 31, 63, 111, 123, 166
Millar, Frederick, 21
Mitchison, Naomi, 89

Moore, Brian, 257, 323
Moore, G E, 32, 197
Morality, 14, 25, 26-27, 28-29, 75, 247-249
  education and, 19-21, 26-27, 89, 129-132, 170, 189
'Mouat, Kit', see Mackay, Jean
Muhammad, 19
Murdoch, Iris, 153, 256
Murray, Gilbert, 116, 329
National Reformer, 9, 12, 23
National Secular Society, 19, 21, 22, 24, 26, 39, 86, 119, 157-158, 180, 182-183, 184-185, 187-188, 207, 230, 237, 257
Naturalism, 36, 82, 197-198, 204-205, 212
Needham, Joseph, 123, 320
Neill, Stephen, 9, 153
Newman, Francis W, 12, 39, 42, 159, 221
New Humanist, 4, 170-175, 176-177, 178-180, 182-184, 186, 191-192, 194, 195, 215, 226, 257, 263
New Zealand, 3, 39, 51, 52, 54-55, 105, 113, 123, 127, 130, 229, 232, 233-234, 262
New Zealand Association of Rationalists & Humanists, 3, 39, 55, 123
Nietzsche, Friedrich, 57, 116, 203-204
Ogden, C K, 116, 178, 257
Open Society, 29, 41, 45, 69, 122, 181-184, 201, 227-230, 242
Owen, Robert, 16, 86, 146
Paine, Thomas, 58, 83, 112, 121, 152
Paranjpye, Sir Raghunath, 190, 320
Passmore, John, 142, 199
Paul Elek Ltd, 178, 253
Pearson, Karl, 13, 22
Pemberton Publishing, 147-148, 167-170, 178-179, 181, 208, 220, 225, 257, 300-303
Penguin, 44-45, 120, 123, 124, 135, 136, 153, 178, 224, 241, 263
Phelips, Vivian, 50, 76, 95, 120
Phillpotts, Eden, 131, 255, 318
Picton, J Allanson, 27, 47
Pike, E Royston, 77, 89, 95-97, 137, 199, 250, 252, 326
Plato, 142, 188
Plumptre, Constance, 15
Pollock, David, 4, 162-163, 187, 191-194, 325
Popper, Karl, 29, 122, 137, 167, 229, 234, 242, 245, 248, 322, 329
Positivism, 18, 31, 47, 94, 218-219
Postmodernism, 166-167, 195, 201, 215, 204, 217-218, 244, 264
  postmodernist historiography, 10, 26, 31, 49
Powys, Llewelyn, 112, 207-208
Poynter, J W, 143
Priestley, J B, 30, 41, 161, 239
Progressive League, see Federation of Progressive Societies and Individuals
Prometheus Books, 36, 169, 177, 180, 208, 244, 264
Propagandist Press Committee, 16-17, 18, 21, 24, 26, 27
Propagandist Press Fund, 15-16
'Protonius', see Whyte, Adam Gowans
Queensbury, Marquis of, 11
Question, 14, 167, 173, 178-180, 214-215
Radcliffe-Brown, A R, 114, 321
Radio Freedom League, 128-129
Raglan, Lord, 112, 114, 136, 321
Rationalism,
  and feminism, 47, 229, 333
  and liberalism, 22, 28-29, 93, 100, 122-123, 143, 166, 200-201

and philosophy, 24, 29, 32, 58, 82, 137, 196-198, 202-205, 209-217
and religion, 18, 25, 28-29, 40, 42, 49, 50-53, 55-64, 89-90, 102, 120-123, 153-156, 160, 164, 175, 181-184, 191, 205-209, 213, 232-233
and science, 36, 47, 71, 88, 114-115, 116-119, 138, 215
and socialism, 22, 93, 102, 105-107, 122-123, 143, 166-167
defections from, 140-143
definition of, 28, 41, 90-91, 173-174, 209-216
meaning of, 23-29, 41, 69-70, 107, 110, 113-114, 116, 176, 209-216
misconceptions about, 31, 36, 40-41, 44, 49, 51, 64, 69-70, 75, 83, 93, 112, 113, 116, 118, 164, 183, 197, 203-204, 216, 225, 236-237, 243-244
nineteenth century, 6-7, 13-14, 18, 22, 23-27, 72, 100, 209-210
value of, 7, 19-21, 36, 82, 113-114, 116, 176, 189
Rationalist Annual, 14, 105-106, 134, 142, 167, 197, 204, 219, 254
Rationalist Council, 104-105
Rationalist Peace Society, 73
Rationalist Press Association
and broadcasting, 44, 91-93, 127-129, 160-162, 186, 193, 247-249
and politics, 30-31, 99-105, 107, 122-123, 129-132, 181-184, 238-239, 242-244
and religion, 26, 30-31, 39, 42, 55-64, 64-65, 83, 113, 181-184, 254
conferences, 137, 152, 167, 194-195, 229, 243, 244, 329-333
disputes within, 52, 64-70, 94-98, 99-107, 146-149, 149-153, 162-163, 171-175, 191-195, 205-209, 222, 227-228, 243
finances of, 31, 33-35, 84-85, 123-124, 146-149, 157-158, 164, 167, 168-170, 171-175, 178-181
First World War and, 71, 72-86, 89
foundation of, 12, 22-23, 26, 27-29, 31
history of, 3, 5, 22, 43-44, 90, 107-108, 140, 249, 262-264
Honorary Associates, 31, 69, 73, 90, 92, 118, 119, 124, 138, 181, 190, 225, 231-261, 318-324
ignoring the history of, 5, 44, 49, 81, 180-181
legacy of, 44-46, 110-111, 244, 262-264
organisation of, 27-29, 33-34, 54-55, 83-84, 92-98, 133-134, 144-149, 156-158, 167, 168-169, 173-174, 177-180, 181, 184-185, 186-188, 191-195, 325-326
publications of, 183, 189, 192, 194-195, 216, 303-304
Second World War and, 125-127
Rationalist Press Committee, 9, 18, 26-28, 31, 32, 33
Rationalist Society, 135-136
Reade, Winwood, 113
Reeves, Joseph, 144, 146-151, 158, 161, 164, 190, 325, 326, 330
Reith, Sir John, 92, 160
Renan, Ernest, 39, 86
'Rhys, Jocelyn', see Major W J R Wingfield
Richards, I A, 257-258, 322
Ritchie-Calder, Lord, 167, 325, 326, 331
Robertson, Archibald, 102-105, 111, 119, 136, 329
publications of, 148, 214
Robertson, J M, 5, 6, 63, 67-68, 84, 102, 108, 115, 180, 198, 207, 250, 318
legacy of, 86, 91, 180-181
publications of, 51-52, 63, 91, 212, 236, 257

Robinson, J A T, 153, 158-160, 167
Roman Catholic Church, 32-33, 42, 121
actions against rationalism, 21, 74, 87, 121-122, 143, 160, 256
Roshwald, M, 224
Ross, William Stewart, 11, 14, 19, 21
Rowland, John, 107, 127, 141
Royle, Edward, 21, 35
RPA Annual, 14, 49, 76, 89, 236
Rushdie, Salman, 181-184
Russell, Bertrand, 58, 82, 92, 99, 109, 120, 122, 137, 142, 151, 196, 235, 236-240, 244, 245, 247, 249, 253, 255, 259, 319, 325
publications of, 88, 122, 161, 202, 204, 236-240, 243
Russell, Dora, 236, 322, 333
Russell, Ivor, 4, 172, 193, 216, 325, 332
Ryle, Gilbert, 137, 329
Sagan, Carl, 36, 233
'Saladin', see Ross, William Stewart
Sartre, Jean-Paul, 135-136, 203-204
Science, 34-36, 40, 58, 63, 71, 88, 114-115, 116-119, 138, 232-236, 261
Secular Humanist Declaration, 226, 245
Secularisation, 6, 7, 44, 161-162, 248-249, 263
Secularism, 10, 16-17, 22, 23-25, 28, 224, 230
Sen, Amartya, 260, 324
September 11 attacks, 191, 195, 229, 230, 245, 259
Shaw, George Bernard, 58, 93, 116, 155, 257
Shelley, Percy Bysshe, 101
Singer, Peter, 82, 231
Sir Isaac Pitman & Sons, 148
Smart, Ninian, 153
Smith, A D Howell, 156, 330
Smith, Grafton Elliot, 88, 319
Smith, W H, 111, 171, 174
Smith, William Robertson, 8
Smoker, Barbara, 183, 188, 333
Snell, Harry, 107-108, 325
Society for the Promotion of Christian Knowledge, 9, 57, 58
Socrates, 24, 82, 181, 204
Sokal, Alan, 199
South Place Ethical Society, 3, 32, 84, 121, 135, 156, 184-185, 191, 221, 235
Southwell, Charles, 9
Spence, Lewis, 115
Spencer, Herbert, 21, 22, 31, 32, 39, 40
influence of, 12, 31, 32, 42, 136, 196-202, 254
publications of, 111, 112, 136, 196-202
Spender, Stephen, 106-107
Spiritualism, 72, 78-82
Stebbing, L Susan, 112, 240-241, 320
Stephen, Leslie, 22, 29, 33, 35, 39, 66, 173, 258, 318
Stewart, D J, 145, 167, 170, 171-173, 178-179, 185, 323, 325, 331
Stopes-Roe, Harry, 222, 223
Strachey, James, 72, 106, 115
Strachey, Lytton, 71-72
Streeter, B H, 60-61
Student Christian Movement, 155, 158-159, 184
Tarkunde, V M, 190, 242, 322
Taylor, A J P, 72, 97, 131-132, 258, 323
Teimourian, Hazhir, 259, 324, 333
Thompson, Iain, 150
Thurtle, Ernest, 109, 125, 130, 325, 326
Trevelyan, G M, 115, 254, 258, 319
Trevor-Roper, Hugh, 181

355

Tribe, David, 4, 178, 230, 253, 324
Tyndall, John, 31, 43
United Kingdom
　Contemporary Britain, 166-167, 177-180, 225, 248, 263
　Edwardian Britain, 6, 30-31, 36, 41, 43-44, 45-46, 53, 57-58, 64, 69, 197
　Inter-war Britain, 71-72, 95, 97-98, 99
　Victorian Britain, 6-7, 36, 71
United States, 76, 101, 163, 177, 222, 226, 230, 244-245
Urwin, Kenneth, 137, 329
Vaughan, Percy, 78
'Vivian, Philip', see Phelips, Vivian
Voltaire, 57, 86, 112, 121, 123
Waddington, C H, 120, 321
Wallace, Alfred Russel, 90
Wallas, Graham, 93-94, 107, 136, 319, 325
Walter, Nicolas, 3
　character of, 177, 188, 194
　contribution to the RPA, 175-177, 181-184, 185, 186-188, 189,191-194, 221-222, 264, 326
　publications of, 175, 183
Watts & Co
　Changing World Library, 117-118, 311
　Cheap Reprints, 37-46, 55-57, 58, 59, 61, 64, 69, 72, 77, 78, 111-112, 197, 263, 305-306
　decline of, 123-124, 136-137, 146-149
　early days of, 10, 14
　Encyclopaedia Biblica, 53, 262
　Extra Series, 47, 53-54, 306-307
　Forum Series, 87-88, 309
　Free Mind, 146
　History of Science Series, 47, 307-308
　Inquirer's Library, 47-48, 112, 308
　legacy of, 43, 44-45, 80-81, 110-112, 227-230
　Library of Science and Culture, 117-118, 310-311
　Life Stories of Famous Men Series, 86-87, 119, 308
　New Thinker's Library, 148-149
　Pamphlets for the Million Series, 76, 308
　People's Platform Series, 86, 309
　publishing policy, 46, 80-81, 97, 147-148, 262
　successes of, 34-36, 43, 44-45, 48-49, 53, 88, 110-112, 113, 124, 138, 155, 262
　Thinker's Digest, 134, 135-136, 146
　Thinker's Forum, 124-125, 212, 315-316
　Thinker's Library, 50, 72, 82, 89, 97, 109, 110-116, 125-126, 135, 136, 140, 178, 195, 197-198, 213, 219, 228, 232, 237, 251-252, 262, 311-315
　Thrift Books, 136-137, 146-147, 316-317
　World of Youth Series, 89, 247, 310
Watts, Charles, 8-10, 11-12, 18, 24, 39, 53, 66, 205-206, 211, 227
Watts, Charles Albert
　as publisher, 14-15, 37, 43, 46, 119, 141, 142, 197, 199
　beliefs, 73-74, 194, 197, 227-228
　character of, 11, 12-13, 16, 22, 28, 31-32, 37, 95, 97, 133, 170
　contribution to the RPA, 3, 16, 22, 28, 31, 33, 37, 43, 97, 103, 109, 132, 133-134, 326
　dispute with T H Huxley, 12-13, 43
　youth, 11
Watts, Frederick Charles Chater
　as publisher, 96, 111, 252
　beliefs, 96
　character of, 96, 133-134, 144, 149-150, 170
　contribution to the RPA, 108, 128, 131, 133-134, 144-145, 149-150, 263, 325, 326
　youth, 96
Watts's Literary Guide, 23, 200
　appeal of, 14
　beginnings of, 14-15
Webb, Beatrice, 45
Wells, G A, 4, 168, 175, 178, 179, 180-181, 215, 323, 325, 326
Wells, H G, 34, 45, 85, 92, 99-100, 102, 105, 109, 120, 141-142, 145-146, 250-253, 258, 319
　publications of, 34, 40, 45-46, 80, 87-88, 100, 106, 111-112, 127, 141, 200, 250-253, 254
West, Rebecca, 102
Whale, George, 85, 92, 118, 258, 259, 325
Whale, Winifred Stephens, 258, 319
Whitehead, A N, 116-117, 203
Whyte, Adam Gowans, 21, 28, 31, 97, 127, 131, 133, 170, 189, 198-199, 210, 263
　legacy of, 97, 140
　publications of, 31, 44, 76, 82, 83, 89, 97, 127, 137, 140, 212-213, 247
Williams, Bernard, 167
Williams, Raymond, 148
Wilson, A N, 112
Wilson, Colin, 141, 153
Wilson, E O, 36, 114
Wingfield, Major W J R, 89-90
Wittgenstein, Ludwig, 71, 122, 241, 242, 259-260
Wood, H G, 120, 237
Wood, Henry J, 131, 258, 320
Wootton, Baroness Barbara, 158, 167, 240, 245-246, 321, 325
Wynne Willson, Jane, 193
Yearsley, Macleod, 227-228
Zola, Emile, 116

356